Computing

Third Edition

Geoffrey Knott BA, AIB, Cert Ed
Nick Waites BSc, MSc, Cert Ed

Business Education Publishers
2000

2000

1901888215

©Geoffrey Knott and Nick Waites 2000

ISBN 1 901 888 21 5

First Published 1992
    Reprinted 1993
    Reprinted 1994
Second Edition 1996
    Reprinted 1997
    Reprinted 1998
Revised Second Edition 1999
Third Edition 2000

Cover Design by Tim Murphy, Creative Solutions

Graphical illustrations by Nick Waites and Geoffrey Knott

Production and Editing by Geoffrey Knott

Published in Great Britain by
Business Education Publishers Limited
The Teleport
Doxford International
Sunderland
SR3 3XD

Tel: 0191 5252400
Fax: 0191 5201815

British Cataloguing-in-Publications Data
A catalogue record for this book is available from the British Library

Printed in Great Britain by Athenaeum Press, Gateshead

To Carolyn and Anne with love

The Authors

Geoffrey Knott and Nick Waites have long experience in Computing and IT education and have been producing highly successful course text books for well over a decade. They are authors of AS/A2 Information and Communication Technology, Computer Studies, GNVQ Advanced Communication and Information Technology, GNVQ Intermediate Information Technology, Information Processing, Small Business Computer Systems, Information Technology Skills - A Student Guide, GCSE Information Systems and co-authors of Business GNVQ Advanced and Core Skills for GNVQ. They are also the authors and developers of the ICT 2000 CD-ROM.

Acknowledgements

We would like to thank Jim Morton for his meticulous proofing of several of the more technical chapters in this book. We also wish to record thanks to the following Examination Boards for their kind permission to reproduce, on the accompanying CD ROM, selected questions set from past papers.

The Associated Examining Board

Joint Matriculation Board

University of Cambridge Local Examination Syndicate

University of London Examinations and Assessment Council

Welsh Joint Education Committee

Acknowledgement is made to the relevant Examination Board beside each question reproduced.

All errors and omissions remain the responsibility of the authors.

NW

GK

Durham, July 2000

Preface

The Third Edition of Computing has been extensively revised and updated to cover the requirements of the new Curriculum 2000 AS/A2 syllabuses from OCR, AQA and Edexcel. This text and the contents of the accompanying CD also contain much supplementary material for students following Higher National and Degree Courses in Computing, Software Engineering and Information Technology, or studying for British Computer Society examinations.

The book is concerned with the science of computing, that is the theory which underpins the internal structure, operation and control of computers, but it also deals extensively with the methods, processes and results of their application in commerce, industry, science and society in general. The Third Edition includes new material to provide even greater coverage of the subject and to keep pace with the developments in computing technology and applications. For example, there are new sections on Internet security and e-commerce, as well as details of the latest communications technologies and applications.

The new chapters on project management and critical path analysis will be particularly useful to those studying software engineering and The CD-ROM materials have been further extended to include a Visual Basic tutorial.

The breadth of topics covered in the book, has led us to divide it into the following sections:

Fundamental Concepts

Hardware

Software

Data Processing

Databases

Programming

>*Programming tutorials for Visual Basic, Pascal, C, COBOL and Assembly language are on the CD ROM*

Applications and Social Issues

The logical grouping of related topics facilitates access to particular areas of interest, as well as providing a framework for a teaching or self-study programme. However, the sequence of the chapters is not meant to indicate the order in which topics should necessarily be introduced.

Many of the chapters are followed by exercises to test the reader's retention of facts or understanding of ideas developed within the text. The sections on Databases and Programming, in particular, are followed by extensive developmental exercises.

Examination practice is also provided through a range of actual examination questions (on CD-ROM), selected from a number of major examining boards. Centres which adopt the book can obtain suggested answers to these questions from the publishers.

Contents of CD ROM

ATL1

A Windows 95/98 application to aid learning about assembly language programming. Based on a hypothetical programming language called ATL1 (Assembler Teaching Language 1), the program has been designed to allow students to investigate the processes involved in assembly language programming and how object programs are executed by a simple processor. Students and lecturers will find it an invaluable aid to investigating this difficult subject. On-line documentation and a printable programming tutorial are included.

Printable programming tutorials in Visual Basic, Pascal, C and COBOL

Each tutorial is stored in .rtf (rich text format) so that it can be printed from any standard word processor. The source listings for illustrative programs used in the tutorials are also stored separately on the CD ROM.

Examination questions

A range of examination questions, selected from a number of major examining boards, are included. Centres which adopt the book can obtain suggested answers to these questions from the publisher.

Contents

Fundamental Concepts

Hardware

Databases

Fundamental Concepts

Chapters

Number Systems

Although the denary number system has proved to be the simplest for people to use, it is more convenient for computers to use the binary number system. The electronic components used in computers can be in either one of two physical states, permitting the representation of 0 and 1, the two symbols of the binary number system. This chapter explains the basis of this and other number systems relevant to the subject of computing.

The base of a number system

The denary system has ten symbols, 0, 1, 2, 3, 4, 5, 6, 7, 8 and 9 and the *base* or *radix* of a number system is identified by the number of different symbols it uses. Thus, the denary number system has base of 10. To identify a number as denary it can be written as, for example, 123_{10}.

Place value

Each symbol can be given a weight or place (or positional) value, according to its position within any given number. In the denary system, each place value is a power of ten. Remember that the base of the denary number system is ten. Thus, for denary integers each place value is ten raised to a power. Starting from the least significant digit on the right, there are units (10^0), tens (10^1), hundreds (10^2), thousands (10^3) and so on. The idea of place value can be illustrated with examples of integer (whole) numbers. Table 1.1 shows that 1263_{10} can be expressed as one thousand, plus two hundreds, plus six tens and three units, or $1 \times 1000 + 2 \times 100 + 6 \times 10 + 3 \times 1 = 1263_{10}$.

power 10^3	10^2	10^1	10^0
thousands	hundreds	tens	units
1	2	6	3

Table 1.1. *Place values example 1263_{10}*

power 10^3	10^2	10^1	10^0
thousands	hundreds	tens	units
0	4	8	7

Table 1.2. *Place values example 487_{10}*

Similarly, Table 1.2 shows that 487_{10} is the same as zero thousands, plus four hundreds, plus eight tens and seven units, or $0 \times 1000 + 4 \times 100 + 8 \times 10 + 7 \times 1 = 487_{10}$. Note that any number ($n$) raised to the power of zero (n^0) is equal to 1. This can be seen from Tables 1.1 and 1.2 and from the place value tables shown later, for each of the binary, octal and hexadecimal number systems. The *fractional* component of a number is also determined by position, except that the power is negative, as shown in Table 1.3.

	10^{-1}	10^{-2}	10^{-3}
decimal point	tenths	hundredths	thousandths
.	6	2	5

Table 1.3. *Fractional place values example 0.625_{10}*

Table 1.3 shows that 0.625_{10}, can be seen as: $6 \times \dfrac{1}{10} + 2 \times \dfrac{1}{100} + 5 \times \dfrac{1}{1000} = \dfrac{5}{8}$

Binary system

The binary system uses only two symbols, 0 and 1. Each digit in a binary number is known as a binary digit or *bit*. An example binary number is 11001_2, which is equivalent to 25_{10}. The binary system has a base of 2, so each place value is a power of two. The next two tables each show a range of integer place values and an example binary number. Table 1.4 demonstrates that the binary number 11101_2 is equivalent to denary $1 \times 16 + 1 \times 8 + 1 \times 4 + 0 \times 2 + 1 \times 1$ or 29_{10}. Table 1.5 shows that the binary number 01100111_2 is equivalent to $0 \times 128 + 1 \times 64 + 1 \times 32 + 0 \times 16 + 0 \times 8 + 1 \times 4 + 1 \times 2 + 1 \times 1 = 103_{10}$.

2^4	2^3	2^2	2^1	2^0
16	8	4	2	1
1	1	1	0	1

Table 1.4. *11101_2 or 29_{10}*

2^7	2^6	2^5	2^4	2^3	2^2	2^1	2^0
128	64	32	16	8	4	2	1
0	1	1	0	0	1	1	1

Table 1.5. *01100111_2 or 103_{10}*

Binary *fractions* can also be represented and an example is shown in Table 1.6.

	2^{-1}	2^{-2}	2^{-3}	2^{-4}
binary point	half	quarter	eighth	sixteenth
.	0	1	1	1

Table 1.6. *Fraction 0.0111_2*

We can see from this that 0.0111_2 is equivalent to $0 \times \dfrac{1}{2} + 1 \times \dfrac{1}{4} + 1 \times \dfrac{1}{8} + 1 \times \dfrac{1}{16} = \dfrac{7}{16}$

Table 1.7 shows the binary equivalents of 0 to 9 in the denary system.

base$_{10}$	base$_2$	base$_{10}$	base$_2$	base$_{10}$	base$_2$	base$_{10}$	base$_2$	base$_{10}$	base$_2$
0	0000	1	0001	2	0010	3	0011	4	0100
5	0101	6	0110	7	0111	8	1000	9	1001

Table 1.7. *Denary symbols and binary equivalents*

Using the place values for the binary system shown in Tables 1.4 and 1.5, it can be seen how each of the denary numbers in Table 1.7 equates with its binary representation.

Rules of binary arithmetic

Addition rules are given, together with example sums, in Table 1.8. The rules for binary addition are needed when studying computer arithmetic in Chapter 3.

addition rules	carry	example sum	example sum
$0 + 0 = 0$		011010	101100
$0 + 1 = 1$		$+110100$	$+000010$
$1 + 0 = 1$		$\overline{1001110}$	$\overline{101110}$
$1 + 1 = 0$	1		

Table 1.8. *Binary addition rules and examples*

Octal and hexadecimal numbers

These number systems are often used as a shorthand method for representing binary numbers. As can be seen from the binary numbers in the earlier tables, they are very confusing to the eye and it is sometimes difficult, even with small groupings, to distinguish one pattern from another. Where it is necessary for the computer's binary codes to be written or read by programmers, for example, it is invariably more convenient to use alternative coding methods. Octal and hexadecimal (*hex*) notations are used in preference to denary because they are more readily converted to or from binary. It must be emphasised that computers can only handle binary forms of coding. Therefore octal and hexadecimal codes must be converted to binary before they can be handled by the computer.

Octal coding

The octal number system has a base of 8, using 0, 1, 2, 3, 4, 5, 6 and 7 as its symbols. Each place value is a power of eight; some of the place values are shown in Table 1.9.

8^4	8^3	8^2	8^1	8^0	8^{-1}	8^{-2}	8^{-3}
4096	512	64	8	1	$1/8$	$1/64$	$1/512$

Table 1.9. *Some octal place values*

Octal coding uses three bits at a time, allowing 8 or 2^3 (see Table 1.10) different patterns of bits.

Binary	0 0 0	0 0 1	0 1 0	0 1 1	1 0 0	1 0 1	1 1 0	1 1 1
Octal	0	1	2	3	4	5	6	7

Table 1.10. *Octal symbols and binary equivalents*

To represent any given value, a binary number can be split into groups of 3 bits, starting from the right-hand side, as the two 16-bit examples in Table 1.11 show. Because the 16 bits will not divide exactly into groups of 3, the left-most or *most significant bit* (MSB) can only take the values 0_8 or 1_8.

0111001101100110_2	0	1 1 1	0 0 1	1 0 1	1 0 0	1 1 0
Octal code	0	7	1	5	4	6
1101010100101011_2	1	1 0 1	0 1 0	1 0 0	1 0 1	0 1 1
Octal code	1	5	2	4	5	3

Table 1.11. *Octal coding examples*

Hexadecimal coding

The hexadecimal number system has a base of 16, and uses the following symbols: 0, 1, 2, 3, 4, 5, 6, 7, 8, 9, A, B, C, D, E and F. The six letters, A to F, are used instead of the denary numbers 10, 11, 12, 13, 14

16^3	16^2	16^1	16^0	16^{-1}	16^{-2}	16^{-3}
4096	256	16	1	$1/16$	$1/256$	$1/4096$

Table 1.12. *Hexadecimal place values*

and 15, respectively. This brings the number of hexadecimal symbols to sixteen. Some place values, each being a power of 16, are shown in Table 1.12.

A group of 4 bits provides 16 unique binary patterns, the number required to represent all 16 symbols of the hexadecimal number system. The symbols and their binary equivalents are given in Table 1.13.

Binary	0000	0001	0010	0011	0100	0101	0110	0111
Hexadecimal	0	1	2	3	4	5	6	7
Binary	1000	1001	1010	1011	1100	1101	1110	1111
Hexadecimal	8	9	A	B	C	D	E	F

Table 1.13. *Hexadecimal symbols and binary equivalents*

Therefore, a binary number can be coded by grouping the bits into groups of four and using the appropriate hexadecimal symbol for each group, as the examples in Table 1.14 show.

1100001111110110_2	1100	0011	1111	0110
Hexadecimal code	C	3	F	6
0101011010111101_2	0101	0110	1011	1101
Hexadecimal code	5	6	B	D

Table 1.14. *Hexadecimal coding examples*

In practice, hexadecimal is used in preference to octal code because computers organise their internal memory in 8-bit groupings (*bytes*) or multiples of bytes. These groupings conveniently divide into 4-bit *nibbles* which can be coded in the shorthand of hexadecimal. A knowledge of hexadecimal is essential for the interpretation of computer manufacturers' manuals, which use the coding system extensively to specify memory and backing storage features. Programmers using low level languages, such as assembly code, also need to be familiar with this number system.

Number base conversion methods

Conversion of binary numbers into their hexadecimal and octal equivalents is described in the preceding section. The following section provides methods and examples of conversion from:

❑ denary to binary;

❑ denary to octal;

❑ denary to hexadecimal.

Denary to binary

Method 1 - using conversion tables

Table 1.15 contains a range of place values for integer conversion; Table 1.16 can be used for fractions.

2^{14}	2^{13}	2^{12}	2^{11}	2^{10}	2^9	2^8	2^7	2^6	2^5	2^4	2^3	2^2	2^1	2^0
16384	8192	4096	2048	1024	512	256	128	64	32	16	8	4	2	1

Table 1.15. *Denary to binary conversion table - integers*

2^{-1}	2^{-2}	2^{-3}	2^{-4}	2^{-5}	2^{-6}	2^{-7}	2^{-8}	2^{-9}
$\frac{1}{2}$	$\frac{1}{4}$	$\frac{1}{8}$	$\frac{1}{16}$	$\frac{1}{32}$	$\frac{1}{64}$	$\frac{1}{128}$	$\frac{1}{256}$	$\frac{1}{512}$

Table 1.16. *Denary to binary conversion table - fractions*

To convert a denary number to binary requires the identification of those place values which, when added together, will equal the denary number. By reference to the appropriate table, a binary 1 is placed in each position, where the value is required and a binary 0 is recorded in each of those remaining. Starting with the largest value in the table, which is less than, or equal to the denary number, successive values to the right are selected and accumulated until the sum is obtained; a binary 1 is placed in each such position. Table 1.17 provides an integer example.

2^{14}	2^{13}	2^{12}	2^{11}	2^{10}	2^9	2^8	2^7	2^6	2^5	2^4	2^3	2^2	2^1	2^0
16384	8192	4096	2048	1024	512	256	128	64	32	16	8	4	2	1
		1	0	1	0	0	1	1	0	0	1	1	1	0

Table 1.17. *Integer 5326_{10} converted to 1010011001110_2*

Obviously, any value which will result in the required sum being exceeded is skipped, a binary 0 being placed in the relevant position. The place values containing a binary 1 can be summed and the result checked as follows.

$$1\times4096 + 0\times2048 + 1\times1024 + 0\times512 + 0\times256 + 1\times128 + 1\times64 + 0\times32 + 0\times16 + 1\times8$$
$$+ 1\times4 + 1\times2 + 0\times1 = 5326_{10}$$

Similarly, Table 1.18, shows a denary fraction converted to binary.

	2^{-1}	2^{-2}	2^{-3}	2^{-4}	2^{-5}
binary point	$\frac{1}{2}$	$\frac{1}{4}$	$\frac{1}{8}$	$\frac{1}{16}$	$\frac{1}{32}$
•	0	1	1	1	0

Table 1.18. *Fraction $\frac{7}{16}$ converted to $\cdot01110_2$*

Again, the binary 1 place values can be totalled and the result confirmed, as follows.

$$0\times\frac{1}{2} + 1\times\frac{1}{4} + 1\times\frac{1}{8} + 1\times\frac{1}{16} + 0\times\frac{1}{32} = \frac{7}{16}$$

Method 2 - successive division by the base

Integers

This technique requires that the denary number is successively *divided by 2*, the base of the binary system, until the result of a division is zero. If a division leaves a *remainder* of denary 1, a binary 1 is placed in the next available position in the binary number being formed; if there is a denary 0 remainder, a binary 0 is entered. Table 1.19 illustrates the process. Note that the binary number should be read, beginning with the most significant bit (MSB), from the bottom of the table, to the least significant bit (LSB).

denary	divided by	equals	remainder	binary	
1273	2	636	1	1	LSB
636	2	318	0	0	
318	2	159	0	0	
159	2	79	1	1	
79	2	39	1	1	
39	2	19	1	1	
19	2	9	1	1	
9	2	4	1	1	
4	2	2	0	0	
2	2	1	0	0	
1	2	0	1	1	MSB

Table 1.19. *Integer 1273_{10} to 100111111001_2*

The binary number is written as follows: $1273_{10} = 10011111001_2$, the last binary 1, at the bottom of Table 1.19, being the most significant bit (MSB).

Real number conversion

Tables 1.20 and 1.21 show how a *real* (having a fractional component) denary number is converted; the integer and fractional parts must be dealt with separately and differently. The *integer* part of 34.375_{10} is converted as shown in Table 1.20, by successive division (as in the previous example in Table 1.19). The *fractional* part is converted by a process of successive *multiplication*, as shown in Table 1.21; this table shows that, if a multiplication results in a 1 appearing before the decimal point, the 1 is placed in the next available place to the right of the binary point; otherwise, 0 is placed there. Note that the binary fraction is read from the top of the table, identified by MSB. The process is

denary	divided by	equals	remainder	binary	
34	2	17	0	0	LSB
17	2	8	1	1	
8	2	4	0	0	
4	2	2	0	0	
2	2	1	0	0	
1	2	0	1	1	MSB

Table 1.20. *Conversion of 34_{10} (integer part of 34.375_{10})*

denary	multiplied by	equals	binary	
0.375	2	0.75	0	MSB
0.75	2	1.5	1	
0.5	2	1.0	1	LSB

Table 1.21. *Conversion of 0.375 (fractional part of 34.375_{10})*

complete when a product of denary 1 is obtained (much of the time, an exact figure will not be achieved and the process is continued until the desired accuracy is reached). Looking at Tables 1.20 and 1.21 together, the result can be seen to be as follows: $34.375_{10} = 100010.011_2$.

Conversion with limited precision

Sometimes, a decimal fraction cannot be converted to its precise binary equivalent (as achieved in Tables 1.20 and 1.21). This topic is dealt with, in more detail, in the section on *floating point arithmetic*, in Chapter 3.

Table 1.22 shows the conversion of denary 0.425 to its binary equivalent, but with some loss of precision. The level of precision is determined by the number of place values allocated for the storage of the binary fraction; more places would allow a greater degree of precision.

Table 1.22 shows that, in this example, absolute precision cannot be achieved (the Product column will continue with the pattern shown and denary 1 will never be reached) and that, using the precision limit in the Table, 0.425_{10} is approximately equal to 0.0110110011_2.

denary	multiplied by	equals	binary	
0.425	2	0.85	0	MSB
0.85	2	1.7	1	
0.7	2	1.4	1	
0.4	2	0.8	0	
0.8	2	1.6	1	
0.6	2	1.2	1	
0.2	2	0.4	0	
0.4	2	0.8	0	
0.8	2	1.6	1	LSB
0.6	2	1.2	1	etc

Table 1.22. *Denary to binary conversion with loss of precision*

Referring to the place values in Table 1.16, it can be seen that the binary fraction is, in fact, equal to the following expression.

$$0 \times \frac{1}{2} + 1 \times \frac{1}{4} + 1 \times \frac{1}{8} + 0 \times \frac{1}{16} + 1 \times \frac{1}{32} + 1 \times \frac{1}{64} + 0 \times \frac{1}{128} + 0 \times \frac{1}{256} + 1 \times \frac{1}{512} = \frac{217}{512} = 0 \cdot 423828125$$

The difference is $0.425_{10} - 0.423828125_{10}$ or 0.001171875_{10}. A greater degree of precision (although not absolute) could be obtained by continuing the process shown in Table 1.22 and using more significant digits.

Denary to octal

Method 2 (successive division by the base), described in the denary to binary section, is also used here, in each case using the relevant base of 8. Table 1.23 shows an example of denary to octal conversion. LSD and MSD stand for least significant *digit* and most significant *digit*.

denary	divided by	equals	remainder	octal	
1273	8	159	1	1	LSD
159	8	19	7	7	
19	8	2	3	3	
2	8	0	2	2	MSD

Table 1.23. *Integer 1273_{10} converted to octal 2371_8*

8^3	8^2	8^1	8^0
512	64	8	1
2	3	7	1

Table 1.24. *Integer 2371_8 and place values*

That $1273_{10} = 2371_8$, is proved, with the following expression (and by reference to the place values shown in Table 1.24).

$$2371_8 = 2 \times 512 + 3 \times 64 + 7 \times 8 + 1 \times 1 = 1273_{10}.$$

Denary to hexadecimal

Method 2 (successive division by the base), described in the denary to binary and denary to octal sections, is also used here, in this case using the relevant base of 16. Table 1.25 shows an example of denary to hexadecimal conversion. Remember that the symbol 'F' is equivalent to denary 15.

denary	divided by	equals	remainder	hex	
1273	16	79	9	9	LSD
79	16	4	15	F	
4	16	0	4	4	MSD

Table 1.25. *Integer 1273_{10} to $4F9_{16}$*

That $4F9_{16} = 1273_{10}$ can be proved by the following expression (the relevant place values appear in Table 1.26).

$$4F9_{16} = 4 \times 256 + 15(F) \times 16 + 9 \times 1 = 1273_{10}.$$

16^2	16^1	16^0
256	16	1
4	F	9

Table 1.26. *Integer $4F9_{16}$ and place values*

✍Exercises

1. Calculate the *denary* equivalents of the following binary numbers:

a. 11001110	d. 00000100	g. 00100000	j. 11111111
b. 10101011	e. 00001000	h. 01000000	k. 11110000
c. 01001100	f. 00010000	i. 10000000	l. 00001111

2. Using the conversion tables provided in the text, write down the *octal* and *hexadecimal* equivalents of the binary values in 1.

3. Using *successive division by the base*, convert 2165_{10} to binary.

4. Convert the real number values 26.325_{10} and 0.4685_{10} to binary. Comment on the results.

5. Use hexadecimal notation to represent the denary numbers 325_{10} and 2967_{10}.

6. Why is hexadecimal notation used in preference to other number bases, to represent binary codes?

Chapter 2
Data Representation

Data, in the context of this chapter, is a general term which covers any data or information which is capable of being handled by the computer's internal circuitry, or of being stored on backing storage media such as magnetic tape or disk. To be processed by computer, data must be in a form which the computer can handle; it must be *machine-sensible*.

Forms of coding

To be machine-sensible data has to be in *binary*, using the digits 0 and 1. Both main memory and external storage media, such as magnetic disk and tape, use electrical/magnetic patterns representing the binary digits 0 and 1 to record and handle data and instructions.

Why binary? - bi-stable devices

Computer storage uses two-state or bi-stable devices to indicate the presence of a binary 0 or 1. The circuits inside a computer represent these two states by being either conducting or non-conducting, that is, current is either flowing or is not flowing through the circuit. A simple example of a bi-stable device is an electric light bulb. At any one time it must be in one of two states, on or off. Magnetic storage media use magnetic fields and the two possible polarities (north and south) are used as bi-stable devices to represent 0 and 1. Denary is not practicable because a computer's circuitry would have to use and accommodate ten clearly defined physical electronic states. Extremely reliable components would be needed to avoid the machine confusing one physical state with another. With bi-stable devices, slight changes in performance do not prevent differentiation between the two physical states which represent 0 and 1.

Character and numeric codes

Much of the data processed by computer and stored on backing storage are represented by *character* codes. The codes used inside the computer are referred to as *internal* codes, whereas those used by various peripherals are termed *external* codes. Data transferred between peripheral devices and the processor may use a variety of binary character codes, but when processing data the processor will tend to use a particular internal code, which will vary with machines of different manufacture. Sometimes, an external character code may continue to be used for storage of data in main memory; alphabetic data remains in character code form during computer processing. On the other hand, numeric data, presented by a peripheral in character code form, is converted to one of a number of numeric codes for processing purposes. Code conversion may be executed within a peripheral, within the *interface* (see Chapter 14) device between a peripheral and the processor, or within the processor itself. Characters may be:

❏   alphabetic (upper and lower case);

❏   numeric (0 to 9);

❏   special characters (apostrophe, comma, etc.);

❏   control characters and codes.

Control characters are used in data transmission, perhaps to indicate the start or end of a *block* of data; *control codes* can be used to affect the display of data on a VDU screen and include those which cause, for example, carriage return, delete, highlight or blinking. Control characters and control codes do not form part of the data which are to be usefully processed, but are needed for control. The range of characters which can be represented by a computer system is known as its *character set*.

The ASCII (American Standard Code for Information Interchange) code uses seven binary digits (*bits*) to represent a full range of characters. Data passing between a peripheral and the computer is usually in character code, typically ASCII or EBCDIC (Extended Binary Coded Decimal Interchange Code). This latter 8-bit character code has a 256 character set and is generally used with IBM and IBM-compatible equipment. Extracts from both the ASCII and EBCDIC character sets are given in Tables 2.1 and 2.2, respectively.

character	ASCII	character	ASCII	character	ASCII	character	ASCII
0	0110000	9	0111001	I	1001001	R	1010010
1	0110001	A	1000001	J	1001010	S	1010011
2	0110010	B	1000010	K	1001011	T	1010100
3	0110011	C	1000011	L	1001100	U	1010101
4	0110100	D	1000100	M	1001101	V	1010110
5	0110101	E	1000101	N	1001110	W	1010111
6	0110110	F	1000110	O	1001111	X	1011000
7	0110111	G	1000111	P	1010000	Y	1011001
8	0111000	H	1001000	Q	1010001	Z	1011010

Table 2.1. *Extract from ASCII character set*

char	EBCDIC	char	EBCDIC	char	EBCDIC	char	EBCDIC
0	11110000	9	11111001	I	11001001	R	11011001
1	11110001	A	11000001	J	11010001	S	11100010
2	11110010	B	11000010	K	11010010	T	11100011
3	11110011	C	11000011	L	11010011	U	11100100
4	11110100	D	11000100	M	11010100	V	11100101
5	11110101	E	11000101	N	11010101	W	11100110
6	11110110	F	11000110	O	11010110	X	11100111
7	11110111	G	11000111	P	11010111	Y	11101000
8	11111000	H	11001000	Q	11011000	Z	11101001

Table 2.2. *Extract from EBCDIC character set*

Parity checking of codes

The ASCII code shown in Table 2.1 is a 7-bit code. An additional bit, known as the *parity bit* (in the left-most or most significant bit position), is used to detect *single bit* errors which may occur during data transfer. Such errors may result from a peripheral fault or from corruption of data on storage media.

The parity scheme used for detecting single bit errors is simple (the detection of multiple bit errors is more complex and is dealt with in the chapter on Data Communications). There are two types of parity, odd and even, though it is of little significance which is used. If odd parity is used, the parity bit is set to binary 1 or 0, such that there is an odd number of binary 1s in the group. Conversely, even parity requires that there is an even number of binary 1s in the group. Examples of these two forms of parity are provided in Table 2.3.

The parity bit for each group is in bold. If even parity is being used and main memory receives the grouping 10010100 then the presence of an odd number of binary 1s indi-cates an error in transmis-

data with no parity	parity bit	data with odd parity	parity bit	data with even parity
1 0 0 1 0 1 0	**0**	1 0 0 1 0 1 0	**1**	1 0 0 1 0 1 0
0 1 0 1 1 0 1	**1**	0 1 0 1 1 0 1	**0**	0 1 0 1 1 0 1

Table 2.3. *Examples of data with odd and even parity*

sion. Provided that the number of bits corrupted is odd, all transmission errors will be detected. However, an even number of bits in error will not affect the parity condition and thus will not be revealed. Additional controls can be implemented to detect multiple bit errors; these controls make use of parity checks on blocks of characters; known *as block check characters* (BCC), they are used extensively in data transmission control and are described in Chapter 11 on Data Communications.

Data storage in main memory

Character codes, such as the ASCII code (Table 2.1), are primarily of use during data transfer between a peripheral and the main memory. They are also generally used to represent non-numeric data inside the computer. Numeric data is usually converted to one of a number of *numeric codes*, including binary coded decimal (BCD) and floating point formats (Chapter 3)

Internal parity checks

Most mini and mainframe computers use parity bits to detect and sometimes correct, data transfer errors within the computer, so the actual length of codes is extended to allow for this. Parity checking, built into the circuitry of the memory chips is a feature of many microcomputer systems. Memory chips can develop faults, so it is important that a user is made aware of parity errors (which may indicate major memory faults), before significant data loss occurs.

Binary coded decimal (BCD)

As the name suggests, BCD uses a binary code to represent each of the decimal symbols. It is a 4-bit code, using the natural binary weightings of 8, 4, 2 and 1 and is only used for the representation of numeric values.

Each of the ten symbols used in the decimal system is coded with its 4-bit binary equivalent, as shown in Table 2.4.

denary	0	1	2	3	4	5	6	7	8	9
BCD	0000	0001	0010	0011	0100	0101	0110	0111	1000	1001

Table 2.4. *BCD equivalents of denary symbols*

In this way, any decimal number can be represented by coding each digit separately. An example is given in Table 2.5.

denary	6	2	4
BCD	0110	0010	0100

Table 2.5. *BCD representation of* 624_{10}

BCD arithmetic

Floating point arithmetic can introduce small inaccuracies which can be a problem in financial data processing applications. For example, an amount of 120.50 stored in floating point form may return a value of 120.499999; although the application of *rounding algorithms* (see Chapter 3) can adjust the figure to the required number of significant figures, the rounding is being carried out on the binary representation, when it is the decimal form which should be rounded.

For BCD numbers, each decimal character is separately coded and their addition cannot be accomplished with the normal ADD instruction (Chapter 4); more complex electronics are needed to carry out arithmetic on data in BCD form than are necessary for pure binary numbers. BCD numbers also take more memory space than pure binary numbers. For example, with a 16-bit word the maximum BCD number is 9999_{10}, while using binary it is 65535_{10}. *BCD arithmetic* is described in Chapter 3. Numbers with a fractional element (*real* numbers) use an implied decimal point which can be located between any of the 4-bit groupings.

Boolean values

Apart from characters and numeric values, binary code can also represent the *Boolean* values of *true* or *false* (Chapter 5), the former by 1 and the latter by 0. Boolean variables can be used to indicate, for example, the condition of a *flag register* (Chapter 7) used to signal the occurrence of an overflow condition after an arithmetic operation, or an *interrupt* from a peripheral indicating its need for servicing by the processor.

Bit-mapped graphics

Chapter 8 refers to bit-mapping for the pixel-level control of displayed output; thus a monochrome VDU screen with a resolution of 720 pixels by 350 rows needs 252,000 bits of memory, each bit capable of being set to 1 for white or 0 for black. Colour screens need to use more bits for each pixel, to allow the setting of a variety of colours; one *byte* (eight bits) per pixel permits 256 (2^8) separate colours to be used. By definition, bit-mapped device control is inflexible and very device-dependent, but its use is essential for graphical work, word processing and text output which uses a variety of sophisticated fonts. Since large amounts of memory are needed, particularly for high resolution colour display, graphics adapter cards provide additional VRAM (*video RAM*) for screen memory.

Gray or cyclic code

Gray code is used in mechanical systems, for example, shaft encoders, which generate a binary number according to the angle of the disk, but is of no use for arithmetic operations. Table 2.6 illustrates a 3-bit Gray code and shows how each grouping is related to its natural binary coding. A normal 3-bit binary number would, according to the place values of each bit and beginning with the most significant bit, have a 421 weighting.

denary	Gray code weighting (2n–1)	converts to	normal binary weighting (n)
	7 3 1		4 2 1
0	0 0 0		0 0 0
1	0 0 1		0 0 1
2	0 1 1	3 – 1	0 1 0
3	0 1 0	3	0 1 1
4	1 1 0	7 – 3	1 0 0
5	1 1 1	7 – 3 +1	1 0 1
6	1 0 1	7–1	0 1 1 0
7	1 0 0	7	0 1 1 1

Table 2.6. *3-bit Gray code conversion*

To produce the Gray codes each of the natural binary weightings of 421 is multiplied by 2 and then 1 is subtracted. This can be written as an expression of the form $2n-1$, n being the normal binary weighting. Thus, the Gray code weightings become 731. The denary values in the leftmost column of Table 2.6 are obtained from each Gray code as follows. Working from the most significant to the least significant bit and ignoring zeroes, the new weighted values are alternately added and subtracted.

An examination of the codes will reveal that if any individual code is incremented or decremented, only one bit changes, thus removing any prospect of ambiguity when, for example, an encoded disk (see later) crosses the boundary between two segments. Obviously, an increased number of bits will allow a larger number of unique codes with the consequent ability to determine the position of an increased number of segments on a shaft encoder's disk. Gray Code can also be used in disk drives for identifying sectors on magnetic disk.

Applications of Gray code

Coded plate transducers

This device uses a plate or disk, such as that shown in Figure 2.1, which contains a number of binary coded concentric tracks. The most widely used code is called *Gray code*, which is shown in Table 2.7 in 3-bit form. Gray code is used in preference to standard binary code because it has the property that each successive value in the sequence of codes changes by only a single bit. In pure binary, also shown in Table 2.7, this is not the case: you can see that, for example, going from 011 to 100, all three bits change, whereas in Gray code the transition is from 010 to 110 in which only the most significant digit changes from 0 to 1. The significance of this can be seen if we consider what might happen if the disk shown in Figure 2.1 were to be 3-bit binary coded rather than 3-bit Gray coded.

The angular position of the disk is determined by the light detectors. They are able to detect the presence of light in the three positions corresponding to the disk's three concentric tracks. However, the disk can stop at any angular position, including the boundaries between two adjacent codes. For example, because of the limited sensitivity of the light detectors, if the disk is at the boundary of 001 and 010, it is possible that two adjacent transparent and opaque areas will be read incorrectly. This means that the position of the disk could be mistakenly read as 000 or 011 just as easily as one of the two correct values.

Figure 2.1. *Coded plate transducer*

value	Gray code	binary	angle
0	000	000	0(360)
1	001	001	45
2	011	010	90
3	010	011	135
4	110	100	180
5	111	101	225
6	101	110	270
7	100	111	315

Table 2.7. *3-bit Gray code and angles represented*

However, using Gray code the equivalent codes to 001 and 010 are 011 and 010 respectively, in which only the least significant bit changes value. Thus the position of the disk cannot be misinterpreted. This is illustrated in Figure 2.2.

(a) Gray code   (b) Binary code

Figure 2.2. *Comparing binary code and Gray code for measuring angle of rotation*

In (a) the Gray coded disk is at the boundary of 001 and 011. The only possible ambiguity is with sensor b, but the three sensors will still only detect either 001 or 011 as required. However, with the binary coded disk shown in (b), sensors a and b could read a zero or a one, possibly providing an erroneous value for the angle of rotation of the disk.

To be able to relate the Gray code output signals from the light sensors to an angular position, the code must be converted into binary. This may be accomplished in two ways:

address	contents
000	000
001	001
011	010
010	011
110	100
111	101
101	110
100	111

1.   Using a logic circuit (Figure 2.3) - the outputs from the sensors are fed into a logic circuit which produces the correct binary outputs which can then be related to an angular rotation (listed in Table 2.7).

Figure 2.3. *Logic circuit to convert Gray code to binary*

Table 2.8. *Look-up table Gray code to binary*

2.   Using a look-up table - after appropriate conditioning, the outputs from the light sensors are used to access a small amount of ROM or RAM containing a table such as that shown in Table 2.8 for a 3-bit code. The memory locations in the first column contain the appropriate binary code allowing any Gray code to be quickly looked up.

Shaft encoders

This type of transducer also uses a rotating disk but this time it has a set of equally spaced radial lines on its surface. A special track on the disk has a zero reference mark on it. An optical sensor is used to detect the radial lines, incrementing a counter each time a mark is detected. This allows the angular position of a shaft to be accurately determined. A typical shaft encoder might have over a thousand radial lines giving a resolution of less than a third of a degree. Some shaft encoders also provide outputs allowing the direction of rotation of the shaft to be determined as well as its current position and rotational speed. By linking the spindle of a shaft encoder to the spindle of another rotating shaft, speed, position and directional data can be accurately obtained.

Figure 2.4 illustrates the operation of a shaft encoder. The rotating shaft of the spindle to be monitored is linked to the shaft of the encoder by means of a suitable shaft coupler. The rotation of the shaft thus causes the shaft of the encoder to rotate at the same rate. An optical sensor uses reflected light to detect the radial lines on the encoder's disk.

Figure 2.4. *Shaft encoder*

The structure of main memory

Main memory is divided into a number of cells or *locations*, each of which has a unique name or *address* and is capable of holding a unit or grouping of bits which may represent data or an instruction. More is said about instructions in Chapter 4. Memory locations are normally addressed using whole numbers from zero upwards. The *size* of memory location used varies from one make of computer to another and is related to the coding methods employed and the number of bits it is designed to handle as a unit.

Memory words and bytes

A *memory word* is a given number of bits in memory, addressable as a unit. The addresses of memory locations run consecutively, starting with address 0 and running up to the largest address. Each location contains a word which can be retrieved by specification of its address. Similarly, an instruction to write to a location results in the storage of a word into the quoted address. For example, the word 01100110 may be stored in location address 15 and the word 11000110 in location address 16. A memory word may represent data or an instruction. The topic of memory addressing is dealt with in Chapter 4. The memory's *word length* equates with the number of bits which can be stored in a location. Thus, memory which handles words of 16 bits is known as 16-bit memory, whilst that which makes use of 32-bit words is known as 32-bit memory (the related topic of *processor word length* is dealt with in Chapter 7). In practice, a machine may use words of different lengths for different operations. Word length is one of the most important design characteristics of computers, in that it can be fundamental to the efficiency and speed of the computer. Generally, the larger and more powerful the computer, the greater the word length. Until recently, 32-bit and 64-bit words were largely used by mainframe and minicomputer systems exclusively. When first introduced, microcomputers were 4-bit or 8-bit machines, but advances in technology have made 32-bit and 64-bit microcomputers commonplace.

Even if a machine normally handles words of 16 or 32 or 64 bits, reference sometimes needs to be made to a smaller unit, the *byte*, which is 8 bits. Programming in a low level language requires separate identification of bytes. Table 2.9 illustrates the formation of a 16-bit word, with byte subdivisions. The leftmost bit in a word is referred to as the most significant bit (MSB) and the rightmost as the least significant bit (LSB). The most significant *byte* in a 16-bit word is identified as the *high order byte*, the least significant byte as the *low order byte*.

high order byte								low order byte							
MSB															LSB
15	14	13	12	11	10	9	8	7	6	5	4	3	2	1	0

Table 2.9. *High and low order bytes*

A 32-bit word would be divided into byte-1 (the lowest order byte), byte-2, byte-3 and byte-4 (the highest order byte). A number of different memory structures have been used, based on different word lengths, which have sufficient flexibility to accommodate the requirements of both numeric and non-numeric data.

✎Exercises

1. Why do computers use binary in preference to, for example, the denary system?
2. (i)   Differentiate between *internal* and *external* codes.
    (ii) When may the ASCII or EBCDIC codes be used both internally and externally?
    (iii) What is the name of a device which converts an external code to its internal equivalent and vice versa?
    (iv) What is the purpose of *parity checking*?
3. Give two examples of the use of *control codes*, one relating to display screens and the other to data transmission.
4. (i)   What is a *coded plate transducer*?
    (ii) Why is *Gray code* used instead of standard binary code, to mark the divisions on a coded plate transducer?
    (iii) Give an example of the kind of read error the transducer may produce if standard binary code is used and explain how Gray code avoids such errors.
5. In the context of computer storage and processing, what does *word length* mean and why is it important?

Internal Numbers and Computer Arithmetic

A number stored without indication as to whether it is positive or negative, but simply as having a given magnitude (25_{10}, 129_{10}, for example,) is known as an *unsigned number*. To be of practical use, a computer must be able to store, manipulate and differentiate between positive and negative numbers (*signed numbers*). There are a number of different ways this can be done. The most common are:

- ❏ sign and magnitude;
- ❏ complementation.

Sign and magnitude

With this method, the MSB position is occupied by an explicit *sign bit*; binary 0 and binary 1 are used to indicate, respectively, a positive and a negative number. The remainder of the binary word holds the *absolute* (independent of the sign) *magnitude* of the number. The examples in Table 3.1 illustrate this method, using a 16-bit word.

	MSB															LSB
$+0_{10}$	0	0	0	0	0	0	0	0	0	0	0	0	0	0	0	0
$+33_{10}$	0	0	0	0	0	0	0	0	0	0	1	0	0	0	0	1
-33_{10}	1	0	0	0	0	0	0	0	0	0	1	0	0	0	0	1
$+85_{10}$	0	0	0	0	0	0	0	0	0	1	0	1	0	1	0	1
-85_{10}	1	0	0	0	0	0	0	0	0	1	0	1	0	1	0	1
bit	15	14	13	12	11	10	9	8	7	6	5	4	3	2	1	0
	sign	<						m a g n i t u d e								>

Table 3.1. *Sign and magnitude format*

Note from the top row in Table 3.1, that the number zero uses a positive sign (0).

Two's complement numbers

To follow the computer arithmetic examples in this chapter, you need to know the rules for binary addition, which can be found in Chapter 1.

A computer can carry out *addition*, using *two's complement* notation. *Subtraction* can also be effected, through addition (by first negating the number to be subtracted). A two's complement number has an *implicit sign bit*. In other words, it has a place value which contributes to the magnitude of the number, as well as indicating its sign (positive or negative). Table 3.2 shows two 8-bit examples. The positive number examples (+33 and +85) contain a binary 0 in the sign bit position, so the place value of -128 does not contribute to the magnitude of the numbers.

	MSB	place values						LSB
	-128_{10}	64_{10}	32_{10}	16_{10}	8_{10}	4_{10}	2_{10}	1_{10}
$+33_{10}$	0	0	1	0	0	0	0	1
-33_{10}	1	1	0	1	1	1	1	1
$+85_{10}$	0	1	0	1	0	1	0	1
-85_{10}	1	0	1	0	1	0	1	1
bit	7	6	5	4	3	2	1	0

Table 3.2. *Examples of two's complement, positive and negative numbers*

The negative number examples (-33 and -85) contain a binary 1 in the sign bit position, so its place value of -128 forms part of each number's value. The negative value is calculated by adding the negative place value of the sign bit to the positive values of the remaining bits, which contain a binary 1.

These points can be illustrated with the following analysis of the numbers.

$$+33_{10} = 00100001_2 = 0 + 0 + 32 + 0 + 0 + 0 + 0 + 1$$

$$-33_{10} = 11011111_2 = -128 + 64 + 0 + 16 + 8 + 4 + 2 + 1$$

$$+85_{10} = 01010101_2 = 0 + 64 + 0 + 16 + 0 + 4 + 0 + 1$$

$$-85_{10} = 10101011_2 = -128 + 0 + 32 + 0 + 8 + 0 + 2 + 1$$

Subtraction, using two's complement numbers uses the following method. The second number (the *subtrahend*) is negated and is added to the first (the *minuend*). This is equivalent to expressing in denary, for example,

$$(+55) - (+25) \text{ as } (+55) + (-25).$$

Conversion of binary to two's complement

The two's complement of a binary number is obtained through the following stages:

Stage 1

The number is converted to its *one's complement* representation by inverting the values of all the bits in the number. In other words all ones are flipped to zeroes and all zeroes are flipped to ones.

The examples in Table 3.3 illustrate the one's complements of some binary numbers.

	Example (i) $+13_{10}$	Example (ii) $+36_{10}$	Example (iii) $+76_{10}$
binary number	00001101	00100100	01001100
one's complement	11110010	11011011	10110011

Table 3.3. *One's complement of binary numbers*

Stage 2

The one's complement of the binary numbers in Table 3.3 can then be converted to *two's complement* by adding 1, as shown in Table 3.4.

	Example (i) $+13_{10}$	Example (ii) $+36_{10}$	Example (iii) $+76_{10}$
one's complement	1 1 1 1 0 0 1 0	1 1 0 1 1 0 1 1	1 0 1 1 0 0 1 1
+	1	1	1
two's complement	1 1 1 1 0 0 1 1	1 1 0 1 1 1 0 0	1 0 1 1 0 1 0 0

Table 3.4. *Converting from one's to two's complement*

The two's complement numbers in each example now represent the following denary values.

two's complement of 13_{10} is $-128 + 64 + 32 + 16 + 0 + 0 + 2 + 1 = -13_{10}$

two's complement of 36_{10} is $-128 + 64 + 0 + 16 + 8 + 4 + 0 + 0 = -36_{10}$

two's complement of 76_{10} is $-128 + 0 + 32 + 16 + 0 + 4 + 0 + 0 = -76_{10}$

Integer arithmetic using two's complement

Binary subtraction

Subtraction can be carried out by negating the second number (the *subtrahend*), in this case by conversion to two's complement form and adding it to the first number (the *minuend*). The ease with which binary numbers can be switched from positive to negative and vice-versa, by complementation, makes subtraction by addition suitable for computers.

Consider the examples in Tables 3.5 and 3.6, assuming a 6-bit word length.

minuend	0 1 1 1 0 1		$+29_{10}$
subtrahend	0 0 0 1 1 1		$+7_{10}$
one's complement of subtrahend	1 1 1 0 0 0		
	1	+	
two's complement of subtrahend	1 1 1 0 0 1	=	-7_{10}
minuend	0 1 1 1 0 1	+	$+29_{10}$
result	1 0 1 0 1 1 0	=	
ignore carry (c)	0 1 0 1 1 0		$+22_{10}$

Table 3.5. *Two's complement arithmetic $29_{10} - (+)7_{10} = 22_{10}$*

The result in Table 3.5 (the carry is ignored) can be proved as follows.

$$0101110_2 = 0_{10} + 16_{10} + 0_{10} + 4_{10} + 2_{10} + 0_{10} = 22_{10}.$$

Now consider the example in Table 3.6, where the minuend is smaller than the subtrahend, resulting in a negative answer.

minuend	0 0 0 1 1 1		$+7_{10}$
subtrahend	0 0 1 0 0 1	−	$+9_{10}$
one's complement of subtrahend	1 1 0 1 1 0		
	1	+	
two's complement of subtrahend	1 1 0 1 1 1	=	-9_{10}
minuend	0 0 0 1 1 1	+	$+7_{10}$
result	1 1 1 1 1 0	=	-2_{10}

Table 3.6. *Two's complement arithmetic example* $+7_{10} - (+9_{10}) = -2_{10}$

The result in Table 3.6 can be proved as follows.

$$111110_2 = -32_{10} + 16_{10} + 8_{10} + 4_{10} + 2_{10} + 0_{10} = -2_{10}$$

Number range and arithmetic overflow

The *number range* for any given word is determined by the number of bits in the word and the fact that the MSB is needed to indicate the sign (unless, of course, the number is unsigned). This applies whatever method is used to indicate the sign of numbers. The number range which can be stored in any given word length can be readily calculated. In an 8-bit word using *two's complement* (Table 3.7), the maximum number which can be represented is either +127 ($2^{n-1} - 1$) or −128 (-2^{n-1}), where n = word length.

$01111111_2 =$	$0_{10} + 64_{10} + 32_{10} + 16_{10} + 8_{10} + 4_{10} + 2_{10} + 1_{10} = +127_{10}$
$10000000_2 =$	-128_{10}
	sign bit (bit-8) implicit (−128)

Table 3.7. *Two's complement number range in an 8-bit word*

With *sign and magnitude*, the range is $\pm 127_{10}$ ($\pm 2^{n-1} - 1$), as shown in Table 3.8.

$01111111_2 =$	$+(64_{10} + 32_{10} + 16_{10} + 8_{10} + 4_{10} + 2_{10} + 1_{10}) = +127_{10}$
$11111111_2 =$	$-(64_{10} + 32_{10} + 16_{10} + 8_{10} + 4_{10} + 2_{10} + 1_{10}) = -127_{10}$
	sign bit (bit-8) explicit (0 = +, 1 = −)

Table 3.8. *Sign and magnitude number range in an 8-bit word*

Detection of overflow

If the result of an operation involving two numbers exceeds the maximum permitted by the word, then overflow occurs. For example, with the use of 16-bit words and two's complement arithmetic, overflow occurs if the result is outside of the range -32768_{10} (-2^{16-1}) to $+32767_{10}$ ($2^{16-1} - 1$). Similarly, a 24-bit word would permit a range of -8388608_{10} (-2^{24-1}) to 8388607_{10} ($2^{24-1} - 1$).

Overflow needs to be detected by the computer so that an incorrect result is not overlooked. The hardware in the arithmetic logic unit (ALU) detects an overflow condition by comparing the states of the *carry in* to, and the *carry out* from, the sign bit. If they are not equal, overflow has occurred and the answer is incorrect.

Consider the two's complement examples in the next two tables, assuming an 8-bit word length. The sum in Table 3.9 shows a correct result, but the example in Table 3.10 appears to result in a negative sum (-96); this incorrect result is a consequence of overflow, indicated by the conflicting *carry in* and *carry out* states. Overflow will also occur when two *negative* numbers are added to produce a sum beyond the range of the word.

	64_{10}	0 1 0 0 0 0 0 0
+	4_{10}	0 0 0 0 0 1 0 0
=	68_{10}	0 1 0 0 0 1 0 0
	carry	0 0

Table 3.9. *Sum with no arithmetic overflow*

	96_{10}	0 1 1 0 0 0 0 0	
+	64_{10}	0 1 0 0 0 0 0 0	
=	-96_{10}	1 0 1 0 0 0 0 0	incorrect answer
	carry	0 1	carries differ - overflow

Table 3.10. *Incorrect sum resulting from overflow*

An *overflow flag* (a single bit) in the *condition codes*, *status* or *flag register* is set as soon as an overflow occurs. Thus, following the execution of an arithmetic process, a low level programmer can include a single test on the overflow flag to determine whether or not incorrect results are due to arithmetic overflow. Other machines may use the flag to implement an *interrupt* (see Chapter 13), which interrupts the CPU operation, to suspend processing and display an error message. The problem of limited number range and the need for accuracy can be overcome by the use of two or more words of memory to store a single number.

Real numbers

The first part of this section has concentrated on the storage and handling of *integers*. Although a programmer could choose to restrict numbers to integer format, all general-purpose computers must be able to deal with *real numbers*. Real numbers include all the integers and fractions of a number system, that is, all numbers above and below zero and including zero. Many computer applications require the use of numbers with a fractional element, that is, real numbers. Clearly, this can provide for a greater level of accuracy than is permitted by integer numbers, but at the cost of increased storage requirements. There are two basic methods of representing real numbers in computer storage:

❑ fixed-point representation;

❑ floating-point representation.

Fixed-point representation

Fixed-point numbers use what can be seen as a conventional format. The binary point is *assumed* to be immediately to the right of the integer part, which is where we would locate the decimal point if we were expressing real denary values. A programmer can require the binary point to be in any position within a memory word, according to the number of bits he or she wishes to assign to the integer and fractional parts. If more bits in a memory word are assigned to the fractional part, greater precision is possible; on the other hand fewer bits are then available for the integer part and this reduces the magnitude range. Conversely, increasing the proportion of a word given to the integer part increases the magnitude range, but reduces the possible level of precision. Table 3.11 illustrates fixed point format.

integer part	.	fractional part

Table 3.11. *Fixed point format*

Of course, a programmer may equally assume a given memory word to be entirely integer, with no fractional part. The binary point is said to have an *assumed* position which gives meaning to a number. Using 8-bit words, the programmer may instruct that the binary points for two numbers, labelled (i) and (ii), are located as shown in Table 3.12.

	integer part	fractional part
(i) 2.75_{10}	0 0 0 0 1 0 .	1 1$_2$
(ii) 28.25_{10}	0 1 1 1 0 0 .	0 1$_2$

Table 3.12. *Fixed point numbers*

If the programmer then relocates the binary points, as shown in Table 3.13, the same binary groupings take on different values. The point for number (i) is shifted one place to the left, which *halves* its value; the point in number (ii) is shifted one place to the right, which *doubles* its value (for clarification of this, refer to Chapter 4). Therefore, a programmer using fixed point numbers must keep track of the point position in order to know their value. This problem is of particular concern to the programmer using low level languages.

	integer part		fractional part
(i) 1.375_{10}	0 0 0 0 1 .		0 1 1$_2$
(ii) 56.5_{10}	0 1 1 1 0 0 0 .		1$_2$

Table 3.13. *Fixed point numbers after moving point*

If a programmer is using fixed point numbers, this simply means that the decisions on the degree of precision are made by the programmer. If no floating point facility is available, the programmer must use integer arithmetic (see earlier) and set the precision after each calculation. The practicalities of this are of concern to the low level programmer, but briefly, involve the *scaling* of numbers to remove any fractional part, carrying out integer arithmetic and then re-scaling the result to the required number of fractional places. Today, all computers provide a floating point number facility, but there was a time when a programmer had to represent all real numbers in fixed point form. As explained later, floating point numbers require a longer word length than 8 bits, which was the norm, for example, for the first generation of microcomputers.

Number range and precision of fixed point numbers

Continuing with the topic of fixed point numbers, consider a 16-bit word with the binary point assumed to be between the bit-4 and bit-5 positions; sign and magnitude format is being used, so the sign bit (shown in bold) occupies the most significant bit position, which leaves 10 bits for the integral part and 5 bits for the fractional part of the number. The number range which can be represented is limited to that given in Table 3.14.

Positive 0_{10} to $+1023.96875_{10}$	Negative 0_{10} to -1024_{10}
00000000000 · 00000$_2$	00000000000 · 00000$_2$
01111111111 · 11111$_2$	10000000000 · 00000$_2$
sign	sign

Table 3.14. *Example sign and magnitude range*

Precision is limited by the number of bits allocated to the fractional part of the number and no matter what word length is used, some loss of precision is, occasionally, inevitable.

Arithmetic overflow

Consider the multiplication of two denary values in Table 3.15, where only 1 place is available for the integer part and 3 places for the fractional part. The maximum positive value the location can hold is $9 \cdot 999_{10}$. Although such a location is large enough to hold each of the two numbers to be multiplied, the product of $11 \cdot 057$ (after rounding to 3 decimal places) results in an arithmetic overflow error. Given a particular word length for *fixed point* numbers, the allocation of more bits to the fractional part improves precision but at the

| $1 \cdot 363_{10} \times 8.112_{10} = 11 \cdot 057_{10}$ | The 10s digit is lost |

Table 3.15. *Multiplication resulting in overflow*

cost of reduced number range. Conversely, the result of the above multiplication could be accommodated if 2 places are given to the integer part, but this would leave one less bit for the fractional element and consequently, reduced precision.

Arithmetic underflow

This condition occurs when a number (a fraction or a negative number) is too small to fit into a given length word. The denary example in Table 3.16 illustrates underflow which results from the smallness of a fraction. Provision is made for a maximum of 3 decimal places. Multiplication of the two decimal fractions gives a product which underflows, giving an erroneous result of zero. Another example illustrates how a

| $0 \cdot 125_{10} \times 0 \cdot 005_{10} = 0 \cdot 000625_{10}$ | underflow error |

Table 3.16. *Arithmetic underflow*

negative number can underflow and result in more serious error; given the provision of only two integer places, $-99_{10} \times 2_{10}$ gives a product of -198_{10}, which does not fit.

The main drawback of fixed point form is the small range of numbers which can be represented. *Floating-point* number representation helps overcome this problem at the cost of slightly slower computation and some reduction in precision; this latter point is discussed later.

Floating-point representation

A *mantissa* and *exponent* (or *index*) can be used to represent a number. Denary numbers, written in *standard index* form, reveal a format similar to that used for the storage of binary floating point numbers.

Examples of binary floating point and denary standard index numbers are given in Table 3.17. Note that the formats are not exactly the same.

binary	binary floating point		denary	denary standard index	
	mantissa *m*	exponent r^e		mantissa	exponent
$101 \cdot 0101_2$	$0 \cdot 1010101_2$	$\times 2^3$	$6,800,000_{10}$	$6 \cdot 8_{10}$	$\times 10^6$
$0 \cdot 0011001_2$	$0 \cdot 11001_2$	$\times 2^{-2}$	$0 \cdot 0000564_{10}$	$5 \cdot 64_{10}$	$\times 10^{-5}$

Table 3.17. *Binary floating point and denary standard index examples*

In floating-point notation, the point is not fixed by the programmer. Instead it remains in a position at the left of the mantissa. Floating-point notation is based on the expression: $m \times r^e$, where *m* is positive or negative and *e* is positive or negative, *m* is the mantissa, *r* is the radix or base and e is the exponent (power). In binary, the radix is 2 (see Chapter 1).

Fixed-point numbers can be converted to floating-point numbers by a process of *normalisation*. As the first example $(101 \cdot 0101_2)$ in Table 3.17 shows, if the number is *greater than* 1_2 then the point floats to the left (actually achieved by shifting the mantissa to the right), to a position immediately before the most significant bit. This part becomes the mantissa (m). The point in Table 3.17 has moved 3 places to the left, the mantissa is now $0 \cdot 1010101_2$ and the exponent (e) is therefore, 3. The second example $(0 \cdot 0011001_2)$ in Table 3.17 shows that, if the number is a *fraction* and a binary 1 does not immediately follow the point, then the point floats to the right (actually achieved by shifting the mantissa to the left) of any leading zeros, until the first non-zero bit is reached; the mantissa becomes $0 \cdot 11001_2$. The point has moved 2 places to the right, so the exponent (e) is -2. Two more examples are given in the next two tables.

fixed point	binary floating point	
	mantissa m	exponent r^e
$1110 \cdot 001_2$	$0 \cdot 1110001_2$	$\times 2^4$

Table 3.18. *Fixed point > binary 1 converted to floating point*

fixed point	binary floating point	
	mantissa m	exponent r^e
$0 \cdot 000111_2$	$0 \cdot 1110000_2$	$\times 2^{-3}$

Table 3.19. *Fixed point < binary 1 converted to floating point*

In Table 3.18, the point moves four places to the left, so the exponent is 4.

In Table 3.19, the fraction is normalised by moving the point three places to the right, so the exponent is -3. The floating point format (there are alternatives) used in this text follows a number of rules.

❏ With normalised *positive* numbers the binary point must not be followed immediately by a binary 0. Only positive, floating point number examples have been provided so far.

❏ Conversely, normalised *negative* numbers require that the binary point is not followed immediately by a binary 1. The next section, on storage of floating point numbers, describes the format for negative numbers in more detail.

❏ Any normalised binary mantissa must be a fraction falling within the range +0.5 to less than +1 for positive values and -1 to less than -0.5 for negative values. The range of possible normalised 4-bit mantissas is shown in Table 3.20.

positive mantissas	denary equivalent	negative mantissas	denary equivalent
$0 \cdot 100_2$	$+\frac{1}{2}$	$1 \cdot 000_2$	-1
$0 \cdot 101_2$	$+\frac{5}{8}$	$1 \cdot 001_2$	$-\frac{7}{8}$
$0 \cdot 110_2$	$+\frac{3}{4}$	$1 \cdot 010_2$	$-\frac{3}{4}$
$0 \cdot 111_2$	$+\frac{7}{8}$	$1 \cdot 011_2$	$-\frac{5}{8}$

Table 3.20. *Range of possible normalised, 4-bit mantissas, with zero exponent*

Storage of floating-point numbers

As already indicated, floating-point numbers are stored in two parts:

❏ The *mantissa*, the length of which is determined by the precision to which numbers are represented. Clearly, if fewer bits are allocated to the mantissa (which is always a left-justified fraction) then less precision is possible.

❏ The *exponent*, which is usually allocated one-third to one-half of the number of bits used for the mantissa.

Table 3.21 assumes the use of a 16-bit word for the storage of each floating-point number, in two's complement form, 12 bits being used for the mantissa and 4 bits for the exponent.

sign	mantissa (fraction)										exponent (integer)			
bit 15	14	13	12	11	10	9	8	7	6	5	4	3	2	1	0

Table 3.21. *Example floating point format using a 16-bit word*

The binary point in the mantissa fraction is immediately to the right of the sign bit, which is 0 for a positive and 1 for a negative floating-point number. Table 3.22 illustrates these points.

positive floating point form		negative floating point form	
12 bits	4 bits	12 bits	4 bits
0 · 1 * * * * * * * * * *	* * * *	1 · 0 * * * * * * * * * *	* * * * *
mantissa	exponent	mantissa	exponent

Table 3.22. *Positive and negative representation in floating point form*

In two's complement form, the most significant digit to the right of the binary point is 1 for a positive and 0 for a negative floating-point number. It should be noticed that the sign bit and the most significant non-sign bit differ in both cases. As explained earlier, any representation where they are the same indicates that the mantissa needs to be normalised. This may be necessary after any floating-point arithmetic operation.

Floating-point conversion

To obtain the denary equivalent of a number held in floating point form requires the mantissa to be multiplied by 2, raised to the *power* of e, which has the value stored in the exponent part of the number. For example, the floating point number in Table 3.23, which uses 8 bits for the mantissa and 4 bits for the exponent, converts to denary as follows.

8-bit mantissa		4-bit exponent
0 · 1 1 0 1 0 0 1	×	0 1 0 1 (2^5)

Table 3.23. *Floating point number*

$$0 \cdot 1101001_2 \times 2^5 = 11010 \cdot 01_2 \text{ (moving the binary point 5 places to the right)}$$

$$= (16 + 8 + 2 + \tfrac{1}{4}) = 26\,\tfrac{1}{4}$$

Therefore, the floating point number $0 \cdot 1101001_2 \times 2^5$ is equivalent to fixed point $11010 \cdot 01_2$. If 4 bits are allocated to the exponent, e can have a value between $+7$ and -8 (assuming two's complement form). Alternatively, in a 16-bit machine, two words with a total of 32 bits may be used to store each floating-point number, the mantissa occupying 24 bits, and the exponent, 8 bits. In such a representation, the exponent e could have a value between +127 and −128 (assuming two's complement). The earlier section entitled Number Range and Arithmetic Overflow gives an explanation of these calculations.

Alternative floating-point forms

Different machines may use different methods for coding floating-point numbers. The mantissa may be coded in two's complement, as described previously, or it may be stored as sign and magnitude. The advantage for machine arithmetic of storing numbers in two's complement form has already been identified, but machines with the circuitry to handle floating-point numbers may also have the facility to carry out subtraction without two's complement representation. The above illustrations of floating-point numbers assume that the exponent is also stored in two's complement form. In practice, the exponent is often stored in sign and magnitude.

Floating-point arithmetic

The floating point addition and subtraction examples used in this section assume the use of a 6-bit mantissa and a 4-bit exponent. Both mantissa and exponent are expressed in two's complement form.

Addition

To add two floating-point numbers, they must both have the same value exponent. If they differ, the necessary *scaling* is achieved by *shifting*, to the right (equivalent to the binary point floating to the left), the mantissa of the number with the smaller exponent and *incrementing* the exponent at every shift until the exponents are equal. The shifting process follows the rules for arithmetic shifts, which are described in Chapter 4.

The addition procedure consists of equalising the exponents by scaling, adding the mantissas and then, if necessary, normalising the result. Tables 3.25 to 3.26 illustrate the floating-point addition procedure with the example sum in Table 3.24.

	mantissa		exponent	
6.75_{10}	$0 \cdot 1 1 0 1 1_2$	$\times$	$0 0 1 1_2$	2^3
$+12.50_{10}$	$0 \cdot 1 1 0 0 1_2$	$\times$	$0 1 0 0_2$	2^4

Table 3.24. *Binary floating point sum $6.75_{10} + 12.5_{10} = 19.25_{10}$*

❏ *Scaling*. In Table 3.25, the mantissa with the smaller exponent is shifted one place to the right and the exponent is incremented. As a result, a binary 1 is lost from the least significant bit position.

mantissa		exponent		mantissa		exponent
$0 \cdot 1 1 0 1 1_2$	$\times$	$0 0 1 1_2$	scales to	$0 \cdot 0 1 1 0 1_2$	$\times$	$0 1 0 0_2$
6.75_{10}		2^3		LSB (1) lost		2^4

Table 3.25. *Equalise the exponents by scaling*

❏ *Add the mantissas.* Table 3.26 shows that this is clearly incorrect, because the sign bit is now 1, indicating a negative value, when the result should be positive. The method by which the computer detects this type of error is explained earlier in the section on Arithmetic Overflow.

	mantissa		exponent	
	$0 \cdot 0 1 1 0 1_2$	×	$0 1 0 0_2$	2^4
+	$0 \cdot 1 1 0 0 1_2$	×	$0 1 0 0_2$	2^4
=	$1 \cdot 0 0 1 1 0_2$	×	$0 1 0 0_2$	2^4

Table 3.26. *Mantissas added*

❏ Normalise the result (1.00110_2) shown in Table 3.26, which is beyond the permitted range (see Table 3.20) for a positive number. Table 3.27 shows the result of shifting the mantissa one place to the right and incrementing the exponent.

mantissa		exponent	
$0 \cdot 1 0 0 1 1_2$	×	$0 1 0 1_2$	2^5

Table 3.27. *Result normalised*

The floating-point result in Table 3.27 can be expressed as follows.

$0 \cdot 10011_2 \times 2^5 = 10011_2$ (moving the binary point 5 places to the right)

$= 16{+}2{+}1 = 19_{10}$

Some loss of accuracy has resulted (19_{10} instead of $19 \cdot 25_{10}$). The loss of accuracy results from the right-shift operation required to equalise the exponents (Table 3.25); a significant bit is lost when the binary value for $6 \cdot 75_{10}$, ($0 \cdot 11011_2 \times 2^3$) becomes $6 \cdot 5_{10}$ ($0 \cdot 01101_2 \times 2^4$). The decimal value of this discarded bit is its fractional value of 1/32, multiplied by the exponent (before scaling) of 2^3(8), giving a result of $0 \cdot 25_{10}$. Although a further right-shift is needed to normalise the result (Table 3.27), the discarded bit is a 0 and does not produce any additional inaccuracy.

Subtraction

The procedures for subtraction are the same as for addition except that the mantissas are subtracted. This can be achieved by negating the subtrahend and then adding it to the minuend. In denary, this is the same as saying $12 \cdot 5_{10} + (-6 \cdot 75_{10}) = 5 \cdot 75_{10}$. Consider

	mantissa		exponent	
$12 \cdot 50_{10}$	$0 \cdot 1 1 0 0 1_2$	×	$0 1 0 0_2$	2^4
$-6 \cdot 75_{10}$	$0 \cdot 1 1 0 1 1_2$	×	$0 0 1 1_2$	2^3

Table 3.28. *$12.5_{10} - 6.75_{10} = 5.75_{10}$*

this example, shown in Table 3.28. The procedures for carrying out this subtraction, using floating point arithmetic are illustrated in Tables 3.29 to 3.32.

❏ Scale the mantissa (Table 3.29) with the smaller exponent and increment the exponent, repeatedly if necessary, until the exponents of the two numbers are equalised. In this case, one right-shift is needed.

mantissa		exponent		mantissa		exponent
$0 \cdot 1 1 0 1 1_2$	×	$0 0 1 1_2$	scales to	$0 \cdot 0 1 1 0 1_2$	×	$0 1 0 0_2$
6.75_{10}		2^3		LSB (1) lost		2^4

Table 3.29. *Scale mantissas*

❏   Negate the subtrahend by finding the two's complement of its mantissa, as shown in Table 3.30.

	mantissa
6.75_{10}	$0 \cdot 0 1 1 0 1_2$
One's complement	$1 \cdot 1 0 0 1 0_2$
+	1_2
Two's complement	$1 \cdot 1 0 0 1 1_2$

Table 3.30. *Convert subtrahend to two's complement*

❏   Add the mantissas, as shown in Table 3.31; the carry of binary 1 is ignored.

	mantissa		exponent	
	$0 \cdot 1 1 0 0 1_2$	×	$0 1 0 0_2$	2^4
+	$1 \cdot 1 0 0 1 1_2$	×	$0 1 0 0_2$	2^4
=	$1 0 \cdot 0 1 1 0 0_2$	×	$0 1 0 0_2$	2^4
	carry ignored			

Table 3.31. *Add the mantissas*

❏   If necessary, normalise the result. In this case, the answer is not in normal form because the sign bit and the most significant bit to the right of the binary point, are the same. The result is normalised by carrying out a left-shift of one on the mantissa and decrementing the exponent accordingly; the result is shown in Table 3.32.

mantissa		exponent	
$0 \cdot 1 1 0 0 0_2$	×	$0 0 1 1_2$	2^3
zero inserted in LSB position			

Table 3.32. *Normalise the result*

The result in denary = $0 \cdot 1 1 0 0 0_2 \times 2^3 = 1 1 0 \cdot 0 0_2$ (moving the binary point 3 places to the right) = $2 + 4 = 6_{10}$. Note that a zero (in bold) is inserted into the least significant bit position of the mantissa. This floating point example has resulted in some significant loss of accuracy (and answer of 6_{10} instead of $5 \cdot 75_{10}$). In reality, inaccuracies of this order would clearly be intolerable and techniques are used to ensure that floating point arithmetic operations produce the degree of precision needed for the most demanding applications. Some aspects of these techniques are introduced in the next section.

Fixed point versus floating point representation

Precision. As stated earlier, given a particular word length, fixed point representation allows greater precision than is possible with floating point form. Consider, for example, a word length of six bits, used to store wholly fractional numbers. In fixed point form, all the bit positions can be used by significant digits, but in floating point form, if two bits are reserved for the exponent, this leaves only four bits for the mantissa and thus a maximum of four figure precision.

Range. As is demonstrated in the previous section, a major advantage of floating point form is the facility for storing an increased number range.

Maintenance of floating point arithmetic precision

Floating-point arithmetic precision can be improved by: increasing the number of bits allocated to the mantissa; rounding; double precision numbers and arithmetic.

Mantissa length

Increasing the number of bits allocated to the *mantissa* will improve precision but inaccuracies can never be completely eliminated. In practice, memory words are much longer than those used for illustration here and where memory words are of insufficient length to ensure acceptable accuracy, two adjacent locations may be used. Machines which make use of this method are providing what is referred to as *double-precision floating-point* facilities.

Rounding

The subtraction example in Tables 3.28 to 3.32 demonstrates a loss of accuracy through *truncation*; a significant bit 1 is lost when the mantissa is shifted one place to the right, in order to equalise the exponents of the minuend and the subtrahend. If a computer process requires a series of calculations, each using the results of previous ones, repeated truncation may accrue considerable inaccuracy and this will be reflected in the final result. As can be seen from the example of floating-point addition in Tables 3.24 to 3.27, the process of normalising the result also requires the shifting or justification of the mantissa.

Consider the example in Table 3.33, which only shows the mantissas to illustrate the normalisation process. In Table 3.33, normalisation has resulted in the loss of a binary 1 from the least significant bit position (a 0 is inserted into the sign bit position) and consequent loss of accuracy. Rounding dictates that, if during an arithmetic shift the last bit to be discarded (the *most significant* of those which are lost) is a 1, then 1 is added to the *least significant* retained bit.

	mantissa	
	0.1001_2	
+	0.1100_2	
=	1.0101_2	sign bit now 1
	0.10101_2	right shift of 1

Table 3.33. *Normalisation of mantissa*

Consider an 8-bit mantissa, rounded as in Table 3.34. The accumulated errors caused by repeated truncation of values during a lengthy arithmetic process can partially, though not entirely, be avoided by rounding. In practice, rounding can sometimes result in greater inaccuracies than would result without rounding. Many rounding algorithms exist to try to overcome this problem and the type of inaccuracy which occasionally occurs will depend on the rounding algorithm.

	7 bits	10101111_2
101011101_2	6 bits	101011_2
rounded to	5 bits	10110_2
	4 bits	1011_2

Table 3.34. *Rounding*

Double precision numbers and arithmetic

As the term (also known as *double length numbers*) suggests, where a single memory word is of insufficient length to accommodate a number, two contiguous words are used. Double precision numbers may be used to increase precision or when the product of a multiplication operation will not fit into a single location. The example addition in Table 3.35 provides a basic idea of double precision arithmetic; in the example, each number occupies two contiguous 4-bit *nibbles*.

most significant half		least significant half		
0	1 0 1	0	0 1 0	$1 0 1 0 1 0_2 = 42_{10}$
0	0 0 1	0	1 1 1	$0 0 1 1 1 1_2 = 15_{10}$
0		1	0 0 1	{1}
0	0 0 1			{2}
0	0 1 0			{2}
0		0	0 0 1	{3}
0	1 0 1			{4}
0	1 1 1	0	0 0 1	{4} $1 1 1 0 0 1_2 = 57_{10}$
sign		carry		

Table 3.35. *Double precision arithmetic*

The procedure is also described with the pseudocode algorithm in Listing 3.1.

Listing 3.1.   Double precision arithmetic

```
{double precision}
add least significant halves of numbers {1}
if carry = 1 then
  add 1 to most significant half {2}
  set carry bit to 0 {3}
endif
add most significant halves of numbers {4}
```

Floating-point multiplication and division

To multiply two floating-point numbers, the mantissas are multiplied and their exponents are added. For simplicity, the multiplication process is illustrated using denary, but the principles are the same for binary floating point numbers. Tables 3.36 to 3.38 illustrate the process.

mantissa		exponent			mantissa		exponent
$0 \cdot 3$	$\times$	10^3	multiplied by		$0 \cdot 2$	$\times$	10^4

Table 3.36. *Floating point multiplication $300_{10} \times 2000_{10}$*

❑   Multiply mantissas and add exponents.

mantissa		exponent
$0 \cdot 06$	$\times$	10^7

Table 3.37. *Result of multiplying mantissas and adding exponents*

❑ Normalise the result; the exponent is decremented each time the mantissa is shifted one position to the left.

mantissa		exponent
$0 \cdot 6$	×	10^6

Table 3.38. *Normalise result*

Tables 3.39 to 3.41 show a second example.

mantissa		exponent		mantissa		exponent
$0 \cdot 237$	×	10^2	multiplied by	$0 \cdot 415$	×	10^3

Table 3.39. *Floating point multiplication $23 \cdot 7_{10} \times 415_{10}$*

❑ Multiply mantissas and add exponents.

mantissa		exponent
$0 \cdot 098355$	×	10^5

Table 3.40. *Result of multiplying mantissas and adding exponents*

❑ Normalise the result; the exponent is decremented each time the mantissa is shifted one position to the left.

mantissa		exponent
$0 \cdot 98355$	×	10^4

Table 3.41. *Normalise result*

Floating-point division is carried out by dividing the mantissas and subtracting their exponents.

Hardware and software control of computer arithmetic

The execution of computer arithmetic operations often involves a mixture of hardware and software control. However, all modern computers are equipped with additional circuitry to handle floating-point numbers directly.

Excess codes

Excess-128

An excess code involves the addition of an excess to the value to be represented. Thus, an 8-bit *excess-128* code would add 128_{10} to each byte. The excess-128 representations for $+26_{10}$ and -42_{10} are shown in Table 3.42.

$+26_{10}$	0 0 0 1 1 0 1 0	-42_{10}	1 1 0 1 0 1 1 0
$+128_{10}$	1 0 0 0 0 0 0 0	$+128_{10}$	1 0 0 0 0 0 0 0
$=154_{\text{excess-128}}$	1 0 0 1 1 0 1 0	$=86_{\text{excess-128}}$	0 1 0 1 0 1 1 0

Table 3.42. *Excess-128 numbers*

The number range for 8 bits, without an excess, is -128 to $+127$. Adding an excess of 128 means the range becomes 0 to 255; effectively, the excess makes all numbers in the range positive and unsigned.

An advantage of the excess code is that no complementation is needed for arithmetic; Table 3.43 provides an example.

$+26_{10}$ becomes $154_{\text{excess-128}}$	1 0 0 1 1 0 1 0
-42_{10} becomes $86_{\text{excess-128}}$	0 1 0 1 0 1 1 0
=	1 1 1 1 0 0 0 0
subtract 128_{10}, as answer is in excess-256	1 0 0 0 0 0 0 0
$= -16_{10}$ or $112_{\text{excess-128}}$	0 1 1 1 0 0 0 0

Table 3.43. *Example $+26-42_{10}$ using excess-128 numbers*

Another advantage stems from the fact that an illegal result, that is one outside of the permitted range, is easily identified. Table 3.44 shows an example sum, with an illegal result; the binary 1 in the bit-8 position indicates a result outside of the number range.

$+122_{10}$ becomes $250_{\text{excess-128}}$	1 1 1 1 1 0 1 0
112_{10} becomes $240_{\text{excess-128}}$	1 1 1 1 0 0 0 0
produces carry of 1 into bit-8 position	1 1 1 1 0 1 0 1 0
subtract 128_{10}, as answer is in excess-256	1 0 0 0 0 0 0 0
carry of 1 into bit-8 signals error	1 0 1 1 0 1 0 1 0

Table 3.44. *Excess-128 sum with result out of range*

Excess-3

Each excess-3 code is 3 greater than its binary-code decimal (BCD) equivalent. For example, denary 2 in excess-3 code is 5 (2+3) or 0101_2. The excess-3 codes for all the denary symbols, are given in Table 3.45.

n_{10}	$n_{10} + 3_{10}$	excess-3	n_{10}	$n_{10} + 3_{10}$	excess-3
0	3	0 0 1 1	5	8	1 0 0 0
1	4	0 1 0 0	6	9	1 0 0 1
2	5	0 1 0 1	7	10	1 0 1 0
3	6	0 1 1 0	8	11	1 0 1 1
4	7	0 1 1 1	9	12	1 1 0 0

Table 3.45. *Excess-3 codes*

Any of the excess-3 binary codes can now be complemented (nine's complement), for the purposes of subtraction, without the production of any invalid codes. The nine's complements of each the excess-3 codes in Table 3.45, are listed in Table 3.46.

n_{10}	excess-3	nine's complement	n_{10}	excess-3	nine's complement
0	0011	1100	5	1000	0111
1	0100	1011	6	1001	0110
2	0101	1010	7	1010	0101
3	0110	1001	8	1011	0100
4	0111	1000	9	1100	0011

Table 3.46. *Excess-3 codes and nines complements*

Before subtraction, 1 is added to the subtrahend, to form the ten's complement. Subtraction can then be carried out, by addition (in the same way as two's complement numbers).

Excess-3 addition

Excess-3 addition requires that: if there is a carry, add 3; if there is no carry, subtract 3.

	carry	excess-3	carry	excess-3	carry	excess-3
746		1010		0111		1001
+168		0100		1001		1011
=		1110	1	0000	1	0100
add carries		1		1		
=		1111		0001		0100
add 3 if carry				+1 1		+1 1
=		1111		0100		0111
subtract 3 if no carry		−1 1				
= 914		1100		0100		0111

Table 3.47. *Excess-3 addition*

BCD arithmetic

The valid BCD (binary-coded decimal) codes are given in Chapter 2. A problem of using BCD numbers is that, using normal integer arithmetic, an addition would sometimes produce invalid BCD numbers; 10 to 15 are illegal codes. So, for example, when 5_{10} (0101_2) is added to 7_{10} (0111_2), the result of 12_{10} (1100_2) is not a valid BCD number. The problem of invalid codes is dealt with as follows.

❑ Six is added to a BCD code if, during the addition process: an *illegal code* is produced; **or** if there is an *overflow carry* from the 4-bit BCD code.

Consider the addition examples in Tables 3.48 and 3.49

	carry	BCD	carry	BCD	carry	BCD
746		0111		0100		0110
+168		0001		0110		1000
=		1000		1010		1110
add 6 if illegal code **or** if carry beyond 4 bits				110		110
=		1000	1	0000	1	0100
add in carries		1		1		
= 914		1001		0001		0100

Table 3.48. *BCD addition $746_{BCD} + 168_{BCD} = 914_{BCD}$*

If both circumstances occur in respect of one BCD code, 6 is only added once. Table 3.49 illustrates such a case.

	carry	BCD	carry	BCD	carry	BCD
269		0 0 1 0		0 1 1 0		1 0 0 1
+549		0 1 0 1		0 1 0 0		1 0 0 1
=		0 1 1 1		1 0 1 0	1	0 0 1 0
add 6 if illegal code or if carry beyond 4 bits						1 1 0
=		0 1 1 1	1	1 0 1 0	1	1 0 0 0
add in carries				1		
=		0 1 1 1		1 0 1 1		1 0 0 0
add 6 if illegal code or if carry beyond 4 bits				1 1 0		
=			1	0 0 0 1		
add in carries		1				
=818		1 0 0 0		0 0 0 1		1 0 0 0

Table 3.49. *BCD addition $269_{BCD} + 549_{BCD} = 818_{BCD}$*

✍Exercises

1. (i) If a computer uses a 16-bit word to represent integers, show how the numbers 30_{10} and 362_{10} would be represented in *binary coded decimal* (BCD).

   (ii) Show how the same computer would represent the values -30, -72 and -473 in (a) *sign and magnitude* and (b) *two's complement*.

2. Using two's complement representation and an 8-bit word, calculate the following:

   (i) $42 + 74$;

   (ii) $74 - 42$;

   (iii) $35 - 46$.

3. Use the addition $75 + 96$ to illustrate *arithmetic overflow* and explain how the computer's circuitry might detect the condition. Assume use of an 8-bit word.

4. What would be the denary, integer *number range*, for a 12-bit word, using two's complement representation?

5. Why is the number range for sign and magnitude different from that for two's complement?

6. If real numbers are to be represented in fixed point format, how does the low-level programmer determine the degree of precision?

7. How does floating point notation allow greater number range, for a given word length, than fixed point notation?

8. Given a particular word length, why does fixed point notation allow greater precision than floating point notation? Use an example to illustrate.

9. A particular computer uses a 16-bit word to store floating point numbers, allocating 10 bits to the mantissa and 6 bits to the exponent; both parts are stored in two's complement notation. Numbers are normalised when the bit immediately to the right of the binary point has a value of 1. The format is illustrated on the next page.

sign	binary point												
		mantissa							exponent				

(i)   Calculate the denary values of:

    a.   0110100101000011

    b.   1010010100100101

    c.   00010101010011101

(ii)   Write down the bit patterns to represent the following numbers, in normalised form:

    a.   +5.4

    b.   − 0.625

(iii) Add the numbers in part (ii), showing each stage, as described in the text.

(iv)   Subtract 4.25 from 10.75, showing each stage as described in the text.

10. In the context of floating point arithmetic, what is meant by *arithmetic underflow*? Give an example of this condition

11. How can the precision of floating point numbers be improved?

12. Convert the following floating point numbers to fixed point notation:

    (i) 0.1101011×0110

    (ii) 0.1001111×1100

    (iii) 1.010011×1010

    (iv) 1.011101×0011

13. Using an 8-bit word, convert the following numbers to excess-128:

    (i) 37_{10}

    (ii) 25_{10}

14. In the context of computer arithmetic, what benefit may derive from the use of excess-128 code?

15. (i)   List the valid BCD codes;

    (ii) Use BCD arithmetic for the following sums:

        a.   347 + 216

        b.   514 + 112

Chapter 4

Computer Instructions

This chapter deals with activity of the Central Processing Unit (CPU) and the ways in which computer program instructions are stored, interpreted and executed in order that the computer can perform its tasks. The various methods for addressing memory are also examined. In Chapter 2 it is stated that data can take various forms when stored as a *memory word*, namely:

❏ pure binary;

❏ coded binary, for example, binary-coded decimal (BCD);

❏ character codes, for example, ASCII.

All the above are considered to be *data* and can be interpreted as such by the CPU, but in order to perform any tasks, it has to have access to computer *instructions*. During processing, data currently being processed and the instructions needed to process the data are stored in main memory. Thus, a memory word can also form an instruction, in which case, it is referred to as an *instruction word*; one formed from data is known as a *data word*.

The central processing unit (CPU)

The CPU has a number of *registers* which it can use to temporarily store a number of words read from memory. These registers are used to apply meaning to memory words. It should be noted that memory words cannot be determined as being data or instructions simply by examination of the code. The CPU differentiates between data and instructions by locating:

❏ instructions in an *instruction register*;

❏ data in *data registers*.

A computer program stored in main memory comprises a sequence of instructions, each of which is transferred, in turn, into the CPUs instruction register, thus identifying the next operation which the CPU is to perform. The instructions are retrieved from consecutive memory locations, unless the last instruction executed requires the next one to be fetched from a different location. Those dealing with the latter circumstance are called *branch* or *jump* instructions. The various types of instruction are described later. The process of fetching, interpreting and executing instructions is called the *fetch-execute cycle* but may also be referred to as the *instruction cycle* or *automatic sequence control*.

As indicated in Chapter 6, the *control unit* has the function of governing all hardware operation, including the activities of the CPU itself. To understand the fetch-execute cycle it is necessary to be aware of the names and functions of the various CPU *registers* used.

The program counter (PC)

The PC keeps track of the locations where instructions are stored. At any one time during a program's execution the PC holds the memory address of the next instruction to be executed. Its operation is possible because, in all computer systems, the instructions forming a program are stored in adjacent memory locations, so that the next instruction will normally (except when a branch instruction is executed) be stored in an address a single increment more than the address of the last instruction to be fetched. By incrementing the address in the PC each time an instruction is received, the PC always has the address of the next instruction to be retrieved.

The program counter is also known by a variety of other names, including the *Sequence Control Register* (SCR) and the *Instruction Address Register* (IAR).

Memory buffer register (MBR)

Whenever the contents of a memory word are to be transferred into or out of main memory, they pass through the MBR. This applies to both data and instructions.

Memory address register (MAR)

The MAR provides the location address of the specific memory word (both instructions and data) to be read from or written to memory via the MBR.

Current instruction register (CIR)

As the name suggests, the function of the CIR is to store the current instruction for decoding and execution.

Accumulators and general-purpose registers

These registers are situated within the arithmetic/logic unit (ALU) and provide a working area for data fetched from memory. Values about to be added or subtracted can be copied, via the MBR, into the accumulators. The arithmetic result can be placed in one accumulator and copied from there into a main memory location.

All communications between the CPU and the memory take place through the MBR, as Figure 4.1 illustrates.

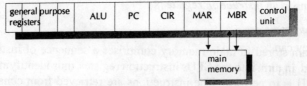

Figure 4.1. *CPU registers used in fetch-execute cycle*

In order to fetch an instruction from memory the CPU places the address of the instruction in the MAR and then carries out a memory read; the instruction is then copied into the MBR and from there, into the CIR.

Similarly, an instruction which itself requires the reading of a particular data word causes the address of the data word to be placed into the MAR. The execution of the memory read then results in the copying of the addressed data word into the MBR, from where it can be accessed by the processor.

❑ The MBR acts as the point of transfer for both data and instructions passing, in either direction, between the main memory and the CPU.

Fetch-execute cycle

The instruction fetch-execute cycle can be described as follows:

Fetch phase - common to all instructions.

❏ the contents of the PC are copied into the MAR. The MAR now contains the location address of the next instruction and a memory read is initiated to copy the instruction word from memory into the MBR.

❏ the PC is incremented and now contains the address of the next instruction.

❏ the instruction word is then copied from the MBR into the CIR.

Execute phase - the action taken is unique to the instruction.

❏ the instruction in the CIR is decoded

❏ the instruction in the CIR is executed.

❏ unless the instruction is a STOP instruction, then the cycle is repeated.

Figure 4.2. *Fetch-execute cycle*

The cycle is illustrated in the flowchart in Figure 4.2.

The fetch-execute cycle is carried out automatically by the hardware and the programmer cannot control its sequence of operation. Of course, the programmer does have control over which instructions are stored in memory and the order in which they are executed.

Types of instruction

All the instructions available on a particular machine are known collectively as the *instruction set* of that machine. There are certain types of instruction commonly available in most computer systems. They can be classified according to their function as follow:

❏ arithmetic and logical operations on data;

❏ input and output of data;

❏ changing the sequence of program execution (branch instructions);

❏ transfer of data between memory and the CPU registers;

❏ transfer of data between registers within the CPU.

Examples of these instructions and their effects are given in Assembly Language Programming (on CD-ROM).

Instruction format

An instruction usually consists of two main components, the *function* or *operation code* (*opcode*) and the *operand*. The opcode part of the instruction defines the operation to be performed, for example to add or to move data and the operand defines the location address in memory of the data to be operated upon.

The storage of a 16-bit instruction word is illustrated in Table 4.1.

bit-15															bit-0
opcode					operands										

Table 4.1. *Instruction format*

Thus, the four most significant bits determine the type of instruction and the remaining twelve bits specify the operand or operands to be used.

Three-address instruction

If an expression requiring the use of three memory variables is to be accommodated by one instruction, then the instruction word will need to contain the address of each variable, that is three operands. An addition instruction can be expressed symbolically as,

        ADD Z,X,Y

that is, add the contents of X to the contents of Y and store the result in Z. The instruction word needs to be large enough to accommodate the three addresses and the format is illustrated in Table 4.2. Because of the large number of bits required this format is not often used.

opcode	operand address	operand address	operand address

Table 4.2. *Three-address instruction format*

Two-address instruction

With this format, only two addresses are available in the instruction, so it is implicit that the result is to be stored in one of the operands (X or Y). This means that one of the original numbers is overwritten by the result. If only one instruction is used, then adding the contents of X and Y and placing the result in X is expressed symbolically as,

        ADD X,Y

The instruction word format is shown in Table 4.3. To place the result in Z (as in the first expression) and to preserve the

opcode	operand address	operand address

Table 4.3. *Two-address instruction format*

original contents of X, a preceding instruction could be used to copy the contents of X to Z. Assuming that a MOVE instruction has this effect, then the following two expressions will effect the addition.

        MOVE Z,X
        ADD Z,Y

One-address instruction

The instruction word format is shown in Table 4.4. It should be obvious that this format only allows an opcode to refer to one operand and that two assumptions regarding storage are implicit. Firstly, as with the two-address format, it must be assumed that the result is to be stored in Z. Secondly, if only

opcode	operand address

Table 4.4. *One-address instruction format*

one operand can be referred to, the addition process must use another storage area for the second operand. Generally, a CPU general-purpose register, called the accumulator, is used. The single-address instruction is used where there is only a single accumulator, so the instruction does not need to refer to the address of the accumulator; it is implicit. The processes needed to achieve the addition are described below.

❑ Copy the contents of one operand, X, into the accumulator. This operation uses a LOAD (accumulator) instruction.

❑ ADD the contents of operand Y, placing the result in the accumulator. At the time of the addition, the contents of operand Y are in the MBR, having been read from memory as part of the instruction. An ADD instruction usually has this effect.

❑ Copy the result from the accumulator into address Z using a STORE command.

An assembly language coding for the above process may be as follows:

```
LDA X     {copies the content of X, via the MBR into the}
          {accumulator}
ADD Y     {reads the contents of Y to the MBR, adds it to the}
          {accumulator and  leaves the result there}
STA Z     {copies the result from the accumulator into memory}
          {address Z, via the MBR}
```

One-and-a-half-address instruction

Where there is more than one accumulator, an instruction using the accumulator must indicate which one is to be used. Since the number of accumulators is generally small, the number of bits needed to refer to a single accumulator is usually less than the number needed for a memory location address. The processes for carrying out the example sum are the same as for the one-address format, except that a specified accumulator is used. Table 4.5 shows the format.

Table 4.5. *One-and-a-half address format*

Zero-address instruction

This type of instruction is particularly popular with small machines because of its economy in size. Many microcomputer systems operate with a combination of one-address and zero-address instructions. A zero-address instruction does not specify any operands within it and relies on the use of a memory-based data structure called a *stack*, to provide the operands. A stack consists of a group of adjacent memory locations, the contents of which are addressed by a *stack pointer*, a register that contains the address of the current top of stack. Values can only be added (*pushed*) to or removed (*popped*) from the top of the stack, which is indicated by the current position of the stack pointer. The value of the stack pointer is incremented or decremented when an item is pushed or popped. A value located below the top item on the stack (as indicated by the stack pointer) cannot be removed until any values above it have been removed. Consider, for example, an ADD instruction which requires the addition of two operands, X and Y. The operands X and then Y are pushed onto the stack; Y is thus at the top of the stack and is the first one which can be removed. The ADD instruction causes the popping of Y and X from the stack; they are added and the sum is pushed onto the top of the stack. Although this instruction format is extremely short, additional instructions are needed in order to transfer operands from memory to the stack and from the stack to memory; obviously these instructions need to be longer in order to allow specification of memory addresses. They are similar to single instruction words, except that operands are copied to and from the stack rather than to and from the accumulator.

Instruction format and memory size

Given a particular word length (the number of bit positions), single-address instructions can directly address (specify the actual memory address) a larger number of memory locations than one-and-a-half or multiple-address formats because all the address bits can be used for one address. Many computers allow a variable length instruction word so that the number of bits available for the address portion of the instruction can be increased, to allow a larger number of memory locations to be directly addressed. If, for example, there are 16 bits for the address, then the highest location which can be *directly* addressed is:

$$2^{16} - 1 = 65,535$$

Therefore, 65,536 locations can be addressed, numbered 0 to 65,535 (computer memory sizes are quoted in nK, K being 1024 and n being a variable) and this example illustrates a 64K memory, that is, 64×1024 which equals 65,536. Clearly, this is insufficient for modern computer systems and a number of approaches are used to extend addressable range.

By increasing the number of bits available for the address to, say, 20, the number of locations which can be addressed is over a million, although in practice, not all memory words need to be addressed directly. For example, to enable the direct addressing of all locations in a 256K ($256 \times 1024 = 262,144$) memory requires the use of 18 bits ($2^{18} = 262,144$). There are addressing techniques to reduce the number of bits needed for a memory address and some of these are described later in the chapter. An increase in word size also allows an increase in the number of bits available for the opcode and the possibility of an increase in the size of the instruction set. It has to be said, however, that a recent development in computer architecture, namely that of the RISC (Reduced Instruction Set Computer) processor, is making this latter benefit somewhat less relevant.

Instruction set

The range of instructions available for any particular machine depends on the machines architecture, in terms of word length and the number and types of registers used. For this reason it is only possible to list some typical types of instruction (the names LOAD etc are not actual mnemonic opcodes) some of which were used in the earlier example:

❑ *Load* - copies the contents of a specified location into a register.

❑ *Add* - adds the contents of a specified memory location to the contents of a register.

❑ *Subtract* - subtracts the contents of a specified memory location from the contents of a register.

❑ *Store* - copies the contents of a register into a specified memory location.

❑ *Branch* - switches control to another instruction address other than the next in sequence.

❑ *Register-register* - moves contents from one register to another.

❑ *Shift* - moves bits in a memory location to the left or to the right for arithmetic purposes or for pattern manipulation.

❑ *Input/output* - effects data transfers between peripherals and memory.

❏ *Logical operations* (AND, OR, NOT, NAND and so on) which combine the contents of a register and a specified memory location or register. These operations are described in Chapter 5 on Computer Logic. The first four instruction types in this list have already been explained in the earlier addition example, so the following sections deal with those remaining.

Branch instruction

These instructions cause the program to divert from the sequence which is dictated by that of contiguous memory locations containing program instructions. A branch instruction causes the value of the Program Counter (PC) to be altered, to direct the next instruction to be fetched from a location which is not physically adjacent to the current instruction. A branch may be *conditional* (dependent on some condition) or *unconditional*. In the latter case, the branch is always made, whereas in the former, the branch only occurs if a specified condition occurs. The conditions tested usually include tests on CPU register contents for zero, non-zero, negative and positive number values. The branch or jump may be to a specified address or simply to skip the next instruction (or several instructions). In either case the program counter must be altered accordingly to change its contents to the address specified by the branch instruction. Branching can be used to repeat a sequence of instructions in a *loop*. Usually this is conditional to avoid an infinite program iteration.

Subroutine or subprogram

As explained in the previous paragraph a branch instruction is used to jump or skip to a specified instruction address, so that the program sequence may continue from that address. On the other hand if the branch is to a subroutine, the original sequence can be restored after its execution.

This requires a special form of branch instruction. It may be necessary, for example, to carry out a particular sequence of calculations at different points in a program. Instead of coding the instructions at each point where they are required, the coding can be written as a subroutine. Whenever a subroutine is used or *called*, there must be a mechanism for returning control to the original program sequence. One method is to save the current contents of the PC in the first location of the subroutine before the branch to the subroutine is made. Upon completion of the subroutine the contents of the first location can be loaded into the PC and control returned to the calling program. The process of branching to a subroutine and then returning to continue the instruction sequence is illustrated in Figure 4.3.

Figure 4.3. *Subroutine operation*

Alternatively, the return address may be placed on a *stack* (a memory facility described earlier in this chapter) and copied back into the PC to allow a resumption of the normal program sequence. The stack is particularly useful where subroutines are nested, which means that a subroutine may be called from within another subroutine. The return addresses are placed onto the stack and removed in reverse order so that the last return address is the first to be removed. The technique is described in detail in the chapter on Data Structures. Subroutines called in this way are referred to as *clos*ed, but where a subroutine is inserted, as and when required, as part of the main program, it is referred to as *open*.

Register-register instruction

As the name suggests, instructions of this type are used to transfer the contents of one register to another. Its format is similar to that of the two-address instruction described in the previous section, and is illustrated in Table 4.6. Although operands to address memory are not used, the instruction allows two operands to address the registers involved. The number of registers available will tend to be small, perhaps two or three, so that a single byte may be sufficient to contain the two operands. In an 8-bit machine, such instructions may be two bytes long, one for the opcode and one for the two register addresses. Data transfers between registers within the CPU are carried out through a communications system which is a subdivision of the computer systems *architecture*.

opcode	reg 1	reg 2

Table 4.6. *Register-register instruction format*

Shift instruction

A shift operation moves the bits in a register to new positions in the register, either to the left or to the right and may be *logical* or *arithmetic*. A shift instruction format is given in Table 4.7.

opcode	register no	no. of shifts

Table 4.7. *Shift instruction format*

Logical shift

Logical shifts are used for pattern manipulation of data and are not concerned with arithmetic operations. Examples of left and right logical shifts are provided in the adjacent tables. Table 4.8 shows an example logical shift left where a 0 is lost from the MSB and a 0 is shifted into the LSB (to fill the vacated position, formerly occupied by a 1).

bit-	5	4	3	2	1	0
initial contents of register	0	0	1	1	0	1
shift 1 place to the LEFT	0	1	1	0	1	0
0 dropped from MSB			0 moved into LSB			

Table 4.8. *Logical shift left of 1*

The example of a logical shift right in Table 4.9 starts with the same register contents as Table 4.8. This time the right shift of 1 moves each bit, one position to the right, causing the loss of a 1 from the LSB and the insertion of a 0 to fill the vacated MSB position.

Another type of logical shift, referred to as *rotational* or *cyclic*, involves rotation of bits in a register or location.

bit-	5	4	3	2	1	0
initial contents of register	0	0	1	1	0	1
shift 1 place to the RIGHT	0	0	0	1	1	0
0 moved into MSB			1 dropped from LSB			

Table 4.9. *Logical shift right of 1*

Rotational logical shift

A rotational shift can be either to the right or to the left, as shown in the next two tables. Table 4.10 shows that for a right shift the 1 in the LSB position is moved to the MSB position, as each bit moves one place to the right.

Table 4.10. *Rotational shift right of 1*

In the left shift example in Table 4.11, the 1 in the MSB position is moved to the LSB position as each bit moves one place to the left.

Table 4.11. *Rotational shift left of 1*

Arithmetic shift

Left and right shift operations are used for multiply and divide operations but arithmetic meaning must be maintained. A left shift of one doubles the number and a right shift of one halves the number. Computer multiplication can be carried out through a sequence of additions and shifts, and division by a sequence of subtractions and shifts. Some examples of

before shift					after shift				
sign					sign				
0	0	1	1	+3	0	1	1	0	+6
1	1	0	0	− 4	1	0	0	0	− 8
1	1	1	0	− 2	1	1	0	0	− 4
0	1	1	0	+6	1	1	0	0	− 4
sign changed to negative, indicating overflow									

Table 4.12. *Arithmetic shift left examples*

arithmetic shifts using two's complement notation are provided in the next two tables. Table 4.12 illustrates an arithmetic shift left of 1 where zeros are inserted into the LSB position. Note that in the last example in Table 4.12, the sign has been changed from positive to negative by the shift left operation. In these circumstances an overflow signal would be set.

Table 4.13 shows two shift right examples. In the second example, a 1 is shifted into the sign bit position to maintain the integrity of the sign.

before shift					after shift				
sign					sign				
0	1	1	0	+6	0	0	1	1	+3
1	1	0	0	− 4	1	1	1	0	− 2

Table 4.13. *Arithmetic shift right examples*

Register transfer language (RTL)

Processor architecture can be described diagrammatically, but RTL is used to define the ways in which data move within it. More particularly, RTL identifies the effects of an instruction by specifying the sequence of data transfers between registers and any arithmetic/logical operations needed for its execution.

The RTL examples used in this section assume knowledge of the fetch-execute cycle and the functions of each of the registers referred to earlier. RTL can be as simple or as complex as is necessary to describe the data transfers within any particular system, but for the purposes of understanding its general function, a number of *primitive operations* are identified.

The *fetch-execute* cycle can be described in RTL as follows:

Fetch phase

        PC ⇨ MAR

specifies that the contents of the program counter (PC) must be copied into the memory address register (MAR), thus ensuring that the next memory word to be fetched is a program instruction;

        PC ⇨ PC + 1

describes the incrementation of the PC to point to the next instruction;

        M [MAR] ⇨ MBR

indicates that the contents of the memory (M) location identified by the MAR are to be copied into the memory buffer register (MBR);

        MBR ⇨ CIR

shows that the instruction is then copied from the MBR into the current instruction register (CIR).

The fetching of any instruction follows this pattern, but the point at which the PC value is changed may vary, provided it occurs after its previous value has been copied to the MAR.

After the fetch phase an instruction must be *decoded* and *executed* and the nature of the instruction will determine the register transfers which are required. The first example which follows relates to a structure which uses *single address* instructions. Later, an example for *two address* instructions is provided.

Single address instructions

As is explained earlier, machines using this type of instruction must make use of an accumulator (ACC) register to perform arithmetic and logic operations and the following addition example illustrates this point.

The fetch phase is common to all instructions.

fetch

	comments
PC ⇨ MAR	{instruction address to MAR}
M [MAR] ⇨ MBR	{copy instruction to MBR}
PC ⇨ PC + 1	{increment PC to next instruction}
MBR ⇨ CIR	{copy instruction to CIR}

decode and thus identify the instruction

execute the instruction

	comments
CIR<adr> ⇨ MAR	{the <adr> indicates the operand portion of the instruction word and this is copied to the MAR}
M [MAR] ⇨ MBR	{read the operand value which is to be added to the contents of the ACC}
ACC + MBR ⇨ ACC	{add operand value to contents of ACC and store in the ACC}

A complete addition process may involve the following operations (expressed in a hypothetical assembly code), assuming that two values are to be summed, that their respective memory addresses are A and B and that the result is to be stored in location C.

LDA A	{copy contents of location A into the ACC}
ADD B	{add the contents of B to those of the ACC, storing the result there}
STA C	{copy contents of ACC to location C}

Remembering that each instruction executed is preceded by the fetch and decode phases detailed previously, it can be described in RTL thus:

execute LDA A

	comments
CIR<adr>A ⇨ MAR	{specifies the operand A to be read}
M [MAR] ⇨ MBR	{operand A copied to MBR}
MBR ⇨ ACC	{operand A copied to ACC}

execute ADD B

	comments
CIR<adr>B ⇨ MAR	{specifies second operand to be read}
M [MAR] ⇨ MBR	{operand B copied to MBR}
ACC + MBR ⇨ ACC	{add operand B to ACC giving result}

execute STA C

```
                              comments
CIR<adr>C ⇨ MAR    {specifies location C as memory location
                    to store result}
ACC ⇨ MBR          {copy contents of ACC to MBR}
MBR ⇨ M [MAR]      {copy result from ACC to location C}
```

Two address instructions

As explained earlier, with two addresses available in the instruction it is implicit that the result of an operation is to be stored in one of the operands, thus overwriting its original contents. For example,

        ADD A, B

would sum the contents of operand addresses A and B, and depending on the architecture, place the result in either the first or second named address.

The addition example which follows is based on the instruction set used in Assembly Language Programming (on CD-ROM). It differs from the single address addition process described earlier, not only in the number of addresses held within the instruction word, but also in the fact that the addresses refer to registers rather than memory locations. This means that the operands have to be moved from memory to their respective *registers* before the operation can be effected. Thus,

```
LDW R1, A     {load word from memory address A into register R1}
LDW R2, B     {load word from memory address B into register R2}
ADD R1, R2    {add contents of R1 and R2, place result in R1}
STW R1, C     {store result from R1 into memory address C}
```

loads the contents of memory location with the *symbolic* address A into a register R1 and similarly, the contents of B into R2. The contents of R1 and R2 are added and the result is placed in R1, the *destination* register. The store instruction completes the process by copying the result from R1 to memory location C.

The data transfers for this operation can be specified in RTL as follows. As before, it is assumed that each instruction is preceded by the fetch and decode phases.

execute LDW R1, A

```
                              comments
CIR <adr>A ⇨ MAR   {specifies operand A to be read}
M [MAR] ⇨ MBR      {operand A copied to MBR}
MBR ⇨ R1           {operand A copied to register R1}
```

execute LDW R2, B

```
                              comments
CIR <adr>B ⇨ MAR   {specifies operand B to be read}
M [MAR] ⇨ MBR      {operand B copied to MBR}
MBR ⇨ R2           {operand B copied to register R2}
```

execute ADD R1, R2

```
                              comments
        R1 + R2 ⇨ R1          {contents of R1, R2 added and result
                              placed in destination register R1}
```

execute STW R1, C

```
                              comments
    CIR <adr>C ⇨ MAR          {Next memory write is to address C}
    R1 ⇨ MBR                  {Copy contents of R1 to MBR}
    MBR ⇨ M [MAR]             {Contents of MBR to memory address C,
                              as indicated by current value of MAR}
```

Input/output instructions

Input/output (I/O) instructions are concerned with the transfer of data between peripherals and memory or between peripherals and registers in the CPU. Chapter 14 on Input/Output Control deals with this topic.

Memory addressing methods

The physical memory addresses ultimately used by the hardware are the *absolute* addresses. As explained earlier, addressing memory locations directly restricts the size of usable memory and for this reason a computers instruction set will normally include facilities for addressing locations beyond those directly addressable with a given address length.

Thus, absolute addresses may be referenced in a variety of ways and the addressing mode used is indicated in the operand of an instruction word.

The format of an instruction word may be as shown in Table 4.14.

opcode	addressing mode	address

Table 4.14. *Instruction with addressing mode*

The following addressing modes are common to most machines:

❑ *immediate*;

❑ *indirect*;

❑ *relative*;

❑ *indexed*.

Immediate addressing

With this method, the operand to be accessed by the instruction is stored in the instruction word or in the word immediately following it in memory. In the former case, the operand would be fetched with the instruction and no separate memory read would then be necessary. In the latter case, an ADD instruction which employed this method of addressing would indicate that the operand is to be found immediately after the opcode in memory.

In a byte organised machine, the first byte would contain the opcode, the execution of which would involve the fetching of the next byte in memory which contained the required operand. Computers based on the Intel 8080 or Motorola 6800 processor series use this latter method for immediate addressing. The Intel 8080 provides the opcode ADI (add immediate) as part of its instruction set. Immediate addressing is useful when small constants or literals are required in a program, for example, a set value of 3 to be subtracted from the contents of a register at some stage in the program. It is inappropriate to use this method if there is any need for the value to be changed as this would require changing the program coding.

Direct addressing

As the name suggests, this addressing mode specifies the actual or effective memory address containing the required operand, in the address field of the instruction word. The addressed memory location specified must be accessed to obtain the operand.

Indirect addressing

With this method, the location address in the instruction word does not contain the operand. Instead, it contains the address of another location which itself contains the address of the data item. Thus, an indirect address is, in effect, a pointer to the address containing the operand. For example, IAD 156 (indirect add) indicates that the address 156 contains the address of the required operand. If specific indirect addressing instructions are not provided, an instruction word may contain a flag bit to indicate whether or not an operand is an indirect or direct address; the flag bit may be set to 1 if the address is indirect and to 0 if it is direct. In this way, an LDA (load accumulator) instruction is able to refer to a direct or indirect address by the appropriate setting of the flag bit. Figure 4.4 illustrates the principle of indirect addressing.

Indirect addressing is generally slower in execution than direct addressing as an extra *memory cycle* is needed each time the actual address is deferred. Indirect addressing is also known as *deferred* addressing and if the address is deferred more than once it is known as a *multi-level* address.

Figure 4.4. *Indirect addressing*

Relative addressing

With relative addressing, the instruction word contains an *offset* address which indicates the location of the operand relative to the position of the instruction in memory (sometimes known as *self-relative* addressing). Thus, if an instruction is stored in address N and the offset is 5, then the operand is in address N + 5. It is a useful technique for branching a program, in which case the offset address will indicate the relative address of the next instruction to be fetched, rather than a data item.

The program counter (PC) is used to calculate the effective address in that it contains the address of the current instruction. By adding the offset to the PC, the address is determined. The instruction set usually contains instructions which allow such program jumps to be made. Absolute addresses may also be determined as being relative to a *base* address and as is explained in the chapter on Operating Systems, by alteration of this base address, programs can be *relocated* rather than be tied to particular absolute addresses each time they are loaded. Multi-programming or multi-tasking techniques demand that programs are relocatable.

Indexed Addressing

With this method, the effective address is calculated by the addition of an index value to the address given in the instruction. The index value is usually stored in either a general-purpose CPU register or a special *index* register.

The method can be employed by a programmer when an ordered block of data is to be accessed and each data item is to be processed in the same way. If the value of the index is N and the address in the instruction is X, then the effective address for an operand is N + X. The register is set to an initial value and incremented as the instructions step through the memory locations. A branch instruction is used to create a program loop to repeat the same set of instructions needed for each item of data in the block.

Exercises

1. How does the CPU differentiate between a *data word* and an *instruction word*?
2. (i)   Which registers are identified by the initials: PC; MBR; MAR; CIR?
   (ii) Briefly explain the function of each of these registers in the *fetch-execute cycle*.
3. Use register transfer language (RTL) to describe the *fetch* and *execute* stages for the following instructions:

   LDA F

   ADD G

   STA H

4. (i)   If an addition is to be expressed as ADD A, B, C and the values in A and B are to be preserved, show how the process would be completed using a:

   a. three address instruction;

   b. two address instruction;

   c. three address instruction.

   (ii) Show the instructions if the result of the addition could be placed in either A or B.
5. (i)   What is meant by the term *absolute* address?
   (ii) Describe the difference between *direct* and *indirect* addressing.
   (iii) What is the main benefit of indirect addressing?
6. What is an *instruction set*?
7. Name two kinds of *branch* instruction.
8. When a *subprogram* is called, what methods may be used to return program control to the normal sequence?
9. An 8-bit word contains the binary pattern 10110010. How does the pattern alter after:
   (i)   a logical left shift of 1 bit;
   (ii) a logical left shift of 2 bits;

(iii) a logical right shift of 3 bits;

(iv) a rotational right shift of 2 bits;

(v) a rotational left shift of 3 bits?

10. An 8-bit word contains the binary pattern 10110010. If the pattern is interpreted as a number in two's complement form, what would the denary value be after an arithmetic right shift of 2 bits?

11. Referring to the opcode and the operand, distinguish between *immediate*, *direct* and *indirect* addressing.

12. If a base address is defined as B and an operand contains an offset of 15, what type of addressing is it?

Computer Logic

In Chapter 2 it is explained that data and instructions in a digital computer are represented by the binary numbering system. Internal registers and locations within the memory of the computer must be able to remember data and instructions as sequences of binary digits. The ALU (Arithmetic and Logic Unit) must be able to perform arithmetic on numbers held in this form, and the decoding circuitry of the Control Unit must be able to recognise and interpret program instructions represented by binary numbers. All of these functions, and many more, are performed by logic circuits. Computer logic is based on a branch of mathematical logic called Boolean Algebra (named after the English mathematician George Boole) which allows the symbolic manipulation of logical variables in a manner very similar to the manipulation of unknowns in an ordinary algebraic expression of the form

$$x.(y+z) \text{ or } x.y + x.z$$

Just as laws are needed for ordinary algebraic expressions, fundamental laws exist for the manipulation of Boolean expressions. By means of these laws, complex logical expressions, representing logic circuits, can be analysed or designed. This chapter introduces the foundations of Boolean Algebra, its relevance to computer circuitry, and the processes by which such circuitry may be designed and analysed. The chapter concludes with a brief discussion of the evolution of integrated circuits.

Boolean variables

A Boolean variable has one of two values, normally represented by 1 and 0. In terms of computer circuitry, a Boolean variable represents a voltage on a line which may be an input to a logic circuit or an output from a logic circuit. For instance, a value of 1 might represent five volts and a value of 0, zero volts. Boolean variables are denoted by letters of the alphabet. Thus the variables X, Y, Z, P, Q, R are each able to represent a value of 1 or 0.

Gates

The term gate is used to describe the members of a set of basic electronic components which, when combined with each other, are able to perform complex logical and arithmetic operations. These are the types of operations associated with the ALU of the CPU. For present purposes, the physical construction of the gates is of no direct concern, and the discussion will be restricted to their functions only.

The OR gate

Gates have one or more inputs but only a single output. The nature of the gate determines what the output should be, given the current inputs. For example, the OR gate could be defined as in Table 5.1 which shows that

❑ the output is 1 if the X or Y input is 1.

X	Y	X OR Y
0	0	0
0	1	1
1	0	1
1	1	1

Table 5.1. *Truth table for OR gate*

X and Y are Boolean variables capable at any time of having the value 1 or 0. Thus at any instant X could have a value of 0 and Y a value of 1, or X could have a value of 1 and Y could have a value of 1; there are four such combinations of the values of X and Y as shown in Table 5.1. With an OR gate, when there is at least one 1 in the input variables, the output is 1. The third column of the table shows the output produced by each combination of the two inputs. The complete table is known as a *truth table* and completely defines the operation of the OR gate for every combination of inputs. As will be shown throughout this chapter, truth tables are extremely useful for describing logic circuits. Symbolically, the combination of X and Y using an OR gate is written

X OR Y or X + Y (read as X or Y)

Both forms mean that X and Y are inputs to an OR gate. The second form is that required for Boolean Algebra and the + is known as the OR operator. The symbol used when drawing an OR gate in a logic circuit is shown in Figure 5.1.

Figure 5.1. *Logic circuit for OR gate.*

Gates are the physical realisations of simple Boolean expressions. The design of logic circuits is performed symbolically using Boolean Algebra. A Boolean algebraic expression can then be converted very easily into a logic circuit consisting of combinations of gates. The OR gate is only one of several which are used to produce logic circuits. The other gates of interest are AND, NOT, XOR, NAND and NOR. The first two, in conjunction with the OR gate, are of the greatest importance since these three are directly related to the Boolean operators used in Boolean Algebra.

The AND gate

The AND gate is defined by the truth table shown in Table 5.2, which shows that

❏   the output is 1 when the X input AND the Y input are 1s.

This time, the gate only produces an output of 1 when both inputs are 1s. The Boolean operator equivalent to the AND gate is the AND operator '.', and is written

X.Y (read as X and Y)

The symbol for the AND gate is shown in Figure 5.2.

X	Y	X AND Y
0	0	0
0	1	0
1	0	0
1	1	1

Table 5.2. *Truth table for AND gate*

Figure 5.2. *AND gate symbol*

The NOT gate

The third important gate is the NOT gate, which has the truth table shown in Table 5.3 and the symbol shown in Figure 5.3.

X	NOT X
0	1
1	0

Table 5.3. *Truth table for NOT gate*

Figure 5.3. *NOT gate symbol*

This gate only has a single input which is inverted at the output. A NOT gate is often called an inverter for this reason and is written $\overline{X}$ or ~X in Boolean expressions.

Example of a useful logic circuit

At this point it is worth considering an example of a widely used logic circuit to illustrate the relevance of this chapter. The circuit, which is called a *half adder*, performs the addition of two binary digits to give a sum term, S and a carry term, C, both being Boolean variables. The inputs to the circuit are X and Y representing the two binary digits to be added. The rules for binary addition are shown in Table 5.4 and the equivalent truth table is shown in Table 5.5.

$0 + 0 = 0$ carry 0 (00)
$0 + 1 = 1$ carry 0 (01)
$1 + 0 = 1$ carry 0 (01)
$1 + 1 = 0$ carry 1 (10)

X	Y	S	C
0	0	0	0
0	1	1	0
1	0	1	0
1	1	0	1

Table 5.4. *Rules of binary addition*

Table 5.5. *Truth table for binary addition*

The requirement is for a combination of AND, OR and NOT gates to give two separate outputs for (S)um and (C)arry given any two binary digits represented by X and Y.

The circuit is shown in Figure 5.4 and the equivalent Boolean expressions for S and C are

$$S = X.\overline{Y} + \overline{X}.Y$$

$$C = X.Y$$

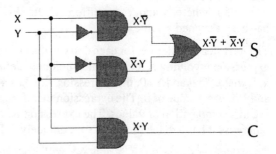

Figure 5.4. *Half adder circuit*

To prove that the circuit actually works a truth table is constructed (Table 5.6) showing the output from every component in the circuit, from stage to stage, given the inputs to that stage.

X	Y	$\overline{X}$	$\overline{Y}$	$X.\overline{Y}$	$\overline{X}.Y$	$X.\overline{Y}+\overline{X}.Y$ (S)	X.Y (C)
0	0	1	1	0	0	0	0
0	1	1	0	0	1	1	0
1	0	0	1	1	0	1	0
1	1	0	0	0	0	0	1

Table 5.6. *Truth table for half adder circuit*

Thus if X=0 and Y=0, $\overline{Y}$=1 and using the truth table for the AND gate (Table 5.2), $X.\overline{Y} = 0.1 = 0$ and $\overline{X}.Y = 1.0 = 0$. The rightmost OR gate in Figure 5.4 has inputs $X.\overline{Y}$ and $\overline{X}.Y$, that is, 0 and 0, and using the truth table for the OR gate (Table 5.1), it can be seen that this results in an output of 0 for S. Similarly, if X=0 and Y=0, the truth table for the AND gate shows that X.Y=0, that is C=0 for this combination of inputs.

Following this type of argument for the remaining rows in the truth table, it can be seen that the circuit produces exactly the right output for each combination of inputs to perform binary addition on the input bits. Thus a combination of a few elementary components has produced a most important circuit. A truth table allowed the operation of the circuit to be confirmed. Later it will be shown how the Boolean expressions representing the circuit can be derived directly from the first truth table defining the required operation of the circuit.

Deriving boolean expressions from truth tables

Suppose that it is required to produce a suitable logic circuit from the following circuit specification:

❏ A circuit has two binary inputs, X and Y. The output from the circuit is 1 when the two inputs are the same; otherwise the output is 0.

X	Y	OUTPUT
0	0	1
0	1	0
1	0	0
1	1	1

Table 5.7. *Truth table for specified circuit*

The first step is to produce a truth table to define the circuit fully and this is shown in Table 5.7. Each possible combination of X and Y has been listed. Where X and Y are the same, OUTPUT has been assigned a value of 1; where X and Y are different, OUTPUT has been assigned a value of 0.

The next step is to define, for each entry in the OUTPUT column having a value of 1, a Boolean expression involving X and Y which uniquely defines that value. So for the first row in Table 5.7, where X=0 and Y=0, the expression $\overline{X}.\overline{Y}$ has a value of 1; for any other combination of X and Y it has a value of 0. The expression therefore satisfies the requirement of uniquely defining this combination of values. The expression X.Y has a value of 1 only when X=1 and Y=1, otherwise it has a value of 0, and so it uniquely defines the last row in the truth table.

Together the expressions $\overline{X}.\overline{Y}$ and X.Y will produce an output of 1 when X=0 and Y=0 or when X=1 and Y=1. Hence

$$\text{OUTPUT} = \overline{X}.\overline{Y} + X.Y$$

X	Y	$\overline{X}$	$\overline{Y}$	$\overline{X}.\overline{Y}$	X.Y	$\overline{X}.\overline{Y}+X.Y$
0	0	1	1	1	0	1
0	1	1	0	0	0	0
1	0	0	1	0	0	0
1	1	0	0	0	1	1

Table 5.8.

The truth table (Table 5.8) confirms this result and the circuit is shown in Figure 5.5.

The process of converting a truth table to a Boolean expression is summarised as follows:

(a) Consider only the rows of the truth table for which the output is to be 1.

(b) Take each of these rows in turn and write alongside the row an expression containing the input variables connected by the AND operator. If the value of an input variable is 0 then it will appear inverted in the expression.

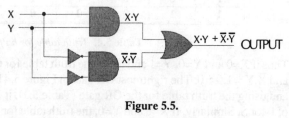

Figure 5.5.

(c)   Combine these expressions using the OR operator.

To provide another illustration of the process suppose that three binary signals, A, B and C, are required to represent a number in the range 0 to 4. The variable A represents the most significant digit of the binary number ABC, B is the next significant digit, and C is the least significant digit. A circuit is required to detect an illegal combination (that is the numbers 5 to 7) by producing an output of 1. The truth table is shown in Table 5.9. Therefore, OUTPUT $=A.\overline{B}.C +$ $A.B.\overline{C} + A.B.C$, and the required circuit is shown in Figure 5.6.

A	B	C		OUTPUT	
0	0	0	(0)	0	
0	0	1	(1)	0	
0	1	0	(2)	0	
0	1	1	(3)	0	
1	0	0	(4)	0	
1	0	1	(5)	1	$A.\overline{B}.C$
1	1	0	(6)	1	$A.B.\overline{C}$
1	1	1	(7)	1	$A.B.C$

Table 5.9.   Figure 5.6.

As an exercise, use a truth table to prove that the Boolean expression above does indeed produce the required outputs.

The laws of Boolean algebra

Though the circuit above does perform as specified, it is very inefficient; it uses more gates than are absolutely necessary to produce the required outputs. In fact rather than six gates, only two are necessary because, as the truth tables in Tables 5.10 and 5.11 show,

$$A.\overline{B}.C + A.B.\overline{C} + A.B.C = A.(B + C)$$

A	B	C	$\overline{B}$	$\overline{C}$	$A.\overline{B}.C$	$A.B.\overline{C}$	$A.B.C$	$(A.\overline{B}.C + A.B.\overline{C} + A.B.C)$
0	0	0	1	1	0	0	0	0
0	0	1	1	0	0	0	0	0
0	1	0	0	1	0	0	0	0
0	1	1	0	0	0	0	0	0
1	0	0	1	1	0	0	0	0
1	0	1	1	0	1	0	0	1
1	1	0	0	1	0	1	0	1
1	1	1	0	0	0	0	1	1
								=OUTPUT

A	B	C	A.(B + C)
0	0	0	0
0	0	1	0
0	1	0	0
0	1	1	0
1	0	0	0
1	0	1	1
1	1	0	1
1	1	1	1
			=OUTPUT

Table 5.10.   Table 5.11.

The circuit for the simplified expression is shown in Figure 5.7.

$A \cdot (B + C)$

Figure 5.7.

The laws of Boolean Algebra enable Boolean expressions such as that in the example to be transformed and, where possible, simplified. The most useful of these laws are as follow:

1. Commutative laws.

    (a) $X+Y=Y+X$; (b) $X.Y=Y.X$

2. Associative laws.

    (a) $X+(Y+Z) = (X+Y)+Z$; (b) $X.(Y.Z) = (X.Y).Z$

3. Distributive laws.

    (a) $X.(Y+Z) = X.Y + X.Z$; (b) $X + Y.Z = (X+Y).(X+Z)$

4. De Morgans laws.

    (a) $(\overline{X + Y}) = \overline{X}.\overline{Y}$; (b) $(\overline{X.Y}) = \overline{X} + \overline{Y}$

5. Laws of absorption.

    (a) $X + X.Y = X$; (b) $X.(X + Y) = X$

6. Laws of tautology.

    (a) $X + X = X$; (b) $X.X = X$

7. Law of complementation.

    $\overline{\overline{X}} = X$

8. Other useful identities.

    (a) $X + \overline{X} = 1$; (b) $X.\overline{X} = 0$

    (c) $X + 1 = 1$; (d) $X.1 = X$

    (e) $X + 0 = X$; (f) $X.0 = 0$

Notice that with each of the first six laws, there is a connection between (a) and (b). Given one of these rules, the other may be derived by replacing the + operator with the . operator or vice-versa. Thus if it is known that $X + X.Y = X$, then the dual of the rule, that $X.(X+Y) = X$, is also true. All identities in Boolean algebra have this useful property. To illustrate the use of these laws in the simplification of Boolean expressions, consider the expression derived earlier:

$$A.\overline{B}.C + A.B.\overline{C} + A.B.C$$

Simplification of this expression could proceed as follows:

(i) $A.\overline{B}.C + A.B.\overline{C} + A.B.C = A.\overline{B}.C + (A.B.\overline{C} + A.B.C)$

Rule 1 allows us to deal with terms in any order.

(ii)   Considering the bracketed pair of terms,

$A.B.\overline{C} + A.B.C = A.B.(\overline{C} + C)$ by rule 3(a)

Here A.B is treated as if it were a single variable, and the expression is therefore of the form

$X.\overline{C} + X.C = X.(\overline{C} + C)$ where X represents A.B

(iii)   Rule 8(a) shows that $\overline{C} + C = 1$, so that

$A.B.(\overline{C} + C) = A.B.1$

and by rule 8(d),

$A.B.1 = A.B$

(iv)   Hence,

$A.\overline{B}.C + (A.B.\overline{C} + A.B.C) = A.\overline{B}.C + A.B$

(v)   Again using rule 3(a),

$A.\overline{B}.C + A.B = A.(\overline{B}.C + B)$

This is of the form

$X.Y + X.Z = X.(Y + Z)$

(vi)   Now consider the term $\overline{B}.C + B$.

Using rule 1(a), this can be rewritten $B + \overline{B}.C$, and now using rule 3(b),

$B + \overline{B}.C = (B + \overline{B}).(B + C)$

As in step (iii), $(B + \overline{B}) = 1$ and $1.(B+C) = (B+C)$.

Hence $B + \overline{B}.C = (B + C)$ and therefore

$A.(B + \overline{B}.C) = A.(B+C)$

Thus the original expression has been considerably simplified and confirms the identity stated earlier.

Fortunately, the process of simplifying expressions involving AND terms separated by OR operators can be performed in a much simpler way using the Karnaugh Map method. This method, as well as being quicker and less prone to error, is also more likely to result in the best simplification possible, particularly where four variables are involved. In certain cases, however, a knowledge of the laws of Boolean algebra is required. Examples of such instances will be provided later.

Karnaugh maps

A Karnaugh map consists of a two-dimensional grid which is used to represent a Boolean expression in such a way that it can be simplified with great ease. For example, consider the expression

$\overline{X}.Y + X.\overline{Y} + X.Y$

This expression involves two Boolean variables, X and Y. The number of different terms possible with two variable is four, and therefore the Karnaugh map for expressions involving two variables is a 2 × 2 grid (Figure 5.8).

Each cell in the grid may be regarded as having a co-ordinate formed from a combination of X and Y. Thus the cell labelled (a) has the co-ordinate $\overline{X}.\overline{Y}$, (b) has the co-ordinate $\overline{X}.Y$, (c) has the co-ordinate $X.\overline{Y}$, and (d) has the co-ordinate $X.Y$. When entered onto the map, the expression quoted above translates to the map in Figure 5.9.

Figure 5.8.

Each 1 on the map indicates the presence of the term corresponding to its cell co-ordinate in the expression, and each 0 indicates its absence. Using a further example, the expression $\overline{X}.Y + \overline{X}.\overline{Y}$ translates to the map shown in Figure 5.10.

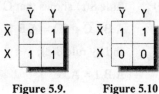

Figure 5.9.   **Figure 5.10**

Having drawn the appropriate Karnaugh map, the next stage is to attempt to identify a simplified expression. The procedure is as follows:

(i)   Identify all pairs of adjacent 1s on the map (horizontally and vertically).

(ii)   Draw loops around each pair.

(iii)   Attempt to include every 1 on the map in at least one loop; it is allowable to have the same 1 in two different loops.

(iv)   The aim is to include each 1 in at least one loop, but using as few loops as possible.

Thus the expression $\overline{X}.Y + X.\overline{Y} + X.Y$ becomes the map shown in Figure 5.11.

(v)   Take each loop in turn and write down the term represented: the loop labelled (a) in Figure 5.11 spans both X and $\overline{X}$, but Y remains constant. The loop is therefore given the value Y. In the loop labelled (b), both Y co-ordinates are covered but X remains constant. This loop has the value X.

(vi)   The loop values are ORed together. In the example, the expression is therefore equivalent to X + Y.

Figure 5.11.

Karnaugh maps take advantage of a small number of the laws of Boolean algebra. The Distributive Law allows terms with common variables to be grouped together:

$$X.\overline{Y} + X.Y = X.(\overline{Y} + Y) \text{ (see rule 3(a))}$$

Another law, 8(a), gives the identity $\overline{Y} + Y = 1$.

And finally, law 8(d) says that $X.1 = X$.

The Karnaugh map allows this sequence of applications of laws to be performed in a single step:

the loop (b) representing $X.\overline{Y} + X.Y$ becomes X.

1s may be included in more than one loop because of the Law of Tautology (Tautology is saying the same thing twice). Thus $X + X = X$, and conversely, $X = X + X$. In other words, any term in an expression may be duplicated as many times as desired without affecting the value of the expression. So, given the expression

$$\overline{X}.Y + X.\overline{Y} + X.Y,$$

the term X.Y may be duplicated to give the equivalent expression

$$\overline{X}.Y + X.Y + X.\overline{Y} + X.Y,$$

where loop (a) is $\overline{X}.Y + X.Y$, and loop (b) is $X.\overline{Y} + X.Y$.

As a further example, the expression

$$\overline{X}.\overline{Y} + \overline{X}.Y + X.Y$$

gives the map in Figure 5.12 and the equivalent expression is $\overline{X} + Y$.

Figure 5.12.

Karnaugh maps for three variables

Expressions containing three variables can contain up to eight terms. The 3-variable map is drawn as shown in Figure 5.13.

Figure 5.13.

This time a co-ordinate pair comprises an X variable and a YZ term. For example, the cell (a) represents the term $\overline{X}.\overline{Y}.Z$, and (b) represents X.Y.Z.

The map in Figure 5.14 represents the expression $X.\overline{Y}.Z + X.Y.\overline{Z} + X.Y.Z$.

Figure 5.14.

In loop (a), X and Z are common factors, but Y changes ($\overline{Y}.Z + Y.Z$). The loop has the value X.Z. In loop (b), X and Y are constant but Z changes ($Y.Z + Y.\overline{Z}$). Thus (b) has value X.Y. The expression therefore simplifies to

$$X.Y + X.Z$$

and a further application of law 3(a) gives the final solution

$$X.\overline{Y}.Z + X.Y.\overline{Z} + X.Y.Z = X.(Y + Z)$$

With a 3-variable map, as well as looping pairs of 1s, it is necessary to look for groups of four 1s. For example, the map shown in Figure 5.15 could represent the expression

Figure 5.15.

$$X.Y.Z + \overline{X}.\overline{Y}.Z + \overline{X}.Y.Z + X.\overline{Y}.Z$$

The single loop spans the X co-ordinate completely, and so X can be removed from the simplified expression. In the YZ terms spanned, Y changes and Z is constant. The simplified expression is merely Z.

Two further examples of groups of four are shown in Figures 5.16 and 5.17.

In Figure 5.18 the group of four is formed from opposite sides of the grid.

Figure 5.16.

Figure 5.17.

Figures 5.19 to 5.22 show some further examples with combinations of different types of loops illustrated.

Note that the largest groups are identified first, and then sufficient smaller groups so that every 1 is in at least one loop.

Figure 5.18.

Figure 5.19.

Figure 5.20.

Figure 5.21.

Figure 5.22.

Karnaugh maps for four variables

With four variables there can be up to sixteen different terms involved, and the 4-variable map is a 4 × 4 grid as shown in Figure 5.23.

It is necessary to look for groupings of 8, 4 and 2 with the 4-variable map. Figures 5.24 to 5.27 illustrate a number of possible groupings, including some that occur on the edges of the maps and which are sometimes difficult to recognise. Again, to determine the term equivalent to the loop, look for the variables that remain common to the co-ordinates of the loop's range horizontally and vertically.

Figure 5.23.

Figure 5.24.

Figure 5.25.

Figure 5.26.

Figure 5.27.

The design of logic circuits

The complete process of designing a logic circuit may be summarised as follows:

(i)   Identify Boolean variables equivalent to the inputs to the circuit required.

(ii)   Identify the outputs from the circuit.

(iii)   Draw a truth table to define the output required for each possible combination of the input variables.

(iv)   Derive an expression from the truth table for the output in terms of the input variables.

(v)   Simplify this expression using a Karnaugh map.

(vi)   Examine the simplified expression for possible further simplifications using direct applications of the laws of Boolean algebra.

(vii)   Draw the circuit using the appropriate gate symbols.

The following problem illustrates the process. Four binary signals A, B, C, D represent a single Binary Coded Decimal (BCD) digit. A logic circuit is required to output logic 1 on the occurrence of an invalid combination of the signals, that is, when they represent a number in the range 10 to 15.

A	B	C	D		OUTPUT	
0	0	0	0	(0)	0	
0	0	0	1	(1)	0	
0	0	1	0	(2)	0	
0	0	1	1	(3)	0	
0	1	0	0	(4)	0	
0	1	0	1	(5)	0	
0	1	1	0	(6)	0	
0	1	1	1	(7)	0	
1	0	0	0	(8)	0	
1	0	0	1	(9)	0	
1	0	1	0	(10)	1	$A.\bar{B}.C.\bar{D}$
1	0	1	1	(11)	1	$A.\bar{B}.C.D$
1	1	0	0	(12)	1	$A.B.\bar{C}.\bar{D}$
1	1	0	1	(13)	1	$A.B.\bar{C}.D$
1	1	1	0	(14)	1	$A.B.C.\bar{D}$
1	1	1	1	(15)	1	$A.B.C.D$

(i)   The inputs to the circuit are clearly defined and it is assumed that A is the most significant digit and D the least significant digit.

(ii)   The single output is to be 1 when the binary number represented by ABCD is in the range 10 to 15, that is, 1010 to 1111 in binary.

Table 5.12.

(iii)   The truth table (Table 5.12) has 16 entries, representing the numbers 0 to 15.

(iv)   The expression for the output is given by

$$\text{OUTPUT} = A.\bar{B}.C.\bar{D} + A.\bar{B}.C.D + A.B.\bar{C}.\bar{D} + A.B.\bar{C}.D + A.B.C.\bar{D} + A.B.C.D$$

(v)   The Karnaugh map is shown in Figure 5.28.

(vi)   Using the Distributive law, 3(a), the expression A.B + A.C may be written A.(B + C).

(vii)   This expression translates to the logic diagram shown in Figure 5.29.

Figure 5.28.

Figure 5.29.

More logic gates

The gates that have yet to be defined are the NOR(Not OR), NAND(Not AND) and XOR (eXclusive OR) gates. The truth table for the NOR gate (Table 5.13) shows that its outputs are the inverse of those for the OR gate.

X	Y	X NOR Y
0	0	1
0	1	0
1	0	0
1	1	0

Table 5.13.   *Truth table for NOR gate*

Algebraically, the NOR gate is written $(\overline{X+Y})$. Thus the gate appears to be formed from one OR gate and one NOT gate inverting the output from the OR gate. In practice, however, the OR gate outputs are generated from a single simple circuit and not by the combination of an OR gate followed by a NOT gate.

The symbol for the NOR gate is shown in Figure 5.30(a).

(a) NOR gate   (b) NAND gate

Figure 5.30.

The truth table for the NAND gate (Table 5.14) shows that its outputs are the inverse of those for the AND gate.

In Boolean algebra, the gate is written $(\overline{X.Y})$. The comments above regarding the construction of the NOR gate similarly apply here; the NAND gate is not constructed from an AND gate followed by a NOT gate, but consists of a single circuit no more complex than the other gates.

X	Y	X NAND Y
0	0	1
0	1	1
1	0	1
1	1	0

Table 5.14. *Truth table for NAND gate*

The symbol for the NAND gate is shown in Figure 5.30(b).

The importance of the NAND gate and NOR gate

The importance of these gates may be attributed to two factors:

(i)   each may be manufactured cheaply and easily;

(ii)   each can be used in the production of any circuit using AND/OR/NOT logical components. In other words, NOR gates and NAND gates can be used in the place of AND, OR or NOT gates.

These two properties mean that a logic circuit using, for instance, NOR gates only, can be produced more easily and cheaply than the same circuit using combinations of three different types of components (AND, OR and NOT gates). A unit using a number of the same component is much easier to manufacture than one using several different components.

Figures 5.31 (a), (b) and (c) show how NOR gates may be used to represent the functions of NOT, AND and OR gates.

Figure 5.31(a). *NOT gate*   **Figure 5.31(b).** *AND gate*   **Figure 5.31(c).** *OR gate*

Figures 5.32 (a), (b) and (c) show how NAND gates may be used to represent the functions of NOT, AND OR gates.

Figure 5.32(a). *NOT gate*   **Figure 5.32(b).** *AND gate*   **Figure 5.32(c).** *OR gate*

(As an exercise, write down Boolean expressions equivalent to the circuits shown above and prove their validity using truth tables).

It may appear from Figures 5.31 and 5.32 that circuits using NAND or NOR gates will generally require more gates than when using AND/OR /NOT components. This may be true on occasions, but at other times fewer gates may be required. The number of gates required often may be reduced by transforming the Boolean expression into a more suitable form. For example, the following expression, when implemented directly using NOR gates, uses more gates than the expression requires using AND/OR/NOT logic:

$$X.\overline{Y} + \overline{X}.Y \ (\text{2 AND gates, 2 NOT gates, 1 OR gate} = 5 \text{ gates})$$

However, it can be shown that the following identity is true:

$$X.\overline{Y} + \overline{X}.Y = \overline{(\overline{X} + \overline{Y}) + (X + Y)}$$

which may not look very helpful but, in fact, shows that the original expression can be transformed into one much more suited to implementation by NOR gates. The circuit based on this transformed expression has only five NOR gates. (See Figure 5.33)

$$X.\overline{Y} + \overline{X}.Y$$

Figure 5.33.

The exclusive OR gate

This is usually abbreviated to XOR or EOR. The truth table for the XOR gate is shown in Table 5.15. The exclusive OR gate is so named because, of its output values, the case where both inputs are logic 1 is excluded; in the OR gate these inputs produce an output of 1. In effect, the XOR gate

X	Y	X XOR Y
0	0	0
0	1	1
1	0	1
1	1	0

Table 5.15. *Truth table for XOR gate*

Figure 5.34. *Symbol for XOR gate*

has an output of logic 1 when the inputs are different; when the inputs are the same, the output is logic 0. Algebraically, the XOR gate is $X.\overline{Y} + \overline{X}.Y$ and the symbol that is frequently used is shown in Figure 5.34. As an example of its use, suppose that it is required to generate an even parity bit for a four bit word ABCD. The truth table for this problem is shown in Table 5.16.

The expression for even parity is thus Parity bit =

$\overline{A}.\overline{B}.\overline{C}.D + \overline{A}.\overline{B}.C.\overline{D} + \overline{A}.B.\overline{C}.\overline{D} + \overline{A}.B.C.D + A.\overline{B}.\overline{C}.\overline{D}$
$+ A.\overline{B}.C.D + A.B.\overline{C}.D + A.B.C.\overline{D}$

and the Karnaugh map representation is shown in Figure 5.35(a). As the map shows, there is no way of simplifying the expression.

	$\overline{C}.\overline{D}$	$\overline{C}.D$	$C.D$	$C.\overline{D}$
$\overline{A}.\overline{B}$	0	1	0	1
$\overline{A}.B$	1	0	1	0
$A.B$	0	1	0	1
$A.\overline{B}$	1	0	1	0

Figure 5.35(a).

However, if the terms are grouped together as follows, a pattern begins to emerge:

Parity bit = $\overline{A}.\overline{B}.(\overline{C}.D + C.\overline{D}) + \overline{A}.B.(C.D + \overline{C}.\overline{D}) + A.\overline{B}.(\overline{C}.\overline{D} + C.D) + A.B.(\overline{C}.D + C.\overline{D})$

Rearranging the terms,

Parity bit = $\overline{A}.\overline{B}.(\overline{C}.D + C.\overline{D}) + A.B.(\overline{C}.D + C.\overline{D}) + \overline{A}.B.(C.D + \overline{C}.\overline{D}) + A.\overline{B}.(C.D + \overline{C}.\overline{D})$

Again, using the Distributive law, the first two and the last two terms can be grouped together to give

Parity bit = $(\overline{A}.\overline{B} + A.B).(\overline{C}.D + C.\overline{D}) + (\overline{A}.B + A.\overline{B}).(\overline{C}.\overline{D} + C.D)$

A	B	C	D	parity bit	
0	0	0	0	0	
0	0	0	1	1	$\overline{A}.\overline{B}.\overline{C}.D$
0	0	1	0	1	$\overline{A}.\overline{B}.C.\overline{D}$
0	0	1	1	0	
0	1	0	0	1	$\overline{A}.B.\overline{C}.\overline{D}$
0	1	0	1	0	
0	1	1	0	0	
0	1	1	1	1	$\overline{A}.B.C.D$
1	0	0	0	1	$A.\overline{B}.\overline{C}.\overline{D}$
1	0	0	1	0	
1	0	1	0	0	
1	0	1	1	1	$A.\overline{B}.C.D$
1	1	0	0	0	
1	1	0	1	1	$A.B.\overline{C}.D$
1	1	1	0	1	$A.B.C.\overline{D}$
1	1	1	1	0	

Table 5.16.

Notice that two of the terms in brackets are immediately recognisable as XOR functions. In addition it can be shown that

$$\overline{X}.Y + X.\overline{Y} = \overline{(\overline{X}.\overline{Y} + X.Y)}$$

Using this identity, the expression for parity becomes

Parity bit = $\overline{(\overline{A}.B + A.\overline{B})}.(\overline{C}.D + C.\overline{D}) + (\overline{A}.B + A.\overline{B}).\overline{(\overline{C}.D + C.\overline{D})}$

Now each bracketed term looks like an XOR gate and, treating each bracketed term as a unit, the complete expression has the form

$$\overline{X}.Y + X.\overline{Y}, \text{ where } X = (\overline{A}.B + A.\overline{B}) \text{ and } Y = (\overline{C}.D + C.\overline{D})$$

Thus the whole expression, and every term within it, represent XOR gates. The equivalent circuit is shown in Figure 5.35(b).

Figure 5.35(b). *Circuit using XOR gates*

Logic circuits for binary addition

The logic circuits which perform the function of addition in the Arithmetic and Logic Unit of the Central Processing Unit are called *adders*. A unit which adds two binary digits is called a *half adder* and one which adds together three binary digits is called a *full adder*. In this section each of these units will be examined in detail, and it will be shown how such units are combined to add binary numbers.

Half adders

Earlier in this chapter, the function of a half adder was explained in order to illustrate the relevance of computer logic. Remember that the function of a half adder is to add two binary digits and produce as output the Sum term and Carry term. The operation of the half adder is defined by the truth table in Table 5.17.

X	Y	Sum		Carry	
0	0	0		0	
0	1	1	$\overline{X}.Y$	0	
1	0	1	$X.\overline{Y}$	0	
1	1	0		1	$X.Y$

Table 5.17.

Thus, the expressions for the Sum and Carry terms are given by

$$\text{Sum} = \overline{X}.Y + X.\overline{Y}$$

$$\text{Carry} = X.Y$$

The circuit equivalent to these expressions was presented earlier in Figure 5.4.

The symbol shown in Figure 5.36 will henceforth be used for a half adder.

Figure 5.36.

Full adders

Table 5.18 shows the truth table for the addition of three binary digits.

Considering the Sum term first, the expression derived from the truth table is

$$\text{Sum} = \overline{X}.\overline{Y}.Z + \overline{X}.Y.\overline{Z} + X.\overline{Y}.\overline{Z} + X.Y.Z$$

Grouping together the first and fourth terms, and the middle two terms gives

$$\text{Sum} = \overline{Z}.(\overline{X}.Y + X.\overline{Y}) + Z.(\overline{X}.\overline{Y} + X.Y)$$

Using the identity

$$\overline{\overline{X}.Y + X.\overline{Y}} = (\overline{X}.\overline{Y} + X.Y)$$

the Sum term can be written

$$\text{Sum} = \overline{Z}.(\overline{X}.Y + X.\overline{Y}) + Z.\overline{(\overline{X}.Y + X.\overline{Y})}$$

which is of the form

$$\overline{Z}.S + Z.\overline{S} \text{ where } S = \overline{X}.Y + X.\overline{Y}$$

X	Y	Z	Sum		Carry	
0	0	0	0		0	
0	0	1	1	$\overline{X}.\overline{Y}.Z$	0	
0	1	0	1	$\overline{X}.Y.\overline{Z}$	0	
0	1	1	0		1	$\overline{X}.Y.Z$
1	0	0	1	$X.\overline{Y}.\overline{Z}$	0	
1	0	1	0		1	$X.\overline{Y}.Z$
1	1	0	0		1	$X.Y.\overline{Z}$
1	1	1	1	$X.Y.Z$	1	$X.Y.Z$

Table 5.18.

In other words, S is the sum term from a half adder with inputs X and Y, and Sum is one of the outputs from a half adder with inputs Z and S.

The Sum term can now be produced using two half adders, as shown in Figure 5.37.

Returning to the Carry term, the expression derived from the truth table is

$$\text{Carry} = \overline{X}.Y.Z + X.\overline{Y}.Z + X.Y.\overline{Z} + X.Y.Z$$

Figure 5.37.

Again gathering terms,

$$\text{Carry} = Z.(\overline{X}.Y + X.\overline{Y}) + X.Y.(\overline{Z} + Z)$$

$$= Z.(\overline{X}.Y + X.\overline{Y}) + X.Y \text{ since } \overline{Z} + Z = 1 \text{ and } X.Y.1 = X.Y$$

Substituting S for $\overline{X}.Y + X.\overline{Y}$ as before, the expression becomes

$$\text{Carry} = Z.S + X.Y$$

Both of these terms look like the carry term from a half adder; Z.S is the carry term from a half adder with inputs Z and S (the carry term from the second half adder in the diagram above); X.Y is the carry output from the first half adder in the diagram.

The two carry outputs merely need to be ORed together, to give the final circuit shown in Figure 5.38.

Figure 5.38.

Adding binary numbers

So far, the circuits for addition have only been capable of adding two or three binary digits; more complex schemes are necessary in order to add two binary numbers each comprising several digits. Two approaches will be considered. The first adds numbers bit by bit, one pair of bits after another and is termed *serial addition*; the other accepts as inputs all pairs of bits in the two numbers simultaneously and is called *parallel addition*.

Serial addition

Suppose that the numbers to be added have a four-bit wordlength, and the two numbers A and B have digits $a_3 a_2 a_1 a_0$ and $b_3 b_2 b_1 b_0$ respectively. The circuit for a four-bit serial adder is shown in Figure 5.39.

In this particular design, a single full adder is presented with pairs of bits from the two numbers in the sequence $a_0 b_0$, $a_1 b_1$, $a_2 b_2$, $a_3 b_3$. As each pair of bits is added, the sum term is transmitted to a shift register to hold the result, and the carry term is delayed so that it is added in to the next addition operation.

Figure 5.39.

Though this method is cheap in terms of hardware requirements, it is not often (if at all) used in modern digital computers because of its slow operation. The degree to which hardware prices have dropped in recent years has resulted in the almost universal adoption of parallel addition.

Parallel addition

In parallel addition, a separate adder is used for the addition of each digit pair. Thus for the addition of two four-digit numbers, one half adder and three full adders would be used.

In this type of circuit, all the digits are input simultaneously, with the carry term from each stage being connected directly to the input of the next stage.

This is shown in Figure 5.40.

Though faster than serial addition, one fault of the type of parallel adder shown above is the successive carry out to carry in connections which cause relatively long delays; more elaborate schemes are capable of overcoming this problem (at the expense of added circuitry).

Figure 5.40.

The efficiency of the addition circuits is of particular importance in microprocessors where the functions of multiplication and division, as well as subtraction, often use these circuits. Larger computers (and many of the more recent 16 and 32 bit microprocessors) have special purpose circuitry for multiplication and division.

Flip-flops

One of the fundamental functions performed by digital computers is the storage of data in memory. The electronic component which is usually used for this purpose is called a *flip-flop*. Other names for the same device are *bistable*, *latch* and *toggle*, but flip-flop is the most commonly used name.

A flip-flop is capable of storing, in electrical form, a single binary digit. Thus, a collection of eight flip-flops can store a byte of data. As well as being used for memory, flip-flops form the basis of other useful CPU components, such as *shift registers* and *binary counters*.

Flip-flops are frequently constructed with gates, but using *sequential logic* rather than the *combinational logic* described in the previous part of this chapter. As we have seen, a combinational logic circuit produces an output which is entirely dependent on the current inputs; with sequential logic, because of the use of feedback, the output from a sequential logic circuit depends on its current state in addition to the current inputs. In other words, the output from a sequential logic circuit is partly determined by the previous inputs it received.

In this section we describe the operational characteristics of the simplest type of flip-flop, the *SR flip-flop*, before going on to show how it may be constructed using NAND gates. We then discuss the synchronous version of the SR flip-flop, the *clocked SR flip-flop* before showing how shift registers, binary counters and memory units may be fabricated using them.

Though there are a number of different types of flip-flops in common use, including JK, Master-Slave and D-type flip-flops, essentially they are all based on the SR flip-flop, and it is beyond the scope of this book to discuss the precise differences between them and why one type is preferred over another for certain types of application.

Operation of the SR flip-flop

The term flip-flop derives from its characteristic of being in one of two stable states at any instant, and hence the alternative name, *bistable*. These two states we conveniently designate 0 and 1. In state 1, the device is said to be *set*, and in state 0, *reset*, hence SR flip-flop. If the flip-flop is in state 1, it will remain in that state until an input causes it to change to state 0, in which state it will also remain until changed. Thus it remembers its current state until some signal causes it to change state.

Figure 5.41(a).
Unclocked

Figure 5.41(a) shows the symbol generally used for an unclocked SR flip-flop.

The two outputs are labelled Q and $\overline{Q}$ because each is the complement of the other. The current state of the device is by convention that of the Q output.

Figure 5.41(b).
Clocked

The input lines, S and R, are used to control the state of the flip-flop. If a signal is applied to the S line, the flip-flop is set (ie Q=1); a signal on the R line resets it (ie Q=0). The absence of any signal leaves the state of the flip-flop unchanged. Applying a signal to both lines simultaneously is not allowed.

Table 5.19 illustrates these rules with a sequence of input signals and the resulting state of the flip-flop.

S	R	Q	effect of input
1	0	1	set
0	0	1	remains in same state
0	0	1	
0	1	0	reset
0	0	0	remains in same state
1	0	1	set
1	0	1	already set so no effect
0	1	0	reset
0	1	0	already set so no effect

Table 5.19.

Construction of the SR flip-flop

A simple form of an SR flip-flop may be implemented using two NAND gates connected as shown in Figure 5.42.

The operation of this flip-flop is defined by Table 5.20.

The current state of the circuit is denoted by Q and the resulting state, due to the two inputs, is Q'. We can verify the operation of the circuit by tracing each pair of inputs and comparing them with the outputs shown:

Figure 5.42.

S	R	Q'
0	0	Q
0	1	0
1	0	0
1	1	not defined

Table 5.20.

(i) $\overline{S}=1$, $\overline{R}=1$ and Q=1. This corresponds to the null input, self-sustaining state. The inputs to the lower NAND gate are both 1, producing an output, Q', of 0. This means that the inputs to the upper NAND gate are 1 and 0, producing an output of 1; no change in the outputs. If the current state is Q=0, the lower gate has inputs 0 and 1, producing an output of 1, and the upper gate now has both inputs at logic-1, producing an output of 0; again no change.

(ii) $\overline{S}=0$ and $\overline{R}=1$. This is the *set* condition. Because $\overline{S}=0$, the upper gate must output logic-1; the inputs to the lower gate both being 1, the output is 0.

(iii) $\overline{S}=1$ and $\overline{R}=0$. This is the *reset* condition. Because $\overline{R}=0$, the lower gate must output logic-1 this time, and the two logic-1 inputs to the top gate produce an output of 0.

(iv) $\overline{S}=0$ and $\overline{R}=0$. In this instance the output from the flip-flop cannot be determined; the resulting state will be unpredictable and will depend on such factors as temperature and component tolerances.

The clocked SR flip-flop

Figure 5.41(b) shows the symbol for a clocked SR flip-flop. It has an additional input designated *clock* or *enable*. The circuit for a clocked SR flip-flop is shown in Figure 5.43.

The extra input allows the operation of the flip-flop to be controlled by a timing signal which is used to synchronise the operation of the separate components of a circuit. Circuits controlled by a clock are called *synchronous* circuits; where a clock is not used the circuit is *asynchronous*.

Figure 5.43.

Because of the added complexity of asynchronous circuits, most circuits are of the synchronous variety.

The effect of the additional gates in the circuit is to hold the S and R inputs at the null state ($\overline{S}=\overline{Q}=1$) until a clock pulse is applied to the first two gates, at which time set and reset signals are applied to the flip-flop. In effect, the clock pulse *enables* the flip-flop to assume a new state.

Shift registers

A four stage shift register is shown in the Figure 5.44.

Figure 5.44.

A sequence of signals representing a binary number is applied to the input. Each input is set up while the clock is at logic-0. When the clock pulse becomes logic-1, each flip-flop is enabled and assumes the value of the signal being applied to the S input. Therefore, the complete contents of the flip-flops are shifted along by one bit at every clock

clock pulse	input	O/P0	O/P1	O/P2	O/P3
		0	0	0	0
1	1	1	0	0	0
2	0	0	1	0	0
3	1	1	0	1	0
4	1	1	1	0	1

Table 5.21.

pulse. The current state of each flip-flop is available on the lines labelled O/P0 to O/P3. Table 5.21 illustrates the process with the binary sequence 1101, assuming that the initial contents of the shift register is 0000.

Binary counters

A binary counter consists of a collection of flip-flops each of which is associated with a bit position in the binary representation of a number. If there are n flip-flops in a binary counter, the number of possible states is 2^n and the counting sequence is from 0 to 2^n-1. If the maximum value is exceeded, the counting sequence starts at 0 again.

A simple form of a binary counter is based on an SR flip-flop connected to act as a *toggle circuit* shown in Figure 5.45.

Each pulse applied to the clock input inverts the output, Q, of the circuit; in effect, this is dividing the input frequency by two by performing alternate *set* and *reset* operations. Table

Figure 5.45.

	input	output (Q)
		0
1	1	1
2	0	1
3	1	0
4	0	0
5	1	1
6	0	1
	etc	

Table 5.22.

5.22 shows how the output changes after each logic-1 input, assuming that the current output is logic-0.

Notice that logic-0 inputs have no effect on the output. A four-bit counter uses four toggle circuits connected in series. (See Figure 5.46)

Figure 5.46.

The output from the first toggle circuit alternates between 0 and 1 as shown in the previous table. Each time a logic-1 is output from the first toggle component, the second one is enabled and its output inverts; each time the output from the second component is logic-1, the third one is enabled and its output inverts, and so on.

Therefore, the first component inverts after each logic-1 input, the second one inverts after two logic-1 inputs, the third after four and the fourth after eight. Table 5.23 shows how the outputs of each of the toggle circuits, A, B, C and D change for a sequence of logic-1 inputs. Thus, A represents the least significant bit of the 4-bit number and D the most significant bit. The counter thus counts up from 0 to 15 cyclically.

input	A	B	C	D
	0	0	0	0
1	1	0	0	0
2	0	1	0	0
3	1	1	0	0
4	0	0	1	0
5	1	0	1	0
6	0	1	1	0
7	1	1	1	0
8	0	0	0	1
9	1	0	0	1
10	0	1	0	1
11	1	1	0	1
12	0	0	1	1
13	1	0	1	1
14	0	1	1	1
15	1	1	1	1
16	0	0	0	0
17	1	0	0	0
etc.				

Table 5.23.

Memory circuits

One of the fundamental characteristics of the digital computer is its ability to store data and programs in random-access memory. We have seen already that sequential circuits are capable of storing binary signals and that collections of such components may be used to store bytes or larger words of data. Large arrays of such circuits constitute the internal memory of a computer. Figure 5.47 shows one possible arrangement for a random-access memory unit. The *Address Lines*, typically 16 or 32 for a microcomputer, specify which particular memory word is to be accessed; a *Chip Enable* line (not shown) enables the chip if it is logic-1, or disables the chip if it is logic-0; when enabled, the chip may be written to, by making *Write=1* and read from, using Write=0.

Each horizontal row of memory elements represents a word of memory which may be selected by an Address Decoder. So for an 8-bit word there will be a row of eight memory elements. When an address is input to the address decoder, it selects the corresponding word. For a 16-bit address, the decoder will select one line from 2^{16} possibilities. If a read operation is required, the word, corresponding to the states of the eight memory elements, will appear on the *Out* lines; a write operation will cause the eight memory elements to take on the binary values on the *In* lines.

Figure 5.47.

The construction of the memory elements, each storing a single bit, is shown in Figure 5.48.

Each element comprises a flip-flop and a number of other gates to control the transfer of data between the flip-flop and the common internal data lines. Notice that the AND gates are used to control the passage of signals; only when all inputs to an AND gate are 1 will the output become 1. Each *word-select* line is used to enable all elements in a row for reading or writing, and each column has two internal data lines, one for reading - data-in - and one for writing - data-out. The data-out line takes the value of the element in the currently enabled word.

Thus, when *Word select=1* the Q output from the memory element is ORed with the data-out line. A word is written into a memory location by presenting the appropriate address to the decoder (which enables the word memory

Figure 5.48.

elements), the bit pattern of the word to the data-in lines and then setting *Write=1*. Two AND gates in each memory element allow its state to be changed to the value on the data-in line providing *Write* and *Word select* are both at logic-1.

Integrated circuits

The logic elements described earlier in this chapter are fabricated using semi-conductors, transistors in particular. The speed of operation of transistors, which act as electronic switches in logic circuits, is dependent on their size; the power consumption, amount of heat generated and cost are also dependent on their size. Since size is such a critical factor, a great deal of research has been done to reduce the size of a transistor as far as possible. The result of this research has been the steady evolution of the Integrated Circuit (IC). Though invented in 1959, integrated circuits were first used in computers in the late 1960s. The PDP-11 was one of the first commercial machines to use such devices. At that time an integrated circuit contained less than one hundred transistors; today, microprocessors can contain one million transistors on a single chip, and it is predicted that by the turn of the century there will be one hundred million transistors on a single microprocessor chip. Electronic devices contain combinations of components such as resistors, capacitors and transistors. The most common material of microelectronic circuits is silicon, the same type that is found in ordinary sand. The silicon is first refined and made into thin discs which form the base material, the substrate, for a number of ICs. The manufacturing process produces several identical ICs, each perhaps only a quarter of an inch square, on one wafer of silicon. The circuit to be set into the silicon is first designed, often with the aid of a computer to minimise the number of components, before being used to prepare a series of masks. After being photographically reduced to the actual chip size, the masks are used in a photographic process which sequentially isolates each chip from its immediate neighbours, defines the position of the components, modifies the structure of the substrate to give it the required semiconducting characteristics and interconnects the components using etched metallic films. Further stages are required to test the circuits, separate them and package them into the familiar 'bug' shape. Table 5.24 is a rough guide to the five generations of ICs, in terms of chip complexity.

Since its invention in 1959, the IC has undergone rapid growth, its complexity following a progression known as Moores Law which states that the maximum number of components on a microprocessor chip dou-

generation	no. of components
Small Scale Integration (SSI)	2 - 64
Medium Scale Integration (MSI)	64 - 2000
Large Scale Integration (LSI)	2000 - 64,000
Very Large Scale Integration (VLSI)	64,000 - 2,000,000
Ultra Large Scale Integration (ULSI)	2,000,000 - 100,000,000

Table 5.24. *Generations of integrated circuits (ICs)*

bles every one and a half years. Currently, the maximum dimension, the *feature* size, of a transistor on a one-million transistor microprocessor is about one micrometre, that is, one millionth of a metre. Such a microprocessor is capable of processing perhaps twenty million instructions per second. It has been estimated that by the year 2000 the norm will be microprocessors containing forty million transistors of feature size 0.25 micrometers processing *one billion instructions per second*. Such a processor would be capable of handling animated graphics of photographic quality in real time. However, as the feature sizes of components approach atomic proportions, stability problems become increasingly problematic; with perhaps only a few hundred atoms separating components, their behaviour can become unusual. This behaviour is referred to as *quantum effects*. Obviously there is a limit to how small a transistor can be made, so continued micro miniaturisation depends on additional innovative research, and in fact quantum effects are providing one such possible avenue of research. When electrons are constrained to move in less than three dimensions, their normal range of energy states is changed. When electrons are confined to two dimensions, in a very thin film of conducting material, certain electron energy states restrict the flow of current through the film, allowing it to act like an electronic switch. Furthermore, when constrained to move in less than two dimensions, in lines or even dots, other quantum effects occur, providing opportunities for multi-state devices and therefore multi-valued logic offering greatly enhanced speeds.

Another quantum effect device is a type of transistor whose operation is based on the charge of a single electron, and yet another invention from IBM scientists is a switch which turns on and off with the motion of a single atom. These new devices are an order of magnitude smaller than those in current use and are capable of operating at much greater speeds, but at the moment there are serious problems to be overcome before they can be implemented in actual machines. The most serious problem is that quantum effect devices will only operate correctly at extremely low temperatures (around $-450°F$). However, experience tells us that apparently insurmountable technological problems remain so for only a short time and that we can expect that the near future will see a new breed of computers having capabilities greatly in excess of those in current use.

✎ Exercises

1. For each of the following, simplify the expression using a Karnaugh map and draw a circuit of the simplified expression:

   (i) $X.Y.\overline{Z} + X.Y.Z + X.\overline{Y}.Z$

   (ii) $A.B.C + A.\overline{B}.C + A.B.\overline{C} + \overline{A}.\overline{B}.C + \overline{A}.B.C$

   (iii) $A.B.C.D + A.B.\overline{C}.D + A.B.C.\overline{D} + \overline{A}.B.\overline{C}.D + \overline{A}.B.C.\overline{D} + A.\overline{B}.\overline{C}.\overline{D}$

   (iv) $\overline{W}.X + X.\overline{Y} + X.\overline{Y}.Z + \overline{W}.\overline{Y}.\overline{Z} + W.X.\overline{Y}.\overline{Z}$

2. Use truth tables to prove the laws of Boolean algebra.

3. Given two binary signals, X and Y, produce a truth table to define the difference of the two digits for every combination. There will be two outputs representing the difference and a 'borrow'. Hence, draw the circuit for a 'half subtractor'.

4. Produce a truth table which defines the 4-bit product when two numbers are multiplied together (the largest number produced will be $3 \times 3 = 9$, which requires 4 bits). Simplify each of the four outputs, using Karnaugh maps and produce a circuit for hardware multiplication of 2-bit numbers.

5. The adjacent figure shows the layout of a seven segment display, commonly used in calculators. Each segment of the display can be emphasised by applying a logic-1 to the input to that segment. By simultaneously emphasising the appropriate segments, the device can be used to display the digits 0 to 9. Design seven logic circuits, one for each segment, such that when four signals representing a binary coded decimal (BCD) digit are applied to each circuit, the appropriate digit is displayed. The truth table has the form shown alongside.

inputs (BCD)	digit	outputs
A B C D		a b c d e f g
0 0 0 0	0	1 1 1 1 1 1 0
0 0 0 1	1	0 1 1 0 0 0 0
etc	....	.....
1 0 0 1	9	1 1 1 1 0 1 1

Hardware

Chapters

Computer Systems

Any system consists of a number of separate components working together to achieve a common aim. A car, for example, is a form of transport system comprising amongst other items, an engine, wheels and a gear box. Its aim is to transport people from one place to another. The system will only operate successfully if all these major components work. An essential additional element is the driver, without whom the car is simply a motionless piece of metal. The components of a system and the ways they interrelate constitute its architecture (Chapter 7). The term *hardware* describes all the physical electronic and mechanical components forming part of a computer system.

Functional components

The hardware components of a computer system can be categorised by function, as follows:

Input

To allow the computer to process data it must be in a form which the machine can handle. Before processing, data is normally in a human-readable form, for example, as it appears on an employee's time sheet or a customer's order form. Such alphabetic and numeric (decimal) data cannot be handled directly by the internal circuitry of the computer. Firstly, it has to be translated into the binary format which makes the data *machine-sensible*; this is the function of an input device. There is a wide variety of such devices, but the most common make use of a keyboard. Data is transferred from the input device to main memory.

Main memory

This element, also commonly known as *RAM*, has two main functions:

- [ ] to temporarily store programs currently in use for processing data;
- [ ] to temporarily store data:
  - entered through an input device and awaiting processing;
  - currently being processed;
  - which results from processing and is waiting to be output.

Central processing unit (CPU)

Often referred to as the *processor*, the CPU handles program instructions and data and consists of two elements:

- [ ] *Arithmetic/logic unit (ALU).* The ALU carries out arithmetic operations such as addition, multiplication, subtraction and division. It can also make logical comparisons between items of data, for example, it can determine whether one value is greater than another. Such logical operations can also be performed on non-numeric data.

❏ *Control unit*. The control unit governs the operation of all hardware, including input and output devices and the CPU. It does this by fetching, interpreting and executing each instruction in turn, in an automatically controlled cycle; this *fetch-execute cycle* is described in detail in Chapter 4.

Output

Output devices perform the opposite function of input devices by translating machine-sensible data into a human-readable form, for example, onto a printer or the screen of a visual display unit (VDU). Sometimes, the results of computer processing may be needed for further processing, in which case, they are output to a storage medium (Chapter 9) which retains it in machine-sensible form for subsequent input.

Backing storage

Backing, or auxiliary, storage performs a filing function within the computer system. In this context it is important to consider a couple of important concepts.

❏ *Memory volatility*. It is not practical to store data files and programs in main memory because of its volatility. This means that the contents of the main memory can be destroyed, either by being overwritten as new data is entered for processing and new programs used, or when the machine is switched off. Such volatile memory is termed random access memory (RAM).

❏ *Retrievable data*. Backing storage media provide a more permanent store for programs (which may be used many times on different occasions) and data files (which are used for future reference or processing).

Peripherals

Those hardware devices which are external to the CPU and main memory, namely those devices used for input, output and backing storage, are called peripherals.

Figure 6.1 illustrates the logical structure of the computer and thereby, the relationships between various hardware elements. It shows the data flow through the system and the flow of control signals from the processor.

Figure 6.1. *Logical structure of computer system*

Computer systems classified

Computer systems can be classified according to the following characteristics: purpose; size and complexity; generation.

Purpose

There are two categories under this heading:

General-purpose computers

As the term suggests, general-purpose machines can carry out processing tasks for a wide variety of applications and most organisations will make use of this type of machine.

Dedicated or special-purpose computers

In their logical structure, these machines are fundamentally the same as the general-purpose machine except that they have been programmed for a specific application. Dedicated word processors provide one example. The advent of cheap, microprocessor-based, special-purpose systems has led to an expansion of their use in controlling machines and many household products, such as washing machines and microwave ovens, are controlled by such systems.

Size and complexity

It should be emphasised that the following categories are only broad guidelines and changes in technology are continually blurring the differences between them. For example, there are now powerful microcomputer systems (often referred to as super-micros) which far exceed the power and flexibility of earlier generation minicomputer systems. However, the generally accepted categories of computer system are as follow:

Mainframe Computers

Such computers are commonly used by large national and multi-national organisations such as banks, airlines and oil companies. They usually support a large number and variety of peripherals and can process a number of applications concurrently (*multi-programming*). The mainframe's power stems from the phenomenal speeds of the processor and the large size of the main memory.

Mainframes may also play a central role in *wide area networks*. Their huge capital cost invariably places them in centralised processing roles; for the same reason, about fifty per cent of the mainframes currently in use are rented or leased from specialist companies.

Mainframe computers are generally accommodated in special-purpose, air-conditioned rooms to ensure trouble free operation.

Supercomputers with processing speeds many times those of mainframe systems are used for scientific and statistical work, being capable of completing such work in a small fraction of the time that a mainframe would require.

Minicomputers (or high-end workstations

The term 'minicomputer' is falling out of use because of its association with rather slow and expensive systems, dependent on the hardware and software products of one manufacturer. A major feature of a minicomputer is its facility for *multiprogramming* and more recently its use of multiple processors for *parallel processing*. Digital Equipment Corporation (DEC) is manufacturer of the VAX, the most popular model of minicomputer. Prime, Data General and IBM also manufacture minicomputer systems. Because the distinction between minicomputer and *high-end workstation* is now blurred manufacturers now use the latter term when referring to their minicomputer range. Frequently they are aimed at computer-aided design (CAD) which needs the vast memory capacity and multiple processors to provide rapid response times. The manufacturers also provide systems based on different *platforms* (operating systems). DEC, for example, offers Unix, Windows NT and VMS alternatives.

The division still exists between these high-end workstations and the standard desktop micro-computer, so describing this separate category is still valid. To emphasise the division and to avoid confusion, we will continue to refer to the term minicomputer.

Minicomputers can support a number of applications concurrently and are often used with *time-sharing* (Chapter 13) operating systems and *intelligent terminals* to provide organisations with decentralised processing facilities. Used in this way, many applications such as word processing, invoicing and customer enquiry can be carried out by users in their own departments. Medium-sized organisations may use minicomputers for their main processing applications. Larger organisations may apply them to *front end processing* (FEP). Employed in this way, a minicomputer handles a mainframe's communications traffic (Chapter 11) with remote terminals or other computers, leaving the mainframe free to handle the organisation's information processing tasks.

Microcomputers

The microcomputer is the smallest in the range and was first developed when the Intel Corporation succeeded in incorporating the main functional parts of a computer on a single *chip* using *integrated circuits* (IC) on silicon. Subsequently, the technique of *large scale integration* (LSI) further increased the number of electronic circuits which could be packed onto one chip. LSI has been superseded by *very large scale integration* (VLSI) which packs even more circuitry onto a single chip thus further increasing the power and storage capacity of microcomputers and computers generally. This type of computer storage is known as *metal oxide semiconductor* (MOS) storage and has completely replaced the *core store* used in earlier mainframe computers.

Originally, microcomputers were only capable of supporting a single user and a single application at any one time. The increase in processor speed and memory capacity now permits their use for *multi-tasking* (the running of several tasks concurrently by one user). *Multi-user* operation is made possible through networking; it is now extremely popular to link microcomputers into a *local area network* (LAN), to allow resource-sharing (disk, printer, programs and data files), as well as electronic communications between users (*electronic mail*). Microcomputers can now support applications packages previously restricted to mini and mainframe systems, including, for example, those used for database and *computer aided design* (CAD) work.

The range of microcomputer software is now extremely wide and the quality generally very high. There are software packages available for most business applications. One area of recent rapid growth has been in the development of graphics-based applications and most popular applications software can now be operated via a *graphical user interface* (GUI) and a *mouse*.

The low cost of microcomputers and the increase in the range of software available, makes their use possible in almost any size and type of organisation. In the small firm, a microcomputer may be used for word processing, stock control, costing, and general accounting. In the larger organisation they may be used as intelligent terminals. Such systems provide the user with the processing facilities of a central mini or mainframe computer and at the same time, a degree of independent processing power through the use of the microcomputers own processor and memory store.

Multi-media systems

The term 'multi-media' is used to describe systems which allow the integration of sound, video, graphics and text in a single software product. Thus, the user of a multi-media encyclopaedia, can not only read about the life of Martin Luther King, but also see video sequences and hear his voice. At present, much multi-media software still leaves the user relatively passive, but future developments are likely to give the user increased flexibility to alter the outputs from a package. The meaning of multi-media has to be frequently updated as advances in software and hardware enable the range of media to be increased. Thus, computer animation may be used to illustrate, for example, the movement of a horse when walking, trotting and galloping, without any interaction with the user, save for the selection of the initial type of movement; the multi-media experience can be enhanced by allowing the user to hear different sounds by selecting the type of ground on which the horse is moving, for example, on a muddy field, on gravel, sand or in shallow water, or a sequence of different surfaces, perhaps over a route planned by the user. Future developments could allow the use of more senses than just sight and hearing, perhaps touch and smell.

At present, microcomputers configured to run multi-media software include a *sound card* (to process sound files), speakers, a microphone (for voice input) and CD-ROM drive. Memory and processor requirements are higher than for routine business machines, because multi-media software has to handle complex graphics, animation and sound files in *real-time*. It should be pointed out that a CD-ROM drive is now a standard component of all microcomputer systems, partly because most software packages are now available on CD-ROM, as well as floppy disk, but also because the storage requirements of packages requires the capacity of CD-ROM.

Portable computers

The first portable computer was developed in the early 1980s, but was nicknamed a 'luggable', because of its size and considerable weight (more than 10 kilogrammes). It also used a CRT (cathode ray tube) screen, which added to its power requirements. Today's portables are worthy of the name. Apart from pen-based, personal digital assistants (PDAs - see earlier), the A4 size notebook computer is the main portable product.Features include:

❑ powerful processor;

❑ liquid crystal display (see earlier) screen. Sometimes, the screen is backlit to improve definition. Colour displays are available, although the resolution cannot match that of conventional screens;

❑ memory is either static RAM (SRAM - see Main Memory) or flash memory. SRAM is volatile and its contents need battery power to be maintained. Flash memory is cheaper and does not require battery power. Unfortunately, flash memory is slower and wears out after, approximately, 10,000 erasures. Flash memory cards can be write protected and include a standard interface, which allows them to appear as hard disks to the rest of the system;

❑ integral hard disk, typically, with hundreds of megabytes capacity;

❑ ports for connection to external devices. These include: serial connections for use with a modem and communications network; parallel printer port; mouse port; external VGA screen connection;

❑   keyboard, sometimes full layout (but no numeric keypad).

Smaller notebooks, often referred to as sub-notebooks and about half the size of the A4 variety, are becoming increasingly popular. Many machines include a number of card slots for the connection of additional devices, such as a modem and network adapter. The most widely used standard for these card slots is PCMCIA (Personal Computer Memory Card International Association). The display size is between 180 mm and 235 mm, across the diagonal. A typical sub-notebook weighs about 1.5 kilogrammes.

Pen-based computers

A pen can be used as an alternative to the mouse but is most effective for handwriting, in conjunction with a digitising tablet, which is either separate or integral to the screen. The latter option is chosen for personal digital assistants (PDAs), pocket-sized computers designed for use on the move; the inclusion of a keyboard would destroy its usefulness as a light, highly portable device. A pen is used to write directly onto the screen. Recognition software attempts to identify and then translate hand-written characters by reference to stored prototypes; some symbols may represent commands, called *gestures*, whilst others may be letters of the alphabet. Hand-written input can then be handled as if it had been keyed in. The system can be trained to recognise how any given user draws a particular shape, if the recognition software cannot read their writing. The pen is the only feasible technology because touch-screens and mice lack the necessary precision, and light pens only function with CRT (Chapter 8) displays.

Generations

Since the first electronic computers were built in the 1940s, a number of developments in electronics have led to computer hardware being categorised by generation, that is, its place in the history of the computer. These generations can be simply defined as follows:

First generation

During the 1940s, this first generation of computers used electronic components including vacuum tubes. The first computer to allow a program to be stored in memory (a stored-program computer) was EDSAC, developed at the University of Manchester. The vacuum tubes were fragile, subject to overheating and caused frequent breakdowns.

Second generation

The introduction of low-cost and reliable transistors allowed the computer industry to develop at a tremendous rate during the late 1950s. The cost and size of the machines were radically reduced so it became possible for large commercial organisations to make use of computers. Examples of such machines include LEO III, UNIVAC and ATLAS.

Third generation

The development of integrated circuit (IC) technology in the mid-1960s heralded the development of more powerful, reliable and compact computers, such as those of the IBM 360 series.

Fourth generation

This generation is typified by large scale integration (LSI) of circuits which allowed the development of the microprocessor, which in turn allowed the production of the microcomputer. All computers used today make use of such silicon chip technology.

Fifth generation

Within this generation, developments are continuing towards expanding memory size, using very large scale integration (VLSI) techniques and increasing the speed of processors. This increasing power is allowing the pursuit of new lines of development in computer systems:

❏ more human orientated input/output devices using voice recognition and speech synthesis allows communication between computers and humans to be more flexible and natural. The aim is to allow computers to be addressed in languages natural to the users. Current techniques on microcomputers allow acceptance of spoken commands and, for example, text entry into a word processor. Another feature of fifth generation computers is the use of graphical user interfaces.

❏ parallel processing techniques.

Analogue computers

Whereas digital computers store numerical information in discrete form, that is, by coded sets of electrical pulses representing digits, analogue computers use physical quantities which are proportional to the numbers involved. Examples of such physical quantities, generically referred to as analogues, include electric current, voltage, temperature, length, or the angle of a shaft. Thermometers, slide rules (obsolete since the advent of the electronic calculator), barometers, pointer instruments such as voltmeters, ammeters, speedometers and the weathervane are typical examples of analogue devices. Analogue information is in continuous form, often depicted on a graph or an oscilloscope screen. Electrical analogue computers use current or voltage as analogues.

Uses. Analogue computers are used by mathematicians and engineers to solve differential equations which occur in science and engineering, for example, in fluid flow, robotics, atomic physics and in the field of simulation. Aircraft and rocket simulation, for example, is useful for training of personnel and as a design aid, particularly where experiments might be too expensive to carry out fully, or where failure may be hazardous to life.

Advantages and disadvantages. The over-riding advantage of an analogue computer, compared with a digital system, is its ability to solve differential equations extremely quickly. Therefore, it is ideally suited to real-time operation, in other words, the performance of operations in the time-scale in which they actually occur. It must be said that the speed and power of modern digital machines permits their application in areas of real-time operation formerly only suited to analogue techniques. Nevertheless, there are a number of situations in control and simulation where analogue computers provide a simpler and less expensive alternative to the digital computer. Analogue computers have a number of disadvantages:

❏ relatively inaccurate, 0.1 percent accuracy being typical;

❏ set-up time can be lengthy and alteration to suit another problem may be difficult;

❏ having no memory, they cannot store problems;

❏ output is only possible in graphical form;

❏ input is only acceptable in the form of dial settings;

❏ extensive maintenance is needed and the user must understand electrical engineering.

Hybrid computers

These were developed to combine the speed of the analogue computer with the flexibility of its digital counterpart. Users must possess skills in both analogue and digital computing. The analogue section of the hybrid computer is used to give an approximate solution, which is then enhanced by the digital section. The latter generates, by table look-up, functions that the analogue part cannot easily simulate. Output from the analogue section is edited by the digital section and printed out in a convenient form. Methods are needed to convert analogue form to digital form and vice versa and these same methods are used to interface a digital computer to the real, physical world. Examples of such interfacing are found in, for example, furnace temperature control systems and image scanners.

✍️Exercises

1. Identify the two main components of the *central processing unit* and describe their functions.

2. Why is *backing storage* an essential component of a computer system?

3. How is the function of an *input* device the reverse of an *output* device's function?

4. In the context of *RAM*, explain the significance of *volatility*.

5. What additional components are needed to ensure that a microcomputer can perform as a *multi-media* machine?

6. Apart from cost and physical size, identify two features of a *mainframe computer* which distinguish it from a *microcomputer*.

7. (i)　What does PCMCIA stand for and to which type of computer does it particularly relate?

   (ii)　Give an example of a PCMCIA product.

8. (i)　Apart from size, what is the main feature of a *PDA*?

   (ii)　In the same context, what is a *gesture*?

9. Identify two features of *fifth generation computers* that did not form part of earlier generations.

Computer Architecture

This chapter looks at a number of aspects of computer systems architecture and builds on some of the basic ideas dealt with in Chapter 6. The technical specification for any particular computer system will not only refer to the types of component, but also their performance and capacity ratings, which individually and in combination with one another contribute to the overall system performance. The following sections explain the operation and function of each component within the architecture of a computer system. Typical capacity and performance ratings are also given.

The components examined are: *memory*; *processor* (including CISC, RISC and parallel processing architectures); *buses* (including standards for bus architecture).

Memory

RAM

RAM constitutes the working area of the computer and is used for storage of program(s) and data currently in use. Computer memory is measured in Kb (kilobytes), where 1 Kb is 1024 bytes; for larger memory, the unit of measurement is Mb (megabyte), which is 1024 Kb. Generally, the performance of a computer system can be improved by the addition of more memory. Other upgrading measures, such as the addition of a hard disk controller (see Chapter 9) will make less impact on system performance if main memory capacity is inadequate. If there is too little memory, more frequent access to disk is required. As a hard disk drive is a relatively slow component, compared with main memory, frequent disk accesses slow down overall system performance. Large main memory enables the system to keep *resident*, all the files it needs for an application. RAM is volatile (the current contents are lost when power is removed or different programs and data are entered), so all programs and data files are held more permanently on a magnetic storage medium; invariably this is floppy or hard disk.

Technical features

RAM is directly accessible by the processor and memory/processor transfers which occur during a program's execution have to be made as quickly as possible to maximise the use of the processor's power. The section on processors describes the use of a 'clock' which generates regularly timed pulses to synchronise the activities of the processor and explains that different activities take different numbers of clock pulses. Memory/processor transfers, although extremely quick, typically 60 to 80 nanoseconds (ns) for a read from RAM, are relatively slow when compared with typical processor speeds. Thus, the quicker the transfer can be carried out, the less time that the processor spends unoccupied. One quality RAM should possess, therefore, is speed. Predictably, the higher the speed, the greater is the cost.

Types of RAM

Broadly, two types of RAM are used in computers. They are: static RAM (SRAM); dynamic RAM (DRAM).

A number of comparisons can be drawn between the two types:

❑   DRAMs are easier to make than SRAMs;

❑   more DRAM can be packed onto a single integrated circuit or 'chip' than is possible with SRAM;

❑   DRAM consumes less power than SRAM;

❑   static RAM, as the term suggests, retains its contents as long as power is maintained, whereas Dynamic RAM needs to be refreshed (the contents of each location are rewritten) at intervals not exceeding 2 milliseconds (ms);

❑   SRAM can be written to and read from more quickly, but is more expensive than DRAM.

The most important features for comparison relate to speed of access and cost. To maximise use of a powerful processor SRAM is the obvious choice. Unfortunately, the needs of modern software for large main memory would make computer systems based wholly on SRAM very expensive. The use of *graphical user interfaces*, such as Windows95 and the increasing sophistication of software packages, calls for a minimum of 16 to 32 Mb of RAM. As software becomes more sophisticated even more memory will be needed. So, for economic reasons, main memory consists of DRAM chips grouped together on a memory board. A conflict exists between processor speed and memory cost. Doubling the clock speed of a processor from 200 MHz to 400 MHz does not necessarily double the speed of the computer's overall operation because of other factors, including *disk access* time and memory read time. To help improve the speed of memory accesses and still keep down the cost of memory, a system of *cache memory* can be used.

EDO (*extended* or *enhanced data out*) RAM, has been used in many of the most recent microcomputer systems because of its superior access times. Despite this performance improvement, *cache memory* is still an essential part of a computer's configuration.

SDRAM (Synchronous DRAM) synchronises with the processor bus and running at 100MHz is around twice as fast as EDO RAM. As processor speeds increase, new memory technologies have to be designed to keep up.

Cache memory

To understand the function of cache memory it is necessary to refer to a feature identified in the section on the processor, namely *wait-state*. A wait-state is an extra clock pulse added to a processor cycle when it accesses memory. The slower the memory, the more wait-states which have to be added to processor cycles to give the memory time to respond. The greater the number of wait-states, the lower the overall computer system performance. Thus, a high performance processor is wasted if it is used with a slow memory system which requires many wait-states. A memory system which requires zero wait-states will allow the system (ignoring peripheral device performance) to function at the maximum performance of the processor. It must be emphasised that overall system performance depends on all components forming a computer system and that *disk access time* also plays a major part in determining such performance. The topic of disk storage is dealt with in Chapter 9.

A cache memory system aims to provide the performance of fast Static RAM (SRAM) but at the lower cost of Dynamic RAM (DRAM). A cache is a small amount of very fast SRAM located between the processor and main memory. Figure 7.1 illustrates the relationship between main memory, the processor and the cache.

Figure 7.1. *Cache memory*

The cache size is typically 256Kb to 512Kb and its purpose is to hold a copy of frequently used code and data. Instead of accessing the slower main memory (consisting of DRAM) for such data, the processor can go directly to the cache memory without incurring any wait-states. The effectiveness of cache memory is based on the principle that once a memory location has been accessed, it is likely to be accessed again soon. This means that after the initial access, subsequent accesses to the same memory location need go only to the cache. Much computer processing is repetitive, so a high hit rate in the cache can be anticipated. The cache hit rate is simply the ratio of cache hits to the total number of memory accesses required by the processor. Systems using cache memory may achieve an 85 to 90 per cent hit rate. Thus, system performance can be radically improved beyond that possible with other systems using the same processor but lacking a cache memory system.

Cache memory aims to improve memory access times and keep down memory costs. The larger the cache, the greater the hit rate but the greater the cost of the memory. For example, a cache the same size as the main memory would obviously give a 100 per cent hit rate but would defeat the object of having a cache. Modern processors have an integral cache (on the same chip) which provides even better cache performance.

ROM (read only memory)

The term *firmware* is used to describe programs and data which are hard-wired into the computer, using integrated circuit ROM chips. ROM is non-volatile, so its contents are not lost when the machine is switched off and the they cannot be overwritten by other programs or data. ROM is normally used to store an initial set of instructions which allow the booting of a computer system and the subsequent loading of the rest of the operating system. ROM (Read Only Memory) is a permanent storage area for special programs and data which have been installed during the process of computer manufacture. The contents are hard-wired and cannot be altered by software.

The software contained within ROM is fairly standard for most machines and generally includes part of the BIOS (Basic Input/Output System). As the name suggests, the BIOS handles the basic hardware operations of input and output. The aim of the BIOS is to provide an interface between the programmer and the computer. The interface relieves the programmer of concern about the physical characteristics of the hardware devices which form the system. As such, the BIOS is machine orientated and will vary from one make of machine to another.

There are two other types of ROM:

❑ *PROM* or programmable ROM chips, which can be purchased content-free and used to store software, such as word processors and spreadsheets, which are used regularly. Plugged into vacant slots inside a computer's system casing, the software they contain can then be accessed without reference to conventional backing storage, but simply by transfer to RAM (Random Access Memory - main memory). It has to be said that this is now less common, and most packages are stored on either a CD-ROM or hard disk drive, from where they can be loaded very quickly. Software is frequently being upgraded and the trouble of replacing ROM chips makes it an unattractive option. Once recorded upon, PROM chips cannot be re-used for any other purpose;

❏ *EPROM* or erasable programmable ROM chips fulfil a similar function to PROM chips, except for the fact that their contents can be erased by exposure to ultra-violet light and then replaced using a special EPROM programmer device.

Flash memory

The main memory in notebook computers is sometimes provided by flash memory, which requires no battery power to maintain its contents. Power is required to read from and write to the memory. Unfortunately, the access times are slower than those available with conventional forms of RAM and a flash memory card will wear out after approximately 10,000 erasures. Of course, they can be replaced when this happens. A flash memory card can be write-protected and because it includes a standard *interface* (see Chapter 14), it can be made to appear as a hard disk to the rest of the computer system.

Associative or content addressable memory

This type of memory allows its addressing according to the *contents* of locations rather than their physical addresses. Apart from Search (or Match) operations, associative memory also allows Reading and Writing according to the addressing principles used in RAM systems. For search operations, the contents of each memory word are compared with a given character string. Each memory word has an associated flag bit and if a match with the search string is found, the relevant flag is set. It is quite possible that the search string will not be unique to one memory location, so multiple matches are likely to be discovered in a single search operation. With the use of a *mask register*, the search string does not have to be compared with the full contents of each memory word; thus, for example, it can be compared with the contents of only the first 4 bits of each 8 bit memory word. Table 7.1 illustrates a masked search operation.

	masked bits							
search register	0	0	1	1	0	1	0	1	
mask register	1	1	1	1	0	0	0	0	logical AND with search register
	0	0	1	1	0	0	0	0	resulting search string
memory word 0	0	1	0	1	0	1	0	1	0 flag (no match)
memory word 1	0	0	1	1	0	1	1	1	1 flag (match)
memory word 2	0	0	1	1	1	1	0	1	1 flag (match)
memory word 3	0	0	0	1	1	1	1	0	0 flag (no match)

Table 7.1. *Use of a mask register on 4 bits*

A *logical AND* operation (Chapter 5) is carried out between the search register and the mask register; this ensures that only those bits in the search register which correspond with bit 1s in the mask register will be used in the search string.

Associative memory has obvious application for on-line information retrieval systems, but to be useful must make use of much longer word lengths to allow for example, search criteria involving names of people or products. To date, high cost has restricted its application.

Processor

The processor is a CPU (Central Processing Unit) on a chip and provides the central base for a machine's power. The following section examines a number of processor features and standards.

Registers

Apart from the registers used in the *fetch-execute cycle* (Chapter 4), most processors have a number which are general-purpose and as such, can be used by the low-level programmer to store intermediate results of processing. *Index* registers can be used to hold offset values to allow indexed indirect addressing methods (Chapter 4) or can be used as counters. Another register contains the *stack pointer*, which is used to store the address of the next available location in a special area of memory called the stack. The operation of the stack is described in the chapter on Data Structures. A *flag* or *status* register is used for the storage of various flag bits which can be set to 1 or cleared to 0 depending on some condition, and typically include:

❑ *sign* flag (positive or negative) indicating the sign of the result of the last arithmetic operation; this would be copied from the sign bit of the result of this last operation;

❑ *carry* flag, set to 1 if the last arithmetic operation produced a carry;

❑ *zero* flag, set to 1 if the result of the last arithmetic operation was zero and to 0 if the result was non-zero;

❑ *overflow* flag to indicate the occurrence of arithmetic overflow in the last operation;

❑ *break* status, set to 1 if a break instruction has been executed;

❑ *interrupt* disable flag, set to 1 if interrupts are disabled (Chapters 13 and 14).

Clock speed

As the initiator of all the activities in a computer, the processor has a wide range of tasks to perform and to ensure that these tasks are properly synchronised, an internal clock mechanism is used. The speed of the clock is one determinant of how quickly a processor can *execute* instructions.

A *program* (a set of instructions designed to make the computer perform in a particular way) is executed by *fetching* each instruction in turn from the computer's memory, *decoding* the operation required and then performing the operation under the direction of the processor. The control of *program execution* is exercised through the processor's *automatic sequence control mechanism*. The activity it controls is known as the *fetch-execute cycle*.

Certain steps in the fetch-execute cycle must wait until the previous step is completed. For example, during the fetching of a program instruction from memory the instruction cannot be moved from the Memory Buffer Register (MBR) to the Current Instruction Register (CIR) until the transfer from memory to MBR has been completed. The time taken for the latter transfer is dependent on the speed of the memory read operation. Not all activities are dependent on the prior completion of another or others. For example, once the value of the Program Counter (PC) has been copied to the Memory Address Register (MAR), the PC can be incremented at any time during the fetch-execute cycle.

Synchronising operations

To synchronise the processor's operations, the clock generates regularly timed pulses, at rates of hundreds of millions per second. A technical specification will express this rating in MHz (Megahertz or million *cycles* per second). For example a 500 MHz processor operates with a clock running at 500 million pulses or cycles per second.

Different processor activities take different times to complete. For example, it takes longer to read the contents of a memory location (a *memory read*) than to increment a value stored in one of the registers within the processor. Any such processor activity must be synchronised with a clock cycle. The number of clock cycles which the processor needs to complete an operation will depend on the type of operation. For example, one operation may be completed within a single clock cycle, whilst another may take several cycles. The most recent processors are able to execute one or more instructions for each clock pulse.

Wait state

When a processor handles data more quickly than it can be accessed from main memory, a memory read may take more than one clock cycle to complete. Each additional clock cycle is known as a wait state. The topic is referred to earlier, in the section on *cache memory*. Subject to certain limitations to be explained later, the greater the clock rate, the quicker the computer system (as a whole) will perform. For example, a 500 MHz processor will carry out processing more quickly than a 200 MHz processor.

Word length

Any given processor is designed to handle a particular number of bits as a unit. The size of this unit is known as the processor's *word length*. A processor with a word length of, for example, 32 bits, uses that unit size during the execution of arithmetic, logic, data transfer or input/output instructions. In addition, any working registers within the processor are also equal to the word length of the processor.

Processor data bus

Within the processor, data are transmitted along a set of parallel lines called an *internal data bus*. An *external data bus* acts as the interface with the system's *motherboard*. The motherboard is a circuit board into which the system components are plugged. If the board is designed for the needs of a particular processor, the data path between the processor and memory components is at least as wide as the processor's internal bus.

Thus, a motherboard designed to take a 32 bit processor has a 32 bit data path to connect it to other processor or memory chips. The processor's external data bus (which connects with the motherboard) is also 32 bits wide. The motherboard is connected to a *system data bus,* which acts as the communication channel between the motherboard and the other system components.

It is worth mentioning that the ISA (Industry Standard Architecture - first used in the IBM AT) design, which is still used in most PCs, has a system data bus which is only 16 bits wide. It also operates at a clock speed of 8 MHz, which is too slow for modern processors. Such imbalance affects the performance of a computer system as a whole (see Bus Architecture).

Table 7.2 shows the word lengths of generations of Intel processors.

Processor	word length	internal bus	external bus
8080	8 bits	8 bits	8 bits
8088	16 bits	16 bits	8 bits
8086	16 bits	16 bits	16 bits
80286	16 bits	16 bits	16 bits
i386	32 bits	32 bits	32 bits
i486	32 bits	32 bits	32 bits
P24T	32 bits	64 bits	32 bits
Pentium	32 bits	64 bits	64 bits

Table 7.2. *Generations of Intel processors showing word lengths and bus widths*

Maths co-processors

Most processors have an associated faster processor (known as a maths co-processor) which can radically improve the performance of processor-intensive applications, such as spreadsheets and computer-aided design (CAD). For example, associated with the Intel processors mentioned earlier are the 8087, 80287, i387 and i487. The Intel i386DX, i486DX and Pentium processors, on the other hand, house a maths co-processor on the same chip; data flow is much faster than is possible with a separate co-processor (the SX versions of the i386 and i486 processors do not incorporate a co-processor, and can be upgraded with the i387 and i487, respectively). The co-processor can only improve system performance if the software recognises and makes use of it.

Processor architecture

The internal structure of a processor is generally referred to as its *architecture*. Within the integrated circuits that form the processor, are contained a complex collection of component units, including registers, counters, arithmetic and logic circuits and memory elements. Although the details of such architecture are mainly of concern to the programmer working at machine code level, two main approaches to processor design are briefly described below. All the instructions available with a particular processor are known as its *instruction set*. CISC is an acronym for *complex instruction set computer* and RISC stands for *reduced instruction set computer*.

CISC architecture

For some time, the view was that longer word lengths should be used to create more complex instruction sets and thus, more powerful processors. This approach has given way to the RISC design, which makes more effective use of the increased word lengths available in modern processors.

RISC architecture

A RISC processor exhibits a number of particular design features:

❑ A reduced instruction set processor is one which provides only a small number of different instructions compared with the prevailing standards for its CISC competitors. Research into conventional CISC architecture has suggested that the average processor spends most of its time executing only a handful of simple instructions. Each instruction type in a RISC processor can be executed in only one clock pulse. More complex instructions can take several clock pulses.

❏   Super scalar execution. This is the ability to execute more that one instruction at once (in parallel pipelines). Thus, for example, a floating point arithmetic calculation can be executed in one pipeline, at the same time as an integer operation in the other. A separate arithmetic unit is available to deal with each. Intel's Pentium processor can, therefore, execute two instructions in one clock pulse, compared with its predecessor's (the i486) one.

❏   Integral cache memory. The topic of cache memory is examined earlier, but the location of this component on the processor provides faster data flow than is possible with a separate cache memory component.

❏   Branch prediction. The processor contains circuitry to predict the outcome of conditional branch instructions (when a certain condition is true, the program branches to an instruction out of the usual sequence) before they even enter the pipeline. Predictions are based on previous execution history. A correct prediction avoids retrieval of irrelevant instructions into the pipeline; instead, the valid instruction is fetched from the branch target address. An incorrect prediction means that the pipeline has to be cleared, but the algorithms for prediction achieve a high success rate, which makes the technique worthwhile.

A British microcomputer manufacturer, Acorn, was among the first to produce a RISC microcomputer called the ARM (Acorn RISC Machine). Now, all the world's major computer manufacturers produce their own RISC-based machines. Notable examples of modern RISC processors include the IBM RISC/6000 series, IBM/Motorola PowerPC601, DEC Alpha AXP and the Sun Microsystems/Texas Instruments SuperSparc. Such processors are designed for high performance systems, to be used as *file servers* or *workstations* in networks (see Chapter 10), rather than as stand-alone machines, where the power would be wasted. Unlike the Alpha, PowerPC and SuperSparc processors, which have been designed purely as RISC processors, the Intel i486 and Pentium processors have had to retain some CISC features, to remain compatible with the huge range of PC software designed for the i386 and its predecessors. The Alpha, PowerPC and SuperSparc processors are pure RISC processors and not compatible with software designed for the Intel range. This means that they are excluded from the lucrative PC software market. Although the Pentium still includes some complex instruction support, its design includes all the RISC features outlined earlier.

Parallel processing architectures

The potential for increasing computation speed through parallelism has long been recognised, its first real manifestation being in the change from computers which handled data serially bit by bit with a single processor to those manipulating parallel bit groupings or words, albeit still with only one processor. Parallelism as described here is concerned with the use, in a variety of approaches, of multiple processors to act upon either single or multiple streams of data. A number of factors have permitted the research and development of parallel processing architectures, which previously had not been cost-effective.

The development of VLSI (Very Large Scale Integration) circuits has allowed tremendous progress to be made in the miniaturisation of computer components, most significantly in terms of processor and memory chips, but although users have felt the benefits of significant speed improvements, they have not been of the same order. They continue to improve, but it has been apparent for some time that the power needs of some applications go beyond single processor systems. It is also recognised that the greatest increases in speed can be obtained through changes in system architecture. The RISC (Reduced Instruction Set Computer) approach is already bringing about significant benefits, but parallel architectures, despite the particular difficulties they present for the design of software which can take full advantage, probably hold the greatest potential for radical performance gains. Parallel hardware is, of course, only half the solution and it must be also possible to write programs that can execute in parallel. The Occam programming language developed by Inmos, addresses the special requirements of writing code for arrays of *transputers* (see later).

Architectural approaches to parallelism

The following sections provide information on some of the ways in which degrees of parallelism may be achieved.

Pipelining

This term refers to the activities of a pipeline of processors each of which performs a mathematical operation on a *single vector stream* of data. The approach is based on the premise that any arithmetic process incorporates a number of distinct stages which can be separately allocated to individual processors.

Each processor has an associated register, isolated from the rest, and permitting parallel computation on the data. A clock pulse synchronises the activities of all processors in the pipeline, so that the data moves through it, step by step with each clock pulse. As an illustrative example, floating point addition requires the performance of a sequence of three operations, namely to: (i) equalise the exponents, adjusting one mantissa as necessary; (ii) add the mantissas; (iii) normalise the result. New sets of numbers to be added can be fed into the pipeline as each set moves through it to produce the sum.

Instruction pipeline

Pipeline processing can also be applied to the instruction stream. Using the buffering principle, consecutive instructions are read from memory into the pipeline, while preceding instructions are executed by the processor. Complications arise when an instruction causes a branch out of sequence, at which point the pipe must be cleared and all instructions read from memory, but not yet processed, are discarded. The overall effect of such *queuing* is to reduce the average memory access time for reading instructions.

Although pipelining can be described as a parallel architecture, the processors are only operating on a single vector stream of data and the acronym SISD (Single Instruction Single Data-stream) is frequently used to describe its mode of operation. A major advantage of pipeline architecture is that program code developed for von Neumann architecture, that is *serial code*, can be run without modification, whilst improvements in the performance of programs particularly suited to pipeline processing can be changed accordingly. This requires the identification of discrete processing stages and the division of particularly processor-hungry sections of code for allocation to separate processors. A number of manufacturers have produced powerful machines of this type.

Processor arrays

Processors connected in a pipeline can be described as forming a linear array, but the following section is concerned with two and three-dimensional processor arrays, for which the Inmos transputer was specifically designed.

SIMD (single instruction multiple data-stream)

In a two-dimensional array, for example, 4096 processors may be connected in a 64 × 64 square, so that each one has 4 neighbouring elements. Known as SIMD architecture, each program instruction is transmitted *simultaneously* to all the processors in the array, so each can then execute the instruction using its *locally* stored set of data. Because all processors are executing the same instruction at any one time, existing serial code can be used, provided the data can be conveniently divided. By the parallel processing of large numbers of data sets at one time, massive increases in job processing speed can be achieved. Of course, not all processors in the array are necessarily concerned with a particular processing stage and data may have to be passed on to the next relevant processor via a number of array elements which have no interest in the data. The length of such communications paths can have a significant effect on system performance and in efforts to reduce the number of processors handling data with which they have no concern, a number of geometrical designs (beyond the requirements of this text) are in use.

MIMD (multiple instruction multiple data-stream)

This also permits the parallel processing of separate sets of data, but each processor is at a different stage in the program's execution. More complex than the SIMD approach, it requires firstly, the vectoring of the program code into separate processes, each with the potential for execution on a separate processor and secondly in some systems, the division of data into *local* (available to a particular processor) and *global* (available to all). Each processor can be viewed as dealing with a particular part of the overall program and a particular data set, as well as having access to certain data available globally to all processors. In order that they can be executed in parallel, each of the processes should be substantially independent of the rest, although in general, they need to communicate with one another. If global memory is used for such communication, co-ordination difficulties can arise. In the Cray 2 system for example, passing data from one processor to another via global memory, requires the synchronisation of the write operation by the transmitting processor and the subsequent read by the receiving one. The *transputer* incorporates serial links which allow communications between processors and the concept of global memory is not used.

Parallel processing applications

A number of applications likely to benefit from parallel processing are outlined below.

- ❑ *Weather forecasting*, which requires number crunching operations on huge volumes of data, gathered globally and from monitoring satellites, in time to produce accurate weather forecasts, rather than comments on existing weather conditions!

- ❑ *Graphics applications*. Ray tracing, for example, where a set of descriptors of three-dimensional objects in three-dimensional space is mapped onto a flat screen complete with shadows, refraction and reflections, needs considerable computation to trace where the light on each screen pixel came from. The application is most easily implemented on pipeline architecture, where it benefits from both the faster maths and the faster communication. With about 10 million calculations to generate a single screen picture, speed is vital when generating sequences of images. A major application is in aircraft flight simulators, where the scenes to be shown are not known exactly in advance, as they depend on the pilot's actions. To be of any use they need to be generated virtually instantaneously in real-time.

❏ *Simulation*. Engineering design problems benefit hugely from computer simulation. The designers of North Sea oil platforms could ill afford to build prototypes to test to destruction, so they carry out all the structural analysis on a Cray supercomputer costing around 20 million; the process only takes about 9 hours, but the time taken still makes extensive prototyping very expensive. A car body designer using a 1 million mainframe has to wait about 20 hours for a typical run to complete. These lengthy run-times mean that computer simulation tends to be used to validate designs already completed, rather than as a development tool.

❏ *Image processing*. A particularly exciting example involves the use of computers to assist the plastic surgeon in the repair of facial injuries or deformities. The patients head is scanned by cameras and the image digitised for display on a computer screen. This image can be rotated or tilted on screen by the surgeon and experimental cuts made, the results of which can then be viewed on screen from any angle. In this way, a plastic surgeon can study the results of a variety of strategies before making a single mark on the patient. The complexity of such image processing requires parallel processing if rapid response to user input is to be achieved. Industrial processes frequently require robots which can recognise different shaped components and possess sufficient spatial awareness to allow accurate assembly to take place. Artificial intelligence techniques are applied to both these areas, so that robots can learn and the power of parallel processing greatly enhances the opportunity for such developments.

❏ *Speech recognition* is an enormously complex process if a system is to be capable of handling a wide range of vocabulary, pronunciation and intonation, let alone the meaning of phrases and even sentences. Artificial intelligence techniques are being applied to the speech recognition process and parallel processing power greatly improves the opportunities for its evolution.

❏ *Financial and economic system modelling*. To make realistic assessments of the effectiveness of various economic strategies requires the processing of huge volumes of raw data.

Multi-processing
Parallel processing should not be confused with multi-processing architectures which allow the simultaneous running of several separate programs, but with each program only having control of one processor at a time.

Transputers
Designed for parallel processing, the Transputer contains its own memory and processing elements and also features unique serial links which allow it to communicate with other Transputers. A matrix of Transputers can be created with each one solving a small part of a complete task. The addition of extra Transputers to a system incrementally adds the full power of each unit to the overall system performance. In theory, if one Transputer operates at 10 million instructions per second (mips), then two will give a system performance of 20 mips, 10 will give 100 mips and so on. In practice, the problem still remains of splitting computer processing problems into separate parts for each of the transputers to handle.

Buses

As explained in Chapter 6, all computers have the same basic functional components, but the architectural details in some are far more complex than in others. A particular area of variation relates to the arrangement of the bus systems which permit communication between the various parts of the computer system. A number of features concerning buses can be identified:

❑   a bus is a group of parallel wires, one for each bit of a word, along which data can flow (as electrical signals);

❑   the *system* bus comprises a number of such communication channels, connecting a computer's processor and its associated components of memory and input/output(I/O) devices;

❑   a single bus may carry data for different functions at separate times or it may be dedicated to one function. A computer will usually have several buses, used for specific purposes, for example, the I/O bus or main memory to processor bus;

❑   some buses are *bi-directional*, that is by the enabling and inhibiting of *gates* (Chapter 5), data can flow in one direction or the other;

❑   the *width* of a bus determines the length of word which can be handled at one time. For example, a processor which used a 16-bit bus, but required a 32-bit word to address memory, would have to concatenate two 16-bit words in two separate fetch operations.

Communication is required within a processor, to allow movement of data between its various registers, between the processor and memory and for I/O transfers. In a *single* bus system, both I/O and memory transfers share the same communication channel, whereas in a *two-bus* system, I/O and memory transfers are carried out independently; similarly, in small systems with few I/O devices, they usually share the same bus, but a larger system requires several I/O buses to ensure efficient operation. Each of the separately identified functions of memory, register-to-register and I/O transfers (assuming that the I/O bus is shared by a number of devices), must have the use of:

❑   a *data bus*, for the transfer of data subject to processing or manipulation in the machine;

❑   an *address bus* which carries the address of, for example, a memory word to be read (the details of memory addressing as part of the fetch-execute cycle are described in Chapter 4), or the output device to which a character is to be transmitted;

❑   a *control bus*, which as the name suggest, carries signals concerning the timing of various operations, such as memory write, memory read and I/O operations (this latter aspect of control is examined in more detail in Chapter 14).

All signals on a bus follow strict timing sequences, some operations taking longer than others.

Bus architecture - a brief history

This concerns the internal structure of a computer, that is the way in which the various components are connected and communicate with one another. As technological advances improve the performance of certain components, so the architecture has to change to take advantage of these improvements. There follows a brief summary of some of the architectural standards used over the last decade.

❏   IBM's Micro Channel Architecture (MCA); despite the commercial power of IBM, this standard did not found general acceptance;

❏   Extended Industry Standard Architecture (EISA);

❏   Local Bus (VESA and PCI).

Micro channel architecture (MCA)

MCA aimed to overcome the limitations of the old, Industry Standard Architecture (ISA), IBM AT (Advanced Technology) machines as well as a myriad of clones produced by IBM's competitors. IBM used MCA in their 32-bit PS/2 (Personal System 2) range.

System bus width and system performance

One of the many differences with the MCA approach concerns the width of the *system bus*. This bus is a communication link between the processor and system components and is an essential, but passive, part of system architecture. The active components, such as the processor, disk controller and other peripherals are the primary determinants of system performance. As long as the data transfer speed along the bus matches the requirements of these devices and does not create a bottleneck, the bus does not affect system performance. The MCA bus is 32 bits, compared with the AT's 16 bits, and the wider data path allows components within the system to be accessed twice as quickly. The MCA bus also uses bus-mastering controllers to handle data transfers more quickly. The wider bus is also compatible with the 32-bit external bus used on more recent processors. The bus can be controlled by separate *bus master* processors, relieving the main processor of this task.

MCA is also radically different from AT architecture in many other respects. For example, the expansion slots in the PS/2 range which allow the user to insert extra features, perhaps for networking or for extra memory, are physically different from those in the AT and PC machines and their expansion cards will not fit in the PS/2 machines. The problem for existing AT and PC users is that they cannot buy new PS/2 machines and still make use of their existing expansion cards. This incompatibility has also meant that few manufacturers have produced MCA versions of their expansion cards. IBM and Apricot are the biggest proponents of the MCA standard, but the fact that IBM is continuing to release ISA models is possibly an admission that MCA is unlikely to become the dominant architecture.

Extended industry standard architecture (EISA)

A consortium of IBM's competitors including Compaq, Zenith, NEC and Olivetti amongst others, established a new architecture (EISA - Extended Industry Standard Architecture) which aims to give the benefits of MCA and to retain compatibility with existing AT expansion cards. EISA also uses a 32-bit bus, thus providing the same data transfer benefits as MCA, particularly for hard disk controllers (a very important contributor to overall system performance).

Both EISA and MCA machines are more expensive than the ISA-based microcomputers, and tend to be used where extra power is needed, as *file servers* (Chapter 10) in networked systems. Most small business users find that ISA machines are adequate for their needs, particularly as the use of *local bus* technology is further increasing their power.

Local bus

A local bus is a high speed data path connecting the processor with a peripheral. Local bus design is used, primarily, to speed communications with hard disk controllers and display adapters. The need for local bus derives from the imbalance between the clock speed of a 32-bit processor (typically, in excess of 100MHz) and the ISA 16-bit system bus (operating at 8 MHz). The ISA system is illustrated in Figure 7.2.

Display   I/O ports   Network   Hard Drive
Adaptor   card   Card   Controller

Figure 7.2. *ISA 8MHz bus and high speed processor imbalance*

This imbalance can result in the processor idling while waiting for data to be transferred from disk, or the display adapter waiting for screen data. The widespread use of Windows, a *graphical user interface* and software packages which make intensive use of the hard disk (such as databases) and screen graphics (computer-aided design), has highlighted the deficiencies of such imbalanced computer systems. A local bus provides a wider data path, currently 32 bits and an increased clock speed, typically 33MHz or more. The first local bus systems appeared in 1992, with manufacturers following a standard referred to as *VL-bus*, developed by VESA (Video Electronics Standards Association). Figure 7.3 illustrates the broad principle of a local bus system. In 1993, Intel backed the development of a new industry standard called *PCI*.

Figure 7.3. *Local bus to high speed display and hard drive devices*

The standard is in competition with VL-bus and aims to encourage the development of computer systems which allow local bus connection to any high-speed peripheral. Apart from speeding communication with screen graphics controllers, PCI local bus can be used with, for example, hard disk, network and motion video controllers (up to 10 devices in total).

Expansion slots

These are slots into which expansion boards or cards can be plugged, to add extra features to a system. For example, a user may wish to install a sound card, to allow full use of multi-media software, or an additional serial port (see Chapter 11) to connect to a modem. Expansion slots are connected to the system bus (it makes electrical contact), so when an expansion card is plugged in, it becomes part of the system.

I/O ports and interfacing

To allow an I/O device to communicate with the I/O bus, for example, to place data entered through a keyboard onto the data bus, requires the use of an I/O port. A number of I/O ports are usually available, the number and types depending on the range of devices which the system is designed to support. Each port has an *interfacing* role which must convert the data signals, as presented by the connected device, into the form required by the processor, as well as the converse for output data. Thus, for example, the *external* ASCII code used for data storage on a particular tape storage system, will probably have to be converted by the interface into the machine's particular *internal* code (Chapter 2).

Exercises

1. What is *cache memory* and why is it used?
2. What do the abbreviations *CISC* and *RISC* stand for?
3. Why may a 'clock-doubled' processor not necessarily double the speed of the overall computer system?
4. What is meant by *parallel processing*?
5. What significance have parallel processing architectures for the way software is designed?
6. What are the functions of the: (i) data bus; (ii) address bus; (iii) control bus?
7. Describe examples of architectural changes which have sought to overcome the performance restrictions of the ISA bus.
8. Research PC magazines for differing computer configurations and draw up a table which compares their specifications (RAM size, type, processor type, speed etc.). Judge the suitability of each for particular kinds of application (graphic design, word processing, accounts etc.).

I/O ports and interfacing

Chapter 8

Input and Output Devices

Input devices

Input devices provide a convenient means of transferring information into a computer so that it may be processed in some way or stored permanently on magnetic media. Whatever its particular purpose, each type of input device is an *interface*, a means of bridging the gap between the human user and the electronic computer. For example, an input device such as computer *keyboard* converts the pressing of a key into an electrical signal representing a particular binary code; this code could represent a character within a word processing document, or it could be part of a response to a question posed by the current computer program. An interactive device such as a *mouse* or a *touch screen* provides a convenient method of communicating actions to a computer. Other input devices, such as *scanners* and *optical mark readers*, allow typed or hand-written documents to be read into a computer. In this section we describe several categories of input devices, namely *interactive devices*, *analogue to digital converters*, and *document readers*.

Interactive input devices

Interactive input devices are used in conjunction with visual display units so that the user is provided with immediate feedback on the task being performed by the computer. For example, the movement of a mouse or tracker ball is shown by a pointer on a display screen, and when a key is pressed on a keyboard, the appropriate character appears on the screen.

Computer keyboard

The main section of a typical computer keyboard is similar to a typewriter keyboard, with the usual alphabetic and punctuation characters. The *shift* keys are used to switch between upper case (capital) letters and lower case (small) letters. The *control* keys are sometimes used to change the operation of a normal key. For example, holding down one of the control keys while hitting the *F* key might activate a menu. The separate *numeric keypad* is useful when data includes a high proportion of numeric characters. The *function* keys are used by application programs for special purposes, so the operation of a function key will often be different from one program to another, but quite frequently function key *F1* is used to gain access to a help facility if one is provided.

A keyboard is usually detachable, enabling the operator to position it to suit personal comfort, but it remains physically connected by a coiled cable. The desirable qualities of a keyboard are reliability, quietness and light operating pressure and in these terms keyboards vary considerably.

Keyboards are commonly used for the following types of tasks:

❑   entering alphanumeric information (that is, combinations of alphabetic, numeric and special characters such as punctuation marks) into the computer. A typical example of this is the use of a keyboard for word processing;

❏ interactively communicating with a program which asks the user questions and responds to the answers. A good example of this is an expert system (see Chapter 12) which provides advice on some area of interest after asking the user a sequence of questions;

❏ controlling animated graphics characters in computer games;

❏ entering commands to an operating system such as MS-DOS.

Concept keyboard

In specialist applications, the standard keyboard is not always the most convenient method of input. In a factory, for example, a limited number of functions may be necessary for the operation of a computerised lathe. These functions can be set out on a touch sensitive pad and clearly marked. This is possible because all inputs are anticipated and the range is small. The operator is saved the trouble of typing in the individual characters which form instructions. Concept keyboards also have application in education, particularly for the mentally and physically handicapped. Instead of specific functions, interchangeable overlays, which indicate the functions of each area of the keyboard allow the user to design the keyboard to particular specifications.

Mouse

A mouse is a small, hand-held device which the user can move on a flat surface to direct a pointer on the computer screen. It has two or more buttons which work in conjunction with software packages, allowing the user to draw, erase, select and format textual and graphical images. The most common type incorporates a ball which makes contact with the flat surface on which the mouse is moved and turns two rollers, one tracking vertical movements on screen, the other horizontal. The movement of the rollers is detected by sensors

Figure 8.1. *How the mouse movement is detected*

which continually send electrical signals through the mouse cable to the computer, reporting the location of the mouse. The software then uses these signals to adjust the pointer's position on the computer screen so that the pointer follows the movement of the mouse. Another type of mouse detects movement purely by optical sensors which work in conjunction with a special mouse pad, and some are cable-less, using infra-red to transfer signals to the computer in a way similar to the use of remote controls for Tvs. Most computer systems are equipped with a mouse facility and many packages, including those for art, design, word processing and desktop publishing can only be operated effectively with a mouse. Graphical user interfaces (GUIs - see Chapter 12) such as Microsoft Windows also depend heavily on its use.

Tracker ball

A tracker ball is another variation of a mouse and is used for the same purposes. A tracker ball is a bit like an upside-down mouse,

Figure 8.2. *Tracker ball*

with the ball visible on the top of the base. To use a tracker ball you simply move the ball in the required direction using your fingers. Buttons are supplied, as with a mouse.

Like joysticks, tracker balls have the advantage over mice, in that a flat surface is not required for its operation, and for this reason they are often used with portable computers.

Touch screen

A touch screen is a touch-sensitive display, used to read the position of a fingertip. The screen displays options which a user can select simply by touching them. The computer detects the position touched and performs the appropriate action. The range of input values which can be selected will normally be small (a finger is not a very precise pointing device), so a touch screen might typically be used by a tourist agency to allow visitors to request information on, for example, local accommodation, entertainment and tourist attractions, or by a bank to allow customers to view details of banking services. The main components of a touch screen are a special film coating on the surface of the screen and a controlling microprocessor which determines the co-ordinates of the finger's contact point and displays the required information.

Digitising tablet

A *digitising tablet* consists of a flat surface, containing an active area, typically 250mm square, which has a grid of very fine horizontal and vertical wires embedded into it. Attached to the tablet is a *stylus* which produces a magnetic field at its tip. The grid of wires allows the position of the stylus on the tablet to be determined very accurately (the grid can contain up to 1000 points per inch), so that the computer can track and store the movement of

Figure 8.3. *Digitising tablet with stylus*

the stylus. As the user draws on the tablet the results appear on the computer screen. Drawings are stored in the computer's memory so that they can be manipulated or displayed.

Digitising tablets are useful for entering drawings consisting of lines - engineering drawings or maps for example - into the computer. The line drawing can be placed on the tablet and the stylus used to trace the outline or locate key points. Usually the tablet can also be used as a device for selecting options in a similar way to the concept keyboard described earlier, but with the capability of providing many more options. Computer-aided drawing programs often allow templates of pre-defined shapes - electrical circuit components for example - to be overlaid on the tablet so that the user can select a shape which will then appear on the screen ready to be used in a drawing.

Light pen

A light pen has an optical sensor in its tip and can only be used in conjunction with a *cathode ray tube* (CRT) display which creates images on screen through the use of a scanning electron beam; as the beam creates the screen images line by line (see the section on Visual Display Units), the light pen's optical sensor detects the exact moment when the beam passes beneath it and, from this, its position at any particular moment. By displaying functions at particular locations on the screen, the controlling program can allow the light pen to be used to make selections from several alternatives. It may also be used in conjunction with a drawing package to create, edit or manipulate images on screen. Though similar to the operation of a graphics tablet and stylus, a light pen is not capable of the same high accuracy, but it is generally cheaper. LCD (liquid crystal display) displays used in laptop, notebook and palmtop computers do not make use of electron beam scanning and cannot, therefore, support the use of light pens.

Analogue to digital converters (ADCs)

Data is often not in *digital* format but is instead a measurement of, for example, temperature or light intensity. These are called *analogue* forms of data and, before they can be used by a digital computer, they must be converted into digital format. A device which converts analogue data into digital data is called an *analogue to digital converter* (ADC).

If, for example, a certain microprocessor-controlled washing machine allowed you to select several temperature settings for the water, it might use a temperature sensor in conjunction with an ADC to convert water temperatures between 0°C and 1000°C to a binary signal in the range 0 to 255, as illustrated in Figure 8.4.

Figure 8.4. *Example of analogue to digital conversion*

The diagram shows a temperature sensor immersed in the water. This will produce a small electrical signal, proportional to the water temperature, which must be amplified so that it produces a voltage in the range 0 volts to 10 volts, for example. The ADC then converts this voltage to a binary signal in the range 0 to 255 (11111111 in binary), so that 0°C is represented by 0 and 100°C is represented by 255. Thus a temperature of 25°C would produce about 2.5 volts from the amplifier and this would translate to binary 63 (00111111).

The term *digitiser* is usually reserved for more complex ADCs used for converting whole frames of photographic film into digital images which, with the aid of suitable software, can be displayed on a computer screen and edited. The output from a video camera, or medical scanning equipment can also be digitised for use in a computer. Digitisers which are designed for textual or graphical documents are usually termed *scanners* and are described in the next section.

Document readers

There are a number of devices designed to capture information, in the form of pictures or text, already printed on paper. Examples of such devices are *scanners, optical character readers* (OCRs), *optical mark readers* (OMRs), *magnetic ink character readers* (MICRs) and *bar code readers*

Scanners

Scanners allow whole documents to be scanned optically and converted into digital images. These vary from small hand-held devices which are manually moved slowly over the document (Figure 8.5), to machines which allow whole sheets of paper to be fed in and scanned automatically (Figure 8.6).

Figure 8.5. *Hand held scanner* **Figure 8.6.** *Flat bed scanner*

Versions of both of these types of scanners are capable of dealing with colour images as well as black and white, though these machines tend to be significantly more expensive. Special scanners are available to convert textual documents, typed or hand-written, into the sort of format used by word processors. These devices perform *optical character recognition* (OCR) and have special software which processes the images once they have been converted into a computer-processable form. The software which can handle handwriting tends to be distinct from that for typed text, and is now commonly available for pen-based portable computers as described in a later section in this chapter.

Optical character reader

As described earlier, these devices perform *optical character recognition* (OCR), the process of converting images of printed or hand-written material into a format suitable for computer processing. Figure 8.7 shows the main components of an optical character reader designed for printed documents.

Figure 8.7. *The components of an OCR system*

The document is illuminated and scanned by a strong light source and the lens concentrates the documents image onto a detector. The detector passes the image data to the OCR software which processes each character of the image, individually matching each character against stored data of the character set. Non-text regions containing graphics for example are often separated out and saved separately from the text which is output in a format which can be processed by an application program such as a word processor. Most commercial general-purpose OCR devices read machine-written text, but a few can cope with hand-printed text. Special-purpose OCR readers are available for such tasks as reading data on pre-printed forms or processing gas and electricity meter readings.

Optical mark reader (OMR)

An OMR is designed to read simple marks placed in pre-set positions on a document. The document is pre-printed and the values which can be entered are usually limited to marks made in specially placed boxes. Thus, a suitable application for OMR is a multi-choice examination paper, where the answer to each question has to be indicated by a pencil mark in one of several boxes located after the question number. The OMR scans the answer sheet for boxes containing pencil marks and thus identifies the answers, allowing the associated software to determine automatically the grade which the candidate has obtained. Optical mark readers can read up to 10,000 A4 documents per hour.

Magnetic ink character reader (MICR)

This particular device is employed almost exclusively by the banking industry, where it is used for sorting and processing huge volumes of cheques. The millions of cheques which pass through the London Clearing System could not possibly be sorted and processed without the use of devices such as MICRs. Highly stylised characters, such as those illustrated below, are printed along the bottom of the cheques by a special printer, using ink containing iron oxide.

The characters are first magnetised as the cheque passes through the MICR which then electronically reads the magnetised characters. A high degree of reliability and accuracy is possible, partly because of the stylised font, but also because the characters are not affected by dirty marks. This is obviously important when cheques may pass through several hands before reaching their destination. Such marks could cause problems for an optical character reader.

Bar code readers

A *Bar code* usually consists of a series of black bars of varying thickness with varying gaps between. These bars and gaps are used to represent data, which are often printed underneath in human-readable form. Using a laser scanner, the beam passes over the code noting the occasions when light is reflected by a bar and when it is absorbed by a space; the feedback is then converted by the scanner to a computer-readable code. Several standard codes are in use, each having particular features which are appropriate to certain application areas. One very common code is the Universal Product Code (UPC), a purely numeric code which, as the name suggests, is associated with supermarkets and general product distribution.

Bar codes are commonly used to store a variety of data such as prices and stock codes relating to products in shops and supermarkets. A sticker with the relevant bar code (itself produced by computer) is attached to each product, or alternatively, the packaging may be pre-coded. By using the data from the code, the cash register can identify the item, look up its latest price and print the information on the customer's receipt. Another useful application is for the recording of library issues. A bar code sticker is placed inside the book cover and at the time of issue or return it can be scanned and the library stock record updated. By providing each library user with a bar-coded library card, the information relating to an individual borrower can be linked with the book's details at the time of borrowing.

Output devices

Just as input devices allow human beings to communicate with computers, so output devices allow computers to present electronically stored, binary coded data in a form which we can comprehend.

In this section we describe *visual display units*, a number of different types of *printers*, two types of *plotters, computer output microform (COM)* and *voice processing* and *synthesis.*

Visual display unit

The most commonly used device for communicating with a computer is the *visual display unit* (VDU). Input of text is usually by means of a full alphanumeric keyboard and output is displayed on a viewing screen similar to a television. The term VDU *terminal* is normally used to describe the screen and keyboard as a combined facility for input and output. On its own, the screen is called a *monitor* or *display*. So that an operator can see what is being typed in through the keyboard, input is also displayed on the screen. A square of light called a *cursor* indicates where the next character to be typed by the operator will be placed. Keyboards are described in the section on input devices.

Dumb and intelligent terminals

A dumb terminal is one which has no processing power of its own, possibly no storage, and is entirely dependent on a controlling computer. Where a terminal is connected via a telecommunications link, each character is transmitted to the central computer as soon as it is entered by the operator, making editing extremely difficult and slow; for this reason, they are not generally used for remote data entry.

An intelligent terminal has some memory and processing power and as such, allows the operator to store, edit and manipulate data without the support of the computer to which it is connected. The processing facility is provided by an internal processor, usually a microprocessor and storage is normally in the form of buffer memory in which numerous lines of text can be held and manipulated before transmission. The facility may also include local backing storage and a printer.

A number of text editing tasks involve the use of control codes and these can be built into ROM (Read Only Memory) or magnetic bubble memory, both of which are non-volatile. Typical control codes are those which, through single key-presses, execute functions such as clearing the screen, moving the cursor up or down, and homing the cursor to the top-left of the screen. Function keys for these and other functions are generally specifically marked. It is also likely that the terminal is programmable thus allowing specific routines to be developed for validation of data. Microcomputer systems are often used as intelligent terminals.

Text and graphics modes

All modern display screens operate in either *text* or *graphics mode*. Text consists of letters (upper and lower case), numbers and special characters such as punctuation marks. Most applications require some text display, although it is safe to say that even basic word processors rely almost entirely on the graphics capability of modern screens to permit the use of various character styles or *fonts*. Despite this, the term *graphics* generally refers to picture images, such as maps, charts or drawings produced using graphic design programs, or even photographic images captured with an appropriate *digitising* device (see section earlier in this chapter).

Text mode dot matrix characters

In text mode (see preceding section), characters are formed using a matrix of pixels, as shown in Figure 8.8, and the clarity of individual characters is determined by the number of pixels used. Selected dots within the matrix are illuminated to display particular characters. A 9 x 16 matrix obviously gives greater clarity and definition than an 8 x 8 matrix. Although both upper and lower case

Figure 8.8.
Dot matrix character

can be accommodated in a particular size matrix, it is usual to add extra rows for the tails of lower case letters such as g, p, y and j. There are two main text modes, each defined according to the number of characters which can be displayed on a single line and the number of rows accommodated within the screen's height; they are, 40 characters x 25 rows and 80 characters x 25 rows. The highest *resolution* (see next section) display standard uses 132 characters by 25 or 43 rows.

Screen resolution and size

A screen's *resolution* determines the clarity or sharpness of the displayed text or graphics characters. The achievement of high quality graphics generally requires a higher resolution or sharper image than is required for text display. Images are formed on the screen with pixels or tiny dots of light and the density with which they are packed determines the screen's resolution. A typical high-resolution screen provides a pixel density of 1024 columns by 768 rows, a total of 786,432 pixels.

Many microcomputer screens are 14-inch (across the diagonal) but larger screens are often used for applications such as computer-aided design (CAD), where the level of detail on some designs cannot be properly seen on a standard screen, and desktop publishing (DTP) to allow a complete page to be displayed at one time using characters of a readable size. Typical screen sizes are 15, 17, 20 and 21-inch.

Graphics display with bit mapping

To provide maximum control over the screen display, each pixel can be individually controlled by the programmer to give maximum flexibility in the design of individual images. Several *bits* of memory store the colour information for each pixel on the screen; the more colours which are required to be displayed, the more bits which are required per pixel, and the total amount of memory needed for a complete screen depends on the screen resolution, that is, the number of pixels to be displayed. An image, built up in memory pixel by pixel, is used to automatically generate the screen display. This is termed *bit mapping*, which is illustrated in Figure 8.9. With black and white images for example, only one bit per pixel is needed: logic 0 to represent black and logic 1 for white; with four colours, black, red, yellow and white for instance, two bits are needed (00=black, 01=red, 10=yellow, 11=white); three bits are necessary for eight colours, and so on.

The memory image is composed of patterns of ones and zeros

The screen image consists of individual dots called *pixels*

Memory

Video hardware

The video hardware maps the memory image to the screen image

Monitor

Figure 8.9. *How a bit mapped image is formed*

Where movement is required, for example in computer games, this is achieved in a similar manner to filmed cartoons - smooth movement is simulated by altering the contents of the appropriate memory locations to make small changes to the shape and location of the image. In addition to animation, bit mapping allows the drawing of extremely detailed and life-like pictures and is therefore used by many graphic design and drawing packages. Even word processors or other text-orientated packages make use of bit mapping to allow the display of different character styles and sizes as well as the *icon* images commonly used in WIMP-based *graphical user interfaces* or GUIs (see Chapter 12).

Monochrome and colour

A monochrome screen uses one colour for the foreground and another for the background. White on black is not generally used because of indications from various research studies which say that users suffer greater eye fatigue than is the case with combinations such as green on black or amber on black.

Colour displays require more memory than monochrome, and as explained earlier, the greater the number of colours available for a particular screen resolution, the more memory that is needed. However, a greater range of colours can obtained by using a process called *dithering*. Close to one another, two different colours appear to merge into a new colour, so by carefully mixing pixels of different colours on the screen, many new colours can be created from the true ones available. Though colour displays require a great deal of memory, over recent years the fall in memory costs and the improvements in screen resolution and quality are making them the norm rather than the exception.

Ferroelectric liquid crystal display (FLCD)

The growing market for portable devices, such as laptop and notebook computers and personal digital devices (PDAs) has increased the need for flat screen displays with low power consumption (portable devices are examined at the end of this chapter). Ferroelectric liquid crystal display or FLCD fulfils these requirements and is the most widely used technology for portable devices. It uses ferroelectric materials as bistable (two state) devices. Computer components use bistable devices to indicate a binary 1 or 0. Binary coding is used throughout a computer system to represent every kind of information which it handles; such information could be, for example, text, numbers or bit mapped (see earlier) screen images. The ferroelectric bistable device remains in one of two stable states until an electric field is applied. The field causes the material to switch to its second state; this state remains until another electric field is applied. The full display consists of FLC cells, sandwiched between two glass plates. When a positive charge is applied to a cell, light is blocked and the image appears dark. A negative charge changes the orientation of the molecules in the FLC cell and light is able to pass through. Cells are arranged in rows and columns, like the pixels (picture elements - the dots which make up the screen image) on a CRT display. Filters are used to provide colour images.

Display quality cannot yet match that of the CRT screen, but power consumption is very low. A CRT screen image is updated (scanned) 50 to 60 times per second (Hz), whereas the refresh rate for an FLC display can be as low as 10Hz. Low power consumption is an important quality for battery powered devices, such as notebook computers. The need for 'greener' (less environmentally damaging) computer systems is likely to advance the cause of this type of display. Larger FLC displays (up to 21 inches) are available, but they are still relatively expensive.

Printers

Printers are classed as being either *impact* or *non-impact* devices, but within these two categories there are large variations in speed of operation and quality of print. Speed of operation is largely dependent on whether the printer produces a character, a line or a page at a time. Impact printing uses a print head to strike an inked ribbon which is located between the print head and the paper. Individual characters can be printed, either by a *dot-matrix* mechanism, or by print heads which contain each character as a separate font (*solid font* type). Non-impact printers do not use mechanical hammers. Though non-impact *ink* and *bubble jet printers* use dot matrix heads similar to some impact printers, the method of transferring the ink to the paper is different, and *laser printers* work on a different principle entirely, a technology closely related to that used in photocopiers.

Dot matrix printers

Characters can be formed from a matrix of dots (see the section on VDUs) and the density of the matrix largely determines the quality of the print. The impact is carried out by a number of tiny pins (typically nine or twenty-four) each of which can be projected or withdrawn according to the pattern which is required. The mechanism is illustrated in Figure 8.10. A *ROM* (*Read Only Memory*) chip inside the printer provides it with one or more character sets, and character styles, or *fonts*. Other fonts may be provided by plug-in cartridge or by software.

Figure 8.10. *How a character is formed by a dot matrix printer*

Most printers now provide a range of print qualities and styles which can be selected through a keypad on the casing.

Increased density of print is achieved by passing the print head over a line twice (*double-striking*). Because the individual pins of dot matrix printers can usually be controlled by software, such printers are capable of producing graphical images as well as text. Some matrix-dot printers have special mechanisms and ink ribbons which enable them to produce colour images.

Barrel printer

The barrel printer has a band with a complete set of characters at each print position, of which there are usually 132. Each print position has a hammer to impact the print ribbon against the paper. The mechanism is illustrated in Figure 8.11. One complete revolution of the barrel exposes all the characters to each print position, so a complete line can be printed in one revolution. The characters on the barrel are arranged so that all characters of the same type are in the same horizontal position. Thus, for example, any required *A*s can be printed,

Figure 8.11. *How a barrel printer works*

then *B*s and so on, until the complete line is printed. The barrel revolves continuously during printing, the paper being fed through and the process repeated for each line of print. Typical printing speeds are 100 to 400 lines per minute. Barrel printers are used for high volume text output.

Line printers are expensive compared with character printers but may be necessary where large volume text output is required. Printing speeds of up to 3000 lines per minute are achieved with impact line printers. Even higher speeds are possible with non-impact printers.

Ink jet printers

Figure 8.12. *Part of the print head of an inkjet*

Ink jet printers spray high-speed streams of ink droplets from individual nozzles in the print head onto the paper to form characters. There are two different approaches to propelling the ink onto the paper. In *thermal* ink jet printers (see Figure 8.12) electric heating elements are used to heat the ink and form vapour bubbles, which force the ink through fine nozzles onto the paper; the empty nozzles then refill. The other main approach is to use the *piezo-electric effect*. Here, a small electrical signal causes a special type of crystal to alter in size, thus creating a pump-like action which forces the ink through the nozzle. Otherwise, the action of this printer is essentially the same as for the thermal type. As for a impact dot matrix printer, characters are formed by the print head printing a number of columns of dots, but because the ink nozzles can be made so small, the separation of the individual dots is much smaller, thus producing much higher quality output. (Typically, there are between 40 and 60 such nozzles). By a series of passes and adjustments to the head's position, graphical images can be produced.

Ink jet printers produce output much more slowly than laser printers. However, printing quality is very high and they provide a relatively cheap alternative to the laser printer, particularly so when colour output is required.

Laser printers

Laser printers use a combination of two technologies: electro-photographic printing used in photo-copying, and high-intensity lasers. Figure 8.13 illustrates the operation of a laser printer.

Once the image to be printed has been transferred to the printer's memory, a microprocessor inside the printer converts the image, line by line, into a sequence of signals which switch a laser beam on and off. Each laser beam pulse, representing a single dot of the image, is reflected by a rotating mirror to the surface of a drum. The special surface of the drum is given an electrical charge wherever the laser beam strikes. After a horizontal line of the image has been transferred to the drum in this way, the drum rotates so that the next line can be built up. As the drum rotates, it comes into contact with plastic ink powder, called *toner*, which is attracted to the electrically charged areas of the drum. Because the printer paper has been given an electrical charge greater than that of the drum, the toner is transferred to the paper as the latter comes into contact with the drum. Finally, the toner is bonded to the paper by means of heated rollers.

Achieving print speeds of 500 pages per minute (ppm), the most expensive laser printers are used in very large systems which require exceptionally high speed output. Effectively, complete pages are printed at one time. Although more costly than dot matrix and ink jet printers, laser printers offer greater speed and quality. Typically, speeds range from 6 to 26 pages per minute. Printing definition, or *resolution*, is measured in *dots-per-inch* or *dpi*; until recently the norm has been 300 dpi but more expensive machines producing 600 dpi are becoming increasingly common. The high quality of the printed image makes the laser printer highly suitable for producing the camera-ready copy used in book and magazine publishing.

Figure 8.13. *How a laser printer works*

Other types of printers

Liquid crystal shutter printer

A liquid crystal shutter uses a very similar technology to that of a laser printer, but instead of a laser it contains a powerful halogen light source. In laser printers, the laser is fixed in one position, so to complete an image the width of a page, the beam is reflected from a rotating mirror which moves the laser beam horizontally across the drum (see previous section). This scanning action involves some complicated mechanical machinery which, together with the laser, form a major part of the component costs. Liquid crystal shutter printers, on the other hand, use a halogen light bulb as their light source and an array of liquid crystal shutters (the same technology used for liquid crystal displays (LCD) on watches and portable computer display screens) to control which positions on the photo-sensitive drum are exposed at any one time. Typically, the array contains 2400 shutters, sufficient to produce a full page-width line of ink dots at one time. In a liquid crystal shutter printer, moving parts are limited to the revolving drum and the paper and this makes the machine simpler and cheaper to service than its laser counterpart.

Chain printer

In a chain printer several complete sets of characters are held on a continuous chain which moves horizontally across the paper. The ribbon is situated between the chain and the paper and an individual hammer is located at each of the 132 print positions. A complete line can be printed as one complete set of characters passes across the paper. Thus, in one pass as many lines can be printed as there are sets of characters in the chain. Printing speeds are therefore very high.

Thermal printers

Characters are burned onto heat-sensitive thermographic paper, which is white and develops colour when heated above a particular temperature. The heat is generated by rods in the dot-matrix print head. By selective heating of the rods, individual characters can be formed from the matrix. Printing can be carried out serially, one character at a time or, by several heads, on a line-by-line basis. Serial thermal printing is slow but speeds of more than 1000 lines per minute are possible with line thermal printing.

Electro-sensitive printers

This type produces characters in a similar fashion to the thermal printer except that the paper used has a thin coating of aluminium which covers a layer of black, blue or red dye. Low voltage electrical discharges in the matrix rods produce sparks which selectively remove the aluminium coating to reveal the layer of dye underneath. Operated as line printers with heads at each print position, printing speeds of more than 3000 lines per minute are achieved.

Summary of printers

Generally, smaller, low-speed character printers are of use with microcomputer systems, but the increasing popularity of the latter has demanded increased sophistication in small printers. Features which have improved speeds of character printers include *bi-directional* printing (in two directions) and *logic-seeking,* which allows the printer to cut short a traverse across the paper if few characters are required on a line. The most popular printers for microcomputers are impact dot-matrix, ink-jet and laser.

Plotters

A plotter is a device designed to produce charts, drawings, maps and other forms of graphical information on paper. The images may be produced by *pens*, *electro-statically* or *ink jets* (see Printers section). Electrostatic plotters are quicker but the quality of the image is inferior to that produced with the pen type. Ink jet plotters, though expensive, produce the best quality drawings. Pen plotters use an ink pen or pens to create images on paper. There are two types, *flatbed* and *drum.*

Drum plotter

A drum plotter has a different drawing mechanism. Instead of the paper remaining still, it moves to produce one of the lateral movements whilst the pens move to execute the other movements. To control the paper, the drum plotter uses sprocket wheels to interlock with the paper. The main advantage of the drum plotter is its ability to handle large sheets of paper. The operation of a drum plotter is illustrated in Figure 8.14.

Plotters are commonly used in conjunction with computer-aided design (CAD) systems for the production of engineering and architectural drawings.

Figure 8.14. *How a drum plotter works*

Flatbed plotter

This type of plotter looks like a drafting board with pens mounted on a carriage which moves along guide tracks. The paper is placed on the bed. The pens can be raised or lowered as the image being created requires and different coloured pens can be brought into use at various stages of the process. Drawing movements are executed by movement of the carriage along the tracks and by the pens along the carriage. The size of paper which can be accommodated is limited by the size of the plotter bed, but this can be extremely large. Figure 8.15 illustrates its principles of operation.

Figure 8.15. *Operation of a flatbed plotter*

Special-purpose output

Computer output microform (COM) recorders

COM recorders record information from computer storage onto microfilm or microfiche, by conversion of the digital information into human-readable images. COM equipment is very expensive, but bureau organisations will generally provide a recording service. Microfilm is a continuous reel, whereas microfiche is a sheet of film with a matrix of squares or pages. Either form can be viewed with a magnifying viewer. COM can result in large savings in paper costs, storage space and handling. For example, a 4 inch × 6 inch microfiche sheet can store the equivalent of 270 printed pages. Computer-aided retrieval (CAR) systems are available to automate the archiving and retrieval of microfiche frames.

COM is particularly useful for the storage of large amounts of information which do not need to be updated frequently. The information can be viewed with the use of a special magnifying projector. Large financial institutions use COM together with CAR to allow rapid retrieval of customer account statements.

Voice processing - recognition and synthesis

The recognition process is used for input and the synthesis for output. Human speech varies in accent, personal style of speech and pitch and the interpretation of the spoken word makes the development of systems capable of handling the full range of spoken communication a difficult process. In normal conversation, humans make assumptions about the listener, often cutting sentences short or emphasising a point with a facial expression. There are however, devices which can be trained to recognise a limited number of words spoken by the individual doing the training. Devices can be used to give commands for machinery control, for example, up, down, left, right, fast, slow etc. Paralysed persons can control a wheelchair or lighting and heating through a voice recognition device controlled by a microprocessor. There are also applications which operate effectively because the communications are highly specialised and the conversation requirements extremely limited. Banks provide telephone banking through interactive voice response (IVR) systems; customers can obtain account balances, order statements or cheque books and make money transfers by spoken commands or by tone entry with the telephone keypad. Interaction is very carefully controlled by the system and callers must be interrogated for precise information, such as their account number. By using a highly structured series of questions and answers, IVR systems only need to recognise key values such as the digits from 0 to 9 and the words 'yes' and 'no'. A caller's spoken request for information is digitised and sent to the host computer; the response is converted into synthesised speech and read out to the caller. IVR systems speak by forming pre-recorded words and phrases into sentences and playing them. For example, a request for an account balance may bring the response "Your balance is", followed by a series of digits which were recorded separately, interspersed by the word "pounds" and "credit" or "debit", as appropriate.

Other systems using voice recognition and voice synthesis include robot operation, telephone answering and information provision concerning the time, share prices, and railway timetables.

Exercises

Exercises for this chapter are combined with those for Chapter 9, Storage Systems.

Chapter 9

Storage Systems

All backing storage systems consist of two main elements, a *device* and a *medium*. For example, a tape drive is a device, but magnetic tape is the associated storage medium. Under program control, the storage device reads from or writes to the medium. The most popular kinds of backing storage devices are those using magnetic tape and magnetic disk, although optical systems are playing an increasingly important role.

Magnetic tape

Despite the continued evolution of disk storage, magnetic tape continues to be used in most large scale computer installations as a cheap and secure method of storing large volumes of data which are normally processed in a serial fashion, as occurs, for example, in the processing of an organisation's payroll. It is also useful for the storage of historical or archival files where rapid access to individual records is not essential. The Police National Computer system in Hendon, for example, stores inactive records off-line on magnetic tape, whilst millions of records of current criminal activities are kept on-line and are directly accessible from magnetic disk. When an archived record needs to be retrieved, the relevant tape is placed on-line and searched until the required record is found. It would be inefficient and expensive to keep all records, no matter how old, on-line all of the time.

General features of magnetic tape

The tapes used on mainframe and minicomputer systems are stored on large detachable reels. Tapes are made of plastic and are covered with a coating which can be magnetised and by which means data is encoded. A particular type of cartridge tape, which looks like a cassette tape but is slightly larger, is often used as a backup for hard disk on microcomputer systems. These *streamer* tapes have huge capacity and can copy the complete contents of a hard disk in several minutes. The rest of this section concentrates on large reel-to-reel systems.

Processing tapes

A tape must be mounted on an on-line tape unit when it is to be used by a computer system. During processing, the tape is propelled past separate read and write heads at high speed. As is explained in Chapter 15 data is transferred between tape and main memory in physical blocks, each one being separated by an inter-block gap (IBG), to allow the tape to decelerate and stop and accelerate again to the correct speed for data transfer. Data transfer has to be carried out in block sizes which can be accommodated by main memory and provide for the quickest possible processing of a complete file.

Data storage on magnetic tape

Figure 9.1 shows how data is stored on magnetic tape. The coding system used is either ASCII or EBCDIC, the latter being used on IBM equipment. The coding systems are binary and in the case of EBCDIC, each character is represented by a group of 8 binary digits (bits), either 0 or 1, plus a parity bit (for checking transmission errors), across the width of the tape. As Figure 9.1

shows, each 0 or 1 bit is accommodated in a single track and each group of bits representing one character occupies one frame across the tape.

Figure 9.1. *Data storage on magnetic tape*

The method of representing a 0 or 1 bit depends on the recording system in use but simplified examples are as follow:

❑   the presence of a magnetic field to represent 1 and the lack of a magnetic field to represent 0;

❑   the 0 and 1 bits are represented by magnetic fields of opposite polarity, say north for 1 and south for 0.

The tape unit reads across the nine tracks in a frame to identify the character represented.

Blocking data on magnetic tape

As explained in Chapter 15, a file is made up of a number of *logical records*. For example, a stock file contains a logical record for each commodity in stock. Generally, a logical record will not be large enough to constitute a physical record or block, so a number of logical records are grouped for transfer at one read or write instruction. The number of logical records in each block indicates the *blocking factor*. Large blocks save space (fewer inter-block gaps) and speed processing, although memory size is a limiting factor on the size of blocks.

Application of magnetic tape

Typically, one magnetic tape reel can store up to 40 million bytes or characters, allowing for header and trailer labels and inter-block gaps; the frequency of the latter will determine the practical capacity of any particular reel. The *data transfer rate*, the rate at which data can be transferred between tape and main memory, is commonly in excess of half a million bytes per second.

These features, together with the media's relative cheapness when compared with magnetic disk, make it appropriate for applications requiring mass storage. However, magnetic tape does not permit direct access to records and this limits its use to applications requiring sequential access only; the most common usage of magnetic tape is for storing back-up files and the archiving of files from magnetic disk storage.

Magnetic disk

Many computer applications require quick, direct access to individual records within a file and this facility is provided by magnetic disk. For this reason, magnetic disks are the most important backing storage media in use today. There are two main types of magnetic disk: *hard* and *floppy*.

Hard disk

The disk is usually made of aluminium with a coating of a magnetisable material on which data can be recorded. Records are stored in concentric rings or *tracks*. The method of encoding is fundamentally the same as that for tape, except that the magnetic states representing binary patterns are stored in single-file around the tracks. Each track is divided into a number of *sectors*, each having the same storage capacity. These features are illustrated in Figure 9.2. Each track and sector has a physical *address* which can be used by

Figure 9.2. *Data storage on magnetic disk*

software to locate a particular record or group of records. A read/write mechanism is provided for each surface of a disk. The central area of the disk is not used, because to do so would necessitate a higher packing density than can be read or recorded by the read/write head. The number of tracks and sectors is known as the disk's *format*. The sector size can either be fixed permanently or can be altered by software. The former is known as hard sectoring and the latter as soft sectoring.

❏ *Hard sectoring*. The position of each sector can be indicated by a slot or reflective marker which can be detected by sensors in the drive unit. As the smallest unit of data transfer between disk and CPU is a sector (block), this means that any application is restricted to the disk's block size. Consider, for example, an application which uses logical records of 64 bytes, stored on a disk with 512 byte hard sectors. A minimum of 8 logical records needs to be transferred to memory even if only one is required out of the sector.

❏ *Soft sectoring*. This method allows the sectors to be set by software. All microcomputer systems use soft sectoring.

Disk pack

To increase storage capacity, disks may be formed into a pack, with a common access mechanism. The disk pack is generally loaded from the top of the disk unit. Because the disk pack can be removed and exchanged, the heads remain in their retracted position when the pack is not in place and when the disks are not revolving at their full operating speed.

Disk cylinder

The concept of the cylinder is explained in Chapter 15. Briefly, if there are ten possible record-ing surfaces with 200 tracks per surface, there are 200 imaginary, concentric cylinders, each consisting of ten tracks. Each vertical plane of tracks is a cylinder and as such is equivalent to a track position to which the heads on the access mechanism can move. All the read/write heads are fixed to a comb so that each is in the same cylinder at any one time. Sequential files are ap-plied to a disk pack on a cylinder-by-cylinder basis so that all records in a cylinder can be processed with the heads in one position.

Single exchangeable disk

Single exchangeable disks are also known as *cartridge* disks and can be inserted into the front of the disk unit, in which case, part of the disk cover automatically slides to one side to allow the read/write heads to move in, or it can be top loaded and the plastic cover removed by the opera-tor once the disk is in place. As is the case with the exchangeable disk pack, the moveable heads remain in the retracted position except when the disk is revolving at full speed.

Winchester disk technology

When first introduced, Winchester disks were designed for large computer systems and are still popular on such systems. They are now an integral component of all microcomputer systems. Winchester disks provide a much greater volume of on-line storage and faster access to pro-grams and data than is possible with floppy disks. Winchester disk systems consist of packs of hard disks, stacked in the same way as the exchangeable disk pack systems described earlier. The disks are not removable and are hermetically sealed in the storage units together with the read/write mechanism. The contamination-free environment in which the disks are stored al-lows very high speeds of rotation, typically, 7200 revolutions per minute. Storage capacities are increasing as technology advances, but commonly available systems for microcomputers can provide almost limitless storage.

Disk access time

Access time is the interval between the moment the command is given to transfer a data block (sector) from disk to main memory and the moment the transfer is completed; three processes can be identified.

❑   *seek time*. Suppose, for example, the read/write head unit is in cylinder 5 and that data is required from cylinder 24. To retrieve the data, the mechanism must move inwards to cylinder 24, the time taken to accomplish this movement being known as the seek time.

❑   *rotational delay*. When a read or write instruction is issued, the head is not usually positioned over the sector where the required data are stored, so there is some rotational delay while the disk rotates into the proper position. On average, the time taken is half a revolution of the disk pack. This average time is known as the latency of the disk.

❑   *data transfer time* is the time taken to read the block of data into main memory.

Various strategies can be used to reduce disk access time. One solution is to store related re-cords in the same cylinder so that head movement is minimised, a strategy usually adopted for sequential files where records are to be accessed sequentially. Even with random files it is sometimes possible to group related records in the same cylinder. Another solution is to use fixed head disks, which provide each track with its own read/write head and involve no seek time. It has to be said, however, that this second option is no longer used in disk drive systems, primarily because of their high manufacturing costs. Other techniques of speeding disk performance are described below.

Storage capacity and performance

Storage capacity is measured in megabytes or Mb (roughly 1 million bytes) or gigabytes (Gb -approximately a thousand million bytes). *Disk array* systems offer extra capacity, measured in hundreds of gigabytes. Traditionally, track recording density (the amount of data packed into a single track) is dictated by the amount of data which can be recorded in the innermost (the shortest) track. All the other tracks then use the same recording density. A technique called *variable zone recording* or *zoned-bit recording* (ZBR) stores more information in the longer, outer tracks. In this way, the storage capacity of the entire hard disk is radically increased.

The performance of a particular drive involves a measurement of its *overall response time*, measured in milliseconds. Different kinds of *disk access* take different times, so a quoted response time should be an aggregate of the time taken for a range of typical operational activities. In practice, this means running a system with a range of commonly used applications.. A typical average seek time is between 7 ms (milliseconds) and 10 ms. The seek time is usually better in systems which use higher spin speeds. This means that the correct sector comes into position more quickly. Hard disk performance may be improved with the use of:

❑   a hardware caching controller;

❑   software caching;

❑   de-fragmentation software;

❑   RAID (redundant array of inexpensive disks).

Hardware caching controller

A hardware caching controller improves the rate at which data can be *written* to or *read* from a hard disk. As an electro-mechanical component of the computer system, the hard disk can access data at speeds measured in milliseconds (thousandths of a second), compared with the processor and main memory speeds, which can be measured in nanoseconds (thousand millionths of a second). A high performance processor may remain idle while waiting for the hard drive to complete a write or read operation. A hardware caching controller uses a separate memory chip, plugged into the drive's controller board. The cache memory is used to store data in anticipation of a read or write operation.

❑   *Write caching* is the drive's attempt to accept data before the write head is correctly positioned to record it. A write operation starts with the computer signalling the drive that it has begun the process. Instantly, the drive starts to move the read/write heads over the correct track. At the same time, the data to be transferred is copied from main memory to the RAM cache within the drive. Once the copy has been completed, the system is free to continue with other tasks, leaving the drive to complete the write operation (using the copy of the data held in the RAM cache). The write operation completed signal is issued while the drive is still recording (as soon as the copy to the cache is completed); otherwise, the system would still be delayed while the cache copy is written to disk. There is a theoretical risk of data loss, but, for most applications, there is none. Write caching is particularly effective for sequential file processing, where data is recorded into contiguous locations on disk (a complete track is filled before the head moves to the next track). Several write operations can be carried out without any head movement and seek time (the most significant contributor to the slowing of access speeds) is minimised. The opportunities for overlapping write operations are maximised.

❑   *Read caching*. The drive attempts to fetch data before the application requests it. The principles are the same as for main memory caching (see Chapter 7).

The memory chip used as the RAM cache is held within the drive unit and does not, therefore, take any part of the system's main memory capacity. A hardware caching controller can radically improve the performance of a hard drive, although other advances in design, such as increased rotation speed may be more significant.

Software caching

A hard disk without a hardware caching controller will probably slow down a system, which in other respects is classed as a high performance system. An effective alternative, commonly used for systems operating Microsoft Windows, is to use a software caching system, such as SmartDrive (Windows 3.1) or Vcache (Windows 95). This uses part of the computer's own main memory as the cache and thus reduces the amount available for applications software and data. Without a hardware caching controller, software caching is an essential component for most business systems.

De-fragmentation and the FAT

Some operating systems keep track of every stored file by following chains of *clusters* through a *file allocation table* (FAT). A cluster is a group of, up to, 32 sectors, which the operating system uses as a file *allocation unit*. A filename entry in the FAT is followed by the address of the first cluster containing the file. If the file occupies more than one cluster, the first cluster contains a pointer to the next, which contains a pointer to the one after that, and so on, until the end of the file is reached (the last cluster contains a special marker). This system was adopted to allow disk space to be taken by new files when old ones are deleted. If a file cannot be fitted into a vacant space, it becomes *fragmented* (distributed over different parts of the disk). The operating system is still able to keep track of the complete file through the cluster linking mechanism, but read and write times become extended. This is because of the increased head movement (see Seek Time).

De-fragmentation software re-organises the disk space, such that each file occupies contiguous (no gaps) clusters. The frequency with which de-fragmentation should be carried out depends on the level of file activity and the application. If the application results in frequent changes to the size of files, system performance may be noticeably affected as fragmentation increases.

RAID (redundant array of inexpensive disks)

RAID systems aim to overcome the performance limitations inherent in single disk systems and to improve reliability. A number of different RAID configurations are commonly in use, each one concentrating on improving either *performance* (speed of access to data) or *reliability*. Five such configurations are known as RAID-0, RAID-1 through to RAID-5.

The idea is illustrated by reference to a RAID-0 system; there are two main parameters which can be adjusted - the *block size* and the *number of disks* (known as the *stripe width*) used. The performance of a RAID-0 system can be set by adjusting the values of these parameters. Data is recorded in the following way; for example, if a company's accounting records are to be spread over several physical disks (a *logical volume*), the data is written to each disk block by block, the first going to the first disk, the second to the second disk and so on. It follows from this that an input-output operation, which requires the accessing of more than one block of data, will need the services of multiple disks. To improve performance, the block transfers are carried out *concurrently*, over multiple data paths. Once all the relevant blocks are transferred the logical input-output operation is completed. Buffers are used to accumulate the blocks and assemble them in the correct order. The improvement in performance is achieved by overlapping the block transfers from several disks, instead of serially from a single disk. A problem with a RAID-0 configuration is that the failure of one disk prevents use of the entire volume. Other RAID configurations use techniques, such as mirroring, which provides an entire duplicate of each disk.

Hard drive interface standards

SCSI stands for Small Computer Systems Interface. It is a high speed, parallel interface (or device controller) standard, defined by ANSI (American National Standards Institute). SCSI interfaces are widely available for connecting microcomputers to a range of peripheral devices, including hard disks and printers; SCSI interfaces are also used for connecting computers to one another, and to local area networks. Separate ports (a port is a location for passing data in or out of a computer) do not have to be used for each attached device. Instead one device can be connected directly to a SCSI port in the computer and other devices (a maximum total of seven) can be linked to the first, in a "daisy chain". Only one device can communicate through the SCSI port at any one time, so each device in a chain is given a separate logical address, which indicates its priority. The device with the highest address is given top priority. Macintosh computers and some computers in the IBM range include an SCSI port as standard.

PCs and 'compatibles' can be upgraded to include an SCSI port, with the use of an expansion card; this is necessary for the connection of a Jaz drive (see later). The SCSI interface was of particular value for the attachment of high speed devices, such as hard disk drives, because it allowed more rapid data transfer than was the norm for the IDE (Industry Device Electronics) based hard drives, used in most PCs. The IDE interface has become most popular with PCs because it is cheaper and easier to install than the SCSI interface. IDE performance has now been increased to that of a SCSI interface. Newer standards, the Enhanced IDE and UDMA (Ultra Direct Memory Access) now provide *data transfer rates* which are superior to those of SCSI and similar to those of the new SCSI Wide.

Application of magnetic disk

On large computer systems, exchangeable disk packs constitute the most popular form of backing storage, because despite being more expensive than magnetic tape, the provision of direct as well as sequential access, gives magnetic disk an overwhelming advantage. Its support of a variety of file and database organisation methods make it appropriate for any application. Typically, a single disk pack can store hundreds of megabytes, or several gigabytes (1 gigabyte = 1024 × megabyte) and although a single CPU can only access one surface in one disk pack at a time, a system may have a number of drive units, each containing a similar disk pack, permanently on-line. Other files may be held on additional disk packs held off-line, but these can be placed on-line as and when required, by exchanging them with those held in the drive units. A multi-processor system could, of course, access several on-line disk packs at the same time. Direct access times will vary, depending on the amount of head movement required (this will depend on the method of file organisation and the mode of access) and the performance characteristics of the disk system in use.

Floppy disks or diskettes

Floppy disks are physically and operationally different from hard disks. They are flexible and encased in a square plastic protective jacket, in which the diskette revolves at approximately 360 revolutions per minute, more slowly than a conventional disk. The jacket is lined with a soft material which helps to clean the diskette as it revolves. The read/write heads make contact with the diskette surface when data transfer is in progress and withdraw at other times to reduce wear, but a diskette will eventually wear out after about 500 to 600 hours of contact. The diskette does not rotate continuously and access times are considerably inferior to those of hard disk systems.

The 3.5 inch disk is stored in a rigid plastic and a metal sliding shutter, which covers the recording surface access slot, slides open when the disk is placed in the drive unit. A diskette has 80 tracks on each side but the number of sectors can be varied (soft-sectoring is used). If a diskette is formatted into 9 sectors, there are 720 addressable locations. Soft sectoring is used because the operating systems of different computers use different addressing formats. Thus, in principle, standard diskettes can be sold which only require formatting to be used on a particular machine (some are pre-formatted). The formatting procedure also sets up a *directory* which is maintained by the computer system to keep track of the contents of each location. Other types of floppy disk, with larger storage capacities and quicker access times are described next.

Application of floppy disk

Storage capacities are only a tiny fraction of the hard disk drive systems which are integral to all microcomputers and their slower revolution rate also makes access times so slow that they are only of use for backup purposes and installation of software packages (see also CD-ROM later). Floppy disk systems have the advantage of providing extremely cheap storage.

Iomega Zip

A Zip disk cartridge holds 100MB or 250MB of data on its single platter. The Zip drive can be attached *externally*, to the parallel printer port or the printer and Zip drive connectors can be 'piggy backed' to allow both to connect to the port. An internal option is also available which allows it to be connected, as another drive, to the hard disk controller. Attached externally, the Zip drive is still relatively slow, but when attached internally to the main hard drive controller, it has a seek time of around 30 ms. This compares with a typical hard drive seek time of between 7 and 12 ms. Its 100MB capacity makes it ideal for users who need to store large files, such as those producing design and multimedia presentations. The quickness of the internal drive encourages regular backup and although not matching the speed of the hard disk drive, it can be effective as an extension to the on-line storage system. Files could be retrieved directly from the Zip without first copying them to the hard drive.

Iomega Jaz

A single Jaz cartridge contains two platters and will store 1GB of data (2GB with data compression). It can be attached internally or externally, but only to a SCSI drive controller. The Jaz drive has an average seek time of between 10 and 12 ms, making it as quick as most fixed hard disks. Its huge capacity and hard drive performance make the Jaz drive a true extension to on-line storage. Files can be retrieved from a Jaz cartridge as quickly as from the main hard drive. It is highly suitable for backing up the contents of the primary hard drive.

Alternative backing storage devices and media

Magnetic tape and disk systems account for a very large proportion of all storage systems in use, but there are a number of alternatives.

Magneto-optical drives

Like conventional disk drives, magneto-optical devices use magnetism to write data onto the disk, but in combination with laser technology. The recording head does not come into contact with the disk surface, but flies above it. This reduces the risk of head crashes and the problem of wear and tear associated with conventional floppy disk systems, which require contact for both reading and writing. Briefly, a magneto-optical drive operates in the following way:

❑   To write to the disk involves a two-stage process. First, the laser is used to heat the surface of the disk to a temperature of about 180°C and the write head is set to record bit-0s in the required location. Once the surface is heated the write head causes the magnetic polarity within the current disk location to change and when the surface cools (which it does quickly), the polarity condition is retained. A second recording pass reverses the polarity of those bit positions which are to represent 1s.

❑   Read operations use the laser at a reduced intensity to detect the bit-1s and bit-0s. They are then translated into the equivalent electrical signals for transmission through the device to main memory. There is no magnetic read head involved in the process.

Disks used in magneto-optical drives require heating before the polarity of stored magnetic fields can be altered. This means that data cannot be corrupted by magnetic fields emanating from, for example, a telephone placed on top of the disks or from nearby electric cabling. Data stored on conventional floppy disks can be corrupted in such circumstances. Reading data only requires the detection of changes in polarised light reflected from the surface of the disk. The manufacturers claim that provided the surface is not scratched, then spilling coffee onto it, for example, would only require that the surface is wiped with a special cleaning kit before it is re-used. To avoid over-heating during the writing process, a small, electric fan is attached to the back of the drive; for the same reason most magneto-optical drives are designed to be attached externally.

The 3.5 inch magneto-optical cartridge has a storage capacity measured in hundreds of megabytes and although the drive units and the media are more expensive than conventional floppy disk (1.44 Mb per diskette) systems, the cost per megabyte of storage is lower. The two-stage writing process means that two revolutions of the disk are required before it is complete and this results in average seek times (see earlier section on disk access time) which are somewhat slower than those for a conventional hard disk drive. Speeds are being improved and because the media are removable, magneto-optical drives could become a cost-effective way of increasing a system's primary backing storage capacity.

Floptical drives

A floptical drive uses floppy disks and makes some use of optical technology. However, unlike the magneto-optical drive, it uses the magnetic heads for both reading and writing and is thus similar to a conventional floppy disk drive. Where the floptical drive differs is in the mechanism which positions the read/write heads over the individual tracks on the diskette; an optical sensor in the drive unit detects an optical positioning pattern on the specially produced floptical diskette, allowing more precise placing of the heads and more densely packed tracks. With the use of very thin heads, data can be packed much more densely and a capacity of 21Mb per disk is typical. A major benefit of the floptical drive is that it is also able to read and write standard 1.44 Mb floppy disks. Unfortunately, the drives revolve the disk at normal floppy drive speeds and provide similar access times. Also, like conventional diskettes, data stored on a floptical disk can be corrupted by nearby magnetic fields. Their storage capacity is small when compared with the magneto-optical variety and their slow access times mean that it is not feasible to use them as an extension to conventional hard disk storage.

Bernoulli drives

The removable disk cartridge used in a Bernoulli drive uses air pressure caused by the disk's revolution to flex the disk towards the read/write head as it passes. It is named after Daniel Bernoulli, an eighteenth century mathematician who first documented the particular airstream effects which are applied in this type of drive. In a conventional Winchester hard disk drive (see earlier section), the read/write heads fly over the surface of the revolving disk and when power is removed may crash onto it, causing severe damage to both and loss of data. Equally, jolting the unit may cause the heads to bounce onto the disk surface and result in similar damage. In the Bernoulli drive, the disk surface is pushed towards the heads which are at a fixed height, so the risk of head crashes is virtually nil. The robustness of the cartridge makes it a popular choice for users wanting removable storage which can be sent through the post. However, the cost per megabyte of storage is relatively high when compared with, for example, magneto-optical drives.

Magnetic-cartridge drives

A magnetic-cartridge drive makes use of a conventional hard disk enclosed in a removable cartridge. The read/write heads are an integral part of the drive and move out over the disk surfaces when the cartridge is inserted. A standard hard drive is sealed and provides a clean operating environment which permits the read/write heads to pass very close to the surface of the disk; this is not the case with a removable cartridge and the dustier environment requires the gap between heads and surface to be greater and this in turn reduces the possible recording density. Nevertheless, a single cartridge can store around 100 Mb and average seek times are better than those for magneto-optical drives (see earlier section).

Docking drives

Docking drives are, effectively, removable standard hard drive units and provide identical access times and storage capacities. However, they are equally delicate, which for a removable device is a significant disadvantage. If security is vital, then the ability to remove and lock up a file storage system is an obvious benefit. Docking drives are expensive and could be used as the primary backing storage facility in place of an integral hard disk system, if the security advantages justify the additional costs.

Optical disk

An optical disk uses laser beam technology to allow data to be recorded and read using bit-densities several times greater than a typical magnetic disk. Data are recorded as bit-patterns, using high-intensity laser beams to burn tiny holes into the surface of the disk. The data can then be read from the disk using a laser beam of reduced intensity.

CD-ROM (compact disk-read only memory)

This type of optical disk uses laser beam technology to allow data to be recorded and read. Data is again recorded as bit-patterns represented by tiny holes in the surface of the disk produced by high-intensity laser beams. The data can then be read from the disk using a laser beam of re-duced intensity. The majority of CD-ROM drives, just like domestic CD music players, are capable only of reading CDs, but much more expensive machines exist which allow reading and writing, and it is likely that in the near future they will become as common as the current read-only drives.

Typically, a single CD-ROM disk can store approximately 600 Mb of data, sufficient space for storing video sequences and digitised sound such as speech. *Multimedia* systems, which use a microcomputer with sophisticated sound capabilities, a CD-ROM drive and a high resolution colour screen, are becoming increasingly popular as a result. These systems use computer pro-grams which combine music and speech with full motion video. They are used for applications such as computer-based training (CBT) and interactive games. CD-ROM is also used for stor-ing and providing access to reference material such as dictionaries, encyclopaedias and graphic images such as clip art. A number of manufacturers are marketing machines specially designed for multimedia applications. Compared to magnetic disk, CD-ROM currently has two major drawbacks: it is significantly slower, and it is read-only. For these reasons magnetic disk drives are preferable in a great number of areas, but it is very likely that further technological advances will increase the popularity of CD-based backing storage in the very near future.

CD-R (recordable compact disk)

This is a CD which can be written to once, but which can be read as many times as required. The CD-R drive is an example of a WORM (write once, read many) drive. The large storage capac-ity of the CD means that the writing facility can be used for a considerable period before all the space is used. Provided the recorded data does not have to be updated, this can be a useful me-dium for *archiving* documentary and other material. The disks are extremely cheap, making cost per megabyte of storage very low. A major advantage, compared with magnetic storage is that the information cannot be erased, making it highly suitable for archiving.

CD-E (erasable compact disk)

When it is generally available, this form of optical storage then has the same facilities presently provided by magnetic media, except that capacities are much greater. Optical storage will then be a viable alternative to magnetic media as the primary form of information storage.

DVD (digital versatile disk)

Using the same basic principles as the CD, DVD packs the data more densely and can store 4.7GB, compared with the CD's 650MB. With this capacity and its quicker data transfer rate, a single DVD disk can hold 133 minutes of video, with Dolby surround sound. It is probable that DVD drives will be an increasingly important removable storage device, particularly with the increasing use of video in multimedia products.

🖉 Exercises

The exercises which follow also refer to topics covered in Chapter 8.

1. What do the following abbreviations represent: OMR; OCR; MICR? Give an example of an application for each.

2. List the names of hand-held, input devices, which provide alternatives to a keyboard. Briefly describe circumstances when each device may be essential or desirable.

3. (i) In the context of screen displays, differentiate between *text* and *graphics mode*.

    (ii) What is meant by *screen resolution*?

    (iii) Explain why colour displays require more memory than monochrome displays.

    (iv) Why is FLCD (ferroelectric liquid crystal display) used instead of CRT (cathode ray tube) for *portable* computers?

4. Research computer magazines for *types of printer* and produce a table comparing costs, speed and quality. Suggest the kind of application for which each type may best be suited.

5. Suggest applications where *voice processing* (recognition and synthesis) is essential.

6. (i) Differentiate between *data storage* on magnetic tape and disk.

    (ii) Which factor is generally the most important when choosing between magnetic tape and disk?

7. (i) Identify the processes which jointly determine to *disk access time*.

    (ii) Which process is likely to most significant in slowing access time:

    a. when randomly accessing a randomly organised file;

    b. when sequentially accessing a sequentially organised file.

8. Explain the role of each of the following in improving disk performance:

    (i) *hardware caching* controller;

    (ii) *defragmentation*.

9. Why is CD-ROM storage vital to multi-media systems?

Chapter 10
Computer Networks

Networking computer systems has the effect of decentralising computer processing and improving communications within and between organisations and between organisations and individuals. Some computer networks use dedicated intelligent terminals or microcomputer systems to permit some independent processing power at sites remote from the *host* computer, to which they are connected. Other networks distribute even more processing power by linking microcomputer, minicomputer, mainframe and supercomputer systems. They are sometimes referred to as *distributed processing* systems. Networks can be configured to suit almost any application, from the provision of a world-wide airline reservation system to home banking. *Nodes* (connection points in the network) may only be a few feet apart and limited to a single building, or they may be several thousand miles apart.

Local and wide area networks

Computer networks can be classified according to their geographical spread. A network confined to, say, one building, with microcomputer workstations distributed in different rooms, is known as a *local area network* (LAN). One particular type, known as a ring network can extend over a diameter of around five miles. A computer network distributed nationally or even internationally makes use of telephone and sometimes, satellite links, and is referred to as a *wide area network* (WAN). In large organisations with several branches, it is common practice to maintain a LAN at each branch for local processing requirements and to link each LAN into a WAN covering the whole organisation. In this way, branches of an organisation can have control over their own processing and yet have access to the organisation's main database at headquarters. In addition, inter-branch communication is possible.

Network architecture

The architecture of any network includes definition of: its *components*, both hardware and software, identified by *name* and *function*; the ways the components are connected and communicate with one another.

The architecture of wide area networks (WANs) is described in Chapter 11 and the following primarily relates to local area networks (LANs). However, the section on Network Topologies does relate, in part, to WANs.

LAN architecture

It is important that the components are combined in such a way that the LAN can be: *extended*. The LAN must be capable of providing for new users and new equipment, as the need arises; *upgraded* to take advantage of new technologies which can improve network performance; *connected* to other LANs, both local and remote and Wide Area Networks.

LAN architecture comprises hardware and software, both for the control of the LAN communications and as an interface between the LAN and its users. In order that all components are compatible and operate as a coherent system, it is important that they conform to agreed standards (Chapter 11). This means that LAN producers have to take account of generally agreed standards for equipment linking and data communications, so that as new products come onto the market, the user is not left with a system which cannot take advantage of them. Unfortunately, a number of different standards exist and this means that the decision on which type of LAN to purchase is not always straightforward.

Hardware components

Figure 10.1 shows a simple *client-server* LAN and identifies the main hardware components: *workstation*; *file server*; *printer server*; network *cabling*. The way in which they are connected defines its general *topology* or physical shape.

Figure 10.1. *Main components of a local area network*

LAN Workstation

A *workstation* gives a user access to a LAN and its facilities. A workstation comprises a *micro-computer* with a *network card*, which fits into an *expansion slot* inside its system casing. The network card enables workstations to communicate across the network, and with the *file server* (see later). The card converts computer-generated data into a form suitable for transmission over the LAN and as such is an *interface* (Chapter 14). The card is operated with a network card *driver*.

Servers

The general function of servers is to allocate shared resources to other nodes on the network. There are a number of different types of server, which can be categorised according to the re-sources they control.

File server

The file server is usually a specially configured microcomputer, with a network card, more memory and disk storage, as well as a more powerful processor than is needed for a worksta-tion. It has to control access to shared storage, directories and files. In addition, it controls the exchange of files between network users. Most network software provides *multiple device* sup-port. This means that file servers can support several disks, allowing file storage capacity on the LAN to be increased beyond that of the file server's integral hard disk. A LAN can also consist of several file servers; indeed except for the smallest of networks, this is normally the case.

Print server

A print server (there may be several) accepts and queues jobs from workstations; the user may be informed when printing is complete. The print server may also provide certain print management functions, for example, to attach priorities to different print jobs so that certain jobs are printed before others, no matter what their positions in the queue. A print server will be configured to:

❑   support the use of particular printers;

❑   service particular printer *queues*; users with the right to use a particular print queue can then place their jobs in that queue.

Communications server

If a LAN is to have access to external networks or databases, a communications server is required. Generally, the communications server can establish a temporary link with remote computers or users on other networks (see Remote Inter-networking).

Network topologies

Computer networks can be categorised according to their physical shape or topology. Each terminal in a network is known as a *node*. If a central computer controls the network it is known as the *host* computer. The topology of a network is the *arrangement* of the nodes and the ways they are interconnected. The communication system within a network is known as the *subnet*. Data can be transmitted around the subnet either on a *point-to-point* basis or through a *broadcast* channel. If point-to-point transmission is used, the data passes through each device in the network. Thus, if two devices wish to communicate, they must do it indirectly, via any intervening devices. Each device must have the facility to store the entire message and forward it when the output channel is free. If a broadcast channel is used, a common communication channel is shared by all devices in the network. This means that any message sent by a device is received by all devices. The message contains the address of the device intended to receive it, so that the other devices can ignore it. There are a number of recognised network topologies and some of the most common are described below.

Star network

A star topology means that each node is connected, by separate connections to a computer at the centre, known as the *hub*. Figure 10.2 shows a LAN in a star topology. It is also a popular topology for a WAN. In this structure, all messages pass through the host (probably a mainframe or minicomputer) computer, which interconnects the different devices on the network. So, in this topology the host computer at the hub has a *message switching* function. Messages are transmitted point-to-point. The topology is particularly useful for intercommunications between pairs of users on the network (via the host). The network may consist of numerous computer systems (the nodes), connected to a larger host computer which switches data and programs between them.

Figure 10.2. *Star topology*

The star computer network is by far the most popular for WANs, because most large organisations start with a central computer at the head office, from which branch computer facilities are provided through the telephone network. The main aim is to provide computer communication between the branches and head office. Most other network topologies aim to provide communication between all devices on a network. The star topology can also be used for a LAN.

The *advantages* of a star network topology are as follow:

❑ It is suitable for WANs where organisations rely on a central computer for the bulk of processing tasks, perhaps limiting the nodes to their local processing needs and the validation of data, prior to transmission to the central computer;

❑ Centralised control of message switching allows a high degree of security control;

❑ Each spoke in the star is independent of the rest and a fault in a link or device in one spoke, can be identified by the computer at the hub;

❑ The data transmission speeds used can vary from one *spoke* (a link from the hub to a node) to another. This is important if some spokes transmit using high speed devices, such as disk, whilst others transmit from low speed keyboard devices. The method of transmission may also vary. For example, one node may only require access to the network at the end of each day, in which case a *dial-up* connection may be sufficient. A dial-up connection uses the public telephone network and the user only pays for the time taken for transmission. Alternatively, other nodes may require the link for most of the working day, in which case a permanent *leased line* is appropriate. Leased lines provide a more reliable transmission medium and also allow higher speeds of data transmission.

The main *disadvantages* inherent in star networks are as follow:

❑ The network is vulnerable to hub failures which affect all users. As a distributed processing system, some processing is still possible at the nodes but inter-node communication is lost when the host computer fails;

❑ For a WAN, the control of communications in the network requires expensive technology at the hub, probably a mini or mainframe computer. Complex operating and communications software is needed to control the network.

Ring network

The ring topology is specifically designed for use with a LAN and is not suitable for a WAN. A ring network connects all the nodes in a ring, as illustrated in Figure 10.3. The *Cambridge Ring*, developed at Cambridge University, has no host computer and none of the nodes need have overall control of access to the network. In practice, a monitoring station is used for the control of data transmission in the network. Messages in a ring network flow in one direction, from node to node.

The ring consists of a series of repeaters, which

Figure 10.3. *Ring topology*

are joined by the physical transmission medium (twisted pair, co-axial, or fibre-optic cable - see Chapter 11). The choice of medium depends on the distances to be covered and the desired transmission rates. Fibre-optic cable allows the greatest distances to be covered and the highest transmission rates. Repeaters are used to regenerate messages as they pass around the network. The use of repeaters allows a ring network to cover larger distances than is possible for other topologies. In fact, recent developments using fibre optic cable allow a ring with a range of about 100 kilometres, which makes it a *metropolitan area network* (MAN). The user devices are connected to the repeaters. A message from one node, addressed to another, is passed continually around the ring until the receiving node flags that it is ready to accept it. Acceptance of a message is determined by its *destination address*, which is examined by each node it passes. If the destination address matches the node's own address, the node takes the message; otherwise, the node repeater regenerates the signal to be passed to the next node in the ring. Data is transmitted in mini-packets of about 40 bits and contains the address of the sending node, the address of the destination node and some control bits. A variation on the Cambridge ring is the IBM ring, which uses a different protocol to allow better control of message flow on the network; the two protocols, *empty slot* and *token passing* are described in Network Access Protocols. The ring network presents advantages:

❑   There is no dependence on a central host computer as data transmission around the network is supported by all the devices in the ring. Each node device has sufficient intelligence to control the transmission of data from and to its own node;

❑   Very high transmission rates are possible; 10 megabits/sec is typical;

❑   Routing between devices is relatively simple because messages normally travel in one direction only around the ring;

❑   The transmission facility is shared equally amongst the users.

The main disadvantages are as follow:

❑   The system depends on the reliability of the whole ring and the repeaters, although it can be designed to bypass any failed node;

❑   It may be difficult to extend the length of the ring because the physical installation of any new cable must ensure that the ring topology is preserved.

Star/ring network - IBM token ring

The *IBM Token Ring* Network is a star-based topology, with a hub or *multiple access unit* (MAU) to which all the workstations are connected. The movement of data is, however in a *logical ring*. All signals between workstations are through the MAU. The star/ring structure has a major advantage over the basic ring. If one workstation breaks down, or the connection with the MAU is broken, other workstations are not affected (except that they cannot communicate with the damaged workstation). Failure of the MAU will prevent operation of the network. The Cambridge ring structure, described earlier, is prone to complete failure if one workstation fails (the continuous ring is broken).

Bus network

With a bus topology, the workstations are connected to a main cable (known as the *bus* or trunk), along which data travels. The ends of a bus are not connected, so that data has to travel in both directions to reach the various nodes on the network. The bus topology makes the addition of new devices straightforward, either by attachment to the existing cable or to cable which can be added at either end. The main bus standard is known as *Ethernet*. The term *station* tends to be used rather than node for this type of network. The communications subnet uses a *broadcast* channel, so all attached stations can hear every transmission. As is the case in the ring network, there is no host computer and all stations have equal priority in using the network to transmit. The maximum length of a single bus *segment* is 500 metres and 100 stations can be attached to it. Segments can be specially linked to form larger configurations, up to a maximum of about 12 kilometres. Transmission speeds of 10 megabits/second are obtainable. The topology is illustrated in the Figure 10.4.

Figure 10.4. *Bus topology*

The bus network provides certain benefits:

❑   If a node malfunctions, it simply stops communicating; it doesn't prevent the rest of the network from working;

❑   The attachment of devices is straightforward and the cable can be extended, if necessary; additional *segments* can be linked to extend the network.

The main drawback is that:

❑   If a part of the Ethernet cabling develops a fault, the whole network (assuming it consists of a single segment) fails.

Mesh network

The nodes of a mesh network are fully interconnected. The mesh topology is not found in LANs, but is typical of the public switched telephone network (pstn) and WANs. Its complexity requires the use of switching techniques to route data through the network (see Packet Switching in Chapter 11).

Network cabling - the transmission medium

In order to share resources on a network, servers, workstations and other devices must be connected; although wireless radio media are possible, most LANs use physical cabling, which acts as the *transmission medium*. The physical layout of the cabling should conform to one of the basic *topologies*: star, ring or bus. The type of cable used depends on the chosen topology and the rules governing the transmission of data through the cable (the *protocol*). The cabling standards of Ethernet and Token Ring, described below, are also LAN protocols.

Ethernet cabling

Ethernet is one the two most widely accepted standards (the other is Token Ring) for specifying how data is placed on and retrieved from a LAN. An Ethernet-equivalent standard is IEEE 802.3 (see Chapter 11), which also uses Ethernet cable, but packets data slightly differently for transmission through the cable. Ethernet cable falls into three main categories:

❑ *Thick Ethernet* coaxial cable, with a diameter of 10mm has a solid copper core conductor. A single network segment can be 500 metres and supports the attachment of 100 devices. The cabling conforms to the IEEE 802.3 Type 10Base5 standard. The transmission rate is 10 megabits (1,000,000 bits) per second (Mb/s).

❑ *Thin Ethernet*, which is 10 millimetres in diameter, has a core of stranded cable. The maximum length of cable which can be used in a single network segment is around 180 metres and the maximum number of workstations is around 30. The cabling conforms to the IEEE 802.3 Type 10Base2 standard. The cable supports a maximum transmission rate of 2 Mb/s.

❑ *10BaseT* Standard Ethernet. The T stands for *twisted pair*. This cable is much cheaper than the thick Ethernet cabling, but provides the same transmission rate of 10 Mb/s; being the same as most telephone cabling, it is easier to install.

Token ring cabling

Used in *IBM token ring* networks use twisted pair cabling, either two pairs or four, depending on data transmission requirements. A single IBM Token Ring network will support up to 260 network devices at rates of 4 Mb/s or 16 Mb/s. Up to eight rings can be connected using *bridges*.

Fibre-optic cabling and FDDI

See Chapter 11. Cable of this type is available for use with any of the network types, but provides greater *bandwidth* and permits transmission over greater distances, without the use of *repeaters*. Fibre Distributed Data Interface (FDDI) is a fibre optic standard with bandwidth of over a Gigabit (1024^3) per second. FDDI is also a token ring standard, but operates with two counter rotating rings and workstations may be attached to one or both rings. FDDI is used widely for network backbones. A *backbone* is the part of a network which carries the main traffic and connects, for example, the LANs in different departments of an organisation.

Cable bandwidth

Digital bandwidth is measured in bits per second and indicates the volume of data which can be transmitted over a communications link in a fixed time. Bandwidth is important because is determines the practicability of using remote communications for modern user applications. High bandwidth is not a crucial consideration for users who wish to exchange the occasional text email, but it is fundamental to the success of businesses with more complex and high volume communication needs. For example, a multi-sited organisation may need use its communications links to the Internet for the transmission of complex documents containing high quality images, voice communications and video conferencing. To meet these requirements the organisation would need dedicated, high speed links from each site to a 'backbone' (a major communications link) in the Internet In summary, bandwidth can be:

❑ Baseband. In a baseband network, a transmitting device uses the whole bandwidth (frequency range), so only one signal can be carried at any one time. This means that, for a brief moment, a transmitting device has exclusive use of the transmission medium. In general, broadband networks are suitable for networks which only transmit data signals.

❑   Broadband. Broadband networks provide a number of frequency bands or channels within the total bandwidth (*frequency division multiplexing*) and thus allow simultaneous use by different devices on the network. Generally, one channel is dedicated to the user workstations, leaving others free for transmitting video pictures for the security system, voice communication, television pictures and so on.

Cable-device connection

A number of different devices are used to make the connection between network devices, such as workstations and servers, and the transmission medium. The particular components used will depend on the type of network (for example, Ethernet or Token Ring); even for the same type of network, there are a range of connection alternatives. This paragraph only details the main categories of connection component, which are:

❑   *network card* (adapter), which is the *interface* for linking a network device to all other resources on the network; this is fitted into an expansion slot inside each workstation and other network devices. A device attaching to a Token ring network needs a different type of network card, from one attaching to an Ethernet network. A notebook or portable computer can be connected using its PCMCIA (Personal Computer Memory Card International Association) slot and a special network adapter;

❑   *Ethernet transceiver*; this device implements the CSMA/CD access protocol (see Access protocols). It is external from the network device and is connected to the network card and the Ethernet network cable. Although most network cards already contain a transceiver chip, *thick* Ethernet connections need an external transceiver. Thin Ethernet connections simply use the transceiver chip on the network card;

❑   *BNC connector*. Figure 10.5 illustrates its appearance; this is one of several types of connector used for *thin* Ethernet cable. There are BNC male and female connectors for linking sections of cable and T connectors for attaching devices to the cable. *Thick* Ethernet cabling uses a stronger screw coupling for cable connections (N-series connectors);

Figure 10.5. *BNC "T" connector*

❑   *Terminator*; this is an electrical resistor which must be attached to each end of an Ethernet network segment (see Bus Topology);

❑   *Multiple Access Unit* (MAU). This is the central component of a star/ring topology and is used in the IBM Token Ring network (see Star/Ring Network).

Connecting and extending LANs

Although there are limitations to the range of a LAN and the number of devices which can be attached, imposed by the performance ability of the network transmission medium, networks can be connected to one another and extended. LANs set up separately can be connected permanently, or data transmission between them can be restricted, for special user or system requirements. The functions of the main devices used in this area of LAN architecture are described below.

Repeater

Figure 10.6 illustrates the role of a repeater in connecting a thick Ethernet *backbone*, to thin Ethernet segments.

Repeaters allow the effective length of an Ethernet segment to be increased. The maximum length of an Ethernet segment is restricted because of signal loss and distortion which occurs as a data packet travels along the cable. A repeater re-strengthens, that is, *re-amplifies* the signal and resets its timing, so that the effective length of the segment can be increased. It is also used to enable a signal to travel to another segment of a network. A repeater can normally connect any kind of cable medium: thick or thin

Figure 10.6. *Use of thick and thin Ethernet*

Ethernet, twisted pair or optical fibre. In relation to the Open Systems Inter-connection (OSI) model, referred to in Chapter 11, a repeater works at the Physical level and only needs to know how to interact with the physical transmission medium.

Bridge

A bridge is used to connect two LANs of the same type, that is, two token ring or two Ethernet LANs. This is known as *local inter-networking*. Packets crossing such a link are *forwarded* by the bridge device. Bridges are *protocol transparent*. Thus, the otherwise similar networks can be using different protocols, for example, IPX (Novell) or TCP/IP (Internet). They can also divide large networks into smaller segments. Segmenting large networks can improve administrative control and the performance of the separate segments. In the latter case, the bridge can be configured such that only data which needs to cross the bridge actually does. For example, if there are two segments, one for the Sales department and the other for Accounts, the data traffic for each function will be isolated within the respective segments, except when data needs to travel between the two. This improves the performance of each segment and thus the effectiveness of the whole network.

Software components

Apart from the physical components identified in the previous section, the following software in needed to run a network (see Chapter 13 for more detail):

❑   a *network operating system* resident in the file server. A major commercial example is Novell Netware;

❑   a *local operating system* within each workstation, for example, MS-DOS, MS Windows, OS/2, UNIX or Apple Macintosh.

❑   *network connection software*; this must be loaded at a workstation before it can communicate with the network.

Network operating system

A network operating system typically includes functional components to set-up, monitor and administer:

❑ The *directory* and *file* system on the server; directories are used to organise the storage of programs and data held on the file server's hard drive(s). Some directories are for the storage of the network operating system; others contain application programs and some directory space is allocated for the storage of user's data. Chapter 13 provides an example of a file server's directory structure; each directory is labelled to identify the nature of the files it contains.

❑ *User login* and activity. A user must be identified by the network operating system before being given access to the network. The supervisor *creates* users and assigns a user-id to each. A user may also be assigned to a *user-group*, for example, Sales or Marketing. To access a network, a user must login at a workstation, which will require the entry of a *user-id* and possibly, a *password*. The precise conditions can be set by the network supervisor; certain time periods can be set when users are not allowed to log into the network; the time restrictions can be applied to all users, specific groups or individuals. The resources available to any given user can also be controlled through the login procedure.

❑ *User access* to applications and data files. Typically, users are assigned *rights*, sometimes as individuals, but more usually as members of a group. These rights relate to directories and files; in other words, the rights determine whether, for example, a user is allowed to delete or copy files in a particular directory. Access rights to *network executables*, that is application programs, only allow the programs to be run.

❑ *Network printing*; users can be given access to a shared printer, through a print *queue*; each queue is controlled by a printer server, which directs the jobs to a network printer under its control.

❑ *Electronic messaging*; this is a LAN version of electronic mail and provides a mailbox facility for inter-user communication.

❑ *Network backup*. This task, although important to users, because it may prevent the loss of important work, or network facilities, is a task carried out on a regular basis by the network supervisor.

All these tasks are the responsibility of the *network supervisor* or *administrator* who has special rights of access, not available to others. Usually, these tasks are carried out through a system console; any computer on the network can be used for this purpose, but, usually it will be secure in a separate location. Although printing, electronic messaging, applications and limited file management are available to users, their rights should not extend to the amendment of these facilities.

Workstation operating system

Each workstation has its own local operating system, such as MS-DOS or Windows95 to control processing; once an application is retrieved from the file server, the workstation must be able to run it.

Network connection software

The network connection software must be loaded into the workstation RAM (usually from the its integral hard drive, during start-up), before the workstation can be logged onto the network. This software remains in the workstation RAM as long as it is logged onto the network. A program which remains resident like this is referred to as a TSR (terminate and stay resident) program. There are usually several components to the connection software, each having a separate function. Two major functional components are the:

❑ *Communication protocol*. This is the set of rules for transmitting data through the network; it ensures that devices can successfully communicate with one another by using the same language. Example protocols are: IPX (Novell Netware); TCP/IP (Internet); SNA (IBM).

❑ *LAN driver*, which controls the network card fixed inside the workstation. LAN drivers which conform to the ODI (Open Data-link Interface) standard can accept data from the network in any of the standard communication protocols, listed in the previous paragraph. This means that workstations of different operating system types (MS-DOS, Macintosh, UNIX etc.) can be attached to the same LAN and share its resources.

Network access protocols

Empty slot technique

This system is appropriate for networks in the shape of rings or loops, where messages are passed point-to-point in one direction. One or more empty *slots* or *packets* circulate continuously around the ring. When a device has information to transmit, it loads it into the slot, which carries it to its destination. At the time of loading, the destination address is placed in the slot and a full-empty flag is set to full. As the slot is passed from one repeater to another, no attempt will be made to load the slot as long as the flag is set to full. When the slot reaches the destination device, the devices repeater reads the information without clearing the slot. Before passing it on, the repeater sets a received message flag in the slot. When the slot again reaches the sending device, the flag is set to empty. The destination device can check that the message was received by checking the received flag. If the message was not successfully received, perhaps because the destination device was not listening, the sender device can check the acknowledgement flag and re-transmit in the next slot.

Token passing technique

This technique is also used for ring networks. An imaginary *token* is passed continuously around the ring. The token is recognised as such by the devices, as a unique character sequence. If a device is waiting to transmit, it catches the token and with it, the authority to send data. As long as one device has the token, no other device can send data. A receiving device acknowledges the receipt of a message by inverting a 1-bit field. Token Ring (IEEE 802.5 Standard) employs this access method.

Carrier sense multiple access (CSMA)

CSMA is used on broadcast systems such as the bus network. Each device is theoretically free to transmit data to any other device at any time. Before attempting to transmit, a device's network card polls the network path to ensure that the destination device is free to receive data and that the communications channel is free. A device wishing to transmit must wait until both conditions exist. Generally such delay will be no more than a few millionths of a second.

❑   CSMA *Collision Detection* (CSMA-CD). Because of the possibility of collision through simultaneous transmission, a collision detection mechanism is used. When collision does occur, the devices involved cease transmission and try again some time later. In order to avoid the same collision, each device involved is made to wait a different time. If a number of retries prove unsuccessful, an error will be reported to the user. Ethernet (IEEE 802.3 Standard) networks (see Network Cabling) use a form of CSMA/CD.

❑   CSMA *Collision Avoidance* (CSMA-CA). This strategy attempts to improve on that of CSMA-CD, which allows a device to place a packet onto the network path as soon as its network card detects it as being free. In the time between the test (measured in fractions of a microsecond) and the placing of the packet onto the path, another device's network card may have detected the path as free and be about to place another packet onto it. CSMA-CA seeks to remedy this problem by requiring a device's network card to test the path *twice*, once to see if the path is free and a second time, after alerting the device that it may use the network, but before the packet is placed onto the path.

Remote inter-networking

The term inter-networking is used to describe the formation of integrated network systems, through the connection of separate networks, locally and remotely. This enables organisations to construct organisation-wide information and communications systems, even if sections of it are a few or thousands of miles apart. This section looks at the devices used to make connections between LANs which are remote from one another and necessarily therefore, between LANs and wide area networks; these may be, for example, public switched telephone and data networks (see Chapter 11). In general, these devices deal with the:

❑   connection of networks operating on different protocols;

❑   connection of LANs to WANs;

❑   connection of networks of different architecture, cabling and protocol;

❑   routing of packets along the most efficient path;

❑   conversion between different packet formats, protocols and transmission speeds.

Computer networking is a relatively new industry and terminology is not entirely standardised. For this reason, definitions of terms, such as bridge, router and gateway can vary from one manufacturer's specification to another. Some devices, for example, combine the features of bridges and routers and are referred to as bridge/routers. Bearing this in mind, the following definitions are generally accepted.

Gateway or router

A gateway, or router, is used to connect two LANs of different (they do not have to be) type ; thus, for example, an Ethernet LAN can be connected to a Token Ring LAN, or the connection may be Ethernet to Ethernet. The LANs may be remotely connected through, for example, British Telecom's Kilostream (Chapter 11) WAN, with a gateway at each LAN's entry point to the WAN. The term *router* is used to signify that the device is more intelligent than a bridge (see Connecting and Extending LANs), in that it makes decisions about the route a data packet (by reference to its destination address) should follow to reach its destination; in this way, packets can be made to take the most efficient path. It may determine an alternative route for a packet, in the event of, for example, congestion or breakdown on a particular link. Networks may have different architectures and protocols.

A LAN using IPX (Novell) protocol can use a gateway to allow users access to, for example, a remote IBM network, which uses SNA protocol, through the Kilostream packet (X.25 protocol) switching network.

Multiplexer

Low speed terminals, such as those with keyboards, transmit at about 300 bps, whereas voice-grade telephone lines can support transmission speeds of up to 14,400 bps. A multiplexer allows a number of low-speed devices to share a high-speed line. The messages from several low-speed lines are combined into one high-speed channel and then separated out at the other end by a demultiplexor.

In two-way transmissions, both these functions are carried out in one unit at each end of the higher speed channel. The operation of a multiplexer linking several remote terminals to a host computer is illustrated in Chapter 11. Multiplexers use different methods to combine signals and separate them out: *frequency division multiplexing* (FDM) and *time division multiplexing* (TDM).

Concentrator

A concentrator greatly increases data throughput by increasing the number of low-speed channels and instead of transmitting a null character, empties the contents of the next full register. The data from each low-speed device is identified by extra identification bits and this constitutes an overhead.

Benefits of computer networks

The general benefits are:

❑ sharing of appropriate *software*, *hardware resources* and common *data*;

❑ sharing of *processing* activity;

❑ *connectivity*; this is a very broad term used to categorise facilities and devices which support connection and communication between otherwise incompatible systems or devices. For example, a *terminal emulation* card, which enables a microcomputer to communicate with a remote IBM host computer, falls into this category;

❑ accessible services for *security*, *user support* and *system maintenance*.

Sharing hardware and software

In a LAN, particularly, there are opportunities to share hardware and software. This is because resources tend to be distributed over a small area; it is reasonable to ask users to share a printing resource if the printers serving them are within the same room, or perhaps in an adjacent room. It could be argued that the rapid fall in hardware costs has, to a certain extent, reduced the need for sharing peripherals, such as hard disk drives and printers. Although the prices of hard drives have fallen, the heavy demands of modern software and the increasing number of applications, ensures matching increases in demand for on-line storage. It is now common for microcomputer systems, even at the cheaper end of the market, to have their own hard disk storage with capacities measured in gigabytes (1024^3 bytes). Although printers are becoming much cheaper, increasing numbers of users are demanding the high quality output (and sometimes colour) provided by top quality printers; printers at the top of the quality range are still relatively expensive.

In summary, a number of factors concerning computer usage, storage and printing confirm that resource sharing remains a major purpose of a LAN.

❑ Applications. The range of computer applications and the number of users is continually increasing.

❑ Software packages. The increasing sophistication of software means that large amounts of disk space are needed for each package. Network versions of a package are cheaper (per user) than those for stand-alone systems.

❑ Storage technologies. Optical storage and high performance hard drives are capable of storing thousands of megabytes (gigabytes or gb) and are still relatively expensive. Individual users, each with their own hard disk-based microcomputer, are unlikely to make use of the several hundred megabytes available on each machine. A shared, large volume, hard or optical drive can satisfy the storage needs of all users.

❑ Printers. Most users require only occasional use of a printer, so there is little point in providing one for each. This is particularly the case for colour printers. A laser printer can produce the high quality output demanded by many applications and it operates at speeds which allow sharing to take place, without unreasonable delay for users.

❑ Other devices, such as scanners and plotters are relatively expensive and are likely to be used only occasionally.

Sharing data

A major benefit of all types of network concerns the sharing of data, frequently from centralised databases. This purpose is made particularly clear by the expansion of *Internet*, the world-wide network described in Chapter 38.

Data can also be regarded as a resource, so sharing it can bring similar benefits to those available from sharing hardware. For example, a common data store supports the use of a *database* system, which itself reduces the need for data duplication. Traditional computer processing methods require that each application has its own files and this results in the duplication of many data items and the updating process. For example, in a retail business both the stock control and purchasing departments make use of commodity details such as Stock Codes, Descriptions and Prices; if separate files are maintained by each department, a change in, for example, the Price of a commodity requires more than one input.

A database system allows these details (a single copy of each commodity's Stock Code, Description and Price) to be shared by all departments that need them. Even if database methods are not used, the storage of the various application files in a common disk store, means that they can, if desired, be made available to all users on a network. For an organisation with numerous branches, each with its own processing facility, there needs to be a central resource, where the results of processing at branches can be merged (and possibly re-distributed) to give corporate (across the organisation, as a whole) information.

Limiting access to shared storage

The sharing of data files presents some problems which need to be tackled. Firstly, access to some data may have to be restricted to particular users. Although the aim of networks is to provide computer access to as many users as possible, procedural and software controls can be built in to limit entry to the system, or to particular files or processes. Network software allows the network administrator to vary the rights of users, according to the kinds of access they require to particular applications or files.

Another problem with sharing files is that several users may attempt to update the same data at the same time. This can lead to corruption of data. To combat this problem, network software usually provides a facility for locking individual records while they are being updated. Thus, if a particular record is being altered, it is locked and made inaccessible by any other user until the updating process is complete.

Sharing processing activity

Host computer with intelligent terminals

A host computer with intelligent terminals allows processing to be carried out at remote sites; as such it comes under the heading of WAN. The distribution of processing work may be very limited, such that the majority is processed by a central computer. For example, terminals connected to a remote host computer often have their own processing power, file storage and printing facilities. Usually, before being transmitted to the host computer for the updating of files, *transaction* data will require some *validation* and other accuracy checks and this can be done at the terminal. Microcomputers equipped with suitable software are often used to *emulate* mainframe intelligent terminals, with the added advantage of being useable as stand-alone systems, when not communicating with the mainframe.

Alternatively, the work may be equally shared amongst a number of powerful computer systems, which then merge the results of their separate efforts.

Client-server network

A *client-server* LAN aims to exploit the full processing power of each computer in the network, including the *file server* and the user workstations or *clients*. This is effected by dividing the processing tasks between a client and a server. The client, a microcomputer in its own right (as opposed to the *dumb* terminal found in older mainframe systems) provides the user with a completely separate facility for running applications. The file server which could be a microcomputer, minicomputer, or mainframe, enhances the client component by providing additional services.

These services are traditionally offered by minicomputer and mainframe systems operating a *time-sharing* operating system; they include shared file management, data sharing between users, network administration and security. The major benefit of a client-server network is that the power of the client and server machines is used jointly to carry out the processing of an application. Interactive activities, for example, construction of a spreadsheet or the word processing of a report, are carried out by the client machine; having logged onto the network, the user can load the required applications software from the file server.

Matters of backup and file sharing security, relating to the application, can be handled by the server. Printing tasks can also be queued and handled as a shared printer becomes available. This task is handled by one or more *print servers*, which can be dedicated devices, or micro-computers assigned to the task. Except for very small LANs, most operate on the client-server principle.

Peer-to-peer network

With a peer-to-peer configuration, it is not necessary to have a file server; instead all the workstations on the network contribute to the control of the network. Thus, any workstation can supply or use resources of others, as required. Unfortunately, this has the effect of slowing performance; in addition it means that files are not held centrally and this complicates file management. *Novell Personal Netware* and *LANtastic 6.0* are popular examples of peer-to-peer networking products.

The peer-to-peer approach is highly suitable for very small networks, but both the products mentioned allow the system to be developed to introduce some file server control. Facilities are also included to allow users to share resources in groups; the name of another peer-to-peer net-working product illustrates this feature: *Windows for Workgroups*; up to 10 users can be networked.

Network administration

Achieving efficiency and reliability

In aiming for such efficiency and reliability, an organisation may use the following guidelines and suggestions for network administration, staff training and the use of fault control systems:

❑ Use hardware and software which conforms to a Standard; this should ensure that equipment from different sources is compatible and works properly with other network components.

❑ Obtain a service and support contract with the supplier of the network, or some other organisation which specialises in the system in use; the call out response times, to attend to faults or repairs, should meet the needs of the network owner.

❑ Ensure that fully trained staff are employed to install, configure, monitor, and develop the network.

❑ Make use of devices to protect against, for example, power failure; an Uninterruptible Power Supply or *UPS* device automatically provides several minutes of power, in the event of a power cut, to allow work to be saved and the network to be shut down safely.

❑ Train users to use the system properly and not to, for example, attempt to reconfigure a workstation's network software.

❑ Employ security to prevent unauthorised access, and entry of viruses to the file server. Virus protection software can help, but users should not be able to bring disks or software from machines at home or other locations; diskless workstations can be used to prevent such abuse of the network.

❑ Ensure regular *backup* of the file server, using, for example, tape streamer devices.

❑ Use a technique, such as *disk mirroring*, whereby two file server disks operate in tandem. Each block of data written to the main disk is also written to the mirror disk; if one fails, the other continues supporting the network without interruption.

Support of mixed traffic

Mixed traffic is a collective phrase to describe the different kinds of information which may be transmitted over computer networks and telecommunications links. These different kinds of information include, audio and video images, as well as computer data (text, numbers and other characters). If an organisation wishes to have a mixed traffic system, it will require a *broadband* (see Broadband) network.

Monitoring activity levels

The word activity is used to refer to various aspects of network use and operation, for example, traffic volumes and patterns. There may be particular times when the volume of data moving around the network significantly reduces its performance; this may indicate a need to re-organise the work patterns of users or to modify the network structure (perhaps by dividing it into smaller segments according to user function, for example Sales and Accounts - see Bridge).

System reporting

A network operating system will normally include various software *utilities* to allow the system administrator or supervisor to monitor and receive reports on various network conditions. For example, the system may report when a workstation has become inoperable or a fault has been detected on the server, or that certain system files have become corrupted and need repair. System reporting can help to ensure network reliability in that the supervisor is notified of such conditions.

Storage control

An important aspect of network management is the control of file storage space on the network. In a client-server (see Client Server Network), applications and data files are held on the file server and its space needs to be managed efficiently to ensure that required files remain accessible and that redundant files are removed (*purged*) and, if necessary, *archived* (copies held on another disk or tape medium, in case they are needed). If redundant files are not removed, space is wasted and the task of retrieving other files becomes more difficult (searching through redundant files for those required).

System configuration

Any network has a particular *configuration*; that is to say, particular types of components are used, they are connected and communicate in a particular way, and particular facilities are provided. The configuration of a network affects the way it works, not only electronically in terms of its hardware and software components, but also in its relationship with users. Thus, the network can be configured concerning:

❑ *User passwords*. A user may be required to enter a *password* before he or she is logged onto the network and given access to its resources.

❑ *User access rights*. The supervisor can assign rights to users in respect of particular directories or files on the file server. Such rights determine what a user can do with those resources. For example, in their own user directories, users may be able to create, copy, delete and rename data files; this would be essential if users were able to store work produced with various applications packages. In contrast, users' rights within the directory containing applications software (*executable* files), would be very restricted and only sufficient to allow them to run the programs. Some groups of users may have no rights to particular applications programs. For example, a sales clerk would be unlikely to have rights to run the personnel management software.

❑ *Job queues.* The shared servers (print and communications servers, for example) can be assigned work from particular users or groups of users, through a system of queues. Thus, a print server manages print queues, which are jobs from users awaiting printing on a shared printer. The configuration determines the printing devices to which jobs are assigned and their priority, if any, in a queue. Access to, for example, a laser printer, may be restricted to a small group of users.

✍️Exercises

1. Identify the main *components* of a LAN and briefly explain the function of each.
2. Identify one advantage and one disadvantage of each of the following network topologies: *star*; *ring*; *bus*.
3. How does the *IBM Token Ring* network overcome a weakness of the basic ring topology?
4. Name the main *Ethernet cable standards*, and the performance specification of each.
5. (i) Differentiate between *baseband* and *broadband* networks.
   (ii) Suggest, by reference to applications, why broadband networks will become increasingly important.
6. Differentiate between the terms *repeater*, *bridge* and *router* (or *gateway*).
7. Identify four functions of a *network operating system*.
8. What is meant by a workstation's *local operating system*?
9. In the context of network connection software, briefly describe the functions of the:
   (i) *communication protocol*;
   (ii) *LAN driver*.
10. Outline the operation of the following network access protocols:
    (i) *empty slot*;
    (ii) *token passing*;
    (iii) *CSMA/CA*.
11. Briefly describe the function of a:
    (i) *multiplexer*;
    (ii) *concentrator*;
12. A major benefit of a network is its facilities for *resource sharing*. Identify the particular resources which can be shared and the benefits such sharing brings for an organisation and its users.
13. Distinguish between a *client-server* and *peer-to-peer* network operating system.

Data Communications

Telecommunications and data communications

The word *telecommunications* can be applied to any system capable of transmitting text, sounds, graphical images or indeed, data of any kind, in electronic form. The signals may travel along wires or they may be radio signals, which require no wires, but can travel through the atmosphere and space. Currently, not all aspects of telecommunications system are digital, so sometimes, data may be transmitted in *analogue* form. Computer data is represented in *digital* form, so where the telecommunications systems support it, data is moved between remote computer systems as digitised signals. The topic of analogue and digital signals is dealt with later. The combination of computer and telecommunications technologies has profoundly affected the way computer systems are used. To a computer, text, sounds and graphical images all constitute data, which it represents digitally, using the *binary* coding system. Although not all transmissions of digital data involve general-purpose computers, they are often generated and controlled by digital computer technology. Data generated by a computer is already in digital form, but other data (the term is used in its broadest sense), such as sounds of human speech, or a photograph, need to be digitally encoded before transmission over a digital network. The term *data communications* can be applied to systems that combine the use of telecommunications and computer technologies.

Standards authorities

The data communications industry has always had to deal with problems of *incompatible* standards. As explained later, standards have to do with all aspects of a communications system, including, for example, the *hardware devices*, the *encoding* of data and the forms of *signals* used. At first, the only computer systems available for use in data communications systems were mainframes and later, minicomputers. These computer systems were produced by a small number of very large manufacturers, the most important being IBM; they also produced the communications devices that worked with their computers. In competition with one another, each manufacturer set the standards for use with its equipment. These *closed* systems prevented a customer from using equipment, produced by different manufacturers, in the same data communications system.

The huge expansion in the uses of data communications, both nationally and internationally has been made possible through the adoption of some common standards. Common standards lead to *open* systems, which allow users to use components from more than one manufacturer. A number of bodies are concerned with the establishment of international standards and these are listed below. Frequently, a standard arises initially from the work of a particular manufacturer, and then, often because of the importance of the manufacturer, it is included in the recommendations of the standards authorities.

❑ CCITT. This is an acronym for Comité Consultatif Internationale de Télégraphie et Téléphonie an organisation that has its headquarters in Geneva, Switzerland. It is part of the United Nations International Telecommunications Union (ITU). The

CCITT makes recommendations on most aspects of data communications, for example, modems (see Data Circuit Termination Equipment), networks and facsimile transmission or FAX and publishes them every four years. These recommendations usually obtain world-wide acceptance. CCITT's 'V' series of standards cover equipment used on telephone lines and its X series relate to digital packet transmission standards. Some examples of these standards are mentioned later in this element.

❑ ANSI is the acronym for American National Standards Institute. ANSI has long maintained a strong influence on standards in the computer and data communications industries. It is formed from industrial and business groups and is a member of the International Standards Organisation (ISO). Examples of its influence can be found in the fields of computer hardware and programming languages. For example, by conforming to ANSI standards, the FORTRAN, COBOL and C languages enable the production of computer software, which is largely *portable*. In other words, because each language is more or less universal, a program written in, for example, COBOL can be readily translated for use on any make of computer. In the area of microcomputer hardware, the ANSI standards define the SCSI (an acronym for Small Computer System Interface) parallel interface, for the connection of peripherals, such as disk drives and printers. The institute is also responsible for the ANSI.SYS *device driver*, a program that provides facilities for greater control of a computer console (screen and keyboard), than is possible with the MS-DOS operating system (see Chapter 13).

❑ IEEE is the acronym for the Institute of Electrical and Electronic Engineers. The organisation has set numerous standards for various aspects of telecommunications and computing. Notably, the IEEE has defined standards for local area network (LAN) protocols (see Chapter 10).

❑ The ISO (International Standards Organisation), has its headquarters in Geneva, Switzerland and is responsible for the definition of the Open Systems Interconnection (OSI) model. This model aims to ensure that any computer terminal is able to connect to any network and communicate with any other terminal, whether it is connected to the same or any other linked network. The OSI model is examined in greater detail in the section on Communications Protocols.

Public telecommunications authorities

The main telecommunications network in the United Kingdom is the public switched telephone network (*pstn*), which is owned by British Telecom (BT). Although BT owns the network, Mercury Communications (a competitor *public telecommunications operator* or PTO), is able to use the pstn to provide telephone and network services. Increasing competition is being provided from the independent providers of cellular telephone services.

Public switched telephone network (pstn)

The *pstn* is the main telecommunications network for the United Kingdom. It was originally designed for voice transmission, using analogue electrical signals; these electrical signals represent what is spoken and heard at each end of a link. A telephone mouthpiece contains a diaphragm, which vibrates when struck by sound waves. The vibrations are converted into electrical impulses and are sent over the network to the earpiece on the receiving telephone; a diaphragm in the earpiece converts the impulses back into sound.

Much of the pstn is now digital, in particular the national trunk network and call switching exchanges; the analogue connections are mainly confined to the pstn's local links to homes and businesses. Digital voice transmission uses coded patterns of digital impulses, which are similar to those used to represent computer data. To transmit computer data over analogue sections of the pstn, requires use of a *modem* (see Data Circuit Termination Equipment or DCE). This device converts the computer's digital signal into an appropriate analogue form before transmission; a modem at the receiving end converts the analogue signal back to the digital form required by the computer.

Types of telecommunications lines

Dedicated lines

These can be leased from British Telecom and provide a permanent connection for devices in a network. They provide high transmission rates and are relatively error-free. They are only cost-effective for high volume data transmission, or when a permanent link is vital to the users. Charging is by a flat rate rather than when calls are made.

Dial-up or switched lines

These are cheaper, but support lower transmission rates than leased lines. They are more cost effective than leased lines for low-volume work and allow the operator to choose the destination of transmissions.

Switched digital network systems

Public switched data network (psdn)

The psdn, owned by British Telecom (BT) is a *packet switching* (see later) service. Modems are not required and transmission performance is better than that achievable over the partially analogue pstn. The service conforms to the CCITT (see Standards Authorities) standard known as the X.25 protocol and for this reason is often referred to as the X.25 network. A major benefit of using this CCITT standard is that the network can be used for international communications. The protocol is steadily being replaced by ATM (see later).

Circuit switching

In any network, setting up a connection between two devices may involve circuit switching. For example, if a network is busy a connection may be established through a series of switches, from one circuit to another, over an alternative route. Thus the actual distance the signals travel may be greatly in excess of the geographical distance between the two points. Charges, whether the connection is for voice or data, will be made according to the geographical distance between the devices (local, medium, long distance), rather than the distance the signals actually have to travel through the various switches.

Packet switching

The main components of a packet switching network are: high speed data lines; packet switching exchanges (PSEs); packet assembler/disassembler (PAD); packet terminal. With the use of a specialised computer, called a *packet terminal*, a customer can create the packets and connect directly to the network through a dedicated dataline.

If the customer is not using a packet terminal, a dial-up connection is used and the data has to go through a *packet assembler/disassembler* (PAD). This device converts data to and from the networks protocol as it enters and leaves the network.

Figure 11.1 illustrates these features.

The principles of packet switching are as follow. Messages are divided into data packets, which are then directed through the network to their destination under computer control. Besides a *message* portion, each packet contains data concerning:

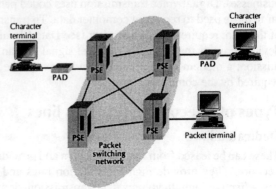

Figure 11.1. *Packet switching network*

❑   the destination address;

❑   the source identification;

❑   the sequence of the packet in the complete message;

❑   the detection and control of transmission errors.

The progress of a packet is monitored and controlled by *packet switching exchanges* (PSE) located at each *node* in the network. A node is a junction of network lines, which could be a computer or a computer terminal or other device.

As a packet arrives at a node, the exchange checks the addressing instructions and unless it corresponds to its present location, forwards it on the most appropriate route. Each node has an *input queue*, into which all arriving packets are entered (even those which are addressed to the node itself) and a number of *output queues* (to allow for the possibility of network congestion).

The route may be determined by one of a number of *routing strategies*:

❑   *hot potato*. The packet is sent as quickly as possible to the shortest output queue; such packets are not unduly delayed, although they may not be transmitted on the most direct route;

❑   *pre-determined routing*. With this method, the routing details are included in the packet itself, each switching exchange forwarding the packet according to the embedded instructions;

❑   *directory routing*. Each switching exchange has a copy of a routing table to which it refers before forwarding each packet. The appropriate output queue is determined from the table and the packet destination.

Network traffic information is continually transmitted between the various nodes, so that each switching computer has information to allow, for example, the avoidance of congested routes. Figure 11.2 illustrates how a network structure provides alternative routes by which a packet may reach its destination.

If a network is structured as shown in Figure 11.2, a packet sent from terminal T(2) to terminal T(6), would go into the input queue of packet switching exchange PSE (a). Depending on the routing strategy and network traffic conditions, the packet could be directed to an output queue leading to any of the other PSEs. If PSE (e) was inoperative, the alternative routes would be cut drastically; in fact the packet would either have to go through PSEs (b), (c) and (d), in that sequence, or direct from PSE (a) to PSE (d). Packet switching allows packets relating to a single message, to be transmitted on different routes. This may be necessary, either because of the breakdown of some routes, or because of variations in traffic conditions over different routes.

Figure 11.2. *Routing in a packet switching network*

The Internet uses TCP/IP, which is a packet switching protocol. In contrast with circuit switching, packet switching is connectionless as packets of data from the same source may travel entirely different routes, rather than via a fixed connection.

Packet switching versus circuit switching

Packet switching networks maximise use of network connections and provide a cheaper, more reliable and efficient, though slightly slower, alternative. Circuit switched connections are ideal for the transmission of data in real-time, when the delays inherent in a packet switching network would not be acceptable.

Message switching

As the name suggests, this type of network deals with identifiable and complete messages, in contrast to a packet switched system where the destination user nodes are responsible for re-assembling their packets into complete messages upon receipt. A number of points can be made when comparing and contrasting packet switching and message switching networks:

❑   both use a store and forward principle; each node in the network has storage facilities for the accumulation of data prior to its onward transmission and the intelligence to examine the destination data before forwarding it;

❑   packet switching networks treat data transparently. Individual packets generally do not contain complete messages and the network does not recognise connections between packets, except from identification of their destination. The destination user nodes are left with the responsibility of re-assembling individual packets into complete messages;

❑   the store and forward facilities in message switching networks need to be much larger than those for packet switching systems, because complete messages must be accumulated at each point of transfer in the network;

❑   message switching requires increased processing time at intervening nodes while messages are accumulated before onward transmission;

❑   message switching provides users with greater confidence that messages will be transmitted and received in complete form.

X.25 protocol

As already mentioned, the psdn uses a packet switching protocol, known as X.25. The CCITT (see Standards Authorities) provide the X.25 protocol for interfacing terminals with a psdn. The protocol provides users with the following facilities.

❑   Division of a message into packets.

❑   Error checking and re-transmission of any packet effected by an error.

❑   An addressing format that allows international transmission.

❑   The PSEs control the transmission of packets through the network.

Integrated services digital network (ISDN)

Many forms of data, including text, voice and video images, can be digitised and an Integrated Services Digital Network (ISDN) is designed to allow the *integrated* transmission of these various data forms over the same network. An Integrated Services Digital Network exists in various forms in different countries, although the ultimate aim is to achieve an international system. It is defined as a wholly *digital* system, with end-to-end digital connections and digital exchanges throughout. ISDN has become achievable because the telephone network has become largely digital. The public telephone network is, by far, the largest communications network, so once it is fully digitised, every business and home user will have access to ISDN services. British Telecom's ISDN began with a pilot scheme in 1985, which was extended in 1986 and has continued to develop since. The network provides three types of access:

❑   *single-line* IDA (integrated digital access). The user gains access with *Network Terminating Equipment* (NTE);

❑   *line adapter module* (LAMs). A LAM allows two terminals to simultaneously share the same, two-wire, connection; this could provide a cheap method of communicating with a remote computer system;

❑   *multi-line* IDA, which provides 30 independent channels, each being capable of transmitting voice or data.

ADSL (Asynchronous Digital Subscriber Line)

ADSL is a relatively new service, similar to ISDN, which operates over standard telephone lines and provides Internet access at around 10 times the speed of a conventional modem. As with ISDN, simultaneous voice communication is also provided. Transmissions are separated at the telephone exchange to channel the voice calls through the standard public switched telephone network and the computer transmissions through fibre optic connection to the user's Internet Service Provider.

Multiplexed network services

Kilostream

An alternative to packet switching is to use *multiplexing*. The Kilostream service uses this technique for data transmission. The service provides a high speed direct link between two points. Data can pass in both directions at the same time; this is known as *full duplex* mode. The main link can transmit data at a rate of 2048 megabits per second (Mbits/s); this allows a number of low speed terminals to be connected to the high speed link through separate low speed links, each transmitting at either 128 kilobits per second (Kb/s) or 64 Kb/s. The signals from each terminal can then be merged for transmission along the high speed link, using a technique known as *time division multiplexing* (TDM).

The process of multiplexing is carried out by a *terminal multiplexer*. At the receiving end of the link, the signals are separated out for transmission along low speed lines connected to their respective terminals. The terminal multiplexer at each end of the link can carry out the functions of multiplexing (combining signals) and demultiplexing (separating the signals). This is obviously necessary for full duplex operation.

Multiplexers fall into two broad categories according to the methods used to combine signals and separate them:

❏ *Time Division Multiplexing (TDM)*, as the term suggests, provides a *time slice* on the higher-speed line for each terminal. The multiplexer has a number of registers, one per low-speed channel. Each register can store one character. The multiplexer scans each register in sequence, emptying the contents into a continuous stream of data to be transmitted. A multiplexer will send a null character whenever it finds an empty slot. TDM is used for digital networks. Figure 11.3 illustrates the time division multiplexing of signals from three terminals to a remote mainframe computer.

Figure 11.3. *Multiplexers to allow several terminal to use a single link*

❏ *Frequency Division Multiplexing (FDM)* differentiates between the data signals sent from different devices by using a different *frequency range* for each. This can be likened to tuning a radio or television to receive particular programmes. So that any given radio programme does not interfere with the transmissions of another (although, they sometimes do), it is assigned a frequency that is not too close to the other assigned frequencies. In the same way, when a data transmission channel is multiplexed to accommodate signals from separate devices, some space must be left between the frequency ranges to avoid confusion of signals. Spaces between the different frequency ranges are know as *guard bands*. FDM relates to analogue signalling.

Megastream

This service is similar to Kilostream, except that no terminal multiplexing equipment is provided. Data can be transmitted at 2.048, 8, 34 or 140 Mbits/s. A user can choose to use the high speed circuit directly or multiplex the circuit, such that a number of low speed channels are made available across the link. Each separate lower speed channel can then be used to carry data or some may be left for the transmission of digitised speech.

Satstream

This digital data service provides customers with a small dish aerial to allow radio transmission of data, through a communications satellite. Customers are thus able to connect with networks in Western Europe.

ATM (Asynchronous Transfer Mode) and virtual networking

ATM evolved partially from the X.25 protocol and offers high bandwidth, packet switching and multiplexing support. ATM's bandwidth can handle data, video and voice transmissions through a single communication link. Its support for TCP/IP and other protocols allows ATM to handle a variety of traffic and services across network backbones, WANs (including the Internet), LANS and desktop computer connections. ATM makes maximum use of the available bandwidth by using virtual networking. This means that different logical networks can be created over the same physical network. For example, if the departments of an organisation are located in different parts of the country and are not connected to the same network segment, they can still be given access to the same set of network resources through a virtual network. Virtual network management software is needed to allow the administrator to view the physical network topology and create the logical views required by the organisation. Graphical user interface (GUI) software allows the administrator to use drag and drop functions to move network nodes and create the desired logical structure.

Optical communications and WDM

Optical fibre cable consists of thousands of clear glass fibre strands which transmit light or infra-red rays instead of electrical signals and is not subject to magnetic interference. The data is transmitted by a light-emitting diode (two-state signals) or injection-laser diode. Bandwidth is measured in gigabits per second and repeaters are only required after around 60 miles (copper cable requires repeaters every 3 or 4 miles). The other end of the cable has a detector which converts the light pulses into electrical pulses suitable for the attached device. Optical fibre cable is slightly more expensive than electrical cable, is used widely in WANs, but is also finding increasing use in LANs, particular for network backbones.

The high bandwidth of optical fibre makes it suitable for multiplexing. WDM (Wavelength Division Multiplexing) modulates signals to create several channels within the light spectrum and is the digital equivalent of FDM (frequency division multiplexing) used with analogue transmissions on coaxial cable. Even greater bandwidth can be obtained with D(Dense)WDM. It is protocol independent and can carry, for example, IP (Internet Protocol), ATM (Asynchronous Transfer Mode) and Ethernet traffic at rates between 100 megabits/sec and 2.5 gigabits/sec.

Connecting to a remote mainframe

In organisations with mainframe computers, it is often desirable for staff with microcomputers on their desks to be able to communicate with the mainframe via those systems. With non-IBM systems, where the host computer uses asynchronous transmission, the connection can be made via the RS232C (this refers to a standard used in most serial communications) serial transmission port, located at the back of the microcomputers system casing. However, the most common mainframe systems, IBM and ICL in particular, use synchronous communications, so special terminal emulation cards are required.

Thus, microcomputer workstations can be converted to mainframe terminals using a technique called emulation. A terminal emulation card is fitted into one of the expansion slots in the microcomputers system casing. If there are a number of terminals to be connected, the microcomputer is then connected, via a coaxial cable, to a terminal cluster controller. The controller is linked to a front-end processor (usually a minicomputer, dedicated to handling incoming and outgoing communications for the mainframe), which is itself connected to the mainframe computer. In this way, a microcomputer can, for example, be converted into an emulation of an IBM 3270 terminal.

The advantage of using a microcomputer as a mainframe terminal is that it can also be used on a stand-alone basis for local processing tasks, such as word processing or spreadsheet work. The terminal emulation package ensures that the mainframe responds in the same way as it would to a dedicated terminal. Security mechanisms, such as passwords, prevent users of emulated terminals from carrying out processes which are forbidden to users of dedicated terminals. However, the microcomputer's facility for local storage and processing can present serious security problems for the mainframes data and various mechanisms have to be included to prevent unauthorised updates. Where emulated terminals are to be linked to a mainframe via a wide area network, adapter cards are available which combine the terminal emulation with the gateway software, to access the intervening network.

Wireless networks

Television and radio broadcasting

When a television studio broadcasts a programme, the signals are carried to television receivers through a network of transmitters; radio programmes are broadcast from a studio in a similar fashion. An out-of-date term for a radio is a wireless; thus the transmissions in these broadcast networks are all carried out without the use of wires, that is, as *radio waves*. Radio waves vary in *frequency* and different frequency bands are used for different kinds of broadcasting. It is beyond the scope of this text to go into detail concerning these frequency bands, but the abbreviations VHF (very high frequency) and UHF (ultra-high frequency) should be familiar. The term *broadcast* is used because the radio wave signals can be received by any number of receivers within the broadcast area. The geographical area which can be reached by a broadcasting station depends on which method is used, namely:

❑ *cable* connections; this is an exception here as it clearly involves the use of wire or cable;

❏   *terrestrial* transmitters;

❏   *communications satellites*

A broadcasting company may use a combination of cable, terrestrial and satellite transmitters to distribute its programmes. For example, the American company WTBS, in Atlanta, Georgia uses satellite to transmit low-cost sports and entertainment programmes to cable systems across the USA. Cable broadcasting, as the term indicates, uses physical cabling and is only economic over a limited area, such as a large city. However, in combination with satellite broadcasting, cable television plays an important role. Although terrestrial transmitters allow a much larger broadcast area than cable, satellites are essential to modern television broadcasting. Within the UK, pictures and monophonic sound are transmitted as analogue signals. The BBC has developed and transmits, NICAM stereo sound and digital aerial services, using digital encoding techniques.

Television broadcasting allows the transmission of *moving pictures*, *sound* and *data* to television receivers within the area served by a broadcasting station. Database services provided by television are *one-way* only, to television receivers and are collectively known as *Teletext* (see Network services). The BBC teletext service is known as Ceefax. To access these services a television receiver must have a Teletext *decoder*.

Microwave transmissions and communications satellites

Microwaves are super-high frequency (SHF) radio waves and can be used where transmitter and receiver are not in sight of one another. The communication path must be relatively obstruction-free. Microwaves can also be transmitted, through earth transmitters, to communications satellites; microwaves can penetrate cloud. Earth stations must be no more than 25-30 miles apart, because humidity in the atmosphere interferes with microwave signals. Each station in a communication path acts as a *repeater* station. Obviously, it is impractical to build sufficient repeater stations to deal with all transmissions, so communications satellites are essential. Once a satellite has received a signal, it amplifies it and sends it back to earth. Satellite communications are now fairly common and provide a cheaper and better trans-ocean transmission medium than undersea cable. Apart from television broadcasting, satellites form an essential part of the international telephone network. Voice and data messages are digitally transmitted as packets (see Packet Switching). There are three basic types of satellite:

❏   GEO (geosynchronous earth orbit). A GEO satellite remains fixed above a given point on the earth's surface. This means that a terrestrial stations, once set to point at the satellite, do not require further adjustment. It is the most expensive to build and launch, but its powerful transmitters mean that few are needed to maintain global coverage. It also has an orbital life in excess of 12 years. A weakness of GEO satellite communication is *latency*, or propogation delay. A transmission passed via a GEO satellite from one terrestrial station to another takes more than two tenths of a second, which may make it unsuitable for use in high speed networks, but perfectly suitable for television broadcasting, mobile communications and global positioning services (GPS).

❏   MEO (medium earth orbit). A MEO satellite moves relative to a point on the earth's surface. This means that ground-based stations must have tracking equipment to maintain contact with a MEO. Global coverage requires the use of more MEOs than is the case for GEOs, but they are cheaper to build and launch and the transmission delay is insignificant. Its orbital life is between 6 and 12 years.

❏   LEO (low earth orbit). A LEO satellite moves quickly relative to a point on the earth's surface and many are needed to provide global coverage. LEOs are the cheapest to build and launch, provide the greatest bandwidth and suffer from virtually no transmission delay. However, a LEO satellite may have a lifespan of only 5 years.

Applications of satellite communication

Undersea cabling used to be the only way of connecting telephone networks on different continents but satellite communication provides a much cheaper alternative. Satellites also make it feasible and cost effective to extend networks to geographically remote and poorer countries which do not have established telecommunications systems. Satellite communications have been used in television broadcasting for over thirty years by traditional aerial delivery networks and cable networks. The bandwidth available through satellite communications allows the transmission of hundreds of television channels. Today, Direct Broadcast Satellite (DBS) allows television networks to transmit direct to individual users. A DBS satellite is geosynchronous and can transmit up to 150 channels, using digital signals to provide high quality reception to consumers.

Satellite communications allow ship to shore communications, linking a ship to a land-based receiver/transmitter anywhere in the world; aircraft use a similar service. A satellite phone can be used, even in the most remote parts of the world for voice and data communications; Inmarsat, for example, provides for ISDN communication. Global positioning services (GPS) can be used by ships, aircraft and land vehicles to determine their precise geographical position. Multiple geosynchronous satellites triangulate their signals to produce geographical coordinates.

Weather forecasting involves reporting, predicting, and studying the weather, including temperature, moisture, barometric pressure, and wind speed and direction. Satellites are vital for the rapid collection and transmission of meteorological data from the many terrestrial and atmospheric sources which contribute to more accurate weather forecasting.

Cellular telephone networks

These networks use *cellular radio* communications, which operate in the UHF (ultra-high frequency) band. Local *base stations* allow cellphone (hand-held or vehicle-based) users to access the pstn. Each base station covers a *cell site*, an area within which it can pick up cellphone signals. Within the UHF band, signals can penetrate buildings and other barriers, but a user must be within a few miles of a transmitter, particularly in urban areas, where the largest numbers of users tend to be found. Thus, a base station in a rural area, serving fewer users, can cover a larger cell site than is possible in an urban area. Computers are used to allow links to be maintained even while the caller is moving from one transmission area to another. Thus, when a base station receives a signal from a cellphone, it monitors the strength of the signal continuously to determine if it is still the most suitable base station to handle the transmission. Obviously, if the user is driving while making a call, a different base station may be handling the call at different points on the journey. The only effect of these changes is a brief (about one-fifth of a second) interruption to the call as the switch is made to a different base station. Two major cellular radio operators in the UK are Cellnet and Vodaphone.

New generation mobile phones

Apart from voice transmission, mobile phones can be used to transmit text messages and those that support Internet Protocol (IP) or the newer WAP (Wireless Application Protocol - see later) can be used to access Internet services, albeit very slowly. The delivery of Internet services through mobile networks is hampered by the mobile phone itself, with its slow processor, poor battery life, mono display and awkward keypad, as well as by limited bandwidth.

The development of broadband mobile networks and more sophisticated phones is vital if the full potential of the Internet's multimedia content is to be made as accessible through a mobile phone as it is through a PC. In the meantime, services are largely text-based and perfectly adequate for the viewing of such information as travel, weather, sport results, share prices and the delivery of bank, ticket and message services.

New generation mobile phones are making use of larger flip-up screens with touch-sensitive input and handwriting recognition as additions to the usual keypad.

WAP and WML (Wireless Markup Language)

Although mobile phones have been able to access Web pages coded in HTML for some time, a WAP-enabled mobile can use its WAP browser to access pages coded in WML, a language specially designed to take account of the limitations of mobile networks and phones. Access to the Internet must be provided through a *gateway* which supports the WAP protocol. All the major cellular networks provide WAP gateways to allow their users to access Internet data services and as the market expands it is likely that conventional Internet Service Providers (ISPs) will provide a similar service.

Once cellular networks are able to provide the bandwidth presently available to PC users, full Java-enabled HTML content will be easily accessible to mobile phone users and the need for WAP and WML is likely to be reduced.

Use of satellites in cellular networks

In common with other communication networks, digital signalling (the European standard for digital mobile communications is GSM - Global System for Mobile communications) has largely replaced analogue signalling. Each cell in a network provides a number of communication channels. In the case of analogue signalling each channel occupies a separate frequency band (frequency division multiplexing or FDM). Digital networks divide the cells into channels by time slot (time division multiplexing). When a network is busy, all the channels in a particular cell may be occupied, preventing other callers from using that cell. Satellites which are operating within a different bandwidth to the cell are able, when they have free bandwidth, to provide extra channel space for overloaded terrestrial cells. Digital cellular networks provide better performance (analogue networks can be subject to cross call interference) and more channels.

Modes of data communication

Direction of transmission

Communications media can be classified according to direction of transmission:

- ❏ *Simplex* mode allows communication in one direction only.

- ❏ *Half-duplex* supports communications in both directions, but not at the same time;

in other words there is only a single channel and the direction is switched after completion of transmission in the other direction.

❏ *Duplex* mode allows communication in both directions at the same time, as there are two channels permanently available. In interactive systems, where two way communication is continuously required, duplex is the only suitable mode.

❏ *Asymmetric duplex* is the same as duplex, except that the transmission speed in one direction is different from that of the other.

Devices differ in the ways they communicate or talk with each other. One such difference is in the number of *conductors* or lines they use to transmit data.

Serial transmission

With serial transmission, the binary signals representing the data are transmitted one after another in a serial fashion. Serial data transmission is normally used, except for very short connections between a peripheral and a computer, where parallel techniques are employed. The technique is illustrated in Figure 11.4.

Figure 11.4. *Serial transmission between two devices*

Parallel transmission

As the term makes obvious, data bits are transmitted as groups in parallel; Figure 11.5 illustrates this form.

Figure 11.5. *Parallel transmission between a computer and a local printer*

This is obviously quicker than sending them serially, but it is only practicable over short distances. Communication between a computer and its nearby peripherals can be carried out using parallel transmission, which is particularly important where high-speed devices, such as disk or tape units, are concerned. Microcomputer systems often use parallel transmission to communicate with a nearby printer. The number of lines needed for a parallel connection defines its *bus width*. As explained in the later section on Connectors or Interfaces, each line has a particular function. Thus, apart from the 8 bits needed for the data (see Data Representation), *handshaking* signals are needed to control the transfer of data between a computer and a terminal, which operate at different speeds. Additional handshake lines are needed to carry these signals.

Asynchronous serial transmission

When a sending device transmits characters at irregular intervals, as does for example, a keyboard device, it is said to be transmitting *asynchronously*.

Although the characters are not sent at regular intervals, the bits within each character must be sent at regularly timed intervals. An example of asynchronous character format is shown in Figure 11.6. It can be seen that the line has two electrical states, representing 1 and 0. Between characters, the line is in the *idle* state, a 1 or *mark* condition.

Figure 11.6. *Asynchronous character format*

The first or *start bit*, set to 0, indicates the start of a character, whilst a *stop bit* marks the end. The receiving machine listens to the line for a start bit. When it senses this it counts off the regularly timed bits that form the character. When a stop bit is reached, the receiver switches back to its listening state. The presence of start and stop bits for each character permits the time interval between characters to be irregular, or asynchronous.

Synchronous serial transmission

The start and stop bits used in asynchronous transmission are wasteful, as they do not contain information. With higher speed devices or *buffered* low-speed devices, data can be transmitted in more efficient, timed, or *synchronous* blocks. Figure 11.7 illustrates the technique.

Figure 11.7. *Synchronous character format*

A variety of formats may be used, each having their operating rules or protocol. Communications protocols are dealt with later in this chapter.

In synchronous transmission, a data stream may be very long, so it is vital that the timing between transmitter and receiver is synchronised and that individual characters are separated. This is done by using a *clock lead* from the transmitter. Synchronisation (*syn*) characters are placed at the beginning of each data block and, in case timing is lost by line disturbance, several syn characters may be situated at intervals within the data block. Thus if timing is lost, the receiver can re-time its bit groupings from the last syn character. Like the start and stop bits used in asynchronous transmission, syn characters constitute an overhead and have to be stripped out by the receiver. Some VDU terminals are designed for high speed data transmission and use synchronous transmission; many others use asynchronous transmission.

Parallel-serial conversion (UART and USRT)

As data moves around a computer system in parallel form, it needs to be converted to serial form for transmission though a telecommunications link and from serial to parallel, when the transmission is inward. These conversion processes are carried out by a hardware device called a *universal asynchronous receiver and transmitter* (UART) or *universal synchronous receiver and transmitter* (USRT), depending on the type of computer being used.

Devices

Data terminal equipment (DTE)

All the external devices attached to a network may be referred to collectively as data terminal equipment (DTE). Examples of DTE equipment are: computer terminals, including microcomputers used for that function; minicomputers; bank cash dispensers; printers.

Dumb terminal

The DTE may be a *dumb* terminal, that is, one which has no processing power of its own, possibly no storage, and is entirely dependent on a controlling computer. As soon as each character is entered by the operator, it is transmitted over the communications link, to the controlling computer; this makes editing extremely difficult and slow. The remote computer, to which the terminal is connected, has to use an *input buffer* (small amount of memory assigned to that purpose) to store characters as they arrive. Because the terminal is dumb, the remote computer must regularly *poll* the line to determine the presence of data.

Intelligent terminal

An *intelligent* terminal (it may be a microcomputer) has memory and processing power, so an operator can use it to store, edit and manipulate data, independently of any other connected computer. For example, a document could be retrieved from a remote computer, be edited within the intelligent terminal and then, in its updated form, be transmitted back to the remote computer. The intelligent terminal's processing facility is provided by an internal processor, usually a microprocessor; its internal memory allows data to be held and manipulated before transmission. The facility may also include local backing storage and a printer. Intelligent terminals can use either EBCDIC or ASCII code (see Standards for Data Representation), but a dumb terminal can only use ASCII. Two points need to be made concerning the methods used to transmit data and the type of terminal used.

❑   Dumb terminals, having no processing power and no buffer memory have to use a *point-to-point* connection with the remote, controlling computer. Such terminals transmit data asynchronously. The characters are not evenly separated, because the transmission of characters is determined by the typing speed of the operator and the characters will obviously not be transmitted at precise, regular intervals.

❑   Intelligent terminals, having a buffer store, can accumulate the keyed characters and send them in blocks or streams. The remote computer signals when transmission of a data stream can begin, thus allowing line sharing by numerous communicating devices. Such line sharing is carried out by multiplexing, a technique described in the earlier section on Packet Switching Networks.

Data circuit termination equipment (DCE)

The intervening connections of a network are leased from the main telecommunications provider, which in the UK is British Telecom. The equipment that allows the DTE to be connected to and interfaced with the network is known as *data circuit termination equipment* (DCE). The CCITT (see Standards Authorities) use the term *data communication equipment* (also DCE). An example of DCE is a *modem*, which allows computer data to be transmitted over sections of the pstn (usually local connections to homes and businesses) which still use analogue signalling.

Modem

Figure 11.8 illustrates the role of the modem in a data telecommunications link.

Figure 11.8. *Modems in a data communcations link*

Even though much of the public switched telephone network (pstn) uses digital transmission techniques, many local connections to homes and businesses still use analogue signals. To allow transmission of computer data (which is digital) over these analogue links, a device called a *modem* is needed to *modulate* and *demodulate* the computers signals. The modem for the transmitter device has to modulate the digital signal into the corresponding analogue form for transmission along the telephone line. The modem at the receiver device has to carry out the reverse operation. Modems are capable of both functions, so that two way communications are supported. Modems are examined in more detail in the section on Protocols.

Telephone-modem connections

To allow computer communication through a telephone line, the user must obtain a modem, of which there are two main types:

❏   asynchronous (irregularly transmitted characters) serial modems. Each character requires *start* and *stop bits* to separate one character from another.

❏   synchronous (regularly timed transmission of data blocks) serial modems. Start and stop bits are not required, because the transmitting and receiving modems are synchronised.

Modem speeds

Baud rate indicates the number of signal changes or pulses per second supported by a communication link. The term used to be synonymous with *bits per second* (bps), but improved data encoding (compression) techniques mean, for example, that a 28,800 baud link can support data transfer rates up to 115,200 bps. Different modems provide different data transmission rates, measured in bits per second (bps). The data compression and error correction standards are set by standards bodies (see start of chapter).

Computer-modem connection

To make use of a modem, the microcomputer should have a serial communication (RS232) port. However, there are two possible alternatives; an adapter card with a serial port capability; a communications board (this fits in an expansion slot, located inside the computer's system casing), which combines the functions of the serial port and the modem.

Interfaces

Interface devices (or connectors - the terms are interchangeable) are designed to allow various pieces of equipment to work with one another. For this reason, they normally conform to certain standards, of which there are a number. For example, to connect a computer to a modem requires an interface that will allow:

❏   the movement of data, in both directions, between the two devices;

❏   selection of the transmission rate for data to pass through the telephone line;

❏   synchronisation of the two devices (with clock timing signals).

Standards (usually recommended by one of the Standards Authorities), applied to the design of the interface, may relate to, for example, the number and arrangement of pins, their functions and the signals that are applied to each. This topic is examined further in the following section. The following sections examine several types of interfaces. Interfaces can be categorised according to whether they are designed to handle *serial* or *parallel* transmission of data.

Data communications standards

Data representation

Before transmission, characters must be coded into a code recognised by the sending and receiving devices. Almost all terminals are designed to use either the ASCII or EBCDIC codes (Chapter 2).

The ASCII (American Standard Code for Information Interchange) code uses seven binary digits (*bits*), plus a *parity bit* (see Error Detection) to represent a full range of characters. It is defined by the International Standards Organisation (ISO). The 8-bit EBCDIC (Extended Binary-coded Decimal Interchange Code) character code has a 256 character set and is generally used with IBM and IBM-compatible equipment.

Communications protocols

A protocol is a set of rules for the transmission of data between two devices. A protocol may include rules to deal with:

❏   the establishment of which device currently has *control of the communications link*;

❏   *error detection and correction*;

❏   *data flow control*; this is to ensure that data transmission flows smoothly, that the communications channel is not overloaded and that the transmitting device does not send data more quickly than the receiver can handle.

Protocols are often developed by manufacturers and then become recommended by Standards Authorities, but sometimes, they are developed by the latter. Not all protocols cover all three items listed above. For example, the V24 (CCITT standard) and RS232 protocols, which are computer-modem interfaces (see Connectors or Interfaces), do not provide error detection facilities; they are *low level* protocols. Similarly, the X25 interface is a protocol and interface standard for connection to a packet switching network; there are a whole series of X protocols established by the CCITT relating to packet switching networks. A higher level protocol, such as V42 (see Example Protocols) includes error detection and correction facilities. The rest of this section aims to give a brief introduction to this very complex area of data communications.

The OSI (open systems interconnection) model

Many computer devices are now designed for use in networked systems. Manufacturers are now tending to conform to standard protocols that make their equipment compatible with a variety of user networks. *Closed* networks, that are restricted to one manufacturer's equipment and standards, are not attractive to the user, because it restricts the choice of equipment which can be used. The aim of standardisation is to achieve more open systems which allow users to select from a wider range of manufacturers' products. A Reference Model for Open Systems Interconnection (OSI) has been under development by the International Standards Organisation (ISO) since 1977. Other standards, including SNA (IBM's System Network Architecture) and Ethernet, are largely incompatible with one another. Certain standards in the OSI model have been set by manufacturers as their commercial products have gained in popularity. The OSI reference model for communications protocol identifies a hierarchy of seven layers. The layers and their functions are briefly described below.

Application layer

This is the highest layer in that it is closest to the user. It supports the transfer of information between end-users, applications programs and devices. Several types of protocol exist in this layer, including those for specific applications and those for more generalised applications, such as accounting, entry control and user identification. The applications layer hides the physical network from the user, presenting a user-orientated view instead. For example, the user need not know that several physical computers are involved when accessing a database.

Presentation layer

This layer covers standards on how data is presented to the end-user devices. The aim is to ensure that different devices, which may be using data in different formats, can communicate with one another. The presentation layer can, for example, handle conversions between ASCII and EBCDIC character codes. It may also carry out encryption to ensure data security during transmission over vulnerable telecommunication links. The presentation layer also attempts to deal with conversions between terminals which use different line and screen lengths and different character sets.

Session layer

The session layer is concerned with the exchange of information between different applications and users; it is the users' interface into the network. When a user requests a particular service from the network, the session layer handles the dialogue.

Transport layer

The data transmission system on any network will have its own peculiarities and the function of the transport layer is to mask out any undesirable features which may prevent a high quality transmission for the network.

Network layer

The function of the network layer is to perform the routing of information around the network and also to connect one network to another. The software can also carry out accounting functions to enable the network owner to charge users.

Data link layer

The physical data transmission media used in a network are subject to interference which can corrupt data and other signals. The data link layer handles data transmission errors and thus improves the quality of the network. The techniques used, for example, for the receipt and acknowledgement of data by a receiver device, are determined by the data link layer. The CCITT V42bis protocol, with its error detection and correction facilities falls into this level.

Physical layer

The physical layer provides the means to connect the physical medium and is concerned with the transmission of binary data within the communication channel. Standards are set regarding the mechanical, electrical and procedural aspects of interface devices. For example, standards are set for the number of pins a network connector should have and the function and position of each pin. The RS232 and V24 protocols are within this level.

Example communication protocols

See also the Chapter 38 on the Internet and Internet Security for explanations of the HTTP and S-HTTP protocols.

TCP/IP

TCP/IP (Transmission Control Protocol/Internet Protocol) is the standard for communication between Internet host computers and is probably the most well known. It is actually a suite of several protocols. The importance of the Internet for network communications means that all modern operating systems provide support for TCP/IP, including those PC and Macintosh computer systems and network operating systems such as Novell Netware. Unix, as the standard operating system for most Internet host computers, has the TCP/IP protocol built in.

SMTP

SMTP stands for Simple Mail Transfer Protocol and is the standard for e-mail transmissions between servers and between clients (user e-mail software) and servers on the Internet.

UDP

UDP or User Datagram Protocol is used for the broadcast of data over IP (Internet Protocol) networks but unlike TCP, does not require that a connection is first established between sender and receiver (point to point). In other words, the data is transmitted without any guarantee that it will reach its destination. For this reason, UDP is referred to as a *connectionless* protocol (TCP is a *connection-orientated* protocol. Ethernet local area networks also operate on a connectionless, broadcast principle.

X.25

This is a CCITT protocol for packet switching networks. X.25 Packet Switched networks allow remote devices to communicate with each other across high speed digital links without the expense of individual leased lines. Packet Switching is a technique whereby the network routes individual packets of data between different destinations based on addressing within each packet.

Handshaking

Synchronisation of data transmission between communicating devices is essential, primarily because they often operate at different speeds, and sometimes, a device may have to wait because the other device is not ready. For example, if a file is being transferred from a remote terminal to a receiving computer, and the file is too large to fit into the computer's memory, then it will have to save sections of the file at intervals. If the computer has no multi-tasking capability, then data may be lost if it is transmitted during a save operation. To prevent such data loss, the flow of data has to be controlled and the activities of the communicating devices need to be properly synchronised.

Handshaking is necessary for both parallel and serial transmissions and involves acknowledgement signals between devices that they are ready to communicate with one another. The process of handshaking can be software or hardware controlled. A hardware handshake, for example, between a computer and a printer, involves the exchange of signals, through dedicated lines or conductors; the signals indicate the readiness of each device to send or receive data. A software handshake, usually employed for serial transmissions through modems, enables each device to establish the particular protocols which will be used for transmissions. Error control and data compression (to improve the transmission rate) can be built into the modems specification and thus be hardware controlled, or they can be provided by a communications package.

Flow control

Flow control enables communicating modems to pause and restart data transmission, as necessary. The need for pauses and restarts stems from the fact that a receiving modem has to use buffer memory (of limited capacity) and may not be able to empty it (pass it on) as quickly as it is being filled. This could be because the computer to which it is connected is busy with another task, such as printing. If transmission is not paused once the buffer is full, data will be lost. To exert flow control, the receiving modem must signal the sending modem that transmission has to be temporarily interrupted. This can be done, either by the modem or the terminal software.

Error detection

Block check characters (BCC)

The idea of even and odd parity bits for each character is introduced in Chapter 2 and is shown to be inadequate for the detection of even numbers of bit errors. Block check characters (BCCs) aim to conquer this problem by checking the parity of blocks of characters within a data transmission stream. BCCs may carry out *longitudinal* or *cyclic* redundancy checks.

Longitudinal redundancy checking (LRC)

By reference to Table 11.1, the principles of LRC can be explained as follows. Each BCC consists of a group of parity bits which carry out LRC. However, each LRC bit is a parity check on the corresponding bits in all the characters in a block. Thus, the first parity bit in the BCC relates to the bits which occupy the first position in each character in the block, the second parity bit in the BCC relates to the second position bits in each character in the block and so on. LRC ensures that multiple errors, whether even or odd, are likely to be discovered, so at the receiver end of the transmission, the parity of individual characters and blocks of characters is checked.

	7	6	5	4	3	2	1	0
	0	1	0	0	1	0	1	1
	0	1	0	0	1	1	1	0
	1	1	0	0	1	1	1	1
	1	1	0	1	0	1	0	0
	1	1	0	1	0	1	0	0
VRC (bit-7) on	1	1	0	1	0	1	1	1
each character	0	1	0	0	0	0	0	1
	1	1	0	0	1	0	0	1
	1	1	0	1	0	1	0	0
	1	1	0	0	0	1	0	1
	0	1	0	1	0	0	1	1
	1	1	0	1	0	1	1	1
	BCC to check LRC parity (per block)							

Table 11.1. *Vertical (VRC) and longitudinal redundancy checks (LRC)*

Cyclic redundancy checking (CRC)

The BCCs described previously treat a data block as a set of characters, whereas cyclic redundancy checking (CRC) uses a BCC which views each data block as a continuous *stream* of bits.

Firstly, the data block is regarded as one large binary number. That number is divided by another agreed binary number, the quotient is discarded and the remainder (sometimes referred to as a *checksum*) is attached to the data block as a BCC. Upon receipt of the data block, the receiver repeats the calculation used to generate the BCC and compares the result with the BCC attached by the transmitter; any difference between them indicates some corruption of the block.

Hamming code

Certain codes can be used, not only to detect the occurrence of an error, but also to identify its precise location. In addition, some errors can be rectified.

The Hamming code described here utilises three *code* bits and four *data* bits, making seven in all, although there are circumstances when more bits may be used.

Table 11.2 illustrates the format which positions each code bit (C_2, C_1 and C_0) in a column position which equates with its binary weight. The data bits (D_3, D_2, D_1 and D_0) occupy the other positions. Thus, C_0 ($2^0 = 1$) is in column 1, C_1 ($2^1 = 2$) in column 2 and C_2 ($2^2 = 4$) in column 4.

Table 11.2. *Hamming code format*

Table 11.2 shows that parity is maintained in sub-groups, such that the C_0 relates to D_3, D_1 and D_0, C_1 to D_3, D_2 and D_0, and C_2 to D_3, D_2 and D_1. Thus, each sub-group of data bits has a single code bit. This is illustrated further in Table 11.3.

group	7	6	5	4	3	2	1
C_0	D_3		D_1		D_0		C_0
C_1	D_3	D_2			D_0	C_1	
C_2	D_3	D_2	D_1	C_2			

Table 11.3. *Association of code and data bits*

The three code bits produce a unique pattern when any single bit is corrupted. A parity output of 000 would indicate the absence of any errors. To correct the word only requires the inversion of the bit position which is in error. The processes are illustrated in Table 11.4.

7	6	5	4	3	2	1	explanation of pattern
D_3	D_2	D_1	C_2	D_0	C_1	C_0	with each group using even parity
1	0	0	1	1	0	0	C_0, C_1, C_2 groups all maintain even parity
0	0	0	1	1	0	0	column 7 error - parity error in each group
1	0	0	1	0	0	0	column 3 error - parity error in C_1, C_0 groups

Table 11.4. *Code patterns with example errors*

Table 11.4 shows three code patterns, the first one being correct and the other two being in error. The location of the erroneous bit is identified by the creation of a 3-bit pattern. Each bit, starting with the least significant is used to flag the parity status of of the C_2, C_1 and C_3 groups, respectively. Even parity is maintained in each group in the first example, so the flag pattern is 000. In the second example, parity is lost in each group, resulting in a flag pattern of 111, which indicates that the erroneous bit is in column 7 (111_2). Checking the third example, reveals that even parity is maintained in the C_2 group, but is lost in the other two; the resulting flag pattern of 011 indicates that the bit in column 3 (011_2) is wrong.

This method does not enable detection of double errors, but the limitation can be removed by the inclusion of a single parity bit across the whole word. However, double bit errors are not correctable.

Echoplex (echo checking)

Echoplex is used in asynchronous communications, for low speed, *dumb* (see Devices) terminals connected to a remote host computer. When a character is transmitted (in other words, when a key is pressed) the host device immediately sends it back to be displayed on the dumb terminal's screen. If the displayed character does not match the character selected from the keyboard, the operator should detect this; the host device can be advised, by the terminal operator, to ignore the incorrect character, by the sending of an agreed *control* character. Clearly, the method is slow and crude. A character could have been received correctly by the host device and an error could corrupt it on its way back. The operator has no way of knowing how and at what point an error occurred. Another disadvantage is that error correction is manual; in an interactive system, the user needs to rely on automatic error control and correction.

Error correction

Automatic repeat request (ARQ)

When a receiver detects an error it must tell the sending device to re-transmit the erroneous data; this is known as *automatic repeat request* (ARQ). The technique is most appropriate to the handling of data streams, that is, synchronous communications, in conjunction with cyclic redundancy checking (CRC - see earlier). ARQ can take one of three forms:

❏ *Stop and wait ARQ* or *ACK and NAK*. With this form the receiver acknowledges every block of data, with ACK if it detects no error and NAK if an error is detected. The sending device cannot send the next block until an acknowledgement is received. Any NAK block is re-transmitted repeatedly, if necessary, until an ACK is received.

❏ *Go-back N ARQ*. With this form, a block is only acknowledged if an error is detected. The sending device can continue transmitting without waiting for an acknowledgement. When a NAK is received, the block in which the error occurred is identified and that block, plus any transmitted since (N blocks), must be re-transmitted.

❏ *Selective-repeat ARQ*. This is the most sophisticated form of ARQ, in that blocks transmitted since the erroneous block (correct ones are not acknowledged), do not have to be sent again. Thus the sender only re-transmits the identified block and then continues from where it left off, when the NAK was received.

File transfer protocols

File transfer is the process of transmitting complete files from one computer to another. To achieve a successful transfer, both sending and receiving devices must establish the protocol (the set of rules) by which they will communicate. Various protocols are commonly recognised, but they vary in their performance and suitability for particular tasks. Some examples are described below.

FTP

File Transfer Protocol (FTP) allows large amounts of information to be transferred between two computers very conveniently. FTP originated with the UNIX operating system and was used to transfer files of all types between remote computer systems. A popular application of FTP is for the uploading and downloading of Web site pages.

ASCII

This is only appropriate for *text* files, which contain no control characters. Thus it cannot be used to transfer files produced with a word processor, spreadsheet or graphics package. Neither can it transfer command (COM) or executable (EXE) files, or files in compressed (ZIP, for example) form. Apart from this, the protocol is not good at controlling errors.

Xmodem

This is a file-transfer protocol used for asynchronous communications. It is commonly used in communications packages. The Xmodem protocol transfers data in blocks of 128 bytes, giving each transmitted *frame* a sequential block number; this number is used to identify the location of errors. A *checksum* (see Block Check Characters) is attached to each block to check transmission errors. Its ability to find and correct errors makes it suitable for the transfer of files, which must retain their integrity, such as program files.

Zmodem

This is one of the most advanced protocols, being much faster than Xmodem. Its error correction controls are absolutely reliable.

CCITT V42bis

This protocol includes a *data compression* (through encoding, data is reduced in volume) technique and error detection and correction. Both the sending and receiving modem must possess the error correction facility.

Transmission media

When data is transmitted between two hardware devices in a network, a communication medium is used. The commonly used media are, *twisted-pair* cable, *coaxial* cable and *optical fibre*. Where a physical connection is not practical, then radio, infra-red, microwave and laser technologies may be used.

Twisted-pair cable

Twisted-pair cable is formed from strands of wire twisted in pairs. It predates any other method and is still extensively used for standard telephone or telex terminals. Each twisted pair can carry a single telephone call between two people or two machines. Although twisted-pair cable is generally used for analogue signal transmission, it can be used successfully for digital transmission. Variation in the lengths of wire within pairs can result in signals being received out of phase, but this can be overcome by the frequent use of repeaters. The repeaters refresh the signal as it passes to maintain its consistency. Although transmission rates permitted by such cable are lower than for some other media, they are acceptable for many computer applications.

Coaxial cable

Coaxial cable is resistant to the transmission interference which can corrupt data transmitted via twisted-pairs cable. It thus provides a fast, relatively interference-free transmission medium. Its construction consists of a central conductor core which is surrounded by a layer of insulating material. The insulating layer is covered by a conducting shield, which is itself protected by another insulating layer. During network installation, the cable can be cut and connections made, without affecting its transmission quality. The quality of cable can vary and some low quality cable is unsuitable for data transmission over long distances. On the other hand, high quality cable can be quite rigid and difficult to install in local networks, where space is limited. Despite this difficulty, it is an extremely popular choice for LANs.

Optical fibre cable

Optical fibre cable consists of thousands of clear glass fibre strands which transmit light or infra-red rays instead of electrical signals. The data is transmitted by a light-emitting diode (two-state signals) or injection-laser diode. Transmission speeds of billions of bits per second are achieved. Repeaters are only required after several miles. The other end of the cable has a detector which converts the light pulses into electrical pulses suitable for the attached device. Optical fibre cable is more expensive than electrical cable but is finding increasing use in LANs. However, its main application is for long-distance communications. See also Optical communications and WDM, earlier in this chapter.

Network services

Many networks, both private and public, provide additional services which give them the collective name of *value-added networks* or VANs. Switchstream, Megastream and Satstream (see Digital Network Systems) are VANs provided by British Telecom. Other VANs provide specific services, such as *videotext* (see later), electronic mail, facsimile transmission, bulletin boards and bibliographic databases, for use by academics and researchers.

Gateways

Gateways allow different types of computer to communicate with one another, even if they use different communications protocols or transfer data at different speeds. For example, the mainframe computers of the main holiday tour operators can be accessed by travel agents, through a Prestel gateway.

Bibliographic databases

These databases provide information on specialised or widely ranging topics. For example, BLAISE, which is provided by the British Library, gives information on British book publications. Euronet Diane (Direct Information Access Network in Europe) provides information extracted from publications, research documents and so on, which may be of interest to specialists, such as scientists, engineers, economists and lawyers. Each extract provides the relevant bibliographic references to allow users to access the original sources more fully.

Bulletin boards

A bulletin board (BB) is simply a means by which, users can, for example, exchange ideas, pass on information and buy or sell items to one another. Frequently, no charge is made. Chat lines are often included; this means that two users can carry on a conversation, through the use of screen and keyboard. Where more than two users are conversing, a form of *teleconferencing* can occur; any user wishing to contribute to the discussion has their contribution placed in a queue, from where it will be displayed on each contributor's screen.

Telex

Telex is a well established communications system which, rather like the public telephone network, allows subscribers to communicate with one another. There are over a million subscribers in this country at present. Each subscriber is given a telex code (you will often see it at the top of business letter headings next to the telephone number) and must have a teleprinter which is a combination of keyboard and printer. There is no screen, so all messages sent or received are printed onto hard copy.

The transmission rate of approximately 6 characters per second is slow compared with more modern telecommunications systems, but the limitations of keyboard entry and printer speed on the teleprinter, make any faster speed unnecessary. The main benefit of telex is that a permanent record of communications is kept and the receiver does not have to be on the spot when the message arrives. Its main disadvantage is that there is no storage facility for messages. Any transmission has to be printed as soon as it is transmitted so that if the receiver is faulty, the system comes to a halt.

Although it is inferior to e-mail (see next section), it is still the only method (apart from telephone) of instant communication with less developed countries, where Telex machines are still widely used.

Electronic mail (e-mail) services

E-mail systems based on computer networks are paper-less (except when a user requires hard copy). A major advantage is the facility for message storage if a destination terminal is busy, or has a temporary fault. When it is free, the message can be transmitted.

Certain basic features can be identified as being common to all e-mail systems:

❏ a terminal for preparing, entering and storing messages. The terminal will be intelligent, possibly a microcomputer, mainframe terminal or dedicated word processor. In any event, it should have some word processing or text editing facilities to allow messages to be changed on screen before transmission. A printer may also be available for printing out messages received over the system;

❏ an electronic communication link with other workstations in the network and with the central computer controlling the system;

❏ a directory containing the electronic addresses of all network users;

❏ a central mailbox facility (usually the controlling computer) for the storage of messages in transit or waiting to be retrieved.

Ideally, the following facilities are available to e-mail users:

❏ messages are automatically dated upon transmission;

❏ messages are automatically acknowledged as being received when the recipient first accesses it from the terminal;

❏ multiple addressing, that is the facility to address a message to an identified group, without addressing each member of the group individually;

❏ priority rating to allow messages to be allocated different priorities according to their importance.

Networks require two particular features in order to support e-mail:

❏ a message storage facility to allow messages to be forwarded when the recipient is available;

❏ compatibility with a wide range of manufacturers' equipment. Devices attached to a network have to be able to talk to the communications network using protocols or standards of communication.

Benefits of e-mail

The following major benefits are generally claimed for e-mail systems:

❏ savings in stationery and telephone costs;

❏ more rapid transmission than is possible with conventional mail;

❏ e-mail can be integrated with other computer-based systems used in an organisation;

❏ all transmissions are recorded, so costs can be carefully controlled;

❏ e-mail allows staff to telework, that is, to work from home via a terminal;

❑   the recipient does not have to be present when a message is sent. Messages can be retrieved from the central mailbox when convenient.

Teletex

Teletex is nothing to do with teletext systems, such as Ceefax and Oracle (see Videotex). Teletex is similar to Telex, except that transmissions are quicker and cheaper and text is not restricted to upper case characters. It uses the pstn, but can also access packet switching networks and the Telex system through *gateways*. Teletex standards have been internationally agreed through the CCITT (see Standards Authorities) and Teletex is now used in many countries throughout the world.

Electronic data interchange (EDI)

Similar to E-mail, EDI allows users to electronically exchange business documents, such as invoices, delivery notes, orders and receipts. EDI can drastically reduce the volume of paperwork and business can be transacted much more quickly than is possible through the normal postal system. UK examples of EDI systems are:

❑   Tradanet, linking manufacturers, wholesalers, distributors and retailers;

❑   Brokernet, which links insurance companies and brokers;

❑   Drugnet, linking medical practices to pharmaceutical companies, allowing the provision of current information on various products;

❑   Factornet allows firms to deal with *factors* who buy outstanding customer bills at a discount; the factors then obtain payment from the debtor. Small firms find this service particularly useful as it enables them to improve their cash flow.

EDI set up costs are quite high and for this reason, is not attractive to the smaller business. The system is typically implemented on private networks and ensures a high level of security for participating organisations. Many such large organisations insist on the use of EDI by their suppliers and business customers. However, the high cost of private networks has led to larger businesses allowing smaller traders to do business with them through their Internet stores. Without such access, these large businesses are denying themselves access to numerous smaller suppliers and business customers.

EFTPOS (electronic funds transfer at point-of-sale)

This service provides for the automatic debiting of customers' bank accounts at the checkout or point of sale. Many garages now have a device for reading the magnetic strip details on bank and credit cards. The system saves considerable time when contrasted with payments by cheque and as an alternative to cash, reduces the likelihood of theft. The retailer also has the assurance that the payment is authorised before the sale is made. Usually, a retailer will have a floor limit, or amount above which a telephone call needs to be made to the credit card company for authorisation of payment.

EFT (electronic funds transfer)

This system is used to transfer money between the branches of the same bank and between different banks. In the UK, the system is known as the Bankers Automated Clearing Service (BACS). The service is not restricted to bank use; organisations can pay their employees salaries directly into their bank or building society accounts. Business accounts can also be settled through this EFT system. Apart from the banks, other users usually link into the pstn through a dial-up connection (unless the volume of data justifies a leased line).

Remote job entry (RJE)

RJE systems make the simplest use of data communications to transmit bulk data rapidly to a central computer; transmission is one-way, from an RJE terminal located at the remote site to the central computer, which is probably situated at the head office of the organisation. In a wholesaling organisation, for example, each distribution warehouse could transmit details of stock changes and requirements via an RJE terminal, at the end of each day via a simplex dial-up communications link. In the 1960s, RJE terminals commonly consisted of a card or paper tape reader and printer; more recently, transmission would be direct from a key-to-disk or key-to-tape system.

Facsimile transmission (FAX)

This service allows the transmission of facsimiles or exact copies of documents or pictures through a data communications network. Using a fax machine connected to a telephone line, the user simply dials the fax number of the recipient, waits for the correct signal and the document is fed though the fax machine and transmitted. The fax machine sends picture elements or pixels obtained by scanning the document in a series of parallel lines; a synchronised fax machine at the other end prints a facsimile from those pixels.

Teletext

Teletext systems, such as Ceefax and Oracle, provide a public service based on a central computer database, which users can access via an ordinary television set with special adapter and keypad. The database consists of thousands of pages or frames of information which are kept up to date by Information Providers. Pages can be accessed and displayed on the television screen through the use of the keypad, directly via page number or through a series of hierarchical indexes. Major subject areas include Sport, News, Business, Leisure and Entertainment, Finance and Travel. Pages are transmitted using spare bandwidth unused by television pictures, in carousels or groups. The user may have to wait some time while the carousel containing the required page is transmitted. Its major drawback is that communication is *one-way*. The user cannot send messages to the database, only receive.

Viewdata or videotex

A viewdata system is based on a central computer database, which provides pages of information on a variety of subjects, including sport, travel and business, for access by subscribers. As an *interactive* system, users typically access services using simple, low cost, viewdata terminals, or microcomputer systems equipped with special software. Users connect with a viewdata *gateway* through the public telephone network. The major public viewdata system in the UK is *Prestel*. It uses the Teletext *alpha mosaic* character set. The graphics it produces appear similar to Lego building blocks. Developed by British Telecom, Prestel is now technologically out of date and is used, mainly, as a *gateway* to third party databases, for example, Electronic Yellow Pages, and CitiService (a financial database). Apart from information provision, the following services may be available through a viewdata system:

❑   Electronic mail. Viewdata users can transmit electronic messages to other users in the system, using such things as bulletin boards and chat lines. The British Campus 2000, which links together schools in Britain and other countries is an example of a viewdata electronic mail system.

❑ Paying bills, purchasing tickets, ordering goods and other such transactions.

❑ The distribution of computer programs. Centrally stored computer programs can be transferred to users' microcomputer systems so that they can later be used independently of the viewdata system. This is sometimes referred to as *telesoftware*.

In France, a combined teletext and viewdata system is called Antiope, and another viewdata system, available since 1984, is called Teletel. The latter system is very widely used, with more than eight million terminals attached to the system. The US service is called Prodigy and in Japan it is called Captain.

File transfer

A file can be a data file or a program file; the data could be a document prepared on a word processor and a program file could be a program of any kind. A file transfer service allows the use of one computer to retrieve a file from another computer, through a telecommunications link. Equally, a file can be transmitted in the opposite direction. E-mail is a special kind of file transfer facility, but to most users, the facility is used to retrieve documentary information from remote databases, or software from, for example, bulletin boards. To be transferred correctly, and this is particularly important in the case of program files (it can not be executed if the code is corrupted), requires the use of file transfer protocols. A modem suited to the purpose will use a particular file transfer protocol and whatever communications package is used, it must be able to use that protocol.

Internet

The Internet (Chapter 38) is a world-wide network derived from DARPANET (Defense Advanced Research Projects Agency Network) which was developed, during the 1960s, initially as a military defence project for the U.S. Department of Defense. Later, with universities and other academic institutions making unauthorised use of the network for private electronic mail, the name was changed to ARPANET. A packet switching protocol called NCP (network control protocol) had its initial development in the UK and this was adopted as the network protocol.

World wide web (WWW)

Although accessing the network is not difficult, finding specific information can be, considering the number of host computers connected to it. In 1990, the European Laboratory of Particle Physics in Switzerland, developed a *hypertext* based user interface. This interface allows a user to move from one Internet resource to another by way of, for example, topic searches, without knowing in advance, the precise location of each piece of information.

Service providers

To gain access to Internet, microcomputer users need to use a *service provider*. These are organisations which not only provide the necessary software to gain access to the network, but provide some of the additional services outlined in the previous section; in particular, the services cover e-mail, file transfer and access to bibliographic databases. Many home users now take advantage of the free Internet access offered by some organisations.

✍️Exercises

1. (i)   Name three *standards authorities* for the data communications industry.

    (ii) What is meant by the phrases *open systems* and *closed systems*?

2. Differentiate between the *pstn* and the *psdn*.

3. What types of user would be likely to use a:

    (i)   *dedicated* line;

    (ii)   dial-up connection.

4. Differentiate between *message* and *packet switching*, identifying any advantages one has over the other.

5. (i)   What is the purpose of *multiplexing*?

    (ii) Name a commercial service which uses multiplexing?

    (iii) Briefly differentiate between *time division* and *frequency division* multiplexing.

6. What is the ISDN?

7. Explain the terms *asynchronous* and *synchronous serial* transmission.

8. Define the terms *simplex*, *half-duplex* and *duplex* transmission.

9. Describe the operation of *cyclic redundancy checking* (CRC).

10. What are the functions of a *modem*?

11. In the context of modem communcations, what is meant by *flow control*?

12. Identify and briefly describe the three main forms of *automatic repeat request* (ARQ), for error checking.

13. Name the seven layer of the *OSI* (open systems inter-connection) model.

14. Identify and briefly describe four *network services*.

Software

Chapters

C hapter 12
Computer Software

The term *software* is used to describe the complete range of computer programs which convert a general purpose digital computer system into one capable of performing a multitude of specific functions. The term software implies its flexible, changeable nature, in contrast to the more permanent characteristics of the hardware or equipment which it controls.

The particular piece of software controlling the computer system at any particular moment determines the manner in which the system functions. For example, a certain type of software might cause the computer to behave like a word processor; another might allow it to perform accounting or stock control functions, or any one of a huge variety of other useful tasks. Whatever the task, it is software which directs the computer system.

Computer programs

The terms software and program tend to be used interchangeably so what precisely is meant by the term *computer program*?

At the level at which the computer operates, a program is simply a sequence of numeric codes. Each of these codes can be directly converted by the hardware into some simple operation. Built into the central processing unit (CPU - the heart of the computer) is a set of these simple operations, combinations of which are capable of directing the computer to perform complex tasks. Computer programs, in this fundamental form, are termed *machine code*, that is code which is directly understandable by the machine.

The numeric codes of the program are stored electronically in the main memory of the computer. Because this memory is volatile (its contents can be changed), it is possible to exchange the program currently held in the memory for another when the computer is required to perform a different function. For this reason the term *stored program* is often used to describe this fundamental characteristic of the modern digital computer.

Programming languages

When it is considered that a typical program might contain tens of thousands of machine code instructions it might seem that programming is a formidable task, well beyond the capabilities of all but the most determined and meticulous of computer professionals. Indeed, if machine code were the only computer language in use, it is extremely unlikely that society would today be experiencing such a widespread presence of computers in almost every aspect of industrial, commercial, domestic and social life.

Fortunately for the computer industry, programming techniques have evolved along with advances in hardware. There is now a proliferation of programming languages designed to allow the programmer to concentrate most of his or her attention on solving the problem, rather than on the tedious task of converting the solution to machine code form. Such computer languages are termed *high-level languages*. High-level languages provide a method of specifying complex processing tasks in a form relatively easy to use and understand by programmers, but not immediately understandable by a computer; the computer itself, using another program called a *language processor* or *translator*, performs the task of converting the high-level instructions into a usable form. Examples of commonly used computer languages are COBOL, Pascal, BASIC and C.

Categories of software

The tree diagram shown in Figure 12.1 below illustrates the different categories of software and, to some extent, their relationships to each other. This section begins by examining the distinction between *systems software* and *applications software*.

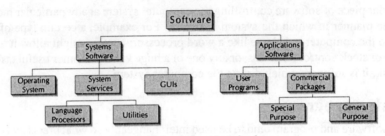

Figure 12.1. *Categories of software*

The term systems software covers the collection of programs usually supplied by the manufacturer of the computer. These programs protect the user from the enormous complexity of the computer system, and enable the computer to be used to maximum effect by a wide variety of people, many of whom will know very little about the inner workings of computers. Without systems software a modern digital computer would be virtually impossible to use; as computer hardware has evolved, so systems software has been forced to become more and more complex in order to make effective use of it.

Broadly speaking, systems software consists of three elements:

❏ those programs concerned with the internal control and co-ordination of all aspects of the computer system, namely the *operating system* (Chapter 13);

❏ a number of other programs providing various services to users. These services include *translators* for any languages supported by the system and *utility programs* such as program editors and other aids to programming;

❏ *graphical user interfaces* (GUIs) providing intuitive, easily learned methods for using microcomputer systems.

Applications software refers to programs which have some direct value to an organisation, and will normally include those programs for which the computer system was specifically purchased. For example, a mail order company might acquire a computer system initially for stock control and accounting purposes, when its volume of business begins to make these functions too difficult to cope with by manual means. Applications programs would be required to record and process customers' orders, update the stock file according to goods sent or received, make appropriate entries in the various accounts ledgers, etc. Commercially produced applications software falls into two main categories:

❏ *special-purpose* packages, such as a company payroll program used to store employee details and generate details of pay for each individual employee;

❑ *general-purpose* packages which may be used for a wide variety of purposes. An example of a general-purpose package is a *word processor*, a program which allows the computer to be used somewhat like an electronic typewriter and is therefore appropriate to numerous text processing tasks.

User programs are written by people within the organisation for specific needs which cannot be satisfied by other sources of software. These program writers may be professional programmers employed by the organisation, or other casual users with programming expertise.

Systems software

First generation computers are normally defined in hardware terms, in that they were constructed using valve technology, but another important characteristic of this generation of computers was the equally primitive software support provided for programmers and other users. Modern computers perform automatically many of the tasks that programmers in those days had to handle themselves: writing routines to control peripheral devices, allocating programs to main store, executing programs, checking peripheral devices for availability, as well as many other routine tasks.

In subsequent generations of computers, manufacturers started addressing themselves to the problem of improving the programming environment by providing standard programs for many routine tasks. Many of these routines became linked together under the control of a single program called the *executive*, *supervisor*, or *monitor*, whose function was to supervise the running of user programs and, in general, to control and co-ordinate the functioning of the whole computer system, both hardware and software. Early programs of this type have evolved into the sophisticated programs collectively known as *operating systems*. Systems software has four important functions:

❑ to make it easier to run user programs;

❑ to improve the performance of the computer system;

❑ to provide assistance with program development;

❑ to simplify use of the computer system for users other than computer specialists.

The operating system takes care of the first two requirements, system services provide assistance with program development and graphical user interfaces (GUIs) simplify the use of the computer system.

Operating systems

If a computer system is viewed as a set of resources, comprising elements of both hardware and software, then it is the job of the collection of programs known as the operating system to manage these resources as efficiently as possible. In so doing, the operating system acts as a buffer between the user and the complexities of the computer itself. One way of regarding the operating system is to think of it as a program which allows the user to deal with a simplified computer, but without losing any of the computational power of the machine. In this way the computer system becomes a virtual system, its enormous complexity hidden and controlled by the operating system and through which the user communicates with the real system.

The main functions of operating systems

Earlier it was stated that the function of an operating system is to manage the resources of the computer system. These resources generally fall into the following categories:

Central processing unit (CPU)

A *multi-user* computer system can be accessed by several users, simultaneously; since only one program can be executed at any one time, access to the CPU must be carefully controlled and monitored. In a *timesharing* multi-user system each user is given a small time-slice of processor time before passing on to the next user in a continuously repeating sequence. Another common scheme is to assign priorities to users so that the system is able to determine which user should have control of the CPU next.

Memory

Programs (or parts of programs) must be loaded into the memory before they can be executed, and moved out of the memory when no longer required there. Storage space must be provided for data generated by programs, and provision must be made for the temporary storage of data, caused by data transfer operations involving devices such as printers and disk drives.

Input/output (I/O) devices

Programs will request the use of these devices during the course of their execution and in a multi-user system conflicts are bound to arise, when a device being utilised by one program is requested by another. The operating system will control allocation of I/O devices and attempt to resolve any conflicts which arise. It will also monitor the state of each I/O device and signal any faults detected.

Backing store

Programs and data files will usually be held on mass storage devices such as magnetic disk and tape drives. The operating system will supervise data transfers between these devices and memory and deal with requests from programs for space on them.

Files

These may be regarded as a limited resource for multi-user systems, in the sense that several users may wish to share the same data file at the same time. The operating system facilitates access to files and ensures restricted access to one program at any one time for those files which are to be written to. Resource allocation is closely linked to one part of the operating system called the *scheduler* (Chapter 13). The term *scheduling* refers to the question of when, in a multi-user system, should a new process be introduced into the system and in which order the processes should be run. Other functions of an operating system include:

❏   interpretation of the command language by which operators can communicate with the operating system;

❏   error handling, such as detecting and reporting inoperative or malfunctioning peripherals;

❏   protection of data files and programs from corruption by other users;

❏   protection of data files and programs from unauthorised use;

❏   accounting and logging of the use of the computer resources.

System services

Often a manufacturer will provide a number of programs designed specifically for program or application development. Some examples of such aids are as follow.

Language processors

These are computer programs designed to convert high-level language programs into machine code, that is, into a form directly usable by a computer. Common types of language processors are *compilers* and *interpreters*.

Utility programs

As part of the systems software provided with a computer system there are a number of utility programs specifically designed to aid program development and testing. These include the following.

Editors

These permit the creation and modification of source programs and data files. The facilities offered by these programs usually include such things as character, word and line insertion and deletion, automatic line numbering, line tabulation for languages which require program instructions to be spaced in a specific manner, the storage and retrieval of files from backing storage, and the printing of programs or other files.

Debugging aids

Programs in which the appropriate translator can find no fault will often contain errors in logic, known as bugs, which only become apparent when the program is run, producing results which are contrary to expectations, or even causing the computer to cease functioning. These bugs are often very difficult to detect and may lead to long delays in the implementation of the program. Debugging aids help programmers to isolate and identify the cause of bugs.

File managers

These simplify and facilitate a number of operations connected with program development and maintenance such as:

- keeping backup copies of important files;
- deleting files and creating space for new ones;
- merging files;
- providing details of current files held on backing storage;
- sorting file names into specified orders.

Without the help of such dedicated programs, operations such as these could be extremely time-consuming and consequently expensive.

System maintenance utilities

These are programs, usually included with the operating system, which carry out routine maintenance tasks on the computer system.

Disk defragmentation

This utility is extremely important for the efficient operation of the main hard drive(s) in a computer system because it optimises the use of disk space and helps to maintain drive performance. To describe its operation, a brief explanation of disk storage is needed.

Disk space is allocated in *clusters*, which are units of disk storage. For example, the cluster size may be 16 kilobytes (KB). When a file is stored on disk it takes up as many clusters as it needs. For example, if a document is of size 525 KB, it will need $525 \div 16 = 33$ clusters (to the nearest whole cluster). When a file is first stored on disk it is given, if possible, a *contiguous* (no gaps between) chain of clusters. Each time it is altered and made larger, it may not fit in its original place, so the extra has to be placed somewhere else. This *fragmentation* of files leads to slower disk performance, because the read/write heads may have to go to several different parts of the disk to retrieve a single file. The defragmentation utility rearranges the disk space so that each file is held in a contiguous set of clusters. The empty space is also organised into a contiguous block of clusters. The Windows 9x defragmentation utility is known as Disk Defragmenter.

Drive compression

This utility is used to increase the amount of disk space, by compressing some of the existing physical space. So, for example, using a compression ratio of 2:1, a disk can be made to hold twice as much data. The Windows 9x drive compression utility is called DriveSpace.

File compression

File compression utilities can be used to reduce the space taken by individual files or groups of files. The storage space taken by bitmap files can be radically reduced through compression by around 95%. Compression programs, such as WinZip allow the creation of *archives* which contain one or more compressed files. The compression program must be available to decompress the files before they can be used again. Compression standards include ZIP, LZH, ARJ, or ARC. Archiving files makes it possible to, for example, backup files to a medium such as floppy disk, which would otherwise have insufficient space. Compression can also reduce the time taken to transmit files over a data communications link, although there is no benefit to be gained if the process is also carried out by the transmitting modem. A compressed file cannot be further compressed.

Disk repair

This vital utility detects and repairs disk recording errors. Some locations on disk may not record data properly and if they are not found and repaired, data may be stored in those locations and be corrupted or lost. The utility also finds 'lost' files. When a program 'crashes', or more seriously, when the operating system crashes, corrupted files, or bits of files, may be left on disk. These lost files take up valuable disk space and often contain meaningless information or 'garbage'. The Windows 9x repair utility is called ScanDisk.

Graphical user interfaces (GUIs)

The vast majority of microcomputer users are interested merely in using a computer as a tool, without any real interest in the technical details of its operation. A typical user will probably want to run one or more common general-purpose applications, organise files into directories, delete files and format disks. Though the operating system will provide these services, the user needs to have a certain amount of technical knowledge to perform these tasks. *Graphical user interfaces* (or GUI, pronounced *Gooey*) provide a more intuitive means of performing common tasks. They usually make use of a pointing device, typically a *mouse* (see Chapter 8), by means of which a *pointer* is moved around the monitor screen on which small pictures (or *icons*) are displayed. These icons represent, among other things, programs which can be run by moving the mouse pointer over the icon and then clicking one of the buttons on the mouse. Applications run in their own self-contained areas called *windows*. In addition, it is usually possible to activate *pull-down menus* which provide access to standard functions. When a GUI uses Windows, Icons, Mouse, Pointers and Pull-down menus, it is referred to as a *WIMP* environment. Figure 12.2 shows an example of a GUI produced by Microsoft, namely, Microsoft Windows.

Figure 12.2. *Graphical user interface for Windows 98 operating system*

The figure shows:

❏   icons (small pictures) representing, amongst other things, programs, which can be run by pointing and clicking the mouse. The recycle bin, browser and system icons are on the right hand side of the figure.

❏   *windows*. Applications run in their own self-contained areas called *windows*. There are two in the figure, one for CorelDRAW, a graphic design program and another for Microsoft's Word, a word processing package. These are all examples of *applications software*.

❏   a Task Bar with *minimised* applications. In the Figure, Windows Explorer is a minimised application, which can be opened as a window merely by clicking its ocon on the Task Bar.

❏   The Start menu gives holds the links to other applications and utilities which can be loaded from the hard drive.

Only Microsoft Word, in the window with the black title bar, is active, that is, currently in use. Any other loaded application can be made the active application by clicking in its window or icon on the Task Bar. Thus it is possible to be working on several applications at the same time, switching from one to the other very quickly and with minimum effort.

All such windows, no matter what the application, have a number of common features, including:

❑   a title bar with the name of the particular application and the name of the document being edited or created by that application;

❑   a menu bar containing the names of a number of pull-down menus;

❑   horizontal and vertical scroll bars providing access to parts of the document not shown in the window;

❑   a number of control icons for sizing, maximising (making the current window occupy the whole screen), minimising (reducing the window to the Task Bar as illustrated by Windows Explorer in Figure 12.2) and closing the window;

❑   a tool bar containing icons which, when selected, perform frequently required tasks, such as saving documents to disk or printing documents as in the case of Word for Windows, or drawing tools in the case of CorelDraw;

❑   a help facility accessed from the menu bar and providing detailed information on the operation of all aspects of the application on the screen while the application is running.

The major advantage of applications having these common features is that, having learned how one application operates, it is possible to use much of the same knowledge with other windows applications, thus significantly reducing the time required to become proficient in the use of unfamiliar applications.

Applications software

An analysis of the uses to which companies and individuals put computers would reveal that the same types of tasks appear time and time again. Many organisations use computers for payroll calculations, others to perform stock control functions, accounting procedures, management information tasks and numerous other common functions. These types of programs are classed as *applications software*, software which is applied to practical tasks in order to make them more efficient or useful in other ways. Systems software is merely there to support the running, development and maintenance of applications software. An organisation wishing to implement one of these tasks (or any other vital to its efficient operation) on a computer has several alternatives:

❑   Ask a software house, that is, a company specialising in the production of software, to take on the task of writing a specific program for the organisation's needs.

❑   Use its own programming staff to produce the software in house.

❑   Buy a commercially available program off the shelf and hope that it already fulfils, or can be modified to fulfil, the organisation's requirements.

❑   Buy a general purpose program, such as a database or spreadsheet package, that has the potential to perform the required functions.

The final choice will depend on such factors as the urgency of the requirements, financial constraints, size of the company and the equipment available. It is beyond the scope of this chapter to enter into a discussion regarding either the strategy for making such a decision or to investigate specific items of software available for specific applications; but, with the immense and growing, popularity of general-purpose packages, particularly for personal microcomputer systems, it is worth looking in more detail at this category of software.

General-purpose packages for microcomputers

Discussion of this class of software will be restricted here to the following headings, though they are not intended to represent an exhaustive list of all the categories of general purpose packages which are available:

❑   word processors;

❑   spreadsheets;

❑   databases;

❑   graphics packages, including desktop publishing (DTP), business graphics, graphic design and computer aided drawing (CAD).

What characterises these software types as belonging to the category of general-purpose packages is that they have been designed to be very flexible and applicable to a wide range of different tasks. For instance, a spreadsheet can be used as easily for simple accountancy procedures as for stock control; a database can be used with equal facility to store information on technical papers from journals, stock item details and personnel details for payroll purposes. In fact, particularly in respect of modern personal computer software, the trend is for general-purpose packages to do more and more. For example, recent word processors, such as Microsoft's Word for Windows and WordPerfect, include facilities, once only found in desktop publishing packages, for drawing diagrams and for producing graphs, in addition to the normal functions associated with a word processor; the graphic design package CorelDraw, includes some word processing functions and graph drawing functions; the spreadsheet Excel has a number of facilities normally associated with database packages. Fierce market competition has resulted in the major software houses continually improving on their last version of a piece of software, attempting to outdo their competitors.

The suitability of a particular general-purpose package for a specific application will be largely dependent on the particular characteristics of the package. Though the general facilities afforded, for instance, by different database packages may be roughly equivalent, each manufacturer will adopt its own style of presentation and will provide certain services not offered by its competitors. A prospective buyer should have a clear idea of the main uses for which the package is to be purchased right at the outset, because some packages may be much more suitable than others. Some advantages of general-purpose software compared to other forms of applications software are as follow:

❑   Because large numbers of the package are sold, prices are relatively low;

❑   They are appropriate to a wide variety of applications;

❑   As they already have been thoroughly tested, they provide a great reduction in the time and costs necessary for development and testing;

❑   They are suitable for people with little or no computing experience;

❏   They are very easy to use;

❏   Most packages of this type are provided with extensive documentation.

Some of the disadvantages are:

❏   Sometimes the package will allow only a clumsy solution to the task in question;

❏   In the case of a spreadsheet or database, for example, the user must still develop the application. This requires a thorough knowledge of the capabilities of the package, which are frequently extensive, and how to make the best use of them;

❏   The user will need to provide his own documentation for the particular application for which the package has been tailored;

❏   Unless the software is used regularly, it is easy to forget the correct command sequences to operate the package, particularly for people inexperienced in the use of computer software of this type;

❏   The user must take responsibility for security measures to ensure that vital data is not lost, or to prevent unauthorised personnel gaining access to the data.

Word processors

The word processor performs much the same function as a typewriter, but it offers a large number of very useful additional features. Basically, a word processor is a computer with a keyboard for entering text, a monitor for display purposes, one or more disk drives for storage of files produced by applications and a printer to provide the permanent output on paper. A word processor is really nothing more than a computer system with a special piece of software to make it perform the required word processing functions; some such systems have hardware configurations specifically for the purpose (such as special keyboards and letter-quality printers) but the majority are merely the result of obtaining an appropriate word processor package.

Word processors can be used to produce:

❏   letters;

❏   legal documents;

❏   books;

❏   articles;

❏   mailing lists;

and in fact any type of textual material.

Here are some of the advantages they have over ordinary typewriters:

❏   typing errors can be corrected before printing the final version;

❏   the availability of such automatic features as page numbering, the placing of page headers and footers and word/line counting;

❏   whole document editing, such as replacing every incidence of a certain combination of characters with another set of characters. For instance, replacing each occurrence of the name Mr. Smith by Mrs. Jones;

❏   printing multiple copies all to the same high quality;

❏   documents can be saved and printed out at some later date without any additional effort.

However, word processors do have some drawbacks. For instance, prolonged viewing of display monitors can produce eyestrain. They are generally considerably more expensive than good typewriters, and to be used properly, a certain amount of special training is required. Word processors are now firmly established in the so-called 'electronic office' and there is no doubt that their use will not continue to expand.

Typical word processor facilities

A typical word processing package will provide most of the following facilities:

Word wrap. As text is typed, a word is moved automatically to the start of a new line if there is insufficient room for it at the right-hand margin. With this facility, the only time that the Enter key needs to be pressed, to move the cursor to the beginning of a new line, is at the end of paragraphs or when a blank line is required.

Scrolling. Once the bottom of the screen is reached during text entry, the top of the text moves, line by line, up out of view as each new line of text is entered. This ensures that the line being entered is always visible on screen. The directional arrow keys on a standard keyboard allow scrolling to be carried out at will to view various parts of the document.

Deletion. This facility allows the deletion of characters, words, lines or complete blocks of text.

Insertion. This is concerned with the insertion of single letters or a block of text.

Block marking. A special function key, or more usually, by dragging the mouse pointer, allows the marking or highlighting of text to be dealt with separately from the rest of the document. The marked text may be moved, deleted, copied or displayed in a different style - in italics or bold print, for example.

Text movement or copying. The user may need to move or copy a marked block of text to a different part of the document.

Tabulation. Markers can be set to allow the cursor to be moved directly to column positions with the use of the TAB key. This is useful when text or figures are to be presented in columns.

Formatting. Text can be *aligned left*, with a straight left margin and a ragged right margin:

XXXX XXX XXXXX X XXXX XXXXXXXXXX XXX XXXXXXX XXXX XXXXXXX XXX XXXXXX XX XXXXXXX
X XXXXX XXXXXXX XX XXXX X XXX XXXXXXXXXXX XXX XXX XXXXXXX X XXXXXXX XXX XXXXXX
XXXXX X XXXX X XX XXXXXX X XXXX XXXXX XXX X XXXXXXXXXX XXXXXX XXX XXXXXXXXX XX
XXXXXXXXXXXXXX XXXX X.

or it can be *justified* so that it has a straight left and right margin:

XXXX XXX XXXXX X XXXX XXXXXXXXXX XXX XXXXXXX XXXX XXXXXXX XXX XXXXXX XX XXXXXXX X
XXXXX XXXXXXX XX XXXX X XXX XXXXXXXXXXX XXXXXXXXXXXXX XXX XXXXXXX XX XXXXX XXX
XXXXXX XXXX XXXXXXXXX XXXX XXXXX XXX X XXXXXXXXXX XXXXXX XXX XXXXXXXXX XX
XXXXXXXXXXXXXX XXXX X.

or it can be *right aligned* with a straight right margin only:

XXXX XXX XXXXX X XXXX XXXXXXXXXX XXX XXXXXXX XXXX XXXXXXX XXX XXXXXX XX XXXXXXX
X XXXXX XXXXXXX XX XXXX X XXX XXXXXXXXXXX XXX XXX XXXXXXX X XXXXXXX XXX XXXXXX
XXXXX X XXXX X XX XXXXXX X XXXXXXXXXXXXXXX XXX XXXXXXX XX XXXXXX XXX XXXXXX XXXX
XXXXXXXXX XXXX XXXXX XXX X XXXXXXXXXX XXXXXX XXX XXXXXXXXX XX XXXXXXXXXXXXXX
                                                                        XXXX.

or it can be *centred*:

XXXX XXX XXXXX X XXXX XXXXXXXXXX XXX XXXXXXX XXXX XXXXX XXX XX XXXXXXX X XXXXX
XXXXXXX XX XXXX X XXX XXXXXXXXXX XXX XXX XXXXXXX X XXXXXXX XXX XXXXXX XXXXX X
XXXX X XX XXXXXX X XXXXXXXXXXXXXX XXX XXXXXXX XX XXXXXX XXX XXXXXX XXXX
XXXXXXXXX XXXX XXXXX XXX X XXXXXXXXXX XXXXXX XXX XXXXXXXXX XX XXXXXXXXXXXXXX
                        XXXX X.

Printing styles

Text can be printed in a variety of styles, including **boldface**, *italic*, ~~strike-through~~, <u>under-scored</u> superscript or subscript. Most word processors allow these styles to be displayed on the screen as well as on the printer and are known as WYSIWYG (What You See Is What You Get) packages.

Various fonts and sizes of characters

Different character fonts, that is variations in the shapes of characters, and sizes of characters can be mixed in the same document:

This is called Dauphin 12 pt

This is Courier New 10 pt

This is Times New Roman 14 pt

This is GoudyHandtooled 14 pt

Mailing lists

This allows a user to personalise standard letters. The mailing list is, in effect, a file of names and addresses, details from which can be inserted into marked points in a standard letter. The word processor prints multiple copies of the standard letter selected by the user and personalises each with data extracted from the mailing list.

Additional features

These include facilities for the checking of spelling (and sometimes its automatic correction as you type) in a document by reference to a dictionary held on disk, the import of text and figures from other packages such as spreadsheets, the incorporation of graphics and the export of text to other packages.

Windows-based word processors

Programs like Microsoft's Word for Windows and other windows-based word processors are have taken over from those that do not operate in a windows environment. These latest word processors allow the use of a mouse to move the cursor around documents quickly, to edit text and to provide easy access to commonly used functions such as saving and printing work, opening existing documents and creating tables. All the other advantages of windows-based programs also apply. To give you an idea of what can be achieved with this type of word processor, Figure 12.2 includes part of a document produced using Word for Windows, .

Spreadsheets

Just as word processors are designed to manipulate text, spreadsheets are designed to do the equivalent with numerical information. A spreadsheet program presents the user with a blank grid of cells each of which is capable of containing one of three types of information:

❑   a label consisting of alphanumeric characters;

❑   a number;

❑   a formula, which usually will make reference to other cells. These allow calculations to be performed on data in other cells, or on the results from other formulae.

These three types of information are sufficient to allow a wide range of applications to be implemented in a very convenient and easily understandable way. For example, suppose that a small business, Acme Computers, dealing in the sale of personal computer systems wishes to use a spreadsheet to record on a monthly basis, the sales of its four salespersons. The spreadsheet might be set up as shown in Figure 12.3.

Figure 12.3. *Excel spreadsheet example*

Column A contains labels describing the systems purchased. Columns C and D, E and F, G and H, I and J show respectively, the sales and commissions for each of the four salespersons. The commission is calculated automatically by means of a formula stored in the commission columns D, F, H and J.

Formulae are used to produce the calculated values. Thus John's sale of the Pentium 233MHz costing £999 is entered in cell C8 and the commission is calculated using the formula '=C8*20/100'. This calculates 20% of the retail price. The actual value of the commission is displayed in cell D8.

The column totals, shown in cells C22 to J22, were calculated using a built-in function '=SUM(range)' which calculates the sum of a range of cells. For example, John's total commission, shown in cell D22, was calculated using the formula '=SUM(D8:D20)'. Note that empty cells are treated by formula as having a value of zero.

Any changes in the data on the spreadsheet would cause all the calculations to be repeated. This automatic calculation facility gave rise to the expression 'what if' which is often used to describe an important capability of spreadsheets. It is possible to set up complex combinations of inter-dependent factors and see what happens to the final result if one or more of the factors is changed. The spreadsheet, once set up, takes care of all the recalculations necessary for this type of exercise.

The earliest program of this form was called 'Visicalc' and it ran on an Apple microcomputer. Many such programs now exist, having capabilities far exceeding those of Visicalc, but they still closely resemble the original concept in appearance and operation.

Typical spreadsheet facilities

Apart from the entry of labels, numbers and formulae, a spreadsheet package normally allows the user to use various facilities from a menu to handle the data stored on the worksheet. Typically, spreadsheets offer the following facilities:

Copying. This allows the copying of fixed values or labels, or formulae which are logically the same in another part of the worksheet. Thus, for example, in the earlier worksheet sample, the formula '=SUM(C8:C20)', which totalled a group of values for John, could be copied to succeeding columns to the right as '=SUM(D8:D20)', '=SUM(E8:E20)', '=SUM(F8:F20)', and so on. The formula is logically the same but the column references change, according to the position of the formula.

Formatting. A cell entry can be centred, or left or right justified within a cell. Numeric values can be displayed in a variety of formats including fixed decimal, integer, percent and scientific or as money values prefixed by a $ or £ sign to 2 decimal places. Individual formats can be selected globally, that is throughout a worksheet or for selected ranges of cells.

Functions. These include =SUM(range) , which adds the contents of a specified range of cells, '=AVERAGE(range)', which calculates the average value in a specified range of cells, '=MIN(range)', which extracts the minimum value held in a specified range of cells, and '=SQRT(cell)', which returns the square root of a value in a specified cell. The full range of functions usually includes those used in mathematics, trigonometry, finance and statistics. These are examples of functions found in Excel.

Macros. Groups of regularly used key sequences can be stored and then executed by one key press in combination with the Alt key, for example, Alt C; alternatively, a macro can be assigned to a new button on the tool bar and executed by clicking it. Macros can be useful when the spreadsheet has been tailored for a particular application which may be used by inexperienced users. Without macros, each user would have to be completely familiar with the spreadsheet commands needed. With macros, one experienced user can tailor the spreadsheet so that training time for other staff is minimised.

Graphs. Numerical data can be displayed in a variety of graphical forms, including bar charts, line graphs, scatter diagrams and pie charts. All modern spreadsheet packages provide graphical output directly and also allow numerical data to be exported to another package for graph production. The range and quality of graphs vary greatly from one package to another. With the use of a colour printer, very attractive and presentable graphs can be produced to illustrate business reports.

Consolidation. This feature allows the merging of several worksheets into a summary sheet, whilst keeping the original worksheets intact. Consolidation adds together cells with the same co-ordinates in the various worksheets.

Other Facilities. These include, amongst others, cell protection facilities to prevent alteration of certain entries, the alteration of individual column widths and the display of cell contents as formulae instead of the results of their calculation.

Spreadsheets have a number of attractive features compared to traditional programming solutions to processing needs:

❑ designed for laypersons;

❑ easy to learn and use;

❑ wide range of uses;

❑ relatively cheap;

❑ easily modified;

❑ well tried and tested;

❑ provide quick development time.

On the debit side:

❑ they tend to be too general-purpose and therefore tend to provide satisfactory rather than ideal solutions;

❑ the problem must still be analysed and a solution method identified.

Database

At one time, database programs, or Database Management Systems (DBMS) as they are often called, were restricted to mainframe computers because of the large memory requirements demanded of such applications. Currently, however, even personal business microcomputers have sufficient internal memory to make such applications not only feasible but also extremely powerful. These programs allow files, comprising collections of records, to be created, modified, searched and printed.

Here are just a few examples of database applications:

❑ names and addresses of possible customers for a mail order firm;

❑ details of the books in a library giving author, title and subject covered by each book, to aid with locating books of a certain type;

❑ details of the items stored in a warehouse, giving location, cost, number currently in stock and supplier;

- ❑   lists of people on the electoral register for a certain region;
- ❑   details of the employees of a large firm.

Typical database facilities

A typical database program will offer, as a minimum, the following facilities:

- ❑   user-definable record format allowing the user to specify the fields within the record;
- ❑   user-definable input format to allow the user to define the way the data is to be entered into the computer;
- ❑   file searching capabilities for extracting records satisfying certain criteria from a file;
- ❑   file sorting capabilities so that records can be ordered according to the contents of a certain field;
- ❑   calculations on fields within records for inclusion in reports;
- ❑   user-definable report formats, so that different types of reports containing different combinations of record fields may be produced.

Database packages for microcomputers

These packages fall broadly into two groups, *card index* and *relational* (Chapters 26 and 27). Generally, card index systems are simpler to set up and operate but they provide less sophisticated data manipulation and search facilities than do the relational type. Further, the relational type provide a programming language which allows the development of user friendly, tailored applications. Thus, a user can be protected from the complexities of package operation by being presented with, for example, a menu-driven system with options for record insertion, modification, deletion and retrieval and perhaps the production of summary reports. The card index type cannot be programmed in this way, so the user must have a more detailed knowledge of package operation.

On the other hand, card index packages tend to be easier to use. The superior data management facilities provided by the relational type tend to be under-used unless professional database designers and programmers are involved in the development of the database application. The business executive who plans to use the database as a personal tool without such professional help, will probably be well advised to purchase a card index package rather than a relational database package.

Another factor to be considered when choosing a database, is disk space and access speed. In contrast with spreadsheet packages, database packages require frequent disk accesses when carrying out sorting and retrieval operations. Floppy disk access times tend to be too slow and their storage capacity inadequate for anything but the simplest application. A package should also allow sorting with the use of indexes, so that files do not have to be physically sorted. Indexed sorts are much quicker and a number of different indexes can be set up so that the database can be displayed in a variety of logical orders without re-organising the data on disk.

Graphics packages

Common types of graphics packages provide facilities for: business graphics; graphic design;

desktop publishing; computer-aided design. Some graphics packages will to a greater or lesser degree cater for all of these applications, but many are designed specifically for one of them.

Business graphics

Business graphics packages allow the production of such things as bar charts, line graphs and pie diagrams, that is, diagrams of a statistical nature likely to be included in business reports. Examples of this type of diagram are shown in Figure 12.4.

Figure 12.4. *Examples of business graphics*

Graphic design

Packages for *graphic design* consist of a collection of special functions aimed at aiding the graphic designer. The artist uses the screen as a canvas and a light-pen, mouse or equivalent device as a brush. They generally allow work of professional quality to be produced in a relatively short amount of time, and include such facilities as:

❑   large colour palette;

❑   geometric figure drawing, e.g. lines, rectangles, circles;

❑   filling areas with colour or patterns;

❑   undoing mistakes;

❑   moving/copying/deleting/saving areas of the screen display;

❑   choice of a variety of character fonts;

❑   printing the finished design;

❑   a large number of pre-drawn pictures for inclusion in designs. This is called 'clip-art'.

Drawing tools are available for:

❑   cutting out rectangular or irregularly shaped areas of the drawing so that they may be moved or erased;

❑   spraying colour;

❑   producing text;

❑   erasing parts of the drawing using a variable-size eraser;

❑   filling areas with colour;

□   brushing colour onto the screen using brushes of different sizes and shapes;

□   drawing filled or unfilled shapes, such as rectangles and circles.

Colours are selected by clicking with the mouse pointer on the colour palette along the bottom of the screen, and other functions can be chosen from the menus along the top of the screen. Drawings can be stored on disk or printed.

Desktop publishing

Figure 12.5 is an example of a poster produced with a DTP program.

Figure 12.5. *Poster produced with a DTP package*

Desktop publishing programs are designed to produce such things as posters, illustrated articles, books and other documents which combine large amounts of text with illustrations. As such they tend to contain a number of facilities in common with graphic design packages, but emphasise layout and printing. These packages place a lot of emphasis on being able to experiment with arranging sections of the document and seeing its overall appearance. Text is also given more importance; a rudimentary word processor may be provided, or text may be imported from a prepared file, and the user is generally able to experiment with different type fonts on text already displayed on the screen. Typically, a DTP package will have facilities for:

□   modifying text by means of using different fonts and type styles;

□   importing text from word processors;

□   displaying text in columns;

□   importing pictures/diagrams from graphic design packages;

□   re-sizing pictures;

□   producing simple geometrical shapes such as lines, rectangles and circles;

□   mixing text and graphics;

□   automatically numbering pages;

□   producing contents pages, lists of figures and indexes.

Notice that the poster contains a mixture of graphics objects and text of various sizes and fonts. All of these components can be repositioned, re-sized and modified very easily using a mouse.

Computer-aided design

Computer-aided design constitutes perhaps one of the most widely used commercial applications of computer graphics. Here the user simulates real-world geometrical objects using various software drawing tools. Often these tools are selected and used in a WIMP style environment. Sometimes a graphics tablet is used in conjunction with a pressure-operated stylus, or a light-pen might be used to draw electronically on the VDU screen. Whatever the physical method of using the system, the types of software tools and facilities available are fairly standard, providing tools for operations such as:

- ❑ drawing common objects (lines, curves, circles, ellipses, rectangles, polygons etc.);

- ❑ editing objects (modifying or deleting objects);

- ❑ filling shapes with patterns or colours;

- ❑ generating three-dimensional objects; Figure 12.6 shows some examples.

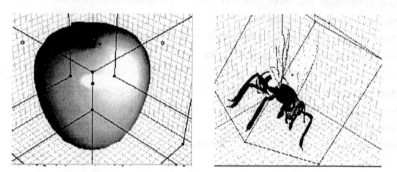

Figure 12.6. *Computer-produced CorelDream ™ 3-dimensional images*

- ❑ rotating two-dimensional and three-dimensional objects;
- ❑ viewing three-dimensional objects from different directions;
- ❑ displaying three-dimensional objects in wireframe or solid form;
- ❑ applying different texturing effects to solid objects.

Applications of CAD programs include: engineering drawing; architectural design; interior design; printed-circuit and integrated circuit design; advertising material; computer animation for tv advertising; special effects in films.

✍️Exercises

1. Why is a *translator program* required for a high-level language?
2. Explain the difference between a *compiler*, an *interpreter* and an *assembler*.
3. Name three *high-level languages*.
4. Define the following terms:
    (i)   *Systems software*;
    (ii) *Operating system*;
    (iii) *GUI*;
    (iv) *Applications software*.
5. Name three main functions of an operating system.
6. What does WIMP stand for?
7. What is an *icon*?
8. Name four commonly used *general-purpose* (that is, content-free) applications packages.
9. List three advantages and three disadvantages of general-purpose software.
10. List four uses of *word processors*.
11. Give three advantages of a word processor over a typewriter.
12. Give two disadvantages of word processors.
13. What three types of information can be stored in a single spreadsheet cell?
14. Give three advantages of a spreadsheet over a specially written program.
15. Give two disadvantages of spreadsheets.
16. List three uses of a spreadsheet.
17. List three applications of a database program.

Operating Systems

If a computer system is viewed as a set of resources, comprising elements of both hardware and software, then it is the job of the collection of programs known as the operating system to manage these resources as efficiently as possible. In so doing, the operating system acts as a buffer between the user and the complexities of the computer itself. One way of regarding the operating system is to think of it as software which allows the user to deal with a simplified computer, but without losing any of the computational power of the machine. In this way, the computer system becomes a virtual system, its enormous complexity hidden and controlled by the operating system and through which the user communicates with the real system.

The central core of an operating system, which remains in memory permanently when the computer is running, is the *executive* (also known as the *supervisor* or *kernel*); as the terms suggest, it has a controlling function, its major function being to carry out system requests from applications programs in such a way that conflicts between them are avoided. The remainder of the operating system is normally held on a direct access medium, from where parts of it can be called as and when required.

Main functions of operating systems

The introduction states that the function of an operating system is to manage the resources of the computer system. These resources generally fall into several categories.

Central processing unit (CPU) or processor

Since only one program can be executed at any one time, computer systems which allow several users simultaneous access (multi-user) must carefully control and monitor use of the processor. In a timesharing multi-user system each user receives a small time-slice from the processor before it passes on to the next user in a continually repeating sequence. Another common scheme is to assign priorities to users so that the system is able to determine which user should next have control of the processor.

Memory

Programs (or parts of programs) must be loaded into the memory before they can be executed, and moved out of the memory when no longer required there. Storage space must be provided for data generated by programs, and provision must be made for the temporary storage of data, caused by data transfer operations involving devices such as printers and disk drives.

Input/output (I/O) devices

Programs will request the use of these devices during the course of their execution and in a multi-user system, conflicts are bound to arise when a device being utilised by one program is requested by another. The operating system controls the allocation of I/O devices and attempts to resolve any conflicts which arise. It also monitors the state of each I/O device and signals any faults detected.

Backing storage

Programs and data files are usually held on mass storage devices such as magnetic disk and tape drives. The operating system supervises data transfers between these devices and memory, and deals with requests from programs for space on them.

Files

These may be regarded as a limited resource in the sense that several users may wish to share the same data file at the same time. The operating system facilitates access to files and ensures that only one updating program can retrieve a particular record at any one time.

The above is by no means an exhaustive list of the functions of an operating system. Other functions include:

- ❑ interpretation of the command language by which operators can communicate with it;

- ❑ error handling, such as detecting and reporting inoperative or malfunctioning peripherals;

- ❑ protection of data files and programs from corruption by other users;

- ❑ protection of data files and programs from unauthorised use;

- ❑ accounting and logging of the use of the computer resources.

Categories of operating system

Single-stream

As the term suggests, single-stream operating systems are designed to handle only one job at a time. Today, the only operating systems which are likely fall into this category are those designed for microcomputer systems, for example MS-DOS (really, it is a *single-user* system- see also *multi-tasking*), but in the late 1950s the then state of the art mainframe systems could only handle jobs singly. These early systems automated the running of their jobs under customised *control programs* (initially punched onto cards), which were the forerunners of operating systems.

Batch processing systems

The concept of batch processing is explained in detail in Chapters 16 and 17. The early single-stream operating system was improved with the use of an *executive* which queues a number of separate jobs, *schedules* them according to allocated *priorities* and *executes* them, one after another. Some jobs will be required more urgently than others and will be allocated priority accordingly; jobs are loaded and executed according to their priority rating, not their position in the queue, so additional jobs can be added at any time.

Such systems are very inefficient for various reasons. Each job must be completed before commencement of the next; the fact that most jobs comprise a great deal of I/O and very little processing means that the processor is idling for much of the time. This feature is exacerbated by the imbalance between the operating speed of the processor and the data transfer rate of the associated disk and tape drives; the imbalance is even greater where printed output is required. Thus, when the overall system's speed is dictated by the speed of the I/O peripheral, rather than the processor, the system is described as being *I/O bound*. The technique of *off-lining* was introduced in the late 1950s to help deal with the problem of very slow peripherals, such as card readers and printers.

Batch multi-programming systems

Optimisation of resource usage

Multi-programming describes the running of several jobs in main memory, apparently simultaneously, although in reality, the processor's attention is being repeatedly switched from one to another under the control of the executive. This makes much better use of the processor's time than the single stream batch processing described previously. Thus, the objective of a batch multi-programming operating system is to *optimise the use of processor time and the rate of system throughput*.

Dynamic resource allocation

With single-stream processing, computer resources (processor time, main memory space, file storage and peripherals) can be allocated to each job and remain fixed for the duration of each job. In contrast, the concurrent processing of several jobs inherent in a multi-programming environment, with the likelihood that the mix of jobs will change as some are completed and new ones are initiated, requires an executive capable of allocating resources *dynamically* to each job.

Job priority

Jobs will vary according to:

❏   the amount of I/O involved;

❏   the types and speeds of I/O devices used;

❏   the amount of processor time needed.

After consideration of these factors, each job is given a *priority rating*, which will determine how frequently and how much processor time it receives. The allocation of priorities can be a complex process but simplistically:

❏   high priority will be given to a job requiring a large amount of I/O and a relatively small amount of processor time. When I/O operations are being carried out, processor attention is not required after the initial I/O command is given. Conversely, when it does require attention, a high priority will ensure that its small processing requirements are attended to promptly and fully, following which it can return to I/O;

❏   a low priority job will tend to be one which requires a large amount of processor time; a high priority would result in it hogging the processor and preventing largely I/O jobs from receiving what little attention they require.

Scheduling

High-level scheduler

It is a function of a high-level scheduler to determine which programs in the job queue should next be loaded into main memory. Before loading a job, the following criteria must be satisfied:

- ❑   there is sufficient room for it in main memory;

- ❑   all associated input files are on-line;

- ❑   the necessary peripherals are also on-line.

If priorities are allocated then, subject to fulfilment of the above criteria, these will be used by the high level scheduler to decide the order in which jobs are removed from the job queue.

Dispatcher or low-level scheduler

The dispatcher allocates the processor amongst the various processes in the system. To understand the operation of the dispatcher, it is useful to differentiate between the concept of a *program* and a *process*. A process is a sequence of actions produced through the execution of program instructions. Processes carried out within the system include, for example, interrupt handling, error handling, I/O control and so on; each process may involve one or more programs.

To do this the dispatcher must record the current *status* of each process selecting from the following possibilities:

- ❑   it is runnable, that is, free to run;

- ❑   it is running; in other words, it has the attention of the processor;

- ❑   it is unrunnable or suspended, perhaps because it is awaiting completion of an I/O operation.

A *process descriptor table* records the status of each process in the *processor queue*. The dispatcher must refer to it before deciding on re-allocation of the processor to a process in the queue; such a decision needs to be made each time there is an *interrupt* (see Chapter 14 and later in this chapter). The dispatcher will choose the process with the highest priority, from those which are runnable, unless the process which was running at the time of the interrupt still outranks them.

The dispatcher is invoked under the following circumstances:

- ❑   whenever the current process cannot continue; this may result, for example, from a programming error or a switch to I/O, **or**

- ❑   when an external interrupt changes the status of a process, for example, following completion of data transfer; it thus becomes runnable.

Batch processing systems collect all input data in a file, from where it is loaded and processed to completion by the relevant application program, storing any output data in another on-line file; the executive then directs the printing program to print any hard copy results from the output file. Prominent features of such systems are:

- ❑   lack of any communication or interaction with the user;

- ❑   the delay in producing results of processing.

The following categories of operating system allow results of processing to be obtained, frequently on a VDU screen, directly after their entry. They are categorised according to the techniques used to manage the computer resources (the ways in which the systems are used are described in the Chapter on Processing Methods):

- ❏ time-sharing;
- ❏ multi-tasking;
- ❏ multi-user;
- ❏ real-time.

Time-sharing

The term time-sharing refers to the allocation of processor *time-slices* to a number of user programs in a multi-programming environment. The aim of a time-sharing operating system is to *keep the users busy*; this contrasts with the batch multi-programming system which aims to keep the processor occupied. The time slices are controlled and synchronised by a real-time clock which generates frequent, regularly timed pulses; each time-slice is extremely short, say 100 milliseconds.

Round robin system

With this method, the operating system works sequentially through the list of programs being run, giving each process an equal slice of processor time.

If all current programs can be accommodated in main memory at one time, users should not experience poor response times. Unfortunately, the total main memory requirements of all current users may exceed the capacity of main memory, making it necessary to swap programs or program segments in and out from backing storage as the processor switches its attention from one to another. The number of such data transfers can be reduced by extending the length of each time slice, but at the cost of reducing the frequency with which the processor transfers its attention from one process to another. Optimising system performance requires a balance to be struck between these two objectives.

Unless the processor is overloaded, perhaps because there are too many users or because the applications require a large amount of processor time (for example, program compilation - see chapter on Language Processing), each user should feel that he or she is the sole user of the system.

Priority system

Instead of giving single time-slices on a round robin basis, they are allocated according to a system of priorities. This means that some programs will receive a number of time slices in succession before another is attended to. The priority rating of each program will not normally remain static but will be adjusted in relation to the relative amount of processing time it receives in comparison with the other programs in operation.

Time-sharing systems are used *interactively* in that users communicate directly with the computer through VDU terminals. A common use of a time-sharing operating system is to provide *multi-access* to one or more programming languages for the purposes of program development. Other systems may provide users with access to various applications programs which can be run apparently simultaneously.

Multi-tasking

Multi-tasking is a technique which allows a computer to carry out tasks in a similar fashion to a human worker. For example, the Financial Director of a business may be composing a financial report which requires the use of a dictaphone, occasional reference to various financial summaries and telephone calls to other executive staff in the business. Although these tasks are not carried on at exactly the same time, the director is rapidly switching from one to another, and they all contribute to the completion of the financial report. At certain times, an unrelated task may have to be completed, for example, the answering of a brief query from a member of staff. This does not require complete abandonment of the other tasks in hand and the main work continues from the point at which it was left.

Computer multi-tasking requires that the system can accommodate several tasks in memory at one time and that these tasks can be run *concurrently* by rapidly switching the processor's attention between them. The principles of resource management are similar to those employed in multi-programming, except that they relate to a *single user*, are controlled interactively and must be executed in ways which maintain response times acceptable to the user.

Multi-user

A multi-user system is invariably multi-access (although it is possible to provide multi-user facilities within a single stand-alone microcomputer, but only one user at a time) in that it provides a number of users with concurrent access to shared computing resources, which may be part of a computer network or may comprise a centralised computer with multiplexed terminals. Additionally however, the multi-user operating system must protect each user's (or user group's) files from access and/or corruption by other users, either within memory or on backing storage. This is achieved through dynamic memory partitioning and directory-based file management respectively. Later in this chapter, the *Novell network operating system* is used to illustrate aspects of a multi-user operation.

Real-time

A real-time system is one which reacts to inputs sufficiently rapidly to permit tight control of its environment. A computer system's environment can be defined as the application or activity it is controlling. Real-time operation is essential for computerised *process control* (see chapter on Industrial and Control Applications), for example, in chemical production. Such activities require continual control so that parameters of, say pressure and temperature, are adhered to. Inputs from the process, collected through *transducers*, are digitised, input and processed, to provide immediate feedback to the system's controllers, which for the previous example may be a heating mechanism and air pressure control.

Some business information systems also require real-time control. Typical examples include airline booking and some stock control systems where rapid turnover is the norm.

The mechanisms used by a real-time operating system to control the system resources are beyond the scope of this text.

Further functions and facilities

Command language interpretation

An important function of the operating system is to interpret the command language which allows the user/operator to communicate with it. Two types of language are generally recognised:

❑   command language;

❏   job control language.

Command language

A *command line interpreter* (CLI) accepts command lines, checks them for syntax errors and passes on the relevant requests to the operating system. Such requests may be, for example, to display directory contents on screen, delete files from disk, or copy them from one disk to another. Simple, ad hoc requests will generally be made via a keyboard but lengthy, regularly used sequences of commands may be stored in a command or batch file. The MS-DOS operating system (see later) provides such a facility.

Today, the *graphical user interface* (GUI) is preferred to the command line interpreter. GUIs are examined in Chapter 12. Operating system utilities are selected, with a mouse, from representative icons on the screen; the GUI communicates these requests in the systems command language and the CLI interprets and passes them on to the operating system in the normal way. The GUI is another level of interface between the user and the CLI.

Job control language (JCL)

Associated with batch processing operating systems, JCLs allow details of job requirements to be specified to the operating system. An example JCL sequence is given below.

```
BEGIN
JOB 3367
COMPILE payroll.cbl (disk 1)
LOAD payroll.obj (disk 1)
RUN
END
```

This sequence of commands identifies the job, compiles a COBOL (cbl) source program, loads the resultant object program and executes it.

I/O handling

The executive part of the operating system controls data transfers to and from peripherals, normally through a system of interrupts. The topic of I/O is dealt with in Chapter 14. Other causes of interrupts are dealt with in the following section.

Interrupt handling

Apart from I/O operations, interrupts are necessary to notify the operating system of a variety of other system events, including:

❏   hardware failure, for example, through power loss or a memory parity error;

❏   program termination;

❏   peripheral data transfer failure, for example, because a printer is out of paper or the directory on a disk has been damaged;

❏   an attempt to access a non-existent memory address;

❏   in a time-sharing or real-time system, a clock pulse indicates completion of time slices;

❏   program instruction error, for example, an attempted division by zero or an attempt to communicate with a non-existent device;

❑   an externally generated command from the operator.

As explained in Chapter 14, when such events occur, the *interrupt handler* routine must establish the cause/source of the interrupt and call the appropriate *interrupt service routine*.

Error handling/trapping

It is important that events which would ordinarily upset or crash the computer system, are *trapped* and handled in an orderly way. Thus, for example, upon encountering an illegal application program instruction, an interrupt is generated, followed by entry to an appropriate interrupt service routine in the executive. The application program is aborted and the service routine displays an error message on screen, detailing the nature of the error. Arithmetic errors, such as an attempt to divide by zero, and I/O errors should also be trapped and treated in a similar fashion. Although data lost as a result of programming errors may not be recoverable by the operating system, any loss caused by abnormal operational interrupt of an I/O activity should be preventable by an appropriate routine to restore the data.

Of course, applications software should, wherever possible, anticipate possible system errors such as disk read errors and other peripheral faults, and protect the user from contact with the operating system by producing its own user friendly messages. Further, in the same way that the operating system prevents system crashes, applications software should, if the fault can be corrected, be robust enough to allow its continuance without loss of data.

File management and security

The major facilities provided by an operating system for file management relate to:

❑   creating and deleting files;

❑   allocating space on storage media;

❑   identifying and keeping track of files on storage media;

❑   editing the contents of files;

❑   protecting files from hardware malfunction;

❑   protecting files from other applications or users;

❑   protecting files against unauthorised access.

More details of file management and security are illustrated by reference to the Novell and MS-DOS operating systems, described later in this chapter.

Accounting and logging

An important part of system control is that the operator should have a record of all operator communications, error conditions and applications which have been run; the operating system keeps a log of such events and either outputs the relevant messages to the operator's console printer or records them on backing storage for later printing. Multi-access operating systems normally provide an accounting facility which identifies and records terminal usage, including basic details such as user-id, time logged on and off, and processor time used; in this way, users or departments of an organisation can be charged for computer time.

Memory management

Single user operating systems such as MS-DOS do not provide particularly sophisticated memory facilities, as only one application is *resident* at one time. There is one special case, that of the graphical user interface (GUI) which stays resident in memory; it must advise the operating system of its storage needs, in order that it is not corrupted by subsequent loading of applications.

Multi-programming and multi-tasking systems require quite complex memory management facilities in order to accommodate and maintain the *integrity* of the several programs and associated data which may be resident at any one time. Memory requirements do not remain static because the mix of programs being run may vary from moment to moment; the space left by a program swapped out of memory may not be large enough to accommodate an incoming program, requiring the *relocation* of programs already there.

Memory partitions and relocatable code

To fulfil these requirements, the operating system must be able to partition memory *dynamically* and adjust those partitions as programs and data are relocated. This latter point means that all software should be capable of relocation and not be tied to *absolute* addresses in memory. This is effected with the use of *relative addressing* instructions which are examined in more detail in Chapter 4. The relocatable code is allocated to the absolute memory addresses by the executive, the relative addresses of each instruction being added to the *base* address of the relevant memory partition. Subsequent relocations can be carried out by re-specification of the base address.

Segmenting and interleaving

Where large programs are concerned, it may be possible to divide them into *segments*, which can be rolled in and out of memory from direct access storage as required. As only one segment of a particular program need be resident in memory at any one time, any replacement segment will simply *overlay* it.

In a multi-programming environment, segments from different programs are in memory at one time and are said to be *interleaved*.

Virtual memory

Although main memory and direct access backing storage are physically separate, it is possible to present their joint capacity as being available to run programs. Such virtual memory can be used to accommodate much larger programs, as well as expand the level of multi-programming. A programmer can regard the addressable memory space as being beyond the physical capacity of main memory. Programs are automatically divided into *pages* (a fixed unit of virtual storage) and when one is loaded, its virtual memory addresses are mapped to the absolute memory addresses by the executive. The addresses of each page are held in main memory and during program execution, they are paged-in and paged-out as required.

Operating system case studies

This section looks at a variety of operating systems which provide a single-user, multi-tasking and/or multi-user environments.

MS-DOS

Although the MS-DOS operating system is rarely used directly, the most recent Windows operating systems still provide access to it through an MS-DOS window, as illustrated in Figure 13.1. Coverage of the operating system is provided here because it aids understanding of operating system functions. GUI-based operating systems are designed to be intuitive and simple to use and quite sensibly, do not require the user to memorise detailed command structures, but they do not provide a 'close-up' view of its basic functions.

```
MS DOS Prompt                                                    _ 8 X
Auto      ▼  □ ▯ ▣ ▣  ▣  ▣  A
VBRUN300  DLL        398,416   05-12-93  12:00a  VBRUN300.DLL
FRUNLOG   TXT          1,494   06-23-99   8:01p  FRUNLOG.TXT
RECBIN    DAT            555   06-24-99   3:49p  RECBIN.DAT
CONFIG    SYS            240   05-05-00  12:56p  CONFIG.SYS
DOSREST   SNP              0   06-24-99   3:42p  dosrest.snp
STRTLOGO  OEM        129,080   05-06-98   8:01p  STRTLOGO.OEM
MYDOCU~1            <DIR>                02-13-99  10:55a  My Documents
PROGRA~1           <DIR>                02-13-99  10:36a  Program Files
NETLOG    TXT          4,107   06-24-99   3:32p  NETLOG.TXT
IDRIVER            <DIR>                06-24-99   3:05p  IDriver
WINDOW~1  BMK             63   07-06-99   4:38p  WINDOWSWinHlp32.BMK
SBPCI              <DIR>                06-18-99   2:20p  SBPCI
ATI                <DIR>                06-18-99   2:20p  ATI
SEARCH    LOG            332   03-09-99  12:27p  search.log
CONFIG    CTL            358   06-18-99   2:23p  Config.ctl
KPCMS              <DIR>                08-20-99   6:41p  KPCMS
USBLOG    TXT            120   08-20-99   6:35p  usblog.txt
AUTOEXEC  001            285   08-20-99   6:31p  AUTOEXEC.001
WINZIP    LOG          6,218   05-10-00   8:41a  winzip.log
CONFIG    TSH            680   05-05-00  12:56p  CONFIG.TSH
AUTOEXEC  TSH            327   05-05-00  12:56p  AUTOEXEC.TSH
          24 file(s)           643,175 bytes
           7 dir(s)        540,278,784 bytes free

C:\>
```

Figure 13.1

Command line interface

All MS-DOS commands can be entered through the *command line* (C:\> prompt shown in Figure 13.1). Commands are available for the control of every aspect of the computer system's resources. The most commonly used commands are concerned with the management of file storage space and the running of applications. The function of some of these commands are described in this chapter. Where example commands are given, they relate to the use of the C:\> prompt, rather than the operating system's shell. All operating system commands are dealt with by the *command line interpreter*. Some commands are *memory resident* or *internal* and are continually available once MS-DOS has been loaded. Other, less frequently used commands, are called from disk as required.

File management and the FAT

Each *filename* is held in a *directory* together with its size (expressed in bytes) and the date and time it was created or last modified (the previous figure shows a typical directory listing). Most microcomputer systems keep track of the current date and time (even when the machine is switched off) with CMOS memory (Chapter 7). Directories are used to divide disk space into a number of user or application areas. A floppy disk with 1.44Mb (megabytes) capacity may contain, say, 60 or 70 files at most, so it is possible for a user to scan a single directory in the search for a particular file name. A hard disk, with a capacity of hundreds of megabytes, may contain thousands of files and managing them all in a single directory is virtually impossible. For this reason, MS-DOS allows the creation of *sub-directories* to which groups of files can be assigned. When the operating system's attention is directed to a particular directory, it is known as the *current* or *working* directory. MS-DOS keeps track of files on disk with the use of a *file allocation table* (FAT). When a disk is formatted, MS-DOS initially sets up two system areas, one for the FAT and the other for the main or *root* directory. The FAT has an entry for each *cluster* (a cluster is group of sectors). Clusters containing only part of a file have a FAT entry which points to the next cluster relating to that file, or, if it is the last part of a file, a special indicator. Thus, MS-DOS can find a complete file by reference to the pointers in each cluster containing a part of it. Empty clusters have a zero entry in the FAT.

File operations

Viewing directories

As explained earlier, it is essential to organise file storage space and to allocate files relating to a single application into, at least, one separate sub-directory. To view the contents of a particular directory may require the entry of commands to:

❑   select the *drive letter*. If a system has a hard disk and two floppy disk drives, these are labelled as C, A and B, respectively. Sometimes, if the hard disk is partitioned into several areas (or there are other drives attached to the system), additional drive letters may be used - D, E, F and so on;

❑   switch to the working directory.

Figure 13.1 shows contents of the C: drive *root* directory. Note that each row details, from left to right, the filename, *extension* (for example, autoexec.bat), size of file in bytes and the date it was last modified. The file extension indicates the file type. For example, BAT indicates a *batch file* (see later) and EXE an *executable* program file. Applications packages add their own file extension to any file created with the package. For example, if a user creates a worksheet with the Excel package and names it BUDGET, the file will appear in the directory as BUDGET.XLS. The details of a named file can also be viewed by the command

        dir a:budget.xls

Using a wild card

A wild card allows the user to broaden the scope of a command. For example, to display details of files beginning with the file name TEST, on drive B, could be entered as

        dir b:test*

The wild card can be used with some other commands, including the COPY command, which is explained in the next section.

Other file and disk commands

❑   erase - to remove a named file (or, using the wild card, group of files) from disk. del has the same effect.

❑   undelete. This command recovers a file which has been accidentally deleted. Deleted files are only marked as such and are recoverable with this command, unless MS-DOS has subsequently used the area for another file. The command cannot be used if the directory which contained the deleted file has been removed.

❑   `copy` - to copy a named file or group of files to another disk and/or directory.

❑   `attrib` - protects a file by making it read only. Thus, `attrib +r budget.xls` prevents any write operation of the named file (`attrib -r budget.xls` removes the protection).

❑   `comp` - compares the contents of two files or two groups of files.

❑   `diskcomp` - compares the contents of two disks on a track-by-track basis, rather than by reference to particular files.

❑   `diskcopy` - allows the copying of a complete disk onto another. It is generally used to carry out security backups.

❑   `format` - formats the disk in the specified drive. All new disks must be formatted to accept MS-DOS files before use (a similar command exists in all operating systems). The command initialises the directory and file allocation tables on disk. It destroys any existing files as the complete disk contents are wiped. File protection attributes provide no protection. The only protection against accidental formatting of diskettes is to use the appropriate write protection mechanism. Hard disks cannot be write-protected but more recent versions of MS-DOS provide more user warnings if the specified drive contains the hard disk. The accidental wiping of a 200 megabyte hard disk could be catastrophic.

❑   `print` - initiates a primitive form of spooling (background printing) and prints a named text file on the attached printer while other commands are processed.

❑   `recover` - recovers a file or entire disk containing some bad or corrupted sectors. The command causes MS-DOS to read the file sector by sector and skips the bad sectors, marking them to ensure that they are not used again. Thus, the uncorrupted parts of a file can be recovered.

❑   `type` - displays the contents of a file on screen. For example, `type A:test.dat`, displays the contents of the file named `test.dat` and stored on drive `A:\>`. A wild card cannot be used with this command.

Directory creation and handling

If a computer is used by more than one user, or a single user is working on a number of different projects, it is advisable to organise work files accordingly into different directories. This is similar to separating manual files by placing them into different drawers or sections of a filing cabinet. Although it may be common practice to maintain all files in the root directory of a floppy disk, it is virtually essential, if any proper control is to be maintained, to organise work files on hard disk into different directories. Systems and applications programs must be installed into separate directories because, in addition to the need for organisation, many have the same filenames and therefore must be separated. For example, there may be one directory (and several sub-directories) for a spreadsheet program, another for the word processing program and another for the accounts programs. Regarding work files, a user has to decide what logical divisions need to be made. MS-DOS organises files in what is termed a *multi-level directory structure*. Figure 13.3 in the Novell Netware section shows this type of structure. Each of the directories and sub-directories may contain a number of files. A multi-level directory structure looks rather like an up-turned tree with a single root at the top and branches growing from it. The root directory is created when the disk is formatted, but other directories have to be created by the user. Any directory with sub-directories beneath it is called a *parent* directory. Once directories have been created, any file can be directed to its relevant directory, either directly with the use of MS-DOS commands or (more usually) through the applications software.

Directory commands

The command mdir (or simply md) stands for make directory and is used for the creation of directories. For example, md\dos creates a directory called dos for the storage of the operating system files. Similar commands can be used to create directories for applications packages (this is usually done automatically when a package is installed) and associated files and the users work files. The backslash (\) symbol is used to separate directories names, the first backslash indicating separation from the root directory which is inferred within the command. The series of directory names and backslashes indicates the path to be taken by the operating system to access particular files. The command chdir (or cd) is used to move from one working directory to another. For example, cd\dos changes to the dos directory. The command cd\ always returns control to the root directory from any point in the structure and cd . . moves back one level in the structure. Directories can be removed with rmdir (or rd). A directory can be deleted only when it is empty.

Accessing external commands

External commands are those operating system commands which have to be called from disk whenever they are required. Internal commands are the most commonly used and remain resident in memory after the operating system has been loaded. A user may be working in any one of a number of directories, so the operating system needs to be given a path to the directory containing the external commands (in case any are needed during processing). If the directory is called dos, then the command path\dos must be executed. This is done automatically at system start-up, by including the command in the autoexec.bat (see later), which is stored in the root directory. The automatic execution of commands through batch files is dealt with in a later section.

Redirecting input and input

Unless commanded otherwise, MS-DOS assumes that input is through the keyboard and that output is to be directed to the screen. With appropriate commands, input can be accepted from a disk file, rather than from the keyboard. Similarly, output can be directed to a printer instead of the screen. Sometimes, output from one process is required as input for another and this redirection of output can be effected with the use of a *pipe*.

An MS-DOS command normally directs output to the screen. For example, dir displays, on screen, the directory listing of the disk in the currently active drive. By adding a greater-than (>) sign and a filename, the directory listing can be written to a disk file of that name. For example, dir >file.lst creates a file called file.lst and writes the directory to it.

To append output to an existing file, two greater-than symbols are used. For example, dir >>file.lst sends the directory listing to the named file and appends the data to the existing file contents. If the file doesn't exist, then MS-DOS creates it.

To call input from a channel other than the keyboard, requires the use of the less-than symbol (<). For example, newfile.txt < input.txt causes newfile.txt to receive its input from the file input.txt, rather than the keyboard.

Filters

Filter commands are used to transform an input file in some way, before it is sent to an output device. For example, filter commands can be used to read a file from disk, sort it and then display the sorted file on screen. MS-DOS provides three commonly used filters:

❏ find, which searches for specified text in a named file;

❏ sort, which sorts a text file. For example, a directory listing could be sorted before being displayed on screen;

❏ more. When displaying a text file on screen, more allows it to be output one screen at a time.

Pipes

Pipes permit the use of more than one operating system command at a time. Each command is separated by a vertical bar sign |. For example, dir|sort|more sorts the working directory and displays it on the screen. If the listing occupies more than the length of the screen, the user is prompted to continue after each section of the list fills the screen.

Batch files

Batch files are special files used for the automatic execution of regularly used sequences of commands. Any valid sequence of commands can be included and the operating system will execute them in the same way as if they had been entered one at a time from the keyboard. To be recognised by the operating system as a batch file, MS-DOS requires the filename extension .BAT to be used. To execute a batch file, only the filename, without the extension .BAT, is typed. One particular type of batch file called autoexec.bat has a special significance which is explained later in this section. A batch file is created with a text editor.

Batch file example - file copying

A batch file called movfile.bat could also be used to automate a file copying operation. The following sequence of commands creates a new directory called second, copies a file bumph.dat from its location in the directory called first, deletes the original and then displays the contents of directory second (which now contains bumph.dat). The word rem means remark or comment and is used to document the file; rem is ignored by MS-DOS.

Listing 13.1. Batch file to copy a specific file

```
rem prevents command execution of screen
@echo off
rem creates the new directory
md c:\second
rem copies the bumph.dat file to the new directory
copy c:\first\bumph.dat c:\second
rem deletes the original file
erase c:\first\bumph.dat
rem displays the contents of the new directory
dir c:\second
rem displays the message shown
echo Here is the file in the new directory
```

The drawback of the batch file shown in Listing 13.1, is that it only deals with two particular directories and one named file. MS-DOS allows replaceable parameters to be entered with the batch file name. This means that movfile.bat can be modified to allow the user to specify directory names and filenames before the batch file is executed. The modified commands are shown in Listing 13.2. The replaceable parameters are represented by %1 and %2.

If the command, movfile c:\second c:\first\bumph.dat, is entered, MS-DOS executes the batch file named movfile and replaces %1 with c:\second and %2 with c:\first\bumph.dat. If these replacements are traced through the command sequence in Listing 13.2, it can be seen that its effect is the same as that in Listing 13.1. Of course, entry of different parameters enables the batch file to be used for any new directory and file, or files to be moved to it. For example, movfile c:\newplace c:\oldplace*.doc would move a set of files, with the same file extension .doc, from the existing directory oldplace to the new directory newplace.

Listing 13.2.   Batch file with replaceable parameters

```
echo off
md %1
copy %2 %1
erase %2
dir %2
echo Contents of new directory
```

Function of autoexec.bat file

An autoexec.bat file can be used to customise a computer for a particular purpose at system start up. Thus, for example, a computer which is used for one particular package can be automated to load that package when MS-DOS is started. Because the autoexec.bat file is executed when the operating system is first loaded, it must reside in the root directory.

Autoexec.bat files can include numerous, advanced command sequences, but a simple example is provided in Listing 13.3.

Listing 13.3.   An example autoexec.bat file

```
echo off
rem loads UK keyboard driver
keyb uk
rem provides path to DOS commands and programs
path c:\dos;c:\word
rem loads mouse driver
mouse
rem opens the MS-DOS shell
dosshell
```

Function of config.sys file

The config.sys file is also stored in the root directory and is automatically executed when the system is switched on. It contains commands which configure the computer system for particular installation requirements. Listing 13.4 shows a sample config.sys file.

Listing 13.4.   Sample config.sys file

```
rem identifies the mouse driver
device=c:\mouse\mouse.sys
rem sets number of files which can be open at any one
```

```
rem time. Normal set-up allows only 8. An application
rem which requires more is likely to indicate the fact.
files =20
rem these are disk buffers in which MS-DOS can hold data
rem being read from or written to disk, when the amount
rem of data is not an exact multiple of sector size. Word
rem processors which use the disk intensively perform
rem better with 10 to 20 buffers. If a large number of
rem directories is created, then 20 to 30 buffers
rem may improve performance.
buffers=20
rem this selects the time, date and currency format.
rem The code 044 is for the UK.
Country=044
```

Windows 9x configuration file

The equivalent configuration file for Windows 9x operating systems is system.ini, an example extract of which is given below.

```
[boot]
oemfonts.fon=8514oem.fon
system.drv=system.drv
drivers=mmsystem.dll power.drv
shell=Explorer.exe
user.exe=user.exe
gdi.exe=gdi.exe
sound.drv=mmsound.drv
dibeng.drv=dibeng.dll
comm.drv=comm.drv
mouse.drv=mouse.drv
keyboard.drv=keyboard.drv
*DisplayFallback=0
fixedfon.fon=8514fix.fon
fonts.fon=8514sys.fon
386Grabber=vgafull.3gr
display.drv=pnpdrvr.drv
SCRNSAVE.EXE=C:\WINDOWS\SYSTEM\BLANKS~1.SCR

[keyboard]
keyboard.dll=
oemansi.bin=xlat850.bin
subtype=
type=4


[boot.description]
system.drv=Standard PC
keyboard.typ=Standard 101/102-Key or Microsoft Natural Keyboard
mouse.drv=Microsoft IntelliPoint
aspect=100,120,120
display.drv=ATI Rage 128 GL AGP (English)
```

OS/2

OS/2 Version 1.0 was announced by IBM and Microsoft in April 1987, as a *multi-tasking* operating system. Since then the collaboration between these two companies has broken down and Microsoft has produced its highly successful Windows GUI. Numerous improvements have been made to the original version of OS/2, but it is still failing to make any significant impression in the PC software market. In an effort to take an increased share of this market, IBM has ensured that OS/2 is able to run applications developed for MS-DOS and Windows, as well as OS/2 itself.

Workplace shell - the OS/2 GUI

Workplace Shell has the main features of a conventional GUI, with windows that can be moved and re-sized, scroll bars (for viewing different areas of work within the available window), dialogue boxes, etc. Unlike the Windows GUI, it does not allocate file management to a separate component. Instead, users are encouraged to view data files as the entry point for applications (rather than the other way around). Workplace Shell can be described as *object orientated*. An object can be a program, a data file, a folder (directory) or device (such as a printer). When an object is selected, a pop-up menu offers options appropriate to the object. For example, a program object menu includes a run option. Similarly, a data file object provides options concerning, for example, the printing or copying of the file. When running Microsoft Windows applications, the desktop is presented accordingly, with the Program Manager window.

32-bit applications

For brevity, OS/2 Version 2.1 is referred to simply as OS/2. As a 32-bit operating system, OS/2 can take full advantage of the current 32-bit processors and 32-bit software. Handling data in 32-bit units, rather than 16 bits at a time, contributes to quicker system performance. To ensure its compatibility with a huge section of the PC software market, OS/2 can run 16-bit software; virtually all MS-DOS and a few Windows applications are designed to retain backward compatibility with the 16-bit 80286 processor. Windows 3.1 also runs 32-bit applications (using an i386, or later, processor), when it is operating in *enhanced mode*.

Multi-tasking

OS/2 allocates a separate, private, area of memory to each application. It also provides facilities to protect one application from the activities of another. Device drivers (disk controllers, screen and printer drivers) operate at a higher level of privilege within memory, because they have to remain accessible to all current applications.

Pre-emptive versus co-operative multi-tasking

Pre-emptive multi-tasking means that the operating system controls the amount of processor time each application receives, giving each application a slice of time before switching activity to one of the others. Windows 9x, Windows NT, OS/2 and UNIX all operate pre-emptive multi-tasking.

An operating system which uses co-operative multi-tasking does not control the amount of time given to an application. Therefore, a processor intensive application will keep control of the processor for as long as it needs it, although when it terminates or switches to an input or output tasks, another application will gain access to the processor. For a co-operative multitasking operating system to be effective, programs must be designed so that they do not control the processor for long periods. Generally, this is achieved by splitting programs into small modules which individually require only short periods of processing before they release the processor.

File management

OS/2 offers two file management systems. Users have to choose which one to install. The choice depends largely on the capacity of the drive and whether or not MS-DOS applications are to be used.

❏   an enhanced File Allocation Table (FAT) system, which can be read by MS-DOS;

❏   a High Performance File System (HPFS).

The HPFS is completely different from the FAT system and is designed to manage, more effectively, the higher capacity (measured in gigabytes) hard drives. HPFS file names can be up to 254 characters in length (compared with the 8 permitted by MS-DOS). Both filing systems allow up to 64Kb of *attribute data* to be attached to each file; the data can comprise text and images. This permits extensive labelling of a file, describing its contents and perhaps associations with other files or applications. Effectively, this means that longer file names can also be used with the enhanced FAT system. Both systems (like Windows 3.x) support *write caching* (see Chapter 9), which means that writing to disk can be delayed if the processor is busy. The mechanism can be disabled, as there is a small risk that data may be lost (while it waits in the cache memory) if there is a sudden power cut.

A short history of Microsoft Windows

Microsoft's Windows was initially developed as a front-end to DOS-based applications. It allowed novice computer users to use an IBM-compatible PC without having to learn the rather cryptic DOS commands. However, it was not really until 1990 that it became a serious alternative to DOS. The history of Windows is briefly traced, from its rather inauspicious first appearance in 1985, to its huge popularity today.

Five releases preceded Windows 95, the latest version of the Microsoft Windows operating system. The first version, version 1.0 released in 1985, was beset with problems. The main reason for this was that the hardware generally available at the time did not lend itself to a graphical user interface. The combination of an under powered processor (the Intel 8086), low-resolution graphics and lack of internal memory conspired to produce a piece of software that was not very well received by the computer industry. Though it did make a PC easier to use for non-technical users, being text-based it was not what is recognised today as a true graphical user interface.

However, the success of Apple's Macintosh personal computer, with its intuitive, graphical user interface, encouraged Microsoft to continue in competition and the result was Windows 2.0. Still text-based, this version was not a great deal better than the previous one, though the Windows/386 version released in 1988 did offer multi-tasking as a direct result of the increased processing power that the Intel 80386 processor provided. It was not until 1990, when Windows 3.0 provided an attractive, user-friendly graphical interface and several other enhancements, that Windows was recognised as providing a real alternative to DOS-based application. Windows 3.0 offered improved memory management so that applications could do more; it made extensive use of icons and it provided the Program Manager utility, which simplified the management of applications.

This version of Windows also allows several tasks to run at the same time. However, partly as a result of its attempt to make Windows 3.0 backwardly compatible with other versions and also with DOS applications, Microsoft introduced too much instability into the operating system. This manifested itself in system crashes which announced themselves with the notorious Unrecoverable Application Error message box. Version 3.1 addressed these problems by fixing known bugs in version 3.0 and, more importantly, by more carefully monitoring the behaviour of applications to trap possible problems before they caused the system to 'hang'. Moreover, in version 3.1 Microsoft introduced the facility to utilise disk space as virtual memory, thus releasing the user from having to be too careful about the amount of memory that was required by an application.

The next main development in the evolution of Windows was the release of Windows for Workgroups 3.11. This release represented Microsoft's efforts to support small organisations using small Local Area Networks. The new features included in Windows for Workgroups allowed a number of PCs to be linked by installing a network card and some cable. Network features such as meeting scheduling and e-mail were also provided. The reliability of Windows was further improved in this version.

Windows NT

Microsoft's Windows NT operating system first became available in September 1993. It is a 32-bit multi-tasking operating system and competes directly with OS/2. Its hardware requirements are greater than those needed for the Windows 3.1 GUI and it is not seen as a replacement for it. Windows NT needs a minimum of 12Mb of main memory and 75Mb of free disk space. Machines based on RISC processors (Chapter 7) require 16Mb of main memory and 92Mb free disk space to run Windows NT. The operating system includes facilities for networking, enabling machines to be used as print and file *servers* (Chapter 10), and *multi-user/multi-access* operation. There are three main parts to Windows NT:

❑ NT *executive*, which is the operating system and controls the hardware;

❑ Win32 sub-system, which the NT executive runs as an application. Win32 provides the Windows GUI;

❑ MS-DOS, OS/2 and Portable UNIX sub-systems, which allows the running of software written for these operating systems. Concerning OS/2, only applications written for the character-based interface are supported. Software written for Windows 3.# will also run under Windows NT. These sub-systems can only operate through the Win32 sub-system.

Figure 13.2 illustrates the main components in the structure and their relationship one with another and to the hardware.

❑ The Virtual Memory Manager controls the allocation of main memory to applications and ensures that each is protected from other processes. When there is insufficient main memory space, some memory contents are paged to disk (*virtual memory*) until room becomes available (when they are paged back in). This protection does not apply to Windows 3.# applications (run through the Windows sub-system) which can, at times, clash for memory space and crash.

❑ The Process Manager controls the multi-tasking process. Windows NT (like OS/2) can carry out fine grained multi-tasking. This enables the concurrent processing of tasks within the same application. For example, new records could be entered into a database, while a database sort is being executed in the background.

❑ The Input/Output Manager handles file reading and writing operations, at the physical machine level. It provides a File Allocation Table (FAT) system, compatible with the MS-DOS system and a High Performance File System (HPFS) to handle OS/2 applications. NT's own file system (NTFS) allows the use of long file names and the storage of files up to 17 billion gigabytes in size.

❏   The *kernel* handles signals from the hardware, indicating conditions such as, the completion of data transfer through a communications port.

Hardware

Figure 13.2. *Windows NT structure*

Portability

The MS-DOS and OS/2 operating systems are designed to make particular use of the Intel series of processors (Chapter 7). Apart from the kernel, the Windows NT operating system does not relate specifically to the architecture of any particular processor; to some extent it is processor independent and can be used on non-Intel processor machines. This independence is achieved with the use of a Hardware Abstraction Layer (HAL), which comes between the hardware and the NT Executive.

Windows 9x

Based on Windows NT, Windows 9x offers a PC operating system that also does not rely on DOS for its operation. Though it is not regarded as a replacement for the more powerful NT operating system, Windows 9x nevertheless has a number of major improvements over previous versions of Windows. These include:

❏   improved speed;

❏   improved reliability;

❏   better user interface;

❏   better networking capabilities;

❏   'plug and play' capability;

❏   support for long file names.

The speed improvement results from the fact that Windows 9x uses 32-bit code to perform much of its work and that it uses *pre-emptive multitasking* to control applications. As mentioned earlier in this chapter, multi-tasking allows several applications, or *tasks*, to be running simultaneously, but with pre-emptive multi-tasking it is the operating system rather than the tasks, that controls the resources that are available. This ensures that each current task is allowed its fair share of the resources that it requests.

Improved reliability has resulted mainly from removing Window's dependence on DOS. Many of the instability problems experienced in previous versions of Windows were directly related to its use of DOS which allowed applications to take complete control of the computer system. When more than one application is running in a multi-tasking environment, then each application must restrict itself to using only certain resources, especially memory, otherwise conflicts arise which cause the machine to crash. DOS applications can still run in Windows 9x, but they are restricted to a virtual machine that emulates earlier processor architectures such as that of the 8086 family. This greatly reduces the possibility of a DOS application 'misbehaving'. Additional stability resulted from more 'bug fixes'. The Windows 98 user interface is shown in Figure 12.2 in Chapter 12.

'Explorer' replaces in a single application the Windows 3.x Program Manager and File Manager utility programs. It provides a very flexible way of organising files and programs using 'folders' which are similar to directories. A *task bar* at the bottom of the screen has a 'Start' button which is used to activate pop up menus, and applications currently available, either running or idle, are shown as separate named buttons. By clicking on the name of an application on the task bar, that application's window becomes the current focus, thereby allowing access to the application's controls. Note also the application shortcuts on the right, represented by icons and the shortcut bar on the left; both features add to the flexibility and ease of use of the system.

Windows 9x provides a form of networking called *Peer-to-peer* (Chapter 10) support. This allows a network to be constructed simply by installing a network card in each workstation and connecting them together with cable. One or more workstations can be configured as servers, without the need to buy extra machines for this purpose. Peer-to-peer networking allows each user to have access to the files on every other machine, providing that they are granted the appropriate rights to do so.

Plug and Play (PNP) is the term given to a computer hardware standard which allows the operating system to detect and to deal with the installation and control of devices automatically. Windows 9x performs the following PNP facilities:

❑   identification of all of the PNP components attached to the system, thus greatly reducing the information that needs to be provided during installation;

❑   determination of the resource needs of each device;

❑   automatic creation of system configuration, thus removing the need for a user-controlled device manager;

❑   device driver loading and unloading as and when required;

❑   notification of configuration changes by displaying a dialogue box on-screen whenever a change in the number or type of devices has changed.

Because of their dependency on DOS, previous versions of Windows required the familiar 8.3 format (*filename.ext*) for file names; Windows 9x now allows filenames of almost any length to be used, including embedded spaces.

Novell Netware

Novell Netware is the most widely used local area network operating system and provides a high level of multi-user provision and security. This section looks in some detail at the filing system and the facilities for multi-user administration.

Filing system

The file server contains the shared file storage system and handles requests for access to it. Like any filing system, it has to be organised to allow efficient access to and management of the resource. Commonly, such organisation is *hierarchical* and the Netware system provides a typical example. Figure 13.3 shows how the file system might be structured.

Figure 13.3. *An example Novell Netware filing system*

Volumes

Referring to Figure 13.3, the server (FS1) disk storage may be divided into *volumes*; a volume is a physical amount of storage, which can be a section of one storage device or it may incorporate several devices. Volumes can be used to divide the network's filing system according to separate organisational requirements. For example, separate volumes may be assigned to Accounts, Manufacturing and Personnel. One reason for such separation is security; security backups can be carried out separately on each volume and allocation of users to the separate organisational functions is made easier. However, these volumes are still part of the same network filing system and a user can be allowed to access more than one, when necessary. For simplicity, Figure 13.3 shows that the server has only one volume (SYS:, which is automatically created when Netware is set up). A workstation accesses a volume by a drive letter (F:\ for example).

Directories and sub-directories

Directories are subdivisions of a volumes space. Referring to Figure 13.3 and volume SYS:, a number of different types of directory can be identified:

❑   *system*; there are four (Login, System, Public and Mail), created when the file server's network software is installed;

❑   *DOS* (a sub-directory of Public). Each version of the MS-DOS operating system, used by workstations attached to the network, has a sub-directory; one workstation may be using version 6.0, whilst others may be using version 5.0 or 4.0 and if applications are to run correctly, they must have access to the appropriate operating system commands;

❑ *applics*; these contain the executable files of applications software. There are three sub-directories within this directory: Word6 (word processor); Pegasus (accounting); Corel50 (graphics);

❑ *users*; the workspace allocated to user data files. Figure 13.3 shows three main sub-divisions of users: Sales; Finance; Design. The Design group has four separate user areas allocated to it: Roberto; Carla; Fabio; Gianna. The other user groups of Sales and Finance may well be similarly sub-divided, but this is not shown in the figure.

The highest level (the top row) in this *tree* structure contains a number of *system* directories. Figure 13.3 shows four:

❑ *login*; this directory contains programs concerning the login procedure;

❑ *public*; this holds Novell network (as opposed to MS-DOS) operating system commands and utilities which can be accessed by users;

❑ *system*; files and programs used by the network operating system and the network supervisor are held in here;

❑ *mail*; this contains a sub-directory relating to each network user and containing their *login script*. A *user login script* can be used to tailor the network environment for a particular user, such as the display of a special applications menu or greeting. More usually, the *system login script* is used for all users; programming statements, such as IF ...THEN ...ELSE can be used to determine the network environment for different users or groups of users. Thus, for example, the Sales, Finance and Design groups may each have a different menu, giving access to a different set of applications.

The *network supervisor* (the person in charge of network administration) needs to create other directories, for the applications and data areas. Figure 13.3 shows an *applics* (applications) directory, which is divided into three sub-directories, one each for word processing, accounting and graphic design packages. The *users* directory is divided into a series of sub-directories, one data or work area for each user; each of these, usually identified by the user name, is the allocated workspace for a user. A data directory may be shared by a number of individual users, belonging to the same group, such as Finance. Alternatively, as in the case of the four Design users, each may have their own data directory. Upon login, the user name is used to *map* the workstation to the user's own data directory; this is done through the *login script* (similar to a batch file in MS-DOS).

User directory and file management

When a user logs in the workstation is *mapped* to their user directory. Thus, at the MS-DOS prompt, user ST001 may see the following.

```
F:\USERS\ST001
```

Within that directory ST001 has full directory and file rights, which means that he or she can:

❑   create and modify a structure of sub-directories, within their user directory, to suit the division of their own work;

❑   read, write, copy, delete or rename any files stored within that structure.

Access rights

Network storage is shared, so access to it needs to be carefully controlled. Thus, users should only be able to gain access to those directories and files which they need and are authorised to use.

There are a number of different rights, each of which permits a certain operation to be carried out in respect of a file or directory. The rights for files and directories are the same. The directory and file operations available to a user are determined by their rights. Rights only relate to the use of network storage and are not relevant to the integral drives of a workstation. The examples given here relate to the Novell Netware operating system.

Every user has certain rights which they can invoke when they login in:

❑   network applications (*executables*), which can only be accessed and run;

❑   access to their default user directory and data files within it. These are broadly unrestricted, although the physical space allocation is likely to be set. Creation and modification of a directory structure is allowed and the user is given full housekeeping rights concerning the files within that structure.

Table 13.1 lists the directory and file rights, which can be assigned with the Novell Netware operating system. Following the table are brief explanations on the significance of each type for network operation and security.

The 8 rights shown in the table can be granted in respect of a given *directory* and will thus be restricted to that directory (except in the case of *inherited rights* - not dealt with in this text). Rights can also be related to specific *files*.

	Right	Meaning
S	Supervisory	Unrestricted in the directory. Can grant rights to other users.
R	Read	Can open files, read contents and run programs in the directory.
W	Write	Can open and alter the contents of files in the directory.
C	Create	Can create new files and sub-directories in the directory.
E	Erase	Can erase directory, sub-directories and files contained in them.
M	Modify	Can alter file attributes or names.
F	File Scan	Can see files and directories covered by this right.
A	Access Control	Can give rights (same as own) to other users in the directory.

Table 13.1. *Novell Netware directory and file access rights*

Table 13.2 gives typical circumstances when a user needs some of the rights in Table 13.1.

Operation	Rights needed
Create a new directory	Create
Execute a program (an *executable* file)	Read, File Scan
Erase a file	Erase

See a filename	File Scan
Look through a directory for files	File Scan
Copy files to another directory	Write, Create, File Scan
Rename a file or directory	Modify
Create a file and write to it	Create

Table 13.2. *Rights needed for example directory and file operations*

Default rights

When a Novell server is set up, a SUPERVISOR user is created, with S(upervisory) rights in all directories. A user group called EVERYONE is also created, to which all new users are assigned, unless the supervisor creates other groups in which to place them. The EVERYONE group members are given the following default rights:

❏ *C(reate)* in the SYS: MAIL directory, which contains a sub-directory for every user (not their data directory). Each sub-directory contains the relevant users *login script* (see Directories and Sub-directories).

❏ R(ead) and F(ile Scan) in the SYS:PUBLIC, which holds the executable network operating system commands for users (for example: NDIR and NCOPY).

Additional rights need to be assigned to allow users to run applications software. From Table 13.2, it can be seen that a user would need R(ead) and F(ile Scan) rights to the directory containing the required applications. The methods by which users can be assigned rights are dealt with in the next section.

User administration

Four categories of *Novell user* need to be identified:

❏ *SUPERVISOR.* This user has unrestricted access and operational power in any part of the network server for which he or she is responsible. The network administrator will be the only SUPERVISOR user.

❏ *Console Operator. Security equivalence* enables a user to be given the same rights as another, so although there is only one SUPERVISOR user for a Novell file server, another person can be given the same rights by being given supervisor equivalence. *Console Operator* is the term given to a person given supervisor equivalence.

❏ *Workgroup Manager.* The network administrator can create this category of user if it is necessary to give another person *supervisory* rights over a particular volume or directory. This is useful if another person is to be given responsibility for their own users and data.

❏ *User.* This is the ordinary user, who has no supervisory rights and whose access to any part of the network is controlled by user *account restrictions*. Accounts also exist for the special users: SUPERVISOR; Console Operator; Workgroup Manager. When a new user is installed, he or she becomes part of the group EVERYONE, every member of which is assigned R(ead) and F(ileScan) rights to the SYS:PUBLIC directory and SYS:MAIL. Additional rights can be assigned directly to the user, or by making him or her a member of a group, which has additional rights. Alternatively, additional rights can be given to all users by altering the rights of the group EVERYONE.

Groups

Network administration can become very complex if file and directory rights are separately assigned to each user. A much better method is to create groups. By making a user a member of a particular group, the rights of that group are automatically assigned to that user. Most users can be dealt with in this way. Suppose, for example that a business allocates directories for Sales, Finance and Design. Clearly, the staff in the Accounts department are going to need access to the same files (customer Sales Ledger, for example), which are held in the Finance directory. Equally, they are likely to need access to the same accounts applications and will need R(ead) and F(ile Scan) rights in the Accounts software directory (this contains executable files for the accounts software). By creating a group called ACCOUNT, and assigning the appropriate rights to it, staff in the Accounts Department can be added to the group and gain the necessary rights automatically. If a member of the Accounts department moves to another job within the business, they can be transferred to another group (with rights to access other directories and files) and their rights will be modified accordingly.

How rights can be assigned

The ways in which a network administrator can assign rights are illustrated in Figures 13.4, 13.5 and 13.6. Unless a user has very particular requirements, then the most appropriate method of giving rights is to assign users to a group which has the assigned rights he or she needs.

user

individually assigned access rights to

directory

Figure 13.4. *Individual rights assigned directly to user*

user

group

made member of

gains access rights of group to

directory

Figure 13.5. *Assigned rights through group membership*

Figure 13.6. *Assigned rights by user/group equivalence*

Another useful method of giving a user or group the same rights as another is to use *security equivalence* (Figure 13.6). This is the method used by the network administrator to give a console operator the same rights as the SUPERVISOR user (the network administrator).

Trustees

Each directory and file on a file server has a *trustee list*, which specifies the users who can use that storage area. The rights granted to a trustee, by whatever method, dictate the kind of access the trustee is allowed to have.

A user or group of users can be trustees of multiple directories and files, but the rights they have in each may be different. Thus, for example, SALES user group may be a trustee of the Accounts directory, but their access rights may be limited to R(ead) and F(ile Scan). This would allow members of that group to view, for example, customer details and amounts owing, but not modify them or erase them. The SALES group may also be trustee of the Orders directory, with the additional rights of C(reate), W(rite) and E(rase). Each member of the user group, would also be a member in his or her own right, and have full rights, within their default data directory. Figure 13.7 shows a directory's trustee list, together with the access rights of each trustee. The letters in the Rights column are the initial letters of the access rights detailed in Table 13.1.

Trustee List	
Trustee	Rights
Artists	[RWCEFMA]
Marketing	[R F]
Peter	[WCE]
Pablo	[RWCEFMA]

Figure 13.7. *A trustee list*

Creating users with SYSCON (system console)

The Novell Netware operating system provides a utility called SYSCON, primarily for use by the network administrator. The opening screen appears as shown in Figure 13.8.

SUPERVISOR user and workgroup managers

SYSCON and other utilities, such as FILER (for network storage management) are held in a Private directory, which is not visible to users generally. The network administrator is a special user, referred to in Novell Netware as SUPERVISOR, who has access to all the network utilities. The network administrator can make the SYSCON utility available to a Workgroup Manager, who is another special type of Novell user. A Workgroup Manager can create users or groups and manage their accounts, but does not replace the SUPERVISOR user, who still has full rights to manage all user accounts. Existing users and groups cannot be controlled by a Workgroup Manager, unless he or she has been given User Account Manager status by the

SUPERVISOR user. The User Account Manager status will only apply to the users and groups assigned by the SUPERVISOR user. For security reasons, a Workgroup Manager is only given S(upervisory) rights in a specific volume or directory, enabling him or her to assign trustee rights to the users in that area only. For example, a Workgroup Manager may have control over the Design directory.

Figure 13.8. *SYSCON utility main menu*

Setting account restrictions

Two options are of particular importance in controlling a users access to the network: *account restrictions*; *change password*. Each user account includes properties which place limits on the user's initial access to the network (during login). Login security is supported through:

❑   the allocation of a user name;

❑   the requirement for a password of minimum length; the settings may also require, for example, periodic password change. A user can be allowed or prevented from making their own password changes;

❑   the restriction of times during which a user can login.

A *change password* option allows the Supervisor to initially set and subsequently alter a user's password. By setting default account restrictions, from the Supervisor options menu, all users can be controlled by basic settings. If special controls are required for individual users, then this can be done separately.

Enabling file sharing

There may be occasions when a user wishes to make their own files available to another user or user group. This can be achieved by making the user or user group a *trustee* of the relevant directory. Normally, a user has all rights in their own directory. To make another user, or group, a trustee of that directory requires use of the A(ccess Control) right. This can be achieved with the GRANT command (at the command line prompt). The format of the command is as shown below.

        GRANT *rightslist* . . . [FOR *path*] TO [USER | GROUP] *name*

The word ALL can follow GRANT, if all rights held by the directory owner (users cannot assign rights they do not have) are to be assigned to the trustee user or group. If the command is being issued from the user's default directory, no *path* needs to be specified. An example command is shown below.

```
GRANT r w c e m TO USER gianna
```

The REVOKE command can be used to remove Gianna's trustee rights, as shown below (specific rights may be listed if some are to remain).

```
REVOKE ALL FROM USER gianna
```

User identification

Before allowing login, the network operating system requires identification of the user, through entry of the user name and password. An organisation can set standards concerning both. These standards will be implemented through user account restrictions, which allow the setting of:

❑   user name formats; standards could determine a strict format for the assignment of user names. For example, each user name may have to begin with a 3 character code, which identifies their department;

❑   a minimum password length. The organisation may set a standard minimum length and this can be enforced through the network user's account. The longer the password, the less likely it is that others will guess it, or identify it from watching the keys that the user presses;

❑   requirement for a periodic password change or a unique password (can only be used once). The organisation may require each user to renew his or her password every week. Infrequent changes increase the likelihood that passwords will not remain secret. Unique (once only) passwords are appropriate for users who only have occasional need to access the network. Each occasion is specially authorised though the assignment of a unique password;

❑   login restricted to certain days or times of day; if the network remains active after normal office hours, for a restricted group of users, other users can be excluded by placing time limits on their accounts;

❑   number of grace logins after expiry of the users password; a user may be allowed, say, three logins after password expiry and if the password is not renewed within that period, the user is locked out. Reference then has to be made to the network supervisor to regain entry. The organisation's standards may require that such circumstances are reported to, for example, the relevant Head of Department, before the user account is unlocked.

✍ Exercises

1.   Briefly describe two functions of an *operating system*.

2.   What is meant by *dynamic resource allocation*?

3.   When jobs are *scheduled* in a batch multi-programming system, what factors regarding each job can be used to determine each job's priority in the schedule?

4.   Distinguish between the *high-level scheduler* and the *low-level scheduler*, or *dispatcher*.

5.   Under what circumstances is the dispatcher invoked?

6. (i) Define the term *time-sharing*;

   (ii) Briefly describe two methods of allocating the processor in a time-sharing environment.

7. Distinguish between a *multi-tasking* and a *multi-user* operating system.

8. Suggest why the *graphical user interface* (GUI) has virtually eclipsed the *command line interpreter* (CLI) as a means of communication between the user and the operating system.

9. (i) Define the term *interrupt*.

   (ii) Identify four *events* which may trigger an interrupt.

10. Why are dynamic *memory partitions* and *relocatable code* essential to a multi-programming operating system?

11. With reference to the MS-DOS operating system, what is a *batch file*?

12. Define the term *pre-emptive multi-tasking*.

13. Identify the various methods used by a network operating system, such as Novell Netware, to *control access* to network resources.

Chapter 14

Input/Output Control

Figure 14.1 illustrates the *architecture* of the communication system which allows data transfers between the various elements of a computer system. This chapter examines the various methods of implementing and controlling input/output (I/O) operations. Some well-known I/O interface standards are also examined. One major problem for I/O control concerns the speed imbalance between the operation of the processor and communicating peripheral devices; various techniques used to compensate for such imbalance are described.

Figure 14.1. *Computer communication architecture*

A number of components can be identified:

❑ *Bus* or *highway*. A bus consists of a number of wires, one for each bit making up the unit of data transfer. A common I/O bus connects all I/O peripherals to the processor, so only one peripheral can use the bus at a time. This is not normally a restriction because the processor can only handle one instruction at a time, but most computers have an I/O bus which is independent of that used for processor/main memory transfers. Those machines using a common bus for I/O and processor/memory data movements are referred to as single bus systems;

❑ *Interface*. This is a hardware device containing electronic components, which connects an I/O peripheral to the computer. The chapter on Data Representation describes the use of internal and external codes for internal computer and external peripheral operations respectively; one of the functions of an interface is to carry out the conversion process between the two codes, according to whether data is being transferred to or from the peripheral;

❑ *Device controller*. This device is fundamentally the same as the interface, except that it is associated with the control of data transfers to and from storage devices, such as magnetic disk and tape drives.

Methods of I/O control

The transfer of data to and from a peripheral device can take place either:

❑   under the control of the host machine's processor; this is *programmed input/output* or *PIO*;

❑   or, under the autonomous control of the device; most commonly, this is *direct memory access* or *DMA*.

Programmed input/output (PIO)

Earlier microcomputers used PIO for the control of data transfers, but this has largely been replaced by DMA. PIO requires that the computer's processor controls each stage of data transfer between the system's hard disk drive and itself. PIO can be effected in one of two ways: *software polling*; *hardware interrupts*.

Software polling

The operating system software regularly polls (checks) each device to see if it requires attention. To achieve I/O transfers by this method, instructions are needed:

❑   for *input* - to transfer data from peripheral to processor;

❑   for *output* - to transfer data from processor to peripheral;

❑   to *set* individual control flags in the I/O interface unit;

❑   to *test* individual flags in the I/O interface unit.

A peripheral device is attached to an interface unit by a cable. The interface unit (usually inside the computer) is connected to one of a number of I/O slots, each of which has a fixed address, by which a peripheral can be identified for input or output. There are 3 basic elements in an interface unit which is polled by software:

❑   a control bit or *busy* flag - used to signal a device to start input or output. This cannot be set by the device as it is under control of the processor;

❑   a flag bit or *done* flag - this is set by the device when the data transfer is complete and can be tested or cleared by program instructions;

❑   a *buffer register* for the storage of data transferred into (read by) or to be transferred from (written by) the device.

When a 'start read' instruction is given, one character is transferred between the interface buffer register and the device. A single character is transferred in the opposite direction if a 'start write' instruction is given. A processor instruction commands the device to operate by setting the busy flag and then repeatedly tests the done flag to discover when the transfer is complete. The major difficulty with software polling is that the repeated testing of the done flag is carried out at the same time as it continues with some other computation. This means that the program instructions currently being executed (probably the program that issued the I/O instruction) must be interleaved with the regular issue of instructions to test for completion of the transfer. The last operating system to use software polling was CP/M (Control Program/Microcomputer) which was used on some early microcomputer systems, but has long been obsolete.

An example instruction sequence for software polling may be as follows:

For *input* from a specific device:

❑ instruction to interface to set the busy flag for 'start transmit';

❑ send instruction to test done flag. If the flag indicates that the transfer is complete, skip next instruction;

❑ branch to previous instruction;

❑ issue instruction to transfer character from buffer register into processor accumulator;

❑ issue store instruction to transfer character from accumulator to main memory.

For *output* to a specific device:

❑ issue instruction to transfer character from processor accumulator into buffer register of interface device;

❑ issue instruction to set busy flag to start transfer;

❑ issue instruction to test done flag and if set, skip the next instruction;

❑ branch to previous instruction.

The repetitive flag-test loop is necessary to ensure that a character transfer is completed before the next one is transmitted. A more efficient method of PIO control is to use hardware interrupts.

I/O using hardware interrupts

An I/O interrupt is a signal from an I/O device to the processor to indicate that:

❑ data is waiting to be read;

❑ an I/O error has occurred;

❑ a previous I/O transfer is complete.

To enable I/O devices to initiate requests for service from the processor, an I/O bus includes interrupt request (IRQ) lines, typically 15. All the IRQ lines go to every expansion slot in the I/O bus, so when a device adapter card (for example, a disk drive controller) is plugged into a slot, the specific IRQ line it is to use can then be set, by configuring the card, either through utility software or by physical switches on the card. The device then uses that IRQ line to signal the processor that it requires service. A processor has only one interrupt pin, which is set when an I/O interrupt occurs, to indicate the presence of an interrupt, but not its source. An interrupt handler routine (part of the operating system software) is executed when an interrupt is detected, to establish its source. On a typical microcomputer, interrupts are used by the keyboard, mouse, disk and the COM ports.

Establishing the source of an interrupt

The source of the interrupt is determined by checking each IRQ line to see if it has been set. If more than one device has set its IRQ line, the handler routine will select the one with the highest priority. Once the source has been identified, the interrupt handler calls the relevant *interrupt service routine.* Following completion of the service, control of the processor must be returned to the original process. The checking of the processor's single I/O interrupt register is carried out at the start of each instruction, as part of the fetch-execute cycle.

Executing the interrupt

Before entry to the relevant interrupt service routine, the current state of the machine must be saved. This includes storing the state of the current process and the contents of the Program Counter (PC) in a separate location; the PC value is then replaced by the starting address of the interrupt service routine and the routine is executed. Once the interrupt has been serviced, control of the processor must be returned to the appropriate point in the original program by copying its stored continuation address back into the PC. An interrupt-on/off flag in the processor must be set to off prior to acceptance of an interrupt and then cleared to on as soon as control has been returned to the original program, in order to prevent an interrupt from another device being accepted until the original program has resumed control.

Interrupt priority

Interrupts may emanate from a variety of sources (I/O and others) and for a number of different reasons (Chapter 13 Operating Systems); the operating system can be used to allocate different priority ratings to particular events and devices.

Nested interrupts

Some systems may leave the interrupt mechanism enabled so that an interrupt service routine may itself be interrupted by a higher priority request; this may happen repeatedly, requiring the nesting of interrupts. A LIFO (Last In First Out) stack (see chapter on Data Structures) can be used to store the return addresses and accumulator contents relating to these nested interrupts so that they can be retrieved in reverse order. If a higher priority interrupt occurs during I/O there is a danger of data being lost. Each peripheral is allocated a given priority rating which must be compared with that of the current process, before the interrupt routine is entered. As a general rule, low speed devices are given high priority, because frequent interrupts to relatively slow data input may result in there being insufficient data to continue processing. Where the interrupting peripheral has a priority rating lower than or equal to that of the current activity, it is kept waiting; otherwise the interrupt takes place.

Masking device interrupts

Where the interrupt mechanism is left enabled, it may be desirable to selectively mask out certain low priority devices from that facility. This can be achieved by using a register as an interrupt mask (Table 14.1), with bit positions corresponding to individual devices in the interrupt request register; devices are masked out by setting the

	interrupt request register						
device	1	2	3	4	5	6	
interrupt status	1	0	1	1	0	1	AND
interrupt mask	1	0	0	0	0	1	
device	1	2	3	4	5	6	
interrupt status	1	0	0	0	0	1	

Table 14.1. *Masking device interrupts*

relevant bits in the mask to 0 and carrying out a logical AND operation between the mask and the interrupt request register.

With the current mask settings, only devices 1 and 6 are allowed to request interrupts.

A number of other system conditions, some with higher priority than I/O requests, may generate interrupts and these are examined in Chapter 13 on Operating Systems.

Direct memory access (DMA)

Not all data transfers between peripheral devices and the processor are carried out under continual program control (programmed input/output or PIO). Other schemes such as DMA allow data transfer to or from high speed storage devices such as tape or disk to be effected without continual processor control.

Data is transferred in blocks, as opposed to character by character. DMA is possible because of the ability of peripheral devices to operate autonomously, that is, after the initial input or output instruction has been given by the processor, the peripheral is able to complete the data transfer independently. To allow the memory to be accessed directly by a peripheral, instead of via the processor, hardware known as a DMA controller is needed. For transfers from main memory to peripheral, the processor supplies the DMA controller with the start address in memory of the data block to be transferred and its length. A transfer from, for example, a disk pack to memory would require the processor to tell the DMA controller the relevant disk address and into which memory locations the data is to be copied.

The DMA controller 'steals' memory cycles from the processor while the data transfer is taking place. Meanwhile, the processor can continue execution of its current program, although its operation is slowed slightly by the cycle stealing. Under these circumstances, DMA is not as quick as PIO, but is an essential component to any computer system working in multi-programming mode.

Recently, the use of 'bus mastering' processors has removed the need for cycle stealing, thereby allowing the main processor to continue work at its normal rate. For this reason, DMA is now widely used.

I/O interface standards

Centronics parallel interface

This interface has become a world-wide standard for parallel data transmission between computers and peripherals. It was originally developed by the American printer manufacturer Centronics, Inc. The Centronics parallel interface includes eight parallel data lines and additional lines for control and status information. The eight data lines are the minimum required for transmission of one complete character at a time; an ASCII coded character consists of 8 bits (including the parity bit). The control and status lines are needed for the 'conversation' between the device and the computer. For example, when a printer is on-line it sends a ready signal to the computer and when the computer is ready to send a character, it initialises the printer, which clears the printer's buffer memory. A character printer (ink jet or dot matrix, for example) has a small amount of memory called buffer memory, which it uses to temporarily store a line of characters, before they are printed. Laser printers, which print a complete page at a time, need sufficient buffer memory to store all the data (both text and graphics) on a page, before the page is printed. The signals and processes that enable printing through a Centronics interface are, briefly, as follow.

❑   Once the printer is on-line, it sends a ready signal to the computer.

❏   The computer sends a response, which initialises the printer; this has the effect of alerting the printer and clearing its small buffer memory.

❏   After the printer is initialised, the computer places the data bits (8), for the first character to be printed, on the data lines.

❏   The computer sends a strobe signal, which sends the 8 data bits, in parallel, to the printer's buffer memory.

❏   Once the data is received by the printer, it is acknowledged with an acknowledge signal to the computer.

The process continues, until the computer has no more characters to send. The printer may, at times, send a busy signal, if it is not ready for the next character; the computer then has to wait for the all clear, before sending the next character. A printer may also interrupt the process, if, for example, it is out of paper.

SCSI and IDE interfaces

SCSI stands for Small Computer Systems Interface. It is a high speed, parallel interface (or device controller) standard, defined by ANSI (American National Standards Institute). SCSI interfaces are widely available for connecting microcomputers to a range of peripheral devices, including hard disks and printers; SCSI interfaces are also used for connecting computers to one another, and to local area networks. Separate ports (a port is a location for passing data in or out of a computer) do not have to be used for each attached device. Instead one device can be connected directly to a SCSI port in the computer and other devices (a maximum total of seven) can be linked to the first, in a "daisy chain". Only one device can communicate through the SCSI port at any one time, so each device in a chain is given a separate logical address, which indicates its priority. The device with the highest address is given top priority. Macintosh computers and some computers in the IBM range include an SCSI port as standard.

PCs and 'compatibles' can be upgraded to include an SCSI port, with the use of an expansion card; this is necessary for the connection of a Jaz drive (see Chapter 9). The SCSI interface was of particular value for the attachment of high speed devices, such as hard disk drives, because it allowed more rapid data transfer than was the norm for the IDE (Industry Device Electronics) based hard drives, used in most PCs. The IDE interface has become most popular with PCs because it is cheaper and easier to install than the SCSI interface. IDE performance has now been increased to that of a SCSI interface. Newer standards, the Enhanced IDE and UDMA (Ultra Direct Memory Access) now provide *data transfer rates* which are superior to those of SCSI and similar to those of the new SCSI Wide.

Serial interfaces

Serial interfaces are used for the connection of modems, terminals and printers. Physically, they are recognisable by the shape of the plug and socket, which are D-shaped. The most common are the 9-pin and 25-pin.

RS232 and V24 serial interfaces

Both these standards (Chapter 11) relate to an interface for serial transmission between a computer or terminal and a modem. RS232 is a Recommended Standard (RS) of the American Electrical Industries Association (EIA). There have been 4 versions of this standard, the most recent being the RS232D (sometimes known as EIA 232D), although the previous version, RS232C is still the most widely used. The main purpose of the revision was to bring it into line with V24, which is the CCITT's equivalent of the RS232C. The V24 standard does not define the physical characteristics of the connection (the RS232 standard does), but only the characteristics of the control signals (see Flow Control) and how they are to be used; the V24 standard is usually used with the 25-pin D-connector. This connector is defined by the International Standards Organisation (ISO - see Chapter 11).

Other I/O techniques

Off-lining

Early computer systems used punched cards as the initial form of input and to speed processing a technique of off-lining was introduced. Data would be transferred from punched cards to magnetic tape under control of a separate processor. The operator could then place the magnetic tape file on-line, from where it could be accessed and processed by the application program. The hugely superior data transfer rate of magnetic tape radically improved processing times and went some way to countering the speed imbalance between the input device and the processor. The same technique was also applied to printed output, which could be directed to magnetic tape and then printed from there under control of a separate processor.

Buffering

Buffering is a technique which helps compensate for the speed differences between the processor and the various input and output devices which communicate with it. To speed processing, many computer systems contain special high-speed memory areas called buffers. An input buffer acts as a waiting area within memory for a block of data transferred from a peripheral; from there it can be quickly accessed and processed by the processor. An output buffer stores data which has been processed by the processor and is awaiting output. Most peripherals have the facility for autonomous operation, leaving the processor free for other tasks; buffering and the use of autonomous peripherals allows the simultaneous operation of several of the latter.

Double buffering

In the case of storage devices, double-buffering makes use of two buffers which work in 'tandem' to speed processing. If the records are blocked the systems software initially places the first block into buffer 1 and the second into buffer 2. Read instructions from the applications program retrieve the data from these buffers. The processor can retrieve logical records faster from the buffer than from tape. As soon as all logical records from buffer 1 have been processed, the reading process transfers to the logical records in buffer 2. Meanwhile, the next block on tape can be transferred into buffer 1 and so on. The principle is also used with peripherals in general, including input and output devices, to help redress the radical imbalance between the processor's speed and that of the device with which it is communicating. This imbalance is less significant in respect of storage devices, which have significantly faster data transfer rates than most input and output devices, particularly where direct memory access (DMA) - see earlier section, is employed.

Spooling (simultaneous peripheral operation on-line)

This is a development of the off-lining technique described earlier and is used to speed data throughput. Multi-programming (Chapter 13 Operating Systems) allows data to be transferred from slow peripherals to fast backing storage devices as a background process. The process is facilitated by autonomous peripherals which can carry out data transfers independently of the processor after it has initiated the read or write instruction.

Multiplexing

Multiplexing is a technique which enables inputs from several devices to be directed through one channel (also see Data Communications - Chapter 11) to a computer; the reverse process is known as de-multiplexing. A multiplexer normally has the facilities to carry out both operations. Figure 14.2 illustrates its principal function.

Figure 14.2. *Multiplexed terminals*

Asynchronous terminal multiplexer

Any multi-terminal computer system will include a local multiplexer to allow a number of terminals to use one interface to the computer. Apart from the benefit of removing the need for numerous separate physical interfaces, a multiplexer can support I/O devices with different data transfer rates.

A multiplexer has buffer registers for the temporary storage of characters before onward transmission, either to or from a connected device. In order to identify individual terminals, each one is given an individual address within the common interface. A multiplexer's operation is based on the realistic assumption that the data transfer rates from the various terminals will be well within the capacity of the computer's I/O interface. Typically, a single local multiplexer will support 16 terminals; even if, for example, each asynchronous (characters are sent at irregular intervals) terminal is transmitting continuously, with a transfer rate of 2400 bits per second (bps), then the resulting 38400 bps from the multiplexer to the interface would be well within the capacity of a typical minicomputer's bus transfer rate of one million bps. In practice, it is unlikely that all terminals would be transmitting continuously at that rate. In order to give attention to each of the transmitting terminals, the multiplexer may address each terminal in a round robin polling sequence. Each terminal is checked to see if there is a character waiting in its buffer and if there is, the character plus the terminal's line number are removed. Once an input character from a particular terminal has been dealt with, the multiplexer checks to see if there is a character to be output to that same terminal and if so the character is fetched from memory and output. The multiplexer then directs its attention to the next terminal in the sequence and repeats the process. The scanning process is implemented by hardware and is, therefore, very quick. Multiplexers can also operate synchronously, that is, transfer characters at a regularly-timed frequency.

BIOS (Basic Input Output System)

A computer system's BIOS holds details of what hardware is installed and settings for individual components. The settings are held in CMOS RAM. This is a special type of RAM, which can retains its contents with only a tiny amount of battery power - the battery is attached to the motherboard and recharged whenever the machine is switched on. The BIOS settings are used to control the *system start-up* and carry out diagnostic checks on the hardware.

System start-up

When a computer system is 'powered on' the BIOS starts the Power-On Self-Test (POST) routine. The POST routine is in two stages:

1. The *motherboard* (also known as the *system board*) and its components (processor, RAM etc.) are checked for their normal operation. The RAM test is visible on screen while it is being carried out.

2. The hardware actually installed is checked to see that it matches with the system's BIOS (Basic Input/Output System) settings.

If an error is identified, the system reports it, either with a 'beep' or an error message on screen. The POST sequence checks the hardware to see that the major components, including RAM, are present and working properly.

BIOS Setup utility

The BIOS Setup utility is held in ROM so that it is not lost when the machine is switched off. The program is used to enter details of the computer system's hardware, that is, the BIOS settings. When a computer is powered on and before the operating system starts to load, the operator has the opportunity to access the BIOS Setup utility, normally by pressing a designated key. Because settings entered through this program are then stored in CMOS RAM, the program menu includes the following two options: Standard CMOS setup; BIOS Features (or Advanced CMOS) setup.

Standard CMOS setup

Standard CMOS Setup is used to record details of the basic hardware in the computer system. The settings are recorded when the motherboard is installed, normally by the manufacturer. This is usually the first BIOS Setup menu option. An example of a Standard CMOS Setup screen is shown in Figure 14.3.

```
                    ROM PCI/ISA BIOS (P155 T2 P4)
                         STANDARD CMOS SETUP

    Date (mm:dd:yyyy) :  Fri, May 15 1998
    Time (hh:mm:ss)   :  8 : 23 : 4      2.5GB Hard Drive
    100MB ZIP Drive
    Hard Disks :       Type   Size  Cyls  Head  Precomp  LandZ  Sector  Mode

    Primary Master   : User   2560  620   128      0      4959    63    LBA
    Primary Slave    : User    100  512   12     65535     511    32    Normal
    Secondary Master: None      0    0     0       0        0      0
    Secondary Slave : None      0    0     0       0        0      0    _____

                          Floppy drive type
    Drive A : 1.44M, 3.5 in
    Drive B : None          Options
    Screen type             All but Keyboard      Base Memory     640K
    Video  : EGA/VGA        All but diskette      Extended Memory 130048K
    Halt on : All Errors    All but Diskette/Keyboard  Total memory  131072K

                                                            128MB RAM
    Esc : Quit
    F1 : Help       ↑↓ → ←  : Select Item   PU/PD/+/  :  Modify
```

Figure 14.3. *Example CMOS setup*

The exact settings will vary according to the computer hardware, but note the following details labelled in the figure.

❑   The Primary Master is the main hard disk drive inside the system unit and in this example, it has a capacity of 2·5 GB.

❑   The Primary Slave, in this example, is a 100MB Zip drive, which uses removable disk cartridges.

❑   There is only one floppy disk drive, designed for 1·44 MB floppy disks.

❑   The 'Halt on' setting specifies that any hardware error will cause the powering up sequence to stop, until the error is corrected. The only other options are to ignore keyboard and/or floppy disk errors. Failure of RAM or the hard disk drive, for example, would always halt the system.

❑   The RAM total is 128 MB.

The screen type is EGA or VGA, which are screen resolution standards. VGA is a minimum 800 × 600 resolution.

The Standard CMOS Settings option would only need to be used if:

(a)   the CMOS contents are corrupted or lost, perhaps through battery failure (as can happen if a machine is switched off for a long period). It is important that the settings are written down, so that if the contents are lost or corrupted, they can be re-entered. Without the correct settings, the machine may not work properly or at all;

or

(b)   the system configuration is altered, perhaps through replacement of the hard disk or installation of a new motherboard.

BIOS Features setup

This option is used to 'fine tune' the hardware configuration, to improve performance and to set certain user preferences. Figure 14.4 shows an example BIOS Features screen. Four features in the previous figure are labelled with comments:

❑   Boot sequence. Following a successful Power-On Self-Test (POST) routine, the BIOS loads the operating system, normally from the hard drive. The boot sequence dictates the order in which the BIOS checks the various disk drives to find the operating system. Setting the A: (floppy) drive as the first to be checked, allows for an emergency 'boot' if the operating system will not load from the hard drive. Windows 9x provides an option to create such a Startup Disk. To carry out the emergency boot, the Startup disk is placed in the floppy drive before the machine is powered up. As soon as the BIOS finds the Startup disk boots the system from there, rather than trying to load the operating system from the hard drive.

❑   Floppy disk access control. The default setting is R/W (read/write), but to prevent users copying files from the hard drive onto floppy disk, it may be set to RO (read only). This may be done for security reasons.

❑   Boot-up NumLock status. Setting the NumLock key to 'On' ensures that it is automatically on when the system is powered up. The keys on the numeric keypad then operate as such. If set to 'Off' the numeric keys have an alternate use as navigational keys (cursor left, right, page up and so on). Whatever the boot setting, the user can switch the NumLock key on or off as necessary.

❏ Security option. As the earlier warning point out, altering BIOS settings has to be carried out with great care and only by someone who knows what they are doing and has the authority to do it. This option allows a password to be set. If a user tries to access the BIOS Setup program during startup, he or she will be asked for the password.

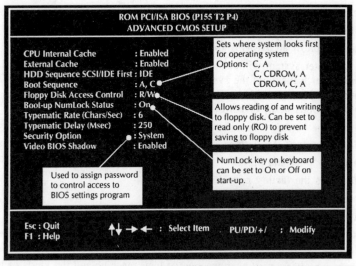

Figure 14.4. *Example BIOS Features setup*

Plug and Play BIOS

Plug and Play operating systems use a BIOS which is automatically updated when a new device is added. On a Windows 98 machine, the BIOS details then appear in the System Properties window, as shown in Figure 14.5.

The Device Manager tab lists all the categories of device attached to the computer system. In the figure, three of the items are expanded, to show details of the actual attached device:

Figure 14.5. *Windows 9x view of BIOS*

❏ The CD-ROM is identified as a TEAC CD-58E;

❏ The display adapter, or graphics card, is a Matrox Millennium;

❏ The monitor is identified as Plug and Play (VESA DDC). 'VESA' indicates that it meets the Video Electronics Standards Association requirements for monitors.

Once a new device, such as a disk drive, or extra RAM, has been connected, the BIOS detects it during the next startup. If the device is not Plug and Play compatible, the installation settings have to be made through the BIOS setup utility.

Exercises

1. Distinguish between *programmed input/output (PIO)* and *direct memory access (DMA)*.
2. What is the main disadvantage of *software polling* to control input/output?
3. What is the function of an *IRQ* line?
4. Define the following terms: *spooling*; *buffering*.
5. What is the function of an *asynchronous terminal multiplexer*?
6. Although a computer system without its operating system is of limited practical use, the various devices which make up the system will operate at a basic level. The BIOS (basic input output system) enables this basic operation. Access a machine's BIOS and note the settings for the various items of hardware.

   Draw up a machine hardware specification based on your findings.

   N.B. Do not alter any of the settings as this may prevent the machine from working.
7. What is meant by 'plug and play'?
8. What benefits does the facility provide for:
   (i)   non-specialist users?
   (ii) technical support staff?
9. Under what circumstances may an operating system be unable to use its plug and play facility?
10. Identify reasons why users may wish to upgrade their machine and the kinds of hardware they may wish to add.

Data processing

Chapters

Data processing

Chapters

Chapter 15

Computer Files

This chapter deals with the ways in which computer files are stored, organised and processed.

Files, records and fields

In data processing, it is necessary to store information on particular subjects, for example, customers, suppliers or personnel and such information needs to be structured so that it is readily controllable and accessible to the user. In traditional data processing systems, each of these 'topics' of information is allocated a file. Figure 15.1 illustrates the structure of a book file.

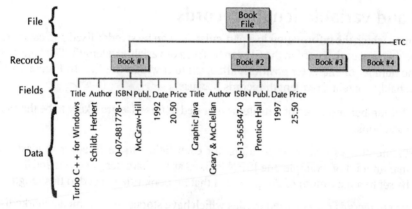

Figure 15.1. *Data file structure*

The *file* is a collection of *records*, one for each book. Each record contains details of the book's title, its author(s), ISBN number, publisher, date of publication and cost; each of these *data items* is allocated physical space, known as a *field*, within the record. Figure 15.1 shows a sample record, with the Title field (each one is identified by its *field name)* containing the value 'Turbo C++ for Windows' and the other fields containing values associated with that book.

Types of file

Files fall into one of four categories, according to use.

Master files

They are used for the storage of *permanent*, or *semi-permanent*, data which is used in applications such as stock, sales or payroll. Some of the fields tend to contain data which is fairly static, for example, customer name and address, whilst data in some fields is continually changing, for example, customer balance, as transactions are applied to the file. Such *updating* is carried out, either through the direct entry (on-line) of individual transactions, or from an accumulated set of entries stored on a *transaction* file.

Transaction files

These are transient and only exist to allow the updating of master files. Each transaction record contains the *key field value* of the master record it is to update (to allow correct matching with its relevant master record), together with data gathered from source documents, for example, invoice amounts which update the balance field in customer accounts.

Reference files

These contain data used for reference or look-up purposes, such as price catalogue and customer name and address files.

Archival or historical files

These contain data which, for legal or organisational reasons, must be kept and tend to be used on an ad hoc basis and may be referred to only occasionally.

Fixed and variable length records

The extent to which the information in a particular file can be standardised and categorised will determine whether each record in the file can be fixed or variable in length. The length of the record is the number of character positions allocated to it within the file. In Figure 15.1 the file would probably contain *fixed* length records because:

❑ the number and types of data items required in this case are likely to be the same for each book;

❑ the number of character positions for each field can be fixed or at least set to a maximum. For example, the ISBN is fixed at 13 character positions and Title could be set to a maximum of 30, provided that no book title exceeded this length.

Variable length records may be used in files which have storage requirements markedly different from those referred to above, for instance:

❑ some records could have more fields than others. In a personnel file, for example, each record may contain details of previous jobs held and as the number of previous jobs may vary considerably from one employee to another, so the number of fields would be similarly varied;

or

❑ the number of character positions used for individual values within a field is variable. For example, in a library system each record may contain a field for data which describes the subject of the book and the amount of text needed to adequately describe this may vary from book to book.

Listed below are some of the advantages of *fixed length* records.

❑ Fixed length records are simpler to process, in that the start and end points of each record can be readily identified by the number of character positions. For instance, if a record has a fixed length of 80 character positions, a program reading the file from the start will assume that the second record starts at the 81st character position, the third at the 161st character position and so on, making easier the programming of file handling operations.

❏   Fixed length records allow an accurate estimation of file storage requirements. For example, a file containing 1000 records, each of fixed 80 characters length, will take approximately 80000 characters of storage.

❏   Where direct access files are being used, fixed length records can be readily updated 'in situ' (in other words the updated record overwrites the old version in the same position on the storage medium). As the new version will have the same number of characters as the old, any changes to a record will not change its physical length. On the other hand, a variable length record may increase in length after updating, preventing its return to its home location.

There are some instances when *variable* length records are more appropriate. For example:

❏   where records in a file contain highly variable quantities of information, variable length records may be more economical of storage space;

❏   when the saving in storage space makes the introduction of more complex file handling techniques worthwhile.

Record identification - primary and secondary keys

In most organisations, when an information system is operational it will be necessary to identify each record uniquely. In a Personnel File, for example, it might be thought that it is possible to identify each individual record simply by the employee's Surname and this would be satisfactory as long as no two employees had the same surname. In reality, many organisations will have several employees with the same surnames, so to ensure uniqueness, each employee is assigned a unique Works Number. The works number field is then used as the primary key in the filing system, each individual having his or her own unique Works Number and so a unique primary key.

There are certain circumstances when the primary key may be a *composite key*, that is, one made up of more than one field and the following example shows how a pair of fields, which individually may not be unique, can be combined to provide a unique identifier.

Table 15.1 shows an extract from a file which details suppliers' quotations for a number of different products. There is a need for a composite key because there may be a number of quotations from one

SupplierNo	PartNo	Price	DeliveryDate
23783	A361	2.59	31/01/96
37463	B452	1.50	29/01/96
40923	A112	3.29	30/01/96
41192	A112	3.29	28/01/96
41192	C345	2.15	30/01/96

Table 15.1. *Extract from quotation file with composite primary key*

supplier (in this case, SupplierNo 41192) and a number of quotations for the same part (in this instance, PartNo A112). It is necessary, therefore, to use both SupplierNo and PartNo to identify one quotation record uniquely.

Uniqueness is not always necessary. For example, if it is required to retrieve records which fulfil a criterion, or several criteria, *secondary keys* may be used. Thus, for example, in an information retrieval system on Personnel, the secondary key Department may be used to retrieve the records of all employees who work in, say, the Sales Department.

File storage media

This topic is examined more fully in Chapter 9. File storage media may be classified according to the kind of access they provide:

❑ serial access;

❑ direct access.

Serial access media

Serial access means that in order to identify and retrieve a particular record, it is necessary to 'read' all the records which precede it in the relevant file. The standard medium for serial access is magnetic tape. One of the difficulties with this medium is that there it has no readily identifiable physical areas which can be addressed. In other words, it is not possible to give a name or code and refer this to a particular location. It is said to be *non-addressable*. To find an individual record, the software needs to examine each record's *key field*, starting from the beginning of the file, until the required record is found.

Direct access media

Storage media such as floppy or hard disks allow *direct* access to individual records, without reference to the rest of the relevant file. They have physical divisions which can be identified by computer software (and sometimes hardware) and are *addressable*, so that particular locations can be referred to by a name or code to retrieve a record which is stored at that location. Retrieval of an individual record stored on such a medium is achieved (depending on the way the file is organised) by specifying the relevant *primary key field value*, thus providing the software with a means of finding and retrieving the specific individual record directly.

File organisation methods

Another function of the *primary key* is to provide a value which can be used by computer software to assign a record to a particular position within a file. The file organisation method chosen will dictate how individual records are assigned to particular *logical* positions within a file. Serial access media are limited in the file organisation methods they permit because they are non-addressable. Direct access media are more versatile in that they allow a variety of file organisation methods, in addition to those allowed by serial access media. The different types of file storage media are discussed in some detail in the next section.

Magnetic tape - a serial access medium

Physical and logical records

Because of the physical characteristics of magnetic tape it is necessary, when processing a file, that the tape unit (the device onto which a tape is loaded for processing) starts to read the tape at the beginning of the reel. The take-up spool receives the tape from the feed spool via a read/write head in the unit which can either record information onto or read information from the tape as it passes. As there are no specific physical locations on the tape which can be identified and referred to by the computer (except of course the beginning and end), the only way it can find a particular record is by reading the whole file. Unless the whole tape is to be processed, it may only be necessary to read up to the point where the specific record it is seeking is found. There may well be more than one logical file on a tape but these will have to be read in the sequence that they appear on the tape. As the tape is read, the computer will compare the key field value of each record which it comes to, with the specified key value, until the required record is found. Figure 15.2 illustrates the way in which a file is arranged on tape both *logically* and *physically*.

Figure 15.2. *Magnetic tape file organisation*

You should note from Figure 15.2 that records R1, R2, R3 and R4 are instances of logical records. For example, if this were a stock file, each logical record would relate to one commodity held in stock. On the other hand each physical record consists, in this illustration, of 4 logical records. The reason for making the distinction between logical and physical records stems from the fact that data is transferred between the computer's internal memory and the tape storage medium in manageable *blocks*, the optimum size of each depending on factors such as the size of the computer's internal memory.

Each physical record is referred to as a block of data. Between each block transfer, the tape has to stop while the previous one is processed by the computer. In order to give the tape time to stop and then restart for the next block, there is an *inter block gap* (IBG), a blank area of tape between each block. It is unlikely that the optimum block size will coincide with the actual length of a single logical record, so it is necessary to transfer a number of logical records between tape and internal memory at one time. Thus, a physical record or block will often consist of a number of logical records.

The example of a stock file is used again to illustrate this point further. Assume that each block contains 3 logical stock records (in other words three individual commodities). If the first record to be processed is stored in the fifth block, then the first four blocks have to be read in sequence into memory and each logical stock record examined for its key field value, without any records actually being used. When the fifth block is eventually read into memory each of the three logical stock records is then examined for its key field value until the required key and thus logical record, is identified.

File organisation methods on magnetic tape

There are two ways in which a file can be organised on tape: *serially*; *sequentially*.

This restriction stems from the fact that magnetic tape is a *serial* access medium. As is noted earlier, this means that it has no addressable locations, so records have to be traced by reading the file from beginning to end.

The processing of tape files can only be carried out satisfactorily if they are organised in the sequence of their primary keys. This restriction applies to both master and transaction files. Serial files, which are out of sequence, are only useful as an interim measure, prior to processing.

Generally, when a transaction file is being created on tape, for example, when customer orders are received, they are written to tape in the order in which they are received, thus creating a serial file. Before the master file can be updated, the serial transaction file has to be sorted by the computer to become a sequential file.

Updating the master file

When a tape file is updated, a new master file must be created on a new reel of tape because the tape drive unit cannot guarantee to write an updated record to the exact position from which it was read (it is *non-addressable*). There is a danger, therefore, of adjacent records being corrupted or completely overwritten.

The following procedures are followed during the update (assuming that no new records are to be inserted). For the sake of clarity, some complexities are not mentioned.

❑   A transaction is read into memory.

❑   A master record is read into memory. If the record keys do not match, the master record is written, unchanged, to the new reel. Master records continue to be read, examined and written in the original sequence to the new reel until a match for the transaction is found.

❑   Once the match is found, the master record is updated in main memory and then written to the new reel.

These steps are repeated until all transactions have been processed and the complete updated master file has been written to the new reel. If the transaction files were not sorted into the same sequence as the master file, it would be necessary to rewind the master file whenever a transaction required a master record which had already passed through the system; clearly, this would be both inefficient and impractical. The process is illustrated in the chapter on System Controls.

Magnetic disk - a direct access medium

Addressing magnetic disk

Magnetic disk provides file storage facilities which are more flexible and powerful than those provided by magnetic tape. As an *addressable* medium, the surface of the disk is divided into physical locations which are illustrated in Figure 15.3. The address of any one physical location on a single disk incorporates a *track* number, and within that track, a *sector* number. A sector is the smallest physical area on the disk which can be

Figure 15.3. *Magnetic disk address structure*

addressed, each addressable unit being referred to as a *block* or *physical record*. The size of the blocks is normally determined by the systems designer through the use of systems software, although some disk storage systems use *hard sectoring* (the block size cannot be altered). The number of logical records which can be accommodated in a particular block obviously depends upon the physical size of the block and the length of each logical record. The maximum number of logical records which can be fitted into a block is known as the *blocking factor*. Considerations regarding the determination of block size are beyond the scope of this text, but some of the design factors can be readily explained as follows.

Example

If a disk's block size approximates to the storage of 500 characters and a stock file has logical records, each with a fixed length of 110 characters, then the maximum number of records which can be stored in a block is 4. To retrieve one logical stock record requires the software to address the relevant block and retrieve the physical record. This means that it will retrieve all the logical stock records in the block. Therefore, the larger the number of logical records stored in any specific block, the less selective the software can be in retrieving them but the faster the complete file is processed.

Operational features of magnetic disk

Although there are many variations in the capacities and sizes of disk that are available, there are certain physical characteristics which are common to all. A computer's hard drive comprises a number of disks may be mounted on a central spindle (Figure 15.4.).

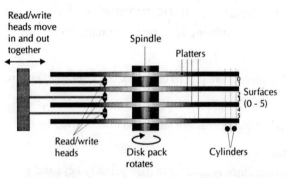

Figure 15.4 *Disk pack illustrating cylinder concept*

To transfer data to or from the disk pack it is necessary to mount it on a disk drive unit which rotates the pack at high speed. Data is recorded magnetically on disk in a similar fashion to the recording on magnetic tape. Special read/write heads are mounted on moveable arms within the disk drive unit in such a way that they move in synchronisation across the disk surface. The software positions the heads for the writing or retrieval of records.

Further disk addressing concepts

Cylinders

Considering Figures 15.3 and 15.4 together it can be seen that, in a disk pack, a specified track on one disk (track 0) is vertically above other tracks on lower disks which are also specified as track 0. In other words, all the track 0s are in the same vertical plane. Such a grouping is known as a *cylinder* or *seek area*. Similarly, all track 1s form another cylinder, as do track 2s and so on. It can be seen therefore, that there are as many cylinders as there are tracks on each disk surface.

The fastest way of reading or writing records on disks is achieved by minimising the movement of the read/write arms. This is achieved by positioning associated records, which are likely to be needed as a group (they may form a complete file), into sequence (as a sequential file) on tracks in the same cylinder. Records are written to the disk pack, such that track 0 on surface 1 is filled first, followed by track 0 on surface 2 and so on, until all number 0 tracks are filled (the first cylinder). Then, if the file requires more than one cylinder, adjacent tracks are filled to form further cylinders, until the file is complete.

When access is required to the file it is quickest, in terms of keeping read/write head movement to a minimum, to deal with one cylinder of records at a time. Thus, a complete cylinder of records is processed before any head movement is required. A cylinder is also known as a seek area, because all records in a cylinder can be accessed by the read/write heads whilst they are positioned in that cylinder.

Buckets

The minimum amount of data which can be transferred between the backing store of the computer and its internal store is the *block*. However, there are occasions when a larger unit of transfer is required and on such occasions the concept of the *bucket* is used; a number of blocks (up to the maximum of one track) is given the same disk address (this is usually the address of the first block in the bucket) and any logical records held within such a bucket are retrieved when that disk address is used.

File organisation methods using magnetic disk

Magnetic disk supports the following file organisation methods.

Serial

As for a serial tape file, records are placed onto disk one after another in no particular sequence.

Sequential

As for a sequential tape file, records are stored on disk ordered by each record's primary key.

Indexed sequential

Records are stored in sequence according to their primary keys and an *index* is produced when the file is created, allowing direct retrieval of individual records. The software searches different levels of the index (a *multi-level index*):

❑ cylinder index;

❑ track index;

❑ bucket (or block index), before positioning the read/write heads to retrieve the block containing the required record.

The indexes may be structured as shown in Table 15.2, using a five-digit primary key in the range 00001 to 50000. The table represents an extract only.

Cylinder index		Track index for cylinder 55		Sector/block index for track 3	
cylinder	highest key	track	highest key	sector	highest key
1	00452	1	26000	1	26071
2	00940	2	26063	2	26076
3	01650	3	*26120*	3	26080
.....	.....	4	26185	4	26087
55	*26500*	5	26242	5	26095
56	27015	6	26320	6	26104
.....	.....	7	26426	7	26112
115	50000	8	*26500*	8	*26120*

Table 15.2. *Extract from multi-level index*

The indexes are constructed as the records are written sequentially (according to the primary key) to the disk pack. As each sector is filled, the primary key of the last record to be placed in the sector (the highest key) is recorded in the *sector index* and once all sectors in a track have been filled, the last key to be entered is added to the *track index*, the completion of a cylinder causing the highest key field in it to be recorded in the *cylinder index*. This process is repeated with subsequent cylinders until the file is complete.

The retrieval of records requires a *serial search* to be made of the cylinder, track and sector indexes respectively, unless a complete track is to be read, in which case the sector index is not used. Referring to the Table 15.2, suppose that the record with primary key 26085 is required; the indexes may be used as follows:

❑   a serial search of the cylinder index is made until a highest key entry is found which is equal to or greater than the required key. The entry which meets this requirement is 26500, indicating that a search of the track index for cylinder 55 is needed;

❑   a serial search of that track index, again looking for an entry greater than or equal to record key 26085, reveals that the record is to be found in track 3, where the highest key field is 26120;

❑   searching the sector index for track 3 returns the entry of 26087, the highest key field entry for sector 4.

Unless record 26085 has been placed in an *overflow area*, owing to a full sector, it can be retrieved by reading in the block of data occupying the address - sector 4, track 3, cylinder 55.

The cylinder index for a given file will normally be read into main memory when the file is first opened and held there until processing is complete. Each track index is normally held in the cylinder to which it relates and will be read into main memory as required. Similarly, the sector index is usually held within its relevant track.

The preceding procedures and mechanisms only illustrate the main principles of index construction and usage, as the detail is likely to vary considerably from one system to another. To facilitate updating, space will normally be left in sectors, tracks and cylinders to allow for the insertion of new records.

This method allows the efficient sequential processing of the file as well as direct retrieval of records using the indexes. Indexes can become quite large and the file may need to be re-organised periodically so that new records can be inserted in the correct sequence. Records which are marked for deletion need to be removed from the file and the indexes then have to be reconstructed. The frequency with which such re-organisation is necessary depends on the level of file activity and the number of insertions and deletions. File re-organisation is a *house-keeping* activity.

Overflow

Where new records, or variable length records which have been extended by updating, cannot be inserted into their correct sequenced positions, they are assigned to overflow areas.

Local overflow areas include any located within the same cylinder as their associated home locations; thus, local overflow areas may be located within each track or sector of a cylinder, or at the end of the cylinder. These overflow areas have the advantage that access to them requires no head movement and therefore, no increase in seek time.

Global overflow areas may be formed from a separate cylinder or cylinders and will tend to be used when local overflow areas are full. The main disadvantage is that access to an overflow record requires additional head movement.

A file may use either local or global overflow areas, or a combination of the two; the use of global overflow only, tends to be less wasteful of space but with the disadvantage that the retrieval of any overflow record will require additional head movement. If frequent reference is required to overflow records, *performance degradation* (a worsening of the system's response times) is likely to be noted by users and file re-organisation will be beneficial.

Random organisation

This is a method which is impractical in any non-computerised situation. However, in a computerised system it is feasible to place records onto disk at random. The procedure for placing specific records in a particular position on disk may simply relate the primary key *directly* to its disk address, for example,

> *disk address = primary key*
>
> *disk address = primary key + index value*

With *absolute* and *indexed addressing*, each record has a unique address and can be retrieved directly with its own primary key. A major disadvantage of this method is its orientation towards the needs of the computer; the values needed for disk addressing may well be inappropriate for use as meaningful (to the user) primary keys for logical records. Further, the unique link between a disk address and a particular logical record means that any vacated space cannot be used by another record unless it adopts the same key as the previous occupant record.

Hashing algorithms

A more usual method of addressing uses a mathematical formula called a *hashing algorithm*, which generates a disk address from the record's primary key. The hashing algorithm operates on the primary keys within a given range to produce pseudo-random numbers which may then be used as bucket addresses, to which the logical records are allocated. Each pseudo-random number could refer to an address where a single record is stored, but it is more economical for it to refer to an area where a group of records is stored; thus a *bucket address* will normally contain a number of logical records.

Overflow

An uneven distribution of records means that some buckets overflow and cannot accommodate all the logical records allocated to them, whilst others remain empty or are seriously under-used. Excessive overflow slows the access time for any record which cannot be allocated to its home address. To achieve a reasonably even spread, the selection of a particular algorithm requires consideration of the following factors:

- ❑ the pattern and range of the primary keys within the file;
- ❑ the size of each bucket and the number available;
- ❑ the *packing density* required (number of records, divided by the total record capacity of the available buckets).

The topics of bucket size and packing density are dealt with in more detail in the section on overflow handling.

Example algorithm

Prime number division. The primary key is divided by the largest prime number which is less than the number of available buckets. The remainder of this calculation is taken as the *relative* bucket number, that is, the number of buckets after the first. For example:

> *available buckets 2000*
>
> *prime number 1999*
>
> *primary key 22316*
>
> *22316/1999 = 11 remainder 327*

The relative bucket number is thus 327.

The same mathematical formula is used to subsequently retrieve records, which is ideal in situations where random enquiries are the norm and there is little need for sequential processing. Randomly organised files can be processed sequentially but with less efficiency than sequentially organised files. An advantage of this method is the lack of large indexes which tend to take up considerable storage space on the disk.

The aim of any randomising or hashing algorithm is to achieve an even distribution of records over the disk space allocated to a file. Most random files allow more than one logical record to occupy a single bucket, as any given algorithm will normally generate the same disk address from several different primary keys; conversely, any hashing algorithm is likely to leave some buckets with no allocated records. Any record which is stored in the address allocated to it by an algorithm is referred to as a *home record*.

Synonyms and collisions

If an address can only hold one record, the first one to be allocated to it, then subsequent records have to be stored elsewhere; such records are referred to as *synonyms* and the circumstances causing their re-allocation, as *collisions*. Synonyms increase access times for affected records, so one aim of an algorithm is to minimise their occurrence. Other factors to be considered by the file designer include, *bucket size* and *packing density* (see previous section). A large bucket size (the maximum is one track) will obviously reduce the number of synonyms, but at the cost of reduced precision in the retrieval of individual logical records. It is fairly unlikely that, in a random file, more than one logical record from the same bucket will be required at the same time, so a number of records are read unnecessarily. In deciding on the packing density (the percentage of the file space occupied) for any particular file, the designer has to consider the *volatility* or activity of the file. It is generally recognised that 50 per cent is probably the minimum packing density and is appropriate only for highly volatile files where a large number of record additions is likely; most files are designed to be 75 to 80 per cent packed when they are set up. A low packing density will further reduce the likelihood of synonyms, but at a cost of increased storage space.

Overflow handling techniques

As can be seen from the previous sections, overflow is a problem encountered with both indexed sequential and random files. There are three methods of tracking the location of overflow records: progressive overflow; chaining; tagging.

Progressive overflow

This is the most simplistic method, in that synonyms are placed in the next available bucket following their home bucket; there are no pointers from home buckets to the appropriate overflow locations. Retrieval of an overflow record requires a serial search of buckets following the home bucket, such simplicity bringing the disadvantage that a request for a non-existent record would not be rejected until the whole file had been searched. Further, if a record is deleted from its home area, a search has to be made to discover if any synonyms of that record exist and if one is found, it must be placed in the vacant home area; if this is not done, and the area is left vacant, it will appear that no synonyms for that address exist.

Chaining

A chain is a data structure which enables items to be accessed by a series of *pointers* leading from the first in the chain, to the second, to the third and so on until the last one is reached. A *link field* in each chained record provides the necessary pointer. Thus, once a bucket is full, the last record to be placed in it is chained to the next record to be assigned to that bucket - the first synonym; each subsequent synonym is linked to its predecessor. Chained overflow records may be held in a separate overflow area, or more efficiently, in the next available bucket. This method combines the benefits of progressive overflow with those of chaining. The main disadvantages of progressive overflow, described in the previous paragraph, are thus removed. Greater efficiency can be obtained by ensuring that chain lengths are kept to a minimum; this can be effected by moving synonyms into home buckets as and when vacancies occur through deletions. Figure 15.5 illustrates the chaining technique.

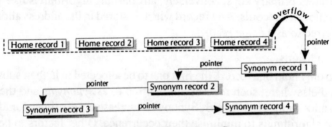

Figure 15.5. *Chained overflow*

Removing and adding synonyms to a chain requires the adjustment of pointers, a process described in the chapter on Data Structures.

Tagging

This method ensures that each synonym can be accessed directly after reference to its home bucket, the address of each overflow record being directly referenced or tagged from its home bucket. The technique is illustrated in the Figure 15.6.

Figure 15.6. *Tagged overflow*

The maintenance of tags in home buckets takes up space, so the number of synonyms should be kept to a minimum. Performance degradation is likely to be minimised with tagging, the most effective of the overflow tracing techniques.

Accessing disk files

Serial files

As with magnetic tape, the only way to retrieve records is serially, in other words, one after another.

Sequential files

The addressing features of disk are not used and the method is the same as that for sequential tape files.

Indexed sequential files

There are 3 methods of retrieving such records:

❑ *sequentially*. Transactions are sorted into the same sequence as the master file. This is suitable when a large proportion of the records in the file are to be processed in one run, that is, when the *hit rate* (the percentage of master records in a file, for which there are transactions) is high. Minimal use is made of the index. The cylinder index and track index may be searched, then the whole track is read into memory, sector by sector, without reference to the sector index;

❑ *selective* or *skip sequentially*. When records are sequentially organised by key, not every record need be read when scanning the file. The transactions are sorted into master file sequence and the indexes are used, so that only those blocks containing master records for which there is a transaction are read into memory. This is suitable when the hit rate is low;

❑ *randomly*. Transactions are not sorted. They are processed in the order in which they occur, the indexes being used to find the relevant master records as they are required. The read/write heads have to move back and forth through the file and so head movement is greater than with sequential methods of processing. This method is appropriate when records are updated immediately after the transaction occurs or, for example, when there is a need for random enquiries of a stock file.

Random files

Transactions or enquiries need not be in any logical sequence. Records are retrieved by generating the physical address from the record key. The software uses the same hashing algorithm it used to assign the record to its address in the first place.

Choice of organisation method and storage medium

Choice should be based on the type and purpose of the system to be used. For example, an on-line enquiry system or stock control system needing frequent, rapid, direct access to individual records within large files will best be served by a randomly organised file, using hash addressing. Very large files, of an archival nature are probably best held off-line on magnetic tape; the medium's lack of an addressing facility would necessitate such files being maintained sequentially. It may be reasonable to hold sections of such archival data, those which are most in demand, on magnetic disk and organised as indexed sequential files. An illustration of this is provided by the Police National Computer system, which holds more recent data on magnetic disk, with older files held on magnetic tape. Systems which do not require direct access, for example, monthly payroll files, can be efficiently stored and processed on magnetic tape and even if the computer system only has disk storage, sequential organisation is still likely to be the chosen method. Applications which require both sequential and direct access are generally best served by indexed sequential files.

Typically, the only files which are held serially, are temporary files, such as transaction files prior to sorting for a sequential update run.

✍️Exercises

1. Distinguish between *master, transaction, reference* and *archival* files.
2. Using a suitable example, illustrate the meaning of the terms: *data; field; record; file.*
3. With the aid of an example, explain when records are likely to be of *variable,* rather than *fixed* length.
4. Using examples, distinguish between the terms *primary key* and *secondary key.*
5. Why are the *logical records* in a sequential file, usually grouped into *blocks?*
6. Why must a *transaction file*, stored on magnetic tape, be *sorted* before it can update the master file? What will determine its sequence?
7. Define the term *blocking factor.*
8. Distinguish between *block* and *bucket.*
9. (i) What is a disk *cylinder?*
   (ii) Why is a *sequential disk file* stored cylinder by cylinder?
10. An indexed sequential file consists of a *multi-level index, home* area and *overflow* areas.
    (i) What *index levels* may exist and what would they contain?
    (ii) Briefly explain how a *new record* would be *inserted* into this file; your explanation should allow for there being no room for the record in its home location.
    (iii) Apart from new records, under what other circumstances may overflow handling be necessary?
    (iv) What housekeeping routine would be needed if numerous records had to be placed outside their home areas.
    (v) Distinguish between *local* and *global overflow.*
11. In the context of *random* file organisation:
    (i) Explain, with the aid of an example, the term *hashing algorithm.*
    (ii) A hashing algorithm should have two main aims. What are they?
    (iii) Define the terms *synonyms* and *collisions.*
12. Compare and contrast the following methods of overflow handling: *progressive; chaining; tagged,* pointing out their comparative benefits and drawbacks.

Chapter 16

Processing Methods

Data handling systems make use of one or more processing methods, depending on the requirements of the application. The methods can be categorised according to the ways in which data is controlled, stored and passed through the system; the major categories are: *batch* processing; *on-line* processing, which includes *real-time* and *time-share* processing; *distributed* processing and *centralised* processing; *database* systems (a separate chapter is devoted to this topic). To allow particular methods of processing a computer must have the necessary *operating system* software (Chapter 13); thus any particular computer system is equipped with, for example, a batch processing or real-time operating system, or even a combination of types, depending on the needs of the user organisation.

Batch processing

Such systems process *batches* of data at regular intervals. The data is usually in large volumes and of identical type. Examples of such data are customer orders, current weekly payroll details and stock issues or receipts. The procedure can be illustrated with the example of payroll, which is a typical application for batch processing. Each pay date, whether it is every week or every month, the payroll details, such as hours worked, overtime earned or sickness days claimed, are gathered for each employee (these details are referred to as *transactions*) and processed in batches against the payroll *master file*. The computer then produces payslips for all employees in the company. A major feature of this and similar applications is that a large percentage of the payroll records in the master file are processed during the payroll 'run'. This percentage is known as the *hit rate*. Generally, high hit rate processing is suitable for batch processing and if, as is usual, the master file is organised sequentially, then the *transaction file* will be sorted into the same sequence as the master file. In the case of magnetic tape, transactions must be sorted because the medium only allows *serial* (one record after another in their physical order) access.

The batch processing method closely resembles manual methods of data handling, in that transactions are collected together into batches, sent to the computer centre, sorted into the order of the master file and processed. Such systems are known as traditional data processing systems. There is normally an intermediate stage in the process when the data must be encoded using a *key-to-tape* or *key-to-disk* system.

A disadvantage of batch processing is the delay, often of hours or days, between collecting the transactions and receiving the results of processing and this has to be remembered when an organisation is considering whether batch processing is suitable for a particular application. Conversely, batch processing has the advantage of providing many opportunities for controlling the accuracy of data (Chapter 17) and thus is commonly used when the immediate updating of files is not crucial.

On-line processing systems

If a peripheral, such as a Visual Display Unit or keyboard, is *on-line*, it is under the control of the computer's processor or Central Processing Unit (CPU). On-line processing systems therefore, are those where all peripherals in use are connected to the CPU of the main computer. Transactions can be keyed in directly. The main advantage of an on-line system is the reduction in time between the collection and processing of data. There are two main methods of on-line processing: *real-time* processing; *time-share* processing.

Real-time processing

Process control in real-time

Real-time processing originally referred only to process control systems where, for example, the temperature of a gas furnace is monitored and controlled by a computer. The computer, through an appropriate sensing device, responds immediately to the boiler's variations outside pre-set temperature limits, by switching the boiler on and off to keep the temperature within those limits.

Real-time processing is now used in everyday consumer goods, such as video cameras, because of the development of the 'computer on a chip', more properly called the *microprocessor*. An important example of the use of the microprocessor is the engine management system, which is now standard on an increasing range of cars. A car's engine performance can be monitored and controlled, by sensing and immediately responding to, changes in such factors as air temperature, ignition timing or engine load. Microprocessors dedicated to particular functions are referred to as *embedded systems*. Further examples of the use of microprocessors can be found on the automated production lines of engineering works and car plants, where operations requiring fine engineering control can be carried out by *computer numerical controlled* (CNC) machines. The important feature common to all real-time applications is that the speed of the computer allows almost immediate response to external changes.

Information processing in real-time

To be acceptable as a real-time information processing system, the *response-time* (that is the time between the entry of a transaction or enquiry at a VDU terminal, the processing of the data and the computer's response) must meet the needs of the user. The delay or response time may vary from a fraction of a second to 2-3 seconds depending on the nature of the transaction and the size of the computer. Any delay beyond these times would generally be unacceptable and would indicate the need for the system to be updated. There are two types of information processing systems which can be operated in real-time: *transaction processing*; *information storage and retrieval*.

Transaction processing

This type of system handles clearly defined transactions one at a time, each transaction being processed completely, including the updating of files, before the next transaction is dealt with. The amount of data input for each transaction is small and is usually entered on an *interactive* basis through a VDU. In this way, the user can enter queries through the keyboard and receive a response, or the computer can display a prompt on the screen to which the user responds. Such 'conversations' are usually heavily structured and in a fixed format and so do not allow users to ask any question they wish. A typical example of transaction processing is provided by an *airline booking system* and the following may describe a client's enquiry for a seat reservation.

(i)   A prospective passenger provides the booking clerk with information regarding his/her flight requirements.

(ii)   Following prompts on a screen, the clerk keys the details into the system, so that a check can be made on the availability of seats.

(iii)   Vacancies appear on the screen and the client can confirm the booking.

(iv)   Confirmation of the reservation is keyed into the system, usually by a single key stroke and the flight seating records are immediately updated.

(v)   Passenger details (such as name, address, etc.) can now be entered.

Such a system needs to be real-time to enable reservations to be made at once, while the client is there (or on the telephone) and so that the seating records accurately reflect availability at all times.

Information storage and retrieval

This type of system differs from transaction processing in that, although the information is updated in real-time, the number of updates and the number of sources of updating is relatively small. Consider, for example, the medical records system in a hospital. A record is maintained for each patient currently undergoing treatment in the hospital. Medical staff require the patient's medical history to be available at any time and the system must also have a facility for entering new information as the patient undergoes treatment in hospital. Sources of information are likely to include a doctor, nurses and perhaps a surgeon, and new entries probably do not number more than one or two per day. This is an entirely different situation from an airline booking system where the number of entries for one flight record may be 200-300 and they could be made from many different booking offices throughout the world.

Time-share processing

The term *time sharing* refers to the activity of the computer's processor in allocating *time-slices* to a number of users who are given access through terminals to centralised computer resources. The aim of the system is to give each user a good *response time*. These systems are commonly used where a number of users require computer time for different information processing tasks. The processor time-slices are allocated and controlled by a time-share operating system. The CPU is able to operate at such speed that, provided the system is not overloaded by too many users, each user has the impression that he or she is the sole user of the system.

A particular computer system will be designed to support a maximum number of user terminals. If the number is exceeded or the applications being run on the system are 'heavy' on CPU time the response time will become lengthy and unacceptable. Time-share systems are possible because of the extreme speed of the CPU in comparison with peripheral devices such as keyboards, VDU screens and printers. Most information processing tasks consist largely of input and output operations which do not occupy the CPU, leaving it free to do any processing required on other users tasks.

Distributed processing

As the term suggests, a distributed processing system is one which spreads the processing tasks of an organisation across several computer systems; frequently, these systems are connected and *share resources* (this may relate to common access to files or programs, or even the processing of a single complex task) through a data communications system (Chapter 11). Each computer system in the network must be able to process independently, so a central computer with a number of remote intelligent terminals cannot be classified as distributed, even though some limited validation of data may be carried out separately from the main computer. Examples of distributed systems include mini or mainframe computers interconnected by way of *wide area networks*, or a number of *local area networks* similarly linked.

Distributed systems provide a number of benefits:

❑ *Economy*. The transmission of data over telecommunications systems can be costly and local database storage and processing facilities can reduce costs. The radical reduction in computer hardware costs has favoured the expansion of distributed systems against centralised systems.

❑ *Minicomputers and microcomputers*. The availability of minicomputer and microcomputer systems with data transmission facilities has made distributed processing economically viable. An increasingly popular option, in large multi-sited organisations, is to set up local area networks of microcomputers at each site and connect them through communications networks to each other and/or to a central mainframe computer at the Head Office. This provides each site with the advantages of local processing power, local and inter-site communications through *electronic mail* (Chapters 11 and 38) and access to a central mainframe for the main filing and database systems.

❑ *Local management control*. It is not always convenient, particularly where an organisation controls diverse activities, to have all information processing centralised. Local management control means that the information systems will be developed by people with direct knowledge of their own information needs. Responsibility for the success or otherwise of their division of the organisation may be placed with local management, so it is desirable that they have control over the accuracy and reliability of the data they use.

Centralised systems

With this type of system, all processing is carried out centrally, generally by a mainframe computer. The continuing reduction in hardware costs and the increase in computer power has led the move towards distributed processing systems. This is achieved through computer networks.

🖉Exercises

1. Define the term *hit rate* and explain its significance in file processing.
2. Distinguish between *batch* and *transaction processing*, using example applications to illustrate your answer.
3. With the aid of an example, describe the main features of an information storage and retrieval system
4. Briefly describe the operation of a *time-sharing* system.
5. Use an example to describe the meaning of *distributed processing*.

System Controls

Computerised information systems present particular problems for the control of data entering the system, because for much of the time this data is not in human-readable form and even when it is stored, the information remains invisible unless it is printed out or displayed on a VDU screen. If proper system controls are not used, inaccurate data may reach the master files or un-authorised changes to data may be made, resulting in decision-making which may be based on incorrect information. System controls can be divided into three main types, according to the purposes they serve: data control; auditing; data security.

Data control

A number of data control mechanisms, including for example, the validation of input data, can be employed. Controls should be exerted at all stages in the data processing cycle, which commonly recognises the following stages: (i) data *collection*; (ii) *input*; (iii) *processing*, including file processing; (iv) *output*. Controls can be implemented by clerical and software procedures. It is only through the combined application of both clerical and software controls that errors can be minimised, although their entire exclusion can never be guaranteed.

Data collection and input procedures

Before describing the controls it is necessary to outline the activities which may be involved in the collection and input of data. Depending on the application these may include one or more of the following:

❏ Source document preparation. To ensure standardisation of practice and to facilitate checking, data collected for input, for example, customer orders, are clerically transcribed onto source documents specially designed for the purpose.

❏ Data transmission. If the computer centre is geographically remote from the data collection point, the source documents may be physically transported there, or be keyed and transmitted through a terminal and telecommunications link to the computer.

❏ Data encoding and verification. This involves the transcription, usually through a keyboard device, of the data onto a storage medium such as magnetic tape or disk; a process of machine verification accompanied by a repeated keying operation assists the checking of keying accuracy. *Key-to-disk* and *key-to-tape* systems are used for encoding, commonly making use of diskette and cassette tape storage, from which media the data is then merged onto a large reel of magnetic tape or a disk pack for subsequent rapid input.

❏ Data input and validation. Data validation is a computer controlled process which checks the data for its validity according to certain pre-defined parameters, so it must be input to the computer first. The topic of validation is examined in more detail later.

❏ Sorting. In order to improve the efficiency of processing, input data is sorted into a sequence determined by the *primary key* of each record in the relevant master file (Chapter 15 Computer Files); this is always necessary for efficient sequential file processing, but direct access files allow records to be processed by transactions in the same order that they are received.

Collection and input controls

Transcription of data from one medium to another, for example, from telephone notepad to customer order form, or from source document to magnetic disk, provides the greatest opportunity for error. A number of strategies can be adopted to help limit data collection and input errors, including:

❏ minimising transcription. This may involve the use of automated input methods such as bar code reading (Chapter 8). Another solution is to use *turnaround documents*, which are originally produced by the computer and later become input documents, for example, remittance advices which, having been sent to customers, are then returned with their payments. Because these remittance advices already show customers' details, including account numbers, only the amounts remitted need to be entered for them to become complete input documents;

❏ designing data collection and input documents in ways which encourage accurate completion;

❏ using clerical checking procedures such as the re-calculation of totals or the visual comparison of document entries with the original sources of information;

❏ using codes with a restricted format, for example, customer account numbers consisting of two alphabetic characters, followed by six digits, permits easy validation;

❏ employing *batch* methods of input which allow the accumulation and checking of batch control totals, both by clerical and computerised methods;

❏ using screen verification before input data is processed and applied to computer files. Screen dialogue (the form of conversation between the computer and the user) techniques, which allow data verification and correction at the time of entry, can be used to provide this facility;

❏ checking input data with the use of *batch* or *interactive* screen validation techniques;

❏ ensuring that staff are well trained and that clerical procedure manuals are available for newly trained staff;

❏ controlling access to input documents. This is important where documents are used for sensitive applications such as payroll. For example, input documents for changing pay rates should only be available to, say, the Personnel Manager.

File processing controls

Once validated data has entered the computer system, checks have to be made to ensure that it is; (i) applied to the correct files; (ii) consistent with the filed data.

Header records

Files can have header records which detail the function, for example, Sales Ledger, *version number* and *purge date*. The purge date indicates the date after which the file is no longer required and can be overwritten. Thus, a file with a purge date after the current date should not be overwritten. Such details can be checked by the application program to ensure that the correct file is used and that a current file is not accidentally destroyed.

File validation checks

Some validation checks can only be made after data input when reference can be made to the relevant master file data. These are described in the later section on data control in batch processing systems.

Data integrity

The printing of all master file changes allows the user department and auditors to check that all such changes are *authorised* and *consistent* with transaction documents. All data used by applications for reference purposes should be printed periodically; price lists, for example, may be held as permanent data on master files or in table form within computer programs.

Output controls

It might reasonably be supposed that input and file processing controls are sufficient to ensure accurate output. Nevertheless, a number of simple controls at the output stage can help to ensure that it is complete and is distributed to the relevant users on time. They include:

- the comparison of *filed* control totals with *run* control totals. For example, when an entire sequential file is processed, the computer counts all processed records and compares the total with a stored record total held in a *trailer record* at the end of the file;

- the *conciliation* of control totals specific to the application, with totals obtained from a related application. For example, the sales transactions total posted to the Sales Ledger for one day should agree with the total sales transactions recorded in the Sales Day Book or Journal;

- the following of set procedures for the treatment of error reports;

- the proper checking and re-submission of rejected transactions.

Data control in batch processing

It is extremely important that all relevant data is processed and that accuracy is maintained throughout the data processing cycle. The controls which are used will depend on the type of processing method in operation, but batch processing provides the greatest opportunity for exerting control over the data, from the input stage through to the output stage.

Amongst the control methods outlined above, there are two which are particularly important - *verification* and *validation*. These control methods can be used to maximum advantage in a batch processing system and typical procedures are described below.

The stages involved in a batch processing *system cycle* are illustrated in Figure 17.1 with a systems flowchart for a payroll run.

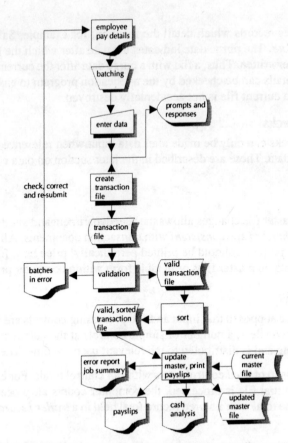

Figure 17.1. *System flowchart of batch payroll system*

The following controls can be used at certain stages within the cycle.

Clerical controls

These can be used at any stage in the cycle when the data is in a human-readable form. The types of check include:

❑ visual checking of source documents to detect missing, illegible or unlikely data values, an example of the latter being a total of 100 in the weekly overtime hours entry for an individual worker;

❑ the verification of entries by checking them against another source, for example, the price catalogue for the price of a stock item on an invoice;

❑ the re-working of calculations on a source document, for example, the checking of additions which make up the total quantity for an item on an order form.

Verification

Before processing, data has to be transcribed from the source documents onto a computer input medium, usually involving a keying operation to encode the data onto magnetic tape or magnetic disk. This stage can be prone to error, particularly if large volumes of data are involved and verification, which is usually a machine-assisted process, can ensure that data is encoded accurately. Magnetic tape encoders (*key-to-tape* systems), for example, can operate in two modes, *record* and *verify*. The operation involves one person keying the data in the record mode, after which a second person re-keys the data with the machine in verify mode. In effect the machine reads the data from the first keying operation and then checks it against the second keying as it occurs. The machine signals if characters do not agree, thus indicating a possible transcription error. *Key-to-disk* systems operate on a similar principle, either with stand-alone workstations or through terminals linked to a minicomputer and usually incorporate some facility for *validation* of data.

Validation

This process is carried out after the data has been encoded onto the input medium and involves a program called the *data vet* or *validation program*. Its purpose is to check that the data falls within certain parameters defined by the systems analyst. A judgement as to whether or not data is valid is made possible by the validation program, but it cannot ensure absolute accuracy. That can only be achieved by the use of all the clerical and computer controls built into the system at the design stage. The difference between *validity* and *accuracy* can be illustrated by the following example.

Example of validation

A company has established a Personnel file. Each record in the file may contain a field for the Job Grade. The permitted values of job grade are A, B, C or D. An entry in an individual's record may be *valid* and accepted by the system if it is recorded as A, B,C or D, but of course this may not be the *correct* grade for the individual worker concerned. Whether or not the grade is correct can only be established by the clerical checks discussed earlier.

Types of validation check

Character, field and record checks

- ❑ *Size*. The number of characters in a field is checked. For example, an account number may require 6 characters and if there are more or less than this, then the item is rejected.

- ❑ *Mode*. It may be that particular fields must contain particular types of character, for example alphabetic or numeric. If the system is programmed to accept only numbers then letters would be rejected.

- ❑ *Format*. This refers to the way characters within a field are organised. For example, an Item Code may consist of 2 alphabetic characters followed by 6 numeric characters, so the system would reject any entry which did not correspond to this format.

- ❑ *Reasonableness*. Quantities can be checked for unusually high or low values. For example, a gas consumer with one small appliance may have a meter reading appropriate to a consumer with a large central heating system and a reasonableness test could be used to reject or highlight it.

- ❑ *Presence*. If a field must always have a value then it can be checked for existence.

For example, the field 'Sex' in a Personnel record would always have to have an M(ale) or F(emale) entry.

❑ *Range.* Values are checked for certain upper and lower limits, for example, account numbers may have to be between 00001 and 10000.

❑ *Check digit.* An extra digit calculated on an account number can be used as a self checking device. When the number is input to the computer, the validation program carries out a calculation similar to that used to generate the check digit originally and thus checks its validity. This kind of check will highlight transposition errors caused by, for instance, keying digits in the wrong order.

The following example serves to illustrate the operation of one such check digit method.

Modulus 11 check digit example

Consider a stock code consisting of six digits, for example 462137.

The check digit is calculated as follows:

(i) Each digit of the stock code is multiplied by its own weight. Each digit has a weight relative to its position, assuming the presence of a check digit in the rightmost position. Beginning from the check digit position (x) the digits are weighted 1, 2, 3, 4, 5, 6 and 7 respectively, as shown in Table 17.1

Stock Code	4	6	2	1	3	7	(x)
multiplied by weight	7	6	5	4	3	2	(1)
product	28	36	10	4	9	14	

Table 17.1.

(ii) The products are totalled. In this example, the sum produces 101.

(iii) Divide the sum by modulus 11. This produces 9, remainder 2.

(iv) The check digit is produced by subtracting the remainder 2 from 11, giving 9.

Whenever a code is entered with the relevant check digit, the validation software carries out the same algorithm, including the check digit in the calculation. Provided that the fourth stage produces a remainder of zero the code is accepted as valid. This is proved in Table 17.2, using the example in Table 17.1.

Stock Code	4	6	2	1	3	7	9
multiplied by weight	7	6	5	4	3	2	1
product	28	36	10	4	9	14	9

Table 17.2.

The sum of the products in Table 17.2 is 110, which when divided by 11, gives 10, with a remainder of 0. Therefore the number is valid.

If some of the digits are *transposed* (swap positions) the check digit is no longer applicable to the code and is rejected by the validation program because the results of the algorithm will not leave a remainder of zero. This is shown in Table 17.3.

Stock Code	6	4	1	2	3	7	9
multiplied by weight	7	6	5	4	3	2	1
product	42	24	5	8	9	14	9

Table 17.3.

The sum of the products equals 111, which when divided by 11, gives 10 with a remainder of 1. The number is, therefore, invalid.

All the above checks can be carried out prior to the master file updating stage. Further checks on data can be made through the use of a validation program at the *update* stage, by comparison with the master file. They are as follow:

❏ *new records*. When a new record is to be added to the master file, a check can be made to ensure that a record does not already use the entered record key .

❏ *deleted records*. It may be that a transaction is entered for which there is no longer a matching master record.

❏ *consistency*. A check is made that the transaction values are consistent with the values held on the master record which is to be updated. For instance a deduction for pension contributions by an employee who is not old enough to be in a pension scheme would obviously be inconsistent.

Validation using batch controls

Batch totals

The purpose of batch totals is to allow a conciliation of manually produced totals for a batch with comparable computer-produced totals. Differences are signalled and the batch is rejected for checking and re-submission. Following the arrangement of source documents into batches of say 30 in each batch, totals are calculated on add-listing machines for each value it is required to control. On an order form, for example, quantities and prices may be separately totalled to provide two control totals. Totals may also be produced for each account number or item code simply for purposes of control although they are otherwise meaningless. For this reason such totals are called hash or nonsense totals.

The totals are recorded on a *batch control slip* (Figure 17.2), attached to the batch, together with a value for the number of documents in the batch and a batch number. The batch number is kept in a register held by the originating department so that missing or delayed batches can be traced. It should be noted that *hash totals* may produce a figure which has a large number of digits, so extra digits over and above the original length of the data item are truncated.

Figure 17.2. *Batch control slip*

Reconciliation of batch totals

The details from each batch control slip are entered with each batch of transactions at the encoding stage. The serial transaction file which results may be arranged as in Figure 17.3.

Figure 17.3. *Arrangement of serial transaction file, with batch totals*

The serial transaction file is processed from beginning to end by the validation program. The sum of the transaction records relating to each batch should match the batch total. If any validation error is detected, either by differences in batch totals or through the character of field checks described earlier, the offending batch is rejected to be checked and re-submitted. Rejected batches are reported on a computer printout.

Validation during updating

Checks can be made in the manner described earlier, on transactions for deleted or new records, or on data which is inconsistent with the relevant record on the master file. These controls can be used in conjunction with proper clerical procedures to ensure that as far as possible, the information stored on the master files is accurate.

File controls

In addition to controlling the accuracy of data entering the system it is essential to check both that the data is complete and that all relevant data is processed. This can be done through the use of file controls on the transaction file.

Following the validation of the batches of transactions, correct batches are written to another file to be sorted and used for updating the relevant master file. During validation, the validation program accumulates totals for all the correct batches. These can be used during the update run to ensure that the whole transaction file is processed.

Validation in on-line systems

On-line systems, as described in the Chapter 16 on Processing Methods, tend to be interactive and transactions are processed immediately against the master files at the data entry stage. The main controls which can be introduced to such systems include:

❑   the character, field and record validation checks described earlier. Error messages are displayed on the screen at the time data is entered and require immediate correction at that time;

❑   visual verification. At the end of each transaction entry, the operator is given the opportunity to scan the data on the screen and to re-enter any incorrect entries detected. This usually takes the form of a message at the bottom of the screen which is phrased in a way such as "Verify (yes or no)";

❑   the use of well-trained data entry operators. They should have sufficient knowledge of the data being entered and the application it serves, to respond to error messages and make corrections to data accordingly.

Auditing

There are two main techniques available for computer system auditing. One technique involves the use of *test data* and the other of *audit enquiry* programs.

Test data method

With this method, the auditor runs the target application with test data, the expected processing results of which are already known. In this way, the computation of for example, payroll figures, can be tested for accuracy in a variety of circumstances. The logical outputs of the program can also be verified. In fact, the method is similar to that used by systems designers prior to a system's implementation. The test data may be recorded on a batch of source documents, in which case, the input will not only test the application's computerised processing and controls, but also the suitability of the source document design for input purposes. The auditing process may also include the testing of batch preparation and input data verification procedures. Software validation checks should be subjected to testing with *normal* and *exceptional* data. Normal data includes the most general data which the software is designed to handle. Exceptional data includes any which the software is not designed to accept. The software should demonstrate that it can reject all such data and continue its normal operation. Test data runs may take one of the following forms.

Live data testing

The auditor selects examples of live data from the system which fulfil the conditions to be tested. The results are calculated manually and checked against the computer-produced outputs. It is essential that manual calculations are made, as a casual assessment of the accuracy of processing can often lead to errors being overlooked. A severe disadvantage of this approach is that the auditor may be unable to find examples of all conditions to be tested in the available live data. It is also quite possible that examples of exceptional or nonsensical data will not be found at the time of the audit and it is important that such conditions are tested. 'Murphy's law' will probably ensure that such exceptional data appears the day after the audit. The testing can only give a 'snapshot' of the system's performance which may be radically different on other occasions.

Historical data testing

Sampling of transactions which have already passed through the system is an important part of internal auditing. It is important that the original transaction documents are made available for inspection to allow the auditor to check their *validity*, *authorisation* and *consistency* with associated results. Results can be calculated manually and then compared with any printed results. If results were not printed at the time, then use may be made of a *file dump utility* to access the appropriate historic file.

Dummy data testing

With this method, the auditor constructs fictitious or dummy data which contains the conditions to be tested. To ensure that such test data is not applied to the application's operational files, it is also usual to set up dummy files, for example, customer or supplier files, specifically for audit purposes. If such data is used in an actual processing run, and the entries are not reversed out in time, there is a danger that the results will be taken as real by users. There are a number of apocryphal stories concerning lorries which delivered goods to non-existent addresses as a result of such fictitious entries. For this reason, it is always advisable to make use of specially created audit files or copies of the master files.

In summary, the test data method is useful for the audit of:

❑   data preparation procedures, such as batching;

❑   data verification and validation controls;

❑   an application's computational and logical processes.

A number of drawbacks and limitations of the test data method of auditing can also be identified:

❑   it only provides a snapshot view of the system at the time of the audit. On the other hand, it may be used repeatedly in order to cover a more extended period of assessment;

❑   it may involve the setting up of dummy files if fictitious data is to be used;

❑   source documents and batch totals have to be prepared for fictitious data which is not of operational use to the business;

❑   the computer system has to be made available to the auditor for the period of the test. During this time it is not available for operational use.

Audit enquiry programs

These programs overcome many of the disadvantages inherent in the test data method and are an essential audit tool, particularly for external auditing which requires the examination of live data already processed. Audit enquiry programs vary in sophistication but generally provide facilities to:

❑   examine the contents of computer files;

❑   retrieve data from computer files;

❑   compare the contents of files. Thus, for example, two versions of identical files may be compared to ensure that the structure has not been altered, perhaps to include an extra field or record type;

❑   produce formatted reports according to the auditor's requirements.

A major benefit to the auditor is that any data stored on computer file can be retrieved. Many financial packages update files 'in situ', so that each updating transaction causes the overwriting of the relevant master record with new values. Thus, there may be circumstances when the results of processing individual transactions can only be established in terms of the cumulative effect of a group of transactions on a particular record. For example, during one day, a stock record may be updated by several transactions but the values held in the stock record at the end will not show their individual effects. However, provided that the source documents are retained or the transactions are logged onto a separate file (see Transaction Logging in the next section on Security), the auditor can still reconcile their expected effect on the master file with the actual values held there.

Audit trails

An audit trail should allow the tracing of a transaction's history as it progresses from input through to output. Computerised systems present particular difficulties in that the trail disappears as it enters the computer system. The auditor may ignore the computer system and pick up the trail at the output stage (auditing around the computer). This has obvious limitations in that the auditor cannot trace a transaction which does not result in printed output. Although audit enquiry programs allow the auditor to examine the contents of files, not every transaction effect is recorded permanently on computer file. Audit trails have to be designed into the system in such a way that intermediate stages of a transaction's progress are recorded for audit purposes.

Data security

The controls used have several main functions:

❑ to prevent loss of data files caused by software or procedural errors, or by physical hazards;

❑ to protect data from accidental or deliberate disclosure to unauthorised individuals or groups;

❑ to protect the data from accidental or deliberate corruption or modification. This is known as maintaining *data integrity*;

❑ to protect the rights of individuals and organisations to restrict access to information which relates to them and is of a private nature, to those entitled or authorised to receive it. This is known as *data privacy*.

Security against data loss

The loss of *master files* can be an extremely serious occurrence for any organisation so properly organised security procedures need to be employed. Among commercial organisations that have lost the major part of their information store, a large percentage subsequently go out of business.

The main causes of data loss are as follow:

❑ environmental hazards such as fire, flood and other natural accidents;

❑ mechanical problems, for example the danger of disk or tape damage caused by a drive unit malfunction;

❑ software errors resulting from programming error;

❑ human error. A wrong file may be loaded, the wrong program version used, a tape or disk mislaid, or physical damage caused to tape or disk;

❑ malicious damage. It is not unknown for staff to intentionally damage storage media or to misuse programs at a terminal.

The standard solution to such problems is to take regular copies of master files and to store the copies in a separate secure location. It is also necessary to maintain a record of transactions affecting a file since the last copy was taken, so that if necessary they can be used to reconstruct the latest version of the file.

Magnetic tape file security

When a tape master file is updated by a tape transaction file the physical nature of the medium makes it necessary for a new tape file to be produced. As Figure 17.4 illustrates, the updating procedure provides a built-in security system referred to as the Grandparent, Parent and Child (*generation*) system.

Figure 17.4. *Generation security system for tape files*

In the first run, Master File 1 is updated by the transactions file to produce Master File 2 as its Child. Master File 1 is the Parent. Should the Child file be damaged and the data lost, it can be re-created from the Parent master file and the relevant transactions. At the end of the second run, Master File 1 becomes the Grandparent, Master File 2 becomes the Parent and Master File 3, the Child. Each generation provides security for subsequent files. The number of generations used will depend on the policy of the organisation. Three generations are usually regarded as providing sufficient security and the oldest files are re-used by being overwritten as each cycle of generations is completed.

Internal header labels

Internal header labels are designed to deal with two major areas of concern:

❑   It is important that the correct file is used in a file processing operation to ensure correct results. Thus, the *subject* of the file and the *version* must be identifiable. For example, it is no good producing monthly payslips using information from a payroll master file three months out of date.

❑   A tape file must be protected against accidental erasure. This may occur because tapes are re-usable and when a file is no longer required it can be overwritten by new information.

To ensure that the correct file is used for any particular job, a tape file usually has an internal header label. The label appears at the beginning of the tape and identifies it. The identifying information in the label is usually recorded under program control or by a data encoding device.

A tape header label usually contains the following items of information:

- ❏ file name e.g. Payroll, Stock, Sales;
- ❏ date created;
- ❏ purge date - the date after which the tape is no longer required and may be re-used.

The label is checked by the program, before the file is processed, to ensure that the correct tape is being used.

File protection ring

A device called a file protection ring can be used to prevent accidental erasure. When tapes are stored off-line, the rings are not fitted. To write to a tape, the ring must first be fitted to the centre of the reel. A tape can be read by the computer whether or not a ring is fitted. The simple rule to remember is 'no ring, no write'.

Magnetic disk file security

Security back-ups

Disk files can be treated in the same way as tape files in that the updating procedure may produce a new master file leaving the original file intact. On the other hand, if the file is updated *in-situ* (which in so doing overwrites the existing data), then it will be necessary to take regular back-up copies as processing proceeds. The frequency with which copies are taken will depend on the volume of transactions affecting the master file. If the latest version of the master file is corrupted or lost, then it can be re-created using the previous back-up together with the transaction data received since the back-up.

Transaction logging

The systems flowchart in Figure 17.5 illustrates the transaction logging procedure.

Figure 17.5. *Backup and transaction logging*

In an on-line system, transactions may enter the system from a number of terminals in different locations, thus making it difficult to re-enter transactions for the re-creation of a damaged master file. One solution is to log all the transactions onto a serial transaction file at the same time as the master file is updated. Thus, the re-creation process can be carried out without the need for keying in the transactions again.

Access controls

Unauthorised access to a system may: provide vital information to competitors; result in the deliberate or accidental corruption of data; allow fraudulent changes to be made to data; result in loss of privacy for individuals or organisations.

To avoid such hasards an information system should be protected *physically*, by *administrative procedures* and *software*. To detect any unauthorised access or changes to the information system:

❑   users should require *authorisation* (with different levels of authority depending on the purpose of access);

❑   the computer should *log* all successful and attempted accesses;

❑   users should be *identifiable* and their identity *authenticated;*

❑   the files should be capable of being *audited;*

❑   the actions of *programmers* should be carefully controlled to prevent fraud through changes to software.

Physical protection

These include the use of security staff, mechanical devices, such as locks and keys and electronic alarm/identification systems.

Computer systems with terminals at remote sites present a weak link in any system and they must be properly protected and here software plays an important protection role. Disk and tape libraries also need to be protected, otherwise it would be possible for a thief to take file media to another centre with compatible hardware and software. A variety of methods may be used to *identify* and possibly *authenticate* a system user. They include:

❑   Identity cards. Provided that they cannot be copied and have a photograph, they can be effective and cheap. The addition of a magnetic strip which contains encoded personal details including a *personal identification number* (PIN), which the holder has to key in, allows the user to be checked by machine. This method is used to allow access to service tills outside banks. Of course, the user of the card may not be the authorised holder, possession of the PIN being the only additional requirement; the following methods allow authentication as well as identification.

❑   Personal physical characteristics. Voice recognition or fingerprint comparison provide effective, if expensive, methods of identification and authentication.

Such methods are only effective if the supporting administrative procedures are properly followed.

Software protection

Ideally, before a user is given access to a system, the log-in procedures should check for: *authorisation*; *identification*; *authentication*.

Authorisation is usually provided by an account code, which must be keyed in response to a computer prompt; similar prompts may appear for a user-id *(identification)* and a password *(authentication)*. Examples of these controls are provided in the section on Novell Netware in Chapter 13.

Further control can be exerted with *fixed terminal identifiers*, whereby each terminal and its location is physically identifiable by the controlling computer, thus preventing access from additional unauthorised locations. Such controls can also be used to restrict particular terminals to particular forms and levels of access.

Password controls

Access to files can be controlled at different levels by a series of passwords, which have to be keyed into the terminal in response to a series of questions displayed on the screen. For example, a clerk in a Personnel Department may be given authority to display information regarding an employee's career record but only the Personnel Manager is authorised to change the information held on file.

Passwords should be carefully chosen, kept secure (memorised and not divulged) and changed frequently. Using people's names, for example, may allow entry by trial and error. Characters should not be echoed on screen as the password is entered.

Handshaking is a technique which requires more than a simple password and may be used between two computers or a computer and a user, as a means of access control. In the latter case, the user would be given a pseudo-random number by the computer and the expected response would be a transform, of that random number. The transform may be to multiply the first and last digits of the number and add the product to a value equal to the day of the month plus 1. Provided the transform is kept secret, handshaking provides more security than simple passwords.

One-time passwords. The computer will only accept a password for *one access occasion*; subsequently, it will expect the user to provide a different password for each additional access, in a pre-defined sequence. Provided the password list and their expected sequence list are kept separate, then possession of one list only will not be of any assistance. The number of attempts at logging-on should be controlled, so, for example, after three unsuccessful attempts, the user should be locked out and a record kept of the time and nature of the attempt.

Authorisation tables

These are held with the relevant files and detail the kinds of access permitted by particular users or groups of users - read only, read and write or delete (see Novell Netware in Chapter 13). Control may also be exerted at a record or field level.

Data encryption

If data signals being transmitted along the telecommunication links are not properly protected, *hackers* can pick up the signals and display them on their own machines. To prevent such intrusion, data encryption methods are used to protect important financial, legal and other confidential information during transmission from one centre to another. Encryption scrambles the data to make it unintelligible during transmission. As the power and speed of computers has increased, so the breaking of codes has been made easier.

Code designers have produced methods of encryption which are currently unbreakable in any reasonable time period, even by the largest and most powerful computers available. An example of such an elaborate coding system is illustrated by the operation of the Electronic Funds

Transfer (EFT) system. This is used by banks and other financial institutions to transfer vast sums of money so these transmissions are protected by the latest data encryption techniques. The Data Encryption Standard (DES) was approved by the American National Bureau of Standards in 1977, but as costs of powerful computers have fallen and come within the reach of criminal organisation, EFT makes use of the DES standard, plus additional encryption techniques.

Security to maintain data integrity

Data integrity refers to the accuracy and consistency of the information stored and is thus covered by the security methods outlined above. A major threat to data integrity comes from a variety of computer viruses.

Computer viruses

A computer virus is program code designed to create nuisance for users, or more seriously, to effect varying degrees of damage to files stored on magnetic media. Generally, the code

❑   is introduced through portable media, such as floppy disks, particularly those storing pirated or shareware programs; files downloaded from *bulletin boards* on the Internet (Chapter 38) may be infected and uncontrolled use of these services is likely to result in the receipt of viruses;

❑   transfers itself from the infected medium into the computer's main memory as soon as the medium is accessed;

❑   transfers from memory onto any integral storage device, such as a hard disk and commonly conceals itself in the boot sector (and sometimes in the partition sector where it is less likely to be traced), from where it can readily infect any other media placed on line in that computer system, whether it be stand-alone or networked. Naturally, any write-protected media cannot be infected.

Some virus codes are merely a nuisance, whilst others are developed specifically to destroy, or make inaccessible, whole filing systems. They pose a serious threat to any computer-based information system, but a number of measures can be taken to minimise the risk:

❑   only use proprietary software from a reliable source;

❑   write-protect disks being used for reading purposes only;

❑   use virus detection software, although this is only effective in respect of viruses using known storage and proliferation techniques;

❑   use diskless workstations on networks;

❑   control access to portable media and forbid employees to use their own media on the organisation's computer system.

Security to maintain privacy of data

The rights of individuals and organisations concerning their confidential records are similarly protected by the security controls outlined earlier. In addition, legislation by parliament (the Data Protection Act- see chapter on Organisational and Social Issues) attempts to exert some control by requiring persons or organisations holding personal information on computer files to register with the Data Protection Registrar. Some countries have 'Freedom of Information Acts' which allow the individual to see any personal information stored in their own files, except where national security is thought to be threatened. It is generally accepted that the Data Protection Act falls far short of complete freedom of information.

✍️Exercises

1. Distinguish between *verification* and *validation*.
2. Using batch order processing as an example:
   (i)   suggest four *data collection controls* to control the accuracy of data entering the system;
   (ii) suggest three *validation checks* which could be applied to customer order details;
   (iii) indicate any *file processing controls* which could be employed.
3. Draw a *system flowchart* to illustrate the batch processing of customer orders and the updating of stock, order and customer files.
4. With the aid of an example, describe how a *check digit* is generated and subsequently used to check the validity of a code number.
5. In the context of auditing, distinguish between *live*, *historical* and *dummy data testing*, pointing out the relative benefits and drawbacks of each.
6. What is an *audit trail* and why is it useful?
7. With the use of an example, describe the *generation system* of security for tape files.
8. What is transaction logging?
9. With the aid of an example organisation, describe methods to prevent *unauthorised access* to data.

Chapter 18

Systems Analysis - an overview

Systems analysis can be defined as *a disciplined process which begins with the establishment of user requirements for a given application and concludes with the implementation of a fully operational system*. The work of systems analysis has been carried out by trained professionals since the introduction of early mainframe computers but its processes are equally appropriate to the task of computerising small business applications. Many businesses will not employ specialist staff capable of carrying out an analysis of their computer requirements and may employ the services of an outside consultant. The main stages of systems analysis are often referred to as the *system life cycle*. The following sections give a brief overview of their functions within the systems analysis process.

Feasibility study

The aim of this stage is to establish whether or not a proposal for the computerisation of a particular application is worthwhile or feasible. In simple terms, the feasibility study has to answer questions such as follow: "Will computerisation achieve the users' objectives?"; "What type of system will be most suitable?"; "Will it be financially worthwhile?"

System investigation and design

Assuming that the feasibility study produces a recommendation to proceed with computerisation of an application (there may, of course, be several), then before any system specification is produced, an analysis has to be made of the processes and procedures involved in the application under consideration. For example, an analysis of Sales Order Processing should identify how orders are received, the order forms used and the procedures necessary to fulfil orders. Analysis is not simply the recording of an application as it currently operates. Through a variety of information gathering methods such as interviewing and observation, the requirements of a new system should be identified.

Although the needs of the organisation are of obvious importance, employees are more likely to be concerned with matters of job satisfaction and working conditions. Successful implementation of a computerised system requires a great deal of work, involvement and willingness to co-operate by everyone concerned. If staff feel that their views have been considered such co-operation is more likely. Although users' views are important an outside observer can often identify problems with current practice which have never been questioned. A systems analyst from outside the firm needs therefore, to possess qualities of tact and diplomacy if his or her views are to be considered.

The process of design should produce a complete picture of the input, processing, storage and output requirements of the new system. The picture will include narrative descriptions, as well as flowcharts illustrating clerical procedures, data flows and the role of the computer in broad outline. The design of a computerised system should include as many improvements suggested in the investigation stage as is practicable and it will almost certainly be necessary to question users further when, for example, problems arise in the implementation of particular system requirements. Compromises will have to be made between what is desirable and what is practicable. Management and users may have specified requirements during the investigation stage which prove either too expensive or extremely difficult to satisfy.

System implementation

System implementation or 'going live' involves a range of preparatory activities, although the importance of each will depend on the type and size of the project and the number of people involved. The main activities are as follow:

❑   Development and/or testing of software. If an 'off the shelf' system is chosen, then no development time is necessary, but testing is still vital.

❑   File conversion. This is probably the most time-consuming activity in that all data relating to the application, which is currently held in manual files, has to be encoded onto the chosen magnetic storage medium. Although a laborious task, accuracy is obviously vital and both software and clerical checking procedures should be employed.

❑   Staff training and education. This may take a variety of forms but may be part of the proposals put forward by the chosen supplier. It is an extremely important activity if the system's effectiveness is to be maximised and if staff are to feel happy and confident in its operation.

❑   Introduction of new clerical procedures. The computer software which has been developed or purchased forms only part of the whole information processing system and if the whole system is to function correctly, the computer processing aspect has to be supported by the clerical procedures designed to work with it. Part of staff training, therefore, has to be dedicated to purely clerical tasks such as the preparation of input data or source documents.

❑   Choice of a changeover or 'going live' plan. A number of alternatives are available and each has costs and benefits associated with it. *Parallel running*, for example, requires that the old and new systems are operated alongside one another until the new system is fully tested. Although this minimises the risks consequent upon system failure, it is an expensive option in that it involves a great deal of staff time. *Direct changeover* is obviously less expensive if the new system works but failure could mean catastrophe for the business. The plan used will depend on a number of factors, for example, the importance of the system to the success of the business.

System maintenance

After its initial introduction a system should be flexible to the changing needs of the business. An allowance for the business's expansion should be made in the original system specification and the supplier should be able to satisfy those expansion needs as and when necessary. Equally, advances in hardware technology and the sophistication of software mean that a system soon becomes outdated. Even if a business chooses not to take advantage of improved software, hardware is likely to become less reliable and will need replacement after about five years of business use. Agreements on software and hardware maintenance should be established with the supplier and formalised in the contract signed by purchaser and supplier.

The Feasibility Study

The traditional purpose of a feasibility study is to determine whether or not the purchase of a computer system can be justified. The study has to answer two fundamental questions: "Can the envisaged applications be carried out by a computer system more efficiently than with existing facilities?"; "Will a computer system be economically viable?". Since the early 1970s, prices of all types of computer system have fallen dramatically and their power has increased to such a degree that, for example, microcomputers challenge the minicomputer in their range of applications. This may be part of the reason why many organisations find it difficult to justify undertaking a detailed feasibility study and argue that no matter how limited their needs there is a computer system to satisfy them at a cost-effective price; it is only necessary to decide on its best application(s). Although this is an understandable view, it should be remembered that any item of equipment should be justified in terms of its costs and benefits to the business and that a computer system should be no exception. Although there are few businesses which cannot benefit from computerisation at all, the process of carrying out a feasibility study disciplines the purchaser to think carefully about how it is to be used.

In modifying the purpose of a feasibility study, the previous questions can be replaced by the following: "Which applications can be computerised to give most benefit to the organisation?"; "What type of computer will be required?"; "What are the likely acquisition and running costs?"; "What are the likely implications, especially those concerning personnel and organisational procedures?".

Pressures for computerisation

There are many and various pressures which can 'trigger' the thought of using a computer, either for the first time or, where a computer is already installed, for other applications still operated manually. Some examples are as follow:

(i)   A business is expanding and to cope with the increased workload it appears that the only the alternative to computerisation is increased staffing.

(ii)   A business is growing at such a rate that more information is needed to manage it properly. To obtain the information manually is too time-consuming and by the time it has been gathered is probably out-of-date.

(iii)   Staff are being asked to work regular and increasing amounts of overtime and backlogs of work are building up.

(iv)   Customers are complaining about the speed and quality of the service provided.

(v)   Where stock is involved, it is difficult to keep track of stock levels and while some customer orders cannot be filled because of stock shortages, other stock is 'gathering dust' on the shelves.

(vi)   A great deal of advertising literature is constantly reminding business management that they are out-of-date and at a disadvantage with their competitors.

(vii)   Other businesses providing a similar service use a computer.

Examples (i), (ii) and (iii) suggest that the business is operating successfully and needs to take on extra staff or streamline its systems. Examples (iv) and (v) may be symptomatic of generally poor business management and in such cases, computerisation alone may not solve the problems. Examples (vi) and (vii) may tempt the management to computerise simply 'to keep up with the Jones's'. Although a computerisation programme resulting directly from one or more such pressures may be completely successful and worthwhile, the pressure itself should not be the reason for computerisation. Instead, management should establish the organisational objectives they wish to achieve through computerisation.

Establishing objectives for computerisation

It is important for management to establish what they are trying to achieve in terms of the overall objectives of the business and in the light of this, the objectives of the systems which contribute to their achievement. For example, two major business objectives may be to improve the delivery of customers' orders and to minimise the stock levels which tie up valuable cash resources. The achievement of these objectives may involve contributions from several different information processing systems and the list may include the following.

❑   Stock Control - records stock movements and controls stock levels.

❑   Purchasing - responsible for the ordering of new supplies from suppliers.

❑   Sales Order Processing - receives customers' orders and initiates the process of order fulfilment.

❑   Purchase Ledger - the accounting record of amounts owed and paid to suppliers of stock.

❑   Invoicing - the production of invoices requesting payment from customers for goods supplied.

❑   Sales Ledger - the accounting record of amounts owing by and received from customers for goods supplied.

These and other applications within a business are interconnected by the information which flows between them. Such connections can be illustrated with the use of data flow diagrams (DFD), which are described in Chapter 25.

Establishing priorities for computerisation

It is not generally advisable or even practicable to attempt the computerisation of more than one or two applications at the same time, even if they are closely linked. In any case, it is likely that some applications make a greater contribution to the achievement of the required business objectives than do others. Thus, the applications which are going to bring greatest benefit to the business should be computerised first.

Establishing individual system objectives

Before any single application can be computerised, it is necessary to establish its objectives clearly because users may have become so used to its procedures that they no longer question their purpose. It is self-evident that before any informed judgements can be made on the design of a computerised system, the objectives of the relevant application must first be clearly understood.

The following list for stock control serves to illustrate the definition of such objectives.

❑ To maintain levels of stock which will be sufficient to meet customer orders promptly.

❑ To provide a mechanism which removes the need for excessive safety margins of stock to cover customer orders. This is usually effected by setting minimum stock levels which the computer can use to report variations below these levels.

❑ To provide automatic re-ordering of stock items which fall below minimum levels.

❑ To provide management with up-to-date information on stock levels and values of stocks held.

The Feasibility Report

The Feasibility Report should contain the following sections:

Terms of reference

These should set out the original purpose of the study, as agreed by management and detail the business objectives to be achieved, for example: (i) the improvement of customer service, such that orders are delivered within 24 hours of order receipt; (ii) the provision of more up-to-date management information on current stock levels and projected customer demand; (iii) a tighter control of the business's cash resources, primarily through better stock management.

Applications considered for computerisation

The applications which may assist the achievement of the business objectives set out in the Terms of Reference are listed, for example: stock control; purchasing; sales order processing; invoicing; accounts.

System investigations

For each application under consideration there should be:

❑ a description of the existing system;

❑ an assessment of its good and bad points. For example, the sales order processing system may be slow to process customer orders and this results in poor delivery times, which in turn causes customers to take away their business;

❑ an estimate of the costs of the existing system. For example, apart from the cost of staffing, an estimate has to be made of the cost of lost business, which could be avoided with an improved system.

Envisaged system requirements

This section should detail, in general terms, those aspects of each application which need to be improved and a broad outline of how each system may operate following computerisation. Of course, it is still possible that not all applications will benefit from computerisation but can be improved by other methods.

Costs of development and implementation

These will include both capital costs and revenue or running costs. Capital costs are likely to be incurred for the following: (i) computer hardware; (ii) systems software and software packages (either 'off-the-shelf' or 'tailor-made'); (iii) installation charges for hardware and software; (iv) staff training. Revenue costs include those for the maintenance and insurance of the system. In addition, unless there are existing computer specialists in the organisation, additional suitable staff may need to be recruited.

Timescale for implementation

This will depend on the scale of the operation, the type of application and whether or not packaged software is to be used.

Expected benefits

These are more difficult to quantify than the costs but may include, for example:

❑   estimated savings in capital expenditure on typewriters and photocopiers;

❑   more efficient stock management allows customer service to be maintained whilst keeping stock levels lower. This releases valuable cash resources and reduces possible interest charges on borrowed capital;

❑   expansion in business turnover, without the need for extra staff and reduced overtime requirements.

Other considerations

The staff have to support any development for it to be properly successful and this usually means consultation at an early stage in the feasibility study and the provision of a proper staff training programme. Customers must also be considered. For example, when a customer receives a computer-produced invoice it should be at least as easy to understand as the type it replaced. Assuming that the feasibility study concludes that the proposed computerisation is worthwhile, according to the criteria set out in the report, then more detailed investigation and design can follow.

Chapter 20

System Investigation and Design

Introduction

If the feasibility report gives the go-ahead to the computerisation project, then a more detailed investigation of each candidate system begins. The facts gathered about each system will be analysed in terms of their bearing on the design and implementation of a computerised version. The objectives of the analysis are to gain a thorough knowledge of the operational characteristics of the current system and to settle, in a fair amount of detail, the way in which a computerised system will operate. It is extremely important that the new system does not simply computerise existing procedures. The design should, as far as possible, ignore existing departmental structures which may inhibit the introduction of different and improved procedures. For example, it may be that customer credit limits are fixed by the Accounts Department and that Sales staff have to refer to the Accounts Department before accepting a customer order. A computerised system may allow Sales staff to access credit limits directly without reference to the Accounts Department. This method could be used in most cases and the computer could indicate any customer accounts which needed to be specially referred to the Accounts staff. The aim of the investigation and design process is to produce a specification of users' requirements in documented form. This is referred to as the Statement of User Requirements and will be used to tender for supply of hardware and software.

Fact-finding methods

There are several methods which can be used to gather facts about a system: (i) interviewing; (ii) questionnaires; (iii) examination of records and procedure manuals; (iv) examination of documents; (v) observation. Each method has its own particular advantages and disadvantages and the method or methods chosen will depend on the specific circumstances surrounding the investigation, for example, the size of the business, the number of staff employed and their location and distribution.

Interviewing

This method has much to recommend it, in that the facts can be gathered directly from the person or persons who have experience of the system under investigation. On the other hand, a business with a number of geographically distributed branches makes the process of extensive interviewing expensive and time-consuming. Further, interviewing skills need to be acquired if the process is to be effective. The interviewer needs to know how to gain the confidence of the interviewee and ensure that the information which is given will be of value in the design of the new system. Questions need to be phrased unambiguously in order that the interviewee supplies the information actually required and a checklist of points will help to ensure that all relevant questions are asked. Of course, the interview may need to stray from the points in the checklist, if it becomes apparent that the interviewee is able to provide relevant information not previously considered. For example, clerical procedures may be designed quite satisfactorily but may be made less effective because of personality conflicts between staff. Such tensions may only be revealed through personal interview.

The interviewer also needs to detect any unsatisfactory responses to questions and possibly use alternative methods to glean the required information. Unsatisfactory responses include:

❑ Refusal to answer. Such refusal may indicate, for example, that set procedures are not being followed and that the member of staff does not wish to be 'incriminated'.

❑ Answer with irrelevant information. It may be that the question is ambiguous and has to be re-phrased in order to elicit the required information.

❑ Answer with insufficient information. If a system is to be designed which covers all foreseeable user requirements and operational circumstances, it is important that the analyst has all relevant information.

❑ Inaccurate answer. The interviewer may or may not be aware that an inaccurate answer has been given but it is important that other sources of information are used to cross-check answers.

Questionnaires

Questionnaires are useful when only a small amount of information is required from a large number of people, but to provide accurate responses, questions need to be unambiguous and precise. The questionnaire has a number of advantages over the interview:

❑ each respondent is asked exactly the same questions, so responses can be analysed according to the pre-defined categories of information;

❑ the lack of personal contact allows the respondent to feel completely at ease when providing information, particularly if responses are to be anonymous;

❑ questionnaires are particularly suited to the gathering of factual information, for example, the number of customer orders received in one week;

❑ it is cheap, particularly if users are scattered over a wide geographical area.

A number of disadvantages attach to the use of questionnaires:

❑ questions have to be simple and their meaning completely unambiguous to the respondents;

❑ if the responses indicate that the wrong questions were asked, or that they were phrased badly, it may be difficult to clarify the information, particularly if the respondents were anonymous;

❑ without direct observation it is difficult to obtain a realistic view of a system's operation. The questionnaire often provides only statistical information on, for example, volumes of sales transactions or customer enquiries.

Examination of records and procedure manuals

If existing procedures are already well documented, then the procedure manuals can provide a ready-made source of information on the way procedures should be carried out. It is less likely, however, that procedures will be documented in the smaller organisation. In any event, it is important to realise that procedures detailed in manuals may not accord entirely with what actually happens. The examination of current records and the tracing of particular transactions can be a useful method of discovering what procedures are carried out.

Special purpose records which may involve, for example, the ticking of a box when an activity has been completed, can be used to analyse procedures which are causing delays or are not functioning efficiently. The use of special purpose records imposes extra burdens on staff who have to record procedures as they happen and the technique should only be used when strictly necessary.

Examination of documents

It is important that the analyst examines all documents used in a system, to ensure that each:

❑ fulfils some purpose, that is, it records or transmits information which is actually used at some stage. Systems are subject to some inertia, for example, there may have been a 'one-off' requirement to record and analyse the geographical distribution of customers over a single month and yet the summary document is still completed because no-one told the staff it was no longer necessary;

❑ is clear and satisfies its purpose, for example, a form may not indicate clearly the type of data to be entered under each heading. In any case, it may well require re-designing for any new system which is introduced.

The documents, which should include, for example, source documents, report summaries, customer invoices and delivery notes, help to build a picture of the information flows which take place from input to output.

Observation

It is most important to observe a procedure in action, so that irregularities and exceptional procedures are noticed. Observation should always be carried out with tact and staff under observation should be made fully aware of its purpose, to avoid suspicions of 'snooping'.

The following list details some of the features of office procedures and conditions which may usefully be observed during the investigation:

❑ office layout - this may determine whether the positioning of desks, filing cabinets and other office equipment is convenient for staff and conducive to efficient working;

❑ work load - this should indicate whether the volume of documents awaiting processing is fairly constant or if there are peak periods of activity;

❑ delays - these could show that there are some procedures which are constantly behind schedule;

❑ methods of working - a trained observer can, through experience, recognise a slow, reasonable or quick pace of working and decide whether or not the method of working is efficient. It is important that such observations should be followed up by an interview to obtain the co-operation of the person under observation;

❑ office conditions - these should be examined, as poor ventilation, inadequate or excessive temperatures, or poor lighting can adversely affect staff efficiency.

Often the observation will be carried out in an informal way but it may be useful on occasion to, for example, work at a user's desk, so as to observe directly the way that customer orders are dealt with. It is important to realise that a user may 'put on a performance' whilst under observation and that this reduces the value of the information gathered.

Documenting the results of analysis

A number of standard approaches, apart from narrative description, can be used to document the result of the system analysis, including: *data flow diagrams* (DFDs); *organisation charts*; *system flowcharts*. Their applications are illustrated in the following section, which examines the categories of information which need to be gathered and recorded during a system investigation; data flow diagrams are further examined in Chapter 25.

Categories of system information

The major categories of information which need to be gathered involve:

- functional relationships and data flows;
- personnel and jobs;
- inputs;
- processes;
- outputs;
- storage.

Functional relationships and data flows

A business has a number of functional areas, such as Sales, Accounts, Stock Control and Purchasing, each having its own information system. However, the computerisation of a system in one functional area cannot be carried out without considering its effects on the rest of the business. Information systems within a business interact with and affect one another. The business, as an entity, also interacts with and is influenced by individuals and organisations in the surrounding environment and the business's individual information systems should be co-ordinated to allow the achievement of overall business objectives. The data flows between individual functional areas can be illustrated with the use of a *data flow diagram* (Chapter 25).

Personnel and jobs

It is possible to design a computerised system without involving staff, but it is likely to be less successful, partly because users can provide valuable insights into the practical aspects of system operation and partly because they will feel less motivated if they have had little or no influence on the final design.

A formal organisation chart can be used to gain an overall picture of staff relationships and responsibilities but it should be borne in mind that designated and actual job responsibilities can differ radically. For example, it may turn out that a junior sales clerk is carrying out the checking of orders, which should be the responsibility of the sales supervisor. Thus, it may be necessary for the analyst to draw an alternative informal organisation chart to show the actual working relationships of staff. An example is given in Figure 20.1.

Apart from identifying working relationships between staff, it is useful to draw up brief job descriptions so that consultation on individual system procedures can take place with the appropriate staff. For example, a job description for a sales clerk may include the following activities: completion of standard order forms; checking stock availability; notification of orders to accounts. Therefore, although the sales departmental manager may have knowledge of such procedures, the sales clerk will have practical experience of their operation and should be consulted.

Figure 20.1. *Organisation chart*

System inputs

A number of details concerning the data inputs to a system need to be established:

❑ *source*. It may, for example, originate from a customer, a supplier, or another department in the business;

❑ *form*. The data may arrive, for example, by telephone, letter, or a standard form such as an order form or supplier's invoice;

❑ *volume* and *frequency*. For example, the number of orders received daily or weekly;

❑ *contents*. For example, the individual items of data which appear on a supplier's invoice.

Such information will allow the analyst to make recommendations on the most appropriate methods of computer input. The design of appropriate input methods also has to take account of several tasks involved with the collection and entry of data to a system:

❑ *recording*. For example, the completion of a customer order form following receipt of a customer order by telephone;

❑ *transmission*. For example, the order details may need to be transferred to another department or branch of the business for encoding and computer processing or they may be keyed in directly at the point of collection;

❑ *visual checking*. It may be, for example, that a customer order has no quantities entered;

❑ *encoding*. Verification procedures need to be designed to prevent transcription errors when data is encoded onto a computer storage medium for processing;

❑ *validation*. Data is checked by a data vet program against set limits of validity, for example, account numbers may have to fall between a particular range of values.

Thus, decisions need to be made concerning: (i) data collection procedures; (ii) methods for the transmission of data to the place of processing; (iii) data entry, data verification and data validation procedures.

Data collection

The designer needs to be aware of the available input technologies. These can be divided into two categories, keyboard entry and data capture technologies such as bar code reading, optical character reading (OCR) and optical mark reading (OMR), which allow direct input to the computer from specially designed input forms.

Keyboard entry

This is the most common method of input and requires the transcription of data from source documents. These can be designed to minimise the possibility of transcription errors at the data collection stage.

Direct input

Bar codes are pre-encoded and are thus immune from errors of transcription (assuming that the bar code is correct in the first place). Optical mark reading requires that pencil marks are used to indicate particular values from a limited set on a pre-designed form. Although no keyboard entry is required, mistakes may be made by the originator of the document and good design is therefore important.

Data transmission

It may be that no data transmission is necessary because the data is processed at the point of collection. For example, customer orders may be recorded on order forms at the sales desk and then taken into the next room for keying into the computer. Alternatively, the data may have to be transmitted some distance, perhaps to another floor of the building or to another building some miles away. A fundamental decision has to be made, whether to localise processing at the points of collection, or to use a central facility with data communications links from each location.

Data entry

The data entry method chosen will depend on the data collection methods used and may involve keyboard transcription from source documents or data may be captured directly from bar codes, OCR or OMR type documents. Where keyboard transcription is used, verification and validation procedures are likely to be interactive, in that the data entry operator has to respond to prompts on screen and make corrections as and when the system indicates

Most small business computer systems will be used for on-line processing, where transactions are processed immediately with master files at the data entry stage. Consequently, validation and verification have to be carried out immediately prior to the processing of each transaction.

On-screen verification

At the end of each transaction entry, the operator is given the opportunity to scan the data on the screen and to re-enter any incorrect entries detected. This usually takes the form of a message at the bottom of the screen which is phrased in a way such as Verify (yes or no).

On-screen validation

Character, data item and record checks, such as range and mode checks, can be made each time the RETURN key is pressed during data entry. For example, the screen may prompt for the entry of an account number, which must be 6 digits long and be within the range 000001 to 500000. Any entry which does not conform with these parameters is erased and the prompt re-displayed for another attempt.

Appropriate screen dialogue to allow the data entry operator to enter into a 'conversation' with the computer is a crucial part of the input design process and is dealt with as a separate topic in Chapter 21.

Batch data entry

The type of keyboard transcription used will be affected by the type of input data. Where, for example, files only need to be updated weekly, transaction data may be batched and entered onto magnetic disk for processing at a later stage in one update program run.

System processes

All the clerical and machine-assisted processes, which are necessary to achieve the desired output from the given inputs, need to be identified. This will allow the systems analyst to determine the role of the computer in the new system, the programs necessary to take over the processing stages and the changes needed to clerical procedures, before and after computer processing.

There are many instances when the processing requires not only the input data but also data retrieved from files. For example, to generate a customer invoice requires:

(i)   input data concerning commodity codes and quantities ordered;

(ii)   data from the stock master file concerning prices of items ordered by reference to the input commodity codes;

(iii)   customer details from the customer master file.

The above processes can be completely computerised but other processes may require human intervention. For example, before a customer order is processed, the customer's credit status may need to be checked and referred to a supervisor before authorisation.

Non-standard procedures

Most processes will follow standards suitable for their particular circumstances. For example, before an order is processed, stock items ordered are checked for availability. It is important, however, that the investigation identifies and notes any non-standard procedures. For example, what procedure is followed when there is an insufficient quantity of an ordered item to completely fulfil a customer order? It may be that some customers will take part-orders, whilst others require the full quantity of an item or none at all. If non-standard procedures are needed, it is important to know their complexity, how often they are used and what extra information is required. Ideally, a system should be designed to cope with all possible circumstances, but cost sometimes forces a compromise. If cost prohibits the inclusion of certain system features, for example, the ability to deal with part-orders, then it is important that the business is aware of such limitations so that it can modify its business objectives.

Document flow

System flowcharts can be used to model the movement and interaction of documents and the data they record, as well as the processes involved, as they pass from one functional area or department of the business to another. In order that the involvement of each section, department or personnel grouping in the processes can be identified, the system flowchart is divided into columns representing these divisions of responsibility.

A system flowchart may use a range of standard symbols which are illustrated in Figure 20.2. A number of standards exist for the drawing of system flowcharts and the range of symbols used depends on which stage of the investigation and design process has been reached. For example, in the early stages of investigation of an existing manual system, there will be no representation of computer methods of input, processing, output or storage. At a later stage, when computer methods are being considered, it will be necessary to use suitable symbols in the flowchart.

Figure 20.2. *Flowchart symbols*

Figures 20.3 to 20.5 show example system flowcharts. Figure 20.3 illustrates a manually operated order processing and invoicing system.

Figure 20.4 represents a batch processing update of a stock master file. Notice the sorting and validation stages, which are essential to batch processing systems. (Chapter 17).

Most business systems require alternative actions to be taken dependent upon some variable condition or circumstance. For example, 15 per cent customer discount may be allowed if the invoiced amount is paid within, say, 14 days of the invoice date, after which time all discount is lost.

In order that computerised and non-computerised processes can be properly designed, the investigation must identify all:

Figure 20.3. *Flowchart of manual order processing and invoicing system*

❏ decisions made during system operation;

❏ conditions and circumstances which lead to alternative decisions;

❏ actions to be taken following a decision.

Figure 20.5 represents the computerised aspects of a similar system, but does not detail procedures needed to prepare, for example, the data for input or the distribution of output. A computerised system must have the necessary clerical procedures to support it. Some decisions and consequent actions will need to be documented for clerical procedure guidelines, whilst others which involve computer processing will form part of program specifications used in program writing or as bases for choice of packaged software.

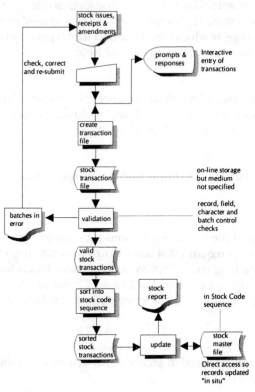

Figure 20.4. *Batch processing stock file update*

Figure 20.5. *On-line order processing*

System outputs

Output design first requires identification of the following:

❏   data items required as output. Some may be revealed in the existing system, whilst others may be requested by users as being desirable in any new system;

❏   form of the output, for example, whether or not printed copy is required;

❏   volume of data with each output and the frequency of the output. This information assists decisions on the type and number of output devices required.

Based on the above information, the following tasks can be carried out: (i) selection of an appropriate output device to display or communicate the outputs. Available technologies are described in Chapter 8; (ii) designing output screen and document layouts. This topic is examined in more detail in Chapter 21.

System storage (files)

The storage of historic and current information is a vital part of any business system. For example, to produce a payslip not only requires transient input data concerning hours worked and sickness days but also data on rate of pay, tax code, deductions of tax and superannuation to date etc., which are held in the payroll master file stored on magnetic disk. Information on the contents of files will be gathered from existing manual files, together with responses from users regarding the output requirements of any new system. If packaged software is to be used then the contents of files will be dictated by the package, in which case some data item types may be surplus to requirements, whilst others which are required may not be available.

File contents

Each file consists of a number of logical records, each of which has a number of associated data items. For example, each stock record in a stock master file may include: Stock Code; Description; Unit Price; Minimum Stock Level; Re-order Quantity; Quantity in Stock.

File organisation and access

This concerns the logical ordering of records within a file. The available file organisation and access methods are described in Chapter 15.

Database management systems (DBMS)

An increasingly popular alternative to traditional file processing systems is to construct databases controlled by a DBMS. The design process requires that data is analysed according to subject area, for example, raw materials or staffing, rather than by department or functional area. The tools and techniques for database design are examined in Chapter 26; the structured analysis and design techniques examined in Chapter 25 are relevant to both database and non-database systems.

Choice of storage device

Choice is concerned with storage capacity, mode and speed of access. A full description of the various storage technologies is given in Chapter 9.

User Interface Design

The movement from centralised to distributed systems and the expansion in microcomputer usage has spawned the need for a variety of approaches to the design of *user interfaces* (UIs) which fulfil the requirements of an increasing population of computer users, the majority of whom are not computer specialists. When all computer processing was controlled by small numbers of experts, in centralised data processing departments, there was little pressure for UI design to be particularly 'friendly'. This is probably a major reason why many people used to regard computers with some suspicion and apprehension. UIs are also variously known as *human-computer* and *man-machine* interfaces. UI design is now recognised as being of critical importance and is usually the yardstick by which a system is judged; poor UI design can seriously affect a user's view of a system's functionality. Several design principles can be identified:

❑   it should be a product of collaboration between the designer and the users;

❑   user, not designer, convenience should be paramount;

❑   the interface should be of consistent design throughout the system;

❑   built-in help and advice should be accessible at different levels, depending on the degree of assistance required.

The technology of the user interface

The typical user interface is supported by hardware devices such as the bit-mapped display, pointing device, microphone, speakers and scanner and software to present various metaphor, menu or command-driven alternatives. These components comprise the technology of the user interface.

Computers are designed to assist humans in the performance of tasks, some of which are simple and some of which are intellectually complex. If we ignore the constraints of processing power and memory capacity, it is the user interface that limits the complexity or sophistication of the problems which can be tackled. For example, with suitable sensor devices, we could ask the computer to use its sense of smell to distinguish between different coffee beans and roasts, or with suitable input and output devices, we could transmit the sense of touch remotely. Video conferencing systems allow meeting participants to hear and see one another, but subtleties of body language and the 'atmosphere' that can be felt in a physical meeting cannot be communicated with current interface technology. A graphical user interface (GUI) undoubtedly makes computers easier to use but it also extends the range and complexity of tasks which can be undertaken by most users. It is doubtful that applications such as desktop publishing and graphic design would be so widely used if the interface was largely command driven and pointing devices did not include the mouse. Similarly, the World Wide Web would not have found such popularity without its multimedia content and hyperlink-driven form of navigation.

Interface metaphors

Through the use of metaphors, an interface can present a system's facilities in a form familiar to the user. A number of metaphors are commonly employed.

Desktop metaphor

As the term indicates, the UI relates everyday desktop or office facilities to routine computer tasks such as loading, saving or deleting files. The following representations are usual:

❑   filing cabinets for disc drives;

❑   documents for files;

❑   folders for directories;

❑   waste paper baskets for the deletion of files from backing storage.

Control panel metaphor

A screen control panel may include a variety of elements, such as:

❑   *buttons* for initiating actions, for example, print;

❑   *switches* for setting options on and off, for example, a grid on a spreadsheet;

❑   *radio buttons* for choosing from ESGs (exclusive selection groups), for example, A5/A4/A3 documents sizes;

❑   *sub-panel menu* of buttons or switches to select, for example, system default settings;

❑   *lights* to indicate some active event, for example, printing;

❑   *signs* displaying, for example, which file is currently active;

❑   *sliders*, to vary for example, RGB (red green blue) colour mixes.

WIMP interfaces

An acronym for Windows, Icons, Menus, Pointing (alternatively, Windows, Icons, Mice and Pull-down menus), the WIMP concept stems from original work by Xerox PARC Laboratories in the mid-1970s and was first employed on Apple Lisa and Macintosh computer systems. Since then a number of WIMP orientated UIs have been developed, notably, GEM, MS-Windows, ARC and Sun. Such interfaces have a number of characteristics and features:

❑   the necessary skills are easy to grasp and the systems are easy to use;

❑   multiple windows for switching between tasks (multi-tasking);

❑   full-screen interaction allows quicker command execution than is usually possible through a *command line interpreter* (Chapter 13);

❑   control panels (see previous section).

However, as a relatively new concept, there are no standards for the design of WIMP-based products. Certain difficulties in their design may be experienced:

❑ although multiple windows are useful for task switching, too many windows can be confusing;

❑ designing icons which unambiguously tell the user of specific functions can be difficult and some may need to be augmented with text support, perhaps in a help window.

Menu systems

A menu of options is displayed, from which a user can make a selection. Menus are only appropriate where a limited range of options is available at any one time, although the selection of an item may cause the display of a further sub-menu. Commonly, each option is identified by a single letter or number which has to be keyed to select the option. Some packages, typically those running under the old MS-DOS operating system, use a menu system which allows selection of an option either by highlighting the option with the cursor and pressing the 'enter' key or simply by keying the first letter of the option (without the need for confirmation). The problem for all such systems is to design each menu such that the first letter of each option is unique in that menu. The use of main menus which give access to sub-menus, each of which in turn may provide access to further sub-menus, follows a hierarchical structure. A number of design principles may be employed:

❑ Provided a simple mechanism is available for the user to return to the main menu, then several levels of menu can be used without the user becoming 'lost'. Commonly, the Esc key allows the user to work backwards from lower level menus to the main menu. Alternatively, each sub-menu may include an option 'Return to Main Menu'.

❑ The designer of a menu structure should limit the number of options displayed in a menu to a maximum of about eight, at which point, a sub-menu should be considered for further options. An excessive number of options on screen at one time looks untidy and may be rather intimidating to the user.

Pull-down menus

This method generally displays the main menu along the top of the screen and is popularly associated with WIMP orientated systems. When an option is selected with the cursor or mouse pointer, the range of sub-options associated with it are 'pulled down' and displayed.

Menu systems provide a number of benefits:

❑ all possibilities are presented as a command list;

❑ minimal typing is required;

❑ error trapping is simple;

❑ inappropriate choices can be withheld from the user;

❑ context sensitive help can be provided.

The drawbacks are that:

❑ they can be tedious for experienced users;

❑   an extended hierarchy of menus can be difficult for the user to follow;

❑   a large number of choices may require the use of several screens, as is the case, for example, with viewdata systems.

Form-fill dialogue

This type of dialogue requires that the screen layout matches the associated input document as closely as possible. The operator is then able to make the entries in the same logical progression as the hand-filled form. A number of features are usually evident:

❑   boxed in areas indicate fields for data entry;

❑   form headings are protected and cannot be overwritten by the user;

❑   cursor movement is restricted to the variable data entry points adjacent to each heading.

A number of design features can be applied to the data entry process:

❑   with fixed length data items, for example, a 6-digit account number, the cursor skips automatically to the next field as soon as the last character is entered;

❑   with variable length data items, the TAB key is pressed by the user when an entry is complete. This causes the cursor to skip to the next field;

❑   when all entries have been made, the user scans the screen to ensure all entries appear correct and the confirms them by pressing 'return';

❑   if errors are discovered before the 'return' key is pressed, a mechanism is available to enable corrections to be made.

The form-fill method is inappropriate when system responses are displayed which may obscure the screen headings or entries. Thus, if an invalid entry is made, the system should 'bleep' to indicate that a correction is required, without displaying an error message or display the message in a status line at the bottom of the screen; users should be well trained and aware of the valid data formats, so the need for help messages should be minimal.

Instruction and response

Examples are given in Figures 21.1 and 21.2.

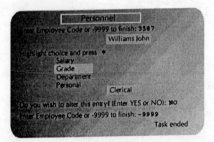

Figure 21.1. *An instruction and response dialogue*

Figure 21.2. *Dialogue for a more experienced user*

This design of dialogue is particularly appropriate for inexperienced users, where the main task is to input data. For more experienced users, the dialogue in Figure 21.1 would seem laboured and extremely frustrating, in which case it could be modified, as shown in the second figure, to omit many of the prompts.

Natural language dialogue

This type of dialogue is frequently used in database systems to allow users to specify their requirements in a 'natural' language style. The construction of the language is a complex process and many systems only allow the use of strictly limited syntax and sentence construction. Thus although the language can be described as 'natural', there is limited flexibility to allow different users to form requests in a way which is natural to each. As a result, the casual user may become frustrated by having to rephrase requests in attempts to resolve ambiguities. Queries tend to be verbose and speech recognition may provide useful support in the future.

Mnemonic driven dialogue

This design is suitable for highly trained users carrying out specialised tasks. Virtually no explanatory prompts are provided. A typical example can be found in airline reservation systems. The operator can carry out a variety of tasks relating to seat reservations using only brief mnemonic (memory aid) representations for the input. For example, in response to a customer enquiry, the operator requests a list of flights which may satisfy the customer's requirements. These may be:

```
Departure Date: 23rd June
Departure Time: 2.30pm
Departure From: London
Destination City: New York, USA
```

The operator's screen entry may appear as follows:

```
? A23JUNLHRNYCJFK1430
```

The string of characters is in strict sequence according to function. Thus: A = Available; 23JUN = 23rd June; LHR = London, Heathrow Airport; NYCJFK = New York City, John F. Kennedy Airport; 1430 = 2.30pm or up to one hour earlier or later. The system then displays any flights which satisfy these criteria, together with details of seats available, arrival times, type of aircraft etc. The operator can, if requested, immediately make a reservation for the customer with a similar mnemonic command.

Command line interface

The user enters a command to initiate action, to access information, or to call up a sequence of other commands. Still available with operating systems such as MS-DOS, a number of advantages and disadvantages are evident.

Advantages

❑   easy to implement with low resolution alphanumeric displays;

❑   the language processing techniques used with the command line interpreter (CLI) are well developed in the related area of compiler design and CLI's are thus cheap to produce;

- ❑ the power of the interface can be extended with macro commands;
- ❑ the brevity of commands, although not particularly user friendly, is ideally suited for rapid expert use.

Disadvantages

- ❑ unsuitable for inexperienced users;
- ❑ the command language must be learned and remembered;
- ❑ system interaction is restricted to the keyboard.

Some design considerations

- ❑ When designing command mnemonics, trying to achieve clarity of meaning tends to conflict with the aim of making them brief enough for rapid use.
- ❑ It may be helpful to use a two-tier system, providing menus for novices, leaving the 'hot key' facilities for experiences users.

Communication of errors

Where data validation is to be performed at the time of data entry, it is important that the interface facilitates error detection and correction. Before designing error dialogues, the following points should be noted.

- ❑ A screen which leaves error messages on screen and re-displays the prompt beneath is untidy and confusing to the user
- ❑ Repeated rejection of data without any explanation can be extremely frustrating. Such systems are only suitable for properly trained users who know the forms of input expected.
- ❑ Validation alone cannot ensure accuracy. Proper input document design, staff training and clerical checking are also vital. Users should be made aware of what validation is and its limitations, otherwise they may come to think of the system as infallible.
- ❑ It can save considerable frustration if the system is 'transparent' in terms of upper and lower case characters. In other words, entries are not made invalid simply because they are upper or lower case. Even if characters are to be output in only one case, the conversion can be carried out by the software.
- ❑ Where inexperienced users are involved, it may be useful if the system produces appropriate help messages from a file on disk. This facility is provided with many general-purpose packages.
- ❑ Error messages should be concise but detailed enough to allow the user to correct the error.
- ❑ Whilst using an application program, the user should not be presented with an error message directly from the operating system; as far as possible, all errors should be capable of being handled by the application and communicated via it to the user.

Other design considerations

It is important that the interface presents screen prompts and responses in a way which aids interpretation and to this end:

❏ any dialogue should follow a logical progression appropriate to the user, the activity and in the case of data entry, to the input document;

❏ spacing is important. Full use should be made of the screen space available;

❏ the interface should, as far as possible, be consistent across all applications in a given user area. This is particularly desirable when several packages are being used in a general application area such as accounts. The dialogue for sales ledger, purchase ledger, stock control and so on, should follow a similar structure. Many integrated packages allow the user to learn basic dialogue structure which allows rapid transfer of skills from one part of the package to another;

❏ techniques of highlighting such as brightness variation, blinking and colour coding should be used sparingly. Brightness variation should be limited to two levels, bold and normal as other variations will be difficult to detect. The blinking of a field on screen to attract the user's attention can be useful provided it does not continue once appropriate action has been taken.

Cognitive theory in interface design

There has been considerable research into cognition, that is the mental processes by which the mind becomes aware of things, as an aid to the interface designer. Card, Moran and Newell published their research findings in 1983 in a book entitled "The Psychology of Human-Computer Interaction".

They divided their examination of the interface into four areas:

❏ the physical interface. This area concerned the input and output devices with which the user communicated with the computer system, for example, the mouse, keyboard and display screen.

❏ the cognitive interface. To allow understanding of this area, the researchers developed the Human Processor Model. The model identifies various human characteristics, such as limited short-term memory, which we use to process information. It also shows how these characteristics and the tasks we undertake, affect they way we work with a computer.

❏ the conceptual interface. This area concerns the presentation of the computer system, which is highly complex, as a model which the user can assimilate and use. The graphical user interface seeks to simplify, for example, many file processing operations with the use of familiar symbols, such as folders and waste bins, and 'drag and drop' operations which avoid the typing of complex and formalised commands. Without an appropriate mental model, a user will find it difficult to make effective use of a computer system.

❏ the task interface.

A mental system model

It is a truism to say that users who understand the general principles of a computer's operation will perform tasks more quickly and effectively than those who do not. Novice users will read a sequence of instructions and follow them blindly, without any idea of how the computer performs the tasks and as a result, may not be able to deal with machine responses which are not identified in the instructions. For example, when a novice user saves a document and has no knowledge of the computer's filing system, it is quite possible that the user will be unable to find it at a later date. Computer use is more effective if the user has a mental model of the system and therefore knows 'how it works'.

A user's mental system model could include knowledge of, for example, RAM, disk storage features, file management software, communication links to remote servers. Apart from this general information, the mental model may include knowledge more specific to the applications. For example, when using a word processor, concepts of 'wrap around', spaces, paragraph alignment and carriage returns are of fundamental importance if the user is to produce the simplest of documents effectively.

Computers would have remained the preserve of specialists if 'user-friendly' interfaces had not been developed. Part of their success stems from their ability to provide the user with appropriate conceptual models of the system. For example, the use of folders for file management, a clipboard for copying and pasting, buttons for opening and saving all help the novice user to understand what the computer is doing. With experience, the mental model and the effectiveness of computer use are improved.

A designer needs to provide the user with a system model which can be easily learned and is appropriate to the type of user and the application.

Design of Help systems

Good design in Help systems is vital if users are to make effective use of an operating system and its interface. In the early days of computing, operating systems were less complex and use of operating systems was largely restricted to experts in centralised computer services departments. The growth of personal computing has required the development of more user friendly systems and on-line Help systems are now an essential part of all operating systems documentation. The Help system is installed as part of the operating system installation and the guidance given in printed documentation tends to be at an introductory "Getting Started" level. Most PCs are now sold with Internet access capability and the Help system will also include links to Web-based support. This is particularly important for the provision of help with system 'bugs' that appear from time to time. The complexity of modern operating systems makes it certain that this will happen for some time after its launch and bug 'fixes' can be placed on the manufacturer's web site for downloading by users. The site may also include FAQs (frequently asked questions) to help users with common problems.

Figure 21.3 shows the on-line Help system which forms part of the Windows 98 operating system.

Typical contents of Help systems include:

❑ Introduction. Figure 21.3 shows the introduction page, which briefly lists the range of help that is provided.

❑ How to use Help. In Figure 21.3 this is within the section "Welcome to Windows 98".

❑ Specific help areas, such as Printing, Networking, Utilities and Accessories, etc. Figure 21.4 shows the "Connecting to Networks" section expanded to reveal help topics on a range of networking facilities.

Figure 21.3. *Microsoft Windows 98 on-line help*

Figure 21.4. *About sharing a network printer*

❑ Getting started. This is a guided tour of the operating system and covers essential areas such as mouse techniques, file and folder management, installation of applications and so on.

❑ Troubleshooting guide. This provides help with common problems and difficulties. A series of multi-choice questions of the form shown in Figure 21.5 take the user through a problem step-by-step. The system works on a process of elimination to identify the user's particular problem and then suggests a solution or refers the user to technical or manufacturer support.

Figure 21.5. *Troubleshooting guide*

On-line Help systems provide different forms of assistance.

❑ Procedural Help. As the name suggests, the user is guided through as series of steps to achieve a particular result. The Help window stays 'on top' so that the user can carry out the steps without losing sight of the Help window.

❑ Conceptual Help, which is designed to explain a technical term or an operating system facility rather than guide the user through a process.

❑ Contextual Help. This is Help in the context of what the user is doing. For example, when dealing with a dialogue box such as Display Settings, the user can use the 'What's this' question mark to click on a particular setting and obtain a 'pop-up' explanation (Figure 21.6).

Figure 21.6. *Example of contextual help*

Chapter 22

System Implementation, Maintenance and Review

There are several clearly identifiable areas which require attention in the implementation of a new system, including: file conversion; system testing; staff training; changeover plan - going live.

File conversion

All records to which the computer requires access must be transferred to the appropriate backing storage medium. Records may include those concerning, for example, customer accounting and stock control. The encoding of large files is a time-consuming process and because live transaction data will be continually changing the values in the master files, they may need to be phased into the computer system in stages. In a stock control system, for example, records for certain categories of stock item may be encoded and computer processed, leaving the remainder to be processed by existing methods and encoded at a later stage. If a business has inadequate staffing to cope with the encoding exercise, a computer bureau may be used. Where possible, the bureau's staff should carry out the work on site because the records will be needed for the continued operation of the business. In favourable circumstances, a large scale encoding exercise may be undertaken to initially create the file and then, through an application program, transactions which have occurred since the encoding began can be used to update the file to reflect the correct values. Users will have to be made aware of which records have already been encoded into the system, so that they can properly update them as transactions occur. An additional problem is that records in their existing state may not conform with the file layouts designed for the new system and the data may have to be copied onto special-purpose input forms to assist with accurate encoding.

System testing

Before a system is made fully operational it should be thoroughly tested, generally in stages. If reputable and popular packaged software is being used, then provided it is being used with a wholly compatible hardware configuration, its reliability can probably be assumed. It is essential, however, that the user tests the system with real data from the business. With tailor-made systems, the testing needs to be more complex and lengthy. Once the reliability of the system has been tested, the user should run it with historical data, for which the results of processing are already known. The computerised results can then be checked for accuracy and consistency against the known manual results; software testing is examined in detail in Chapter 32.

Staff training

The education and training of the users of a system is vital if it is to be operated correctly and the full benefits are to be obtained.

Generally, although managerial staff will not carry out routine data entry, except in the event of staff sickness, they should possess skills in the operation of a terminal, desk-top or notebook microcomputer, to allow them, for example, to make database enquiries. The supplier should provide training for everyone connected with the computer system, so that they are aware of its functions and are confident in its use. In the main, this will consist of computer operating skills for data entry staff, but those receiving computer output need to know what to expect and to be able to interpret it readily. Deciding when to carry out the training can be difficult. If too early, some staff will have forgotten what they have been taught by the time the system is introduced. If too late, staff may feel panicked because they have not been properly prepared.

System changeover

Switching from the old to the new system can be carried out in stages or all at once. There are three generally recognised approaches to going live: parallel running; pilot running; direct changeover.

Parallel running

With this approach, the old and new systems are run concurrently and the results of each are compared with the other for accuracy and consistency. The old system is not abandoned until the user has complete confidence in the reliability and accuracy of the new one. Obviously, parallel running places a great administrative strain on the business, in that staff are effectively doing many of the jobs twice. Any inconsistencies in results have to be cross-checked and the source of errors located (they may result from the old or the new system). The major advantage of parallel running is that the old system can be used whenever the computer system crashes or fails to function as it should. However, the two systems cannot operate together indefinitely and "Murphy's Law" will probably ensure that some errors only become apparent after the old system has been abandoned. In conclusion, it can be said that parallel running provides a safe, but expensive and time consuming, method of switching systems. It is unlikely that many businesses will use it for any extended period, except where system failure would be completely catastrophic.

Pilot running

This strategy requires that only a portion of live transactions go through the new computerised system, the rest being processed by the old method. Thus, for example, the transactions for one section of the business, or a sample of transactions from the whole business, could be used to test the system. This is a reasonably safe strategy but again, the transactions which cause errors may be amongst those which do not pass through the computer system.

Direct changeover

This is the riskiest option in that the new system completely replaces the old, without any interim parallel or pilot running. Its major benefit is the lack of administrative costs experienced with the other two methods. The potential costs can be severe, in that system failure could mean complete loss of data access and business failure. To minimise these risks, changeover should be preceded by careful system testing and thorough staff training. It is also helpful if the changeover is carried out during a slack period so that staff are not under pressure. The considerable cost of parallel and pilot running mean that this, the riskiest strategy, is often used in small businesses.

System maintenance

Following its initial introduction, a system will not remain static and dealing with the necessary changes is termed *system maintenance*. Problems will probably become apparent as the system is operated but even if they do not, the information needs of the business will probably change after a time. Some changes will come from within the business, as staff and management identify new possibilities for the system, whilst others may be forced upon the organisation because of changes in the strategies of competitors or government legislation. The most important catalyst for change is probably the desire for better and more timely information by management, to assist their decision-making and planning. Maintenance may concern updating of hardware or amendment of software. The hardware purchased should be expansible and the software should, ideally, be flexible enough to allow amendments to be made. Often, where packaged software is used the manufacturer provides, either free or more usually for an additional payment, upgraded versions of the software with extra features (this can be a supplier-led method of system maintenance).

System review

The final phase of the system development process is the assessment of the completed system. In this *review*, or *evaluation*, a number of factors are examined, including:

❑ How well the system is performing with reference to the needs that were initially identified.

❑ The final cost of the system compared to its original budget.

❑ The time taken to complete the work.

Even after the system is fully operational its performance is continually *monitored* throughout its life. At some stage, monitoring will identify needs that are no longer satisfied by the current system, and the system development process will begin once more with a preliminary study.

📖 Case Study

This case study is the basis for the systems analysis exercise, which follows it.

Barford Properties is a small firm of estate agents, with three partners, each one specialising in a particular aspect of the business. The specialisms are:

❑ property valuation;

❑ mortgage, insurance and conveyancing;

❑ marketing.

There are five sales negotiators and a potential buyer or vendor is assigned to one sales negotiator. The partner responsible for marketing has an assistant. These staff are directly responsible to the partners. An office manager is responsible for two accounts staff and one administrative clerk. Two secretaries are also employed, with a range of duties including general correspondence, and the production of property descriptions (including photographs).

The agency operates a number of functions, as follows:

❑ Property valuations. When a client first approaches the agency with a request to handle the sale of their property, the responsible partner visits the property to assess its market value. The establishment of a selling price is usually a matter for negotiation. The client has a minimum figure in mind, which may coincide with the valuation assessment by the agency. If the valuation is less than the minimum figure put forward by the client, they are advised to lower the asking price accordingly. However, the final decision is made by the client. The asking price may be reviewed, depending on the response or otherwise of potential buyers. In making the assessment, the agency draws on its local experience, but also on data concerning regional and national trends in the housing market.

❏   Property sales. Once an asking price is agreed, fees are settled. Charges vary according to the value of the property, as the agency takes a percentage of the ultimate selling price, plus costs of advertising. Other charges for conveyancing work are also made. The sales negotiator assigned to a vendor handles their routine enquiries and correspondence to keep them informed of progress. If a client is not satisfied with progress and wants a different asking price, for example, he or she is referred to one of the partners.

❏   Marketing. This section deals with the placing of advertisements in local and national newspapers and property journals. It also organises the window displays and property details leaflets which are given out to interested buyers.

❏   Mortgage, conveyancing and insurance services (the agency acts as a broker). Buyers of properties handled by the agency are offered these services, and many clients make use of them, particularly if they are first-time buyers. The agency does not have Independent Financial Adviser status and mortgages are arranged with the Barford and Bamford Building Society. Property, mortgage protection and endowment insurances are obtained from the Buzzard Life Insurance Company.

❏   Financial accounting. This section handles all the customer accounts and deals with receipts and payments flowing between the agency, building societies, solicitors and insurance companies.

A brief outline of the procedures involved in a property sale is given below.

1. The initial request from a client wishing to sell a property is dealt with by the responsible partner, who makes an appointment to visit the property. Details of location, type, agreed asking price, number of rooms and so on are recorded. Photographs are also taken.

2. The property details are transcribed onto one of two standard forms, depending on whether the property is residential or business. This process is carried out in the Property Sales section.

3. The staff categorise the property according to basic criteria, including property location, type, size, quality, number of rooms and price range. These basic details are transcribed onto record cards, which are the initial point of reference when a potential buyer makes an enquiry.

4. To match prospective buyers with properties for sale, a Buyer Clients file is maintained. Details of suitable properties are sent (using a mailing list) to potential buyers.

5. When a buyer expresses an interest in a property, a viewing appointment is arranged between the buyer and the vendor (if the property is empty, one of the partners will accompany the buyer).

6. If a buyer expresses interest, they are asked to make an offer, which is then put to the vendor for consideration. Apart from the offer price, other factors are considered; for example, whether, the buyer has a property to sell.

7. Once a sale is agreed, solicitors take over the process of carrying out the various conveyancing operations and agreeing a completion date, when payment is made and the property ownership changes hands. When this is completed, the agency requests payment of the fees by the vendor. Buyers are not charged by the agency, although they do incur conveyancing costs.

✍Exercise

This *systems analysis* exercise relates to topics covered in Chapters 18 to 22 and is based on the preceding Barford Properties case study. To extend the exercise, you may carry out some additional research into the operation of an estate agency in your area. It is proposed that the Property Sales system is computerised.

1. Produce a plan of the *systems analysis stages*, which you will need to follow. Explain the purpose of each stage and the general activities it involves.
2. Identify the users who would be expected to have access to the records and assess their requirements.
3. Undertake a *feasibility study* of the proposal. Define the *purpose* of the Property Sales System and establish its *objectives*. Other systems within the estate agency, which may interact with it, also need to be identified.
4. Briefly describe the standard techniques for gathering users system requirements. Select the technique(s) you consider most appropriate for the estate agency proposal and your choice. Prepare a *questionnaire* for gathering information from buyers. The aim of the questionnaire is to establish which types of information on houses they most need, in the initial stages of an enquiry and the form(s) in which they would like the information to be presented to them. You also want to know which types of house and price ranges are most in demand and the number of houses each respondent has bought. Most people have bought at least one house, so you should obtain around 20 *responses*.
5. Draw an *organisation chart* to represent the divisions of responsibility in the agency.
6. Analyse the Property Sales system, and a produce a *systems analysis report* on the existing manual system. Use systems flowcharts, where appropriate. Your analysis should detail the current:

- ❑ data collection methods and inputs;
- ❑ documents used;
- ❑ operations and decisions;
- ❑ storage;
- ❑ system outputs.

Also, include in your report, *recommendations* for a computerised system. These should:

- ❑ describe the different types of system (for example, batch processing, transaction processing, information storage and retrieval) and make an argued recommendation for a particular type;
- ❑ detail *input* (including form, source and collection method), *processing* (form of processing activity), *storage* and *reporting* requirements of the system; you should also

detail expected *volumes* of data and *frequency* of input and outputs;

❑ identify *expectations* of the system.

❑ assess likely *costs* and *savings* of a new system, identifying necessary resources.

Chapter 23

Project Management

A project is a relatively short-term activity (weeks, or months usually), designed to achieve specific objectives. Working on a project team, therefore, is not usually a person's main job. So, programmers, systems analysts and other computing and user specialists are assigned to a project team as and when the need arises. Examples of computer-based projects are:

❑   implementation of a new computerised payroll system;

❑   extension of a local area network to a new laboratory;

❑   introduction of a products database, through which customers can browse.

The stages which lead to the completion of a project are formally described in Chapters 18 to 22 and include, for example, a preliminary study, systems analysis and design, implementation, maintenance and review.

Project teams

A project team should comprise people with the necessary mix of personal qualities, skills and knowledge to achieve the objectives of the project. Departmental barriers should not restrict the choice of team members and where appropriate they should be selected from across the organisation and, if necessary, from outside it, as consultants. Apart from the project manager, a project team is likely to include systems analysts and designers, programmers and depending on the type of system, database administrators and network engineers. The team may also include specialists from the particular function for which the system is being developed, such as the Head of Department. If departmental representatives are not included in the team they will have a considerable consultancy role to play.

Project activities

Identifying a project

Very often the need for a major new system, product or facility is identified by corporate management. This is because management has the benefit (or should have) of a 'bird's eye' view of the organisation, are responsible for decisions to move it in one direction or another, and control its resources, including finance, staffing, equipment and so on. Thus, a decision to computerise a personnel management system and the initiation of a project to achieve that objective is likely to be 'top-down'. Occasionally, needs are identified by staff working at an operational level, precisely because they have a more intimate understanding of the day-to-day problems they experience.

Identifying project objectives and scope

The objectives of a project need to be clear, because they describe its main functions and what it seeks to achieve. Without objectives, the tasks of team members will be unclear. The scope of a project identifies its boundaries, so the limits of the project are set. Formally, the objectives of a project are detailed in a document titled the Statement of Requirements.

Planning the project

Before starting any project, a number of questions need to be asked: What results are wanted? When does it have to be completed? What resources, including accommodation, equipment, finance, components and people are needed to carry out the project? What are the main tasks? Can some tasks be progressed at the same time or be overlapped? Which tasks have to be completed before which others? In what order do the tasks have to be completed? When does each task have to be started and completed? How do the tasks relate to one another and contribute towards the successful completion of the project? Who needs to be on the team? Who is responsible for dealing with each task? Is best use being made of each member's personal qualities, knowledge and skills?

All these questions point to the need for *planning* a project before it is started. Perhaps the most important questions are:

❑   What has to be done?

❑   What is the sequence of tasks and events?

❑   What time is needed to complete the tasks?

Why plan?

Asked the question, "Why plan?", you would probably say something like, "It's obvious. If you plan something, you're more organised and more likely to achieve what you want." Figure 23.1 illustrates the main purposes of planning.

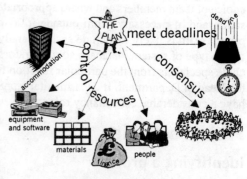

The Figure shows that *resources* include: people (members of the team and users and managers involved in the project); finance; materials (such as paper and other consumables); equipment (IT and any other special equipment); software (for example, word processor, charting and critical path analysis packages); accommodation (for planning work and team meetings). *Control* is needed, not only to ensure that necessary resources are made available, but also to promote efficiency in their use and keep the project within the planned budget.

Figure 23.1. *Purposes of project planning*

Consensus shows a two-way arrow between the plan and the people involved in the project. To achieve consensus, requires that when feedback on progress is provided by participants, their comments are properly considered and, if necessary, used to modify the plan.

A plan also sets *deadlines*, dates or times when particular tasks should be completed. It is important that team members keep to deadlines. Each team member is given a role and some responsibilities and lateness is likely to prevent progress of dependent tasks, for which other team members are responsible. This delays the project and probably causes discord and resentment within the team. However, difficulties, unanticipated problems and modifications to the plan, are bound to result in changes to deadlines, hence the two-way arrow in Figure 23.1.

Analysing the project

This requires a detailed analysis of the project objectives, to determine the solutions to achieve them. The detail of this work is covered in Chapter 20. To summarise, team members need to break the problem down into smaller component parts, suggest possible solutions, evaluate them and either accept or reject them. This will be an *iterative* process, as decisions on one aspect of the project may require a re-examination of other aspects. The formal method of analysing a problem into progressively smaller components is known as *top-down design*. Analysis also requires that a sequence of activities is identified for the achievement of each project component, as well as the resources which are needed at various points in the sequence. This is known as *scheduling*.

Co-ordinating and integrating the project

The aim of a schedule is to plan the timing of events, activities and resource usage, such that a particular aspect of a project is competed at a particular time. A project is likely to consist of several separate 'strands', each occupying different members of the team. The work of team members needs to be co-ordinated, or properly related. If we say that someone is uncoordinated, we mean that their various physical movements do not properly relate to one another. Lack of physical co-ordination manifests itself in clumsiness, and for example, an inability to dance or do gymnastics. Co-ordination of a project, therefore, means ensuring that the activities of team members and the tasks on which they are working, are related and complement one another. Loss of co-ordination may manifest itself in a team member working hard on a task, which bears little relation to and does not properly contribute to, the progress of the project. Co-ordination is necessary between team members, but also between the team and others who may contribute to the project (in other departments or from other organisations). For this reason, there should be *team* and *steering group meetings* (with user and management representatives and perhaps consultants from outside the organisation). Integration is the fitting together of separate components.

Budget monitoring and control

Every project has a budget, that is, a limited amount of money allocated for its development. The amount depends on the importance of the project to the organisation and the type of project. Not all projects proceed, perhaps because it is not seen to give value for money, or another project, viewed as more important, gains priority. For example, in a college, it may be highly desirable for maths and science students to have a new computer laboratory, but the travel and tourism courses attract far more students and their project for a travel agency office gains priority. The computer laboratory project may be cancelled or scaled down to half the number of computer workstations.

Cost control

Given a financial budget, it is necessary to control money costs to stay within it. Careful thought needs to be given to what constitutes a cost. If you were asked to estimate the costs of installing a computer network, you may check catalogues for the prices of computer file servers, workstations, desks, printers, cabling, connectors and so on and come up with a total cost.

You may also consider the costs of software and installation charges. Obviously, these are major items, but they do not reflect the complete cost of the project. You also need to consider staffing costs, not only those of the team, but also the salary of a technician or network administrator who is to manage the network. If users are unfamiliar with the software, training charges will be incurred.

If the members of the project team are salaried employees of the organisation, the difficulty arises of separating their responsibilities to the project, from their other work. Members of a project team are rarely fully occupied by the project, and have other responsibilities. For example, a sales supervisor may be seconded to a sales marketing project team and spend approximately two days per week working on the project. It is more likely that the time given to the project will be highly variable, for week to week, depending on the stage reached. Despite this difficulty, efforts have to be made to calculate the cost of the sales supervisor's (and any other team members) secondment to the project. Otherwise, the actual cost may, in reality, veer drastically from the budgeted cost (although this may not be apparent at the time).

A large project will probably need a complex accounting and cost control system, but a smaller project can be measured by the number of people and the hours they spend working on it. To summarise, in seeking to control costs, you need to recognise what they are and the items in Figure 23.1 provide a useful checklist. Using the example of a computer network, we can identify the following likely costs:

- ❏ project team members' time, costed according to their hourly rate of pay;

- ❏ consultancy charges, both from outside the organisation and from other departments (if charged by them); this will be a corporate decision. If a department has a budget, it will need to charge other departments for work they do for them;

- ❏ computer and network hardware;

- ❏ software licences;

- ❏ carpets, air conditioning, blinds; tables, chairs, cable conduit.

- ❏ installation charges (unless carried out by the project team);

- ❏ training costs for users on use of new software;

- ❏ training/employment of network manager;

- ❏ accommodation, both for the project team and for location of the new network.

The team member with budget monitoring responsibility must record and monitor these costs as the project progresses. Costs give a guide to progress, in the sense that it is a measure of the value of work done. This is particularly so with tangible items, such as computer equipment. The accountant must also monitor the costs against the allocated budget and report to the project manager, or member of senior management, if the project is going over budget.

Project implementation

This includes systems analysis, design, implementation and review, all of which are covered in Chapters 18 to 22.

Evaluating the project

This activity is associated with the monitoring and review of the project, during and after its completion. Evaluation should include the following.

❑ Measuring progress against schedules and budgets. Has the planned stage been achieved at the budgeted cost?

❑ Are resources being used economically and effectively? If not, this may be because the strengths of team members are not being used in the most effective way. One person may be particularly skilled in one area, but is assigned a role, in which they are under-used or inadequate to the task.

❑ If the project is behind schedule, what are the causes? The problem may be inadequate definition of project, unclear solutions, lack of suitable resources, weakness of team member(s), either in commitment, knowledge or skills. Evaluation will tackle these problems and examine remedies which allow the project to progress (or if it is supposedly completed, correct the deficiency).

❑ The identification of potential problems and ways of avoiding them. In this way, the team should avoid 'management by crisis', by ignoring potential problems, hoping they will simply go away and only re-acting when forced.

❑ Analysis of alternative courses of action, referred to in spreadsheet jargon as 'what if' analysis. In this way, likely effects of different approaches to the project can be anticipated. For example, during a project to install a computer network, consideration may be given to alternative shared printer solutions. The costs of these alternatives can be projected and a judgement made as to the project budget's sufficiency. If a more expensive printing solution is chosen, it may be that savings can be made in other areas of the project. Alternatively, an approach may be made to the project sponsor for an increase in the budget. However, this would require a submission of arguments as to the cost effectiveness of the change.

❑ Quality assessment. Measuring the quality of a product, such as a car, is fairly straightforward. The number sold in comparison with other cars in the same category and continuance of good sales over a long period indicates a high quality product. Measuring the quality of a service is much more difficult. Information systems provide services to fulfil the needs of various organisational functions and assessment of quality is sometimes highly subjective. The most important quality assessment is that of the project's customers; has the project achieved its objectives?

People, roles and responsibilities

Another word for 'role' is 'function'. Put another way, if your function is to take the minutes of team meetings, your role is 'minutes secretary'; in that role, it is your *responsibility* to take the minutes. The range of roles needed for a project will depend on its size, complexity and scope. Some roles can be regarded as *internal* and relate to the project team, whilst others are external; the latter may relate to people who are not directly involved in the project, but are affected by it, have an interest in its outcome and may be of occasional assistance to the project team. For example, a similar project may have been completed elsewhere (within the organisation, or outside it) and it makes sense to consult the people involved. If the project is being financed by a bank or other external agency, clearly the role of bank manager is going to impinge on the work of the team. Other team responsibilities include: resource allocation, monitoring of resource usage (records need to be kept) and monitoring of progress against schedules.

Team building

Building a team involves the development of: ways of working to improve efficiency and productivity; relationships among members; mutual respect of each others' strengths; the team's adaptability to changes in circumstances, such as a cut in budget, or a reduction in the time allocation.

If a team works successfully over a longer time (perhaps months, or years), or on different successful projects, the initial stages of team building should be unnecessary.

Achieving consensus

Making decisions by consensus is desirable, but not always achievable, at least in the sense of absolute and unreserved agreement. Consensus can only be obtained when each member has clearly expressed his or her views and disagreements, listened to and understood those of the others, and presented any alternatives they wish to be discussed. When, through discussion and negotiation a decision, which everyone understands, is reached then we can say a consensus decision has been made.

Measuring team performance

Leadership

A team does not always have the same leader. Any team member must be willing to take that role. This is because, as a project progresses, different specialisms are needed. Thus, for example, during the analysis stage, when questionnaires are being drawn up and user interviews conducted, the team has a particular leader. When the project moves onto the production stage, entirely different talents are called for, such as technical knowledge of project equipment and computer software, and another member takes the team leader role. Teams should be democratic, so leaders should lead, not dictate.

Team leader role

A team leader should:

❑   gain consensus on the project objectives and clarify members' expectations of the project. If all the team are clear about the objectives, in the short and longer term, they are more likely to be able to co-ordinate and integrate their activities;

❑   make the best use of the available skills and talents. This means that task assignment must be carefully considered, so members work to their strengths and not their weaknesses;

❑   hold regular meetings to discuss progress and problems as they arise;

❑   monitor and give feedback on team and individual performance;

❑   ensure co-ordination and integration of separate tasks;

❏   ensure that the project is completed (as explained earlier, this is likely to be a stage or one aspect, as the team leader role may be occupied by different members, as appropriate).

Leadership styles

Various leadership styles can be adopted, depending on the experience, competence and confidence of the team's members (and the team leader):

❏   lead by good example (but don't do it all);

❏   delegation and trust (assign tasks and leave them to get on with it, until the next review meeting);

❏   participate and support; this style may be appropriate where none of the members have strong experience of leading a team and need extensive support from one another. The team leader must still lead, otherwise direction and momentum are lost.

Co-operation, enthusiasm and adaptability

Co-operation means working together to achieve common objectives. It does not mean obeying orders from dictators! Enthusiasm comes from genuine interest in the work, so although people cannot always do what they most enjoy, they tend to be more enthusiastic when using their talents, rather than struggling with weaknesses. Enthusiasm also tends to come from previous success and recognition by others of achievement. Adaptability is important, because a project will not go absolutely as planned. Members may have to learn new skills or extend existing ones (for example, a new version of a software package may be provided), work with different team members at various times and possibly, take the role of team leader.

Technical knowledge and competence

It is not necessary for every member of a team to be expert in the same technical areas. Each person is assigned to a team because they have a particular contribution to make; this contribution is likely to be a mix of the personal qualities already mentioned and competence in a particular area. For example, a team member with good communication skills may chair meetings, take minutes, or take the role of team leader. Of course, a team leader has to have the technical knowledge to understand the task or tasks for which they have responsibility. Some members of the team are likely to be, for example, better programmers and some may have highly developed design skills. The assignment of people to particular roles should take account of a range of factors, but technical knowledge and competence are fundamental to the production of a good product. It is useless to compose a team of good communicators, if their knowledge of the project subject is sketchy.

Effort and efficiency

Non-productive effort is wasted. However, this does not mean that every effort should achieve instant success. By working on a task, finding that the results are unsatisfactory and repeating or modifying the work, we can learn and ultimately improve the end product. Of course, with proper preparation and planning, the chances of success are increased. For example, a programmer should not tackle a problem by immediately coding the program, but should follow a disciplined program design method. Without this preparation, the program is likely to be difficult to debug and modify. Efficiency comes from properly channelled effort. To carry out a task efficiently requires that all the components (materials, tools, technical knowledge, accommodation and so on) are available as and when they are needed.

✍️Exercises

1. A large organisation is planning the development of a new computer-based system.
    (i)   Identify the main categories of staff who ought to be members of the *project management team*.
    (ii)   Why is it important to define the *scope* of a project?
    (iii) List the main *resource categories* which may be required for the development of the project.
    (iv)   Why is it important to set various *deadlines* during the project?
    (v)   Many processes within a project will tend to be *iterative*. Why is this?
    (vi)   Describe the main *categories of cost* which may be incurred during the project and following its implementation.
    (vii) Describe three criteria for the *evaluation* of a project.
    (viii) Using a suitable example, explain why *consensus* is important but not always achievable.
2. (i)   Identify two qualities which are desirable in a *project leader*.
    (ii)   "All members of a project team should have sufficient technical knowledge to understand and sufficient competence to play an active role in, all aspects of the project."

    To what extent do you regard this statement to be true or false? Explain your answer.
    (iii) Why is important that project team members are able to distinguish between *effort* and *efficiency*?

Chapter 24

Critical Path Analysis

Techniques such as PERT (*Project Evaluation and Review Techniques*) and CPA (*Critical Path Analysis*) use a branch of mathematics called *network analysis* to systemise and aid project management. Networks allow projects to be represented graphically as a series of activities connected by nodes representing their start and end points. Network analysis allows the crucial activities which determine the total duration of the project to be identified. Project management software is available for all these techniques. The following case study uses a network to perform a critical path analysis of a project involving the installation of a LAN in a college.

Case study: installing a local area network

A college has decided to install a local area network of PCs in a classroom. As well as obtaining and installing the network, the project involves refurbishing the classroom to be used - replacing the ceiling, redecorating, providing blinds on the windows, new carpets, air conditioning, benches for the workstations and chairs - and also appointing a technician who will help with the installation and testing of the network. It has been decided that tenders will be invited for suppliers of the network system and for the classroom conversion work. The suppliers of the office furniture and application software required - word processors, spreadsheets etc - will be selected and ordered by the college's computer manager directly. One of the first duties of the newly appointed technician will be to test the computer equipment before it is installed in the network room. Once the classroom has been converted the office furniture and computer hardware will be installed and then the system will have to be tested and any faults corrected. Documentation will need to be provided for users of the network - one type for students and another for teaching staff - and finally, before staff start to use the network, they will need some training.

Identifying activities

The first stage in managing a project such as this is to identify the activities involved and to assign a letter to each one. The list of activities for this project is as follows:

	Activity		Activity
A	Carry out initial study of needs	I	Test computer hardware
B	Invite tenders from suppliers	J	Procure office furniture
C	Appoint suppliers	K	Install furniture and network system
D	Obtain computer equipment	L	Procure network application software
E	Convert classroom	M	Prepare documentation for network users
F	Advertise for technician	N	Test network
G	Shortlist candidates & invite for interview	O	Correct system faults
H	Interview candidates	P	Train staff

At this stage it is not possible to assign a precise order to the activities since some of them can occur in parallel with others. The next stage is to estimate the length of time required to complete each activity. These estimates may be based on experience, discussions with prospective suppliers and building contractors, information obtained from equipment suppliers regarding probable delivery times, or from other sources. It should also be possible at this stage to identify, for each activity listed, which activity or activities must be completed before it can commence. For example, before tenders can be invited from network suppliers, the college must have conducted a study of its requirements so that the type and size of the network could be specified precisely. Similarly, before the network can be installed, the room must be ready and the equipment must have been delivered.

Activity dependence tables

An *activity dependence table* lists each activity together with activities that must be completed before this particular one can begin. The activity dependence table for our case study is shown below. Included in the table is a column which shows the estimated amount of time required for each activity.

	Activity	Duration (Days)	Preceding activity
A	Carry out initial study of needs	15	None
B	Invite tenders from suppliers	19	A
C	Appoint suppliers	5	B
D	Obtain computer equipment	10	C
E	Convert classroom	40	C
F	Advertise for technician	21	A
G	Shortlist candidates and invite for interview	10	F
H	Interview candidates	2	G
I	Test computer hardware	10	H
J	Procure office furniture	20	A
K	Install office furniture and network system	15	D, E, I, J
L	Procure network application software	28	A
M	Prepare documentation for network users	15	K, L
N	Test network	10	K, L
O	Correct system faults	6	N
P	Train staff	10	M, O

Network analysis

A common method of representing activities and how they relate to each other is by means of a *network* in which each activity is represented by an arrowed line and the starting point and finishing point are each represented by a circle called a *node*. The nodes are numbered such that the node at the start of an activity is always lower than the node at the end of the activity. The following diagrams illustrate how nodes and activities are drawn.

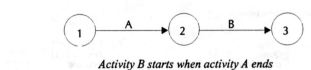

Activity B starts when activity A ends

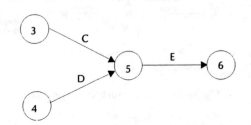

E begins when both C and D have finished

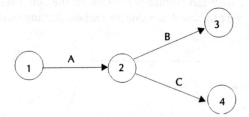

B and C can start when A is complete

Drawing the Network

A network diagram illustrates how all of the activities identified depend on each other. Note, however, that there are a number of rules to be observed when drawing the network:

1. There must be only one start node and one finish node.

2. No activities are allowed to have the same start and finish node.

To avoid this, dummy activities, which have a duration of zero, are introduced as shown above.

3. Arrows should go from left to right.

Using these ideas, we can produce the network shown in Figure 24.1 for our case study project. The diagram clearly shows the order of the activities, which ones can be undertaken at the same time and dependencies between activities. What we now need to determine is how long the project will take overall.

Figure 24.1. *The network for the project*

Earliest starting times

Remembering that no activity can commence before all the activities which converge on its start node have finished, we can now determine the earliest starting times for each activity. This is shown in Figure 24.2.

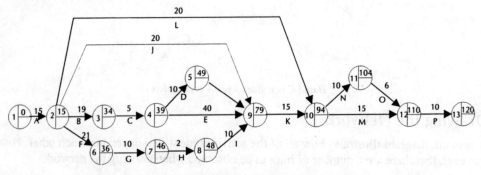

Figure 24.2. *Earliest starting times for the project*

The time taken for each activity is shown above the activity letter. The extra figure inside the node now shows the earliest day on which the project can start. Thus B starts 15 days after A has commenced, and since B requires a further 19 days for completion, C starts on the 34th day. Where two or more activities finish on the same node, for example on node 9, the highest accumulated figure is always shown. Thus, although activity I finishes after 48 days, D finishes after 49 days, and J after 35 days, it is the finish time of activity E, that is 79 days, which is recorded in node 9.

The diagram shows that the *total project time* is the longest path through the network, and it amounts to the figure shown in the last node, namely 120 days.

Latest starting times

We are almost at a position now to determine the *slack time*, or *total float*, for each activity (see Figure 24.3). This will tell us by how many days each activity could be extended, or delayed, without delaying the whole project. In order to do this we must first calculate the latest starting time for each activity.

Starting with the figure in the last node (120 days in this case), we work backwards through the network calculating the latest possible time each activity could commence without overrunning the time shown in its finish node. In practice this involves subtracting the duration of the activity from the latest starting time shown in its finish node and writing this in its start node. If a choice of two values occurs, the smallest figure is always chosen.

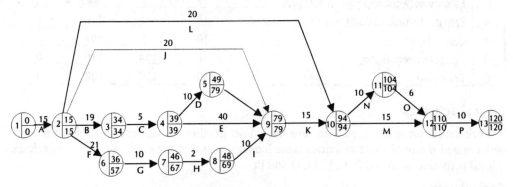

Figure 24.3. *Latest starting times for the project*

For example, the latest start time of activity P is found by taking its duration of 10 days from the value 120 in its finish node. This gives a latest starting time of 110. For activity O, we subtract 6 from 110 to give 104; for N 10 from 104 gives 94. When we get to M, subtracting 15 from 110 gives 95, but activity N gave a value of 94, which is smaller, so we use 94 as node 10's latest starting time.

Slack time

Slack time is the extra time that the activity could take without delaying the whole project. The diagram below illustrates how it is calculated.

Slack time = L - D - E

Thus the slack time for activity I is 79 - 10 - 48 = 21 days. This means that testing the hardware could be allowed to take up to 21 days more to complete than was originally estimated without affecting the total project time. The following table shows the slack times for all the activities.

	Activity	Duration (Days)	Latest start time	Earliest start time	Slack time
A	Carry out initial study of needs	15	0	15	0
B	Invite tenders from suppliers	19	15	34	0
C	Appoint suppliers	5	34	39	0
D	Obtain computer equipment	10	39	79	30
E	Convert classroom	40	39	79	0
F	Advertise for technician	21	15	57	21
G	Shortlist candidates and invite for interview	10	36	67	11

H	Interview candidates	2	46	69	21
I	Test computer hardware	10	48	79	44
J	Procure office furniture	20	15	79	44
K	Install office furniture and network system	15	79	94	0
L	Procure network application software	28	15	94	51
M	Prepare documentation for network users	15	94	110	1
N	Test network	10	94	104	0
O	Correct system faults	6	104	110	0
P	Train staff	10	110	120	0

Critical activities

The critical activities are those with zero slack time. In other words, the total project time will be increased if any of these activities takes longer than was anticipated. For our network the critical activities are A, B, C, E, K, N, O and P.

Critical path

This is the path, or paths, through the network consisting of only critical activities. In our example there is only a single critical path, but it is possible for other projects to have more than one critical path. The critical path is shown by the heavy line in Figure 24.4.

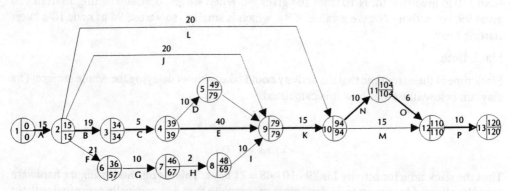

Figure 24.4. *The critical path*

The critical path is always the longest path through the network, and it tells us what the total time will be for the project. During the course of a project, the critical activities will need to be monitored very carefully to ensure that they do not overrun and thereby increase the total project time. If this is in danger of occurring, it may be possible to divert manpower from non-critical activities in order to ensure that critical activities are completed on time.

Gantt charts

A Gantt chart is a diagram which clearly illustrates when activities can start and finish. Each activity is represented by a solid line and any associated slack time by a dotted line as shown in Figure 24.5. The start, end and duration of every activity can be read from the horizontal axis which shows the time scale in days.

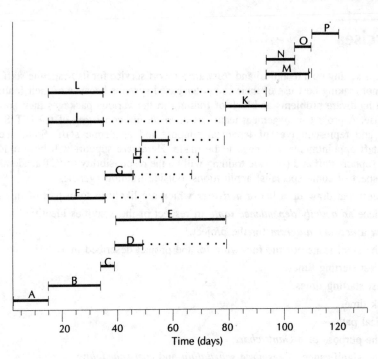

Figure 24.5. *The Gantt chart for the project*

Resource scheduling

Resource scheduling is concerned with minimising the numbers of people required at any one time for the project. The Gantt chart shows us where overlapping activities can be moved to reduce the amount of overlap. For example, each of the activities D, E, G, H and I overlaps with one or more of the others, but D, G, H and I each have a considerable amount of slack time allowing them to be delayed. So, if, say D and G could each be carried out by one person, but not at the same time, then D could be delayed so that it starts when G finishes, thus allowing the person to do both jobs but one after the other.

In projects involving large numbers of human resources, this type of adjustment can result in a significant reduction in the number of people who need to be employed, and consequently result in a large reduction in cost.

Cost scheduling

Cost scheduling uses the network to find the cheapest means of reducing the total project time. Activities can be shortened by, for example, using extra personnel, or by paying them overtime to work longer hours. This invariably incurs a cost penalty, but shortening some activities may be cheaper than others. The average cost of shortening each activity on the critical path by one time unit (a day for instance) can be calculated - this is called the *cost slope* of an activity - assuming accurate costing information is available. By repeatedly finding the critical activity with the least cost slope and reducing its duration, the overall project time can be shortened for the least cost.

✍️Exercises

1. A college is setting up a technical and software support service for its academic staff. Some staff are not making best use of their computer-based systems because of their inability to deal with hardware problems and lack of training in the various packages they are called upon to use. A project management team has been set up, consisting of the ICT Services Manager and representatives of technical support and academic staff. Some technical support staff appointments will need to be made. Hardware support will be provided by technical support staff and software training will be the responsibility of ICT academic staff and in respect of some specialist applications, outside training agencies.

   (i) Suggest and draw up a list of *activities* which are likely to form part of this project.

   (ii) Produce an *activity dependence table* in respect of the activities identified in (i).

   (iii) Draw a *network diagram* for the project.

2. Explain the significance of the following for the project described in 1.

   (i)   Earliest starting times.

   (ii) Latest starting times.

   (iii) Slack time.

   (iv) Critical path.

3. Explain the purpose of a *Gantt chart*.

4. Explain the significance of *resource scheduling* and *cost scheduling*.

Databases

Chapters

Databases

Chapter

Chapter 25

Structured Systems Development Techniques

The value of structure and methodology in programming is well recognised. Jackson's Structured Programming (JSP), is one such methodology which defines the structure of the data to be processed, determines the programming processes based on those structures and then defines the necessary tasks to be performed in more detail.

The task of analysing and designing a complete system comes within the framework of the system life cycle, described in Chapter 18 Systems Analysis - an Overview. The main drawback of the traditional analysis and design approaches, is that progress tends to be incremental and problems discovered at one stage frequently necessitate a return to an earlier stage to deal with them.

The data modelling techniques described in this chapter and in Chapter 26 on Databases seek to improve on the traditional approach and like JSP, the approach described here is data-driven and typified by Entity-Relationship Modelling (ERM), which forms part of the data analysis technique developed by Chen in 1976. Methodologies developed since then have adopted the data driven approach or used ERM as a basis for another, such as the SSADM (Structured Systems Analysis and Design Methodology).

The following sections describe the main tools and techniques used in data-driven methodologies.

Database modelling tools and techniques

Data analysis

Data analysis is a technique primarily concerned with determining the *logical structure* of the data, its *properties* and the *processes* needed to make use of it. Its objective is to produce a model which represents the information needs of a particular information system or sub-system and it should be understandable by users as well as analysts, in order to provide a basis for discussion and agreement.

The main tool used within data analysis is the *Entity-Relationship Model (ERM)*, which classifies information into:

❑   entities;

❑   attributes;

❑   relationships.

Entities are objects which are of interest or relevance to the organisation, for example, Supplier, Customer, Stock. An entity will normally equate with a database table; an *entity occurrence* is normally synonymous with a *record* within that table.

Attributes comprise those properties of an entity which are identified as being of interest to users. It may be helpful to equate attributes with fields in a conventional record, but it is important to note that in database systems (where the term data item type is sometimes used), it is not always necessary to have all the attributes for an entity stored in the relevant record in the database; it is necessary, however, to ensure that all attributes relevant to a particular entity can be associated with it. This point is explained in Chapter 26.

Relationships exist between entities. For example, an Employee works for a particular Department and a Purchase Order is sent to one particular Supplier.

The degree of the relationship may be: one-to-one; one-to-many; many-to-one; many-to-many.

One-to-one relationship

Figure 25.1 provides an example of a one-to-one relationship. Each hospital patient develops a unique medical history and each medical history can only relate to one hospital patient.

Figure 25.1. *One-to-one relationship*

One-to-many relationship

Figure 25.2 illustrates that an order may comprise one or many order lines, but each order line will be unique to a particular order. Note the double arrow head to indicate the *many* side of the relationship. By many, we mean one or more, whereas one means one only.

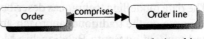

Figure 25.2. *One-to-many relationship*

Many-to-many relationship

A stock item may be ordered in a number of purchase orders and a single purchase order may include a number of stock items. This is symbolised in Figure 25.3.

Some of the practical implications of these relationship types are explained in the *Stock Control* case study in Chapter 27 (Editing Tables through Query Dynasets).

Stock item — is ordered in — Purchase order

Figure 25.3. *Many-to-many relationship*

An ERM for a given information system or sub-system may consist of a number of entities, the attributes associated with each and the relationships between those entities. The modelling process requires that any given model is continually refined until its efficiency in satisfying users' needs is optimised and its structure is in a form dictated by the requirements of the RDBMS in use.

An ERM for an Academic database

Figure 25.4 shows a normalised (3NF) entity relationship model (ERM) for the *Academic* database outlined in Chapter 26.

Figure 25.4. *Normalised ERM for Academic database*

The diagram can be interpreted as follows.

❑ Each student registers for one or more enrolments, but each enrolment relates to only one student. This is a one-to-many relationship, the enrolments being the many side. The single arrow head indicates the one side and the double headed arrow, the many side.

❑   Each tutor is named in many enrolments, but each enrolment only names one tutor; this is also a one-to-many relationship. Although tutors are assigned students, the process is carried out through the enrolment entity, so there is no direct relationship between the Student and Tutor entities; instead the connection is through the Enrolment entity. This structure is arrived at through the normalisation process.

❑   Each course has many enrolments, but each enrolment only concerns one course. Therefore, there is a one-to-many relationship between the Course and Enrolment entities.

An ERM for a Personnel database

Figure 25.5 is an ERM for the *Personnel* database, used as a case study in Chapter 27.

The diagram shows the following relationships between the three entities.

Figure 25.5. *Normalised ERM for Personnel database*

❑   Each department contains many staff, but each member of staff is based in a single department - a one-to-many relationship between Department and StaffMember.

❑   Each job (job title or grade) is held by one or more members of staff, but each member of staff has only one job title. The relationship between Job and StaffMember is also one-to-many.

The ERMs shown in Figures 25.4 and 25.5 illustrate database structures after data normalisation. They can be drawn at various stages of the modelling process, to help clarify the entities which are needed and the relationships which arise between them. Thus, an ERM drawn for the Academic database after the first stage of normalisation (1NF), would only show the Student and Enrolment entities (see Chapter 26). The second and third stages of normalisation are fine-tuning the structure, but it must be in first normal form (no repeating groups) before you can attempt to construct a database. Entity relationship modelling can be a complex process, which requires much training and experience, so at this stage, you are likely to be constructing databases from fully normalised ERMs.

Functional analysis

This activity is concerned with identifying the data requirements, processes and activities relevant to each business function which is to use the data model established in the data analysis stage.

Data flow diagrams (DFDs)

Figure 25.6 shows some typical, standard symbols for the drawing of data flow diagrams. DFDs are used to illustrate, in a diagrammatic form, the logical data flows between entities, accompanying processes and any file storage or data stores.

DFDs can be used at various stages in the analysis and design process. In the early stages, they will be at a high level and may, for example, show little detail except for a department's general function, such as sales accounting or stock control; later, DFDs may be drawn at a lower, more detailed level, to show for example, the checking of a customer's account before sending an invoice reminder or statement of account.

Figure 25.6. *DFD symbols*

Figure 25.7 shows a *high level* DFD for a typical trading organisation. More details on the data flows in its Sales Order Processing system are shown in the low level DFD in Figure 25.8.

Figure 25.7. *High level DFD for trading business*

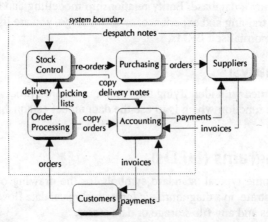

Figure 25.8. *Low level DFD showing detail of Order Processing System*

Normalisation

Normalisation (see Chapter 26) is a technique which is particularly useful in the design of relational database models. It is used to determine the validity of the logical data model produced in the data analysis stage and is particularly concerned with:

❑ minimising data redundancy or duplication;

❑ establishing dependencies between data items and grouping them in the most efficient way;

❑ obtaining a measure of data independence, such that a database can be supplemented with new data without changing the existing logical structure and thus the applications programs.

Prototyping

A prototype is, in effect, a first try at manufacturing a newly designed product; it is not expected to be perfect, but will form a basis for future development and design improvements. Car manufacturers do this when trying to incorporate revolutionary features and technologies into a new car. A prototype of an information system allows users to test it for achievement of their desired objectives. Prototyping can take place at various stages of the system development cycle, but its use must be planned and anticipated to ensure maximum feedback is obtained from users. In the early stages, a prototype may be developed to test the appropriateness of screen dialogues, without constructing the main files, whilst later it may include a section of database and some applications software. Prototyping is expensive, in terms of time and resources and is unlikely to be used where user requirements are well established or the system is fairly standard.

CASE (computer-aided software engineering) tools

Software engineering is a concept which recognises the fact that the principles of engineering normally applied to other disciplines, can be highly relevant to the 'engineering' of information systems; the parameters for the effectiveness and quality of an information system have to be set at the design stage, if users' needs are to be properly met.

A CASE tool can loosely refer to any software tool used in the development of information systems, for example:

❑ language processors (compilers and interpreters);

❑ fourth generation languages (4GLs);

❑ graphics programs to allow analysts to draw DFDs or ERMs.

A more precise definition of the term requires reference to the typical features of CASE proprietary software; complete CASE packages or toolkits are commercially available to aid the systems analyst and/or programmer in system development. A CASE toolkit would normally contain components for:

❑ diagram construction;

❑ data dictionary development and control;

❑ interface generation;

    ❑   source code generation;

    ❑   project management.

Diagram construction

This tool is essential for the support of a structured systems methodology. The graphical facilities allow the drawing, storage and modification of diagrams and charts, such as data flow diagrams (DFDs), entity-relationship models (ERMs) and data structure diagrams (for program development).

Data dictionary

Being particularly important in the development of database systems for the control and consistency of data, the function of data dictionaries is described in Chapter 26 on Databases.

Interface generation

Interface generators support the preparation of prototypes of user interfaces, such as screen dialogues, menus and reports.

Source code generation

These tools allow the automated preparation of computer software, in other words, the conversion of a system specification into the source code of a chosen programming language, which can then be compiled into executable object or machine code. CASE tools for code generation are general purpose and are, as a consequence less efficient in the production of source code than specialised applications generators; most code generators will only produce, say, 75% of the code automatically, leaving the rest to be hand-coded by a programmer.

Project management

Such tools support the scheduling of analysis and design activities and the allocation of resources to the various project activities.

Integrated CASE tools

CASE tools can be used as separate, discrete elements or as a complete system. The integrated use of CASE tools can best be managed through windowing software, which allows, for example, the simultaneous viewing of data flow diagrams and data dictionary entries on screen. Integration also has the benefit of allowing data from one component of the toolkit to be transferred to another, for example, data dictionary entries to entity-relationship diagrams.

✍️Exercises

1. Identify the *entities*, *attributes* and *relationships* in each of the applications:
    (i)   patient records in a General Medical Practice;
    (ii)   a library lending system;
    (iii) an estate agency's 'houses for sale' monitoring system.
2. Draw an *entity-relationship model* (ERM) for each application.
3. Define the terms: *prototyping*; *normalisation*; *data dictionary*.

Chapter 26

Database Design and Construction

The term database is often used to describe any large collection of related data, but to understand the concepts which follow, it is necessary to establish a more precise definition. More specifically a database is *a collection of data, generally related to some subject or topic area and structured so as to allow relationships to be established between separate data items according to the various needs of users*. From this definition it is possible to identify specific features of a database:

❑ A database contains data of use in a *variety* of applications.

❑ The data is *structured* to allow separate data items to be connected, to form different *logical* records according to the requirements of users and hence, to applications programs.

❑ A database will normally be used for different applications, but those applications must have some *common interests* concerning the data items they use. For example, sales, purchasing, stock control and production control applications are likely to use common data in respect of raw materials or finished goods. On the other hand, a database containing data on both materials and personnel may be difficult to justify; even then connections between the separate databases can be facilitated if the information requirements so justify.

Basic principles

Controlled redundancy

One feature which is not specifically referred to in the definition is that of *controlled redundancy*. Effectively, this means reducing to a minimum the number of data items which are duplicated in a database. In traditional computerised filing systems, each department in an organisation may keep its own files, which results in a massive amount of duplication in the data that are stored. Although the removal of duplicated items is a desirable aim in terms of keeping database volume to a minimum, there are occasions when duplication is necessary to provide efficient access to the database.

Physical storage and data independence

Periodically, the *physical* database needs to be changed to accommodate variations in user requirements. However, there is no need to alter all applications programs, because the way the data is *physically* stored on the storage medium is independent of the *logical* record structures required by applications programs. In a traditional computerised system, if a data file is changed, then any program accessing it needs to be changed also. In a database, records can be stored essentially in two different ways.

❑ Independently - the primary key is used to decide the physical location of a record; frequently this is effected through a *randomising* process to distribute records efficiently on the storage medium.

❏   In association - records are stored according to their relationship with other records and connections may be made between them with the use of *pointers* (see chapter on Data Structures). A *physical pointer* gives the address where a record is stored and can be used to relate records anywhere in the database; a *logical pointer* is a value from which the physical address can be calculated.

The physical and logical database

A database has to satisfy the differing information needs of many users, generally through specially written applications programs. Therefore, it is often necessary to add further data items to satisfy changes in users needs. The software which controls the database must relate to the data at data item rather than at record level, because one programmer's logical record requirements may contain some data items which are also required for another programmer's logical record description. The physical database must allow for both. It must be possible for data items to be connected into a variety of logical record forms.

Creating the database

A special language called a *data description language* (DDL) allows the database to be created and changed and the logical data structures to be defined.

Manipulating the database

A *data manipulation language* (DML) enables the contents of the database to be altered by adding, updating or deleting records. The language is used by programmers to develop applications programs for users of the database. The functions of both these languages are combined, together with a query language facility in *Structured Query Language* (SQL), which is dealt with later in the chapter.

Database storage

Because the database must allow for various user applications programs accessing it at the same time, direct access storage must be used. There are many ways of physically organising the data which are dealt with in the chapter on Data Structures, but whatever method is used it must allow for the variety of logical record forms needed by applications programs. The applications programmer does not need to know how the data is physically stored. The programmer's knowledge of the data held in the database is restricted to the *logical view* required for the program. The complete or global logical database is termed the *schema.* The restricted or local logical views provided for different applications programs are termed *subschemas.*

Database management systems (DBMS)

So that each application program may only access the data which it needs for processing or retrieval (that data which is defined in its subschema), a suite of programs referred to as the Database Management System (DBMS) controls the database and prevents accidental or deliberate corruption of data by other applications programs. An application cannot access the database without the DBMS. Figure 26.1 illustrates the relationship between users, application programs, the DBMS and the database. A DBMS has the following functions.

❏   It is the common link between all applications programs and the database.

❏   It facilitates the use and organisation of a database and protects the database from accidental or deliberate corruption.

❏   It restricts a programmer's logical view of the database to those items of data which are to be used in the applications program being written.

Figure 26.1. *Relationship between database, DBMS, applications and users*

Types of database

The logical structure of a database can be based upon one of a number of natural data structures which the Database Management System (DBMS) uses to establish links between separate data items. Physical pointers inform the DBMS where the next logical record is to be found. In certain types of database the logical organisation of the database is constrained by whatever data structure is used and can therefore be described as *formatted*. Two main categories of data structure are used in such databases: (i) *Hierarchical* or *tree* structure; (ii) *complex* and *simple plex* structure (often called *network* structures). To avoid some of the restrictions inherent in formatted databases, a popular method of database management is to use a *relational* approach. To provide a basis for comparison with relational databases it is useful first to examine the data structures used in formatted databases.

Hierarchical or tree structure

A hierarchical or tree structure is illustrated in Figure 26.2. Each element is called a *node* and the only node which is not a *member* in any relationship is the *root* at the top of the tree. Three features of this structure need to be identified:

Figure 26.2. *Hierarchical structure*

❏   only *one-to-many* relationships are supported;

For example, in the Figure 26.2, each Department can have many Employees, but each Employee can only belong to one Department. Similarly, each Employee may have more than one Task but each Task can only be carried out by one Employee.

❏   the highest level in the hierarchy has only one node called the *root;*

❏   each node is a member in exactly one *relationship* with a node on a level higher than itself, except for the root node at the top of the tree.

For example, Job and Employee each relate to only a single *parent node* (Department); the root node, Department, is not a member in any relationship. The main problem with the hierarchical structure is that not all databases fit naturally into it; a record type may require more than one parent. For example, a library database may require a book to be a member in more than one book category, say, Geology and Geography.

Network data structures

There are two types of network or plex data structures: *complex*; *simple*.

Complex plex structure

A complex plex structure is illustrated in Figure 26.3. This structure supports *many-to-many* (complex) relationships. Thus, a Student may be enrolled on one or more (many) Courses and each Course may have many Students.

Figure 26.3. *Complex plex*

Whether or not such data structures can be used depends on the data description language (DDL) being used. IBM's DDL called DL/I supports any plex structure but the Codasyl DDL (described later) does not and cannot therefore, be used to describe complex plex structures.

Simple plex structure

A simple plex structure is illustrated in Figure 26.4. This structure supports *one-to-many* or simple relationships and unlike the tree structure, a node can have more than one parent. Thus, for example, a Quotation record may be owned by both one Builder and one Job record, but each Builder and Job record could own many Quotation records.

Figure 26.4. *Simple plex*

A complex plex structure can be reconstructed if the available software does not support such a structure. For example, the complex plex structure in Figure 26.3 can be converted to a hierarchical structure or to a simple plex structure. These reconstructions are shown in the Figures 26.5 and 26.6 respectively.

Complex plex to hierarchical

The structure in Figure 26.3 can be converted to two hierarchical or tree structures by duplicating Course and Student as follows in Figure 26.5; the course and student data will only be duplicated *logically*, not physically.

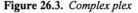

Figure 26.5. *Complex plex to hierarchical*

Complex plex to simple plex

The simple plex structure in Figure 26.6 is achieved through the creation of another record, which avoids the need to duplicate the Student and Course data. The relationships are now one-to-many rather than many-to-many.

The new record Enrolment must contain the information necessary to establish the relationship

Figure 26.6. *Complex plex to simple plex*

between the original Course and Student records; as in this example, the record identifiers are generally used for this purpose.

An example of a DBMS which supports *simple plex* structures is the CODASYL database management system.

The Codasyl logical schema in Figure 26.7 serves to illustrate this method of database organisation.

Codasyl database schema for a large company

The schema can be explained in terms of *sets* as follows.

There are 4 record types:

1. DEPARTMENT
2. STAFF MEMBER
3. SECTION
4. PREVIOUS JOBS

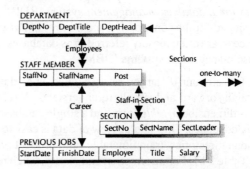

Figure 26.7. *Example Codasyl schema*

Each of 1, 2 and 3 can be retrieved directly by its *record key*, DeptNo, StaffNo and SectNo respectively. Record type 4 is only accessible through the STAFF MEMBER type record. This is reasonable as it would be unusual to search for a PREVIOUS JOBS record without first knowing the identity of the member of staff.

There are 4 *sets*, each of which has an *owner* record and one or more *member* records. For example, one DEPARTMENT will have a number of STAFF MEMBERs (a one-to-many relationship). The sets are:

Employees   *(owner*, DEPARTMENT/ *member*, STAFF MEMBER)

Sections   *(owner*, DEPARTMENT/ *member*, SECTION)

Staff-in-Section *(owner*, SECTION/ *member*, STAFF MEMBER)

Career   *(owner*, STAFF MEMBER/ *member*, PREVIOUS JOBS)

Diagrammatically, a set can be pictured as shown in Figure 26.8. For example, referring to Figure 26.7, Department 4 (an owner record) may have a number of Section (member) records. Data Manipulation Language statements could be used to retrieve a Section record directly using its SectNo or through its Sections Set (owned by Department Record). For example, if the section is in Department No 12, it may be found through the following steps.

Figure 26.8. *Codasyl set*

```
1 move 12 to DeptNo
2 find any Department
3 show Section
4 find next Section
5 show Section
```

Steps *4* and *5* are repeated until the correct Section record is found or the end of set is reached. It should be noticed that a PreviousJobs record can *only* be found through the Career set and the appropriate StaffMember record. As with any database, a Codasyl DBMS organises and accesses the logical database through the schema description. In all formatted databases, the structure defines the route which can be taken through the database, but the programmer/user must know what linkages have been established to be aware of how and what data can be accessed.

Relational database management systems

This section examines the principles of database design and definition, as well as the role of a *relational database management system* (RDBMS) package. RDBMS software packages are designed for the construction and control of *databases*. Packages, such as dBase, Paradox and Access, are often loosely referred to as databases. Strictly and to avoid confusion, they are database management systems (DBMS).

A fair amount of jargon is associated with database theory but the ideas represented are straightforward and simple to understand. A relational DBMS is designed to handle data in two-dimensional, *table* form and a single database is likely to contain a number of separate, but related, tables. This tabular view of data is easy to understand; everyday examples include telephone directories, train timetables and product price lists. An example of tabular data is given in Table 24.1. For information and clarity, when referring to other texts on relational databases, some of the jargon is defined below, by reference to Table 24.1. The underlined terms are not used further in this text.

❏   A table is sometimes referred to as a *relation* and each entry in the table is a single data item value. For example, PartCode 012 is a data item value consisting of 3 characters.

PART_SUPPLIER		
PartCode	**Price**	**SupplierNo**
012	3.25	14
015	0.76	07
016	1.26	14
018	7.84	05

Table 26.1. *Tabular data*

❏   Each column in the relation contains values for a given *data item type*. We will use the word *field*. The set of values for a given data item type is called its *domain*. A domain is identified by its description, that is, the name for the data item type. For example, in Table 24.1 the set of values in the second column is called the Price domain.

❏   Each row in a relation is a record occurrence and is called a *tuple*; we use the more usual word, *record*. The terms record and field are defined in Chapter 15.

Establishing relationships

The power of a relational DBMS lies in its facility to allow separate tables to be manipulated and combined in a variety of ways to establish new tables. Thus, for example, a table containing details such as the names and addresses of a firm's employees can be combined with a table detailing the make and registration numbers of cars owned by the employees, to produce a new table containing the names of employees owning, say, Ford cars.

In a formatted database using a simple plex structure, for example, connections between such data would have to be established when the database is constructed; a relational database can leave this task to the programmer or the Database Administrator (DBA).

It is important to realise that the existence of a relationship depends on the presence in both tables of a field value or values; they may not necessarily have the same field name. Tables in a relational database are related dynamically through the values of the information found within them, rather than through inbuilt physical links. In the simplest types of relational DBMS, that is those used on small business systems, it is the responsibility of the programmer or user to be aware of the existence of common values to link tables together. In a mini or mainframe system owned by a larger organisation, this responsibility may lie with the DBA, whose task is to control database usage by programmers and users.

The need for common values to establish relationships requires some duplication of data (see later examples) and thus some *controlled redundancy*.

Benefits of a relational DBMS

The attraction of the relational approach is that logical record structures and connections between them are not constrained by pointers using rigid formats such as those provided by the tree and plex structures described earlier. Instead, with some duplication of data or controlled redundancy, a programmer can establish any relationships that need to be made for output specified by users. New relations can be added or existing relations modified as user requirements change.

Database design

Design is an important pre-requisite for database construction. For example, a common mistake is to create one table, containing all the data items required by the applications programs.

Consider the Product table in Figure 26.9. Additional fields could be included for suppliers' names and addresses, but, on the assumption that many products come from one supplier, much data would be needlessly duplicated. It is more useful to create a separate table for the suppliers' names and addresses, as shown in Figure 26.10. Note that the Supplier table also contains a Supplier Code field; this allows a *relationship* to be established with

PartCode	Description	Price	Quantity	SupplierCode
A123	Table (Cottage)	£23.50	15	KSU518
A124	Chair (Cottage)	£42.23	36	KIT518
A125	Stool (Cottage)	£28.15	6	KIT518
A133	Bar Stool	£33.55	4	KSU518
A136	Bread Bin (wood)	£14.25	4	KIT518
A139	Bread Bin (metal)	£10.25	6	KSU518
B122	Spanner (adjustable)	£8.25	4	BCS436
B126	Step Ladder (small)	£19.50	6	PAR116
B129	Screw Driver (ratchet)	£15.55	13	BCS436
B133	Ladders (aluminium)	£85.66	2	STA436
B136	Spirit Level	£13.55	6	STA436
B145	Step Ladder (medium)	£31.25	4	PAR116
B181	Hammer (medium claw)	£6.75	12	STA436

Figure 26.9. *Product table*

the Product table. Similarly, a database for the maintenance of student records, may contain a single table consisting of twenty or thirty data items ranging from student name, address, and date of entry, to all assignment and exam grades for all subjects studied within a given course. Clearly, such a database is unwieldy when, for example, a list of student names and addresses is all that is required by a particular user. The following sections describe some of the more important concepts and techniques relating to proper database design.

Figure 26.10. *Product and Supplier tables*

Entities

A database should contain a number of logically separate tables, each corresponding to a given subject or part-subject (an *entity*). In the example of the product database (Figure 26.10), two logically separate tables (one for the Product entity and the other for the Supplier entity) are constructed.

Entities are the objects of the real world, which are relevant to a particular information system.

Attributes

An entity has a number of related *attributes*, which are of interest to users. Consider, as an example, a Personnel database (see also *Personnel* case study in Chapter 25). An entity, StaffMember, may have the attributes of StaffCode, Name, JobCode, JobTitle, DeptCode, DepartmentName. These attributes determine the *fields* which are associated with the StaffMember *table*. Some attributes may be kept in a separate table. For example, JobTitle and DepartmentName are likely to contain the same values in numerous records in the StaffMember table. In other words, some employees work in the same department and some have the same job title.

With an RDBMS, it is more efficient to separate these attributes, through the creation of separate tables (one for Department and the other for Job). Although an employee has a given job title and works in a particular department, these attributes are also of separate interest; each is a separate *entity*. For example, a new job title may be identified before an employee has been assigned to it. Figure 26.11 shows the tables which represent these entities.

Identifying and non-identifying attributes

Some attributes, for example, Name and JobTitle, are descriptive. Another (StaffCode) may serve as a unique identifier. Attributes can be classified, therefore, as being either *identifying* or *non-identifying*. In Figure 26.11, StaffCode acts as the unique identifier (or *primary key field*) for a StaffMember record; Department and Job records use DeptCode and JobCode, respectively. These entity and attribute structures can be expressed in the form shown in Figure 26.12.

Figure 26.11. *Tables for StaffMember, Department and Job entities*

Unique identifiers are underlined.

```
StaffMember (StaffCode, Name, JobCode, DeptCode)
Job(JobCode, JobTitle)
Department(DeptCode, DepartmentName)
```

Figure 26.12. *Entity structures*

Sometimes, more than one attribute is needed to uniquely identify an individual record; such attributes form a *composite identifier* or *key*. An example of such a key is given below.

```
Order Line (OrderNo, ItemNo, Description, Price, Quantity)
```

Figure 26.13. *Entity structure using composite primary key*

An order form usually has several lines, each relating to a separate item which a customer wants. The same item may be ordered by other customers, so the OrderNo and ItemNo are needed to identify a particular order line, relating to a particular customer order.

Relationships, link fields and foreign keys

Notice that, in Figure 26.12, the JobCode and DeptCode fields also remain in the StaffMember table. This is necessary to allow relationships, or links, to be established between the tables. Suppose, for example, that a user wishes to view a list of employee details, which includes Name, DepartmentName and JobTitle. The list is obtained by *querying* (see Database Construction and Operation) the database.

To process the query, the RDBMS needs to extract information from more than one table. An examination of the entity structures in Figure 26.12 reveals that all three are needed (StaffMember, Job and Department). The user must specify which fields are used to link the tables to one another.

Figure 26.14 illustrates these links.

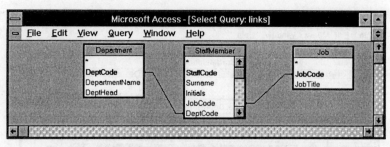

Figure 26.14. *Link fields to establish relationships between tables*

DeptCode is the primary key for the Department table, but the same attribute also appears in the StaffMember table. When the two are linked, DeptCode in the StaffMember table is acting as a *foreign key*. JobCode in the StaffMember table also serves as a foreign key when it is used to link with the Job table.

Data analysis

This process (see Chapter 25) is concerned with establishing what the entities, attributes and links (*relationships*), for any given database, should be. To make such an analysis, it is obviously necessary to have knowledge of the organisation to which the information relates, because there will be certain items of information which only have significance to that particular organisation. For example, in an Academic database, the following entities may be identified and a table established for each.

     Student; Course; Tutor; EducationHistory; ExamGrade

Normalisation

Normalisation is a technique established by E.F. Codd to simplify the structure of data as it is *logically viewed* by the programmer or user. The data requirements for a database are systematically analysed to establish whether a particular attribute should be an entity in its own right, or simply an attribute of some other entity. When an attribute is identified as a separate entity, the link or relationship must be maintained with the original entity. Normalisation is a step-by-step process for analysing data into its constituent entities and attributes. Its main aim is to improve database efficiency. There are three stages of normalisation described here, though there are others which are beyond the scope of this text. To illustrate the process of normalisation, the example of an *Academic* database is used. When a student enrols for one or more courses, a registration form is completed. An example is shown in Figure 26.15.

Malverley College
Wareham   Principal: Peter Ansell, BA, PhD
Dorset
DO5 3DD

Student Registration Form

Student Number	G234563
Surname	Harrison
Forename	Pauline
Address	123 Newcastle Road, Sunderland, SR3 2RJ
Sex	Female

Course Code	Course Title	Tutor Code	Tutor
4PDCS1	Computing	124	Watkin
4PDNE1	Electronics	133	Parks
4PDFR1	French	118	Teneur
4PDGE1	German	166	Roberts

Figure 26.15. *Extract from student registration form*

First normal form (1NF)

Treated as a single entity, the structure could be described, initially, as shown in Figure 26.16.

```
Student (StudNo, Surname, Forename, Address, Sex, [CrseCode,
CrseTitle, TutNo, TutName])
```

Figure 26.16. *Structure of Student entity*

The unique identifier (primary key), StudNo, is underlined. Each student registration form (see Figure 26.15) may show enrolments on several courses. Thus, the attributes [CrseCode, CrseTitle, TutNo and TutName] can be identified as a *repeating group*.

The first stage of normalisation demands the removal of any repeating groups. This is achieved by creating a new entity. The attributes in question relate to the activity of enrolment, which is of separate interest and an entity in its own right. The new entity is called Enrolment-1 and is used to store details of individual enrolments; each enrolment will be a separate record in the Enrolment table. Neither StudNo nor CrseCode, on its own, uniquely identifies an individual enrolment. A *composite key*, using both attributes, is used to uniquely identify a single enrolment. The two entity descriptions are shown in Figure 26.17.

```
Student-1 (StudNo, Surname, Forename, Address, Sex)
Enrolment-1 (StudNo, CrseCode, CrseTitle, TutNo, TutName)
```

Figure 26.17. *Entity structures after conversion to first normal form (1NF)*

The entities are now in first normal form (1NF) and this is indicated by suffixing each entity name with a 1. The unique identifier is underlined in each entity description. Note the *composite key* in the Enrolment entity.

To relate the Enrolment records to the relevant Student records requires that StudNo (as the link field) appears in both the Student and Enrolment tables in the Academic database. Thus, to ensure that entities and attributes are in first normal form requires the removal of repeating groups of attributes, rewriting them as new entities. The identifier of the original entity is always included as an attribute of any such new entity, although it is not essential for it to form part of the identifier of the new entity (it could be a non-identifying attribute). Some necessary *data redundancy* is created by including StudNo in both entities, to allow a given student to be connected with a particular enrolment. Such duplication of data does not necessarily mean an increased use of storage because normalisation is concerned with the *logical structure* of the data and not with the ways in which the data is physically organised.

Second normal form (2NF)

The second stage of normalisation ensures that all non-identifying attributes are *functionally dependent* on the unique identifier (the primary key); if the identifier is composite (comprising more that one attribute), then non-identifying attributes must be functionally dependent on the whole of the identifier. This rule is best explained by example. Consider the 1NF entity descriptions, produced from the first stage of normalisation (Figure 26.17). Referring to the Enrolment entity, it can be seen that TutNo and TutName each depend on both parts of the composite identifier. For example, if a student enrols on more than one course, he or she has a different tutor for each course. To identify a tutor in an enrolment record, requires specification of both values (StudNo and CrseCode). However, CrseTitle is not functionally dependent on the whole of the composite identifier, only on CrseCode; the title of a course could be found through entry of the

CrseCode value alone. Figure 26.18 illustrates both these points with a diagram. An arrowed line connects the box, which surrounds the composite identifier, to TutNo and TutName. CrseTitle is connected only to CrseCode. The second stage of normalisation is achieved by the creation of a new entity, Course-2, with the attributes CrseCode (the identifier) and

Figure 26.18. *Functional dependency*

CrseTitle. The entity descriptions now appear as in Figure 26.19. The suffix 2 indicates that all entities and attributes are now in second normal form.

```
Student-2(StudNo, Surname, Forename, Address, Sex)
Enrolment-2(StudNo, CrseCode, TutNo, TutName)
Course-2(CrseCode, CrseTitle)
```

Figure 26.19. *Entity structures in second normal form (2NF)*

Benefits of 2NF

Conversion of entities and attributes to second normal form brings advantages apart from the avoidance of some data duplication. The entry of new data into the database is also facilitated. Suppose, for example, that a new course is to be added to the database and that the data is stored as arranged after the first stage of normalisation. The new course entry could not be made until the first enrolment for that particular course. Also, if a particular course has no enrolments, then information concerning the course is not held in the database.

Third normal form (3NF)

At this stage we are concerned with finding any *functional dependencies* between non-identifying attributes. These can be identified from Figure 26.19 as TutNo and TutName and are illustrated in Figure 26.20. Again, the problem is solved by the creation of a new entity, Tutor-3. The entity contains TutNo as the identifier and TutName as a non-identifying attribute. The entities are in third normal form (indicated by the suffix, 3), as shown in Figure 26.21.

Figure 26.20. *Functional dependencies*

```
Student-3(StudNo, Surname, Forename, Address, Sex)
Enrolment-3(StudNo, CrseCode, TutNo)
Course-3(CrseCode, CrseTitle)
Tutor-3(TutNo, TutName)
```

Figure 26.21. *Entity structures in third normal form (3NF)*

Defining a database structure

Each entity structure, shown in Figure 26.21, must be defined as a table in the *Academic* database. In the case of Student-3, it would be beneficial to sub-divide Address into separate attributes of, say, Street, Town and PostCode. Each definition includes reference to *primary keys*, *field names*, *data types* and *field lengths*. All these terms are explained, through examples, in Chapter 27 on Database Case Studies, but are briefly defined below.

Primary keys

In the Academic database, for example, StudentNo, CrseCode and TutorNo, act as primary keys for the Student, Course and Tutor tables, respectively. Although an Enrolment record can be identified through the combined use of StudNo and CrseCode, you could add an additional field, such as EnrolmentNo, to act as the primary key.

Data types

A typical RDBMS provides the following data types.

Character, text or alphanumeric

This is for a field which may contain text, or a mixture of text, symbols and numbers. Sometimes a field may only contain numeric digits, perhaps an account number or telephone number. If it is not treated numerically, but as text, character type is normally used.

Numeric

This type must be used for fields containing numerical values (such as money amounts or quantities) to be used in calculations.

Logical (yes/no)

This type allows the entry of two possible values, indicated by *true* or *false*. Sometimes, *yes* and *no*, respectively, may be used instead. For example, the Student table in the academic database contains a field to record the sex of a student. Use of the field name Male means that Yes is entered for a male student and No for a female. If the field name Female is used, No is entered for a male and Yes for a female student. The name of the field determines whether an affirmative or a negative (Yes or No) is entered.

Date

Although character type may be used for the storage of dates, the *date* type allows the correct sorting of dates. Also, in defining queries, date type fields enable the database to compare dates held in records, with a specified date. This is not practical with a character type field.

Field lengths

Logical and *date* type fields invariably have a pre-determined length, typically, 1 and 8 respectively. For a character field, a maximum length must be specified (allowing for the number of digits, letters or symbols to be accommodated within it). Numeric fields are defined according to the number range which needs to be accommodated and the number of decimal places.

Abbreviating and coding data

There are a number of benefits to be gained if data can be abbreviated or coded, without obscuring its meaning. Some are described below.

❑ *Saving space*. Codes and abbreviations take up less space, but must be of sufficient length to allow the entry of unique values. The minimum length of such a field is determined by the number of different values which need to be represented.

❑ *Query expressions* can be shorter. As long as users are aware of what the codes mean and are happy with using them, much time and keying effort can be saved.

❑ *Data entry*. If there are a large number of records to be keyed in, the procedure is extremely time-consuming and tedious. Coding and abbreviating data may reduce the time and labour requirements considerably.

Querying a database

A query is a request for information from a database. Queries can include *criteria* for the selection of information. For example, the Academic database could be queried for details of all male students, or students on a particular course. If the query requires that the RDBMS takes data from more than one table, appropriate link fields must be indicated.

Suppose, for example, that a report is required listing the names of all students, together with the name(s) of the course(s) on which they are enrolled. It is assumed that no criteria are specified. Student names are held in the Student table, the course code is in the Enrolment table, and the name of the course is in the Course table. Therefore, to process the query requires that these three tables are used. The QBE form of the query is shown in Figure 26.22.

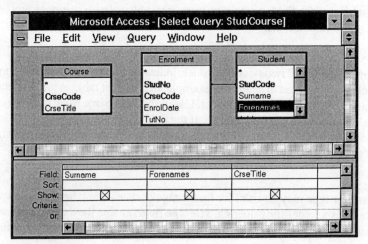

Figure 26.22. *Query (QBE form) using three tables from Academic database*

The query can also be expressed in *Structured Query Language* (SQL), as shown in Figure 26.23.

```
SELECT DISTINCTROW Student.Surname, Student.Forenames,
Course.CrseTitle
FROM Student INNER JOIN (Course INNER JOIN Enrolment ON
Course.CrseCode = Enrolment.CrseCode) ON Student.StudCode =
Enrolment.StudNo;
```

Figure 26.23. *Structured Query Language (SQL) form of query in Figure 26.22*

The use of SQL and QBE is dealt with in Database Construction and Operation. The query produces more than one record per student, but this is because a student may be enrolled on more than one course. The output appears in Figure 26.24.

Figure 26.24. *Output from query in Figure 26.22*

Secondary keys

Apart from the primary keys, which are used to identify records uniquely, an important function of an RDBMS is to allow the querying of the database, by reference to *secondary key* values. Thus, in the Academic database, useful secondary keys could be CrseTitle, and TutName (if neither code was available). Secondary keys can also be used as foreign keys (see Relationships and Link Fields), when joining tables in a query.

Structured query language (SQL)

Many new RDBMS packages provide a Structured Query Language (SQL). Practical examples of SQL are given earlier in this chapter and in Chapter 25. Developed by IBM, SQL is a *non-procedural* language and as such belongs to the group of programming languages known as 4th Generation Languages (4GLs); this means that programmers and trained users can specify what they want from a database without having to specify how to do it. Procedural languages such as COBOL, Pascal and C, require the programmer to detail, explicitly, how a program must navigate through a file or database to obtain the necessary output. The programmer must, for example, code procedures such as read the first master record, process it, read the next, process it and so on until the end of the file is reached. As explained below, SQL is an attempt to provide a language which includes the facilities normally provided separately by a *data description language*, a *data manipulation language* and a *query language* (to allow on-demand queries by users).

Features of SQL

The example database extract in Figure 26.25 is used here to illustrate some of the main features of SQL by showing how a programmer or trained user could use SQL to access a database without specifying procedures.

Figure 26.25. *Extract from company database*

Selection by criteria

Referring to Figure 26.25, if the Name and Salary of EMPLOYEE 124 is required, the SQL statements may take a form similar to the example in Figure 26.26).

```
SELECT Name, Salary
FROM EMPLOYEE
WHERE EmpNum = 124
```

Figure 26.26. *SQL statement to extract details of Employee 124*

The output would be as in Figure 26.27.

Name	Salary
King, H	12000

Figure 26.27. *Output from query in Figure 26.26*

SQL supports all the functions expected of a *relational* language including, for example, the operators, JOIN and PROJECT.

Updating the database

SQL can also change values in a database; for example, to give all employees in the A5 (Sales) department a 6 per cent pay increase, the statements shown in Figure 26.28 may be used:

```
UPDATE EMPLOYEE
SET Salary = Salary * 1.06
WHERE DeptCode = A5
```

Figure 26.28. *SQL update query*

SQL has built-in functions and arithmetic operators to allow the grouping or sorting of data and the calculation of, for example, average, minimum and maximum values in a particular field.

Defining the database

As a multi-purpose database language, SQL can be used to define, as well as manipulate and retrieve data. This definition function is traditionally carried out using a separate data description language (DDL) but SQL incorporates this facility for implementing the logical structure (*schema*) for a database. For example, to create a new table called QUALIFICATIONS the statements in Figure 26.29 may be entered:

```
CREATE TABLE QUALIFICATION
(EmpNum CHAR (3)
Qual VARCHAR (20));
```

Figure 26.29. *SQL statement to create a table*

The table would contain two fields, namely, EmpNum with a fixed length of three characters and Qual with a variable number of characters up to twenty. Following creation of the table, data can be entered immediately if required.

Modifying the database definition

Tables can be modified to allow for the removal or addition of fields, according to changes in user requirements. Existing data does not have to be re-organised and applications programs unaffected by data changes do not have to be re-written. The independence of the logical database from the applications programs is known as *logical data independence* and constitutes one of the main features of a relational database.

Two major aims are inherent in the design of SQL:

❏   As a non-procedural language it is expected to increase programmer productivity and reduce the time and costs involved in application development.

❏   SQL allows easier access to data for the purposes of on-demand or ad hoc queries.

Techniques for Database Administration

Database administrator (DBA)

A database administrator (DBA) appointed with a corporate function has special responsibility for:

❏   database design and development;

❏   selection of database software;

❏   database maintenance;

❏   database accuracy and security.

A DBA should have a working knowledge of both the DBMS and the organisation. A DBA will supervise the addition of new data items to the database (changes to the schema). Supervision of the data dictionary is also the DBA's responsibility (see next paragraph). The DBA has to ensure the consistent use of data across the whole database. For example, a functional area may request new data to be added to a database, when it already exists. This can happen when different departments in an organisation refer to a field by different names. For example, a Sales department may refer to the name Product Code, whilst the Warehouse staff may use the term Stock Code, when referring to the same field. During database development, it is easy to forget the precise definitions given to a field and when adding the field to another table, introduce inconsistencies.

Data dictionaries

A data dictionary system is a data processing department's own information system, with the database administrator, systems analysts and programmers as the main users.

An essential part of the database design process is to maintain a data dictionary. Its main function is to store details of all the data items in a database. Such details can be wide ranging, but should include, as a minimum:

(i)   field names and the table(s) in which they occur;

(ii)   field definitions, including field types and lengths;

(iii)   additional properties, concerning, for example, data formats and validation controls;

(iv)   synonyms. Sometimes, the same field occurs in more than one table, but using different names. Generally it is better not to use synonyms.

The dictionary's main role is to ensure consistent data usage; if synonyms are used (different data names may be used by different functional areas of an organisation to refer to the same field), the dictionary must record their use accordingly to prevent duplication.

Database recovery

Recovery techniques can be used in certain circumstances to recover lost data when a database is corrupted. Most recovery techniques depend on making a *dump* (copy) of the whole (or a selected part) of the data in the database. Recovery of a database requires:

❑   that the cause of the failure be diagnosed and remedied;

❑   replacement of the corrupted database with the most recent dump of the database;

❑   updating of the database with all the transactions and amendments which occurred since the last dump until the time of the database's failure.

Difficulties are apparent in this procedure; re-processing may take a long time and all updating transactions which have taken place since the last dump must be recorded, together with their sequence of entry, since the order of processing can determine the eventual state of the database. To allow for this, a DBMS will record each entry in a sequential file or transaction log; re-processing can then take place in the correct sequence, without any re-keying of data.

Data sharing and data integrity

Sharing of data by different users is fundamental to the database concept and the DBMS has to allow for it, whilst at the same time protecting the *integrity* of the database. Such access may be through different applications programs or through the same one. Database integrity is not affected by accesses which only read data; no matter how many users are reading the same data, its integrity will not be affected. *Concurrent* updates present the possibility of updates being lost.

Consider, for example a database schema which held the following stock record type.

```
STOCK(Item#, Item-Description, Quantity-held)
```

Two applications programs PR1 and PR2 are updating the Quantity-held for Item# 3254; following the delivery of units of that item, PR1 is to increase the balance by 200, whilst PR2 is to reduce it by 150 in respect of stock issues. If the initial value of Quantity-held is 200, then the following sequence of events could occur:

(i)   PR1 reads Stock record, Item# 3254;

(ii)   PR2 reads Stock record, Item# 3254;

(iii)   PR1 increases Quantity-held by 200 and re-writes the record to the database;

(iv)   PR2 decreases Quantity-held by 150 and re-writes the record to the database.

At this stage, Stock record, Item# 3254, would show a Quantity-held value of 50, when it should be 250. This error has occurred because PR2 read the record before PR1 had re-written its updated version to the database.

With the use of *integrity locks*, a DBMS can ensure that any program which reads a record for the purpose of updating, must result in the *locking* of that record against access by any other updating program, until the updated version has been re-written to the database. Programs accessing the record for *reading purposes only*, are not prevented access by an integrity lock.

Integrity locks can be implemented through the use of an additional data item within a record, the value of which can be set to *on*, as and when required. Integrity locks can present their own problems, but they are not of concern in this text.

Database security

Security is concerned with controlling access to data, both to prevent its accidental or deliberate corruption and, in the case of confidential data concerning individuals or organisations, to maintain appropriate privacy.

Access control mechanisms

Identification, authentication and authorisation

Before being granted access to a database, users must identify themselves, normally with an assigned account number or identification code. Authentication of a user's identity normally requires provision of a password, known only to the system and its legitimate users; the Chapter on System Controls examines the topic of passwords in more detail. The system holds information, supplied initially by the database administrator (DBA), on each user or category of user. This information is held to allow the system to carry out its identification and authentication procedures and to determine the level of authorisation - the kinds of access any particular user is permitted.

Another mechanism for controlling access uses access control locks and access control keys. Consider the following example of how a very simple access lock could work; the extracts of a schema description and application program are coded in the Codasyl Data Description Language and Data Manipulation Language.

Schema extract

```
RECORD NAME IS CLIENT
CLIENT-NUM PICTURE 9 (8)
DATE-OF-BIRTH PICTURE 9 (6)
BALANCE PICTURE 9 (6) V99
ACCESS CONTROL LOCK FOR GET IS `ZEBRA'
```

Program extract

```
MOVE `ZEBRA' TO KEY-CHECK
USE FOR ACCESS CONTROL ON GET FOR CLIENT
```

The character string 'ZEBRA' is declared as being the access control lock on the command GET for the data item BALANCE, only. Thus, the Balance data cannot be used by an application program unless the access control key 'ZEBRA' is provided and transferred to the location called KEY-CHECK, where it is compared by the DBMS with the access control lock. If the values do not agree then access is prevented to the Balance data. This is a fairly trivial example and not particularly secure, as a glance at the schema listing would reveal the access control lock's value; more sophisticated ways of assigning the access control lock are generally used.

Levels of authorisation

A fundamental principle of security is that access is limited to those persons who require it and that the degree of access is limited to that which is necessary to their jobs. For example, authorisation to alter schema or sub-schema descriptions may be limited to the DBA; user A may be given access to particular data for enquiry, but not for alteration purposes, whilst User B may be the only person authorised to change prices in the Stock File.

Benefits and drawbacks of databases in general

The following list details some of the generally accepted advanatages and disadvantages.

❑ Apart from controlled redundancy, there is no unnecessary duplication of data as occurs in traditional filing systems. Apart from the economic advantage, this means that transactions can update all affected areas of the database through a single input.

❑ Because of the single input principle, there is less chance of inconsistency as may occur if the same transaction is keyed in several times to different files. Equally, of course, an incorrect entry will mean that all applications programs using the data will be working with the wrong data value.

❑ The opportunities for obtaining comprehensive information are greatly improved with a central pool of data.

❑ On-demand or ad hoc enquiries are possible through the use of a query language.

❑ Security opportunities are enhanced because access to a single database can be more readily controlled than is possible with a system based on numerous separate files. On the other hand, database design and creation is a complex process and the failure of a database affects all applications which make use of it.

✍️Exercises

1. Distinguish between the *physical* and *logical* database.
2. Define the terms *schema* and *subschema*, illustrating your definition with examples.
3. Suggest three applications for which a *hierarchically* structured database would be unsuitable.
4. (i)   If the relationship between 'cinema' (with multiple screens) and 'film' is *complex plex*, what does this mean?

    (ii) Illustrate a method of converting the relationship in (i) to a *simple plex* structure and explain the new structure.

    (iii) Why would the conversion in (ii) be necessary for a relational database structure?
5. What kind of structure is supported by a Codasyl database management system?

Chapter 27

Relational Database Case Studies

The Overview section takes you through the main facilities provided by an RDBMS (relational database management system), using a simple database example. Then there are three database case studies to provide varied illustrations of RDBMS usage. They are: *EuroTent*, holding information on European campsites; *Personnel*, which stores staff details for Pilcon Electronics; *Stock Control*, which records details of products and suppliers. In Chapter 26, another case study, *Academic*, is used to illustrate the design process for a relational database.

Overview of RDBMS operation

When you use an RDBMS, you need to be familiar with the purpose and functioning of a number of components, which are described in the following paragraphs. A simple Products database is used to illustrate the descriptions.

Tables

An RDBMS is designed to handle data structured in two-dimensional *table* (the term relation is also used) form. A single database may contain one or more tables. The *EuroTent* database has only one table, which holds all the information on the European campsites it has in its brochure.

The *Personnel* database separates the data into three separate tables, each being concerned with a different aspect of staff information. Thus, there is a table holding staff names, department codes, job codes and salaries; the other two tables contain further information on jobs and departments.

Stock Control is a database comprising two tables, one for product and the other for supplier details.

The *Academic* database (see Chapter 26) places information on enrolments, students, courses and tutors into four separate tables. The idea of dividing information into separate tables is fundamental to the operation of an RDBMS and is explained fully, in Chapter 26.

Although the information may be in more than one table, it is related and can be brought together as and when you require, by linking or joining the tables. It is anticipated that you will work through the EuroTent example first, as this will allow you to develop your skill in the practical operation of the RDBMS package, without concern for relational database theory. To fully understand the Personnel and Stock Control examples you should first have studied Chapter 26.

You will use tables in two ways:

(i)   to *define the structure* of the data which is to be held within it; you need to do this before you can enter any data into the database;

(ii)   to *enter* and subsequently *view* and *edit* the data within a table.

Figure 27.1 shows data held in a Product table. Each column in Figure 27.1 corresponds to a particular type of data and is referred to as a *field*. A name which identifies a particular field is known as a *field name*. There are five fields in the Product table, called PartCode, Description, Price, Quantity and SupplierCode, respectively. Each row in the table is a *record* occurrence. The PartCode field is used to uniquely identify an individual product and is know as the *primary key* field. For example, PartCode 'A125' al-

Figure 27.1. *Product table with sample records*

lows unique identification of the 'Stool(Cottage)' record and the information contained within it. The Product table will contain a record for each product. Figure 27.2 displays the definition of the Product table.

Figure 27.2. *Definition of Product table*

A number of table features can be identified from Figure 27.2. There are three columns in the upper part of the window. From left to right, the columns are used for:

❑ *Field names*. You enter a field name for each item of data you are going to store concerning the table topic. In Figure 27.2, the table defines a product *record* which comprises five fields: PartCode; Description; Price; Quantity and SupplierCode.

❑ *Data types*. You can define the kind of data which is to be stored in a field. For example, in Figure 27.2, you can see that the Description field allows the entry of *text*; this means any characters, alphabetic or numeric. Obviously, the Quantity field is defined as *number*, because it will contain numeric quantities only. The definition of the Price field as *currency* ensures that a £ sign and 2 decimal places are automatically assigned to each price entered. Thus, for example, if you enter the value 3.5, it will be altered to £3.50. Other data types include date and logical, but these will be described in more detail later.

❑ *Field descriptions*. These are not used by the RDBMS and are simply there to allow you to document some aspect of the field.

Field properties

The lower half of the window is for the specification of *field properties*. Figure 27.2 displays the additional properties set for the SupplierCode field:

❑   *field size* has been restricted to 6 characters;

❑   an *input mask* ensures that each supplier code is entered as 3 letters followed by 3 digits. You should also note that *validation* parameters can also be set. For example, the Quantity field prevents entry of values less than zero.

Forms

You can use a form to tailor your view of information held in a table. A form is always associated with a particular table and allows you to enter, edit and view the data held within it. A form is not a separate store of data, but simply an alternative view of its associated table. A major benefit of a form is that it allows you to view or edit one record at a time; a table displays as many records as can be accommodated within its window.

Figure 27.3 shows a form associated with the Product table in Figure 27.1. It was created with Form Wizard, in the Access RDBMS.

Figure 27.3. *A form for Product records*

You can begin with a blank form and design your layout, or more easily, you can produce one with a wizard and then modify it to your requirements.

Figure 27.4 shows the Product Record Form in design mode, with the 'Description' field label selected. You can see from the figure that a form consists of a number of objects, including field labels and data entry points. Each data entry point uses the field name defined in the table definition and ensures that each entry point on the form is associated with the correct field in a record. As a consequence, field names should not be altered on the form (unless they are also altered in the table definition). Field labels, on the other hand can be altered; the field names are used by default, unless you specify otherwise.

The form design is divided into sections: *header* (for titles); *detail* (for the field names and data entry points); *footer* (for additional comments, perhaps to guide the data entry process).

Figure 27.4. *Product record form in design view*

Queries and dynasets

A query is a request for information from a database. You can use a query to:

(i)   display all the records in a table;

(ii)   display information from several tables by *joining* them (see Personnel, Stock Control and Academic Case Studies);

(iii)   display limited information by specifying that only certain fields are displayed;

(iv)   use *criteria* to *filter* records from one table or from several joined together.

The data extracted by a query is known as a *dynaset*. Referring to (iv), you may want to query, for example, a Product database for all products supplied by a particular supplier; alternatively, you may wish to identify products within a particular category. Each of these is an example of a *criterion*. If you specify more than one requirement, such as products from a particular supplier, under a particular price, then you are using two *criteria*. When criteria are used in a query, a filter is being applied; only those records which satisfy the criteria pass through the filter. If you want to identify an individual record, you will normally use the primary key; in the case of the Product table, this would be the PartCode.

To retrieve groups of records, such as products from a particular supplier, you can use the SupplierCode, which is an example of a *secondary key*. You can only identify products within a particular category if there is a field in the table which allows for it. In the Product table in Figure 27.1, you can see that the PartCodes beginning with 'A' are connected with items of furniture, whereas, the 'B' items are do-it-yourself or DIY items. Assuming this is the intended categorisation, you could use the first letter of the PartCode for such a query. In this case, the PartCode field will be serving as a secondary key; this is because only part of it (the first character) is being used. A query can be made on a single table or, as demonstrated in the Personnel, Stock Control and Academic examples, on more than one.

Queries can be expressed in one of two forms:

(i)   *query by example (QBE)*. With this method, queries are carried out according to the criteria you provide, in the form of examples. The query in Figure 27.5 uses the Product table from Figure 27.1. By entering the expression '<10', which means 'less than 10', under the Quantity field, you are effectively applying a filter; only records which satisfy the criterion pass through the filter and are selected by the query.

Figure 27.5. *Query by example to retrieve products with quantity less than 10*

Figure 27.6 shows the query result . Compare it with Figure 27.1 to see the effect.

Figure 27.6. *Dynaset from query in Figure 27.5*

(ii)   *structured query language (SQL)*. This method requires that you know the form of the language, to write the query expressions. However, if you create a query using the QBE method (which is the simplest), you can request the RDBMS to show you the SQL equivalent. Figure 27.7 displays the SQL equivalent of the QBE example in Figure 27.5. For most queries you will use QBE, but SQL is needed if the query you want to make is not possible with QBE.

Figure 27.7. *SQL for query in Figure 27.5*

A number of component parts can be identified in the SQL statement in Figure 27.7. The lower case words are table and field names. The upper case words: SELECT; DISTINCTROW; FROM; WHERE, are all SQL *reserved words*. Like any programming language, they have a particular meaning to the language processor and can only be used for a specified purpose. Briefly, each has the following use:

❑   SELECT. This is used to select individual or groups of records from named table(s); it is followed by the fieldnames (each prefixed by its table name) to be displayed when the query is executed;

❑   DISTINCTROW. This prevents the selection of duplicate (values are the same in the fields selected for the query) records;

❑   FROM is used to identify the table(s) to which the query is directed; in Figure 27.7, the named table is Product;

❑   WHERE is followed by the criterion which, in Figure 27.7, is that the Quantity is less than 10. The field name is prefixed by the name of the table (Product). This is because a criterion can be directed at a different table from the one identified in the FROM clause.

Sorting

Although a table or query output may have a particular sequence, perhaps in the order of the primary key, there will be occasions when you want to change the sequence. If for example, you are viewing a list of personnel, you may wish the list to be in alphabetical order by surname. Alternatively, you may prefer to see them first grouped into departments (which you also want in alphabetical order) and then, within each department, ordered alphabetically by surname. Before executing a sort, you need to indicate which column or field is to dictate the sequence; apart from this, you can choose ascending or descending order. Indexing can be used to speed the sorting process.

Indexes

Indexes are used to speed the sorting and retrieval of records. If you index (see Table definition in Figure 27.1) a field, this speeds the sorting and retrieval of records, using that field as a key. The effect will only be noticeable with databases containing hundreds of records. The RDBMS creates an index file for each field you index and has to update it every time you modify the contents of the table to which it relates. Indexes take up space and because of the need for their updating, may have the effect of slowing data entry and editing. For this reason, you should avoid using them indiscriminately.

An index file contains all the values taken from the indexed field. For example, if you indexed the SupplierCode field in the Product table in Figure 27.1, each value in that column would be in the index file. Each value would then have a pointer which indicated the physical location of the record containing that value. Referring to Figure 27.1, you can see that some supplier code values are duplicated; this is necessary because numerous products may be supplied by a single supplier. You can choose that the index allows for duplicates. The primary key in the Product table is indexed and duplicates are not permitted; this is obvious, because the purpose of the primary key is to uniquely identify a record.

Reports

Report facilities allow you to decide what information from a table or query is visible when you view it or print it. Reports are usually categorised as:

❏ *Single column.* Records are displayed in full down the side of the page or screen, rather than across the page in columns.

❏ *Multiple column.* A column is provided for each field you specify and records are placed one after another. You can allow the field names to be used as column headings, or design your own.

❏ *Grouped.* If the information can be grouped into different levels, then the report can be presented in this way, with sub-totals or other calculations on numeric or currency fields, at the end of each group or subgroup.

Figure 27.8 shows a report on screen, generated with a 'report wizard', using the Product table from Figure 27.1. The sequence is by Description and this was specified as part of the report construction process. Like *forms*, you can design reports from scratch or use a wizard and then modify the design (see Figure 27.4 for Form design) as necessary.

PartCode	Description	Price	Quantity	SupplierCode
A124	Chair (Cottage)	£42.23	36	KIT518
B181	Hammer (medium cl	£6.75	12	STA436
B145	Step Ladder (mediu	£31.25	4	PAR116
B126	Step Ladder (small)	£19.50	6	PAR116
A125	Stool (Cottage)	£28.15	6	KIT518
A123	Table (Cottage)	£23.50	15	STA436

Product Listing

12-May-95

Figure 27.8. *Column report on contents of Product table*

EuroTent database case study

EuroTent is a small holiday agency, specialising in a range of French campsites, details of which are published in its brochure. It also provides a ferry and site reservation service. Some clients have no clear idea about the sites they wish to use and sometimes are not even sure which region they want to visit. For these clients, the main criteria for selection are price and campsite rating. Campsites charge on a nightly basis, but the price varies according to the season. There are two charging periods: Low Season (March to May and September to October) and High Season (from June to August). Most campsites are closed outside those periods. A computer database would allow flexible retrieval of information, using criteria, such as price range or region. Also, amendments, perhaps to site ratings or prices, could be recorded. This would allow checks to be made on the current situation, where the printed brochure may be out of date. EuroTent decide to create a single table database to manage the campsite information.

A database named EuroTent is created and the task for defining the campsite table begins.

Defining the Campsite table

Figure 27.9 shows the table definition, including field names, data types and field descriptions. The lower half of the figure, shows the field properties chosen for the Pitches field.

Figure 27.9. *Definition of Campsites table in Eurotent database*

Note that:

(i)   you can see that the selected data type is number and that the field size is *integer* (whole number only). Other optional field sizes allow for the storage of *real* numbers (they can have a fractional element) at different levels of precision (more or fewer significant digits);

(ii)   a validation rule has been set, using the expression '>=30 And <=500'. This ensures that only values between 30 and 500 are accepted; the validation text is the message which appears when an attempt is made to enter a value outside this range.

The properties for three of the other fields are shown in Figure 27.10 and the entries are explained below. The Name, Place and Region fields are all text fields of varying lengths, with no other properties specified.

	Code	Star	Low
Field size	4	1	Currency
Format			
Input mask	LL00	0	
Validation rule		='3' Or '4' Or '5'	>=7 And <=25
Validation text		Characters 3, 4 or 5	Must be £7 to £25
Required	Yes	No	No
Indexed	Yes (no duplicates	No	No

Figure 27.10. *Field properties for Code, Star and Low fields*

(i)   Code field. As you can see from Figure 27.9, this is a text field. Figure 27.10 shows that the size has been set to 4. If no other controls are exerted, any four characters can be entered. However, an *input mask* ensures that the data must have a particular pattern of entry. 'LL00', in the Access RDBMS, ensures that the first two characters are letters (A-Z) and that the last characters are digits (0-9). You can only use an input mask to set patterns for a *text*, *date* or *time* field. The field is indexed, but as the primary key for the table, it allows no duplicates (each campsite has a unique code).

(ii)   Star field. This stores a 'star' rating for a site. You can see from Figure 27.9 that this is a text field, even though the input is apparently numeric (sites are rated as '3', '4' or '5' Star). This enables an input mask to be used (0) which ensures entry of a single digit between 0 and 9. You cannot do this with a numeric field. A byte field, for example, which allows storage of values between 0 and 255 (an integer field allows −32,768 to 32,767) will not prevent the entry of real numbers, but will simply round them to the nearest whole number. The validation control for the Star field is completed by the expression = '3' Or '4' Or '5'. A suitable error message is set to display if any other characters are entered.

(iii)   Low field. This stores the price of a pitch (per night) during the less popular seasons. The High field stores the high season price. It will hold prices in sterling and the currency format ensures that if values are entered without a £ sign or without 2 decimal places, it is altered to this format. A validation rule is included to restrict values to the range 7 to 25 (you do not enter the £ sign in the expression, but it is shown in the validation text message). The High season price field has similar settings except that the prices are from £10 to £28.

Form data entry

Figure 27.11 shows some sample records in the Campsite table. As explained in the Overview section, you can use a *form* to enter, view and edit records. You can do the same in the table's 'data view', but you have no control over the layout or the fields which are displayed.

Code	Name	Place	Region	Pitches	Star	Low	High
DR13	Camping De Roffy	Sarlat	Dordogne	200	3	£10.00	£14.00
DR14	La Palombiere	Sarlat	Dordogne	150	4	£15.00	£19.00
DR19	St. Avit Loisirs	Le Bugue	Dordogne	180	4	£10.00	£14.50
DR22	Les Hauts De Ratebout	St. Foy	Dordogne	180	5	£17.00	£24.50
DR23	Camping Limeuil	Limieul	Dordogne	80	3	£9.00	£14.50
HP11	Camp Du Verdon	Castellane	Haute Provence	300	5	£16.50	£19.50
HP12	Les Lacs Du Verdon	Regusse	Haute Provence	150	3	£16.00	£22.00
MC11	Camping L'Ardechois	Vallon	Massif Central	120	4	£11.00	£14.50
MC16	Val De Cantobre	Cantobre	Massif Central	200	3	£9.50	£12.00
MC19	Les Tours	St Amans	Massif Central	130	3	£7.00	£10.50
MC21	Camping L'Europe	Murol	Massif Central	175	4	£13.00	£17.50
RV13	Camping De La Baie	Cavalaire	French Riveria	350	4	£14.00	£19.00
RV14	Domaine Des Naiades	Port Grimaud	French Riviera	200	4	£13.00	£16.00
RV15	Camping Des Pecheurs	Roquebrune	French Riviera	100	3	£10.00	£14.50
RV16	L'Etoile D'Argens	St. Aygulf	French Riviera	300	5	£16.50	£22.00
RV17	Residence Du Campeur	St. Aygulf	French Riviera	300	4	£13.00	£18.50
RV19	Camping De La Baume	Frejus	French Riviera	400	4	£13.50	£17.00
RV22	Les Pins Parasols	Frejus	French Riviera	80	4	£10.00	£14.50

Record: 1 of 18

Figure 27.11. *Sample records of Campsite table*

Figure 27.12 shows a form generated with a form wizard; it has then been modified, in design mode, to include different entry labels. Unless you specify otherwise, the field names from the table definition are used.

Figure 27.12. *Form with modified entry labels*

Database queries

EuroTent query 1 - Low Season Prices

The design of the first query, 'Low Season Prices', is shown in Figure 27.13.

Figure 27.13. *Design of Low Season Prices query*

A customer is visiting France during March, which is part of the low season and is willing to consider any area at the moment. Therefore, a list of all sites is appropriate, but only showing the prices for the relevant season. As the figure shows, the Campsites table is selected for the query (as it happens, the database only has one table at present). Then the fields to be included in the query (Name, Place, Region, Star and Low) are placed in the relevant row in the QBE grid. If the query is to be used in a report, you can alter the order of the fields through the report design.

This query does not filter records with criteria, because a list is required of all sites in the database. However, not all details are needed and as Figure 27.13 reveals, only five field names have been placed in the QBE grid. The query is also sorting the records into ascending alphabetical order, by region.

The query, expressed in SQL, is shown in Figure 27.14.

```
SELECT DISTINCTROW Campsites.Name, Campsites.Place,
Campsites.Region, Campsites.Star, Campsites.Low
FROM Campsites
ORDER BY Campsites.Region;
```

Figure 27.14. *SQL form of Query 1 to display low season prices of sites*

The SQL reserved words 'SELECT', 'DISTINCTROW' and 'FROM' have already been used and defined in the Overview. The phrase 'ORDER BY' means sequence, or sort, using the named field; in this case it is 'Region' and is prefixed by the name of the table. Every time you use a field name in an SQL statement, you need to prefix it with its table name. This is despite the fact that the EuroTent database has only one. Note from Figure 27.13 that the table used in the QBE query has to be selected first. The table must always be named, because you can use the same field name repeatedly, provided each occurrence is in a different table. The output from the Low Season Prices query is shown in Figure 27.15.

Microsoft Access - [Select Query: Low Season Prices]				
File Edit View Format Records Window Help				
Name	**Place**	**Region**	**Star**	**Low**
Les Hauts De Ratebout	St. Foy	Dordogne	5	£17.00
St. Avit Loisirs	Le Bugue	Dordogne	4	£10.00
Camping Limeuil	Limieul	Dordogne	3	£9.00
La Palombiere	Sarlat	Dordogne	4	£15.00
Camping De Roffy	Sarlat	Dordogne	3	£10.00
Residence Du Campeur	St. Aygulf	French Riviera	4	£13.00
Camping Des Pecheurs	Roquebrune	French Riviera	3	£10.00
Camping De La Baie	Cavalaire	French Riviera	4	£14.00
Camping De La Baume	Frejus	French Riviera	4	£13.50
Les Pins Parasols	Frejus	French Riviera	4	£10.00
L'Etoile D'Argens	St. Aygulf	French Riviera	5	£16.50
Domaine Des Naiades	Port Grimaud	French Riviera	4	£13.00
Les Lacs Du Verdon	Regusse	Haute Provence	3	£16.00
Camp Du Verdon	Castellane	Haute Provence	5	£16.50
Les Tours	St Amans	Massif Central	3	£7.00
Camping L'Europe	Murol	Massif Central	4	£13.00
Val De Cantobre	Cantobre	Massif Central	3	£9.50
Camping L'Ardechois	Vallon	Massif Central	4	£11.00
Record: 2 of 18				

Figure 27.15. *Dynaset from Low Season Prices query*

EuroTent query 2 - Pitches 150 or less, Low Season, 4 to 5 Star

Customers visiting France when campsite prices are lower can afford to be more selective and frequently choose small, but good quality sites. This query (Figure 27.16) is designed to produce the kind of information they require.

Figure 27.16. *Design of Query 2*

The SQL form of Query 2 is shown in Figure 27.17.

```
SELECT DISTINCTROW Campsites.Name, Campsites.Place,
Campsites.Region, Campsites.Pitches, Campsites.Star, Campsites.Low
FROM Campsites
WHERE ((Campsites.Pitches<=150) AND (Campsites.Star="4" OR
Campsites.Star="5"))
ORDER BY Campsites.Low DESC;
```

Figure 27.17. *SQL form of Query 2*

The meaning of the SQL statement, shown in bold, should be quite clear when you compare it with the criteria used in the QBE form in Figure 27.16. The reserved word WHERE is followed by two criteria; the first is that the Pitches field must contain a value of 150 or less; the second criterion is that the Star field must contain either '4' OR (used as a *logical operator*) '5'. The AND logical operator means that both criteria must be satisfied, before a record is selected. The final statement in this SQL query contains the reserved word DESC, which means *descending* (order). The output from Query 2, showing the smaller, better quality sites, with low season prices, is shown in Figure 27.18.

Figure 27.18. *Dynaset from Query 2*

EuroTent query 3 - French Riviera £14 to £19

This query is in response to a more precise request for information. A family wish to stay in the Riviera region during the High season and are willing to pay between £14 and £19 a night. The query design is displayed in Figure 27.19.

Figure 27.19. *Design of query for Riviera sites between £14 and £19*

The main point to note is that there are two criteria, one concerning the Region and the other, the High season price. The latter is similar to the criterion used in Query 2. The criterion that the Region should be the French Riviera could have been expressed fully, in the form ='French Riviera'. QBE does not require the use of an '=' sign, so you could simply type 'French Riviera' as the criterion. In Figure 27.19, a wild card (*) is used, thus: *Riviera. The RDBMS takes this as being a request for any string of characters which ends with 'Riviera' and prefixes it with 'Like', which is the proper form of the expression.

If there were other occurrences of the string 'Riviera' in the Region column, such as 'Italian Riviera', you would have to be more specific.

The SQL form of Query 3 is displayed in Figure 27.20.

```
SELECT DISTINCTROW Campsites.Name, Campsites.Region,
Campsites.Place, Campsites.Pitches, Campsites.Star, Campsites.High
FROM Campsites
WHERE ((Campsites.Region Like "*Riviera") AND (Campsites.High>=14
And Campsites.High<=19))
ORDER BY Campsites.High;
```

Figure 27.20. *SQL form of Query 3*

The results of running Query 2 are displayed in Figure 27.21.

Figure 27.21. *Dynaset from query for Riviera sites at £14 to £19 per night*

A grouped column report

Query 1 produces the full list of campsites, ordered alphabetically by Region. Since there are several sites in each region, each regions name is repeated. A grouped column report only displays each group name once. Figure 27.22 shows a grouped report on the output from EuroTent's Query 1.

EuroTent		14-May-95	Low Season Prices	
Region	Name	Place	Rating	Price
Dordogne				
	Camping Limeuil	Limieul	3	£9.00
	St. Avit Loisirs	Le Bugue	4	£10.00
	Camping De Roffy	Sarlat	3	£10.00
	La Palombiere	Sarlat	4	£15.00
	Les Hauts De Ratebout	St. Foy	5	£17.00
French Riviera				
	Camping Des Pecheurs	Roquebrune	3	£10.00
	Les Pins Parasols	Frejus	4	£10.00
	Residence Du Campeur	St.Aygulf	4	£13.00
	Domaine Des Naiades	Port Grimaud	4	£13.00
	Camping De La Baume	Frejus	4	£13.50
	Camping De La Baie	Cavalaire	4	£14.00
	L'Etoile D'Argens	St. Aygulf	5	£16.50
Haute Provence				
	Les Lacs Du Verdon	Regusse	3	£16.00
	Camp Du Verdon	Castellane	5	£16.50
Massif Central				
	Les Tours	St Amans	3	£7.00
	Val De Cantobre	Cantobre	3	£9.50
	Camping L'Ardechois	Vallon	4	£11.00
	Camping L'Europe	Murol	4	£13.00

Figure 27.22. *Grouped report on output for Query 1*

Personnel database case study

This case study demonstrates the use of a relational database by using multiple tables to store the information. Pilcon Electronics is organised into the following departments (the abbreviation in brackets is used in the database as the DeptCode):

- Accounting and Finance (ACC);

- General Office Services (GOS);

- Management Information Services (MIS);

- Personnel (PER);

- Production (PRO);

- Purchasing (PUR);

- Research and Development (RAD);

- Sales and Marketing (SAL);

- Warehousing (WAR).

The Personnel database holds basic information on individual staff, departments and job grades; the database has three tables, one for each of these categories of information. They are named: StaffMember; Department; Job. The database allows the staffing in the departments to be monitored, in terms of salary costs and the individuals who are employed in them. It is also useful to be able to monitor the structure of staffing by grouping staff according to job titles; this analysis can be carried out across Pilcon Electronics, as a whole, or it can be specific to one department. Each table has to be separately defined, in the same manner as the Campsites table in the EuroTent case study.

The definition of the StaffMember table is displayed in Figure 27.23.

Figure 27.23. *Definition of StaffMember table*

StaffMember definition

The field properties of the StaffMember table are shown in Figure 27.24.

property	StaffCode	Surname	Initials	JobCode
field size	3	25	4	3
input mask	000			LL0
validation rule	>=100And<=200			
validation text	Range 100 to 200			
required	No	No	No	No
indexed	Yes(no Duplicates)	No	No	No
property	DeptCode	Salary	StartDate	Superann
field size	3			
format			Medium	Yes/No
input mask	LLL			
validation rule		>=8000 And <=45000	<=Now()	
validation text		Range 8000 to 45000	Invalid date	
required	No	No	No	No
indexed	No	No	No	No

Figure 27.24. *Field Properties in Staff Member table*

The lower half of Figure 27.23 shows the field properties chosen for the StartDate (the date a member of staff's employment with Pilcon began) field and you should note the following:

(i)   The data type is *date/time* and the format is *medium date*. This means that data can be entered as, for example, 1/4/95 and it will be displayed as 01-Apr-95, or similar. Formatted as long date, it would appear as 1 April 1995.

(ii)   A validation rule is used to ensure that the starting date for an employee must not be in the future. A function 'Now()' returns the system date (the current date and time is stored in the computer) and the expression '<=Now()' means 'less than or equal to today's date'.

Most of the other field properties, shown in Figure 27.24, have already been introduced in Figure 27.10 and are explained thereafter.

One detail not given in Figure 25.24 is the validation rule for DeptCode. It is as follows.

```
=ACC Or GOS Or MIS Or PER Or PRO Or PUR Or RAD Or SAL Or WAR
```

The expression checks that the DeptCode is one of the three character strings listed; these are the abbreviations for each of the departments (see earlier). The Superann (Superannuation Scheme Member) field is a *logical* or *yes/no* field. It is used as a true/false indicator. Thus, with a field name Superann, 'yes' indicates that the person is a member of the company superannuation scheme; 'no' obviously means he or she is not a member.

Department definition

The DeptCode and DepartmentName fields in Figure 27.25 need little explanation. You should notice that the DeptHead field has the same format as StaffCode in the StaffMember table definition; the same input mask is used. DeptHead and StaffCode are *synonyms*; they are different names, but they have the same meaning. You could make the DeptHead field size, say 25, and store the names of heads of departments in the Department table. There is no point however, because as members of staff, their names are already held in the StaffMember table.

Microsoft Access - [Table: Department]		
File **Edit** **View** **Window** **Help**		
Field Name	Data Type	Description
DeptCode	Text	Primary key, 3 alpha validated for all department codes
DepartmentName	Text	one of nine departments, not validated
DeptHead	Text	Synonym for Staff Code in Staff Member table

Field Properties

Field Size	3	
Format		
Input Mask	000	
Caption		
Default Value		A field name can be up to 64 characters
Validation Rule	>="100" And <="200"	long, including spaces. Press F1 for
Validation Text	Range 100 to 200	help on field names.
Required	No	
Allow Zero Length	No	
Indexed	No	

Figure 27.25. *Department definition showing properties for DeptHead*

As shown later, information can be drawn from several tables in a database, provided there are *link fields* to establish *relationships* between them.

Job definition

In Figure 27.26, you can see that JobCode is the primary key for the Job table. You should recognise that the field of the same name in the StaffMember table enables access to the job titles in the Job table. The fields have exactly the same pattern, so the same input mask is used (LL0 - two alphabetic and one digit) to control input to the JobCode field.

Microsoft Access - [Table: Job]		
File **Edit** **View** **Window** **Help**		
Field Name	Data Type	Description
JobCode	Text	Primary key 2 alphabetic and 1 digit
JobTitle	Text	Up to 30 text characters

Field Properties

Field Size	3	
Format		
Input Mask	LL0	The field description is
Caption		optional. It helps you
Default Value		describe the field and is
Validation Rule		also displayed in the status
Validation Text		bar when you select this field
Required	No	on a form. Press F1 for help
Allow Zero Length	No	on descriptions.
Indexed	Yes (No Duplicates)	

Figure 27.26. *Definition of Job table*

Contents of Personnel database

Figures 27.27, 27.28 and 27.29 show contents for StaffMember, Department and Job Tables.

Microsoft Access - [Table: StaffMember]

File Edit View Format Records Window Help

StaffCode	Surname	Initials	JobCode	DeptCode	Salary	StartDate	Superann
100	Picket	W.	CL2	ACC	£15,000	23-Jan-77	Yes
101	Ringwood	K.	HD1	PRO	£33,000	14-May-95	Yes
103	Clacket	D.	CL0	GOS	£13,500	01-Jan-86	No
106	Boreham	L.	SS1	ACC	£23,000	23-Sep-72	Yes
108	Winkle	R.V.	SU1	WAR	£18,000	01-Sep-88	Yes
110	Dickens	C.	OP1	PRO	£8,000	14-May-95	No
115	Cratchit	B.	CL2	ACC	£8,500	01-May-94	No
118	Boffin	C.	HD1	RAD	£38,000	01-Sep-66	Yes
123	Heap	U.	HD1	SAL	£37,500	31-Oct-93	Yes
124	Miggins	M.	SU1	GOS	£14,500	31-Oct-93	Yes
126	Squeers	W.	SS1	PER	£17,500	13-Jun-88	Yes
128	Chiseller	M.	HD2	ACC	£43,000	01-Apr-83	Yes
131	Marley	J.	OP1	PRO	£8,600	16-Jun-91	No
133	Server	I.	HD1	WAR	£32,000	01-Sep-60	Yes
136	Grabbit	U.	HD2	PUR	£45,000	12-Apr-66	Yes
138	Stackit	I.	OP1	WAR	£9,200	03-Apr-68	No
139	Broaket	H.E.	OP2	PRO	£13,000	17-Apr-76	Yes
145	Ramidos	Z.	SU1	MIS	£17,900	12-Jun-88	Yes
149	Machem	I.	HD2	PRO	£40,000	01-Apr-90	Yes
155	Pusher	P.	HD2	GOS	£44,000	01-Feb-60	Yes
159	Nervey	M.	OP1	WAR	£10,000	01-Apr-95	No
160	Surcoat	I.	HD2	MIS	£40,000	02-May-66	Yes
168	Sached	U.R.	HD2	PER	£38,000	01-May-82	Yes
172	Tefal	B.	HD2	RAD	£37,000	02-Mar-66	Yes
180	Leavmey	B.	HD2	SAL	£42,000	01-Oct-72	Yes
187	Lostem	I.	HD2	WAR	£32,500	31-Oct-88	Yes

Record: 11 of 26

Figure 27.27. *StaffMember records*

Microsoft Access [Table: Department]

File Edit View Format Records Window Help

DeptCode	DepartmentName	DeptHead
ACC	Accounting and Finance	128
GOS	General Office Services	155
MIS	Management Information Services	160
PER	Personnel	168
PRO	Production	149
PUR	Purchasing	136
RAD	Research and Development	172
SAL	Sales and Marketing	180
WAR	Warehousing	187

Record: 3 of 9

Figure 27.28. *Department records*

Microsoft Access [Table: Job]

File Edit View Format Records Window H

JobCode	JobTitle
CL0	Clerical - Trainee
CL1	Clerical - Junior Grade
CL2	Clerical - Middle Grade
CL3	Clerical - Senior
HD1	Assistant Head of Department
HD2	Head of Department
LS1	Production Line Supervisor
OP1	Machine Operator
OP2	Machine Maintenance Technician
SS1	Section Supervisor
SU1	Supervisor
SU2	Supervisor - Senior

Record: 4 of 12

Figure 27.29. *Job records*

Database queries

Queries can be applied to single tables or to more than one. Multiple tables can be queried because *relationships* exist between the tables. For example, the relationship between the Department table and the StaffMember table is through the DeptCode field, which exists for that purpose in both tables. The relationship is *one-to-many*; this means that each StaffMember record relates to only one Department, but each Department record relates to many StaffMember records. Similarly, the relationship between Job and StaffMember is one-to-many. There is no direct relationship between Job and Department; this is only possible through the StaffMember table, which relates to both.

Personnel query 1 - Department Heads and Salaries

In preparation for a meeting of Pilcon's Board of Directors, details of the salaries earned by the Heads of Department are required. The information should comprise, each Head's surname, salary and their Departments name; the output is to be in descending numerical order, by Salary. The names and salaries of Heads of Department are held, with those of the rest of the staff, in the StaffMember table and the Department names are in the Department table. This means that the query has to join these two tables. The full details of the query design (using QBE) are shown in Figure 27.30.

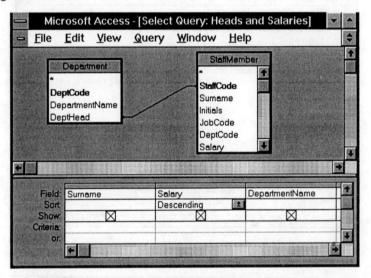

Figure 27.30. *QBE to extract Heads of Department details*

You might be surprised that no criterion is necessary to select the JobCode 'HD2', which identifies Heads of Department. This can be explained as follows. You can see from Figure 27.30 that a *relationship* is established between DeptHead in the Department table and StaffCode in the StaffMember table (remember these field names are synonyms). This ensures that, when the tables are *joined* in the query, data is only used from those records where the value in StaffCode matches with the value in its synonym, DeptHead. The latter field is an example of a *secondary foreign key*. A link could also be established between the DeptCode fields in each table, but it is unnecessary; having linked the tables through StaffCode and DeptHead, the DepartmentName details are made accessible. The query, in SQL is displayed in Figure 27.31.

```
SELECT DISTINCTROW StaffMember.Surname, StaffMember.Salary,
Department.DepartmentName
FROM Department INNER JOIN StaffMember ON Department.DeptHead =
StaffMember.StaffCode
ORDER BY StaffMember.Salary DESC;
```

Figure 27.31. *SQL form of Query 1 to display Heads of Department details*

Much of the SQL in Figure 27.31 is used in earlier examples. The new points to note relate to the second statement. Joining tables establishes relationships or links between them. Figure 27.31 shows two such relationships. 'INNER JOIN' is the most commonly used operation which merges information from two tables where values in the link fields are common to both tables. The SQL word 'ON' is followed by the table names and fields to be joined. As can be seen from the QBE form of the query in Figure 27.30 and the SQL statement in Figure 27.31, records are combined when the DeptHead (Department table) value equals the StaffCode (StaffMember table) value. The dynaset from Query 1 is shown as a report in Figure 27.32 (see Figure 27.33 for report design screen).

Pilcon Electronics
Salaries of Heads of Department
17-May-95

Surname	Salary	DepartmentName
Chiseller	£43,000	Accounting and Finance
Grabbit	£45,000	Purchasing
Leavmey	£42,000	Sales and Marketing
Machem	£40,000	Production
Pusher	£44,000	General Office Services
Surcoat	£40,000	Management Information Services
Tefal	£37,000	Research and Development
Sached	£38,000	Personnel
Lostem	£32,500	Warehousing
	£361,500	

Figure 27.32. *Column report on Heads of Department query*

Figure 27.33. *Design screen for report in Figure 25.32*

Note that the report design process automatically inserts a SUM formula to calculate and display the total for the Salary column. Note also the use of the *Now()* function to display the current date.

Personnel query 2 - Non-HODs in Superannuation scheme

This query uses the criterion '<>HD1' And '<>HD2', which means 'staff who are not Heads or Assistant Heads of Department', to extract records of other staff. There are two other criteria: member of Superannuation scheme; appointed on or before 1st January 1990. To produce this information requires the joining of the StaffMember and Department tables. Figure 27.34 shows the QBE form of this query.

Figure 27.34. *QBE form of Personnel Query 2*

Note that the JobCode and Superann fields are needed in the QBE grid to allow entry of the appropriate filter criteria. However, they do not need to displayed, so the 'Show' check boxes are deselected. The SQL form of the query is shown in Figure 27.35. All the SQL features in this query have already been met, so it should be self-explanatory. Note that the deselected fields are not included in the first statement.

```
SELECT DISTINCTROW StaffMember.Surname, StaffMember.Salary,
Job.JobTitle, StaffMember.StartDate
FROM Job INNER JOIN StaffMember ON Job.JobCode =
StaffMember.JobCode
WHERE ((Job.JobCode<>"HD2" And Job.JobCode<>"HD1") AND
(StaffMember.Superann=Yes) AND (StaffMember.StartDate<=01/1/90#));
```

Figure 27.35. *SQL form of Personnel Query 2*

The simple table form of output for this query is shown in Figure 27.36.

Figure 27.36. *Dynaset for Personnel Query 2*

Personnel Query 3 - Operator and Clerical Staff

This query (see Figure 27.37) involves the use of all three tables. To enable selection of operators and clerical staff, the JobCode is needed. Using a wild card, *Like 'CL*'*, finds CL0, CL1 and CL2. Similarly, *Like 'OP*'* picks out OP1 and OP2.

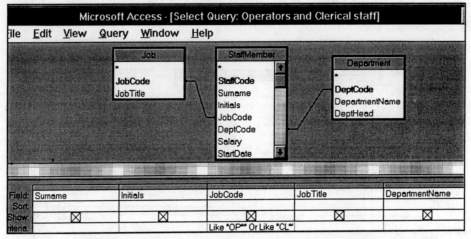

Figure 27.37. *QBE form of query to identify operator and clerical staff*

The SQL form of the query is shown in Figure 27.38.

```
SELECT DISTINCTROW StaffMember.Surname, StaffMember.Initials,
StaffMember.JobCode, Job.JobTitle, Department.DepartmentName
FROM (Job INNER JOIN StaffMember ON Job.JobCode =
StaffMember.JobCode) INNER JOIN Department ON StaffMember.DeptCode
= Department.DeptCode
WHERE ((StaffMember.JobCode Like "OP*" Or StaffMember.JobCode Like
"CL*"));
```

Figure 27.38. *SQL form of Personnel Query 3*

The output is displayed in Figure 27.39.

Microsoft Access - [Select Query: Operators and Clerical staff]				
File Edit View Format Records Window Help				
Surname	**Initials**	**JobCode**	**JobTitle**	**DepartmentName**
Picket	W.	CL2	Clerical - Middle Grade	Accounting and Finance
Clacket	D.	CL0	Clerical - Trainee	General Office Services
Dickens	C.	OP1	Machine Operator	Production
Cratchit	B.	CL2	Clerical - Middle Grade	Accounting and Finance
Marley	J.	OP1	Machine Operator	Production
Stackit	I.	OP1	Machine Operator	Warehousing
Broaket	H.E.	OP2	Machine Maintenance Technician	Production
Nervey	M.	OP1	Machine Operator	Warehousing
Record: 5	of 8			

Figure 27.39. *Dynaset for Query on operator and clerical staff*

Personnel query 4 - updating Salaries

Figure 27.40 is an example of an *update query*. Using this type of query you can update groups of records with a single operation. Of course, the update has to be of a form which allows group updating, such as a percentage increase in salaries. The salary increase of 10% is effected with the expression *[Salary]*1.1*. On performance, Pilcon have decided not to increase the salaries of Heads and Assistant Heads of Department (see criteria in Figure 25.40). If you did increase their salaries, you would first have to alter the validation rule for the Salary field, which restricts values to the range 8000 to 45000.

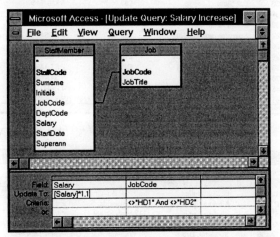

Figure 27.40. *Update query to increase salaries by 10%*

The SQL form of this update query is displayed in Figure 27.41.

```
UPDATE DISTINCTROW StaffMember INNER JOIN Job ON
StaffMember.JobCode = Job.JobCode SET StaffMember.Salary =
[Salary]*1.1
WHERE ((StaffMember.JobCode<>"HD1" And
StaffMember.JobCode<>"HD2"));
```

Figure 27.41. *SQL form of update query*

The main points to observe from Figure 27.41 are as follow:

(i)   Instead of SELECT, the first SQL word is UPDATE;

(ii)   The INNER JOIN is carried out ON a SET of records, WHERE JobCode is not equal to 'HD1' and not equal to 'HD2'.

Viewing the StaffMember table would reveal that all salary figures (except those of Heads and Assistant Heads) are increased by 10%.

Stock Control database case study

This example makes use of the Product table, used for illustration in the Overview, plus a Supplier table. The full definitions of the database are not given here. The main purpose of the Stock Control case study is to illustrate editing tables through a query dynaset and further aspects of *forms*.

Editing tables through query dynasets

The contents of the Product and Supplier tables are shown in Figures 27.42 and 27.43, respectively.

PartCode	Description	Price	Quantity	SupplierCode
A123	Table (Cottage)	£23.50	15	KSU518
A124	Chair (Cottage)	£42.23	36	KIT518
A125	Stool (Cottage)	£28.15	6	KIT518
A133	Bar Stool	£33.55	4	KSU518
A136	Bread Bin (wood)	£14.25	4	KIT518
A139	Bread Bin (metal)	£10.25	6	KSU518
B122	Spanner (adjustable)	£8.25	4	BCS436
B126	Step Ladder (small)	£19.50	6	PAR116
B129	Screw Driver (ratchet)	£15.55	13	BCS436
B133	Ladders (aluminium)	£85.66	2	STA436
B136	Spirit Level	£13.55	6	STA436
B145	Step Ladder (medium)	£31.25	4	PAR116
B181	Hammer (medium claw)	£6.75	12	STA436

Figure 27.42. *Sample contents of Product table*

SupplierCode	SupplierName	SupplierAddress
BCS436	BCS Supplies	Imperial Buildings, Darlington DL3 4ST
KIT518	Kitchen Systems	28 Holmeside, Sunderland, SR3 4ST
KSU518	Kitchen Supplies	112 High Street, Darlington, DL1 4SJ
PAR116	Parsons Ltd	Parsons House, Market Place, York YO4 3NS
STA436	Stapleton Bros	36 Warwick Place, Darlington, DL4 6AJ

Figure 27.43. *Sample contents of Supplier table*

Suppose, for example, that you wish to view and edit the combined information from both tables. You could join the tables in a query, the design of which is shown in Figure 27.44.

Figure 27.44. *Query to join information from Product and Supplier tables*

The simple datasheet view of the resulting dynaset is shown in Figure 27.45.

PartCode	Description	Price	Quantity	SupplierCode	SupplierName	Su
B181	Hammer (medium claw)	£6.75	12	STA436	Stapleton Bros	36 Warwick Place, Dai
B133	Ladders (aluminium)	£85.66	2	STA436	Stapleton Bros	36 Warwick Place, Dai
B136	Spirit Level	£13.55	6	STA436	Stapleton Bros	36 Warwick Place, Dai
A124	Chair (Cottage)	£42.23	36	KIT518	Kitchen Systems	28 Holmeside, Sunder
A125	Stool (Cottage)	£28.15	6	KIT518	Kitchen Systems	28 Holmeside, Sunder
A136	Bread Bin (wood)	£14.25	4	KIT518	Kitchen Systems	28 Holmeside, Sunder
B126	Step Ladder (small)	£19.50	6	PAR116	Parsons Ltd	Parsons House, Marke
B145	Step Ladder (medium)	£31.25	4	PAR116	Parsons Ltd	Parsons House, Marke
A123	Table (Cottage)	£23.50	15	KSU518	Kitchen Supplies	112 High Street, Darlir
A133	Bar Stool	£33.55	4	KSU518	Kitchen Supplies	112 High Street, Darlir
A139	Bread Bin (metal)	£10.25	6	KSU518	Kitchen Supplies	112 High Street, Darlir
B129	Screw Driver (ratchet)	£15.55	13	BCS436	BCS Supplies	Imperial Buildings, Dai
B!45	Spanner (adjustable)	£8.25	4	BCS436	BCS Supplies	Imperial Buildings, Dai

Figure 27.45. *Dynaset from query joining Product and Supplier tables*

You should notice that each supplier name and address is repeated several times. The relationship between the Supplier and Product tables is one-to-many, which means that many products are bought from a single supplier, but each product is ordered from a single supplier. Although the information from both tables can be viewed, only certain fields can be edited to update the tables, upon which the query is based. In the case of a one-to-many relationship, changes can only be made to dynaset fields which come from the *many* side of the relationship. Two important points need to be understood.

(i)   Referring to Figure 27.44, if the query uses the SupplierCode from the Product table, you will be able to alter the Supplier codes in the dynaset shown in Figure 27.45. The name and address will then change accordingly (by using the relationship established with the Supplier table). The changes to the supplier details will be applied to the underlying Product table. Changes affect the many side of the relationship, only. Figure 27.46 shows that the supplier of the 'Hammer (medium, claw)' is now 'Parsons Ltd', instead of 'Stapleton', as shown in Figure 27.45. This is achieved by altering the SupplierCode for that record.

	Description	Price	Quantity	SupplierCode	SupplierName	Su
	Hammer (medium claw)	£6.75	12	PAR116	Parsons Ltd	Parsons House, Marke
	Ladders (aluminium)	£85.66	2	STA436	Stapleton	36 Warwick Place, Dai
	Spirit Level	£13.55	6	STA436	Stapleton	36 Warwick Place, Dai
	Chair (Cottage)	£42.23	36	KIT518	Kitchen Systems	28 Holmeside, Sunder
	Stool (Cottage)	£28.15	6	KIT518	Kitchen Systems	28 Holmeside, Sunder
	Bread Bin (wood)	£14.25	4	KIT518	Kitchen Systems	28 Holmeside, Sunder

Figure 27.46. *Change of Supplier for Hammer (medium, claw) record*

(ii)   If, in designing the query in Figure 27.44, you use the SupplierCode from the Supplier table, the RDBMS would not let you edit it through the dynaset. In this example, this means that you can edit the Product table (the *many* side), but not the Supplier table (the *one* side), through the query dynaset.

If the underlying tables have a one-to-one relationship there are no editing restrictions through the dynaset. If you want to prevent any editing through a dynaset, the RDBMS provides an option to disable the facility. There are other circumstances when dynaset editing is restricted, but they are beyond the scope of this text.

Viewing and editing with main/sub forms

Figure 27.45 shows a dynaset which provides a view of all the information in both the Product and Supplier tables. The main drawback is that the suppliers' names and addresses are repeated several times. In addition, as a dynaset, the Supplier table (the *one* side of the one-to-many relationship) cannot be edited through it. Editing could be carried out using a separate form for each table, or more effectively, with the main/sub form shown in Figure 27.47.

Figure 27.47. *Main/sub Form showing one Supplier record and the associated Products*

The form can be created using a form wizard, but you can start with separate forms and then combine them, making the Product form the sub. As you scroll through each Supplier record (you can see that there is a scroll bar for each part of the form), all the associated (through the SupplierCode relationship) Product records appear in the lower, sub form. You can edit or add new Supplier Records, by using the upper, main form.

Figure 27.48 shows a new supplier record entered within the main form, but before entry of any product records for that supplier. Entry of a new supplier code would mean that there would be no Product records in the sub form; you could then enter any details of products supplied by the new supplier. Similarly, you can edit or add new Product records in the sub form, for an existing supplier. Remember, changing a SupplierCode in the Product section of the form (the *many* side) will not affect records in the Supplier table (the *one* side).

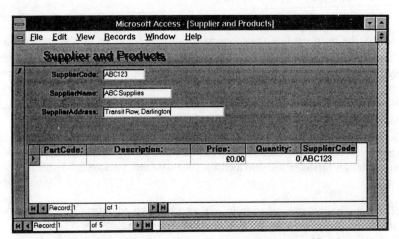

Figure 27.48. *Entry of new Supplier, but before entry of Products*

Forms for dynasets

The rules which apply to dynaset editing, detailed already, also apply to editing through a form. Thus, creating a form for the dynaset shown in Figure 27.45, does not alter the restrictions concerning the editing of any underlying table on the 'one' side of a one-to-many relationship.

✍️Exercises

Each of the following exercises is to be implemented with a relational database. In each case, ensure that the data is in third normal form (3NF) and produce an entity-relationship model (ERM).

1. As a member of local botany group, you have been given the task of designing and creating a wild flowers database. It will be used as a central resource for members. Details of flowers will be added as they are spotted by members. The following sample data is provided.

    Chaffweed. Primrose family. Latin name Centunculus. 1 inch high. Pink flower. Grows in damp gravelly places. Flowers June to August. Annual.

    Chickweed. Primrose family. Latin name Trientalis. 4-6 inches high. White flower. Abundant in Highlands of Scotland. Flowers June. Perennial.

    Sea-Milkwort. Primrose family. Latin name Glaux. 3-6 inches high. Pink flower. Common on sea shore and salt marshes. Flowers June to August. Perennial.

    Viper's Bugloss. Borage family. Latin name Echium. 1-2 feet high. Red then blue flower. Walls, old quarries and gravel pits. Flowers June to August. Biennial.

    Lungwort. Borage family. Latin name Pulmonaria. 1 foot high. Pale purple flower. Woods and thickets, rare. Flowers April, May. Perennial.

    Comfrey. Borage family. Latin name Symphytum. 1-3 feet high. White, pink or purple flower. Water places and banks of rivers, common. Flowers May to August. Perennial.

    Borage. Borage family. Latin name Borago. 1-2 feet high. Deep blue flower. Waste ground. Flowers June to September. Biennial.

    St. John's Wort. St John's Wort family. Latin name Hypericum. 1 foot high. Yellow flower. Gardens and shrubberies. Flowers July to September. Perennial.

(i)   Identify the main entities, their associated attributes and set up the appropriate tables.

(ii) Consider the different kinds of reports which could be generated from this database and design and construct it accordingly. If you can gather information concerning other wild flowers, it would help to expand the database.

(iii) Print the complete database and check the information against your manual lists. Use the database editing facilities to correct any errors.

(iv) Generate a number of reports, which you think may be useful to the botany group. For example, you could list those flowers which fall into the same family. Make use of whatever report design facilities are provided by your database package.

2. The following description is taken from a brochure which advertises hundreds of holiday properties (throughout Europe) for rent. Several different agents are represented.

> *Casa Girasole, Castagneto, Tuscany, Italy. Sleeps 6. This delightful farmhouse, set amid 8 acres of rolling pasture land and terraced olive groves, is 2 miles from the quaint hilltop village of Castagneto Carducci and only 9 kilometres from the nearest beach at Marina di Castagneto. The owners live in one part of the property and guests have their own entrance and terrace. The accommodation, comfortably furnished, is on two floors with a large, fully equipped kitchen and spacious living room. The bedrooms, on the first floor, are small. Children would delight in exploring the estate and discovering the livestock on this small working farm. There are very good views from the bedroom windows. The unmade road to the property is rough in parts.*
>
> *Accommodation. Ground floor: Entrance from terrace into kitchen/dining room. Shower/WC, washing machine. Sitting room, fireplace. First floor: 2 bedrooms: 1 double, 1 small room with bunkbeds. Bathroom/WC.*
>
> *Situation/facilities. Castagneto Carducci 2 km. All facilities. Seaside 9 km. Volterra 70 km. San Gimignano 95 km. Pisa 70 km.*
>
> *Agent: Italia Vita, 23 Hemingway Road, Malvern, Worcestershire, WR13 9PN. Tel. 0435 364782*

(i)   Identify the main entities, their associated attributes and set up the appropriate tables.

(ii) Analyse the description and define a suitable database structure. Use similar property descriptions to create a holiday home database.

(iii) Identify and generate reports which may be useful for clients who are seeking property to rent.

3. This activity concerns the patient records held by a medical practice. Information is held concerning: patient name and address; date of next visit; details of visits over the past five years; doctor to whom the patient is assigned; current medication (if any); medical history, including stays in hospital and medication given by the practice; allergies to medication; risk factor to particular illnesses, such as heart disease.

(i)   Identify the main entities, their associated attributes and set up the appropriate tables.

(ii) Design and construct a suitable database structure. You should be able to identify further entities or attributes to extend the database.

(iii) Enter sufficient records to allow demonstration of the database.

(iv) Generate those reports which you think may be of use to the medical practice. Make use of any report design facilities provided by the package.

4. Borsettshire College of Further and Higher Education runs a wide range of vocational and non-vocational courses for both full-time and part-time students. It is generally accepted and generally stipulated by external course validating bodies such as BTEC, that full-time vocational courses should include a period of relevant work experience for each student. Borsettshire College offers full-time vocational courses in, for example, catering, hotel management and reception, computing, business studies, nursery nursing and social work. During the year, the total number of students requiring work placement of one sort or another is around 500. Approximately 30 academic staff are involved in organising the work placements, and many use the same employers.

It has been agreed that, as a first step, information on work placements should be centrally available to all interested staff. Before approaching an employer, a member of staff would be expected to refer to the centrally held information, to see who else used the employer and to determine if there are likely to be any clashes. If any further information is required, the other member(s) of staff responsible for work placements with the same employer, can be consulted directly.

The database is to contain information concerning the employer, the type of work placements offered, official contacts and details of the relevant college staff.

(i) Identify the entities, attributes and primary keys. Ignore any requirement for the identification of college tutors with particular employers.

(ii) Define and save the database structure.

(iii) Enter sufficient records to illustrate the operation of the database. Print the contents of each table.

(iv) Query the database, for three useful output reports, establishing any necessary links between the tables in the database. Save each query.

(v) Define a suitable report layout for each query and execute the queries. Print the results of each query, using the appropriate report layout.

Chapter 28

Distributed Databases

Put simplistically, a database is a central store of information accessible by multiple applications. A <u>distributed</u> system subdivides the database over multiple computer systems, but it still appears as a single database to applications and users. When a complete database is replicated at different sites, it is still referred to as a distributed database because the technical problems of database management are similar to those of a truly distributed database. We will look at the principles of and options for database replication and then examine true distributed database systems.

Database replication

Copies of a database or partial database may be held on multiple servers to improve performance and ensure access to data is maintained.

Single master replication

Figure 28.1 illustrates a replication model which allows read-only access to distributed copies, only allowing updates to be effected on the master database. For example, an application can access a local version of the database for enquiry purposes if the communications link to the master database is temporarily unavailable. Depending on the method used to maintain consistency between the various copies and the master database, such local access may mean that data is not entirely up-to-date. For reasons which will be explained later, updates must be effected through the master database only.

Application

Following an update to the master database, the changes are copied to the local database(s). The replication may not be immediate, either because the process is only carried out periodically, or because the network connection to a local database is temporarily unavailable. Provided that the organisation plans for such differences in data values and absolute currency is not essential to applications, the model may work perfectly well. For example, supermarket chain may only make price changes every two days, which it applies to the master database at its headquarters and then replicates to the copies at supermarket branches. This is, in effect, batch processing.

If updates are carried out in realtime and replication required more or less immediately, network links or a high volume of update transactions may prevent local copies from being properly updated. This could have serious consequences for some applications. For example, suppose that enquiries are made locally on stock levels and orders to customers are agreed on the basis of those enquiries. If there have been numerous stock issue updates without frequent replication orders may not be met, resulting in the loss of valuable custom.

The model is useful for systems where the high volume of updates to the master makes it difficult to handle queries efficiently. If enquiry-only applications use the local copies this removes the burden from the master database. The more copies there are, the more the load is shared.

Peer-to-peer replication

In this model, there is no master and all replicas (copies infer use of a master database) are treated as equal for the purposes of enquiry and updates, hence the term peer-to-peer. The database management system (DBMS) software must ensure that an update of one replica is then copied to the other replicas. Updates at each site may be queued and replicated at set intervals (a kind of batch processing known as *store and forward*) or, if the application requires it, they may be applied immediately to all replicas in *real-time*. Replication is essential to maintain consistency of database values across all database replicas. Figure 28.2 illustrates a peer-to-peer replication model.

Figure 28.2. *Peer-to-peer database replication*

Application

Peer-to-peer replication can be used to

❑   distribute the load in a high volume, transaction processing, system.

❑   ensure continued database access, a vital feature for many applications including, for example, those of the emergency services. In the event of failure of a replica, its users can be automatically switched to another.

❑   updating a centralised database from a number of locally held databases. This is a common requirement for organisations with sales or servicing staff whose jobs depend on the use of, for example, notebook computer systems. For example, following completion of a servicing job, a gas engineer will update the customer record on a notebook computer. At the end of the day, the database changes can be uploaded to the centralised database.

Replication update conflicts

The consistency of database replicas can be lost when updates can be applied to different replicas of the same database. The problem does not apply to single master replication because updates are only applied to the master database - copies cannot be updated, except by replication from the master database. Real-time replication is not subject to conflicts because all replicas are immediately updated and at the time that a record is being updated at one site, it is *locked* to other sites. As soon as the update has been completed and replicated to all sites, the record is unlocked. Real-time replication relies entirely on the continued availability of the high-speed network connections which are need to connect the sites to one another. However, the following types of conflict can occur when replication is not immediate, that is for peer-to-peer, store and forward replication:

❏   primary key duplication, as illustrated in Figure 28.3;

❏   simultaneous updating of the same record at different database sites (Figure 28.4);

Figure 28.3. *Potential duplicate primary key conflict*

Figure 28.4. *Conflicting attempts to update the same record at the same time*

❏   attempt to delete or update a record already deleted at another site (Figure 28.5).

Figure 28.5. *Conflicting attempt to update a record already deleted at another site*

Detecting and resolving conflicts

The database management system (DBMS) must be able to detect and resolve any of the conflicts outlined above. Fore example, in the case of the attempt to update or delete a record which has already been deleted at another site, this can be resolved by only setting record deletion markers, rather than physically removing records from the database. Periodically, such marked records can be permanently removed or *purged*.

Distributed databases

A true distributed database partitions an organisation's 'global' database into a number of individual databases, perhaps one or two for each branch or division. Figure 28.6 provides an example.

Each database contains network links to connect it with other databases (not necessarily all) to form the global database. Each link needs to indicate the location of the database and the relevant table. For example, the Sales database in London may include a link to the JobHistory table in the Personnel database in Manchester, as follows.

```
jobhistory.personnel@manchester.abcengineering.co.uk
```

The Figure illustrates an example structure of a distributed database but does not attempt to show the network connections which would be needed to connect the various databases.

Database transparency

Although there is not replication in this model, individual transactions will sometimes affect more than one table. A transaction may affect local

Figure 28.6. *Example hierarchy of a distributed database*

or remote tables, but to retain database consistency the updates must be applied to all affected tables simultaneously. Usually, the physical location of individual databases will be hidden from both applications and users. A programmers can develop an application according to the restricted logical view or sub-schema provided by the database administrator (DBA). This *transparency* allows a distributed database to appear as a single, global database. Distributed databases reduce central processing requirements, but can be vulnerable when network links are unavailable. For databases which are updated in real-time, uninterrupted network communications are essential.

The security issues relating to distributed databases are similar to those for the control of access to computer networks. Levels of access are controlled through the use of user accounts. A database administrator (DBA) is given *global* or *supervisor* user status and has unrestricted access to a local, and possibly, the global database. The DBA must be able to modify database definitions as the application and user requirements change. For a fuller description of the DBA's role, see Chapter 26. Programmers and users are restricted to the database areas they need and are given access rights appropriate to their tasks. For example, staff who respond to customer enquiries should have read-only access, whereas, supervisory staff may be able to modify data.

✍️Exercises

1. (i)   Distinguish between database *replication* and *distribution*.

    (ii) A wholesaler has a single central orders database which it *replicates* to each of its distribution warehouses at the end of each day.

          Comment on the quality of information which will be held by the branches.

    (iii) Explain the problem of *update conflicts* when *peer-to-peer* replication is used.

2. (i)   Examine Figure 28.6 in this Chapter and comment on the benefits and drawbacks of the *distributed* system it represents in comparison with a wholly *centralised* system.

    (ii) Use the example in Figure 28.6 to explain the term *database transparency*.

Programming

Chapters

Programming in High-level Languages

The general characteristics of high-level languages (HLLs) are discussed briefly in Chapter 12. Here we consider the common characteristics of HLLs in more detail before examining a number of languages in depth. Like computer hardware, computer languages can be categorised according to *generations*, from the first to the latest fifth generation languages. The five generations may be summarised as follow.

First generation

Appearing in the 1960s, these languages were based on the architectures of the current computers. Control structures were very basic, closely related to the instruction set of machines such as the IBM 704. Data structures were similarly based on the internal representations used for numbers and characters. The rather rigid syntactic structure of first generation languages was influenced by the constraints arising from the use of punched cards as the main input medium for programs. Fortran is typical of this generation of languages.

Second generation

These elaborated on the structure of first generation languages in a number of important ways. Firstly, block structuring (see later) was introduced, facilitating program design. Secondly, there was a move towards structured programming by the introduction of more structured control constructs. Thirdly, the syntax of the languages became more flexible, allowing statements to be expressed in a freer format. Algol-60 is typical of this generation.

Third generation

User-defined data structures became available, allowing a more application orientated approach to programming to be adopted. Control structures were modified to make them simpler and more efficient than those of the previous generation, and new, application oriented control structures such as the case statement, were added. These changes resulted in third generation languages becoming much more independent of computer hardware. Pascal is a good example of third generation languages.

Fourth generation

Such languages continue the tradition of reducing the work of the user and increasing the load on the computer. The terms Fourth Generation Language, and its contraction, 4GL, are subject to a wide variety of interpretations and definitions, but they all have a number of characteristics in common:

❏ easier to use than existing high-level languages, particularly by non-specialists;

❏ allow quick solutions to data processing tasks;

❏ more concise than existing high-level languages;

❏ the language is closer to natural language;

❑   user-friendly;

❑   non-procedural.

Two examples of current software systems which fit this loose definition of a 4GL are Structured Query Languages (SQLs) and Program Generators.

Fifth generation

These languages break away from the conventional imperative language format in ways which facilitate implementation on alternative computer architectures. For example, the declarative nature of the fifth generation language PROLOG allows programs to be implemented using parallel processing techniques. Object oriented languages and functional languages also allow this possibility, while still usable on conventional computers. LISP and Smalltalk are two further examples of fifth generation languages. Though all HLLs can be applied to a wide variety of programming tasks, and are in that sense general-purpose languages, most high-level languages have been designed specifically for particular application areas. For example, Fortran's syntax facilitates modelling mathematical problems, COBOL allows data processing and file handling applications to be coded in a convenient manner, and LOGO was written to encourage children to approach problem solving logically and to explore mathematical concepts. Table 29.1 summarises the characteristics of a number of well-known languages. All of the languages below are to a greater or lesser extent general-purpose, so only special application areas are mentioned. The code c means Compiled, i means Interpreted and t means Threaded Interpretive Language.

language	date	type	application areas
Ada	1979	c	Real-time systems programming; embedded systems.
ALGOL	1960	c	General-purpose.
APL	1966	i	Scientific/mathematical problems inc vectors and matrices.
BASIC	1963	i,c	Teaching programming; for casual users rather than serious professional programmers.
C	1972	c	Systems programming.
COBOL	1960	c	Data processing.
Forth	1969	t	Control of servo-driven devices.
FORTRAN	1954	c	Mathematical/scientific problems.
LISP	1960	i	Artificial intelligence.
Logo	1967	i	Helping children with problem solving;artificial intelligence.
Modula-2	1979	c	Systems programming.
Pascal	1970	c	Teaching program/algorithm design.
PL/1	1965	c	General-purpose.
PROLOG	1972	i	Artificial intelligence.
Smalltalk	1972	c	Object oriented programming.
SNOBOL	1966	i	Text processing.

Table 29.1.

All of these languages, and many others, have a considerable number of similarities; most programming problems require data to be stored, calculations to be performed, values to be read from some external source or displayed in some form, alternative sets of operations to be executed depending on some condition arising, sections of programs to be repeated a specified number of times, and so on. For convenience, these similarities can be grouped under a number of headings:

- ❏   reserved words and keywords;

- ❏   identifiers;

- ❏   data structures;

- ❏   operations on data;

- ❏   input/output operations;

- ❏   control structures;

- ❏   file handling;

- ❏   functions and procedures;

- ❏   reserved words and keywords.

All high-level languages contain a number of words having special meanings. For example, in Pascal begin, end and while are such words. These are called *reserved words* because the programmer is not allowed to use them as identifiers; they are used only in specific contexts and their meanings are recognised by the language compiler. In languages such as COBOL, having over 300 reserved words, this constitutes something of a problem for programmers.

An alternative approach, one used by some early HLLs, notably Fortran, is to use keywords which are only recognised by the compiler as being special words if they are used in prescribed circumstances; used in any other context they are assumed by the compiler to be identifiers. Most modern HLLs use reserved words as this method is less prone to ambiguity.

Identifiers

In addition to reserved words or keywords, programs contain names created by the programmer. Names are given to program variables or constants; names are assigned to subprograms or program modules; names are given to user-defined data structures. These names are collectively called *identifiers*. They comprise groups of alphanumeric characters, typically beginning with a letter, which allow programmers to give convenient names to program items.

Data items whose values are allowed to change during the execution of a program are called variables; constant data items retain their values throughout the execution of the program. In some HLLs, variables, constants, procedures and functions have to be declared before they can be used, usually at the start of the program or subprogram in which they appear. Declarations are used to define the form or type of identifiers.

Scope of variables

The term scope refers to the degree of accessibility of a variable. For example, variables declared within the main program are often accessible to any part of the whole program, whereas the accessibility of variables defined within a subprogram (see later) is restricted to that subprogram only. The former are termed *global* variables, and the latter *local* variables. The precise rules governing scope vary according to the particular language.

Data structures

The commonest data types are:

❑   *numerics*, either Integers (e.g. 255) or Reals (e.g. 1.45);

❑   *characters* (e.g. a) and Character Strings (e.g. Freddy);

❑   *booleans*, which can take only one of two values (e.g. TRUE or FALSE);

❑   *pointers*, which contain the location of other data items.

These *primitive* data types can be combined to form data structures, the commonest of which are:

❑   *arrays* or lists of data of one specific type, with individual elements referenced by means of one or more subscripts;

❑   *records*, which allow collective names to be assigned to groups of variables of different types;

❑   *files*, which are collections of identically structured records.

A number of HLLs, notably Pascal and C, allow new user-defined data types to be constructed from primitives or other (previously declared) user-defined data types, in order to create data structures of almost any complexity.

Operations on data

The operations available in an HLL normally include:

❑   arithmetic operations involving addition, subtraction, multiplication and division;

❑   logical operations, usually the operations AND, OR, NOT and EOR(exclusive OR).

Results of such operations may be stored in variables by means of assignment statements taking the form of mathematical identities. For example, an assignment statement in Fortran looks like this:

```
Sum = A + B
```

The variable Sum would be assigned the value corresponding to the sum of the values of the variables A and B. The normal rules of precedence apply, and brackets may be used freely as in ordinary algebra.

Input and output operations

Most HLLs provide special input statements for capturing data from a standard input device such as a keyboard for allocation to a specified variable, and special output statements for displaying data on a standard output device such as a VDU.

Control structures

Control structures are the means by which the normal top to bottom execution order of statements may be modified. The basic control constructs are:

❑   *Selections*, such as IF..THEN..ELSE, CASE, ON X..GOSUB, allowing the current states of specified variables to determine the next action to be taken by the program; in other words, the means by which alternative courses of action may be taken.

❑ *Iterations*, such as FOR..NEXT, REPEAT..UNTIL, WHILE..DO, allowing blocks of instructions to be repeated.

Note that certain HLLs, for example Prolog, do not explicitly have the above types of control structures; the reason for this is explained later in the section on Logic Programming.

File handling

High-level languages invariably provide a set of instructions for manipulating files held on backing storage devices such as magnetic disks. By means of these types of instructions, blocks of data may be transferred to and from backing storage. A typical set of file-handling instructions might include instructions for:

❑ opening files ready for use;

❑ closing files;

❑ reading records from a sequential file;

❑ writing records to a sequential file;

❑ reading records from a random file;

❑ writing records to a random file.

Other languages, COBOL for example, provide facilities for processing indexed-sequential files. Sometimes a language will provide low-level file-handling instructions for reading/writing single bytes, single numbers or strings from backing-storage. C is such a language.

Functions and procedures

Languages such as Pascal and C allow the programmer to create subprograms (also called subroutines or modules) which may be referenced by name in the main program. Broadly speaking, a subprogram is a self-contained section of program code which performs some identifiable task. This facility is invaluable when designing large programs because it allows the programmer to split a large, complex task into a collection of smaller, simpler tasks.

Subprograms are usually allowed to contain local variables, which are declared within the subprogram, and whose scopes are restricted to the extent of the subprogram. These variables are usually dynamically created when the subprogram is invoked and are destroyed, that is, their memory areas are released, on completion of the subprogram.

Subprograms, are frequently called procedures or functions. Simply speaking, a procedure is a subprogram which when invoked, or called, from the main program (or another subprogram) performs some task and then returns control to the place from which it was called; a function does much the same thing but, in addition, returns a value to the calling program or subprogram.

The difference between procedures and functions is best illustrated by means of an example. Suppose, as part of a large program which has been produced as an aid in the design of buildings, a subprogram is required to display a rectangle, of given dimensions, on the VDU. Then this would probably be written as a procedure invoked by a statement such as

```
procedure draw_rectangle(10, 5)
```

where the numbers in the brackets are parameters specifying the dimensions of the rectangle to be drawn. The code for the procedure `draw_rectangle` would exist either within the program or on some backing storage medium, such as a magnetic disk, accessible to the language compiler. The code would be executed, causing a rectangle of the required dimensions to be drawn, and the program would continue with the next instruction following the call.

Suppose now that another subprogram is required to calculate the area of building material required to produce a rectangular shape of the same dimensions. This task would most probably be implemented as a function of the form

```
area = function calc_area(10, 5)
```

Again two parameters are passed to the function, but this time it is expected to calculate and, on completion, return a value which is to be stored in the variable area.

This is a rather simplistic view of procedures and functions; in practice there are many variations and enhancements of these basic ideas. Pascal and C both make extensive use of subprograms assuming a variety of different forms.

Block structuring

Earlier it was mentioned that some languages require that variables are defined prior to their use by means of declarations. When such declarations are made in subprograms, the declared variables are usually termed local variables. This means that their values are defined only when the subprogram is being executed, and otherwise, as far as the main program is concerned, they do not exist. The scope of these variables, depends on the language. In C, the scope of such variables, that is the area of the program able to recognise them, is restricted to the subprogram only; in Pascal it is restricted to that subprogram and any other subprograms defined within it. Variables which are defined in the main program have global scope, that is they are accessible to the whole program, including its subprograms. Such variables are called global variables.

A number of languages allow the use of compound statements, where a number of statements can be grouped together to form a block. For example, in C a block starts with the delimiter { and ends with the delimiter }. Within these block delimiters it is possible to declare variables whose scope is restricted to the block, as if they had been defined as local variables within a subprogram. Indeed, a block in this context is a kind of open subroutine, that is a subprogram which is inserted where it is required rather than being referenced by name, with the actual code appearing elsewhere in the program. Blocks may be nested to any depth.

Languages which exhibit these types of structures, that is nested subprograms or compound statements containing declarations of variables in addition to program statements, are called block-structured languages. In Pascal, Modula-2 and Ada the block-structuring is implemented by means of nested procedure definitions, whereas in C nested compound statements, with similar scoping rules, are used.

Parameters

An important characteristic of procedures and functions is the ability to pass parameters to and from them. Parameters are frequently shown as variables enclosed within brackets after the name of the procedure/function, as illustrated in an earlier section. Parameters allow the programmer to use the same subprogram to process different values, without the necessity of repeating the code for the subprogram wherever it is needed. Two types of parameters are in common use: *value* parameters and *variable* parameters.

With value parameters, the transfer of data is one way only - from the calling program to the subprogram. A copy of the value to be passed to the subprogram is made before transfer takes place, and therefore the original is unchanged by whatever processing occurs within the subprogram. This is often termed a *call by value*.

In the case of variable parameters, the subprogram uses an alias (ie a different name) for the variable passed as a parameter; this means that the subprogram can alter the value of the variable even though it may use a different name for the variable. This is often termed a *call by value-result*. Pascal supports both of these systems of parameter passing.

Summary of high-level languages

The following sections give a brief introduction to a number of well-known high-level languages. A number of other languages, PROLOG as an example, are dealt with elsewhere because of their special natures. All of the languages in this section are conventional high-level languages in the sense that they were designed for use on computers based on Von Neumann's model of a digital computer. A growing number of other high-level languages, regarded as being fourth or fifth generation, have been developed with other computer architectures in mind. Languages such as PROLOG, Ada, and Modula-2 fall into this category.

BASIC

BASIC was developed at Dartmouth College, in the USA, in 1963 and was intended to be easy to learn and appropriate for a wide variety of applications. Its popularity has been largely the result of its ease of implementation on microcomputers, and it is frequently supplied with them. There is a standard for BASIC, just as there are standards for Fortran and COBOL, and most versions of BASIC adhere to this standard, but each version usually has additional features, many of which are specific to the particular version. Fortunately, however, having learnt one version makes it easy to adapt to a different one.

In the past, BASIC has been heavily criticised for its tendency to encourage bad programming habits. Initially, few versions of BASIC had control structures to encourage or facilitate the use of structured programming techniques, and consequently large programs tended to be difficult to understand and modify. Some recent versions, however, have rectified this deficiency to greater or lesser extents by incorporating Pascal-like facilities.

Originally BASIC was an interpreted language, a feature which contributed to its suitability for novices, but over the past few years, such has been its popularity, that a significant number of software houses have produced BASIC compilers which allow programs to be run independently of an interpreter and with the usual speed and security benefits provided by compiled languages.

C

C is a programming language developed by Bell Laboratories of the USA around 1972. It was designed and written by Dennis Ritchie who was at the time working on the development of the UNIX operating system. UNIX was designed to be particularly useful to the software engineer by providing a wide variety of software tools. In fact, the UNIX operating system was written in C, and even the C compiler is now written in C.

It was designed to be easy to learn and use, powerful and reliable and it has many characteristics of structured languages such as Pascal. Its roots are based in the language Algol, and C retains many of its features, but Cs strength lies in its simplicity, the facility with which complex programs may be built from simple building blocks.

Because Dennis Ritchie worked in the field of systems software, C is orientated to such applications as operating systems, computer language development and text processing. Its suitability for these areas is largely attributable to the fact that it is a relatively low-level language which facilitates very efficient programming, yet at the same time it retains the advantage of high-level languages to hide the details of the computer's architecture.

COBOL

On the whole, data processing applications involve a great deal of input and output operations with a relatively minor amount of calculation in between. The data operated upon generally consists of files comprising a large number of records. For example, a computerised stock control system for a wholefood warehouse would contain details of each item held: description of item, sale price, unit size, number currently in stock etc. This collection of data is termed a record, and together all these records form the stock file. Each time an item of stock is sold, the record for that item would need to be changed by reducing the stock level for that item. In terms of the data processing requirements of this type of operation, it would be necessary for the computer to read the details of the sales, find the appropriate stock records, subtract the appropriate amounts from the current stock levels and store the modified records. This sequence would be necessary for each sale recorded on a sales file.

COBOL is ideally suited to this type of application; it was designed to facilitate the manipulation of large amounts of data requiring fairly simple processing operations. Programs written in COBOL tend to be lengthy compared to other languages capable of performing similar processing tasks, the reason being that it requires the programmer to identify the purpose of the program, the computing equipment to be used, and the format of the files to be processed, as well as the procedure to be adopted for processing the files. All this information must be contained within the program itself. Subsequently, COBOL is often criticised for being very cumbersome, but on the credit side, all this detail helps to make a COBOL program easy to read and understand.

A COBOL program is divided into four areas termed DIVISIONS which appear in the order IDENTIFICATION division, ENVIRONMENT division, DATA division and PROCEDURE division. Each division comprises a number of SECTIONS and these are further divided into SENTENCES.

The IDENTIFICATION DIVISION allows the programmer to describe the whole program in general terms by supplying, under appropriate headings, such information as the name of the program, its author, when it was written and what it does. Some of this information is optional and none of it has a direct effect on the program's operation.

In the CONFIGURATION SECTION of the ENVIRONMENT DIVISION are details of the computers on which the program was developed and is intended to be run, and the INPUT-OUTPUT SECTION specifies the peripheral devices to be used for reading or writing the files which will be defined later in the program.

The DATA DIVISION contains a FILE SECTION in which each file named in the INPUT-OUTPUT SECTION is given a File Description (FD). The FD contains the file name and one or more record names. The structure of a record is defined hierarchically using LEVEL numbers starting at 01 and getting progressively bigger for finer definitions. The WORKING-STORAGE SECTION of the DATA DIVISION contains definitions of other data items specifically referenced in the PROCEDURE DIVISION of the program but which are not part of any file.

Finally, the PROCEDURE DIVISION defines precisely how the processing is to be performed. The programmer may give PARAGRAPH names to groups of SENTENCES to which reference may be made from other parts of the program, and these paragraphs may be grouped together into SECTIONS.

Each SENTENCE, terminated with a full stop, defines one or more basic operations to be performed on data; in keeping with the general philosophy of making a COBOL program easily readable, the instructions often read like ordinary English sentences as, for example, the SENTENCE

```
ADD vat TO cost GIVING total
```

Java

Java is programming language for the Internet. It allows programs to be transferred over the Internet in the same way as web pages - Java programs are executed by browsers just as web pages are displayed by browsers. Programs downloaded and executed in this way are called 'applets', that is small applications. Java was developed by Sun Microsystems Inc in the USA.

The team of developers designed Java to be:

Simple. They designed it to look like a simplified form of C++, a widely used programming language. Although it looks very much like C++, it lacks a number of features which are rarely used, can lead to poor programming practices , or are prone to introducing program 'bugs'. As a result, Java is relatively easy to learn, particularly for experienced programmers.

Distributed, so that it could support applications on networks, and in particular the Internet. With Java it is just as easy for a program to access a file on a remote computer anywhere in the world as one on your own computer.

Portable. A Java compiler is initially used to produce program object code in the form of 'byte-codes', a neutral form of code that is later run by a Java interpreter. This means that any computer system, no matter whether it is a mainframe, IBM PC or Macintosh, can download and run a Java applet if the browser is 'Java enabled' (which all of the latest browsers are).

Secure. Because Internet users can download and run Java programs from random sites on the Internet, Java has safeguards against such things as computer viruses or other programs that attempt to alter files.

FORTRAN

FORTRAN was designed by John Backus of IBM in 1953 for the science and engineering field. A compiler for the language first appeared in 1955 for an IBM machine, and since that time it has enjoyed widespread popularity as a powerful software tool. Since its introduction, FORTRAN has steadily evolved, giving rise to such versions as WATFOR (developed at the university of WATerloo, Canada) and WATFIV as well as FORTRAN IV. Mainly orientated towards scientific/mathematical/engineering applications, many of its statements resemble and provide for numerical calculations. A FORTRAN program may be defined as a subroutine (subprogram) which may be referred to (called) by other programs in order to perform some standard or common operation. By forming libraries of these subroutines a programmer is able to reduce the amount of work required to write a new program; where possible, his program will make reference to these pre-written modules which will be combined with his code when the program is compiled. The language has many standard mathematical functions, such as SIN, COS, and SQRT, built in.

Pascal

Devised by Professor Niklaus Wirth in 1970 and named after the gifted 17th century mathematician and philosopher Blaise Pascal, Pascal is a general-purpose language based on Algol-60. Because Pascal, like BASIC, was designed as a teaching language, it is a very easy language to learn. Moreover, being orientated towards structured programming, it encourages the clear expression of the logical structure of the program. This makes Pascal a very easy language to write programs in, and is particularly suitable for the development of large programs. For these reasons it is widely used in teaching, and is being adopted by more and more establishments of further and higher education as the main programming language for computing courses.

Many people believe Pascal to be superior to any other general-purpose programming language in use today, and its expanding use in all sectors of industry is evidence in support of this claim. Each Pascal program consists of a declarations section in which the structure of the data to be processed and produced is defined, a section for the definition of functions and procedures which are referenced in the program body section. The program body defines the operation of the program in a precise series of steps. Functions and procedures may be called from the program body whenever required.

Recursive programming

The term recursion is used to refer to the process of subprograms calling themselves. This is best explained by means of an example. The pseudocode program in Listing 29.1 uses a recursive call to print integers starting at 1 up to a given value.

Listing 29.1.

```
{Print consecutive integer values}
  read number
  call print_upto(number)              {call the
                                        procedure}
{end}

Procedure print_upto(N)
  select
    when N > 1
      call print_upto(N-1)             {procedure calls
                                        itself}
    when N <= 1
      next statement                   {ie do nothing}
  endselect
  write N
  return
```

The recursive procedure is called `print_upto(number)` taking, as a parameter, the integer variable `number` which is read at the start of the program and is the upper limit for the integers to be printed.

Notice that, in the procedure `print_upto(N)`, the parameter N enclosed in brackets is automatically local to the procedure; this property of procedures, vital to recursive programming, is illustrated by the program trace which follows (the value of `number` is taken to be 3).

Depth of Recursion

Step		0	1	2
1	call	print_upto(3)		
2		when 3 > 1 call	print_upto(2)	
3			when 2 > 1 call	print_upto(1)
4				write 1
5				return
6			write 2	
7			return	
8		write 3		
9		return		
10	end			

Step 1:   the procedure is called from the main program passing as a parameter the value of number (taken to be 3 in this example).

Step 2 :   the first line of the procedure tests the value of the parameter (called N in the procedure) and, because it is greater than 1, calls itself, this time passing a parameter value of N-1, that is 2. Because the procedure has not yet been completed, local variables (in this case just N) are saved to a stack so that when control eventually returns, the values of the local variables can be restored.

Step 3 :   the process is now at a recursion depth of 1 because the procedure has called itself once. The parameter N now has a value of 2, which is still greater than 1. Because the condition tested is true, the procedure calls itself once more. The current value of N (i.e. 2) is saved to a stack before the procedure is called.

Step 4 :   the process is now at a recursion depth of 2 because the procedure has called itself twice. The parameter N now has a value of 1, which is not greater than 1. Because the condition N >1 is not true this time, the procedure ignores the call statement and goes on to the next statement in the procedure which prints the current value of N (i.e. 1).

Step 5 :   the return statement causes local variables to be discarded and their memory space reclaimed before program control is returned to the calling (sub)program. This process of returning back through recursive calls is often termed *bottoming out*.

Step 6 :   the process resumes at recursion depth of 1 having returned from the call statement invoked in Step 3. The values of all local variables are restored from the stack. The write statement displays the value of local variable N (i.e. 2).

Step 7 :   this is identical to step 5.

Step *8* :   the process arrives at the first invocation of the procedure having returned from the call statement in Step *2*. The values of all local variables are restored from the stack. The print statement prints the value of local variable N (i.e. 3).

Step *9* :   this is identical to steps *5* and *7*.

Step *10*:   finally, the program terminates.

Problems that lend themselves to recursion are often definable in terms of simpler versions of themselves as illustrated above: printing the numbers 1, 2, 3, 4 is just a simpler version of the problem of printing the numbers 1, 2, 3, 4, 5; printing 1, 2, 3 is just a simpler version of the problem of printing 1, 2, 3, 4, and so on. A number of data structures, including trees and linked lists, lend themselves to recursive processing techniques for this reason. The next examples further illustrate the point.

Two simple examples of recursive algorithms

The algorithm in Listing 29.2 calculates the value of an integer number, base, raised to certain positive integer power, exp.

Listing 29.2

```
{Calculate base raised to power}
   read base, exp
   write power(base,exp)
{end}

function power(b,e)
   local v
   select
     when e = 0
       v = 1
     when e <> 0
       v = b * power(b,e-1)
   endselect
   return(v)
```

Table 29.1 contains examples of the values returned by the algorithm in Listing 29.2.

base	exp	result	
10	0	1	$=10^0$
10	3	1000	$=10^3$
2	0	1	$= 2^0$
2	5	32	$= 2^5$

Table 29.1

The example in Listing 29.3 uses a very similar method to calculate the factorial of a positive integer.

Listing 29.3.

```
    {Calculate a factorial}
      read fac
      write factorial(fac)
    {end}

    function factorial(f)
      local v
        when f = 0
          v = 1
        when f <> 0
          v = f * function factorial(f-1)
        endselect
    return(v)
```

Table 29.2 shows some factorials calculated by the algorithm in Listing 29.3.

factorial	result	
0	1	
1	1	
2	2	$= 2 \times 1$
3	6	$= 3 \times 2 \times 1$
4	24	$= 4 \times 3 \times 2 \times 1$
5	120	$= 5 \times 4 \times 3 \times 2 \times 1$

Table 29.2.

Tracing through these algorithms in the same way as illustrated for the first example in this section should help to clarify the mechanisms used to obtain the desired results.

Advantages and disadvantages of recursive programming

Recursive solutions to programming tasks are often elegant and concise. They tend to be most effective when the solution to a problem may be expressed in terms of a simpler version of itself.

When a subprogram is executed, its data area is stored on a stack, so that if a subprogram calls itself a number of times, there will be a number of similar data areas on the stack at the same time, one for each recursive call. Therefore there is always the possibility of running out of stack space when executing recursive programs.

Another not insignificant problem with recursive programming is understanding how it works sufficiently well to be able to write programs which use recursion; being able to appreciate a recursive solution to a programming task is often very much easier than originating such a solution. Furthermore, detecting and correcting bugs in recursive programs may not be as straightforward as debugging more traditional, iteration-based programs.

Recursion is one of the central features of logic and functional programming languages both of which are discussed in later sections.

Declarative vs imperative languages

The languages discussed so far are often classified as *imperative* or *procedural* languages. These terms are used to describe high-level languages which require the programmer to show explicitly the order in which program statements are to be executed, and precisely how the programming solution is to be reached. The sequence of commands in a program is a key feature of imperative languages such as Pascal, FORTRAN and COBOL, since they are based on the Von Neumann computer model in which a stored program is executed by sequentially stepping through instructions stored in the main memory of a computer. Store locations are modified as a direct result of the action of the program. Similarly, imperative languages achieve their objectives by modifying program variables using assignment statements, and by causing sequential execution of program statements. Because imperative languages are so closely related to the operation of conventional computers, they are relatively efficient. However, other computer architectures, such as those using parallel processing, give rise to different types of programming languages.

Declarative languages rely on a different mechanism for solving programming problems. In these languages the emphasis is on defining the problem to be solved, not on the detailed sequence of instructions that are required in order to achieve the desired solution. It can be argued that a language such as Pascal is less procedural, and therefore more declarative, than an assembly language because there is less need for the programmer to define precisely how to do standard processing tasks such as input/output or arithmetic operations. For example, in an assembly language, it would require quite a complex sequence of instructions to perform the Pascal floating point calculation

```
x := (-b + sqrt(det))/(2.0*a);
```

Yet in Pascal it is merely a matter of specifying the calculation to be performed and allowing the compiler to determine how to organise the instructions required to do it. Thus languages that are predominantly procedural have elements of non-procedural characteristics. Declarative languages take this a stage further, allowing the language translator to do much more of the work, so that the programmer can concentrate on specifying what the problem is rather than how to solve it.

Because declarative languages do not rely on the programmer specifying precisely in which order instructions are to be executed, it is often possible to process a number of instructions in parallel if the mechanism exists to allow this. In the next section we examine the logic programming language PROLOG which is generally regarded as a good example of a predominantly declarative, or non-procedural, language. Functional languages, LISP for example, also essentially declarative, are described in a later section. Both PROLOG and LISP have features which allow them to take advantage of alternative computer architectures.

Logic programming

PROLOG, PROgramming in LOGic

Invented by Alain Colmerauer in the early 1970s, PROLOG was first implemented in Marseilles in 1972. It provided a means of allowing the programmer to specify a problem in terms related to formal logic rather than procedures.

The language has been adopted as the basis of software development for the Japanese fifth-generation project because of its relevance to research in artificial intelligence. It has been used extensively in the development of expert systems because it includes facilities ideal for this type of application.

PROLOG is said to be goal oriented, that is to say the programmer specifies the problem to be solved in terms of a goal, and is not expected to provide detailed instructions regarding the achievement of the goal. A goal is defined in terms of subgoals, the achievement of which will lead to the final solution. A subgoal may be a simple statement which evaluates to logical true or false, or may depend on its own subgoals which PROLOG will try to evaluate. Since there may be alternative sets of subgoals for a particular goal, PROLOG may, having failed to successfully resolve one combination, backtrack and try another combination. It will continue to try different combinations until either a solution is reached or there are no further combinations of subgoals to try. The power of PROLOG lies in its built-in ability to select goal combinations and to backtrack; in other languages this would have to be programmed explicitly.

Programming in PROLOG involves defining objects to be manipulated and relationships between them. A program consists of facts and rules (or clauses): facts are taken to be true statements about objects and rules declare that statements about objects are true if certain conditions (subgoals) are true. Executing a PROLOG program involves stating a goal to be achieved and allowing PROLOG to determine whether the goal can be achieved with the current facts and rules.

As an example, to represent the relationships between the members of a family spanning three generations as illustrated by the family tree shown in Figure 29.1.

Figure 29.1. *Family tree*

This shows that Harry and Dorothy had two daughters, Anne who married Ken, and Barbara who married Nick. Anne and Ken had a son, Stuart, and a daughter, Sally. Barabara and Nick had two sons, Daniel and Matthew. Not shown on the diagram are Nicks parents, Raymond and Margaret.

These facts could be represented as follows in PROLOG:

```
male(raymond).
female(margaret).
male(harry).
female(dorothy).
male(nick).
female(barbara).
male(ken).
female(anne).
female(sally).
male(stuart).
male(matthew).
male(daniel).
```

```
parent(raymond,nick).
parent(margaret,nick).
parent(harry,barbara).
parent(dorothy,barbara).
parent(harry,anne).
parent(dorothy,anne).
parent(nick,daniel).
parent(nick,matthew).
parent(barbara,daniel).
parent(barbara,matthew).
parent(anne,sally).
parent(anne,stuart).
parent(ken,sally).
parent(ken,stuart).
```

The first type of fact concerns the sex of each member of the family:

```
male(raymond).
```

This asserts that `raymond` belongs to the set `male`. Similarly, `barbara` belongs to the set `female`. The other type of fact, `parent`, asserts that, for example, `nick` is a `parent` of `daniel`.

At this point we could ask PROLOG questions, in the form of simple goals, about this small database. For example, at the PROLOG prompt, ?, we could type

```
?- parent(X,barbara).
```

PROLOG would search its collection of facts and respond

```
X = harry
More(y/n)?
```

Having found one value of variable X satisfying the goal, PROLOG displays this and asks if the search is to continue for another fact satisfying the goal. If we answered 'y', PROLOG would respond

```
X = dorothy
More(y/n)?
```

This is the only other solution to the goal and if we responded 'y' again, PROLOG would answer with 'No', indicating that there were no more solutions to the goal.

The goal

```
?- parent(anne,X).
```

would return values 'X = stuart' and 'X = sally', that is, the children of Anne.

Moreover, the goal

```
?- parent(X,Y).
```

would return all of the parent/child pairs in the database in the form

```
X = nick, Y = daniel
```

Rules could be added to the database in order to establish connections between facts. For example, the rule

```
childof(Y,X) :- parent(X,Y).
```

says that Y is a `childof` X if X is a `parent` of Y.

If we wanted to find out from the collection of facts all the children of Dorothy, at the PROLOG prompt (?-) we would type

```
?- childof(y,dorothy).
```

PROLOG would regard this as a goal to be achieved and would try to find a fact or rule satisfying this goal. Because `childof` is a rule consisting of one subgoal, `parent`, PROLOG tries to find a value of X such that `parent(X,dorothy)` succeeds. It therefore produces 'Y = anne' and 'Y = barbara' as solutions to the goal.

The slightly more complex rule

```
mother(X,Y) :- parent(X,Y), female(X).
```

establishes that X is the `mother` of Y if X is the `parent` of Y and X is also `female`.

Suppose we wished to establish whether Barbara is the mother of Matthew. We would pose the question

```
?- mother(barbara,matthew).
```

Substituting for X and Y, PROLOG would generate the two subgoals

```
parent(barbara,matthew), female(barbara).
```

Since both of these facts exist in the database, both goals could be achieved and PROLOG would answer Yes.

Posing the question

```
?- mother(X,sally).
```

would again generate two subgoals, this time of the form

```
parent(X,sally), female(X).
```

PROLOG would first find a solution to the first subgoal in the form `parent(ken,sally)`, and then attempt to satisfy the second subgoal, `female(ken)` which would fail. PROLOG would then backtrack to search for another solution to `parent(X,sally)`. It would find `parent(anne,sally)` as a solution and then search for `female(anne)`, this time succeeding. Finally, PROLOG would respond with 'X = anne'.

As a further example, the rule

```
grandparent(X,Z) :- parent(X,Y), parent(Y,Z).
```

establishes the condition for X to be the `grandparent` of Y.

Recursion plays a prominent role in PROLOG programs. Consider, for example, a rule which generalises the previous rule for a `grandparent`:

```
predecessor(X,Z) :- parent(X,Z).
predecessor(X,Z) :- parent(X,Y), predecessor(Y,Z).
```

This time there are two clauses associated with the same definition: the first is necessary to halt the recursion exhibited in the second. To understand how this works, suppose that we posed the question

```
?- predecessor(X,daniel).
```

We would expect the solutions to be X = nick, X = barbara (these are parents), X= raymond, X = margaret, X = harry and X = dorothy (grandparents).

PROLOG would start by finding solutions to the first rule and simply find X = nick and X =

barbara. The second rule would also be used as a goal, generating the subgoals

```
parent(X,Y), predecessor(Y,daniel).
```

One solution to parent(X,Y) is parent(raymond,nick), so PROLOG would try to find predecessor(nick,daniel).

This recursively generates the subgoal parent(nick,daniel) from the first rule for predecessor, and this succeeds producing in effect

```
parent(raymond,nick), parent(nick,daniel)
```

allowing PROLOG to exit from the recursion. PROLOG would therefore state 'X = raymond' as another solution.

PROLOG has been used extensively as a database language and in AI (artificial intelligence) for natural language processing, expert systems and applications requiring knowledge representation.

PROLOG's suitability as a database language can be attributed to three main characteristics:

❑   A database defined in Prolog can be extended readily without any special provision for this growth needing to be made. This is in contrast to languages such as BASIC and COBOL where new information or requirements might necessitate a complete software revision.

❑   Databases can be merged or pooled with great ease; systems can be extended without the necessity for extensive forward planning.

❑   The language has, built in, the facility for drawing logical conclusions from a user's inputs, and for extracting information embedded in complex sequences of rules. This obviates the need for a special database query language.

Since natural language has a large number of rules regarding the composition of sentences, PROLOG is well suited to natural language processing where it is necessary to reduce sentences into their constituent parts. For example, in BNF notation a simple sentence can be represented by

```
<sentence> ::=<noun phrase><verb phrase>
<noun phrase> ::=<determiner><noun>
<verb phrase> ::=<verb><noun phrase>
<determiner> ::= the|a|an
<noun> ::= dog|man
<verb> ::= bit|fed
```

This is sufficient to successfully parse the sentences

```
The dog bit the man,
A man fed the dog
```

Notice the close similarity with PROLOG: the facts are <determiner>, and <noun>, and the rules are <sentence>, <noun phrase> and <verb phrase>. Natural language is of course much more complex than shown by this example, but PROLOG's suitability for this type of problem should be quite obvious.

Expert systems and other knowledge-based systems also require collections of facts combined with rules for establishing connections between them, again just what PROLOG is designed to handle.

Knowledge-based systems

A knowledge-based system embodies human knowledge in a form amenable to processing by a computer program. Such a system will store facts about a certain subject area, and relationships, often in the form of rules, which will allow conclusions to be drawn from the facts. A PROLOG program such as that provided in the previous section is a good example of a knowledge base, and a PROLOG translator executing such a program could be classed as a knowledge-based system.

The most common type of knowledge-based system is the expert system, and this is discussed in some detail in the following section.

Expert systems

Pure research in the field of artificial intelligence has had a number of practical spin-offs. One such spin-off has been the development of programs known as Expert Systems, or Intelligent Knowledge Based Systems. These are programs designed to be able to give the same sort of help or advice, or make decisions, as a human expert in some narrow field of expertise. For instance, a program called PROSPECTOR is capable of predicting the existence of mineral ores given various pieces of information gathered from physical locations. In the same way that, given certain evidence, an expert might say that a particular site looked favourable for containing ore, PROSPECTOR indicates the probability of the existence of the ore. PROSPECTOR is in fact attributed with the discovery of an extremely valuable quantity of molybdenum which had previously been overlooked by human experts. Expert systems have been developed in numerous areas which traditionally have been the province of human experts. For example, several expert systems have been developed to aid medical diagnosis and treatment. However, decisions in areas such as this are often so critical that it would be foolish to blindly accept the pronouncement of a computer. For this reason, expert systems have the built-in ability to justify the chain of logical reasoning leading to any conclusion, so that it can be checked and verified (or rejected) by a human. Another characteristic of many expert systems is the use of *fuzzy logic* which allows degrees of uncertainty to be built in to logical deduction processes. Such expert systems are able to state conclusions which are qualified by a probability value indicating the probability of the conclusion being correct.

Other successful expert systems include:

> MYCIN - diagnosis of infections;
>
> HEURISTIC DENDRAL - identifies organic compounds;
>
> XCON - for configuring (VAX) computer systems;
>
> SACON - for advice on structural analysis.

An expert system has three main components:

- a *knowledge base* consisting of rules which use facts supplied by some external source, typically a user;
- an *inference engine* which processes the knowledge base;
- a *user interface* to facilitate communication with the user.

As an example, the following knowledge base is for a simple botanical expert system to identify whether a particular plant is a shrub, tree, herb or vine. Four rules are to be used:

```
1   IF        STEM IS GREEN
    THEN      TYPE IS HERB.
2   IF         STEM IS WOODY
    AND       ATTITUDE IS CREEPING
    THEN      TYPE IS VINE.
3   IF        STEM IS WOODY
    AND       ATTITUDE IS UPRIGHT
    AND       ONE MAIN TRUNK IS TRUE
    THEN      TYPE IS TREE.
4   IF        STEM IS WOODY
    AND       ATTITUDE IS UPRIGHT
    AND        ONE MAIN TRUNK IS FALSE
    THEN      TYPE IS SHRUB.
```

This forms the knowledge base.

The inference engine starts by attempting to satisfy a primary goal, in this instance to determine the TYPE of the plant. To this end, it searches its knowledge base for the goal by looking for a rule containing the word TYPE in the conclusion part of the rule (after the THEN part of a rule). This process of examining conclusions to rules while attempting to resolve goals is called *backward chaining* (or *goal-driven inference*).

Rule 1 satisfies this requirement, but in order to establish if the plant is a HERB, the system must obtain information regarding the STEM. Initially this information will not be available and must be supplied by the user. Consequently, obtaining the STEM information is added to a list of subgoals to be evaluated, along with rule 1, and the system looks for another rule containing the goal in its conclusion. The subgoal list also notes the rule which generated the subgoal in question.

After the remaining rules have been processed in a similar fashion, the system must then attempt to satisfy the subgoal list. Consequently, the user interface is invoked. This generates a question of the form

        IS THE STEM OF THE PLANT GREEN?

Let us suppose that the plant is a SHRUB (which has a woody stem, grows upright, and has more than one main trunk). The user answers NO which is stored as a fact relating to the stem of the plant.

Having succeeded with a subgoal, the inference engine again searches for a rule conclusion containing TYPE. It can attempt to evaluate the first rule now that it has all the necessary information. The rule does not produce a conclusion since the STEM is not green. This rule is therefore discarded since it can never cause the primary goal to succeed in this particular consultation.

Examination of the second rule reveals to the inference engine that it cannot be resolved until the ATTITUDE of the plant is in its list of facts, so this is added to its list of subgoals.

Eventually, all the necessary facts are available and the inference engine is able to discard all rules except rule 4 which establishes that the plant is a SHRUB.

In the course of a consultation the user might wish to know why the system is asking a certain question. The information required to answer this question is easy to find: the subgoal generating the question being asked was stored along with the rule from which it came, and this contains all the necessary information. For example, if the inference engine was attempting to resolve rule 4 by asking about the number of TRUNKS, the user interface might respond,

```
I am trying to determine the TYPE. I know that the STEM is
woody. I know that the ATTITUDE is upright. If ONE MAIN
TRUNK is false then I will know that the TYPE is SHRUB.
```

Expert system shells

The term Shell is given to expert systems which have been given no specific knowledge base, only the inference engine and user interface; the knowledge base has to be provided by the user. A single expert system shell can thus be used to provide advice or help in a number of areas of expertise, providing it is given the appropriate knowledge base for each area.

For example, an expert system shell could be used to give advice on the procedures and sequence of steps necessary for selling a house (what solicitors call conveyancing), or to give advice about possible causes and cures of diseases in houseplants, or diagnosing faults in cars. Not only could these applications be of practical use, but they could also be instructive because the user could ask for and obtain the reasons behind any conclusions.

One of the problems of using such shells is the determination of the rules which represent the wisdom of a human expert; many experts are not consciously aware of the precise reasoning processes they themselves use in order to come to some conclusion, yet in order to produce an expert program, these processes must be defined in a form that is usable. The process of determining the knowledge base rules is known as knowledge elicitation or knowledge acquisition and is performed by knowledge engineers.

Functional languages

The pseudocode function, range, shown in Listing 29.4 determines the range of three numbers by finding the difference between the largest number and the smallest number.

Listing 29.4.

```
function range(x, y, z)
    a = max(x, y)
    b = max(a, z)
    c = min(x, y)
    d = min(c, z)
    r = b - d
return(r)

function max(m, n)
  select
    when m > n
        return(m)
    when otherwise
        return(n)
  endselect
{end}

function min(m, n)
```

```
    select
      when m < n
          return(m)
      when otherwise
          return(n)
    endselect
  {end}
```

Notice that function range uses a number of assignment operations for intermediate calculations, and that these calculations must be executed in the order specified because they occur on consecutive lines. In fact, all of these assignment statements can be eliminated by writing the range function in the following way (the word function has been omitted from functions max and min for the sake of clarity);

```
function range(x, y, z)
return(max(max(x, y), z) - min(min(x, y), z))
```

This is the function-based version which eliminates all assignment statements and no longer specifies the order in which intermediate calculations are to be executed. Moreover, the max and min functions may be executed in parallel since neither depends on the other.

Functional languages such as LISP and, to a lesser degree, LOGO use this nested function approach, thereby allowing more flexibility in the implementation of programs. However, these languages take the use of functions a stage further than that shown in the example. In LISP, for instance, the same program might appear as shown in Listing 29.5.

Listing 29.5.

```
(defun max(m n)
   (cond((greaterp m n) m)
 (t                    ) n)


]
(defun min(m n)
   (cond((lessp m n) m)
   (t                  ) n)


]
defun range(x y z)
(- (max (max x y) z) (min (min x y) z))
]
```

All functions, which are defined using defun, are enclosed in brackets and return a value. Thus the built-in function greaterp returns t (true) if m is greater than n.

The selection function, cond, takes the form

```
(cond (exp₁ val₁)
      (exp₂ val₂)
        . .
      (expₙ valₙ))
```

and it returns the value (val) corresponding to the first true expression (exp) in the list of value/expression pairs. So, for example, the pseudocode

```
select
  when exp
     return(val₁)
  when otherwise
     return(val₂)
endselect
```

translates in LISP to

```
(cond (exp val₁ )
      (t    val₂ ))
```

where t is boolean true. Thus if exp is true, val$_1$ is returned from cond, else val$_2$ is returned since t is always true.

The subtraction function is merely the '−' sign. So, to subtract the two values a and b we would write

```
( a b)
```

where a and b could be numbers or functions returning values.

As a final note of explanation, the terminating square bracket,], is used to represent any number of close parentheses,) ; with complex nested expressions it is quite difficult sometimes to determine the correct number of) , and easy to get it wrong, so the] is provided to prevent this occurring.

The following two sections describe in very general terms the main characteristics of LISP and LOGO as examples of functional languages.

LISP

Though LISP is one of the oldest computer languages (nearly as old as FORTRAN) it is used extensively in one of the most innovative of today's research areas: artificial intelligence. As its popularity increases it is becoming available on more and more machines; most mainframes and an increasing number of micros support a version of the language.

LISP was designed as a purely functional language. By this we mean that statements in LISP look like functions. For instance, the function which adds numbers in LISP is called PLUS and is written

```
(PLUS 2 3)
```

The function PLUS operates on the arguments 2 and 3. All statements are written in this way.

However, LISP is primarily a language for manipulating symbols rather than performing complex numeric calculations. It treats all forms of data as being elements of lists and has facilities for conveniently manipulating these lists in various ways. Moreover, the language is extensible in that the user is able to create his own functions to be used like any of those supplied.

Programs in LISP are developed interactively. Typing the name of a function, followed by its arguments, causes the function to be performed and the result displayed. In the addition example above, LISP would return the number 5 as soon as the function had been entered. This characteristic is one of the strengths of the language in that programs are written in small, easily testable steps, the effects of which can be seen immediately.

LOGO

Designed as a language to provide a very early and easy route into programming, LOGO is probably best known as the first language to use turtle graphics. When running LOGO, the turtle appears as a graphics cursor which can be instructed to move across the screen using commands such as FORWARD 20 or RIGHT 30. Remotely controllable devices can also be connected to the computer and controlled by the same commands.

The turtle commands have been designed to be appealing and to motivate children to write programs to make the turtle perform visually pleasing manoeuvres. Seymour Papert, the American mathematician who designed the language, was largely influenced by Piagets well-known ideas on intellectual development in children. Consequently LOGO is emerging as an important educational tool. Unlike much educational software currently available in which the computer is the teacher, and the child reacts to it, LOGO offers a completely different approach to computer assisted learning. With LOGO the roles are reversed, the child teaching the computer what to do.

In his book, Mindstorms, Seymour Papert explains the philosophy of LOGO, how it was developed and how it works. LOGO, however, is more than a language just for children. It is based on LISP and shares many of its features. Like LISP it is extensible, based on list processing, and allows recursion. Because it is interpreted, it is easy to use and allows programs to be edited without difficulty. In fact it is a surprisingly powerful language, as well as being easy to learn. It is by no means a toy language and is attracting much interest in all kinds of areas, including artificial intelligence applications. Here are two simple subprograms in LOGO to enable the turtle to draw a box of side L screen units.

```
TO SIDE :L
FORWARD :L
RIGHT 90
END


TO SQUARE :L
REPEAT 4 [SIDE :L]
END
```

The first subprogram, SIDE, instructs the turtle to move forward L units and then turn right by 90 degrees.

The second subprogram, SQUARE, draws a square of side L by repeatedly calling SIDE.

The turtle would be instructed to draw a square of side 100 units with the command

```
SQUARE 100
```

The functional nature of the language is illustrated by the manner in which arithmetic is performed. For example, to add two numbers and store them in the variable, S, we would write:

```
MAKE S SUM :A :B
```

where SUM is the function taking two arguments, in this case the values of variables A and B.

As a second example, the calculation x = a + b*c would become

```
MAKE X SUM :A PROD :B :C
```

Object oriented programming (OOP)

Object oriented programming attempts to simulate the real world by means of objects which have characteristics and functions. Object oriented languages are classed as fifth generation languages.

As its name suggests, object oriented programming is based on the idea of an object. An object is a combination of local variables and procedures, called *methods*, together forming a self-contained programming entity. The term *encapsulation* is sometimes used to describe the combination of a data structure and the methods which manipulate it in an object. Invoking a method is called passing a message to an object.

The individual variables in an object together form a data structure which exists intact throughout program runtime. This is not the case with similar structures such as subprograms whose variables are in effect destroyed on completion of the subprogram. An object can retain *state information* even while it is inactive.

Information hiding is another characteristic of object oriented programming. The idea is that the programmer needs to know only what an object does, not how it does it, in order to use it in a program. By means of *inheritance*, new objects may be derived that inherit data and methods from one or more defined objects. Further data structures and methods may be redefined or added to the derived objects, hence forming a hierarchy of structures and reducing the code required to define a new object.

These ideas need to be clarified by means of an example. Borland's Turbo C++, an object oriented extension of C, will be used as the vehicle for the example which involves part of an interactive drawing program. Suppose that we wish to provide a facility for drawing a dot of a certain colour. The dot object could be defined as shown in Listing 29.6.

Listing 29.6

```
class point
  {
   private:
     int X,Y;
     int colour;
   public:
     int getX() {return X;}
     int getY() {return Y;}
     int getcolour() {return colour;}
     void setcolour(int c) {colour=c;}
     void plot() {putpixel(X,Y,colour);}
  }dot;
```

The declarative class allows objects to be defined. In addition, class allows the use of the word private, which restricts access to the variables (X, Y and colour in this case) exclusively to the objects methods, and public which allows access to variables and methods by functions external to the object being defined. Five methods are defined: the first three allow external functions to obtain the position of the point and its colour, the fourth allows the point's colour to be set at some integer value, and the final one displays the dot using a predefined function, putpixel(). Notice that the methods are defined within the object, that is in-line, though C++ also allows them to be defined elsewhere if required. In order to obtain dot's X co-ordinate we would invoke method getX() using a statement such as

```
x_coord = dot.getX();
```

To change its colour to 1 would require

```
dot.setcolour(1);
```

and it could be displayed using

```
dot.plot();
```

It is important to note that the only way to use the dot object is by means of the appropriate method; this means that if any of the methods are changed, there will be no need to alter any other part of the program which makes use of the object. This is a very important characteristic of object oriented programming. Furthermore, there is no possibility of an objects variables being corrupted inadvertently elsewhere in the program since, having been declared as private, the only functions allowed to access them are the objects methods. Together, these two features characterise information hiding mentioned earlier.

Notice also that the dot object's state information, that is, its co-ordinates and colour, is retained throughout the execution of the program, unlike local variables within a subprogram.

Object oriented programming languages usually allow defined objects to be the basis of derived objects, in which variables and methods may be inherited. For example, we could use the point object as the basis of a more general dot which would allow its co-ordinates to be changed. This would involve defining the new dot in terms of point and adding two more methods, one to set X and the other to set Y.

This type of situation, where a base object may be used to derive a special object, occurs frequently in programming tasks. A car object, for instance, could be the basis of a number of different types of cars, such as sports, saloon, hatchback, and so on, each inheriting the basic car characteristics and adding to or modifying them according to special data/functional requirements. A convenient way to start when using object oriented design is to state the system requirements in narrative form and identify key nouns which relate to object classes, and key verbs which correspond to object methods. For example, consider the outline system specification below:

> The temperature control system regulates the temperature of a number of <u>rooms</u> in the building. Each room has a <u>minimum temperature</u> and <u>maximum temperature</u> and the system **keeps** the temperature of the room between these two limits. The limits may be **changed** by means of the <u>system console</u>, which also **shows** the <u>current temperature</u> of each room in the form of a <u>dynamic display</u>.

Nouns are shown underlined and **verbs** in bold.

Thus the nouns identify a room object which requires temperature regulation, and a system console object for data input and display purposes. As a preliminary step we might therefore identify the following object classes and associated operations.

```
Object class:      Room
Operations:        Detect temperature
                   Increase temperature
                   Decrease temperature

Object class:      System Console Keyboard
Operations:        Get new/initial temperature limits
                   Communicate with user

Object class:      System Console Display
Operations:        Update room temperatures
                   Display room temperatures
```

This would provide a reasonable starting point for the detailed design which would follow.

Implementation languages

A number of computer languages have features which facilitate object oriented design without having been specifically written for this purpose. These languages include Simula, Ada, Modula-2, C++ and some versions of Pascal. Smalltalk on the other hand was designed specifically as a language which could be used to implement an object oriented design directly.

Smalltalk was developed by the Xerox Corporation following an idea by Alan Kay regarding the development of personal computers. The original research in the 1970s involved the development of a notebook computer called a Dynabook. To this end, a windows-based, graphical user environment was developed, with the underlying control of the system being achieved by Smalltalk. The system was highly interactive, having been influenced by the type of user interface employed by Logo.

Since object oriented design encourages software re-usability, Smalltalk provides a large library of basic object classes which may be used directly or tailored to specific needs. Since it was originally designed to be used with powerful personal computers supporting WIMP environments, its use is likely to increase, particularly with the increasing speed and memory size of personal computers we are currently experiencing.

Advantages of object oriented programming

We have already seen that communication between objects is via messages, eliminating the need for shared data areas such as sets of global variables, and removing the possibility of accidental modification to data shared by a number of functions or programs. This is particularly important when a large programming project is being developed by a team of programmers simultaneously working on different aspects of the job, because it ensures that the work of one programmer will not interact in unforeseen ways with that of any other.

Furthermore, access to an objects methods are exclusively by means of a well-defined, unchanging interface. The way that an object performs its characteristic functions is of no interest to users of the object, and any internal changes to its structure will be invisible. This ensures that modification of an object, being independent of other objects, will have no effect whatsoever on any other part of the program.

The inheritance property of object oriented programming languages allows the hierarchical structuring of objects, reducing coding effort and simplifying the program structure. Because objects are self-contained entities which may be used sequentially or in parallel, an object oriented design offers substantial flexibility in its implementation; decisions regarding the use of processing method, whether serial or parallel, need not be made immediately, and programs may be converted to a different processing method without the necessity for a complete rewrite.

Disadvantages of object oriented programming

Object inheritance can produce significant run-time overheads, reducing the execution speed of a program. A complex hierarchical object structure might involve a substantial number of cross-referenced objects, giving the program extra work to do.

An object oriented design is not always the most appropriate solution. Sometimes a more functional approach can simplify the programming task, particularly where system state information does not need to be retained by a program. Remember that an object can retain state information during the execution of a program, unlike the values of variables in subprograms which are lost as soon as the subprogram is exited; in certain applications this may not be required. For example, the common cash dispenser comprises a screen, a numeric keypad and a number of function keys such as Withdraw cash, Obtain balance, Proceed, Cancel request. The customer, having entered his or her PIN (personal identification number), selects a function by pressing the appropriate function key. A natural program design would be to assign a subprogram to process each function. Since each function operates independently of the others, there is no need to retain any sort of state information. An object oriented approach could of course still be used, but there would be no particular advantage in doing so.

Exercises

1. Briefly describe the main characteristics of the five generations of computer languages.
2. What are reserved words and how do they differ from keywords?
3. The text describes the main features of a number of popular languages. Research and summarise, in a similar fashion, the following languages, which are not covered in the text:
   (i)   C++;
   (ii)   Visual C++;
   (iii) Visual Basic;
   (iv)   Delphi;
   (v)   Java;
   (vi)   Perl;
   (vii) Python.
4. Explain the difference between Declarative and Imperative computer languages. Give an example of each of these two types of languages.
5. What is meant by recursive programming?
6. What are the main components of an expert system?
7. Name two languages associated with artificial intelligence work.

Chapter 30

Language Processing

The definition of computer languages

Fundamental to the design of a computer language is the idea of a grammar which precisely defines the syntax of program statements. This section describes two notations commonly employed to specify such grammars; they are *Backus-Naur form* and *syntax diagrams*. All languages, whether computer languages such as Pascal or Prolog, or natural languages such as English or Japanese, have a number of rules governing the syntax of well-formed statements or sentences. The collection of these syntax rules is called the grammar of a language. The grammar of a natural language is very difficult to state precisely, and might require several hundred syntax rules to define it even approximately, but, because computer languages are relatively simple and unambiguous, they can be defined exactly using a relatively small set of rules. Two common methods of describing the grammar of languages are:

❑ Backus-Naur Form (BNF), named after the two men that developed this notation for defining Algol;

❑ syntax diagrams.

These are examples of *meta-languages*, that is, languages which are used to describe other languages.

Such formal definitions of computer languages are useful for a number of reasons:

❑ they provide the means to determine whether a given sequence of characters constitutes a valid statement in the language;

❑ they allow us to break down a statement into its constituent parts, that is, parse the statement, so that it can be converted into a machine-sensible form;

❑ they can be used to generate well-formed statements.

Backus-Naur form (BNF)

As a simple example of the use of BNF notation, consider a grammar which defines the form of integers of any length:

        <integer>::=<digit>|<integer><digit>

        <digit>::= 0 | 1 | 2 | 3 | 4 | 5 | 6 | 7 | 8 | 9

<integer> and <digit>, are called *non-terminals* because they are defined in terms of other non-terminals or elementary symbols called *terminal* symbols. Thus the symbols 0 to 9 are terminal symbols. The ::= notation is read as 'is defined as' and the symbol | means 'or'. So the first rule reads

        '*integer* is defined as a *digit* or an *integer* followed by a *digit*'.

The second rule reads

'*digit* is defined as the symbol 0 or 1 or 2 ... or 9'.

integer and *digit* are termed *syntactic entities* since they each define a separate part of the grammar.

We can use these rules to generate integers by repeatedly replacing the left-hand syntactic entities by the right-hand terminals and non-terminals. For example, replacing *digit* by 5 produces

                              <integer>::= 5   (from the rule, <integer>::=<digit>)

This is one instance of an integer, according to our grammar. But the grammar also states that <integer>::=<integer><digit>, so we can replace <integer> on the right-hand side by 5 and <digit> by, say, 2 to give

                              <integer>::= 52

By repeating this procedure we can produce any integer value; for this reason, rules are also called *productions*. Notice that the *recursive* nature of the first rule enables this simple grammar to generate an infinite number of integers. Not all grammars are recursive, but those that are describe infinite languages. A (simplified) recursive grammar for an arithmetic expression in a high-level language such as C could be expressed as:

<expr>	::=<term> | <expr><expr operator><term>
<term>	::=<factor> | <term><term operator><factor>
<factor>	::=<variable> | <integer> | (<expression>) | –<factor>
<variable>	::= A | B |..... | Z
<integer>	::=<digit>|<integer><digit>
<digit>	::= 0 | 1 | 2 | 3 | 4 | 5 | 6 | 7 | 8 | 9
<expr operator>::= + | –
<term operator> ::= * | /

Using this grammar, examples of valid arithmetic expressions are:

A + B

P – Q/2

X + Y*(Z + 1) – W

L*M + 3*(A*A – B/4)

A compiler could use this grammar to determine the syntactic validity of an expression within a program statement by attempting to establish that the expression conforms to the rules of the grammar. *Parsing*, this process of analysing a string of symbols using the production rules of the grammar, is discussed later in the section devoted to the structure and function of compilers.

Syntax diagrams

A more graphical approach to language definition is the use of *syntax diagrams*. For example, the BNF definition of an unsigned integer given in the previous section is equivalent to the syntax diagram shown in Figure 30.1. The different paths that may be taken through the diagram are indicated by the arrows.

Figure 30.1.

Here, *digit* represents one of the symbols 0–9 as before and shown in Figure 30.2.

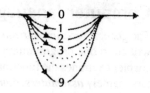

Figure 30.1 shows that, by following a single left-to-right path, an integer can be a single digit; by following the loop path two or more times, an integer can contain two or more digits.

The arrows in Figure 30.2 indicate that only one of the digits 0-9 may be selected in going from left to right, meaning that a digit is one of the symbols 0,1,2...9. Syntax diagrams are read by fol-

Figure 30.2.

lowing the routes indicated by arrows, adding the symbols indicated in the circles or oval boxes to build up strings representing valid syntactic structures. So, in the example above, we could select '8' as the first digit, and by following the loop back around once more, and this time choosing '5', we would have generated the integer 85. Figure 30.3 defines the rules for the formation of the Roman numerals for 1-10:

Figure 30.3.

The ten possible different routes through the diagram generate the numerals: I, II, III, IV, V, VI, VII, VIII, IX, X. As a final example, the syntax diagram in Figure 30.4 shows the overall structure of a Pascal program. When used for this purpose, three different symbols are used:

Figure 30.4.

Examples of valid program identifiers, according to this definition, are

    program example1(input,output);<block>.

where *example1*, *input* and *output* are identifiers and <block> is a non-terminal which is defined by its own syntax diagram.

    program eg2(file1,file2,file3);.

Here *eg2*, *file1*, *file2* and *file3* are identifiers and <block> is again a non-terminal.

Syntax diagrams have the added advantage of succinctly describing the complete set of syntactic constructs of a computer language, thus providing a convenient source of reference for programmers.

Computer language translators

The general function of *translators* (or *language processors*) is to convert program statements written in one programming language into another, most commonly into machine code. This chapter examines the function and operational characteristics of the three main types of translators, namely *assemblers*, *compilers* and *interpreters*.

Assemblers

In the history of programming languages, one of the first significant innovations was the development of assembly languages. A program written in an assembly language is much more readable and understandable than its equivalent in machine code; the problem arises, however, that it is no longer directly executable by the computer. An *assembler* is a computer program which carries out the necessary translation.

The assembler accepts an assembly language program as data, converts *mnemonic* operation codes (op-codes) to their numeric equivalents, assigns *symbolic addresses* to memory locations and produces as output the required machine code program.

The assembly language program is termed the *source program* and the final machine code program is the *object program*.

Though it is true that by far the majority of computer programming today is in high-level languages such as Pascal, C or COBOL, programming in assembly languages is still essential for certain tasks. The reason for this, despite continual improvements in compiler design, is simply that the programmer, having total control over the structure of the machine code generated by the assembler, is able to write much faster and more efficient code than that produced by a compiler. The very nature of high-level languages, allowing us to deal with a greatly simplified, virtual machine, often precludes the programmer from being able to fine-tune code according to particular circumstances.

For example, a commonly used method of increasing the speed of a machine-code program is to utilise internal registers as much as possible in preference to memory locations, in order to minimise relatively slow memory accesses. While this type of code optimisation is perfectly feasible in any assembly language, most high-level languages do not allow the programmer this degree of control (C is a notable exception, allowing identifiers to be specifically allocated to general purpose registers).

A consequence of the one-to-one correspondence between an assembly language instruction and its equivalent machine-code instruction is that assemblers are *machine dependent*, producing machine code for a specific type of processor. For instance, the machine code generated by an Intel 8086/88 assembler could not be used directly by a computer with a Motorola 68000 processor. For this reason, there is no single, archetypal assembler; rather, each assembler is related to the architecture of the processor for which it has been designed. Thus, if the processor supports two-address machine-code instructions (Chapter 4), this will be reflected in the format of the assembly language instructions.

In the following sections a number of fundamental characteristics, common to most assemblers, are introduced. Assembly language programming is described on the companion CD-ROM. It uses a hypothetical microprocessor and associated assembly language to illustrate simple programs and includes an example program to illustrate the assembly process.

Assembler tasks

Early assemblers did little more than convert instruction mnemonics to their equivalent numeric machine codes, but current assemblers do much more. Some of the most common assembler tasks are described below:

❏ *Op-code translation*. Numeric operation codes replace the mnemonic op-codes used in the source program.

❏ *Absolute address allocation*. Each instruction or data word in the source program must be allocated an absolute machine address (its physical location). The assembler maintains a *location counter* (sometimes referred to as a *load pointer*) which, having been set to an initial base address, is incremented by the length of each data or instruction word as it is assembled.

❏ *Symbolic operand conversion*. This refers to the assembly process of substituting any symbolic addresses, that is, user identifiers used in place of memory locations, with numeric machine addresses. A symbol table records each symbolic operand together with its corresponding absolute address; a similar table logs labels and their machine addresses. If relative addressing is used, labels and symbolic addresses are converted to offsets from the location counter; this enables a program to be relocatable (See Chapter 4).

❏ *Converting constants to their internal forms*. This will involve conversion from textual (ASCII, for example) representations of decimal, hexadecimal, octal or binary to pure binary.

❏ *Replacing identifiers by user-defined macros*. If the assembly language supports the use of *macro* instructions (a shorthand used by a programmer to express sequences of regularly used instructions by a macro name), any such macro must be expanded by the assembler and inserted into the source program prior to assembling it.

❏ *Obeying directives*. Many assemblers support the use of *pseudo-operations*, or *directives* which are instructions not directly translatable into machine instructions. These involve such things as reserving space for data, defining the values of identifiers used in the program and defining where the program is to be located in memory.

❏ *Generating error messages*. If the assembler detects any syntax errors in the source program, it must be able to issue a message indicating the source and nature of the problem.

❏ *Producing source-code listings*. These may take various forms including listings of the source-code, object-code and symbol table.

Assembly

The assembly process usually involves the assembler in executing several passes of the program's source code, each one carrying out certain of the tasks described above. The problem of forward referencing (an instruction uses a symbolic operand which is not defined until later in the program, so its address has not been allocated at that point and cannot be included in the instruction) means that assemblers usually carry out a minimum of two passes.

Two-pass assembly

Pass 1. Any macro instructions are expanded as part of the pass or as a separate initial pass, making three in all. All instructions are examined and checked for syntactical correctness; any errors are recorded in a table. After each instruction has been dealt with, the location counter is incremented, and a symbol table is constructed to link any symbolic operands and labels with their corresponding absolute addresses.

Pass 2. By reference to the symbol tables, the assembler generates and outputs the object code.

In the Assembly Language chapter on the CD-ROM, a three-pass assembly is illustrated with a simple program, showing how the object program is generated at each stage in the assembly process.

Cross assembler

This is an assembler which carries out the translation of an assembly program on one machine to produce object code for execution on another. For example, a certain cross assembler running on an IBM PC might assemble a source program to produce Motorola 68000 machine code for use on an Apple computer.

Compilers and interpreters

There are two main types of high-level language translators (or language processors as they are often known): (i) compilers; (ii) interpreters. Since the choice of translator has implications regarding program development time, debugging and testing, memory requirements, execution speed and program security, it is important from a programming point of view to be quite clear about the difference between the two types.

A compiler accepts a *source program*, that is, a program written in some high-level language, Pascal for instance, checks that it is correctly formed and, if so, generates the equivalent *object program* in a low-level language. The translated program may be in the form of an assembly language, in which case it must first be assembled before it is executed, or it may be in machine code, allowing it to be executed directly without further modification. If any errors are detected during compilation, they will be reported and, if serious enough, may prevent the compiler from completing the translation process.

A compiler will often have access to a library of standard routines and special routines appropriate to the application area for which the source language was designed; this collection of subroutines is called the *run-time library*. Included in this library of machine code subprograms will be routines for performing arithmetic operations, input/output operations, backing storage data transfers and other commonly used functions. Whenever the source code refers to one of these routines specifically, or needs one to perform the operation specified, the compiler will ensure that the routine is added to the object program.

Note that the final object code is independent of both the source code and the compiler itself. That is, neither of these two programs needs to be resident in main store when the object code is being executed. Any alterations to the program subsequent to its compilation will necessitate modification and re-compilation of the source code prior to executing the program again.

An interpreter uses a different method to translate a source program into a machine-sensible form. An object program is not generated in this form of translation, rather the source program, or an intermediate form of it, is scanned statement by statement, each in turn immediately being converted into the actions specified.

The source code statements are translated and executed separately, as they are encountered, while the source code is being processed by the interpreter. The object code actually executed is held within the interpreter; the latter merely identifies from the source statement which piece of machine code is relevant and causes it to be performed. On completion of a statement, control returns to the interpreter which then processes the next logical statement in the program sequence.

It might seem, therefore, that an interpreter has a big advantage over a compiler. In terms of the amount of effort required in obtaining an executable program, this is certainly true, but there are a number of other factors which favour the use of a compiler. For example, an interpreter must do a considerable amount of work before it can even begin to cause a source statement to be executed (error checking, for instance); on the other hand, a compiler has already done this work during compilation. Moreover, should a section of source code be repeated one or more times, an interpreter must re-interpret the section each time. Consequently, interpreted programs tend to run significantly slower than equivalent compiled programs, and for time-critical applications this might be a major concern. Furthermore, because the translation and execution phases are interwoven, the interpreter must be resident in memory at the same time as the source code. If memory space is at a premium, this can be a severe limitation of an interpreted language. Languages designed for use by children or for teaching purposes are often interpreted. Logo, for example, originally designed as a language for children, is interpreted to facilitate its interactive nature. Similarly, BASIC is interpreted in order to simplify its use for programming novices. A possible compromise is to provide both an interpreter and a compiler for the same language; this allows rapid development time using the interpreter, and fast execution obtained by compiling the code.

Compilers

The compilation process can be broken down into a number of stages:

(i)   lexical analysis - the source code is scanned and converted into a form more convenient for subsequent processing, and a symbol table is partially constructed;

(ii)   syntax analysis and semantic analysis - the output from the lexical analyser is analysed for grammatical correctness, the symbol table is completed, error messages are generated if errors have been detected, and the program is further transformed ready for the next stages;

(iii)   intermediate code generation - the output from the parser is put into an internal form permitting easier conversion into object code;

(iv)   code optimisation - the intermediate code is made more time or space efficient using a number of different techniques;

(vi)   code generation - the object code, which may be either machine code or assembly language, is generated.

These stages are discussed in more detail in the following sections.

Lexical analysis

Most programming languages allow a certain amount of redundancy in the preparation of the program. For example, spaces can often be inserted to aid readability of the source code, and comments are used to explain the function of the program and sections of code. A section of the compiler, called the *lexical analyser* or *scanner*, removes such redundancies and performs other modifications of the source code prior to passing it to the next stage of compilation.

The lexical analyser takes the source code and translates it into a string of characters, which is to be passed to the *syntax analyser*, or *parser*. The process of lexical analysis identifies *lexemes*, that is, the basic lexical units of the source language, such as reserved words, operators, identifiers, constants and literals, and associates them with specific integer values or *tokens*. For example, each reserved word would be represented by a unique integer, say in the range 256-511, all identifiers would have a certain code such as 512, constants perhaps 513, and special symbols such as '(' or '*' would probably retain their ascii values. Additionally, each identifier would be replaced by a pointer to its position in a *symbol table* containing details of its characteristics. The lexical analyser thus preprocesses the source code to facilitate subsequent stages in the compilation process. In addition, it provides an interface between the programmer and the computer, allowing some limited flexibility in the layout of the source code.

Syntax and semantic analysis

These analysers do the actual hard work of breaking the source program into its constituent parts. The complete source program is analysed into blocks, which are then broken down into statements, which are further analysed into instruction words, variables and constants. Each variable used in the source program is placed in a symbol table, together with a declaration of its attributes - type (numeric, string etc.), where it is to be located in memory (its object program address) and any other information required for object code generation. The syntax analyser, or parser, takes the output from the lexical analyser and determines syntactic correctness of the program using the grammatical rules for the language.

The *syntax* or grammar of a programming language consists of a set of rules which define a legal program statement, as opposed to a meaningless string of characters. The rules determine correct sentence structure; the process of checking the validity of sentence structure is known as *parsing*. In English, for example, the sentence

>   the monkey ate the banana

can be determined as grammatically correct by reference to the rules of English grammar. Conversely, the rules can be used to determine that

>   *monkey the ate banana the*

is grammatically incorrect.

Similarly, the grammar or syntax of the Pascal programming language can be used to determine that the program statement

```
        net := gross - deductions;
```

is correct, and that

```
        gross - deductions := net;
```

is not.

However, even the first statement, though syntactically correct, might still be invalid on *semantic* grounds. For instance, if any of the variables `net`, `gross` or `deductions` had not been previously declared, or if any of them had been declared as having type char (character), the statement would be meaningless. Returning to our English example, the sentence

The banana ate the monkey.

is still grammatically correct but semantically very suspect because we are aware that one of the attributes of an ordinary banana is that it is a non-carnivorous fruit.

Semantic analysis is therefore concerned with checking the meaning or interpretation to be placed on words in the particular context of their use. Once the parser has confirmed the grammatical validity of a program construct, the semantic analyser can use the symbol table to check that an operation is semantically valid. In addition, the semantic analyser may supplement the work of the parser by using the symbol table to guide the generation of intermediate code. For example, a number of languages use different routines for arithmetic, depending on whether the arithmetic expression involves integer or real values, or a mixture of the two. The semantic analyser will examine the data types of the variables in the expression and determine the appropriate routines to use.

Sometimes the parser contains semantic routines which are invoked as the parsing process progresses, sometimes semantic analysis forms a distinct stage after the parser has completed its analysis, but frequently the two methods are combined. During the course of this stage in the compilation process, a number of data structures may be created to facilitate code optimisation and generation. The symbol table has already been mentioned, but in addition a *parse tree* will be created, representing the structure of the complete program split into a hierarchy of its components, and arithmetic expressions may be converted into a more convenient internal form such as *postfix*, also known as *Reverse Polish*, notation. The next few sections examine these data structures in more detail.

Parsing techniques

To determine whether a string of symbols such as $P - Q/2$ represents a valid expression in a simplified version of the grammar defined in the section on BNF:

<expr>   ::=<term> | <expr><expr operator><term>

<term>   ::=<factor> | <term><term operator><factor>

<factor>   ::=variable | integer | (<expr>) | –<factor>

<expr operator> ::= + | –

<term operator> ::= * | /

Here 'variable' and 'integer' are named terminals, so called because they are identifiers which represent actual terminals. The analysis could proceed as shown below, repeatedly scanning the string from left to right, replacing (at appropriate points) terminals and non-terminals by higher level non-terminals:

1.   P - Q/2

2.   variable<expr operator> variable <term operator> integer

3.   <factor><expr operator><factor><term operator><factor>

4.   <factor><expr operator><term><term operator><factor>

5.   <factor><expr operator><term>

6.   <term><expr operator><term>

7.   <expr><expr operator><term>

8.   <expr>

This process of *bottom-up parsing* repeatedly examines the string of symbols and at each pass determines whether a group of syntactic entities may be combined to form another syntactic entity. Thus the group, <term><term operator><factor>, can be replaced by <term>, which is a higher level syntactic entity. Since, at stage 8, we arrive at the highest level, that is, <expr>, an expression, the string must be a well-formed arithmetic expression in this grammar. Here is another example, this time illustrating the recursive nature of the grammar: the string to be parsed is X*(Y + Z).

1.   X*(Y + Z)

2.   variable<term operator>(variable<expr operator>variable)

3.   <factor><term operator>(<factor><expr operator><factor>)

4.   <factor><term operator>(<term><expr operator><factor>)

5.   <factor><term operator>(<expr><expr operator><term>)

6.   <factor><term operator>(<expr>)

7.   <factor><term operator><factor>

8.   <term><term operator><factor>

9.   <term>

10.   <expr>

Though we have used an intuitive method to determine at what point in the parse to make substitutions for syntactic entities, in practice the process is based on precedence relations between adjacent symbols which precisely determine the order in which the components of the input string are processed. However, the precise details of the process are quite complex and they are beyond the scope of this text. An alternative approach is to use a *top-down* parser such as that employed in *recursive descent parsing*. Such a parser uses a set of recursive functions to represent the syntactic structure of the source program. The outline pseudocode for such a recursive descent parser might take the form shown in Listing 30.1.

Listing 30.1.   Recursive descent parse

```
function expression()
   token := function term()
   while token = expression_operator
      select
         when "+": token := function term()
            call addition()
         when "-": token := function term()
            call subtraction()
      endselect
   endwhile
   return(token)
```

```
function term()
  token := function factor()
  while token = term_operator
    select
      when "*": token := function factor()
        call multiplication
      when "/": token := function factor()
        call division
    endselect
  endwhile

function factor()
  token := function get_next_token()
  select
    when variable: call variable_found()
      token := function get_next_token()
    when integer: call integer_found()
      token := function get_next_token()
    when "(": token := function expression()
      if token < > ")": token := brackets_err
        call error(token)
  endselect
  return(token)
```

The parser assumes that the expression to be parsed is in token form, and that the function get_next_token() takes care of keeping track of the next token to be processed and returns this token when called. Each of the three functions, expression, term and factor corresponds to the appropriate syntax diagram, and each returns a value corresponding to the next token available. The process terminates when a NULL (terminating) token is encountered, or when an error arises during the parse.

The first function, expression(), immediately calls term(), which immediately calls factor() which identifies the current token as being either a variable, an integer or an expression enclosed in parentheses. Appropriate procedures (not detailed here) deal with each of these cases, storing the identified item in a parse tree. Function factor() then returns the next token available, or an error code if an invalid token has been detected. Function term() then looks for a term operator, '*' or '/' and calls factor() again to provide the next operand. This repeats until there are no more factors in the term being processed. A term having been identified, control returns to expression() which looks for an expression operator, '+' or '–', to be returned from term(). If this is the case, expression calls term() again to identify the next term in the expression; the process terminates if a NULL token is returned, or some other token signifying an error condition. In recursive descent parsing, control continually descends through the function nesting to obtain operands, and ascends through the functions in reverse order. The recursive nature of the parse results from the definition of a factor which may be a parenthesised expression, thus causing expression() to call itself. These parsers are relatively simple to implement, being based directly on the language definition.

BASIC interpreters frequently use recursive descent to evaluate arithmetic expressions, since such interpreters need to do no preprocessing of expressions (see the case study in the section on interpreters following).

Parse trees

The following Pascal program calculates the area of a rectangle, given its length and width:

```
program pteg (input, output);
var area, len, wid :integer;
begin
   readln (len, wid);
   area := len*wid;
   writeln ('The area is', area)
end.
```

When the program above is processed, the parser builds up a parse tree which identifies all the grammatical categories it encounters. The leaves of the tree are the tokens, that is the smallest grammatical entities, and the interior nodes represent non-terminals. As each non-terminal and token is identified, it is added to the parse tree being constructed until, finally, the whole program has been transformed into an intermediate representation. The parse tree is shown in Figure 30.5.

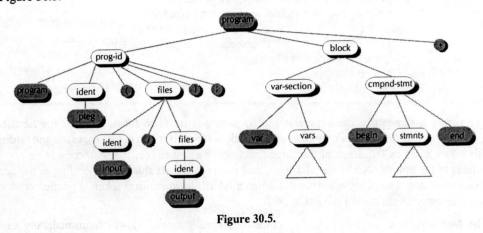

Figure 30.5.

The parts of the tree shown as shaded triangles are expanded in Figures 30.6 and 30.7.

Figure 30.6

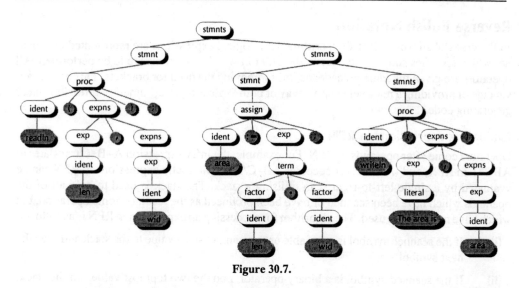

Figure 30.7.

Notice that the parse tree has the same form as the syntax diagrams for the same structures, but it is specific to this program rather than being a generalised specification of Pascal. The parse tree could be conveniently implemented as a tree data structure (see Chapter 33) with each node identifying the appropriate grammatical structure and with pointers to other nodes identifying substructures. In this form, the source program is much easier to handle in the code generation phase of the compilation process.

Symbol tables

Checking for semantic correctness and generating code requires knowledge of the attributes of the identifiers used in the source program. This information is stored in a data structure known as a *symbol table* which plays a central role in the translation process. For each occurrence of an identifier in a source program, the table will be searched for its symbol table entry, new identifiers will be inserted into the data structure, and new information regarding known identifiers will be added.

Typically, the information stored in the symbol table for each variable will comprise:

❑ name;

❑ type, for example, integer, real, character etc.;

❑ memory location allocated.

Subprograms will require additional information related to parameters to be stored.

Because of its importance to the translation process, the symbol table needs to be structured in a manner which allows efficient insertion and extraction of information. Numerous strategies for structuring the symbol table are possible. One commonly used method is to use a *binary tree* organised alphabetically to facilitate access to identifiers and insertion of new nodes. Another method uses *hashing* to speed access to symbol table entries. Yet another approach is to use a combination of *hashing* and *linked lists*. The principles of these three techniques are discussed in Chapter 33.

Reverse Polish Notation

In Reverse Polish Notation (RPN), arithmetic or logical expressions are represented in a manner which specifies simply and exactly the order in which operations are to be performed. All operators are given the same precedence, thus removing the need for brackets. This has the advantage of providing a relatively simple way of both evaluating an arithmetic expression and of generating code.

Evaluating expressions in RPN

Operators come after operands in RPN. For example, the infix expression A+B*C translates to ABC*+ in RPN, and (A–B)/C+D becomes AB–C/D+. Arithmetic expressions in RPN can be evaluated by a single left-to-right scan utilising a stack. The stack is used to hold all of the operands which have been scanned or have been produced as the result of some operation, but which have not yet been used. The algorithm for processing an expression in RPN is as follows:

(i)   If the scanned symbol is a variable or constant, push its value to the stack and scan the next symbol.

(ii)   If the scanned symbol is a binary operator, pop the two topmost values on the stack, apply the operation to them and then push the result to the stack.

(iii) If the scanned symbol is a unary operator, pop the top of the stack, apply the operation to this item and then push the result to the stack.

[Note that the term *binary operator* refers to an arithmetic or logical operator which requires two operands, such as * in the expression $a+b*c$; the two operands are b and c. The term *unary operator* refers to an arithmetic or logical operator which requires a single operand, such as '–' in the expression $-b+c*d$; the single operand is b in this case.]

For example, suppose that we wish to evaluate the RPN expression

   ab~cd*++

equivalent to $a+(-b+c*d)$ in usual infix notation, where ~ represents unary –. Table 30.1 illustrates how the evaluation would be handled with values $a=2$, $b=3$, $c=-4$ and $d=5$.

scanned symbol	old stack contents	operation	new stack contents
ab~cd*++		push a	[2]
ab~cd*++	[2]	push b	[2,3]
ab~cd*++	[2,3]	–b	[2,–3]
ab~cd*++	[2,–3]	push c	[2,–3,–4]
ab~cd*++	[2,–3,–4]	push d	[2,–3,–4,5]
ab~cd*++	[2,–3,–4,5]	c*d	[2,–3,–20]
ab~cd*++	[2,–3,–20]	–b+c*d	[2,–23]
ab~cd*++	[2,–23]	a+(–b+c*d)	[–21]

Table 30.1.

Table 30.1 shows the symbol being scanned (underlined), the stack contents prior to this symbol being processed, the operation performed on the appropriate operands and, lastly, the contents of the stack after processing the scanned symbol.

Converting arithmetic expressions from infix to RPN

An algorithm for converting from infix to RPN is as follows. Firstly, we associate numerical values with the relative precedences of arithmetic operators according to Table 30.2.

operator	precedence level
unary + and −	4
^ (exponentiation)	3
*, /	2
+, −	1

Table 30.2.

The method also uses a stack, this time for the temporary storage of operators while processing the infix input string. The output from the algorithm is the equivalent string in RPN. The algorithm is based on the following rules which are applied as each symbol in the input string is scanned in turn:

(i) If the incoming symbol is a variable or a constant, copy it to the output string directly.

(ii) If the incoming symbol is an operator, and it is of higher numerical precedence than the operator currently on top of the stack, or if the stack is empty, push it to the stack.

(iii) If the incoming symbol is an operator of equal or lower precedence than the current top of the stack, pop the top of the stack to the output string and go to step (ii) using the current symbol.

(iv) Left parenthesis, '(', goes on top of the operator stack regardless of the current contents of the the stack, and remains on the stack until released by right parenthesis, ')'.

(v) Right parenthesis, ')', releases all operators on the stack to the output string until a ')' is encountered, at which point the ')' is removed from the stack.

(vi) When the end of the input string is reached, any operators remaining on the stack are released to the output string, and the process terminates.

Table 30.3 traces the conversion of the expression a*(b+c)−d/g to RPN.

scanned symbol	current stack	new stack	output string
a*(b+c)−d/g	[]	[]	a
a*(b+c)−d/g	[]	[*]	a
a*(b+c)−d/g	[*]	[*,(]	a
a*(b+c)−d/g	[*,(]	[*,(]	ab
a*(b±c)−d/g	[*,(]	[*,(,+]	ab
a*(b+c)−d/g	[*,(,+]	[*,(,+]	abc
a*(b+c)−d/g	[*,(,+]	[*]	abc+
a*(b+c)−d/g	[*]	[−]	abc+*
a*(b+c)−d/g	[−]	[−]	abc+*d
a*(b+c)−d/g	[−]	[−,/]	abc+*d
a*(b+c)−d/g	[−,/]	[−,/]	abc+*dg
a*(b+c)−d/g	[−,/]	[]	abc+*dg/−

Table 30.3.

Intermediate languages

Having completed the parsing phase, it is quite common for a compiler to produce an intermediate language prior to generating code. One reason for doing this is to facilitate code optimisation by tailoring the intermediate code to the needs of the optimisation phase. Another reason is that it allows compilers for different target machines to use the same 'front end' stages and machine specific 'back end' stages for code optimisation and generation, the intermediate code being the interface between the two ends. One type of intermediate language consists of a set of *three-address statements*. For example, the C fragment

```
if ( a > max +1 ) a = max + 1;
b = b + 1;
```

might be transformed into

```
    T1 := max + 1
    if a < T1 goto L1
    T2 := max + 1
    a := T2
L1:T3 := b + 1
    b := T3
```

where T1, T2, T3 are temporary variables which are added to the symbol table.

Code optimisation

The example of intermediate code shown in the preceding section provides a number of opportunities for optimisation. If, for instance, one or more of the variables referenced were allocated to internal CPU registers, the code would become more time efficient since fewer memory accesses would be required. In fact some high-level languages (C for instance) allow the programmer to explicitly allocate variables to registers with declarations such as

```
register int i;
```

Another opportunity for optimisation is to use increment/decrement operations rather than addition/subtraction operations. For example, it is faster to increment b in the statement b := b + 1 rather than perform the addition if the target language contains an increment instruction. Other common optimisation techniques include:

❑ *Constant folding* - where arithmetic operations can be executed at compile time rather than run time. For example, if the term 20*3 appears in an arithmetic expression, it can be replaced by 60 by the compiler, thus removing the need for the multiplication when the program is executed.

❑ *Algebraic identities* - code can be simplified by taking advantage of a number of algebraic identities such as

$$x + 0 = x$$

$$0 + x = x$$

$$x*0 = 0$$

$$x*1 = x$$

$$0/x = 0$$

$$x - 0 = x$$

- ❑ *Dead code elimination* - the compiler detects code that can never be reached during execution.

- ❑ *Loop-invariant expressions* - an expression within a loop may be exactly the same each time through the loop, so evaluating it only once outside of the loop will reduce execution time. For example, `for i := 1 to m*4 do procX`, could be compiled as if it had been written

```
T1 := m*4;
for i := 1 to T1 do procX;
```

Machine-specific compilers may use other techniques which are dependent on the target language, but, though optimisation is desirable, care must be taken that optimisation does not alter the original intention of the programmer; most compilers are therefore conservative with optimisation, and several give the user the option of what optimisations the compiler is to attempt at compile time. As a final note, probably the best optimisations are those produced by careful algorithm design on the part of the programmer, rather than those of the compiler.

Code generation

The final phase of the compilation process translates the optimised intermediate code to either machine code or to assembly language, depending on the particular compiler. Here the actual sequences of code necessary to, for example, call subprograms, add two floating-point numbers, and multiply two integers are emitted.

Because the intermediate form of the source program will be only slightly more abstract than assembly language, a table lookup process can be used to replace each three-address instruction by the equivalent assembly language code. At this time the compiler must determine whether a variable is to be allocated to a register or to main memory, and also take into account the context in which variables are referenced; the symbol table will contain information regarding the nature of each variable, whether it is global or local for instance.

Types of compilers

It is possible to write a compiler that works its way through the source code once only and produces the object code at the end of the pass. This is called a *single-pass compiler*, for obvious reasons. The main problem with this approach is the necessity to deal with *forward references*. For example, the compiler may have to compile an instruction such as

```
goto L1
```

without yet knowing the location of the label L1. The solution is to leave a gap for the address of the label, note that the information is missing by adding an entry to a special list reserved for this eventuality, and then when the information becomes available, filling in the gap after consulting the list.

However, it is generally more convenient to process the source program using a multi-pass compiler in which there are number of passes, each pass performing certain functions and producing a modified version of the program to be used in the next pass. Such compilers have two major advantages over the single-pass compilers:

- ❑ The compiler can be written in a modular manner rather than as a monolithic program.

❑   Decreased memory requirements, since the code for the current pass is all that needs to be memory resident.

The chief disadvantage of the multi-pass compiler is the probable necessity to make frequent disk accesses to read and write the intermediate files required to allow the separate phases to communicate with each other.

Linking

Frequently, the object code produced by the compiler comprises separate modules of machine code which are related to each other via call and return addresses; the separate modules may also share common data. The object code may also make reference to library routines, held externally from the main program block. The function of the linker program, or *linkage editor*, is to incorporate the absolute call and return addresses of any external routines (*closed subroutines*) which are to be used by the program, as well as those needed to link the various modules of machine code produced by the compiler. Sometimes, linking is carried out as part of the compilation process.

Interpreters

Because interpreters do not produce stand-alone object code, they use a number of special processing techniques to optimise the speed at which a program executes. For example, before starting to execute a source statement, an interpreter might first convert it into a more convenient internal form by tokenising keywords as they are entered so that they are more readily recognisable at run time. Rapid methods of accessing variables must be devised since this will be a major task of the interpreter.

These and other issues are addressed in the following sections using interpreted BASIC as a case study.

A case study - BASIC

The interpreter described here is based on one of Acorn's early BASIC interpreters. It consists of a number of functional components:

❑   command handler;

❑   tokeniser;

❑   statement interpreter;

❑   expression evaluator;

❑   heap/stack handler.

These are described in the following sections.

Program statements in BASIC start with a line number and contain one or more keywords such as PRINT or INPUT. These statements are tokenised before being inserted into the current program at the position determined by the line number. The program is executed when the command RUN is entered. However, if a statement is entered without an initial line number, BASIC assumes that the statement is to be treated as a command and executed immediately. Thus the line

```
    PRINT 'Hello there'
```

would be treated as a command causing the computer to display 'Hello there' on the monitor, whereas

```
100 PRINT 'Hello there'
```

would cause this line to be inserted at the appropriate point in the current program.

Heaps and stacks

As well as the space required for the program, a BASIC interpreter must also be able to allocate dynamic storage for variables and other needs that arise during the running of a program. BASIC uses two data structures, a *heap* and a *stack* for such purposes.

The BASIC heap is explained in the chapter on Data Structures, as an application of a linked list. Briefly, the heap consists of an interwoven set of linked lists, one list for each set of variables starting with the same letter. The heap is located in the memory area just above the program storage area, and it increases in size each time a variable is allocated a value for the first time. A special pointer keeps track of the next free location available for the storage of a *variable information block* which contains the details of a variable. A variable information block contains a pointer to the location in the heap of the next variable with the same initial letter, the name of the variable (except for its initial letter which does not need to be stored) and its value. Locating an established variable involves accessing each node of the appropriate linked list until the required variable information block is located.

Two additional linked lists are included in the heap: one for procedures and the other for functions. The value field in this instance contains a pointer to the location of the start of the procedure or function definition.

The main BASIC stack is used for three main purposes:

(i)   As a temporary storage area for storing intermediate values while the expression evaluator is processing an expression.

(ii)   To store the processor stack when procedures or functions are called. This is necessary if the processor's stack is limited in size because recursive subprograms might cause it to overflow very quickly.

(iii)   As a temporary storage area for parameters and local variables associated with procedures and functions so that they may be restored to their original values when calls are completed.

Two other smaller stacks are used for repeat...until and for...next loops. These are used to store the locations of the first statements in such loops so that control can repeatedly return to them while loops are in operation.

Tokens and links

When a line has been typed at the keyboard, the command handler sends the line to the tokeniser so that keywords can be *tokenised*. This involves replacing the keyword by a single byte containing a unique value. Tokens serve the dual function of reducing the size of a program by replacing multi-character keywords with a single character, and of speeding up program execution by proving an efficient method of invoking the appropriate keyword handler.

When a keyword token is recognised, it is used as an offset to the start address of a table of pointers to keyword-handling routines. For example, assuming 16-bit addresses, suppose that the keyword FOR had a token value of 5 and the keyword address table started at address 1000, as shown in Table 30.4.

address	keyword handler address(hex)	keyword
1000	BF50	ABS
1001	AEEF	COS
1002	AEE3	DEG
1003	AF32	EVAL
1004	BF78	FN
1005	BF47	FOR
1006	AD45	GET

Table 30.4

Then, in order to access the subprogram that deals with FOR statements, the interpreter needs only to add 5 to the base address of 1000 to obtain the starting address (BF47) of the FOR handler.

The tokeniser will also tokenise initial line numbers, again to save space but also, more importantly, to speed up the location of destination line numbers in statements such as

```
200 GOTO 4560
```

which will entail searching each line number in the program in turn from the start until 4560 is located; tokenised line numbers significantly reduce the amount of time spent in comparing line numbers with the one required, particularly when a large number of statements are involved.

Another device for speeding up searching for particular lines is by using links inserted into program lines. These links are offsets to the start of the next instruction. Thus a program line might have the following format:

> *tokenised line number*
>
> *length of line*
>
> *first character of statement*
>
> *second character of statement*
>
> *etc*
>
> *end of line character*
>
> *start of next line*

The *length of line* item allows the line to be skipped by adding its value to the address of the start of the line - this gives the start of the next line. Thus the body of unwanted lines may be ignored, saving a relatively large amount of time when searching for a particular line.

Statement interpreter

When a program is executed, after it has been entered and tokenised, the *statement interpreter* then decides how to handle the line. If it finds a keyword, then it will call the appropriate keyword handler; if it finds a variable name, it calls the assignment handler which in turn calls an *expression evaluator* to provide a value to be assigned to the variable. Failing it finding any valid construct, the statement interpreter will generate an error message to indicate that an unrecognisable instruction has been located at this current line.

Most of the keyword handlers will also call the expression evaluator to obtain the values they require in order to perform their functions; it is therefore one of the major sections of the interpreter.

Expression evaluation

In the earlier section on parsing, a technique called *recursive descent* parsing was described. It was described as being used by a compiler to analyse a source statement and to convert it into an intermediate form. The same method is often used by interpreters to evaluate expressions. The *expression evaluator* divides the expression into several processing levels according to the priorities of the operators it encounters as it scans the expression. Low priority operations are dealt with by the top levels which call lower levels to deal with higher priority operations. High priority results are passed back to the top levels for low priority operations to be completed. So, for example, in the calculation 5 – 8/2, the subtraction is a lower level operation than the division, so the division would be performed first and the result would be passed back to the subtraction routine to complete the evaluation of the expression.

This is exactly the same process as recursive descent parsing, but the interpreter evaluates the expression as it is analysing the expression rather than using it as a compiler would to produce a data structure for use later. Tracing the expression above, (that is, 5 - 8/2), and using a simplified scheme, would produce the following steps:

(i) the *expression* evaluator calls a routine *term* to obtain a value corresponding to a term in the expression;

(ii) *term* calls *factor* to obtain a value;

(iii) *factor* gets the value 5 which it pushes to a stack before returning to term ;

(iv) since there are no more factors in the first term, *term* has completed its task and returns control to *expression*;

(v) *expression* then finds a '-' so it calls *term* again;

(vi) *term* calls *factor* to provide a value;

(vii) *factor* obtains the 8 and then pushes it to the BASIC stack;

(viii) *term* needs another factor because of the '/' it finds, so it calls *factor* again;

(ix) *factor* gets the 2 which it stacks and then returns to *term*;

(x) *term* performs the division 8/2 and stacks the result, 4, before returning to *expression*;

(xi) *expression* then pops the 4 and the 2 from the stack and completes the subtraction to give an answer of 1.

The section on recursive descent parsing earlier in this chapter contains an algorithm (Listing 30.1) for the process outlined above.

It is worth mentioning at this point that although interpreters and compilers are the main types of translators used for high-level languages, there are several variations on this theme, two of which are described below.

Threaded interpretive languages (TILs) allow the programmer to define operations in terms of sequences of predefined, primitive operations, called *words* in TIL parlance, such as add, subtract, multiply, divide and many of the operations found in other languages. Words may refer to other user-defined (secondary) words which then become new commands extending the language. In fact, typical TIL programs consist of short, progressively defined new words. The final word of the program is entered, to perform the required task.

In one variation of this type of language, the words are linked together using pointers to the location of either a primitive word or a secondary word, depending on how the word has been defined. When executed, an interpreter controls this process by getting the next pointer, jumping to the location pointed to and either executing the machine code found there if the routine is a primitive or repeating the process if it finds another secondary word. Usually there is no theoretical limit to the depth to which these secondary levels may be nested. Because the interpreter must perform this function at run-time, it must be co-resident with the program in memory, taking up space and slowing down execution time. Other TIL variations overcome the speed restriction to some degree but still operate in much the same way. An example of a TIL is Forth.

Some languages are processed using a combination of compiler and interpreter. The compiler operates in the normal way, but instead of producing machine code it produces *p-code* (pseudo-code) which is a refined form of the source code. The interpreter must then be used to actually execute the program by interpreting the p-code at run-time. Because the compiler has already performed most of the analysis and error checking of the source code, the interpreter has much less work to do than in a conventional system and can execute the p-code very efficiently.

One of the main advantages of this system is that the language is easier to implement on a variety of different computer systems since the relatively simple interpreter can be tailored to the particular machine. Again, however, the penalty in using an interpreter is loss of speed; machine code will execute more quickly than p-code. Some versions of Pascal produce interpreted p-code and BCPL also works on this principle.

✏️Exercises

1. Name and briefly describe two common methods of defining computer languages.
2. Explain the difference between the following types of language translators:
   (i)   assembler;
   (ii) compiler;
   (iii) interpreter;
3. With the aid of examples explain the following terms:
   (i)   lexical analysis;
   (ii)   semantic analysis;
   (iii) bottom-up parsing;
   (iv)   recursive descent parsing;
   (v)   parse tree;
   (vi)   symbol table;
   (vii) Reverse Polish Notation.

Chapter 31

Program Design

The single most important requirement of a computer program is that it runs without error at all times, since a program that either produces erroneous results or hangs up under certain circumstances is almost useless. Because of this stringent requirement, computer program design and production is a very skilled activity demanding meticulous attention to detail. It is not sufficient to address only the relatively easy problem of designing and implementing a program which produces the correct output when provided with ideal data. Rather, the program must be able to cope with non-ideal data such as that provided by a user who may be unfamiliar with its operation or data input requirements. Such a user might supply inappropriate input by, for example, entering alphabetic instead of numeric characters, and even experienced operators of the program might accidentally enter invalid data on occasions.

In fact there are many ways that a program could be presented with exceptional - that is, invalid or unreasonable - data and it is the responsibility of the program designer to allow for such. Consequently, the program design stage of program production, in which possible problems - and their solutions - are identified, is of vital importance. As a result, there are now a number of established program design methodologies to aid the program designer to produce well-crafted, error-free programs. The design method described here is a form of *structured programming* using *top-down*, *stepwise refinement*.

Two forms of notation that we will use to express solutions to design problems are *pseudocode* and *structure charts*; these are called *program design languages* (PDLs). Structure charts provide a graphical representation of a program, allowing its logical structure to be easily appreciated, whereas pseudocode, having a form similar to program instructions, aids program writing and testing.

Problem solving

Whether a problem is computer-related or otherwise, the strategy for solving it has essentially the same three main stages:(1) *understand the problem*, (2) *devise a solution*, and (3) *test the solution*. In addition, for program design tasks there is a further stage which is to (4) *document the solution*.

1. Understand the problem

This first stage requires a *thorough* understanding of the problem being addressed so that you can identify what assumptions can be made and what can't in order to test your solution in the correct context.

Some problems are apparently straightforward but, when analysed with a view to producing a program design, become much more complex. As an example, consider the following outline program specification:

> *Write a program to read in a date and convert it to the number of days from the start of the calendar year.*

It sounds simple enough until you start to consider what the problem implies. For example, what format is to be used for the date? - 15th January, 1995 or 15 Jan 95, or 15/1/95, or 15-01-95 or 150195, or 950115, and so on. Is a particular format to be adopted and incorrectly formatted dates to be rejected, or is the program to attempt to interpret different formats? Are leap years to be considered when calculating the day number? Do you assume that the date is for the current year or can the date be for a different year? You may be able to think of more problems that could arise.

2. Design a solution

The method adopted here to design the solution involves tackling the problem in a number of steps. An outline program is designed first, showing the main modules of the program, and the order in which they are to be executed. Each main module is then reduced to a number of smaller, simpler, and more manageable components, and this process of refinement continues until the program designer judges that there is sufficient detail in the design for a programmer to be able to convert the design directly into a programming language. The process of reducing components into sequences of smaller components in stages is often termed *stepwise refinement*. Top-down, stepwise refinement encourages program design to be tackled methodically in a number of stages of increasing detail. Although structure charts and pseudocode are both suitable program design languages, we recommend that you adopt our approach of first using structure charts to produce your program designs in outline form and then translating them into detailed pseudocode prior to testing and subsequent conversion to program code.

An example of a simple structure chart and the equivalent pseudocode for the addition of two real numbers are shown in Figure 31.1. (Note that a *real* number is a number with a fractional part such as 23·456, whereas an *integer* is a whole number such as 32). An-swer, a and b are called variables

Structure chart

Pseudocode
1. read a, b
2. Answer = a+b
3. write Answer

Figure 31.1. *Simple program design for addition of two real numbers*

which serve a similar function to the symbols used in algebra - they are general, symbolic representations of data that is to be processed. Thus, the pseudocode statement 1 in Figure 31.1 means 'read two values from the input device (such as a keyboard) and call them a and b respectively'. Statement 2 adds the two values and calls the result Answer. Statement 3 displays Answer on the output device (such as a display screen). By using variables rather than actual numbers, this sequence of statements defines how a computer is to deal with the addition of *any* two numbers. In addition to the problem solution itself, another part of the design is a *data table* which defines the purpose and type of the variables used in the solution. The data table (Table 31.1) would identify whether these variables were integers or real numbers and their purpose.

name	description	type
Answer	Holds the sum of the two numbers	real variable
a	First number entered	real variable
b	Second number entered	real variable

Table 31.1

3. Test the solution

This involves using test data to manually step through the solution statements so that the computed output can be compared with the expected output. For instance, the date example mentioned above should give an answer of 69 for 10th March 1995, assuming that the days are calculated from 1st January, 1995. This value would be compared with that provided by the design - if the answer was different then the apparent design fault would need to be investigated and corrected before continuing with further testing. The design of test data is considered in Chapter 29.

4. Document the solution

The documentation contains the following: (i) the problem statement; (ii) the top-level program design; (iii) the final detailed program design; (iv) the data table. These are produced during the course of the first three stages of program design. The examples in later sections show the form of this documentation.

Structured programming

Most current program design methodologies are based on *structured programming* concepts. Structured programming is generally associated with certain basic principles:

1.   **Restricted use of control structures**. These are limited to three types: *sequence* consisting of instructions which are performed one after the other in the order that they appear in the program; *selection* of one set of instructions from several possible sets of instructions so that the program is able to deal with a number of different circumstances; *repetition*, or *iteration*, of a set of instructions using some kind of program loop. Restricting design to using only these three constructs does not necessarily produce error-free code, but it does help to produce a program which is clear and relatively easy to test.

2.   **Modularity**. This is the subdivision of a program into easily identifiable and manageable segments, or *modules*. Each module should require no more than about one page of code. A module may be realised in the final program as one or more small subprograms. Using modules helps to clarify the logical structure of a program for human readers and, by incorporating subprograms, aids its construction.

3.   **Top-down, stepwise refinement**. This program design method was described in the earlier section *Problem Solving*.

4.   **Clear program format**. This is concerned with the layout of the program instructions. Each page of coding should contain clearly identifiable control structures and blocks of code. One main method of achieving this clarity of structure is by the consistent use of indentation showing the limits of loops, selections and blocks of instructions. Formatting standards apply both to pseudocode and actual program code.

5.   **Comments**. The thorough use of comments within the pseudocode design and the actual program in order to explain the purpose of each variable and each few lines of logically related code.

6.   **Simplicity**.Where there is a choice between a simple solution to a problem and a slightly more efficient solution which perhaps uses less code, then the simple solution

is to be preferred. Straightforward, simple code is easier to test, modify and understand than obscure, 'clever' code.

Basic control structures

As explained earlier, structured programs are constructed using the three control structures sequence, selection and iteration. In order to illustrate how each of these is expressed and used in program design, consider the following programming problem:

> *Read a set of ten positive and negative numbers entered from a keyboard and find the separate totals of the positive numbers and the negative numbers. Print the two totals.*

It is assumed that only valid real numbers such as $1 \cdot 2$, $-7 \cdot 3$, 25, -6 will be entered. The program can be considered to be a *sequence* of three simple modules:

1. **Initialise variables.** Two variables will be required: one for the total of the positive numbers and the other for the total of the negative numbers.

2. **Process the numbers.** This involves a loop to read numbers typed in from the keyboard until ten values have been entered. A count will be incremented every time a number is read in.

3. **Display the results.** This will involve writing out the two totals.

This top-level design is illustrated by the structure chart shown in Figure 31.2.

The equivalent pseudocode for the top-level design is shown in Listing 31.1.

Figure 31.2 *Top level design as sequence of three modules*

Listing 31.1.

```
{Totals}
1    Initialise
2    Process numbers
3    Display results
```

The first refinement of the design results in the structure chart shown in Figure 31.3.

Figure 31.3. *First refinement showing an iteration*

The loop that reads the ten numbers, in other words the *iteration*, is indicated in the structure chart by an asterisk in the top right-hand corner of the component that is to be repeated.

The condition governing the loop is written above this component; in this case the loop continues while the count variable has a value less than ten.

The equivalent pseudocode is shown in Listing 31.2.

Listing 31.2.

```
{Totals}
1.1   PosTot=0
1.2   NegTot=0
1.3   Count=0
2     while Count < 10
2.1       Process Number
2     endwhile
3.1   write PosTot
3.2   write NegTot
```

Each of the Listing 31.1 statements, numbered *1*, *2* and *3*, have all been refined in Listing 31.2; statement *1* (initialise) has been replaced by three detailed instruction, *1.1*, *1.2* and *1.3*. Similarly, statements *2* and *3* in Listing 31.1 have also been refined in Listing 31.2. (These statement level numbers reflect the depth of the structure diagram; a single statement level such as *1* indicates a top-level module, a statement number such as *1.2* indicate the second step of a refinement of level *1*. Number *2.3.1* indicates the first step of a refinement of statement *2.3*, and so on. A refinement of a statement is denoted by adding another level to the statement number.) Notice that the end of the loop is indicated by endwhile and the instruction inside the loop, Process Number, is indented. A loop thus translates into three pseudocode statements: one statement for the type of loop and the condition that governs it, another for the item that is to be repeated, and the third for the end of the loop. The final refinement is to expand Process Number, since this is the only statement that has not yet been fully defined: we need to show *how* a number is to be processed. The full design is shown in Figure 31.4.

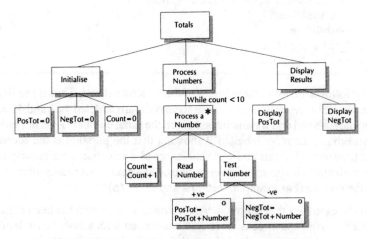

Figure 31.4. *Final refinement showing a selection*

The structure chart shows that the repeated component `Process Number` involves three steps: increment the count, read a number, and test the number to determine its sign. Positive numbers are to be accumulated in `PosTot` and negative numbers are to be accumulated in `NegTot`. The test involves a *selection*, each independent choice being indicated by a small circle in the top right-hand corner of the box. The condition governing each choice is written above the appropriate box as shown. This version of the design needs no further refinement since it is now in a suitable form for conversion to pseudocode and subsequently to a programming language such as COBOL or C.

The pseudocode in Listing 31.3 uses a `select` statement for the selection. If the condition following the first `select` is true, the statement or statements following are obeyed, otherwise the next `select` is considered. The `endselect` statement must be used to terminate the `select` statement.

Note that the number of alternative sets of statements is not limited to two - as many as necessary can be chained together in this way. If some action is necessary when none of the `select` statements is true then the `select when otherwise` statement can be included before `endselect`.

Listing 31.3.   Totalling positive and negative numbers

```
{Totals}
1.1        PosTot = 0
1.2        NegTot = 0
1.3        Count = 0
2          while Count < 10
2.1          Count = Count + 1
2.2          Read Number
2.3          select
2.3.1a         when Number > 0
2.3.1b            PosTot = PosTot + Number
2.3.2a         when Number < 0
2.3.2b            NegTot = NegTot + Number
2.3          endselect
2          endwhile
3.1        write PosTot
3.2        write NegTot
```

The numbering follows the refinement levels of the structure charts. Thus if the first module is refined as a sequence of two statements, these statements are labelled *1.1* and *1.2*. In the case of an iteration, the start and end statements are given the same number. Thus in Listing 31.3, the `while` and `endwhile` both are labelled *2* showing that the iteration is the second top-level module in the program. The start and end statements of a selection are similarly labelled, but each option, which might involve a number of steps, has a small letter added to indicate that it is a step within the option. (For example, *2.3.1a* and *2.3.1b*).

In addition, in the examples that follow, where a structure chart step has been expanded in the pseudocode, each part of the expansion is also designated with a lower case letter. This frequently occurs when the structure chart shows that a value is to be entered by a user through a keyboard; the pseudocode might be expanded thus: *5.1* read Number becomes

```
5.1a  write 'Enter a number'
5.1b  read Number
```

This helps to prevent the structure chart from becoming too detailed and thus unclear. To complete the design, the three variables must be defined in a data table (see Table 31.2).

name	description	type
Count	Counts how many numbers have been entered	integer variable
PosTot	The sum of the positive value numbers	real variable
NegTot	The sum of the negative value numbers	real variable

Table. 31.2. *Definition of variables*

Summary

Figure 31.5 summarises the structure chart and pseudocode notation used for the three basic control structures, sequence, selection and iteration. Iteration is shown in a commonly used alternative form in which the condition is expressed as `repeat..until <condition>`. In this form the condition is tested at the end of the loop rather than at the beginning; this means that the statements within the loop will be repeated at least once. The `repeat..until` loop is illustrated in the worked examples.

Figure 31.5. *The three basic control structures used in structured programming*

Worked examples

The worked examples presented in the next sections use a combination of structure charts and pseudocode to arrive at the final program design. Structure charts are used for the design refinements in order to express the overall logic in a clear, easily understandable form. The design is then presented in pseudocode, a form more suitable for testing and subsequent conversion to a programming language. At this stage some fine detail may also be added to the design.

The program design technique presented here, rather than being targeted at a particular programming language such as COBOL, is in a form suitable for conversion to any one of a number of quite different high-level languages.

Each of the following worked examples is in the format:

(i)   the problem statement;

(ii)   any assumptions that have been made;

(iii)   structure charts showing the top-level design and any further refinement stages;

(iv)   pseudocode for the final design;

(v)   the data table for the complete design;

(vi)   comments.

Reading and displaying information

Problem statement

Design a program which will accept from the keyboard a value representing a number of inches and display the equivalent number of centimetres.

Assumptions

1.   The input is a valid real number.

2.   There is no preferred format for the output.

Top-level design

The top-level design, shown on the right, now requires only minor refinements concerned with the precise form that the output is to take.

This can be accomplished conveniently in pseudocode without the need to draw another structure chart.

Pseudocode

```
{Convert inches to centimetres}
1a   write 'Enter the length in inches: ', <newline>
1b   read Inches
2    Centimetres = Inches*2.54
3a   write <newline>
3b   write 'A length of ', Inches, ' inches is equivalent to ',
                    centimetres, ' centimetres', <newline>
```

Data table

name	description	type
Inches	Value entered at the keyboard and converted to centimetres	real variable
Centimetres	The value to be output	real variable

Comments

`<newline>` indicates that the cursor is to move to the beginning of the next line.

Loops - Running totals

One very frequent programming task is to keep a running total when a number of values are read within an iteration (that is, *loop*). This next example illustrates the technique usually adopted to accumulate a total in a variable.

Problem statement

Design a program to read ten numbers from a keyboard and display their sum.

Assumptions

1.   Exactly ten valid real numbers will be entered using a keyboard.

2.   The sum of the numbers is to be accumulated as the numbers are entered, and thus there is no requirement to store them.

Top-level design

The top-level design is a simple sequence of three modules. The second module, `Process Numbers`, involves a loop which is to repeat a known number of times (namely 10). It can therefore be implemented using a count variable as shown in refinement #1.

Refinement #1

The variable `Total` is to be used to accumulate the sum of the ten numbers and therefore must start with an initial value of zero. `Count` is to start at 1 because it must be increased by one each time a new number is read. Each time through the loop a new number is read into the variable `Number` and then added to `Total` which accumulates the numbers. When `Count` reaches 10, the loop terminates.

Refinement #2

The statements required for processing a number and incrementing the loop control variable have been added; this represents the final structure chart form of the design.

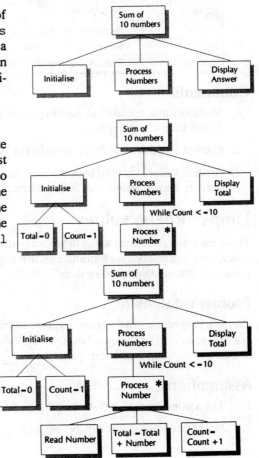

Pseudocode

```
{Sum of 10 numbers}
1.1    Total = 0
1.2    Count = 1
2      while Count <= 10
2.1a     write <newline>, 'Enter number #', Count
2.1b     read Number
2.2       Total = Total + Number
2.3      Count = Count + 1
2      endwhile
3      write <newline> , 'The sum of the 10 numbers is: ', Total
```

This pseudocode form of the final refinement is to make the program a little more user friendly by adding some text to prompt the user to enter a number - this is much better than presenting the user with a blank screen and expecting him/her to know exactly what to do. The final instruction adds some text to announce the answer.

Data table

name	description	type
Total	Accumulates the ten numbers	real variable
Number	Stores the latest number input	real variable
Count	The control variable for the loop	integer variable

Comments

1. Variables that are used as running totals and counts must always be initialised before a loop commences.

2. Control variables for loops are always of type integer.

3. A count variable is used to control the duration of a loop when the number of repetitions is known before the loop commences.

Loops - Rogue values

There are many occasions when the exact number of repetitions of a loop is not known in advance. Frequently loops are terminated when a special value is entered by the user. Such special values are often called 'rogue values'.

Problem statement

Design a program to read a set of numbers representing the cost of some purchased items. The end of the list is to be indicated by entering 0 for the cost. Display how many items were purchased and the total cost of the items.

Assumptions

1.   The values entered will be valid real numbers

2.   No negative numbers will be entered

Top-level design

The strategy used in this instance is to read a value before the loop represented by the module, Process Items, is started. The condition governing the continuation of the loop will be While Amount > 0 and this means that Amount must have been assigned a value before the loop starts. (*Reading ahead* is a common method of reading files (see later in this chapter).

Refinement #1

This refinement now shows that if the user initially enters zero for the amount, the loop is not executed at all because the condition, Amount > 0, is false. This is a very important characteristic of the while loop and a reason for not using the repeat..until loop construct in this instance.

Refinement #2

Processing an item requires a sequence comprising incrementing a count for the number of items, adding the current item's cost to the running total and finally obtaining another item cost. Again, if this latter amount is zero, the condition for continuing the loop becomes false and the loop is terminated. The results are then displayed.

Notice that the last statement executed in the loop is a read statement which obtains the data to be processed next. Since no further detail is required for the structure chart, this is the final refinement before writing the pseudocode.

Pseudocode

```
{Enter and total costs}
1.1    Total = 0
1.2    Count = 0
2.1a   write 'Enter the cost of the first item, or 0 to end'
2.1b   read Amount
3      while Amount > 0
3.1       Count = Count + 1
3.2       Total = Total + Amount
3.3a      write <newline>, 'Enter cost of next item, or zero to end'
3.3b      read Amount
3      endwhile
4.1a   write   <newline>,
4.1b   write   <newline>, Count, 'items were purchased'
4.2a   write <newline>
4.2b   write 'The total cost was: £', Total
```

The detail added to the pseudocode is again to improve communication with the user by displaying prompts such as that in statement 2.1a and by using blank lines (that is, write <newline>) to improve the clarity of the output.

Data table

name	description	type
Total	Accumulates the cost of the items	real variable
Amount	Stores the current item's cost	real variable
Count	Counts the number of items	integer variable

Comments

Try to avoid using a while condition such as Amount <> 0 (not equal to zero) instead of Amount > 0 because real numbers may not be represented exactly within a computer; the representation of zero might not be **exactly** zero and the condition Amount <> 0 may still be true even when zero is entered for Amount.

Making decisions - the select statement

This example introduces the idea of taking one of several courses of action depending on the value of a variable read in from the keyboard. A loop is again terminated by testing for a rogue value, this time a negative value.

Problem statement

Design a program to accept a number of values representing student examination marks. Each mark is to be displayed as a grade as follows:

Mark	Grade
80 or over	Distinction
60 or over	Merit
40 or over	Pass
less than 40	Fail

A negative value is to be used to indicate the end of the set of marks.

Assumptions

The marks are entered as valid integers.

Top-level design

The third module in this sequence is an iteration which repeatedly reads and grades a mark until a negative mark is entered.

Refinement #1

The threshold values for the grades are assigned to integer constants. Any negative value entered will be regarded as the signal to terminate the program.

Refinement #2

The four actions comprising the selection statement, Grade, which determine the message to be displayed should not be considered as a sequence of tests; the selection notation simply shows which action is to be taken depending on the one condition which is true, and as such the four actions could have been drawn in any order.

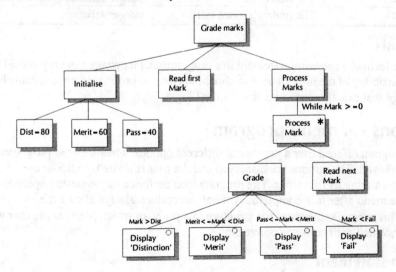

Pseudocode

```
{Grade marks}
1.1        Dist = 80
1.2        Merit = 60
1.3        Pass = 40
2.1a       write 'Enter the first mark(-1 to end):'
2.1b       read Mark
3          while Mark >= 0
3.1          select
3.1.1a         when Mark >= Dist
3.1.1b            write 'Distinction', <newline>
3.1.2a         when Mark >= Merit and Mark < Dist
3.1.2b            write 'Merit', <newline>
3.1.3a         when Mark >= Pass and Mark < Merit
3.1.3b            write 'Pass', <newline>
3.1.4a         when Mark < Pass
3.1.4b            write 'Fail', <newline>
3.1          endselect
3.2a         write 'Enter the next mark(−1 to end):'
3.2b         read Mark
3          endwhile
```

The three thresholds for the grades are stored in the integer constants Dist, Merit and Pass. The advantage of doing this rather than using the actual values 80, 60 and 40 respectively is that if any of these values need to be modified, they need only be changed in the initialisation module and nowhere else.

Data table

name	description	type
Dist	The distinction mark	integer constant = 80
Merit	The merit mark	integer constant = 60
Pass	The pass mark	integer constant = 40
Mark	The student's exam mark	integer variable

Comments

The precise form of a selection statement in a programming language can vary considerably; it is the responsibility of the programmer to choose the most appropriate form available in the target language that exactly represents the required logic.

Decisions - A menu program

Where a program offers a user a number of different options, a menu-based program structure is often employed. The options are displayed and the user is invited to choose one of them by, for example entering its first letter. The program then performs the requested operation and re-displays the menu after it is completed. One of the options always allows the user to exit the program. This example illustrates the structure of a program which presents the user with four options concerned with currency conversion.

Problem statement

Design a menu-based program to allow a user to choose between converting pounds sterling to

German marks, American dollars or French francs. The program will ask the user to enter the number of pounds and it will display the equivalent amount in the chosen currency before returning to the menu. The menu is to appear at the top of a blank screen and appear as follows:

```
Currency conversion program

(M)arks
(D)ollars
(F)rancs
e(X)it

Which currency do you want to convert to Pounds?
```

Assumptions

1. Invalid choices (that is entering a letter other than M, D, F or X) will produce an error message and an invitation to try again.

2. Upper and lower case letters will be allowed.

3. The amount in pounds entered by the user will be a valid real number.

4. A single statement, ClearScreen, is available to blank the display screen.

Top-level design

The top-level design in this instance is very simple: the initialisation module sets the values for the three currency conversion factors and the remaining module, Main, repeatedly displays the user options and executes the one chosen.

Refinement #1

Three constants used for the currency conversion calculations are defined at this point (don't rely on these figures for holiday plans!).

Further, the iteration is defined as a repeat..until loop with condition c1. Logical conditions governing loops and selections can be coded in this way so that defining their precise form can be deferred until the design has been completed. We will see later in refinement #3 that c1 is the condition that indicates the user has chosen the exit option. Remember that the repeat loop causes the statements within the loop to be repeated at least once, and that the test for continuing to repeat the statements is made at the end of the loop.

Refinement #2

This refinement now shows that the loop controls a sequence of two modules. The

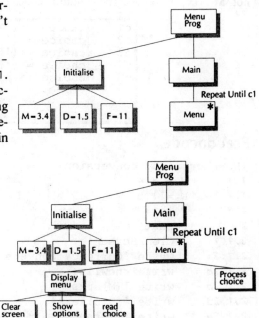

first, Display menu, repeatedly clears the display screen, shows the menu of options and then reads the user's choice. The second module is a selection statement which processes the option chosen. The final refinement defines the operation of each of the options and under what circumstances each is chosen.

Refinement #3

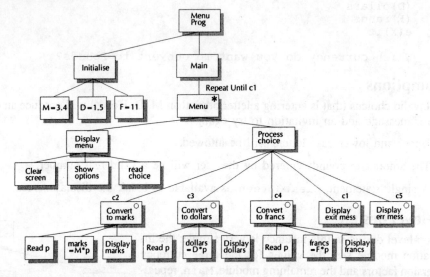

The first three options are concerned with the actual currency conversions. The fourth option displays a message to confirm that the user has chosen to exit the program. The final select statement is only invoked if the user has entered an invalid choice, that is, the letter entered is not 'M', 'D', 'F' or 'X'. The condition codes c1–c5 are defined in the next table.

c1	choice = ('X' or 'x')
c2	choice = ('M' or 'm')
c3	choice = ('D' or 'd')
c4	choice = ('F' or 'f')
c5	choice <> ('X' or 'x')or ('M' or 'm')or ('D' or 'd')or ('F' or 'f')

Pseudocode

```
{Menu currency conversion}
1.1       M = 3.4
1.2       D = 1.5
1.3       F = 11
2         repeat
2.1.1       ClearScreen
2.1.2a      write 'Currency conversion program', <newline>
2.1.2b      write <newline>
2.1.2c      write '(M)arks'
2.1.2d      write '(D)ollars'
2.1.2e      write '(F)rancs'
```

```
2.1.2f        write <newline>
2.1.2g        write 'Which currency do you want to convert to pounds?'
2.1.3         read Choice
2.2           select
2.2.1a          when Choice = ('M' or 'm')
2.2.1b             write <newline>, 'Enter amount'
2.2.1c             read p
2.2.1d             Currency = M*p
2.2.1e             write ' = ', Currency, ' Marks'
2.2.1f             write <newline> 'Press <Enter> to return to menu'
2.2.1g             read key
2.2.2a          when Choice = ('D' or 'd')
2.2.2b             write <newline>, 'Enter amount'
2.2.2c             read p
2.2.2d             Currency = D*p
2.2.2e             write ' = ', Currency, ' Dollars'
2.2.2f             write <newline> 'Press <Enter> to return to menu'
2.2.2g             read key
2.2.2a          when Choice = ('F' or 'f')
2.2.3b             write <newline>, 'Enter amount'
2.2.3c             read p
2.2.3d             Currency = F*p
2.2.3e             write ' = ', Currency, ' Francs'
2.2.3f             write <newline> 'Press <Enter> to return to menu'
2.2.3g             read key
2.2.4a          when Choice = ('X' or 'x')
2.2.4b             write 'Exiting program...'
2.2.5a          when otherwise
2.2.5b             write 'Invalid option. Please try again'
2.2.5c             write <newline> 'Press <Enter> to return to menu'
2.2.5d             read key
2.2           endselect
2.3           until Choice = ('X' or 'x')
```

Data table

name	description	type
M	Conversion factor for pounds to marks	real constant = 3.4
D	Conversion factor for pounds to dollars	real constant = 1.5
F	Conversion factor for pounds to francs	real constant = 11
p	The number of pounds to convert	real variable
Choice	The user's menu choice	character variable
Currency	The equivalent value in the currency chosen	real variable
key	Dummy variable to accept the <Return> key	character variable

Comments

1. This is a good model for constructing menu-driven programs.

2. The manner of implementing the `select` statement can vary considerably with the

target programming language. COBOL provides `if` and `evaluate` statements which each have their particular advantages and disadvantages. The programmer is responsible for choosing the most appropriate selection construct from those available.

File handling

The term *file* can be used to describe a number of different forms of storing data on backing storage. Here are some examples of different types of files:

❑ *Program source file* - the source code for a program written in a high-level language such as COBOL or C. This is usually a text file such as that produced by an editor or word processor.

❑ *Executable, or binary, file* - a file, containing compiled program code, which is in a form suitable for running. It could be a word processor or spreadsheet program or a scientific program, for example.

❑ *Picture file* - a collection of data representing a coloured or black and white picture which can be displayed on a computer screen with the aid of suitable software, such as a graphic design program.

❑ *Data file* - a file organised as a collection of *records*, each record comprising a number of fields. Such files are commonly used in data processing applications such as payroll, stock control and accounting.

We will be concerned with this last type of file. Most general-purpose high-level programming languages are able to create, read and modify files organised as collections of records; they provide single program instructions to transfer a complete record as a unit from backing storage into memory, at the same time splitting the record into separate data items called *fields*. The data in the fields are automatically allocated to variables declared for this purpose. This is the process of *reading a record* from a file. Another instruction allows the programmer to transfer a single, complete record as a unit from memory to a backing storage medium. This is the process of *writing a record*. Two other important file-handling operations are (1) *opening a file* in an appropriate mode and (2) *closing a file* which previously has been opened. The open file statement usually involves naming the file to be opened and specifying whether it is to be opened for input (that is, for reading records) or output (that is, for writing records).

The program designs which follow are concerned only with reading and writing sequential files, that is, where the records can be read only in a fixed sequence. Simple examples illustrate the logic required to create, read and search sequential files.

Creating a sequential file

Problem statement

Design a program to create a sequential file of car details. Each car record will contain:

Make	*: maximum of 10 characters*
Model	*: maximum of 10 characters*
Insurance group	*: an integer value*
Cost	*: a real value*

Assumptions

1. The data will be stored in the form that it is entered - no validation checks will be performed.

2. A backing storage device such as a hard disk drive or a floppy disk drive is available to store the records of the file.

Top-level design

The top-level design is a sequence of a statement to prepare the file for output, followed by an iteration which allows the user to keep adding records to the file, and finally a statement which closes the file.

Refinement #1

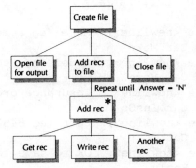

The iteration is implemented as a `repeat` loop which terminates when the user answers 'no' to the opportunity to add another record to the file.

The loop repeatedly

1.   requests the user to enter a set of car details (that is, a car record),

2.   stores the record if the user consents to it, and

3.   then asks if another record is to be entered. The character variable, `Answer`, will contain 'N' if the user wishes to discontinue adding records to the file and this will cause the `repeat` loop to terminate.

Refinement #2

In this final refinement, the detail of the Add rec module is added. The selection statement, `Write action`, shows that we are interested only in `Reply` containing the character 'Y' indicating that the car record is to be stored; any other character simply results in no action being taken, which is indicated by the dash in the box.

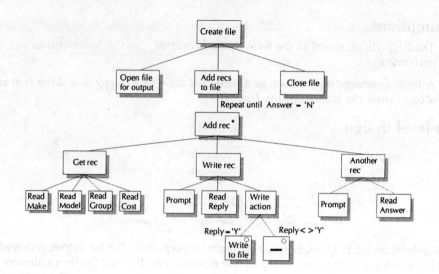

Pseudocode

```
{Create sequential file}
1             fopen output, Carfile
2             repeat
2.1.1a          write <newline>, 'Make (eg Ford):'
2.1.1b          read Car.Make
2.1.2a          write <newline>, 'Model (eg Escort):'
2.1.2b          read Car.Model
2.2.3a          write <newline>, 'Insurance group (eg 7):'
2.1.3b          read Car.InsGp
2.1.4a          write <newline>, 'Cost (eg 8450.50):'
2.1.4b          read Car.Cost
2.2.1           write <newline>, 'OK to save this record(Y/N) '
2.2.2           read Reply
2.2.3           select
2.2.3.1a          when Reply = ('Y' or 'y')
2.2.3.1b            fwrite CarFile, Car
2.2.3.2a          when otherwise
2.2.3.2b            next statement
2.2.3           endselect
2.3.1           write <newline>, 'Another record to file?(Y/N)'
2.3.2           read Answer
2             until Answer = ('N' or 'n')
3             fclose CarFile
```

The data table in the next section shows that `Car` is a record data structure with fields `Make`, `Model`, `InsGp` and `Cost`. The *dot notation* is used to specify a field within a record, so that, for example, the insurance group variable is designated `Car.InsGp`. This same notation is used in the pseudocode listing on the previous page. This allows a complete record to be treated as a unit for the purposes of reading and writing records. Thus the file write statement, *2.2.3.1b* `fwrite CarFile, Car` specifies that the current `Car` record is to be written to `CarFile`.

The list of file-related commands used in this chapter have the following general formats:

```
fopen output, FileName          Opens named file for writing
fopen input, FileName           Opens named file for reading
fwrite FileName, RecordName     Writes named record to the named file
fread FileName, RecordName      Reads named record from named file
fclose FileName                 Closes named file
```

Finally, note that following statement from the pseudocode listing, *2.2.3.2b* next statement means, in effect, that no action is to take place at this point and control passes to the next available statement. It is included to make the logic of the selection statement clear and consistent with the structure chart component that it represents.

Data table

name	description	type
`Car`	A car record	record
`Car.Make`	The manufacturer of the car	string field
`Car.Model`	The model of the car	string field
`Car.InsGp`	The insurance group of the car	integer field
`Car.Cost`	The price of the car	real field
`CarFile`	Sequential file of car records	file of Car record
`Reply`	Holds the user's answer (Y or N) regarding whether a record is to be written to the file	character variable
`Answer`	Holds the user's answer (Y or N) regarding whether another record is to be entered	character variable

Comments

This program creates the car file; each time that it is used, the car file would be re-created. A technique for extending a sequential file is presented in a later example.

Reading sequential files

Two variations of reading records in a sequential file are presented here. The first design is the most general form which assumes that a programming language will detect the end of a file when an attempt is made to read a record after the last one in the file. The read file statement in this instance has an `at end` clause which allows some action (in our case, setting a flag called `EOF` to boolean true) if an end-of-file condition has arisen. Languages such as C and COBOL handle sequential files in this way.

The second design assumes that EOF is a built-in system function which detects the file and returns a value of true if there are no more records to be read. This is how Pascal handles sequential files.

Problem statement

Print in tabular form the contents of the car file created in the previous progam.

Assumptions

1.   The file is to be printed in the same order in which it was created.

2.   Version A assumes that the variable EOF is set to true when an attempt is made to read past the last record in the file.

3.   Version B assumes that the function EOF becomes true when there are no records in the file remaining to be read.

Top-level design

This shows that in version A the first record is read outside the loop, and the final operation within the loop is to read the next record (see refinement #1). In version B, this first read is unnecessary.

Refinement #1

Processing a record in version A requires the current record to be printed before an attempt is made to read the next record. If there are no more records remaining to be read, EOF becomes true and the loop is terminated. With version B, a record is read and then printed. If it is the last record, EOF becomes true and the loop exits.

Pseudocode for version A

```
{Read file version A}
1.1    fopen input, Carfile
1.2    EOF = false
2a     fread CarFile, Car
2b        at end set EOF = true
3      while not EOF
3.1       write <newline>, Car.Make, Car.Model, Car.InsGp, Car.Cost
```

```
3.2a       fread CarFile, Car
3.2b           at end set EOF = true
3          endwhile
4          fclose CarFile
```

Note the at end option used with the read file statements - if an attempt is made to read past the last record in the file, EOF is set to true.

Pseudocode for version B

```
{Read file version B}
1          fopen input, Carfile
3          while not EOF(CarFile)
3.1            fread CarFile, Car
3.2            write <newline>, Car.Make, Car.Model, Car.InsGp, Car.Cost
3          endwhile
4          fclose CarFile
```

Here, EOF(CarFile) checks CarFile and if there are no more records remaining to be read, it returns boolean true, otherwise it returns boolean false. When available, this facility simplifies sequential file processing.

Data table for version A

name	description	type
Car	A car record	record
Car.Make	The manufacturer of the car	string field
Car.Model	The model of the car	string field
Car.InsGp	The insurance group of the car	integer field
Car.Cost	The price of the car	real field
CarFile	Sequential file of car records	file of Car record
EOF	Boolean variable used to detect the end of the file	boolean variable

Data table for version B

This is the same as for version A except that the variable EOF is not used; instead EOF(CarFile) is a system function which returns true if there are no more records to be read in CarFile, otherwise it returns false.

Comments

These two versions should be sufficient to describe the logic of sequential file processing for the majority of commonly used high-level languages.

Searching sequential files

This example illustrates the logic of extracting details from all records in a file that satisfy some criterion. In this instance we want to find all the cars that are within a certain price range, but the logic would be the same if we were searching for any other characteristic of the data held in the car records. The structure of the design is very similar to that for reading a sequential file, and the structure diagrams should be self-explanatory.

Problem statement
Produce a report of all cars which are within £1000 of a price which the user enters.

Assumptions
1.   The EOF (FileName) function described in Version B of the previous example is available. Follow the guidelines given for Version A if the target programming language does not offer this facility.
2.   The complete record of cars matching the criterion will be printed.

Top-level design

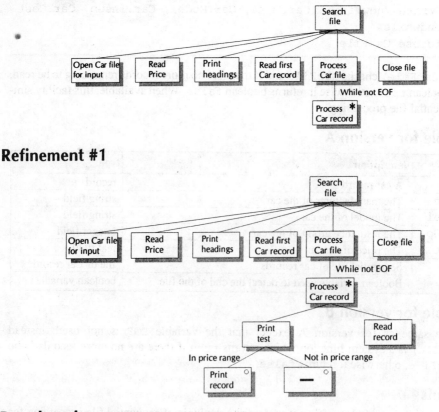

Refinement #1

Pseudocode
```
{Sequential search}
1        fopen input, Carfile
2a       write <newline>, 'Enter approximate price of cars to list'
2b       read Price
3        write <newline>,'Cars within £1000 of £', Price,':'
4        fread CarFile, Car
```

```
5          while not EOF(CarFile)
5.1          select
5.1.1a       when Price-1000 <= Car.Cost <= Price+1000
5.1.1b         write <newline>,Car.Make, Car.Model, Car.InsGp,Car.Cost
5.1.2a       when otherwise
5.1.2b         next statement
5.1          endselect
5.2          fread CarFile, Car
5          endwhile
6          fclose CarFile
```

Data table

name	description	type
Car	A car record	record
Car.Make	The manufacturer of the car	string field
Car.Model	The model of the car	string field
Car.InsGp	The insurance group of the car	integer field
Car.Cost	The price of the car	real field
CarFile	Sequential file of car records	file of Car record
Price	Approximate car price entered by the user	real variable

Comments

If the target programming language does not deal with sequential files in the same way as Pascal, remember that you must use a variable in the `while` condition to register the end of the file and terminate the iteration.

Subprograms

One of the characteristics of programming in high-level languages is the use of *subprograms* such as *procedures* or *functions* to allow a large program to be separated into a number of independent units. These subprograms are connected together by means of a main program. A subprogram usually communicates with the main program with the aid of *parameters* which allow data to be passed to and from the main program. Here we show how subprograms can be represented by structure charts and pseudocode.

Structure chart symbols and pseudocode

Figure 31.6 shows the symbols used for subprograms in structure charts and the equivalent pseudocode statement. Diagram (a) shows the simplest case in which component `Sub 1` is a procedure which has no parameters. The subprogram has its own structure chart which is drawn separately from the main program. The pseudocode statement which invokes the subprogram is `call Sub1`. Again, the content of the subprogram is defined as a separate piece of pseudocode.

In diagram (b), `Sub 2` has a single value parameter to which the variable X is passed. In pseudocode, brackets indicate that the variables inside are parameters. `Sub 3` returns a value to the main program variable Y; in pseudocode this is indicated by putting the variable after the colon, as in `call Sub3:Y`. Diagram (d) shows how a subprogram which has a variable parameter Z is depicted; the double arrow indicates that Z is passed to the subprogram and that it is also returned to the main program. In pseudocode, a variable parameter is indicated by preceding it with var, as in call sub4(var Z). Finally, diagram (d) shows how a subprogram with more than one parameter and more than a single return value is represented. Notice that in the pseudocode statement call Sub5(var W, X):Y, Z, var only refers to W; X is a value parameter because it is not immediately preceded by var.

Figure 31.6. *Symbols for subprograms*

In a structure diagram these new symbols appear as illustrated in Figure 31.7.

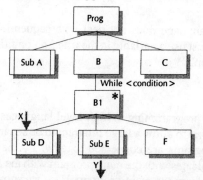

Figure 31.7. *Use of subprogram symbols in structure charts*

The diagram shows that component A is a simple subprogram with no parameters, subprogram D has a value parameter and accepts a variable X from the main program, and subprogram E returns a value to variable Y. The equivalent pseudocode is shown in Listing 31.12.

Listing 31.12.

```
{Prog}
1       call SubA
2       while <condition>
2.1       call SubD(X)
2.2       Y = call SubE
2.3       F
2       endwhile
```

Notice line *2.2*, in which the call to subprogram E results in a value being returned to the main program variable, Y.

The adjacent data table for the main program needs to contain entries defining each subprogram. The table shows that SubA is a procedure which has no parameters; SubD is a procedure which requires a string type to be passed as a parameter; SubE is a function which has no parameters but which returns an integer type.

name	description	type
SubA	Procedure to	proc
SubD	Procedure to	proc(string)
SubE	Function to	func:integer

Defining subprogram structures

Figure 31.8 shows the structure chart for a subprogram called Sub 2. It shows that a value is passed into value parameter P from the main program and that it returns a value in variable R to the main program (or subprogram) that called it. Notice that a subprogram can itself also contain further subprograms (component D).

Figure 31.8. *Subprogram*

Listing 31.13 shows the pseudocode equivalent to this subprogram.

Listing 31.13.

```
Function Sub2(P)
1    process B
2    process C
3    call D(X)
4    return R
```

The parameters to which values are passed are shown inside the brackets after the name of the subprogram. The value that is returned is named after the word return at the end of the subprogram. Each subprogram must also have its own data table which must define all of the parameters of the subprogram and any other variables used. For example, the subprogram in Listing 31.13 would require that P and R have entries such as those shown in Table 31.13.

Function Sub2(P):R		
name	description	type
P	Parameter used for ...	integer value parameter
R	Returns ..... to main program	real value parameter
etc.		

Table 31.13

The following worked example shows the complete design of a program which uses subprograms to extend a sequential file.

Extending a sequential file

We mentioned earlier that when a sequential file is opened for output it must be re-created. In the next example we examine a general method of extending a sequential file without using a special extend-file command. (Some languages, notably COBOL, allow you to open a sequential file in a mode especially for extending it, but this is not generally the case). The method uses a temporary file to which the sequential file is copied. While this temporary file is still open for output, the additional records are added and then the complete temporary file is copied back to the original file.

Problem statement

Design a program to enable car records to be added to the car file.

Assumptions

1.   Any number of extra records can be added to the car file.

2.   The EOF(FileName) function described in previous examples is again available.

Main program

Top-level design

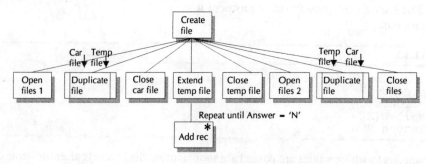

The procedure Duplicate file copies the first-named file to the second file. Thus it appears twice here: the first time to copy the current car file to a temporary file to which the extra records are to be added; the second time to copy the temporary file, now containing the extra records, back to the original file.

Refinement #1

The further detail shows the order in which the two files need to be opened and closed, and also that two further subprograms are used. Get rec is used to get the details of a new car and return this record to the main program. Write rec writes the record to the temporary file.

Both the record and the name of the file to which it is to be written are passed as parameters to this procedure.

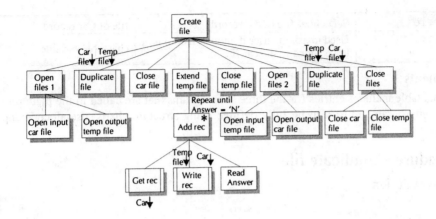

Pseudocode

```
{Extend sequential file}
1.1     open input CarFile
1.2     open output TempFile
2       call DuplicateFile(CarFile, TempFile)
3       close CarFile
4       repeat until Answer = 'N'
4.1       Car = call GetRec
4.2       call WriteRec(TempFile, Car)
4.3a      write <newline>, 'Add another record to the file?(Y/N):'
4.3b      read Answer
4       until Answer = ('N' or 'n')
5       close TempFile
6.1     open output CarFile
6.2     open input TempFile
7       call DuplicateFile(TempFile, CarFile)
8.1     close CarFile
8.2     close TempFile
```

Data table

name	description	type
DuplicateFile	Procedure to copy one sequential file to another	proc(file of Car record, file of Car record)
GetRec	Function which gets and returns a car record	func:Car
WriteRec	Procedure to write a car record to a car file	proc(file of Car, Car)
Car	A car record	record
Car.Make	The manufacturer of the car	string field
Car.Model	The model of the car	string field
Car.InsGp	The insurance group of the car	integer field
Car.Cost	The price of the car	real field

CarFile	Sequential file of car records	file of Car record
Answer	Used to ask the user if another record is to be added to the car file	character variable

Comments

The data table includes entries for the three subprograms that are called in the main program. These subprograms must also be fully defined using structure charts, pseudocode and data tables.

Procedure - Duplicate file

Top-level design

Pseudocode

```
Procedure DuplicateFile(SourceFile, DestFile)
1       while not EOF(SourceFile)
1.1        fread SourceFile, Rec
1.2        fwrite DestFile, Rec
1       endwhile
2       return
```

Data table

Procedure DuplicateFile(Sourcefile, DestFile)		
name	description	type
SourceFile	The file to be copied	file of Car records
DestFile	The copy file	file of Car records
Rec	A single car record from the file	Car record

Function - Get rec

Top-level design

Pseudocode

```
Function GetRec:Crec
1a      write <newline>, 'Make:'
1b      read Crec.Make
2a      write <newline>, 'Model:'
2b      read Crec.Model
3a      write <newline>, 'Insurance Group:'
3b      read Crec.InsGp
4a       write <newline>, 'Cost:'
4b      read Crec.Cost
5       return Crec
```

Data table

Function GetRec:Crec		
name	description	type
CRec	A car record	record
CRec.Make	The manufacturer of the car	string field
CRec.Model	The model of the car	string field
CRec.InsGp	The insurance group of the car	integer field
CRec.Cost	The price of the car	real field

Procedure - Write rec

Top-level design

Pseudocode

```
Procedure WriteRec(File, CarRec)
1a      write <newline>, 'OK to save this record?(Y/N) '
1b      read Reply
2       select
2.1a      when Reply = ('Y' or 'y')
2.1b        fwrite File, CRec
2.2a      when otherwise
2.2b        next statement
2       endselect
3       return
```

Data table

Procedure WriteRec(File, CRec)		
name	description	type
File	The file to be written to	value parameter file of Car records
CRec	A single car record from the file	value parameter Car record
Reply	User reply	character variable

Exercises

Program design, programming and program testing

For each of the following problems, design and implement a program. Also create test classes and test cases as detailed in Chapter 32 and test each program accordingly.

Decisions

1. Read a number and display a message which states whether the number is positive, negative or zero.

2. Read a number and print it only if it is between 10 and 20.

3. Read a number followed by a single letter code. The number represents the price of an item and the code indicates whether tax is to be added to the price. If the code is 'V' then the tax is 20% of the item's cost. If the code is 'X' then the item is not taxed. Print out the total cost of the item.

4. Read three positive, non-zero integers which may represent the sides of a triangle. The numbers are in ascending order of size. Determine whether or not the numbers do represent the sides of a triangle.

5. Extend the previous question to determine the type of triangle if one is possible with the values provided. Assume that the only types of triangles to consider are: *scalene* - no equal sides; *isosceles* - two equal sides; *equilateral* - three equal sides.

6. Read in a single character and print a message indicating whether or not it is a vowel.

Loops

7. Write separate programs to produce conversion tables for:
    (i)   Inches to centimetres (1 to 20 inches, 1 inch = $2 \cdot 54$ centimetres);
    (ii) Pounds to kilograms (1 to 10 pounds, 2.2 pounds per kilogram);
    (iii) Square yards to square metres: 10, 20 , 30,...., 100 sq yds (1yd = $\cdot 91$ m)

8. The cost and discount code of a number of items are to be entered by a user. The program must print out each item's cost, discount and cost less discount. The discount codes are as follows:

   The program will terminate when the user enters 0 for the cost of the item. The program must then print the total cost of all the items entered.

9. Write a program to repeatedly display a menu containing a number of options for converting between different units, plus one option to exit the program. The user must enter a number or letter corresponding to a menu item. Valid entries are to accept a numeric value from the user and apply and display the appropriate conversion, invalid entries are reported and the user is reminded about what choices are valid, and the exit option terminates the program. An example is given below.

Menu
1   **Inches to centimetres**
2   **Centimetres to inches**
3   **Pounds to Kilograms**
etc
4   **Exit**
Please enter option number :

10. A program reads an integer representing the number of gas bills to be processed, followed by that number of customer details. Each set of customer details consists of a customer number, a single character code representing the type of customer and the number of units used. Customers are of type 'D' (domestic) or 'B' (business). Domestic customers are charged 8p per unit and business customers are charged 10p per unit. For each customer print the customer number, the number of units used and the cost of the gas used. Print the total number of units used for this batch of customers and the total amount charged.

11. Repeat the previous question assuming that all the domestic users are first and that separate totals are required for domestic and business users.

Chapter 32

Program Testing, Debugging and Documenting

Introduction

Once a program has been written, it must go through two stages in order to remove errors which almost inevitably will be present. No matter how much care has been taken in the design and coding of a program, it is still very likely to contain *syntax* errors, that is incorrectly formed statements, and probably errors in *logic* as well. *Debugging* is the term given to the process of detecting and correcting these errors or *bugs*.

The first stage in the removal of errors is the correction of syntax errors. Fortunately for the programmer, modern interpreters and compilers will provide a large amount of assistance in the detection of syntax errors in the source code. Badly formed statements will be reported by a compiler after it has attempted to compile the source code; an interpreter will report illegal statements as it attempts to execute them.

Logic errors, however, are largely undetectable by the translating program. These are errors which cause the program to behave in a manner contrary to expectations. The individual statements in the program are correctly formed, but when executed it does not operate correctly; it may give incorrect answers, or terminate prematurely, or not terminate at all. Hopefully, even the most puzzling logic errors, having been detected, eventually can be removed. But how can the programmer be confident that the program will continue to behave properly when it is in use? The answer is that the programmer never can be absolutely certain that the program will not fail. However, by the careful choice of test data in the second stage of the debugging process, the programmer can test the program under the conditions that are most likely to occur in practice.

Test data is designed to determine the robustness of the program: how well it can cope with unexpected or spurious inputs, as well as those for which it has been designed specifically to process.

The purpose of *documentation* is to provide the user with all the information necessary to fully understand the purpose of the program and how that purpose has been achieved.

The precise form that the documentation takes will be determined by a number of factors:

❑ The type of program.

❑ Who is likely to use the program.

❑ Whether it will be necessary to modify the program coding after it has been finally tested and accepted.

General guidelines for the contents of program documentation are given at the end of this chapter.

Detecting logic errors

If after examining program code for a reasonable amount of time the cause of an error remains a mystery, there are a number of courses of action which probably will be much more productive than continuing to pore over the listing:

1. Ask a fellow programmer to listen while you explain the operation of the program and the way it is behaving. Quite often you will see the cause of the error as you are making the explanation. Alternatively, your helper might recognise the type of error and its probable cause from his/her own experience, or might ask a question which makes you reconsider some aspect of the program which you have assumed to be correct or had no direct bearing on the problem. It is surprising how often this simple approach works.

2. Examine the values of key variables while the program is running by inserting temporary lines of code throughout the program to display the values of key variables. Comparison of the values actually displayed with expected values will normally identify the likely source of the error.

3. Use debugging utilities provided in the language itself or separately in the system software. Most high-level language development systems provide debugging aids. These allow the programmer to do such things as step through the program line by line and display the value of variables, or to insert break-points to interrupt the execution of the program so that the state of variables can be examined. It is the responsibility of the programmer to investigate the debugging aids available and make good use of them.

Test data

When the programmer feels that the more obvious program errors have been detected and removed, the next stage is to test the program using carefully selected data. The nature of the test data should be such that:

❑   every statement in the program is executed at least once;

❑   the effectiveness of every section of coding devoted to detecting invalid input is verified;

❑   every route through the program is tried at least once;

❑   the accuracy of the processing is verified;

❑   the program operates according to its original design specification.

In order to achieve these aims, the programmer must be inventive in the design of the test data. Each test case must check something not tested by previous runs; there is no point in proving that a program which can add successfully a certain set of numbers can also add another similar set of numbers. The goal is to strain the program to its limit, and this is particularly important when the program is to be used frequently by a number of different people. There are three general categories of test data:

1. *Normal data*. This includes the most general data for which the program was designed to handle.

2.   *Extreme values.* These test the behaviour of the program when valid data at the upper and lower limits of acceptability are used. The process of using extreme values is called 'boundary testing' and is often a fruitful place to look for errors. For numeric data this could be the use of very large or very small values. Text could be the shortest or longest sequence of characters permitted. A program for file processing could be tested with a file containing no records, or just a single record. The cases where zero or null values are used are very important test cases, frequently highlighting programming oversights.

3.   *Exceptional data.* Programs are usually designed to accept a certain range or class of inputs. If invalid data is used, that is data which the program is not designed to handle, the program should be capable of rejecting it rather than attempting to process it. This is particularly important when the program is to be used by people other than the programmer, since they may be unaware of what constitutes invalid data. A programmer should from the outset assume that incorrect data will be used with the program; this may save a great deal of time looking for program errors which may actually be data errors.

Two commonly used approaches to the generation of good test data, namely *black box testing* and *white box testing*, are described in the following sections. Note, however, that good program testing will use a combination of testing techniques to generate test data, since no single method is sufficient to test a program thoroughly.

Black box testing

In *black box testing*, test data is created from a knowledge only of the function of the program module in terms of its inputs and outputs. In other words, only a knowledge of what it is supposed to do is required, not how it has been written. This approach allows people with no knowledge of the actual program code or of programming languages to be able to derive test data.

A frequently used form of black box testing is *boundary value analysis*, but before describing this technique in more detail it is necessary to consider the concept of *equivalence classes*.

Equivalence classes

Suppose that a program accepts an input in the range 1 to 10. Suppose also that we use the values 2, 6, 7 and 8 to test the program. The test cases 2, 6, 7 and 8 are all values from a single equivalence class, that is, the class of numbers within the range 1 to 10. Each of these test cases is equivalent to all of the other test cases and so there is little point in using more than one or two such values, since if the program functions correctly with one of them, it most probably will work for the others. (Note, however, that this is never absolutely certain, which is why it is impossible to be sure that a program is completely error-free). Two types of equivalence classes are always considered, namely those that are *valid* and those that are *invalid*; it is essential that the program is executed with both good and bad data.

To be clear about valid and invalid equivalence classes, Table 32.1 shows a number of examples of programs which require simple inputs. For each input we can identify both valid and invalid equivalence classes.

Input	Class	Description	Type
Integer in range 0 to 99	1	All values between 0 and 99 inclusive	Valid
	2	Values less than 0	Invalid
	3	Values greater than 99	Invalid
	4	Non-integer	Invalid
	5	Non-numeric	Invalid
Between 2 to 8 characters	1	2 to 8 characters	Valid
	2	Less than 2 characters	Invalid
	3	More than 8 characters	Invalid
Between 2 to 6 values	1	Between 2 and 6 values	Valid
	2	Less than 2 values	Invalid
	3	More than 6 values	Invalid
One of the set of single	1	'A'	Valid
letter codes, 'A', 'B', or	2	'B'	Valid
'C'	3	'C'	Valid
	4	Any other input	Invalid

Table 32.1. *Examples of programs requiring simple inputs*

Test cases

Having established the classes of test data, the next stage is to identify suitable test cases according to the following rules:

1. Create as many test cases as necessary in order to cover all the *valid* classes of test. This means that a single test case may cover more than one valid class.

2. Create a *separate* test case for each *invalid* class of test.

The following example illustrates the procedure for deriving test cases.

Example

A program requires the following three inputs to be entered:

`Quantity`	Integer in the range 1 to 99
`Item Code`	Single letter followed by any three numeric digits
`Payment Code`	Single letter code: 'P', 'C' or 'D'

The valid and invalid equivalence classes for the three inputs are shown in Table 32.2.

Input condition		Valid	Class No	Invalid	Class No
Quantity			**Class No**		**Class No**
	Value	1-99	*1*	<1	*8*
				>99	*9*
				non-numeric	*10*
				non-integer	*11*
Item code					
	1st character	Alphabetic	*2*	non-alphabetic	*12*
	Size	4 chars	*3*	< 4 chars	*13*
				> 4 chars	*14*
	Last 3 chars	Numeric	*4*	non-numeric	*15*
Payment code					
	Value	'P'	*5*	not 'P', 'C' or 'D'	*16*
		'C'	*6*		
		'D'	*7*		

Table 32.2. *Equivalence classes for three inputs*

The next stage is to devise test cases according to the two rules given earlier for valid and invalid classes. The test cases are shown in Table 32.3.

Test case	Inputs			Classes covered	Type
	Quantity	**Item**	**Payment**		
1	25	r123	'P'	*1,2,3,4,5*	Valid
2	33	X345	'C'	*1,2,3,4,6*	Valid
3	44	G786	'D'	*1,2,3,4,7*	Valid
4	0	h123	'D'	*8*	Invalid
5	123	D123	'C'	*9*	Invalid
6	1ab	S123	'P'	*10*	Invalid
7	1.26	f123	'P'	*11*	Invalid
8	25	0123	'P'	*12*	Invalid
9	36	e1	'P'	*13*	Invalid
10	65	a12345	'C'	*14*	Invalid
11	33	abcd	'D'	*15*	Invalid
12	10	v123	'B'	*16*	Invalid

Table 32.3. *Test cases for valid and invalid classes*

Twelve test cases have been created. Notice that the first three test cases for valid inputs test several equivalence classes at once. The remaining test cases for invalid data only test a single equivalence class as required by the rules described earlier.

Note that this set of test cases represents the *minimum* set of values required to test the program; additional test cases could be easily justified. For example, in order to test Invalid class 16, that is, a Payment code other than 'P', 'C' or 'D', we have entered the letter 'B'. It would be advisable also to try entering numeric characters and other special characters such as '!' or '%' found on keyboards.

Boundary value analysis

Observation has revealed that many programs fail when data are at the extreme edges, that is *boundaries*, of expected input. For example, if a program is designed to accept a single numeric input in the range 1 to 10, what happens when values at the boundaries of these values are entered, that is, such values as 0 and 1 around the lower boundary and 10 and 11 around the higher boundary? Such test data are more likely to reveal problems than several values such as 2, 6, 7, 8 which are all within the expected input range.

Boundary value analysis is the name given to a commonly used black box testing procedure for the identification of classes of test data at the boundaries of expected inputs and from which test cases can be created. Boundary value analysis extends the idea of equivalence classes by concentrating on the values at the boundaries of equivalence classes rather than those within them. For example, with a test class for a numeric value in a certain range, values at both ends of the range and just below and above the range would be selected for test cases.

Where a number of values are to be entered, test cases would be chosen for the minimum number of values, the maximum number of values, one less than the minimum and one more than the maximum.

The rules for applying boundary value analysis are:

1.   Identify the valid and invalid equivalence classes.

2.   Identify boundary values for the valid and invalid equivalence classes.

3.   Produce test cases using the rules for equivalence classes.

The procedure for determining test cases using boundary value analysis is illustrated in Table 32.4, using the same example provided earlier for equivalence classes. Note that sometimes a boundary value for a class does not exist; where this occurs there is no entry in the table.

Since the first character of Item can be either upper or lower case, there are in effect two lower boundaries, 'a' and 'A', and two upper boundaries, 'z' and 'Z', for the valid equivalence class. However, there are no boundary values for the invalid equivalence class; we can simply choose a non-alphabetic character as an invalid test case.

Input condition	Valid			Invalid	
Quantity		BV	Class No		BV	Class No
Value	1-99	1	*1*	< 1	0	*13*
		99	*2*	> 99	100	*14*
				Non-numeric		
				Non-integer		
Item						
1st character	Alphabetic	'a' 'A' 'z' 'Z'	*3* *4* *5* *6*	non-alphabetic		*17*
Size	4 chars	4 chars	*7*	< 4 chars	3 chars	*18*
				> 4 chars	5 chars	*19*
Last 3 chars	Numeric	'000' '999'	*8* *9*	Non-numeric		*20*
Payment						
Value	'P', 'C' or 'D'	'P' 'C' 'D'	*10* *11* *12*	Not 'P', 'C' or 'D'		*21*

Table 32.4. *Determining test cases for boundary analysis*

These boundary values lead to test cases such as those shown in Table 32.5.

Test case	Inputs			Classes covered	Type
	Quantity	Item	Payment		
1	1	a000	'P'	*1,3,7,8,10*	Valid
2	99	A999	'C'	*2,4,7,9,11*	Valid
3	44	z678	'D'	*5,12*	Valid
4	7	Z123	'D'	*6,12*	Valid
5	0	D123	'C'	*13*	Invalid
6	100	s345	'P'	*14*	Invalid
7	lab	S123	'P'	*15*	Invalid
8	1·26	f123	'P'	*16*	Invalid
9	25	0123	'P'	*17*	Invalid
10	36	el	'P'	*18*	Invalid
11	65	a1234	'C'	*19*	Invalid
12	33	abcd	'D'	*20*	Invalid
13	10	v123	'B'	*21*	Invalid

Table 32.5. *Test cases for boundary values*

White box testing

Here the program code is examined in order to determine the various routes that can be followed through the program. This approach requires a knowledge of the language being used, and in particular being able to recognise and understand conditional and looping instructions. The following example illustrates the process for dealing with conditional instructions within a program.

Covering multiple conditions in a program

Suppose that a mail order firm supplies goods to locations all over the world. An order from a customer is given a code, and if this code is of type A, B or C a discount on the total cost of the order is given. In addition, providing the order exceeds a minimum value, postage is free for customers within the UK.

The pseudo-code in Listing 32.1 illustrates typical instructions which might be used to determine the total charge to the customer. It is assumed that the variables Quantity and UnitCost have already been assigned values.

Listing 32.1   Calculate total customer charge for order

```
1     {Calculate the order value}
2     TotalCost = Quantity * UnitCost
3
4     {Determine whether any discount can be allowed}
5     select
6       when OrderCode = 'A' or OrderCode = 'B' or OrderCode = 'C'
7          Discount  = TotalCost * DISCOUNT_RATE
8       when otherwise
9            Discount = 0
10    endselect
11
12    {Adjust the order value to allow for discount}
13    TotalCost = TotalCost − Discount
14
15    {Determine whether postage and packing needs to be charged}
16    select
17      when TotalCost > MIN_ORDER-VALUE and Country = 'GB'
18          Postage = 0
19      when otherwise
20          Postage = PP_RATE
21    endselect
22
23    {Adjust the order value to allow for postage and packing}
24    TotalCost = TotalCost + Postage
```

The code shows how the discount and the postage might be calculated given the three constants DISCOUNT_RATE, PP_RATE and MIN_ORDER_VALUE (assumed to be £100).

We need to ensure that the compound conditional instructions on lines *6* and *17* are fully tested. This is accomplished by identifying test classes which cause each part of the conditional instruction to be true and false. For instance, on line *6* we must use test data such that the order code is of type 'A' (so that the condition OrderCode = 'A' is true), and also such that the order code is not of type 'A' (so that the condition OrderCode = 'A' is false). The same applies to the other two order codes, 'B' and 'C'. A *truth table* of the type shown in Table 32.6 is a convenient way to organise these requirements.

| | Order type | | |
Class no.	'A'	'B'	'C'
1	T	F	F
2	F	T	F
3	F	F	T
4	F	F	F

Table 32.6. *Truth table for OrderCode types*

The entries under the column headings 'A', 'B' and 'C' show that for the first class, the order will be type 'A', in the second class test the order type will be 'B' and in the third class, the order will be of type 'C'. In addition, we must also use a fourth test for the case where the order type is other than these three types in the table. The same procedure needs to be used for the second conditional statement on line *17*. The truth table is shown in Table 32.7.

| Class No. | Condition | |
	TotalCost > MinOrderValue	Country = 'GB'
5	T	T
6	T	F
7	F	T
8	F	F

Table 32.7. *Truth table for second conditional statement on Line 17*

Again, all of the possible combinations of the two conditions are covered, adding a further four test classes.

Having identified all of the paths through the program, we must now devise test cases using data which ensures that all of the paths are covered. Table 32.8 shows the data for four test cases which accomplish this requirement.

Test case	OrderCode	TotalCost	Country	Classes covered
1	'A'	123	'GB'	1, 5
2	'B'	720.45	'USA'	2, 6
3	'C'	62	'GB'	3, 7
4	'D'	27.34	'XXX'	4, 8

Table 32.8. *Data for four test cases*

Notice that this table illustrates that we can cover more than one test class with a single set of test data as long as all of the classes are covered by the total set of tests.

Covering loops within a program

We need to create test data, where possible, to cover the following situations:

- ❏ Going through the loop the minimum number of times (which may mean skipping the loop entirely).

- ❏ Executing the loop once (if not covered above).

- ❏ Executing the loop the maximum number of times.

- ❏ Executing the loop one less than the maximum number of times.

- ❏ Executing the loop several times (between the maximum and minimum number).

For example, consider the pseudocode program fragment in Listing 32.2.

Listing 32.2   Pseudocode program fragment to illustrate testing of loops

```
Total = 0
Count = 0
write 'Enter the cost of the first item, or 0 to end'
read Amount
while Amount > 0
    Count = Count + 1
    Total = Total + Amount
    write <newline>, 'Enter the cost of the next item, or 0 to end'
    read Amount
endwhile
write <newline>
write   <newline>, Count, 'Items were purchased'
write   <newline>
write 'The total cost was: £', Total
```

Suitable test data for the program fragment may be as shown in Table 32.9.

Test case	Test data (Amount followed by 0)	Comment
1	0	Minimum number of times through loop, i.e. none
2	12·23, 0	Once only through loop
3	25·67, 17·99, 222·05, 123·45, 6·91, 0	Several times through loop

Table 32.9. *Test data for program fragment*

In this instance, because there is no maximum limit to the number of amounts that can be entered, we cannot devise test data for the maximum repetitions or for one less than the maximum, but in the case of the next example this is possible. In this example the loop is set to repeat a fixed number of times determined by the constant, LoopLimit. To change the number of times the loop is repeated, we simply alter this constant in the program as shown below.

```
LoopLimit = 10
Count = 0
while Count < LoopLimit
    {Instructions to be repeated are here}
    . . . . . . . .
    . . . . . . . .
    Count = Count + 1
endwhile
```

The test cases for `LoopLimit` are shown in Table 32.10.

Test case	LoopLimit value	Comment
1	0	Minimum number of times through loop, i.e. none
2	1	Once only through loop
3	5	Several times through loop
4	9	One less than maximum
5	10	Maximum

Table 32.10. *Test cases for* `LoopLimit`

Test logs

Once the test cases have been devised, the program must be executed using the test data. The effect of using the test data is recorded in a *test log*. Since the point of program testing is to find errors, the log will indicate a <u>successful</u> test <u>if an error is found</u>, and an unsuccessful test otherwise.

The test log will form part of the documentation of the program so that if the program is subsequently modified, the same test data can be re-applied to ensure that no program errors have been accidentally introduced by the modifications. For each set of test data, the expected output must be determined before running the program so that it can be compared with the actual output produced by the program.

The test log could be set out in tabular form as follows.

TEST LOG

Date:

Program name:

Version:

Author:

Tested by:

Test case	Expected output	Observed output	Result	Comments
1				
2				
3				
4				
etc				

Validation

At some point the programmer must decide that the program has had sufficient testing. He or she will be confident that the program will operate according to specification and without 'crashing' or 'hanging up' under extreme or unexpected circumstances; the reputation of a professional programmer relies on this. Prior to release, the final testing is then performed by the user for whom the program was developed. The programmer may have overlooked areas of difficulty because it is often hard to consider a problem objectively or entirely from the viewpoint of the user. If this is the case, that the operation of the program is not entirely satisfactory, the program will be modified and re-tested until all user requirements are met.

Program documentation requirements

The documentation produced for a program will depend on a number of factors. For instance, a program which validates a temporary file prior to creating it permanently will probably require a minimum of user interaction and only a small number of user instructions. However, at some later date, it might be necessary for the author of the program, or a different programmer, to modify it. This possibility means that the structure of the program will have to be explained in great detail, and test procedures to ensure its correct operation will need to be provided.

A general purpose program such as a spreadsheet, designed for people who just want to use the computer as a tool, will require extremely detailed instructions regarding its function and use. Such programs are generally accompanied by detailed user manuals and tutorials. On the other hand, users would not be expected (and definitely not encouraged) to modify the program coding; thus no details would be provided regarding the way the program has been written. This latter type of documentation would only be required for the people responsible for producing the program. In addition to the documentation requirements of users and programmers, there is a third category of person to be considered. These are people such as managers who are neither likely to use programs extensively nor want to attempt to modify them. They merely need to have an overview of the program - its function, capabilities, hardware requirements etc.

Thus there are many factors governing the coverage of documentation, and for this reason in the next section it is only possible to provide a checklist of items which might reasonably be included.

Documentation checklist

The documentation for a simple program generally falls into four sections:

❑   Identification.

❑   General specification.

❑   User information.

❑   Program specification.

Most users will need access to the first three sections; in general the fourth section will only be needed if the program is to be modified. The amount of detail in each section will depend entirely on the particular application and, to some extent, the implementation language. COBOL, for example, is largely self-documenting: it contains an Identification Division containing all the information listed in the first section below; the Data Division of a COBOL program contains precise details regarding all of the files used by the program and which devices are required; the Procedure Division is written in 'English-like' sentences which are generally easy to understand, even by a non-programmer. Consequently, a program written in COBOL will generally require less documentation than one written in Pascal or C, languages which are not self-documenting. The following checklist is a guide to what might reasonably be included in the documentation for a program.

1. Identification.

❑   Title of program.

❑   Short statement of its function.

❑   Author.

❑   Date written.

❑   Language used and version if relevant.

❑   Hardware requirements.

2. General specification.

❑   Description of the main action(s) of the program under normal circumstances.

❑   File specifications.

❑   Restrictions and/or limitations of the program.

❑   Equations used or references to texts explaining any complex procedures /techniques involved.

3. Program specification.

❑   Structure charts/flowcharts/decision tables.

❑   Annotated listing.

❑   Testing procedure including test classes and test data with expected output and a test log.

4. User Guide.

❑   Installation instructions

❑   Detailed explanation of the operation of the program

❑   Tutorial

❑   Screen shots

❑   Troubleshooting guide

✍️Exercises

1. Explain the difference between white box and black box testing.

2. What valid and invalid equivalence classes would you define for programs which accept the following inputs:

    (i)   a single integer value in the range 1 to 99;

    (ii)   a single name containing only alphabetic characters;

    (iii) a single numeric digit;

    (iv)   an integer representing the number of units of a certain item sold, followed by the unit cost of the item;

    (v)   three names separated by commas;

    (vi)   a post code of the form *AA99 9AA*, where *A* represents any alphabetic character and *9* represents any numeric digit;

    (vii) a telephone number which starts with an area code followed by a space.

    Devise test cases for your test classes.

3. Use white box testing methods to devise test classes and test cases for the following fragments of pseudocode:

(i)

```
if (Letter = 'a') or
   (Letter = 'e') or
   (Letter = 'i') or
   (Letter = 'o') or
   (Letter = 'u')
then
   VowelCount:= VowelCount + 1
endif
```

(ii)

```
if a > b then
   Temp:= a
   a:= b
   b:= Temp
endif
if b > c then
   Temp:= b
   b:= c
   c:= Temp
endif
```

(iii)

```
Count:= 0;
if a = b then
   Count:= Count + 1
endif
if b = c then
   Count:= Count + 1
endif
if c = a then
   Count:= Count + 1
endif
select
  when Count = 0
    TriangleType:= 0
  when Count = 1
    TriangleType:= 2
  when Count = 2
    {not possible}
  when Count = 3
    TriangleType:= 3
endselect
```

(iv)

```
repeat
  {get character from keyboard using}
  {readkey function                  }
   key:= readkey

  {check that character is a numeric}
  {digit                            }
   if (key >= '0') and (key <= '9')
      then
         write(key)   {echo to screen}
   endif

until key = ' '{exit loop only when }
              {spacebar pressed     }
```

Chapter 33

Data Structures

A sound knowledge of basic data structures is essential for any computer programmer. A programming task will almost invariably involve the manipulation of a set of data which normally will be organised according to some coherent structure. It could be that the data is to be read in and processed, in which case a detailed knowledge of its structure is essential. Furthermore, processing the data might involve organising it in a way that facilitates its subsequent retrieval, as in information retrieval applications. Output from the program might require that the data is presented in yet another form. So a single program might be required to handle a number of data structures; only by having a thorough knowledge of basic data structures can the programmer choose, or design, the structures most appropriate to the problems being addressed.

From a programming viewpoint, the study of data structures involves two aspects, namely, the theoretical principles upon which the structures are founded, and the practicalities of implementing them using a computer. This chapter addresses both of these considerations by describing a number of important data structures and their applications to programming tasks.

A data structure is essentially a number of data items, also called elements or nodes, with some relationship linking them together. Each item consists of one or more named parts called fields occupying one or more memory locations in the computer. In its simplest form, an element can be a single field located in a single word of memory. A list of numbers occupying consecutive memory locations in a computer is a simple data structure called an *array* and an example is shown in Table 33.1.

memory location	contents
1000	56
1001	34
1002	123
1003	11
1004	77

Table 33.1. *Array data structure*

The relationship linking the individual elements is merely the order in which they are stored in memory. In order to access the next element in the list (that is, an element's successor) it is necessary only to increment the memory address; the previous element at any point in the list (that is an elements predecessor) is found by decrementing the current memory address. This simple structural relationship allows the list to be accessed in sequential order.

Data structures such as *linked lists* provide pointers linking elements together. So, for example, to access the above numeric list in ascending order of magnitude, an extra field could be added to each element to point to the next element in the sequence, as shown in Table 33.2.

memory location	link field	value
1000	1004	56
1001	1000	34
1002	0000	123
1003	1001	11
1004	1002	77

Table 33.2. *Linked list*

Now, starting with location 1003 and following the links, the list can be accessed in ascending order: the link contained in location 1003 indicates that the number succeeding 11 is in location 1001; location 1001 contains the number 34 plus a pointer showing that the next number in the sequence is to be found at location 1000; the list terminates at location 1002 which contains the final number, 123, and a zero link indicating that there are no more elements in the list. Linked lists make it easier to insert or delete elements at any position in the sequence of items, at the cost of increased complexity and increased memory demands. Other data structures such as *stacks* and *queues* restrict access to elements to certain points of a sequential data structure, normally the start or end. With stacks, elements may only be added or deleted at one end of the list; queues allow items to be added at one end and deleted at the other.

The attraction of using a simple array data structure is that a data item may be accessed by means of a simple key which specifies its position within the array. So, for example, if we used an array to store details of a collection of 30 videos, and we assigned to each of them a different code number in the range 1 to 30, searching the array for the details of a particular video would merely entail entering the code number; the required details would be obtained in a fixed length of time by using the code number as an index value.

However, if for a video hire shop we also wanted to use an array to store its videos, so that any one could be accessed in the shortest possible time, the amount of storage space required would be prohibitive. For instance, using a six-digit key would require 1,000,000 digits to be stored for the keys alone, and then the video details would be in addition. If the key was to be used to encode information concerning the video - how many duplicates, children's or adult's for example - then we would expect that out of these 1,000,000 possible keys only a relatively small proportion of them would be used. Suppose that this proportion is 10%, that is, the system is only intended to cope with a maximum of 1,000 videos. Then 90% of the space allocated to the storage of video details would be wasted. What is required is a method of mapping the 1,000,000 keys to a table containing only 1,000 keys. Hashing allows us to do this by applying a *hash function* to the key to produce an integer, in a much smaller range, which is used as the actual index to the table containing the records. The chief disadvantage of this scheme is that the hashing function will most probably generate non-unique index values, that is, two different keys could easily produce exactly the same index. This is termed a *collision*, and any hashing process must allow for this occurrence and cope with it using a *collision resolution strategy*.

Where a data structure is to be searched using an alphabetic key such as a surname, which could be incorrectly spelled, a useful method of coping with this problem is to use *Soundex Coding*. This allows words which sound alike, though spelled differently, to be given an identical code.

Arrays

Storage of arrays

High-level procedural languages such as BASIC, COBOL and Pascal allow programmers to manipulate tabular data stored in *arrays*. The programmer merely declares the name, size and dimension of the array and the language processor takes care of allocating memory for it. The immediate access store (memory) of a computer consists of a large number of memory locations, each with its own unique address (see Chapter 4). Memory locations have addresses ranging from 0 to $n-1$, where n represents the total number of memory locations available in the computer. For example, in a computer which has 640K bytes of user memory, byte addresses will range from 0 to $(640 \times 1024)-1$, that is, 0 to 655359. If a programmer defines a one-dimensional array of, say, twenty integers each occupying a single word, then the language processor must assign sufficient storage space for the array in user RAM and be able to find any array element as quickly as possible. Locating an array element requires a small calculation involving the starting address of the array, which is termed the *base address*, and the number of bytes per array element. For example, suppose we have a one-dimensional array A_k of single byte words, where k is over the range 0 to 20, with base address b. Then element A_0 will have address $b + 0 = b$. Element A_1 will have address $b + 1$ and, in general, element A_k will have address $b + k$.

Figure 33.1 shows the relationship between array elements and memory locations.

Figure 33.1. *Array-memory relationship*

Because the memory of a computer is essentially a one-dimensional array of memory locations, when it is required to represent a two-dimensional table, a slightly more complicated calculation is necessary: the language processor must convert the subscripts of two-dimensional array element into a one-dimensional physical memory address. Consider the storage requirements of a two-dimensional array, $T_{j,k}$ single word integers and size 10×6 that is, a table with 10 rows (j=0 to 9) and 6 columns (k=0 to 5) as shown in Figure 33.2.

Figure 33.2. *Two-dimensional array*

If the base address is at location b, and the array is stored row by row, then the elements of the array might be stored in memory as shown in Figure 33.3.

Figure 33.3. *Storage of array in memory*

The positions marked by an × in Figures 33.2 and 33.3 show the correspondence between a two-dimensional array element and the same element's memory address. The calculation required to convert the position of a two-dimensional array element $T_{j,k}$ to a memory location, M, is

$$M = b + j \times 6 + k$$

For example, element $T_{0,3}$ would occupy the location

$$M = b + 0 \times 6 + 3 = b + 3,$$

and element $T_{3,2}$ would be at location

$$M = b + 3 \times 6 + 2 = b + 20$$

The calculations above assume that the array is of size 10×6. In general, if the array is of size $m \times n$, then an element Tj,k would translate to the location

$$M = b + j \times n + k$$

This is called a *mapping function*, a formula which uses the array size and the element subscripts to calculate the memory address at which that element is located.

Note that if the array is stored column by column rather than row by row, the mapping function becomes

$$M = b + k \times m + j$$

Extending this scheme to an array, $D_{i,j,k}$, of three dimensions and size $l \times m \times n$, the conversion calculation becomes,

$$M = b + i \times m \times n + j \times n + k$$

Figure 33.4 illustrates the correspondence between array elements and memory locations for a three-dimensional table of size $3 \times 5 \times 6$.

Here, i can be considered to be the subscript which specifies a number of tables, each of size j × k. Thus, $D_{2,3,5}$ references element (3,5) of the third table (for which $i=2$). This corresponds to the location

$$M = b + 2 \times 5 \times 6 + 3 \times 6 + 5 = b + 83$$

Further application of the principles explained above allow arrays of any number of dimensions to be handled.

Figure 33.4. *Three-dimensional array and memory mappings*

Iliffe vectors

When speed has a higher priority than memory requirements, a *table look-up* scheme is sometimes adopted for accessing array elements. The main drawback of using a mapping function is the time taken to perform the address calculation, which will generally involve one or more relatively slow multiplication operations.

The number of calculations can be significantly reduced by pre-calculating row or column addresses and storing them in another table. For example, suppose that we have

k j	0	1	2	3	4
0	b	b+1	b+2	b+3	b+4
1	b+5	b+6	b+7	b+8	b+9
2	b+10	b+11	b+12	b+13	b+14

Figure 33.5. *3 × 5 array*

a 3 × 5 array as illustrated in Figure 33.5. We first calculate, and then store in three consecutive memory locations, the starting address for each of the three rows. This is called an Iliffe vector (see Figure 33.6).

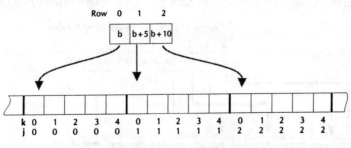

Figure 33.6. *Use of Iliffe vector*

So, given the row subscript for the array element to be accessed, the Iliffe vector is consulted for the starting address of that row, and the location of the required element is found by using the column subscript as an offset to be added to this row address.

When implemented in assembly language or machine code using appropriate addressing modes, this scheme virtually eliminates the necessity for any address calculations.

Access tables

The principle of using a table containing the starting addresses of data items is particularly useful for accessing elements of string arrays. Figure 33.7 shows how an access table is used to point to the starting locations of string array elements stored in memory.

Figure 33.7. *Access table for string arrays*

The array S_k (k= 0 to 4) to be represented consists of a number of string elements of variable sizes, each terminated by a special character indicating the end of the string. In this instance, the strings, with their subscripts, are:

```
0 CPU
1 Disk Drive
2 Printer
3 Random Access Memory
4 Monitor
```

The access table contains entries which point to the starting locations of each of the strings in order. For example, if the element S_3 was to be accessed, the entry in the access table corresponding to this element (that is, the element with subscript 3) provides the starting address for S_3 which has a value Random Access Memory. Sometimes, rather than indicating the end of a string element by means of a special character, such as an ASCII carriage return code, the access table is used in conjunction with another table giving the length of the string (Figure 33.8).

Figure 33.8. *Access table and string length table*

This scheme improves access speed but at the expense of additional storage requirements.

Search strategies

Having stored a number of data items in an array, it is more than likely that it will be necessary at some time to search the data structure for the occurrence of specific items of data. For example, suppose that an array A_k (k=0 to 9999) is being used to store stolen credit card numbers, and it is to be searched in order to ascertain whether a shop customer is using a stolen credit card. The search algorithm might be as shown in Listing 33.1.

Listing 33.1.   Sequential search

```
{search_array}
k:= 0
pos:= -1
card_found: = FALSE
while k < array_size and not card_found
   if S(k) = Card_number
      then card_found:= TRUE;
      pos:= k
   endif
k:= k+1
endwhile
if card_found
   then card number is located in S(pos)
          else card number is not in stolen cards list
endif
```

Each element in the list is compared with the number of the customer's card; if a match is found, the iteration is terminated by setting the boolean variable card_found to true, and the position of the value in the array is stored in the variable pos; if the loop ends and the variable card_found still has a value of false, then the customer's card is not in the list of stolen credit cards. The technique is called a *sequential search*. Though very straightforward, a sequential search can be very time consuming, since it could necessitate the complete list of 10,000 elements being searched. A faster method is possible if the list of card numbers is in ascending or descending numerical order. This alternative method is called binary search, or sometimes binary chop. For example, suppose that the list of stolen card numbers is in ascending numerical order, then a binary search proceeds as follows:

1. Set the array subscript to mid, middle value. In this case, mid is 9999/2, which is 5000 to the nearest integer.

2. Compare required card_number with S(mid).

3. (a) If card_number<S(mid) then card_number can only be in the first half of the array.

   (b) If card_number>S(mid) then card_number can only be somewhere in the latter half of the array.

(c)   If card_number=S(mid) then the card number has been found.

4.   If the card number has not yet been found, repeat from step 1 using mid as the size of the array.

The procedure successively reduces the size of the array to be searched by a factor of two. For an array of size 10,000, this means that only a maximum of 14 elements need to be examined in order to determine whether a particular element is a member of the list. Thus, for 10,000 elements, the search size reduces as shown in Table 33.3.

number of comparisons	array size to be searched
0	10,000
1	5,000
2	2,500
3	1,250
4	625
5	313
6	157
7	79
8	40
9	20
10	10
11	5
12	3
13	2
14	1

Table 33.3. *Array sizes and number of comparisons in binary chop*

Notice that 2^{14} is the smallest power of 2 which exceeds the maximum array size of 10,000:

$2^{13} = 8,192$ which is less than 10,000;

$2^{14} = 16,384$ which is greater than 10,000.

This is how the maximum figure of 14 comparisons has been derived. A more formal version of the binary search algorithm can be stated as in Listing 33.2.

Listing 33.2.   Binary chop

```
{binary}
low:= 0
high:= array_size - 1
pos:= -1
card_found:= FALSE
while low < high and not card_found
```

```
    mid:= int((low + high))/2
    select
      when S(mid) = card_number
        card_found:= TRUE
        pos:= mid
      when S(mid) > card_number
        high:= mid - 1
      when S(mid) < card_number
        low:= mid + 1
    endselect
  endwhile
  if card_found
    then stolen card number is located in S(pos)
        else card number is not in list
  endif
```

In order to select the appropriate part of the array to be searched, the algorithm uses two variables, `low` and `high`, to store the lower and upper bounds of that part of the array. They are used to calculate the mid point, `mid`, (rounded to the nearest integer value), so that the value stored there can be compared with the value required (the card number, in this example). Each time the comparison fails, the lower or upper bound is adjusted and the procedure is repeated. The process continues until either the value is located or the lower and upper bounds coincide, in which case the value does not exist in the array. The variable `pos` is used to store the position of the value if it exists in the array; a negative value for `pos` indicates that the search was unsuccessful. The binary search method will usually be employed when the array size is large, otherwise the processing overheads caused by the algorithm's increased complexity make it unsuitable.

The stack

A *stack* is a data structure characterised by the expression Last In First Out (LIFO), meaning that the most recent item added to the stack is the first one which can be removed from the stack. A *stack pointer* is used to keep track of the last item added to the stack, that is, the current top of the stack. Suppose that we wish to implement a stack using a one-dimensional array, S_i where $i=1$ to 5. A special register, sp, must be reserved as the stack pointer, and this will have an initial value of 0 indicating that the stack is empty. To add, or *push*, an item to the stack, the following steps are required:

1.   Check that there is room in the stack to add another item. In this case, the stack is full when sp has a value of 5, that is, when all of the elements in the array S_i have been used to store items. When the stack pointer is at its maximum value, and another item is required to be stored on the stack, a *stack overflow* condition has occurred, and it will not be possible to push the item onto the stack.

2.   If an overflow condition does not exist, the stack pointer is incremented and the item is transferred to the array element pointed to by the stack pointer.

For example, suppose that the number 15 is to be pushed to the stack. After completing the operation the state of the stack will be as shown in Table 33.4, *sp* having a value of 1.

i	S_i
1	15
2	-
3	-
4	-
5	

⇐*sp=1*

i	S_i
1	15
2	6
3	21
4	-
5	

⇐*sp=3*

Table 33.4. *One item pushed to stack*   **Table 33.5.** *Stack with three items*

After adding two more numbers the stack will contain three elements and the stack pointer will have a value of 3, as shown in Table 33.5. The algorithm for pushing a value to a stack can be summarised as follows:

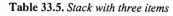

```
algorithm push              {add item to top of stack}
  if sp < maximum stack size  {test for overflow}
    then sp := sp + 1;         {increment stack ptr}
      S(sp) := item           {push item}
    else Stack overflow
  endif
end
```

To remove an item from the stack, often called *pulling* or *popping* a value, requires the reverse procedure:

1.   Check that the stack is not empty, that is, sp is greater than zero. If the stack is empty, an attempt to pull a non-existent value causes a *stack underflow* condition to arise.

2.   If the stack is not empty, the item on the top of the stack, as shown by the stack pointer, is transferred to its destination and the stack pointer is decremented.

i	S_i
1	15
2	6
3	21
4	-
5	

⇐*sp=2*

Thus, after pulling a value from the stack S_i, it would be in the state shown in Table 33.6. Notice that the value pulled from the stack, 21 in this instance, still exists in the stack; it is not necessary to actually remove a value from the stack since, by decrementing the stack pointer, this is effectively what has happened. Pulling a value from a stack is effected by copying the value to its destination before decrementing the stack pointer. The top of the stack is now the second element of the array which contains the value 6. To summarise, the algorithm for pulling a value from a stack is:

Table 33.6. *One item pulled from the stack*

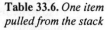

```
algorithm pop               {remove item from top of stack }
  if sp > 0                   {that is, stack is not empty   }
    then item := S(sp);        {transfer item to destination  }
      sp := sp - 1            {decrement stack pointer       }
```

```
        else stack underflow
    endif
end
```

Application of stacks

The stack is used frequently in programming languages for control structures. In some versions of BASIC, for example, GOSUB, FOR...NEXT, REPEAT...UNTIL and procedure /function calls all use stacks in their implementation.

The GOSUB instruction causes control to be transferred to the line specified in the instruction. Subroutine instructions are executed as normal until a RETURN instruction is encountered, whereupon control returns to the instruction following the last GOSUB instruction executed. Thus, with the fragments of BASIC code illustrated in Listing 33.3, the subroutine starting at line 1000 is called at line 100 by the GOSUB 1000 instruction.

The BASIC interpreter must store its current position in the program so that after executing the subroutine it can return control to this same position when a RETURN instruction is encountered. This is accomplished by pushing the return address to a stack prior to jumping to the start of the subroutine.

Listing 33.3.

```
10 REM *** Mainline program ***
. . . . . . . . . . . .
. . . . . . . . . . . .
90 REM Call subroutine at line 1000
100 GOSUB 1000
105 REM Program contines here after completing subroutine
110 LET a = x + 1
120
990 STOP
999 REM *** End of Mainline program
REM *** Subroutine code goes here
1010
. . . . . . . . . . . .
etc
. . . . . . . . . . . .
1490 RETURN
```

When a RETURN instruction is executed, the top of the stack is pulled and the interpreter continues from that address. In this way the same subroutine can be called from different parts of the program and control will always return to the instruction following the GOSUB instruction. Another reason for using a stack is that it facilitates the use of nested control structures. In the example shown in Listing 33.3 it is possible to have another GOSUB instruction in the subroutine at line 1100. (See Listing 33.4).

Listing 33.4.

```
10 REM *** Mainline program ***
. . . . . . . . . . . .
. . . . . . . . . . . .
90 REM Call subroutine at line 1000
```

```
100 GOSUB 1000
105 REM Program continues here after completing subroutine
110 LET a = x + 1
120
............
etc
............
990 STOP
999 REM *** End of Mainline program ***
1000 REM *** Subroutine code goes here ***
1010
............
1100 GOSUB 2000
1200
............
1490 RETURN
2000 REM *** Code for second subroutine goes here ***
2010
..........
etc
2490 RETURN
```

In this instance the stack is used twice: the return address appropriate to the subroutine call at line 100 is pushed to the stack, then the return address for the second, nested, subroutine call is pushed to the stack during execution of the first subroutine at line 1100. When the RETURN statement at line 2490 is executed, BASIC pulls the top of the GOSUB stack causing control to return to line 1200, the line following the most recent GOSUB instruction. The RETURN statement at line 1490 causes BASIC to pull the new top of the stack which provides the return address for the first GOSUB call at line 100. This technique allows subroutines to be nested to any depth, subject to the size of the GOSUB stack.

The same principle applies to the management of FOR..NEXT loops in BASIC. A separate stack is used to store information regarding the FOR..NEXT control variables. The BASIC interpreter stores on the stack five pieces of information when it encounters a FOR statement:

(i)   the address of the control variable;

(ii)   the type of the control variable;

(iii)   STEP size;

(iv)   TO limit;

(v)   the address of the next statement following FOR.

The stack pointer is incremented by the number of words occupied by this information, and then the statement following the FOR instruction is executed. A NEXT instruction will cause BASIC to use the information on the top of the stack to either repeat the statements between the FOR and NEXT instructions, or to exit the loop if the control variable has exceeded its maximum value. If the latter is the case, the FOR...NEXT stack pointer will be decremented to remove the top of the stack thus terminating this loop. The use of a stack again allows nesting of FOR..NEXT loops, subject to a depth governed by the size of the FOR..NEXT stack. A REPEAT..UNTIL stack is used in a similar way to that of the FOR..NEXT stack, though the procedures for managing `REPEAT..UNTIL` loops are simpler. Procedures and functions in BASIC are handled in a similar manner to the `GOSUB` structure, but the BASIC interpreter has to cope with additional problems associated with passing parameters and saving the values of local variables so that they can subsequently be restored. These extra problems are once again overcome by the use of stacks.

The queue

The data structure known as a *queue* has the same characteristics as the queues we encounter in everyday life. For instance, a queue at the checkout counter of a supermarket increases at its rear as customers join the queue to have their purchases totalled, and only reduces in size when a customer is served at the head of the queue, the checkout counter. A queue of cars at traffic lights behaves in a similar manner, with cars exiting the queue only at its head and joining the queue only at its rear. A *queue* is a data structure in which elements are added only at the rear of a linear list and removed only from the front, or head, of the list. A queue is often given the name FIFO list, from the initial letters of the words in the phrase First In First Out which describes the order of processing the elements of the list.

Suppose that an array, Q_k ($k=0$ to 31), is to be used as a queue. `Head` will be used to keep track of the front of the queue and `Rear`, the end of the queue as shown in Figure 33.9.

Figure 33.9. *Queue*

Initially, the queue is empty so that `Head` = `Rear` = 0. When an item is added to the queue, `Rear` is incremented; when an item is removed from the list, `Head` is incremented. Assuming that the queue is simply storing single alphabetic characters, Table 33.7 illustrates the operation of the queue for ten queue operations.

operation	item	Head	Rear	state of queue
		0	0	empty
1. Add item	A	0	1	A
2. Add item	C	0	2	AC
3. Add item	G	0	3	ACG
4. Add item	E	0	4	ACGE
5. Remove item	A	1	4	CGE
6. Add item	F	1	5	CGEF
7. Remove item	C	2	5	GEF
8. Remove item	G	3	5	EF
9. Remove item	E	4	5	F
10. Remove item	F	5	5	empty

Table 33.7. *Queue operations*

The following algorithms show how items are added to a queue and removed from a queue, assuming array_size is the maximum size of the array Q used for storing the queue.

```
algorithm queue {Add item to queue}
   if Rear <= array_size - 1
      then Q(Rear):= item
         Rear := Rear + 1
      else Queue is full
   endif
end
```

```
algorithm dequeue {Remove item from queue}
   if Rear <> Head
      then item := Q(Head)
         Head := Head + 1
      else Queue is empty
   endif
end
```

Notice that the queue is empty when the head pointer has the same value as the rear pointer. Notice also that, unlike a queue in real life, as items are added and removed, the queue moves through the array since both the head and rear pointers are incremented. This means that eventually the queue will run out of space, at which time an overflow condition will occur. One solution to this problem is to implement a circular queue which reuses array elements that are empty.

Circular queues

Figure 33.10 illustrates the principles of a circular queue. The circular arrangement of the array elements is merely a means of illustrating the principles of operation of a circular queue; the data structure used to store the queue is physically the same as before, that is, a one-dimensional array. Head and Rear are again used, but this time when either of them reach a value equal to m, the upper bound of the array, they start again at the beginning, using up elements which previously have been removed from the queue. The diagram shows the queue in a state where ten items have been added to the queue and three items have been removed.

Figure 33.11 shows that the queue has completely traversed the array such that Rear is equal to m, and there are five items in the queue. The next item to be added to the queue will be inserted at position 1, so that Rear has a value of 0 rather than m + 1. In other words, when Rear exceeds the upper bound reserved for the queue, it takes the value of the lower bound. The same thing applies to the Head of the queue.

Figure 33.12 shows the queue, having traversed all the elements of the array, starting to reuse unoccupied positions at the beginning of the array. A slight difficulty with a circular queue is being able to differentiate between an empty queue and a full queue; the condition for a non-empty queue can no longer be that Rear < Head since, depending how many items have been added and removed, it is possible for a non-empty queue to be such that Rear has a larger value than Head. Figures 33.11 and 33.12 illustrate both queue states, the first where Head < Rear and the second where Head > Rear.

Figure 33.10. *Principles of circular queue*   **Figure 33.11.** *Circular queue with Rear at upper bound*

One solution to this problem is to adopt the convention that Head always points to the array element immediately preceding the first item in the queue rather pointing to the first item itself; since Rear points to the last item in the queue, the condition that Head = Rear indicates an empty queue. Head and Rear are initialised to be equal to the array's upper bound rather than zero. Thus, initially, the queue is empty.

The queue becomes full only when the rear pointer catches up with the head pointer.

Figure 33.12. *Circular queue re-using deleted elements*

The algorithms shown in Listing 33.5 define the processes of adding an item to a circular queue and removing an item from a circular queue.

Listing 33.5.   Algorithms for adding and deleting queue items

```
algorithm c_queue {Add item to circular queue}
temp:= Rear {Copy Rear Pointer}
  if Rear = Upper_bound {check for upper limit}
    then Rear := Lower_bound {start at beginning or..
      else Rear := Rear + 1  .. increment rear pointer}
  endif
  if Rear <> Head {check for queue full}
    then Q(Rear) := item {add item to queue}
      else Queue is full{overflow condition}
        Rear := temp{restore Rear pointer}
  endif
end

algorithm c_dequeue{Remove item from circular queue}
  if Head <> Rear{check for queue not empty}
    then
```

```
    if Head = Upper_bound    {check for upper limit}
      then Head := Lower_bound{start at beginning or..
        else Head := Head + 1.. increment head pointer}
    endif
    item := Q(Head){remove item from queue}
  else Queue is empty{underflow condition}
endif
end
```

Applications of queues

Most printers in common use today contain a quantity of RAM for the purpose of temporarily storing (or *buffering*) data transmitted from a computer. The buffer allows the computer to transmit, for example, a few kilobytes of data to the printer very quickly and allows the printer to print it autonomously, (that is, without further intervention from the computer). This allows the computer to continue processing other tasks while the relatively slow printer deals with the data it has received. The printer buffer must operate as a queue, because the data must be printed in the same order as it was transmitted from the computer. As data is received by the printer, it is added to the buffer queue until either the computer stops transmitting data or the queue is full. The printer then commences to process the data in the queue, starting at the head of the queue and ending when the queue is empty. This process of filling up the buffer quickly and then emptying it at the speed of the printer, continues until the computer ceases to transmit data. Buffers may range in size from a few kilobytes to several megabytes of RAM. A microprocessor in the printer itself deals with the way the data queue is processed.

Circular queues are frequently used by operating systems for spooling operations. For example, in a multi-user system in which a printer is shared between a number of users, print jobs may be spooled to a disk drive. The queue thus formed on the disk will be processed by the printer in the order the jobs were received (unless a priority system is in operation). As one job is printed, room will be available on the disk area allocated to the printer for another job; the circular queue principle applied to spooling will allow optimum use of the disk area allocated to print jobs. The operating system keeps track of the appropriate queue head and rear pointers required to operate the circular queue.

Linked lists

element	data
0	Aaron
1	Abelson
2	Bateman
3	Craddock
4	Dunfy
5	Eastman
6	
7	
8	
9	

Suppose that an array stores a number of items in alphabetical order as shown in Table 33.8. Adding a new item such as Gregory, while maintaining the alphabetic ordering, is easy, as Table 33.9 shows. The item is added to the end of the list. However, to insert Crawford requires more effort: all of those entries after Craddock must be moved down the array so that Crawford may be inserted immediately after Craddock. The list is then as shown in Table 33.10.

For a list containing hundreds or thousands of entries, this process could be considerably time-consuming.

An alternative approach is to introduce a second array containing pointers which link the elements together in the required order. Now an element, or *node*, contains a pointer in addition to the data.

Table 33.8. *Array with items in alphabetical order*

So, returning to the original list in Table 33.8, it would be represented as follows in Table 33.11.The original list is now in *linked list* form. Given the start position of the list, stored in Start, the pointers link the items together in the correct alphabetical order. The end of the list is indicated by a *null pointer*, in this case −1. Another pointer, Free, keeps track of the next free location for storing new items, and it is incremented whenever a new item is inserted or added to the list.

element	data
0	Aaron
1	Abelson
2	Bateman
3	Craddock
4	Dunfy
5	Eastman
6	Gregory
7	
8	
9	

element	data
0	Aaron
1	Abelson
2	Bateman
3	Craddock
4	Crawford
5	Dunfy
6	Eastman
7	Gregory
8	
9	

	node	data	pointer
start	0	Aaron	1
	1	Abelson	2
	2	Bateman	3
	3	Craddock	4
	4	Dunfy	5
	5	Eastman	−1
free	6		
	7		
	8		
	9		

Table 33.9. *Adding an item to the end*   Table 33.10. *Inserting an item to maintain*   Table 33.11. *Linked list*

Adding Gregory to the list would entail changing the Eastman pointer from 1 to 6 (that is, the value currently given by Free) and putting Gregory at the position indicated by Free (Table 33.12).

	node	data	pointer
start	0	Aaron	1
	1	Abelson	2
	2	Bateman	3
	3	Craddock	4
	4	Dunfy	5
	5	Eastman	6
	6	Gregory	−1
free	7		
	8		
	9		

Table 33.12. *Adding Gregory to the linked list*

Gregory is given a null pointer (−1) to indicate that it is the last item in the list, and Free is incremented.

In pseudocode form, the steps illustrated above to add an item to the end of a linked list are as shown in Listing 33.6.

Listing 33.6.   Adding a node to a linked list

```
algorithm add_node
  i := Start;              {copy start pointer                          }
  while ptr(i)<> null  {follow pointers until null pointer found}
    i := ptr(i)
  endwhile
  ptr(i) := Free           {link new item to current last node          }
  data(Free) := item       {store new data in next free node            }
  ptr(Free) := null        {store null pointer in next free node        }
  Free := Free + 1         {increment next free ptr                     }
end
```

The notation ptr(i) is used for the pointer located at node i, and data(i) represents the data at node i. For example, in the alphabetical list above, ptr(2) = 3 and data(2) = Bateman.

Now, to add Crawford only one pointer is altered, rather than rearranging the items in the array, and the new node is added to the end of the list (Table 33.13).

	node	data	pointer	
start	0	Aaron	1	
	1	Abelson	2	
	2	Bateman	3	
	3	Craddock	7	
	4	Dunfy	5	
	5	Eastman	6	
	6	Gregory	−1	
	7	Crawford	4	inserted node
free	8			
	9			

Table 33.13. *Inserting a node into the linked list*

Thus, the order of accessing the array in alphabetical order is 0 - 1 - 2 - 3 - 7 - 4 - 5 - 6.

In pseudocode, the algorithm for inserting a node to maintain the alphabetic ordering, is shown in Listing 33.7.

Listing 33.7.   Algorithm for insertion of node into linked list

```
algorithm insert_node
  i := Start {copy start pointer}
  found := FALSE
    repeat
      if data(i) > item{ie alphabetically}
              or Start = null {allow for empty list}
```

```
        then found := TRUE{insertion position found}
        else p := i {save current node}
           i := ptr(p) {next node in list}
    endif
  until found {insertion position located}
         or i = null {reached end of list}
  if i = start
      then data(Free) := item {insert at head of list}
        ptr(Free) := Start
        Start := Free
      else ptr(p) = Free; {insert in body of list}
        data(Free) := item
        ptr(Free) := i
  endif
  Free := Free + 1 {increment next-free pointer}
end
```

The increased complexity of the algorithm arises partly from the necessity to allow for the list being initially empty, this state being recognised by Start containing a null pointer. If the list is empty initially, then Start is set equal to Free which contains a pointer to the first available node, and the new data together with a null pointer are stored in this node. To delete a node merely entails ensuring that its predecessor's pointer links the node following it. For example, to delete Bateman, the pointers would be adjusted as shown in Table 33.14.

	node	data	pointer	
start	0	Aaron	1	
	1	Abelson	3	
	2	**Bateman**	3	deleted node
	3	Craddock	7	
	4	Dunfy	5	
	5	Eastman	6	
	6	Gregory	−1	
	7	Crawford	4	
free	8			
	9			

Table 33.14. *Adjustment of pointers after deletion of node*

The pointer order is now 0 - 1 - 3 - 7 - 4 - 5 - 6, which misses out the third item in the array containing Bateman. The pseudocode algorithm is shown in Listing 33.8.

Listing 33.8. Algorithm for deleting node from list

```
algorithm delete_node
  i := Start                              {copy start pointer}
  found := FALSE
  repeat
```

```
      if data(i) = item or Start = null {found node or empty list}

          then found := TRUE                {deletion position found}
          else p := i                       {save current node}
            i := ptr(p)                     {next node in list}
      endif
   until found or i = null                  {deletion position located
                                             or reached end of list}

    if Start = null or i = null             {ie empty list or reached
                                             end of list without
                                             finding node}

      then node does not exist!             {impossible to delete node}
      else if i = start
              then Start := ptr(i)          {delete head of list}
              else ptr(p) := ptr(i)         {skip node in body of list}
           endif
    endif
 end
```

The algorithm allows for three special cases:

(i)   the list is empty - this means that it is not possible to delete an element;

(ii)   the item to be deleted is not in the list - it is impossible to delete this item;

(iii) the item to be deleted is the first one in the list - this requires that Start must be set to point to the second node in the linked list.

With a linked list it is possible to locate any element by following the pointers, irrespective of the physical location of the item. Rather than storing the list in consecutive elements of an array, confined to a certain range of memory locations, it is perfectly feasible to store the elements of the linked list anywhere in the memory space allocated to a user program. For this reason, an alternative, and more general, diagrammatic form is often used for linked lists, in which each node contains one or more pointers and one or more words of data. For example, the linked list in Table 33.14 might be represented as shown in Figure 33.13.

Figure 33.13. *Representation of linked list*

Arrowed lines are used to show the order in which nodes are linked together, and special nodes indicate the start point of the list and the next free node.

Linked lists have a number of advantages over arrays :

❑   Greater flexibility for the location of nodes in memory (it is even possible for nodes to be located on auxiliary storage, such as magnetic disks, rather than in main memory).

❑   The ease with which nodes may be added or deleted from the list.

❑   By adding more pointers, the list may be traversed in a number of different orders.

On the debit side for linked lists:

❑   Locating specific items necessitates searching the list from the start node, whereas arrays allow direct access to elements.

❑   Linked lists require more memory because of the need for pointers.

❑   Linked lists involve more housekeeping operations because of the necessity to change pointers when adding or deleting nodes.

Applications of linked lists

With an interpreted language such as BASIC, variables must be accessed as quickly as possible so that program processing speed is acceptably fast. One method of ensuring this is by the use of linked lists. In one such scheme, used by Acorn BASIC, variables starting with the same character are given their own linked list, so that there is a linked list for each possible starting character. Though the lists are quite separate, each with its own start pointer, they occupy a common area of memory and link around each other. Each node in the linked lists contains the name and value of the variable, plus a pointer to the next variable with the same starting letter. Figure 33.14 illustrates this scheme at the stage where a number of variables with starting letters A, B or C have been created.

Figure 33.14. *Creation of BASIC variables in linked list*

The start pointers for the linked lists are stored in a table in a specific area of memory. The first pointer in the table contains the address of the node for the first variable starting with the letter

A to be created in the current program, in this case AX. This node contains a pointer to the second variable created, AY, and its node contains a pointer to AZ, the last variable created starting with the letter A. Similar lists occur for the variables starting with B (B1 and B2) and C *(CostP, CostS, CV* and *C12)*. Because the lists link around each other, there is a common free-space pointer for all the lists.

To find a particular variable's node, the starting letter of the variable is converted into an address giving the start pointer for its linked list, and the nodes of this list are traversed in pointer order until the variable is located. For example, suppose that the table of start pointers was at memory location 1000, and the variable *BZ* is to be accessed. The letter *B* is first converted into a number indicating its position in the alphabet, that is 2, and this is added to the start address of the table.

Thus, 1000 + 2 = 1002 is the location of the start pointer for the linked list of variables beginning with B. The first node in the list is for variable B1, which is not the one required, so its pointer is used to access the next node in the list. This time the variable found is *BZ* as required.

For a program containing many variables, this scheme can dramatically reduce the time required to locate a certain variable, provided variable names are chosen with different starting letters. It is worth noting that in this instance, a knowledge of the internal organisation of an interpreter can help the programmer to write more efficient programs.

Linked lists are also used for procedures and functions so that they can be located as quickly as possible no matter where in the program they are referenced. Otherwise, a program would have to be searched sequentially from the beginning every time a procedure or function was invoked.

The tree

The term *tree* refers to a non-linear data structure in which nodes have two or more pointers to other nodes, forming a hierarchical structure as illustrated in Figure 33.15.

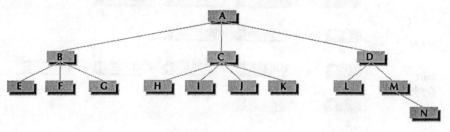

Figure 33.15. *Tree structure*

Node A is the *root* node of the entire tree with pointers to three *subtrees*. *B, C* and *D* are known as *children* of the *parent* node *A*. Similarly, *E, F* and *G* are children of *B*. Nodes *B* to *N* are all descendants of *A*, just as nodes *L* to *N* are all descendants of *D*. Nodes such as *H, I* and *L*, which have no children, are known as leaves or terminal nodes.

Trees are useful for representing hierarchical relationships between data items, such as those found in databases. For example, a record in an employee file might have the structure shown in Figure 33.16.

Stored as a tree, the data can be accessed in a number of ways. For example, extracting the first level of the tree provides a summary of the employee, giving Name, Home county, Sex, Post and Holidays taken; accessing only the fourth subtree provides details of the employee's current position; accessing the tree in order of the five subtrees provides all the employee's details.

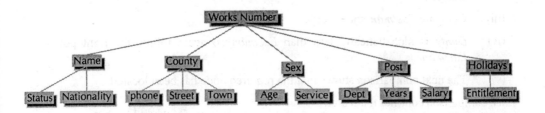

Figure 33.16. *Tree showing hierarchical structure of fields in an employee record*

A binary tree is a particular type of tree which has more uses than a general tree as described above, and is also much easier to implement. Binary trees are described in the following two sections.

Binary trees

A binary tree is a special type of tree in which each parent has a maximum of two children which are linked to the parent node using a left pointer and a right pointer. The general form of a binary tree is shown in Figure 33.17.

Figure 33.17. *Binary tree*

Binary trees have many important applications, a number of which are described in the next section. This section explores the nature of binary trees, how they are created, modified and accessed.

In the previous section we saw that in order to locate a specific node in a linked list it is necessary to search the list from the beginning, following the pointers linking the nodes together in the appropriate order. For a list containing a large number of elements, this process could be very time consuming.

The solution to the same problem with an array structure was to use the binary search technique (see section on Search Strategies); the same principle can be applied to a linked list if the list is in the form of a *binary tree*. Consider the alphabetically ordered linked list described earlier in the section on linked lists and shown in Figure 33.18.

Figure 33.18. *Alphabetically ordered linked list*

Now suppose that the same list is represented as a binary tree with two pointers in each node, one pointing to an element alphabetically less than the node data (a *left pointer*) and the other pointing to an element alphabetically greater than the node data (a *right pointer*). (See Figure 33.19).

If we were looking for *Eastman*, the procedure would be as follows:

(i)   Compare *Eastman* with the *root* node, *Craddock*.

(ii)   Because *Craddock* is alphabetically less than *Eastman*, follow the right pointer to *Dunfy*.

(iii)   Compare *Eastman* with *Dunfy*.

(iv)   *Dunfy* is alphabetically less than *Eastman* so again follow the right pointer to *Eastman*.

(v)   The next comparison shows that the required node has been located.

Each comparison confines the search to either the upper or lower part of the alphabetic list, thus significantly reducing the number of comparisons needed to locate the element required.

Figure 33.19. *Alphabetic list as binary tree*

To add an element, *Crawford* for example, to the configuration shown above, whilst retaining the alphabetic ordering, is merely a matter of searching for the new item until a null pointer is encountered. In this example, a null pointer occurs when attempting to go left at *Dunfy*. *Crawford* is installed in the next free node and *Dunfy's* left pointer points to it. The new tree is shown in Figure 33.20.

Figure 33.20. *Adding the node, Crawford*

Unfortunately, deleting a node is not quite so simple. Three cases can arise, and these are described with reference to Figure 33.21 which is an extended form of the binary tree shown above.

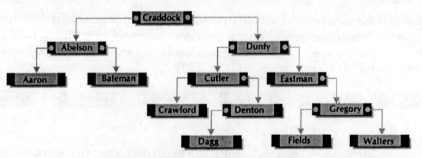

Figure 33.21. *Extended form of binary tree*

(i)   The node to be deleted is a terminal node, or leaf, having null left and right pointers. *Bateman* is an example of such a node. Deleting it is simply a matter of setting

Abelson's right pointer to the null pointer (Figure 33.22).

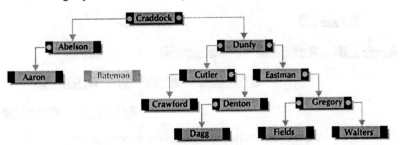

Figure 33.22. *Deletion of Bateman node which has null left and right pointers*

(ii)   The node to be deleted contains one null pointer. *Eastman* is an example of this type of node. This is handled in the same way as deleting a node from a linked list - *Dunfy's* right pointer is replaced by *Eastman's* right pointer (Figure 33.23).

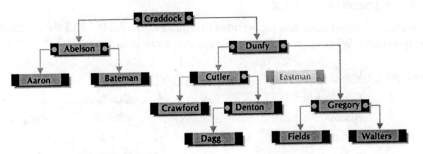

Figure 33.23. *Deletion of Eastman node which contains one null pointer*

(iii)   The node to be deleted contains no null pointers. There are two possibilities here: re-place the deleted entry with an entry from its right subtree, or an entry from its left subtree. We will consider both of these using Dunfy as the item to be deleted from the original tree.

Taking the left subtree first, the procedure is to search the left subtree for the alphabetically largest entry by following the right pointers at each node until a null pointer is found. The left subtree of *Dunfy* is shown in Figure 33.24 and the largest value is *Denton*.

Figure 33.24. *Left subtree*

In order that *Dunfy* can be deleted whilst still retaining the correct ordering, it is replaced by *Denton* and a number of pointers are adjusted as shown in Figure 33.25.

Figure 33.25. *Adjustment of pointers to delete Dunfy*

Denton's pointers are replaced by *Dunfy's* pointers; *Craddock's* pointer now points to *Denton*; *Cutler's* right pointer now points to *Dagg*.

Note that for clarity Figure 33.25 above gives the impression that nodes have been moved around, but all that occurs in practice is that pointers are changed to alter the nodes that are to be linked together or deleted; the *Dunfy* node still exists in the tree but is effectively deleted because no node pointers reference it.

This is made clear when the tree is represented in tabular form. Table 33.15 shows the structure of the original tree. With the node *Dunfy* deleted, the result is as shown in Table 33.16.

node	left	data	right
0	1	Craddock	4
1	2	Abelson	3
2	-1	Aaron	-1
3	-1	Bateman	-1
4	5	Dunfy	9
5	6	Cutler	7
6	-1	Crawford	-1
7	8	Denton	-1
8	-1	Dagg	-1
9	-1	Eastman	10
10	11	Gregory	12
11	-1	Fields	-1
12	-1	Walters	-1

node	left	data	right	
0	1	Craddock	7	
1	2	Abelson	3	
2	-1	Aaron	-1	
3	-1	Bateman	-1	
4	5	Dunfy	9	deleted
5	6	Cutler	8	
6	-1	Crawford	-1	
7	5	Denton	-1	
8	-1	Dagg	-1	
9	-1	Eastman	10	
10	11	Gregory	12	
11	-1	Fields	-1	
12	-1	Walters	-1	

Table 33.15. *Structure of original tree*   **Table 33.16.** *Tree with Dunfy deleted*

If the right subtree of *Dunfy* is selected rather than the left subtree to search for a replacement, then the procedure is very similar; this time the left pointers are followed in order to find the alphabetically smallest item, which then replaces *Dunfy*. In this case the smallest item is *Eastman* and the tree becomes as shown in Figure 33.26.

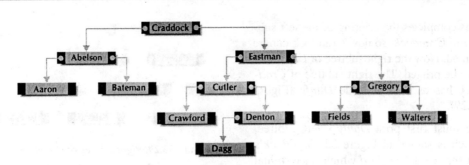

Figure 33.26. *Use of Dunfy's right subtree to find a replacement*

Methods of tree traversal

Having created a binary tree, it is likely that it will need to be accessed in some particular order, alphabetically for example. The algorithm for visiting the data items of a binary tree in alphabetical order is an example of *in-order* traversal and can be stated quite simply:

```
In-order traversal:
    visit the left subtree in in-order then
    visit the root node then
    visit the right subtree in in-order.
```

Notice that the algorithm makes reference to itself. In other words, the algorithm for visiting a subtree is exactly the same as that for visiting a tree. The seemingly endless process of visiting trees within trees within trees etc. continues until a null pointer is encountered, allowing the process to terminate, or *bottom out*. The operation of the algorithm is best illustrated by means of an example. Consider the tree shown in Figure 33.27.

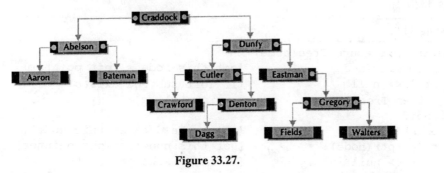

Figure 33.27.

Suppose that this tree is to be printed in alphabetical order, that is, an in-order traversal is to be performed. Then the procedure would be as follows. The left subtree of the *root node, Craddock* is shown in Figure 33.28.

Figure 33.28. *Left subtree of Craddock*

To print this subtree, we must first print its left subtree, which is just the entry *Aaron* which has no descendants. We therefore print Aaron. Now we can print the node data, Abelson and turn to the right subtree of *Abelson*. This right subtree is simply *Bateman*, which is then printed.

This completes the printing of the left subtree of *Craddock*, so now Craddock can be
printed. Now the right subtree of *Craddock*
is to be printed. The right subtree of *Craddock* has as its root node *Dunfy* (Figure
33.29).

We must first print *Dunfy's* left subtree,
which is shown in Figure 33.30. *Cutler's*
left subtree is *Crawford* which is a terminal

Figure 33.29. *Right subtree of Craddock*

node and is therefore printed. Cutler is then printed, followed by Dagg then Denton. This completes the printing of *Dunfy's* left subtree, so Dunfy is printed followed by its right subtree
(shown in Figure 33.31).

Figure 33.30. *Dunfy's left subtree*   **Figure 33.31.** *Dunfy's right subtree*

In order, this subtree would be printed: 'Eastman'- ' Fields'- 'Gregory'- 'Walters', which completes the process.

The simplicity of this method is also reflected in the pseudocode version of the algorithm. We
begin by defining a procedure called `Tree` which prints a tree starting at a specified node (Listing 33.9).

Listing 33.9.

```
define procedure Tree(node)
   l := lptr(node)          {get this node's left pointer}
   if l <> null             {if left subtree exists,
     then Tree(l)             print it}
   endif
   print(node)              {print the data at this node}
   r := rptr(node)          {get this node's right pointer}
   if r <> null             {if right subtree exists,
     then Tree(r)             print it}
   endif
endprocedure Tree
```

Notice that this procedure calls itself; this is termed *recursion*, a very useful programming device. The procedure `Tree` is invoked to print the left subtree at a particular node by passing the
left pointer as a procedure *parameter*, or to print the right subtree by passing the right pointer as
a procedure parameter. A procedure parameter allows values to be transmitted to the procedure
which are local to the procedure, having no existence outside the procedure.

In Listing 33.9, `node` is a parameter which initially points to the root node. By making the procedure call, `Tree (root)`, the procedure is invoked with the value of `root` passed to the parameter `node`. In the procedure, `node` is used to get the value of the left pointer using `1 = lptr (node)`. If it is not a null pointer, `1` is now passed to the procedure recursively using `Tree (1)`, and now `node` has the value of the pointer for the left subtree. In this way, the procedure `Tree` is used recursively to process subtrees, only printing a node and going on to the right subtree when a null pointer is encountered.

To illustrate the operation of the pseudocode, consider the binary tree shown in Figure 33.32 which is to be processed in alphabetical order.

Figure 33.32. *Binary tree to be processed in alphabetical order*

The equivalent table is Table 33.17.

node	left	data	right
0	1	Leeds	6
1	4	Bradford	2
2	5	Halifax	3
3	−1	Hexham	9
4	−1	Batley	−1
5	−1	Dewsbury	−1
6	10	Wakefield	7
7	8	York	−1
8	−1	Wetherby	−1
9	−1	Hull	−1
10	−1	Malton	11
11	−1	Stoke	−1

Table 33.17. *Table representation of binary tree in Figure 33.32*

Table 33.18 traces the pseudocode in Listing 33.9, indicating the action taken at each invocation of `Tree`. Only the pointer currently relevant is indicated in the two pointer columns. The process is started by the call `Tree (0)`.

node	left	data	right	action
0	1	Leeds		call Tree(1)
1	4	Bradford		call Tree(4)
4	−1	Batley		print 'Batley'
4		Batley	−1	exit Tree(4)
1		Bradford		print 'Bradford'
1		Bradford	2	call Tree(2)
2	5	Halifax		call Tree(5)
5	−1	Dewsbury		print 'Dewsbury'
5		Dewsbury	−1	exit Tree(5)
2		Halifax		print 'Halifax'
2		Halifax	3	call Tree(3)
3	−1	Hexham		print 'Hexham'
3		Hexham	9	call Tree(9)
9	−1	Hull		print 'Hull'
9		Hull	−1	exit Tree(9)
3		Hexham		exit Tree(3)
2		Halifax		exit Tree(2)
1		Bradford		exit Tree(1)
0		Leeds	6	call Tree(6)
6	10	Wakefield		call Tree(10)
10	−1	Malton		call Tree(11)
10		Malton	11	print 'Stoke'
11	−1	Stoke		exit Tree(11)
11		Stoke	−1	exit Tree(10)
10		Malton		print 'Wakefield'
6		Wakefield		call Tree(7)
6		Wakefield	7	call Tree(8)
7	8	York		print 'Wetherby'
8	−1	Wetherby		exit Tree(8)
8		Wetherby	−1	print 'York'
7		York		exit Tree(7)
7		York	−1	exit Tree(6)
6		Wakefield		exit Tree(0)
0		Leeds		

Table 33.18. *Tracing action of Listing 33.9 in printing an alphabetically ordered list*

As each invocation of Tree is completed, control is returned to the point where the procedure was called. For example, if currently the root node of a subtree is node 7, York, then exit Tree(7) returns control to the instruction following call Tree(7) which happens to be the end of Tree(6), Wakefield; similarly, exit Tree(6) returns control to the point where

`Tree(6)` was called, the end of `Tree(0)`. Successively returning to parent nodes is the bottoming out process referred to above, and it relies heavily on the use of a stack (see the earlier section on applications of stacks).

Using the recursive procedure, `Tree`, hides the use of the stack because of the way that procedure parameters are handled. On entering a procedure, the current values of its parameters are pushed to a stack and are replaced by the values passed to the procedure; the original values of the parameters are restored only when the procedure is exited. For example, the procedure call `Tree(2)` passes the value 2 to the parameter node. At this point, `Tree(1)` is being processed with node having a value of 1. So before node takes the value 2, its current value, that is 1, is pushed onto the stack. Then node is given the value 2 and the procedure is executed. When control returns to the point following the `call Tree(2)`, the top of the stack, the value 1, is pulled and copied to node thus restoring it to its local value.

The tree traversal algorithm given above is called in-order tree traversal, one of three main methods of accessing trees. The other two methods are called *pre-order* and *post-order* traversal. These are defined as follow:

```
Pre-order traversal:
visit the root node, then
visit all the nodes in the left subtree in pre-order, then
visit all the nodes in the right subtree in pre-order
```

With reference to the tree above, pre-order traversal would produce the list:

> Leeds Bradford Batley Halifax Dewsbury Hexham Hull Wakefield Malton
> Stoke York Wetherby

```
Post-order traversal:
visit all the nodes of the left subtree in post-order, then
visit all the nodes in the right subtree in post-order, then
visit the root node
```

This would produce the list:

> Batley Dewsbury Hull Hexham Halifax Bradford Stoke Malton Wetherby
> York Wakefield Leeds

Notice that the definitions of pre-order and post-order traversals again are recursive, allowing them to be handled in the same way as the in-order traversal.

Applications of binary trees

Sorting

A binary tree can be used to order a set of integers using the algorithm given in Listing 33.10.

Listing 33.10.

```
algorithm tree_sort
  repeat
    read num                {get next number}
    addnode(0)              {call procedure}
  until no_more_numbers     {continue until all
                             numbers read}
  end
```

```
define procedure addnode(node)
  if data(node) > num
    then if lptr(node) = null
           then createnode(num)
           else addnode(lptr(node))        {recurse using lptr}
         endif
    else if rptr(node) = null
           then createnode(num)
           else addnode(rptr(node))        {recurse using rptr}
         endif
  endif
endprocedure addnode
```

Initially, the first number in the list is stored in the root node. Then, in turn, each of the remaining numbers is compared with the current root node (that is, data(node)) to determine whether the number should be in the left subtree or the right subtree. If the number is greater, then it must go somewhere in the right subtree, otherwise it must go somewhere in the left subtree. If the appropriate subtree pointer is null, a new node is created containing the number and the subtree pointer links it to the tree; when the subtree pointer is not null, the process calls itself (recurses) using the pointer as the new root node.

The procedure createnode(num), referred to in the algorithm merely allocates space for new nodes, stores the number in the new node and links it to the tree by adjusting the parents left or right pointer.

As an example, suppose the following list of numbers is to be used to created an ordered tree as described above: 57 10 26 13 85 2 30 63 120

The tree would assume the form shown in Figure 33.33.

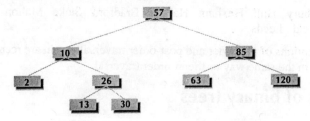

Figure 33.33. *Ordered tree of number list*

The numbers could be visited in ascending order using in-order traversal, as described in the previous section, to give the list

    2 10 13 26 30 57 63 85 120

Representing arithmetic expressions

Compilers often transform arithmetic expressions into more manageable forms prior to generating object code. A binary tree representation of an arithmetic expression is one such transformation. Consider the expression B + C*D.

The equivalent binary tree representation is shown in Figure 33.34.

$B + C*D$

An in-order traversal of the tree produces the original expression. This type of representation is relatively easy to handle by a compiler: if a node contains an operator, the left subtree is evaluated, the right subtree is evaluated and the two values obtained are the operands for the operator at that node. If a subtree also contains an operator node,

Figure 33.34. *Tree representation of B + C*D*

the same procedure is used recursively to produce the intermediate result. In the example above, + at the root node causes the left subtree to be evaluated, resulting in the value assigned to B; however, the right subtree contains the operator node * (multiplication) causing a recursive call to its left and right subtrees before the multiplication, C*D, can be evaluated. Figures 33.35 to 33.37 provide further examples of expressions represented as binary trees.

Figure 33.35. *Tree of (A+B)*C*

Figure 33.36. *Tree of A+B−C/2*

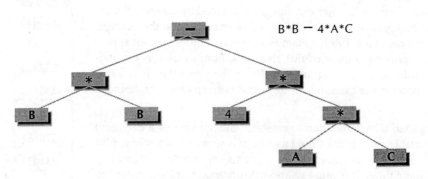

Figure 33.37. *Tree of B*B − 4*A*C*

All of these expressions are in *infix notation*, that is, with the arithmetic operators positioned between the operands. Thus, to add two numbers, A and B, using infix notation we would write A + B. There are two other standard notations for arithmetic expressions, namely, *postfix* and *prefix* notations. In postfix notation, A + B is written AB+ and in prefix, +AB.

By traversing the binary tree in in-order we saw that the infix expression resulted. Perhaps unsurprisingly, traversing the tree in post-order gives the postfix expression, and traversing the tree in pre-order gives the prefix expression.

Table 33.19 shows the same expressions in the three different forms.

Infix	Postfix	Prefix
B+C*D	BCD*+	+B*CD
(A+B)*C	AB+C*	*+ABC
A+BC/2	ABC2/+	+AB/C2
B*B−4*A*C	BB*4AC**−	−*BB*4*AC

Table 33.19. *Expressions in three different forms*

Postfix notation is also known by the name Reverse Polish notation, extensively used in the programming language Forth and of general importance in computing.

Hash functions

A hash function takes a numeric key lying within a certain range of values and transforms it into a table index which is within a smaller range of values. For example, if we have, say, under 200 data items with keys in the range 135246 to 791824 which are to be stored in a table of size 200, the mapping function will need to perform some mathematical operation on any given key to convert it to a number in the range 0 to 198. This number produced by the hash function is an index to the table. Furthermore, it is desirable to use a hash function which evenly maps key values to table index values in order to avoid two keys producing the same hash value.

A commonly used method of producing this even spread of hash values is to use the MOD function. This is simply a function which returns the integer remainder after one integer is divided by another. For instance, $MOD(11,4) = 3$, since $11/4 = 2$ remainder 3. In the example above we could use 199 (prime numbers give a more random spread than non-primes) as the modulus, that is the number used as the divisor, in order to generate an index value in the range 0 to 198. Table 33.20 shows some examples of keys and corresponding table index values.

Having used a hash function to establish the position of a data item within a table, and having stored it there, it is simply a matter of applying the same hash function again to the items key in order to locate it at some future time. This allows almost direct access to items stored in this manner. Notice that the third and the eighth keys both give an index value of 91. This is termed a *collision* and some method of coping with this eventuality must be devised; *collision resolution strategies* are discussed in the next section.

key	index
123456	76
232345	112
232324	91
436170	161
660912	33
376888	181
234023	198
456000	91
345999	137

Table 33.20.

As another example of hash functions, suppose that this time the keys of the data items are alphanumeric, containing up to eight characters, and that there are no more than, say, 50 items to be stored in a table of size 60. The first step is to convert the key to an integer; an easy way to do this is to sum the ASCII values of the characters in the key. Table 33.21 illustrates this procedure:

key	ASCII values								sum	MOD59
williams	119	105	108	108	105	97	109	115	866	40
knott	107	110	111	116	116				679	30
smith	115	109	105	116	104				668	19
jones	106	111	110	101	115				662	13
waites	119	97	105	116	101	115			772	5
craven	99	114	97	118	101	110			758	50
gold	103	111	108	100					541	10
collins	99	111	108	108	105	110	115		875	49
bates	98	97	116	101	115				646	56

Table 33.21.

The ASCII values are then summed, and finally they are expressed as a MOD 59 number which is, as before, the index of the data item in the storage table.

Collision resolution strategies

When a hash function produces the same value from two different keys, a *collision* is said to have occurred. Two common methods of coping with collisions are:

- ❑ direct chaining;
- ❑ open addressing.

In *direct chaining* each data item is extended to include a pointer to another item. Initially this pointer is a null pointer, but if a collision occurs, it is used to record the location of a collision item in some overflow area. Thus each element in the storage table is either empty, or contains the first item of a linked list of items all having the same hash value. Where collisions have not occurred, these linked lists contain only one item. Figure 33.38 illustrates this data structure.

KEY

empty element

single element

elements in linked list with same hash value

Figure 33.38.

With *open addressing*, collision items are stored in the next available location in the storage table. Thus, if the table element for a particular item is already occupied, the remaining table is searched sequentially until a vacant slot is found for it. The table is searched circularly. That is, if the end of the table is reached before a vacant slot is found, the search continues at the beginning of the table.

Applications of hash tables

Earlier in this chapter we saw that linked lists could be used for dynamic allocation of variables by an interpreter. In fact, this particular application of linked lists also incorporates an elementary form of hashing using direct chaining: the first letter of an identifier is used as an index to a table of pointers to linked lists of all identifiers starting wih the same letter.

Another application of hash functions is described in Chapter 15. In address generation a hash function is used to determine the disk block address for a record to allow the record to be accessed as quickly as possible.

A third application of hash functions is in the production of symbol tables by compilers. In this instance, as identifiers are encountered in the source code, a table containing details of their type and value must be consulted. If an identifier does not have an entry in the symbol table, one must be inserted; if it does have an entry already, further information may need to be added. Because of the frequency with which the symbol table needs to be consulted, and because of its central role in the compilation process, it is important that accessing it is made to be as efficient as possible; the use of hash functions is a possible solution.

Soundex coding

If the user of a personnel records system were to be asked to locate a record having the key Waites, then it is unlikely that the record would be retrieved if the user typed in Whaites or Waits. A possible solution is to convert the name to a *Soundex Code* defined as follows:

❏ the first letter of the name is the first letter of the code

❏ all vowels and the letters H, W and Y are ignored

❏ double letters are replaced by a single instance of the letter

❏ the remaining letters are replaced by values according to Table 33.22.

❏ the code is restricted to four characters in length

❏ if the code contains less than four characters, it is padded with trailing zeros.

letter	code
B F P V	1
C G J K Q S X Z	2
D T	3
L	4
M N	5
R	6

Table 33.22.

Table 33.23 provides some examples of names converted to soundex codes.

Soundex coding techniques are used extensively by the police force for searching criminal records. It is important to find all similar sounding names from their files because of the high probability of a name being reported incorrectly.

Soundex coding is also very useful for helping to make interactive information retrieval systems more user friendly. For example, rather than the computer saying, "There are no personnel records with the name JOHNSON", it reported, "There are no personnel records with the name JOHNSON, but here is a list of records closely matching this name: A. JONSON, B.

JOHNSEN... etc", this would be much more useful to the user.

name	Soundex Code
Waites	W320
Whaites	W320
Waits	W320
Williams	W452
Johnson	J525
Jonson	J525
Johnsen	J525
Morton	M635
Morten	M635
Summerville	S561
Sommerset	S562

Table 33.23.

✍️Exercises

1. Explain the purpose of:
   (i)   Iliffe vectors;
   (ii) access tables.
   Illustrate your answer with examples.

2. Calculate the number of comparisons required to find a particular item using binary search for the following lists:
   (i)   1000 numbers;
   (ii) 2542 numbers;
   (iii) 20,333 numbers.

3. With the aid of an example show how a new number would be inserted into an array containing numbers that are stored in ascending order of magnitude. Write a pseudocode algorithm for the procedure.

4. State the main characteristics of the following types of data structures:
   (i)   stack;
   (ii)   queue;
   (iii) circular queue;
   (iv)   linked list;
   (v)   binary tree.
   Illustrate your answer with examples to show how items are added and removed from them.

5. For each of the following situations described below suggest an appropriate data structure to

use. Justify your choice of data structure in each case.

(i)   A simulation of the flow of traffic at a set of traffic lights.

(ii)   The storage of the names and values of variables used by a program written in an interpreted language such as BASIC.

(iii) Storing return addresses in a programming language that permits the use of subroutines.

(iv)   A college enrolment system which records the names of people who apply in advance for places on evening classes. Places are allocated on a 'first come, first served basis'.

(v)   A list of names which must be maintained in alphabetical order. New names are frequently added to the list and existing names are frequently deleted from the list.

(vi)   A train arrivals and departures system that provides information for passengers. The information is displayed on monitors which show (in separate lists) the next ten train arrivals and departures.

6. Draw a binary tree which would allow the following list of numbers to be visited using in-order traversal:

    55   23   78   13   122   61   3   321   8   43

7. Draw a binary tree for each of the following arithmetic expressions:

    (i)   (A+B)*(A-B)

    (ii)   B*(C+D) - C*D

    (iii) A*(B-C/D) + E

    (iv)   (X+N/X)/2

    (v)   2*X*X - 5*X + 7

    Use the trees to convert the expressions into postfix and prefix notation.

Sorting Techniques

For computing purposes, a distinction has to be made between internal and external sorting. Where large volumes of data have to be sorted, such as entire files held on magnetic tape or disk, an external sort is used; this involves repeated transfers of data between memory and backing storage media. The basis of all such external sorting is *merging*, a process of forming one single sorted sequence from two previously sorted sequences.

Merging

The pseudocode, Merge in Listing 34.1 describes the process of merging two files, File1 and File2, into a new file, File3. If the files were held on magnetic tape, then three tape drives would be needed to effect the merge.

Listing 34.1.   Merging two files into a third

```
{Merge}
open File1, File2, File3                      {initialise}
read File1
read File2
while not eof(File1) and not eof(File2)       {start of main
                                              processing
                                              loop}

  if RecordKey(File1) < RecordKey(File2) then
       write Record(File1) to File3, read File1
     else write Record(File2) to File3, read File2
  endif
endwhile                                       {one file is
                                               now empty}

while not eof(FileN)
   write to File3, read FileN
endwhile
```

Merge sort

The merge algorithm assumes that the two files to be merged are already sorted, but the same process, used repeatedly, can be used to sort a completely unsorted file. The following example presupposes the use of three files, File1, File2 and File3, and a set of record keys with no repeated values.

Stage 1

File3 contains the sequence

       (18 26) (3 9 34) (5 21) (14) (6)

The brackets denote that there are already groups of values in ascending sequence, referred to as *runs*.

Place alternate runs into File1 and File2, thus

```
File1: (18  26)  (5  21) (6)
File2: (3  9  34)  (14)
```

Stage 2

Using the following procedure, File1 and File2 onto File3: compare the leading values from File1 and File2 and write to File3 the smallest of the two which is also greater than the immediately preceding value written to File3. If both are smaller than the latter, write the smaller of the two.

Thus, proceeding with the values currently in File1 and File2, the first pair for File1 and File2 are 18 and 3, respectively; 3 is the smaller value and since File3 is, at present, empty, 3 is selected.

```
File1: (18  26)  (5  21)  (6)
File2: (9  34)  (14)
File3: 3
```

Next, 18 and 9 are compared and 9 is selected because it is smallest and also greater than 3, the last value written to File3.

```
File1: (18  26)  (5  21)  (6)
File2: (34)  (14)
File3: 3  9
```

Of the next pairs 18 and 34, 18 is smaller but greater than the trailing value, 9, in File3.

```
File1: (26)  (5  21)  (6)
File2: (34)  (14)
File3: 3  9  18
```

Comparing the next pair, 26 and 34, the former is selected.

```
File1: (5  21)  (6)
File2: (34)  (14)
File3: 3  9  18  26
```

Comparison of 5 and 34 results in the selection of 34, because 5 is less than 26, the trailing value in File3.

```
File1: (5  21)  (6)
File2: (14)
File3: 3  9  18  26  34
```

The next comparison reveals that 5 and 14 are both less than 34, so 5 is selected.

```
File1: (21)  (6)
File2: (14)
File3: 3  9  18  26  34  5
```

14 is the next chosen value.

```
File1: (21)  (6)
File2:
File3: 3  9  18  26  34  5  14
```

File2 is now empty and the remaining values in File1 are transferred to File3.

```
File3: (3  9  18  26  34)  (5  14  21)  (6)
```

Stage 1 is repeated.

The runs have increased in length and are directed alternately to File1 and File2

```
File1:  (3 9 18 26 34)  (6)
File2:  (5 14 21)
```

Stage 2 is repeated, merging the runs in `File1` and `File2` back to `File3`, to produce

```
File3:  (3 5 9 14 18 21 26 34)  (6)
```

Stage 1 is repeated and runs are written alternately to `File1` and `File2`

```
File1:  (3 5 9 14 18 21 26 34)
File2:  (6)
```

Stage 2 again merges `File1` and `File2` onto `File3`, this time as a completely sorted sequence.

```
File3:  3 5 6 9 14 18 21 26 34
```

The algorithm in Listing 34.2 describes the process. X denotes the most recent value written to `File3`, A is the smaller of the two leading values in `File1` and `File2` and B the larger.

Listing 34.2.   Merge sort

```
{mergesort}                                    {open File1,
                                                File2, File3}

  repeat
    procedure split_and_merge                  {split File3 into
                                                File1 and File2,
                                                putting alternate
                                                runs into
                                                alternate files}

    while not eof(File1)and not eof(File2)
        if eof(File3) or (X < A) or (B < X) then
            write A to File3
        else write B to File3
        endif
    endwhile                                   {one of files is
                                                now empty}

    while not eof(FileN)
        write to File3
    endwhile
  until File3                                  {consists of only
                                                one run}
```

4-file merge sort

The efficiency of a merge sort can be increased with the use of four files as follows.

The following values are to be sorted

```
21 14 54 6 87 15 32 76 38 23 44 16 17
```

This time, single values are written alternately to `File1` and `File2`

```
File1:  21 54 87 32 38 44 17
File2:  14 6 15 76 23 16
```

The values are successively merged in pairs using `File3` and `File4` alternately.

```
File3:  (14 21)(15 87)(23 38)(17)
File4:  (6 54)(32 76)(16 44)
```

These runs are now merged alternately to `File1` and `File2`.

```
File1: (6 14 21 54) (16 23 38 44)
File2: (15 32 76 87) (17)
```

The extended runs are merged alternately to `File3` and `File4`.

```
File3: (6 14 15 21 32 54 76 87)
File4: (16 17 23 38 44)
```

A final merge back to `File1` only, produces the final sorted sequence.

```
File1: 6 14 15 16 17 21 23 32 38 44 54 76 87
```

Internal sorting, which is the subject of study in the following sections, involves the sorting of items entirely within memory into a strict ascending or descending order. For programming purposes, the items to be sorted are held in a one-dimensional array. The purpose of the data items will vary according to the application, but they may serve, for example, as keys to logical records. Direct access files frequently make use of indexes to identify the locations of individual records on a storage medium. Searching such an index for a particular record key value is often more efficient if the index is sorted into a particular sequence. The study of sorting algorithms is a long standing area of research in computer science and many highly efficient but complex methods have been developed. In order that the main principles of sorting can be understood, this text provides a detailed description of three relatively simple sorting techniques: *exchange* or 'bubble' sort; *selection* sort; *insertion* sort; and two more complex methods: *shell* sort; *quicksort*.

Each narrative description is followed by:

❑   an outline of the main programming requirements needed to implement the sort in a high level language;

❑   pseudocode with detailed annotation of the main processes;

❑   annotated sample programs implemented in Turbo Pascal.

Exchange or bubble sort

If it is assumed, for example, that items are to be sorted into ascending sequence, then the idea of the bubble sort is that, firstly the smallest value 'bubbles' to the top or beginning of the list, followed by the second smallest into the second position, the third smallest into third position and so on. The process can best be illustrated by a practical example as follows.

Consider a one-dimensional array of 5 elements, each containing an integer value. The array is known by the symbol M and each element in the array is identified by its subscript. The array elements and their contents are shown in Table 34.1.

The bubble sort requires that the array of values be scanned repeatedly and that with each scan, or more properly, *pass*, adjacent pairs of numbers are compared to see if they are in the required order; if necessary they swap positions. In the example in Table 34.1, the first pair, 3 and 6, are compared and found to be in the correct order; no exchange is necessary. Then the second and third items, 6 and 2, are compared, found to be in the incorrect order and are exchanged. The array now appears as in Table 34.2. The first pass continues with the comparison of the third and fourth items, 6 and 1; these require exchanging and the list is as shown in Table 34.3. The first pass ends with a comparison of the fourth and fifth items, now 6 and 5 respectively; again, an exchange is required. At the end of this first pass, the sequence appears as in Table 34.4.

elements	M(1)	M(2)	M(3)	M(4)	M(5)
contents	3	6	2	1	5

Table 34.1.

elements	M(1)	M(2)	M(3)	M(4)	M(5)
contents	3	2	6	1	5

Table 34.2.

elements	M(1)	M(2)	M(3)	M(4)	M(5)
contents	3	2	1	6	5

Table 34.3.

elements	M(1)	M(2)	M(3)	M(4)	M(5)
contents	3	2	1	5	6

Table 34.4.

The sort is not yet complete and further passes are needed. The complete process is illustrated in Table 34.5, below (continues onto next page). Shading indicates those values currently being compared and, if necessary, exchanged.

array elements	exchange	M(1)	M(2)	M(3)	M(4)	M(5)
begin Pass 1	no	3	6	2	1	5
	yes	3	6	2	1	5
	yes	3	2	6	1	5
	yes	3	2	1	6	5
end Pass 1		3	2	1	5	6
begin Pass 2	yes	3	2	1	5	6
	yes	2	3	1	5	6
	no	2	1	3	5	6
	no	2	1	3	5	6
end Pass 2		2	1	3	5	6
begin Pass 3	yes	2	1	3	5	6
	no	1	2	3	5	6
	no	1	2	3	5	6
	no	1	2	3	5	6
end Pass 3		1	2	3	5	6
begin Pass 4	no	1	2	3	5	6
	no	1	2	3	5	6
	no	1	2	3	5	6
	no	1	2	3	5	6
end Pass 4		1	2	3	5	6

Table 34.5.

A number of features can be identified in the above process:

❏ with each pass, the smallest value moves one position towards the beginning (the left) of the array;

❏ after the first pass, the largest value is at the end of the array. At the end of each subsequent pass, the next largest number moves to its correct position;

❏   the sort has been completed before the final pass.

Referring to this last feature, the sort is complete by the end of Pass 3. Why then is a further pass necessary? The answer is that the first comparison in Pass 3 results in an exchange between the values 2 and 1. If it is assumed that the occurrence of an exchange indicates that the sort is not complete, then a further pass is needed to determine that the array is sorted; that is, there have been no exchanges. The maximum number of passes required is always N−1, N being the number of items in the array. Frequently, the sort is complete well before this maximum is reached and any further passes are wasted. Consider the sequence in Table 34.6

array elements	exchange	M(1)	M(2)	M(3)	M(4)	M(5)	M(6)
initial contents		3	1	2	6	7	9
begin Pass 1	yes	3	1	2	6	7	9
	yes	1	3	2	6	7	9
	no	1	2	3	6	7	9
	no	1	2	3	6	7	9
	no	1	2	3	6	7	9
end Pass 1		1	2	3	6	7	9
begin Pass 2	no	1	2	3	6	7	9
	no	1	2	3	6	7	9
	no	1	2	3	6	7	9
	no	1	2	3	6	7	9
	no	1	2	3	6	7	9
end Pass 2		1	2	3	6	7	9

Table 34.6.

The maximum number of passes necessary should be N−1, that is, 5. Instead, the sort is completed by the end of the first pass and confirmed by the lack of exchanges in the second pass.

Program requirements

Comparison of adjacent values in an array. Assuming that the values are held in a one-dimensional array, reference is made to elements within the array by subscript. For example, the 4th element in an array called List, is addressed by List(4). To carry out a pass of all the elements in an array requires the use of a program loop to increment the subscript from 1 to N, the variable N being the size of the array. This can reduce by 1 after each complete pass, because the largest number 'sinks' to the bottom of the list and therefore need not be considered in subsequent passes; the efficiency of the algorithm is thus improved. For the sake of simplicity, this particular feature is not used in the illustrative algorithm or programs.

Exchanging the positions of adjacent values. Assuming that the programming language in use does not provide an 'exchange' or 'swap' instruction, then a temporary store is required to allow the exchange to take place.

For example, to exchange the contents of two variables, first and second, using a temporary store, hold, requires the following processes:

1.   Copy contents of First into Hold;

2.   Copy contents of Second into First;

3.   Copy contents of Hold into Second.

This is illustrated in Table 34.7, with some example values.

location	First	Second	Hold
initial contents	6	3	
after process 1	6	3	6
after process 2	3	3	6
after process 3	3	6	6

Table 34.7.

Detecting completion of the sort. A flag or sentinel variable, initialised for example, to 0 at the beginning of each pass and set to 1 if any exchanges take place during a pass, can be used to detect the completion of the sort before the maximum number of passes has been completed. For simplicity, the pseudocode in Listing 34.3 does not include this feature, although it is used in the sample Pascal program.

Listing 34.3.   Bubble sort pseudocode

```
{Bubble sort}
Number:= N                          {number of values and
                                     subscript of last item}
Passes:=1                           {initialise passes}
while Passes <= Number - 1 do       {control number of
                                     passes}
  Item := 1                         {set array subscript}
  while Item <= Number - 1 do       {loop for one pass}
    if M(Item) > M(Item + 1) then
      swap                          {swap if necessary}
    endif
    Item := Item + 1                {increment subscript}
  endwhile                          {end of single pass}
  Passes := Passes + 1              {increment passes}
endwhile                            {end of all passes}
```

Listing 34.4.   Bubble sort in Turbo Pascal

```
program Bubble (input, output);
const                               {number of values}
  number = 20;                      {to sort}

var
  M :array[1..number] of integer;   {declare array}
  Exchange :boolean;                {flag for swap}
  Item, Passes, Spare :integer;
begin
  for Item := 1 to Number do        {fill array M}
    begin
      writeln('number');
      readln(M[Item]);
```

```
      end;
    Passes := 1;                                    {initialise to}
                                                    {first pass}

    Exchange := true;
    while (Passes <= Number - 1) and                {control passes}
(Exchange) do
      begin
         Item := 1;                                 {initialise element}
                                                    {pointer}

         Exchange := false;                         {initialise swap}
                                                    {flag before each}
                                                    {pass}

         while Item <= Number - 1 do                {control number of}
                                                    {comparisons}
            begin
               if M[Item] > M[Item +1] then         {compare adjacent}
                                                    {values}
                  begin                             {swap elements}
                     Spare := M[Item];
                     M[Item] := M[Item + 1];
                     M[Item + 1] := Spare;
                     Exchange := true;              {set flag to}
                                                    {indicate swap}

                  end;
                  Item := Item + 1;                 {move pointer to}
                                                    {next element}

            end;
            Passes := Passes + 1;                   {increment pass}
                                                    {counter}

      end;
    for Item := 1 to Number do                      {display sorted}
                                                    {array}

      begin
         writeln(M[Item]);
      end;
end.
```

Selection sort

This method also requires the comparison and exchange of elements in a list. It is based on the principal that the item with the lowest value is exchanged with the item at the beginning or head of the list and that the process is repeated with N-1 items, N-2 items and so on, until only the largest item is left. Table 34.8 shows array M containing six, unsorted, integer values.

M(1)	M(2)	M(3)	M(4)	M(5)	M(6)
15	8	-3	62	24	12

The list is to be sorted into strict ascending sequence, as shown in Table 34.9.

M(1)	M(2)	M(3)	M(4)	M(5)	M(6)
−3	8	12	15	24	62

Table 34.9.

Table 34.10 shows the scanning process, the shaded values indicating the length of the list to be examined in each scan.

M(1)	M(2)	M(3)	M(4)	M(5)	M(6)	action
15	8	−3	62	24	12	starting sequence
−3	8	15	62	24	12	3 exchanged with 15 at head of list
−3	8	15	62	24	12	no exchange needed
−3	8	12	62	24	15	12 exchanged with 15 at head of list
−3	8	12	15	24	62	15 exchanged with 62 at head of list
−3	8	12	15	24	62	no exchange needed

Table 34.10.

The first pass of N items returns the value of −3 as being the smallest value in the list; this value moves to the head of the list and the previous head, 15, is moved to the position formerly occupied by −3. The list to be scanned is now N−1 items and has the value 8 at its head. The next pass reveals 8 as the smallest value, but no exchange is made because it already heads the shortened list. The next pass examines N−2 items and returns 12 as the lowest value, which is exchanged with 15 at the head of the shortened list. The process continues until only two items remain, 24 at the head and 62 at the rear; no exchange is needed and the list is sorted.

Program requirements

Certain features are similar to those of the bubble sort described earlier.

❑ Comparison of values in different locations in an array.

❑ Exchange of values in different, although not necessarily adjacent, positions in the array.

❑ The use of a pointer to allow element positions to be stored and incremented and also to be used as a subscript to refer to the contents of an individual location.

❑ The use of a temporary store to enable an exchange of element positions.

Listing 34.5. Selection sort pseudocode

```
{Selection}
Number:= N                            {number of values to sort}
for Head := 1 to N - 1                {increment head}
  PresentValue := M(Head)             {value of current head}
  PresentPntr := Head                 {position of current head}
  for NextOne := PresentPntr + 1 to N {increment search pointer}
    if M(NextOne) < PresentValue then
      PresentValue := M(NextOne)      {store smaller value and
      PresentPntr := NextOne           its position in the list}
  endif
```

```
          endfor
          if PresentPntr <> Head then        {check smallest value not
                                              already at head}
             Temp := M(Head)                 {temp is a temporary store
                                              for the swap}
             M(head) := M(PresentPntr)       {exchange smallest/head
                                              values}
             M(PresentPntr) := Temp
          endif
       endfor
```

The use of a temporary location Temp in the above algorithm is not strictly necessary, since the smallest value is assigned to PresentValue at the end of a pass and as the following program implementation illustrates, the swap could be implemented with:

```
    M(PresentPntr) := M(Head);
    M(Head) := PresentValue;
```

Listing 34.6.   Selection sort in Turbo Pascal

```
program Selection (input, output);
const
  Number = 20;
var
  M :array[1..Number] of integer;
  Head, NextOne, PresentValue,
  PresentPntr :integer;
begin
  for NextOne := 1 to Number do
    begin
       write ('number');
       readln (M[NextOne]);
    end;
  for Head := 1 to Number - 1 do
    begin
       PresentValue := M[Head];
       PresentPntr := Head;
       for NextOne := PresentPntr + 1 to Number do
         begin
            if M[NextOne] < PresentValue then
              begin
                 PresentValue := M[NextOne];
                 PresentPntr := NextOne;
              end;
         end;
       if PresentPntr <> Head then
           begin
              M[PresentPntr] := M[Head];
              M[Head] := PresentValue;
```

```
            end;
      end;
      for NextOne := 1 to Number do
         begin
            writeln(M[NextOne]);
         end;
end.
```

Insertion sort

This method can best be illustrated with the example of an unsorted pack of playing cards. Assuming that the cards are to be put into a row of ascending sequence (the least value on the left), the procedure may be as follows:

(i)   take the first card from the source pile and begin the destination row;

(ii)   continuing with the rest of the source pile, pick one card at a time and place it in the correct sequence in the destination row.

The process of finding the correct point of insertion requires repeated comparisons and where an insertion requires it, movement of cards to make space in the sequence. Thus, the card to be inserted, x, is compared with successive cards in the destination row (beginning from the largest value at the right hand end of the destination row) and where x is less than the card under comparison, the latter is moved to the right; otherwise x is inserted in the next position to the right.

Program requirements

The procedures are fairly simple, although a practical exercise with a pack of cards should help to clarify them. As with previous sorts, reference to array subscripts is required to allow comparison with different elements in the array. Nested loops are needed; the outer one for selecting successive values to be inserted into a destination sequence and the inner for allowing the insertion value to be compared with those already in sequence. Control of the outer loop does not present a problem as it simply ensures that all values are inserted, starting with the second; the first obviously needs no comparison as it is the first to be inserted. The inner loop controls the movement of values through the destination list to allow insertion of new values at the appropriate points. This loop may be terminated under two distinct conditions:

(i)   a value in the destination sequence is less than the value to be inserted;

(ii)   there are no further items to the left in the destination sequence.

To ensure termination under these conditions, a *flag* or *sentinel* is used. In the pseudocode and program implementations, array element (0) is used to store the value to be inserted, thus ensuring that when the left hand end is reached, no further comparisons are made. The pseudocode in Listing 34.7 illustrates the procedure; the analogy of a pack of cards is continued.

Listing 34.7   Insertion sort pseudocode

```
{Insertion sort}
for PickCard = 2 to NumInPack  {pick cards singly, starting with
                                second}
   InHand := M(PickCard)        {store value of card to insert}
```

```
    M(0) := InHand                  {to prevent insertion beyond left
                                    end of destination sequence}
    J := PickCard - 1               {ensures comparison with first
                                    card}
    while InHand < M(J) do          {card to insert < next card to the
                                    left in destination sequence}
      M(J + 1) := M(J)              {move card > card to insert, to the
                                    right}
       J := J - 1                   {pointer to next card compared with
                                    card to insert}
    endwhile
    M(J + 1) := InHand              {insert card into destination
                                    sequence}
  endfor
```

Listing 34.8.   Insertion sort in Turbo Pascal

```pascal
program insertion (input, output);
  const
    CardsInPack = 20;
  var
    M :array[0..NumInPack] of integer;
    Card, PickCard, InHand, J :integer;
  begin
    for Card := 1 to NumInPack do
      begin
        write ('number');
        readln (M[Card]);
      end;
    for PickCard := 2 to NumInPack do
      begin
        InHand := M[PickCard];
        M[0] := InHand;
        J := PickCard - 1;
        while InHand < M[J] do
          begin
            M[J + 1] := M[J];
            J := J - 1;
          end;
        M[J + 1] := InHand;
      end;
    for Card := 1 to NumInPack do
      begin
        writeln (M[Card]);
      end;
  end.
```

Comparative efficiency of sorting methods

The sorts described so far are not the most sophisticated, and in many cases, are not very quick.
They are, however, relatively simple to understand and they have been chosen for this reason.

More efficient, and consequently more complex, sorting algorithms include the Shell sort and Quick sort.

Shell sort

Named after its designer, D.L. Shell in 1959, it is a refinement of the insertion sort and divides the list into groups which are sorted separately. For example, with an array of eight items, those which are four positions apart are sorted first; the four groups will each contain two items. A second pass groups and sorts afresh the items which are two positions apart; this involves two groups, each with 4 items. Finally, all items (only one position apart) are sorted in a final pass. With each pass, the *distance* between the keys is halved, effectively changing the contents of each group. Successive passes continue until the distance between the elements in a group is one. The idea of the Shell sort is that the early passes compare items which are widely separated and thus remove the main disorders in the array. Later passes may then require fewer movements of items. The Turbo Pascal programs for the Shell sort (Listing 34.10) and the Quicksort (Listing 34.12) include routines for the generation of random numbers and the calculation of execution times. These routines can be used in all the Pascal sort programs in this chapter to test the effectiveness of each on various sets of random numbers. The performance of the Quicksort is particularly impressive, with the Shell sort taking a close second place.

Listing 34.9   Shell sort pseudocode

```
{Shell sort}
NumKeys := N
Gap := NumKeys                          {set gap to full
                                         list}

repeat
  Pntr1 := 1                            {set pointer to top
                                         of list}

  Gap := trunc(Gap/2)                   {calculate gap
                                         between keys}

  Pntr2 := Pntr1 + Gap                  {set pointer to 2nd
                                         key}

  repeat
    if M(Pntr1) > M(Pntr2) then         {compare keys}
      Exchange                          {call procedure
                                         Exchange}

    endif
    Pntr1 := Pntr1 + 1                  {move pointers down
                                         the list}

    Pntr2 := Pntr2 + 1
  until Pntr2 > NumKeys                 {test for bottom of
                                         list}
                                        {sort completed}
until Gap =1

procedure Exchange
Temp := M(Pntr1)                        {swap keys using
                                         temporary location}

M(Pntr1) := M(Pntr2)
M(Pntr2) := Temp
```

```
Pntr4 := Pntr1                                        {set pointers for
                                                       pass}
Pntr3 := Pntr1 - Gap
while (Pntr3 > 0) and (M(Pntr3) > M(Pntr4)) do {not top of list
                                                       and swap needed}
  Temp := M(Pntr3)                                    {swap keys}
  M(Pntr3) := M(Pntr4)
  M(Pntr4) := Temp
  Pntr3 := Pntr3 - Gap                                {move pointers up
                                                       the list}
  Pntr4 := Pntr4 - Gap
endwhile
```

Listing 34.10   Shell sort in Turbo Pascal

```
program Shell (output);
uses dos;
const
  NumKeys = 1000;
var
  M :array[1..NumKeys] of integer;
  I, Item, Gap, Pntr1,
  Pntr2, Pntr3, Pntr4, Temp :integer;
  Hrs, Min, Sec, Sec100 :word;

procedure Exchange;
begin
  Temp := M[Pntr1];
  M[Pntr1] := M[Pntr2];
  M[Pntr2] :=Temp;
  Pntr4 :=Pntr1;
  Pntr3 :=Pntr1 - Gap;
  while (Pntr3 > 0) and (M[Pntr3] >M[Pntr4]) do
  begin
    Temp := M[Pntr3];
    M[Pntr3] :=M[Pntr4];
    M[Pntr4] :=Temp;
    Pntr3 :=Pntr3 - Gap;
    Pntr4 :=Pntr4 - Gap;
  end;
end;

procedure SortList
begin
  settime(0, 0, 0, 0);
  Gap :=NumKeys;
  repeat
    Pntr1 :=1;
    Gap :=trunc(Gap/2);
```

```
        Pntr2 := Pntr1 + Gap;
        repeat
          if M[Pntr1] > M[Pntr2] then
             Exchange;
          Pntr1 :=Pntr1 + 1;
          Pntr2 :=Pntr2 + 1;
        until Pntr2 > NumKeys;
      until Gap =1;
      gettime(Hrs, Min, Sec, Sec100);
    end;

    procedure ShowTime;
    begin
      writeln(Hrs:10, Min:15, Sec:20, Sec100:25);
    end;

    begin
      write('Creating', NumKeys, 'random numbers');
      randomize;
      for I:=1 to NumKeys do
        begin
          M[I]:=random(30000);
        end;
      writeln;
      write('Sorting', NumKeys, 'random numbers');
      SortList
      writeln;
      for I:=1 to NumKeys do
        begin
          write(M[I]:8);
        end;
      ShowTime;
    end.
```

Quicksort

This *partition* sort was invented by C.A.R Hoare, who called it 'Quicksort' because of its remarkable speed. It is based on the exchange principle used in the bubble sort described earlier and is one of the fastest array sorting techniques, for large numbers of items. Quicksort is based on the general principle that exchanges should preferably be made between items which are located a large distance apart in an array. Initially, the array is divided into two partitions, using the mid-point. Beginning at the left-most position in the array, the item in this position is compared with the item at the mid-point position. If the former is less than the latter, the next item in the partition is compared with the mid-point element. The comparisons with the mid-point item are repeated with successive items in the partition until one is found which is greater than or equal to the mid-point item. The same process is used on the right-hand partition until an item is found which is less than or equal to that at the mid-point position. Once items are found in both partitions which satisfy these respective conditions, they are swapped. Successive comparisons and swaps are carried out until each item in each partition has been compared with the mid-point item. The whole process continues *recursively* (it calls itself repeatedly), further sub-dividing the partitions, until each sub-partition contains only one item, when the array is sorted. The topic of recursion is dealt with the chapter on Data Structures.

Listing 34 .11.   Quicksort pseudocode

```
{Quicksort}
NumKeys := N                             {number of keys to sort}
Lo := 1                                  {store lower limit of array}
Hi := NumKeys                            {store upper limit of array}
Qsort(Lo, Hi)                            {call recursive sort}
                                         procedure passing initial
                                         parameters}
end

procedure Qsort(LowEnd, TopEnd)          {recursive sort procedure}
LeftPntr := LowEnd                       {set pointers to current}
                                         left and right partition}
                                         limits}
RightPntr := TopEnd
MidValue := M((LowEnd + TopEnd)/2)       {store value at mid point
                                         between new left and right
                                         partitions}
repeat
  while M(LeftPntr) < MidValue do        {continue pass of left
                                         partition while mid value
                                         greater than each key
                                         examined}
    LeftPntr := LeftPntr + 1
  endwhile
  while MidValue < M(RightPntr) do       {continue pass of right
                                         partition while mid value
                                         less than each key examined}
    RightPntr := RightPntr - 1
  endwhile
  if LeftPntr <= RightPntr then          {provided the pointers have
                                         not yet crossed, swap the
                                         smaller key from the right
                                         partition with the larger key
                                         in the left}
    Temp := M(LeftPntr)
    M(LeftPntr) := M(RightPntr)
    M(RightPntr) := Temp
    LeftPntr := LeftPntr + 1
    RightPntr : = RightPntr - 1          {move left pointer one right}
                                         {move right pointer one left}
  endif
  until LeftPntr > RightPntr             {until pointers cross}
if LowEnd < RightPntr then               {if left partition still has
                                         more than one element}
  Qsort(Lowend, RightPntr)               {procedure calls itself to
                                         sort left partition with new
                                         parameters}
endif
```

```
if LeftPntr < TopEnd then          {if right partition still has
                                   more than one element}

  Qsort(LeftPntr, TopEnd)          {procedure calls itself to
                                   sort right partition with new
                                   parameters}

endif
```

Listing 34.12. Quicksort in Turbo Pascal

```pascal
program Quicksort(output);
uses dos;
const
  NumKeys = 1000;
var
  M :array[1..NumKeys] of integer;
  I, Lo, Hi :integer;
  Hrs, Min, Sec, Sec100 :word;

procedure Qsort(var LowEnd, TopEnd :integer);
var
  leftpntr, rightpntr, midvalue,
  temp :integer;
begin
  LeftPntr := LowEnd;
  RightPntr := TopEnd;
  MidValue := M[(LowEnd + TopEnd) div 2];
  repeat
    while M[LeftPntr] < MidValue do
      LeftPntr := LeftPntr + 1;
    while MidValue < M[RightPntr] do
      RightPntr := RightPntr - 1;
    if LeftPntr < RightPntr then
      begin
        Temp := M[LeftPntr];
        M[LeftPntr] := M[RightPntr];
        M[RightPntr] := Temp;
        LeftPntr := LeftPntr + 1;
        RightPntr := RightPntr - 1;
      end;
  until LeftPntr > RightPntr;
  if LowEnd < RightPntr then
    Qsort(LowEnd, RightPntr);
  if LeftPntr < TopEnd then
    Qsort(LeftPntr, TopEnd);
end;

procedure ShowTime;
begin
  writeln(Hrs:10, Min:15, Sec:20, Sec100:25);
```

```
end;

begin
  write('Creating', numkeys, 'random numbers...');
  randomize;
  for I:=1 to NumKeys do
    begin
      M[I]:=random(30000);
    end;
  writeln;
  write('Sorting', numkeys, 'random numbers...');
  settime(0,0,0,0);
  Lo := 1;
  Hi := NumKeys;
  Qsort(Lo, Hi);
  gettime(Hrs, Min, Sec, Sec100);
  writeln;
  for I:=1 to NumKeys do
    begin
      write(M[I]:8);
    end;
  ShowTime;
end.
```

Quicksort's speed stems from the fact that the early passes bring items close to their final sequence, leaving the last few passes to make only minor changes.

Tree sort

This is a selection sort and is described in the chapter on Data Structures. Like Quicksort, the binary tree sort uses the technique of recursion.

Comparison of sorting methods

Comparing the efficiency of various sorting algorithms with one another requires careful use of 'bench test' data to ensure that comparisons are fair and specialists in the subject of sorting have spent a great deal of time analysing the various methods. It is beyond the scope of this text to pursue such analysis in detail, but some broad comparisons can be made of the relative efficiency of the simple sorts described so far. It must be said that where only a few items are to be sorted, little tangible benefit will be gained from using a sophisticated sort, as opposed to a simple one. With a larger number of items, the limitations of simple sorting algorithms, such as the bubble sort, soon become apparent. Another factor which may affect a sort's performance is the degree to which items are out of order to begin with.

The bubble sort is probably the least efficient and is rarely used by experienced programmers. It is, however, a simple sort to understand and provides a good introduction to any programmer wishing to develop their skill in this area. The selection sort generally performs better than the insertion sort, except when the items are almost in order to begin with.

Applications and Social Issues

Chapters

Chapter 35

Business Applications

Financial accounting is largely concerned with past events. *Cost and management* accounting aims to provide management with information to support their decisions on the planning of future business activity. Accounting systems should provide management with information to:

❑ establish and monitor the financial targets of the business. One target may be to increase sales of a particular product by 10 per cent over the next six months. A parallel target could be to cut, by 5 per cent, its unit production cost. Targets are usually fairly specific so that their achievement, or otherwise, can be determined;

❑ control income and expenditure within the business. Financial accounting is concerned with the whole of the business whereas cost accounting identifies cost centres (for different parts of the business). Analysing costs and revenues in this way allows a business to allocate financial budgets for various areas of the business and determine the contribution of each area to the profitability of the business.

Numerous commercial software packages are available for both financial and cost accounting applications, but this chapter concentrates on financial accounting systems and related applications.

Financial accounting systems

The following section describes the various financial accounting systems of a typical business and the main features of accounting software. To begin with some associated terminology is defined and some basic concepts are explained.

The ledgers

Business accounts are needed to record:

❑ *debtor* transactions; debtors are people or organisations who owe money to the business for goods or services provided (credit sales);

❑ *creditor* transactions; creditors are people or organisations to whom the business owes money, for the supply of goods (credit purchases).

These transactions are recorded in the *sales ledger* and the *purchases ledger* respectively. A third ledger, the *nominal* (or *general*) *ledger* is used to record the overall income and expenditure of the business, with each transaction classified according to its purpose.

Sales ledger

General description

The purpose of the sales ledger is to keep a record of amounts owed to a business by its trading customers or clients. It contains a record for each customer with a credit arrangement. Most businesses permit their customers to buy goods on credit. The goods are usually supplied on the understanding that, once payment has been requested, the debt will be paid for within a specified period of, for example, 14 or 30 days. Payment is requested with the use of a customer addressed *invoice*, which contains details of goods supplied, the amount owing and credit days given. Once a customer order has been accepted and processed, the total amount due for the order is recorded in the relevant customers account in the sales ledger and the balance owing is increased accordingly. When a payment is received from the customer, the amount is entered to the customer's account and the balance owing is decreased by the appropriate amount.

There are two main approaches to sales ledger maintenance, *balance forward* and *open item*.

❑   Balance forward. This method provides: an opening balance (the amount owing at the beginning of the month); the transactions for that month, giving the date, type (for example, goods sold or payment received); the amount of each transaction; a closing balance. The closing balance at the end of the month is carried forward as the opening balance for the next month. A *statement of account*, detailing all the transactions for the month will normally be sent to the customer and a copy filed away for business records. The customer's account in the sales ledger will not then contain details of the previous month's transactions so any query will require reference to the filed statements of account.

❑   Open item. The open item method is more complicated in that each invoice is identified by a code and requires payments from customers to be matched against the relevant invoices. All payments received and relating to a particular invoice are recorded against it until it is completely paid off. This method can make control difficult as some customers may make part payments, which cannot be tied to a particular invoice. If a customer does not specify to which invoice a particular payment relates it is normally assigned to the oldest invoice(s). Once an invoice has been completely settled it is cleared from the ledger and any subsequent statements of account.

Package requirements and facilities

Customer master file

When setting up the Sales Ledger system, one of the first tasks is to open an account for each customer. These accounts are maintained in a sales ledger *master file*, which is updated by sales and account settlement transactions. A typical package should provide as a minimum, the following data item types for each customer record:

❑   *account number* - used to identify uniquely a customer record;

❑   *name and address* - this will normally be the customers address to which statements of account and invoices are sent;

❑   *credit limit* - the maximum amount of credit to be allowed to the customer at any one time. This is checked by sales staff before an order is authorised for processing;

❑   *balance* - this is the balance of the customer's account at any one time.

A choice is usually provided to select the form of sales ledger required, either *open item* or *balance forward* (see previous section). Normally, when the file is first created, a zero balance is recorded and outstanding transactions are entered to produce a current balance. An open item system stores details of any unpaid invoices. Each invoice can be associated with a particular customer account through the account number.

Transaction entries

Transactions may be applied directly to customer accounts in the sales ledger (*transaction processing*) or they may be initially stored as a transaction file for a *batch* updating run. Whichever method the package uses, it should allow for the entry of the following transaction types:

❏ *invoice* - this is sent to the customer requesting payment concerning a particular order. The amount of the invoice is debited to the customer's account in the sales ledger, thus increasing the amount owing;

❏ *credit note*. If, for example, goods are returned by a customer or there is a dispute concerning the goods, a credit note is issued by the business to the customer. The amount of the credit note will be credited to the customer's account in the sales ledger, thus reducing the balance owing. Credit notes are often printed in red to distinguish them from invoices;

❏ *receipt* - this is any payment or remittance received from a customer in whole or partial settlement of an invoice. Such an entry will be credited to the customer's account and reduce the balance owing accordingly.

The following data may be entered with each type of transaction:

❏ *account number* - essential to identify the computer record. Although some packages allow for the entry of a shortened customer name (if the account number has been forgotten) the account number is still necessary to identify uniquely a record;

❏ *date of transaction*;

❏ *amount of transaction*;

❏ *transaction reference* - this is the invoice number to which the transaction relates.

Outputs

The following facilities may be expected:

❏ *single account enquiry* - details of an individual customer's account can be displayed on screen. Retrieval may be by account number or a search facility, using a shortened version of the customer name. If more than one record is retrieved by this method they may be scanned through on screen until the required record is found;

❏ *customer statement printing* - it is essential that the system can produce monthly statements for sending to customers;

❏ *debtors age analysis* - this provides a schedule of the total amounts owing by customers, categorised according to the time various portions of the total debt have been outstanding (unpaid). It is important for a business to make financial provision for the possibility of *bad debts*. These are debts which are unlikely to be settled and may have to be taken out of business profits. From their own experience of the trade, the proprietor of a business should be able to estimate the percentage of each debt that is likely to become bad. Generally, the longer the debt has been outstanding, the greater the likelihood that it will remain unpaid;

❏ *customers over credit limit* - this may form the basis of a black list of customers. Any new order from one of these customers has to be authorised by management. On the other hand, the appearance of certain customers on the list may suggest that some increased credit limits are needed. When a business is successful, it often needs more credit to expand further;

❏ *dormant account list* - if there has been no activity on an account for some time, it may warrant removal from the file. Alternatively, it may be useful to contact the customer to see if further business may be forthcoming.

Validation and control

The package should provide for careful validation of transactions and the protection of records from unauthorised access or amendment. Generally, for example, a customer record cannot be removed from the sales ledger while the account is still live (there is a balance outstanding). More details of validation and control are given in Chapter 17.

Purchase ledger

General description

The purchase ledger function mirrors that of the sales ledger, except that it contains an account for each *supplier*, from whom the business buys goods. When trading with a supplier, it is usually through credit arrangements, similar to those provided by the business for its own customers. Thus, the business receives an invoice requesting payment, within a certain period, for goods purchased. The amount of the invoice is credited to the supplier's account and the balance owing to the supplier is increased accordingly. When payment is made to a supplier, in full or part settlement of an invoice, the supplier's account is debited by the appropriate amount and the balance is decreased. Most purchase ledger systems operate on an open item basis. Each supplier invoice is given a reference number and when payment is made to a supplier, the reference number can be used to allocate the payment to a particular invoice.

Package requirements and facilities

Supplier master file

The supplier master file contains the suppliers' (*creditors'*) accounts. It is updated by supplier invoices and payments to suppliers. A typical package should provide, as a minimum, the following data item types for each supplier record:

❏ *account number*- used to identify uniquely a supplier record;

❏ *name and address* - the name and address of the supplier business;

❏ *credit limit* - the maximum amount of credit allowed to the business by the supplier at any one time. A check should be kept on this to avoid rejection of orders;

❏ *settlement discount* - this is the amount of discount given by a supplier if an invoice is settled within a specified discount period;

❏ *due date* - the system may issue a reminder when payment is due. A report may be printed, on request, listing all invoice amounts due for payment within, say, 7 days;

❏ *balance* - the current balance on the account.

A choice is usually provided to select the form of purchase ledger required (either open item or balance forward).

Transactions

Transactions may update the supplier accounts directly (transaction processing) or they may be initially stored as a transaction file for a later updating run. A purchase ledger package should allow for the following transactions:

☐ *supplier invoices* - before entry, each invoice must be checked against the appropriate order and then against the relevant delivery note, for actual receipt of goods. The balance on a supplier's account (the amount owed to the supplier) is increased by an invoice entry. Some packages allow unsatisfactory (there may be doubt about the delivery of the goods) invoices to be held in abeyance until cleared;

☐ *approved payments* - once an invoice has been cleared for payment, a voucher may be raised to ensure payment, on or before a due date, and discount for prompt payment. The entry of the payment value decreases the balance of a supplier's account and thus the amount owed by the business to the supplier. Cheques may be produced automatically on the due date, but there should be some checking procedure to ensure that payments are properly authorised;

☐ *adjustments* - to reverse entries made in error.

Outputs

The following output facilities may be expected:

☐ *single account enquiries* - details of an individual supplier's account can be displayed on screen; retrieval may be through a supplier code;

☐ *payment advice slip* - this may be produced to accompany a payment to a supplier. Each payment slip details the invoice reference, the amount due and the value of the payment remitted. Payment advice slips help the supplier, who may be using an open item sales ledger system;

☐ *automatic cheques* - the package may, with the use of pre-printed stationery, produce cheques for payment to suppliers, as and when invoices fall due. There must be a careful checking and authorisation procedure to prevent incorrect payments being made;

☐ *unpaid invoices* - a list of all outstanding invoices, together with details of supplier, amount owing and due date;

☐ *creditors' age analysis* - this is the supplier equivalent of debtors' age analysis. The report provides a schedule of total balances owing to suppliers, analysed according to the time the debt has been outstanding. The report may be used to determine which payments should be given priority over others.

Nominal ledger

General description

The nominal ledger is used to record the income and expenditure of a business, classified according to purpose. Thus, for example, it contains an account for *sales*; sales totals are entered on a daily basis. The sales ledger analyses sales by customer, whereas the *sales account* provides a cumulative total for sales, as the accounting year progresses. The *purchases account* in the nominal ledger fulfils a similar purpose for purchases by the business. Other income and expenditure accounts recorded in the nominal ledger may include, for example, *rent, heating* and *wages*. If some items of income and expenditure are too small to warrant separate analysis, there may also be *sundry income* and *sundry expenditure* accounts. The information held in the nominal ledger accounts is used to draw up a *profit and loss account*. This account provides information on the trading performance of the business over the year. A *balance sheet* can then be produced to give a snapshot view of the assets and liabilities of a business, on a particular date.

Package requirements and facilities

Nominal accounts master file

When an account is opened in the nominal ledger, the following data item types should be available:

- ❑ *account code* - each account is given a code, to allow the allocation of transactions. For example, an entry for a gas bill payment may be directed to the Heating account by the code 012;

- ❑ *account name* - for example, Sales, Heating, Rent;

- ❑ *balance*.

Associated with each account are a number of transactions processed during the current accounting period.

Transactions

- ❑ *sales and purchases* - these may be entered periodically as accumulated totals or, in an integrated accounts system, values may be posted automatically, at the same time as they update customer and supplier accounts in the sales ledger and purchase ledger;

- ❑ *other income and expenditure* - entries concerning, for example, wages, rent, rates or heating.

Outputs

Typical output facilities include:

- ❑ *trial balance* - this is a list of debit and credit balances categorised by account. The balances are taken from the nominal ledger and the total of debit balances should agree with the total of credit balances;

- ❑ *transaction report* - a full list of transactions which may be used for error checking purposes, or as an audit trail, to allow the validity of transactions to be checked by an external auditor. The topic of auditing is described in more detail in Chapter 17;

- ❑ *trading and profit and loss account* - a statement of the trading performance of the business over a given period;

- ❑ *balance sheet* - a statement of the assets and liabilities of a business, at a particular date.

The major benefit of the computerised nominal ledger is that these reports can be produced easily and upon request. The manual production of a trial balance, trading and profit and loss statement and balance sheet can be a laborious and time consuming task. Many small businesses, operating manual systems, have difficulty in completing their annual accounts promptly for annual tax assessment.

Apart from the basic ledgers described in the previous section, there are other applications which can benefit from computerisation. They include:

- ❏ stock control;
- ❏ sales order processing and invoicing.

Stock control

General description

Different businesses hold different kinds of stock. For example, a grocer holds some perishable and some non-perishable stocks of food and a clothing manufacturer holds stocks of materials and finished articles of clothing. Any trader's stock needs to be controlled, but the reasons for control may vary from one business to another. For example, a grocer wants to keep the full range of food items that customers expect, but does not want to be left with stocks of unsold items, especially if they are perishable. A clothing manufacturer's stocks will not perish if they are unsold, but space occupied by unwanted goods could be occupied by more popular items. On the other hand, if the manufacturer runs out of raw materials the production process can be slowed or even halted. Apart from such differences, there are some common reasons for wanting efficient stock control:

- ❏ excessive stock levels tie up valuable cash resources and increase business costs. The cash could be used to finance further business;
- ❏ inability to satisfy customer orders promptly because of insufficient stocks, can often lead to loss of custom.

It is possible to identify some typical objectives of a stock control system and these can be used to measure the usefulness of facilities commonly offered by computer packages:

- ❏ to maintain levels of stock which will be sufficient to meet customer demand promptly;
- ❏ to provide a mechanism which removes the need for excessively high safety margins of stock to cover customer demand. This is usually effected by setting minimum stock levels which the computer can use to report variations outside these levels;
- ❏ to provide automatic re-ordering of stock items which fall below minimum levels;
- ❏ to provide management with up-to-date information on stock levels and values of stock held. Stock valuation is also needed for accounting purposes.

Stock control requires that an individual record is maintained for each type of stock item held. Apart from details concerning the description and price of the stock item, each record should have a balance indicating the number of units held. A unit may be, for example, a box, 500 grammes or a tonne. The balance is adjusted whenever units of that particular stock item are sold or purchased. Manual or computerised records can only give recorded levels of stock. Physical stock checks need to be carried out to determine the actual levels. If there is a difference between the recorded stock level of an item and the actual stock of that item, it could be because of pilferage or damage. Alternatively, some transactions for the item may not have been applied to the stock file.

Package requirements and facilities

Stock master file

The stock master file contains records for each item of stock and each record may usefully contain the following data item types:

❑ *Stock code or reference* - each stock item type should have a unique reference, for example, A0035. The code should be designed so that it is useful to the user. For example, an initial alphabetic character may be used to differentiate between raw materials (R) and finished goods (F) and the remaining digits may have ranges which indicate particular product groupings. The stock file may also be used to record any consumable items used by a business, for example, stationery and printer ribbons. The initial character of the stock code could be used to identify such a grouping. The number and type of characters in a code, as well as its format, are usually limited by the package because the code will also be used by the software to determine a record's location within the file;

❑ *Description* - although users may become used to referring to individual products by their codes or references, a description is needed for the production of, for example, purchase orders or customer invoices;

❑ *Analysis code* - this may be used in conjunction with sales orders so that they can be analysed by product group. If, for example, a clothing manufacturer produces different types of ski jacket, it is important for production planning purposes to know the relative popularity of each type;

❑ *Unit size* - for example, box, metre, tonne, kilo;

❑ *Re-order level* - this is the stock level at which an item is to be re-ordered, for example, 30 boxes. Reaching this level may trigger an automatic re-order when the appropriate program option is run. Alternatively it may be necessary to request a summary report which highlights all items at or below their re-order level. The decision on what the re-order level should be for any particular item will depend on the *sales turnover* (the number of units sold per day or week) and the *lead time* (the time taken for delivery after a purchase order is placed with a supplier). Seasonal changes in sales figures will require that re-order levels for individual items are changed for time to time;

❑ *Re-order quantity* - this is the number of item units to be re-ordered from a supplier when new stock is required;

❑ *Bin reference* - this may be used to indicate the physical location of stock items within, for example, a warehouse;

❑ *Minimum stock level* - when an item falls to this level, a warning is given that the stock level of the item is dangerously low. As with the re-order level, the warning may be produced by a request for a special summary report which highlights such items. Even though the re-order level warning may have already been given, it is possible that no new stocks were ordered or that the supplier was unusually slow with deliveries;

❏ *Cost price* - the price paid by the business for the stock item;

❏ *Sale price* - the price charged to the customer. The package may allow the storage of more than one sale price to differentiate between, for example, retail and wholesale customers;

❏ *VAT code* - different items may attract different rates of Value Added Tax (VAT);

❏ *Supplier code* - if orders can be produced automatically, then the supplier code may be used to access a supplier file, for the address and other details needed to produce an order;

❏ *Quantity issued* - generally, several values may be entered, so that the turnover of an item can be viewed for different periods, for example, from 3 months ago to date, the preceding 3 month period and so on;

❏ *Stock allocated* - a quantity may not have been issued but may have been allocated to a customer order or factory requisition;

❏ *Quantity in stock* - the current recorded level of stock. This will change whenever an issue, receipt or adjustment transaction is entered.

Transactions

❏ *Goods received* - stock received from a supplier;

❏ *Goods returned* - for example, stock returned by a customer or unused raw materials returned from the factory;

❏ *Goods issued* - this may result from a customer order or from a factory requisition, if the business has a manufacturing process;

❏ *Stock allocated* - this will not reduce the quantity in stock figure but the amount allocated should be used to offset the quantity in stock when judging what is available;

❏ *Amendments* - for, example, there may be amendments to price, re-order level or supplier code.

The method used to update the stock master file will depend on how up-to-date the figures need to be (this will depend on how tight stock levels are) and how often the data entry operator can get at the computer. To keep the file up-to-date throughout the day, physical stock changes have to be notified immediately to stock control and the transactions have to be entered as they occur. Unfortunately, this means that a single-user system would be unavailable to any other users, such as sales staff, who needed to know quantities in stock. A networked system with central file storage, would allow continual updating and enquiry access. If the stock levels are sufficiently high to allow differences to arise between physical and book totals without risking shortages, then daily batch updating may be acceptable. In such a situation, an enquiry on a stock item may reveal, for example, a book stock of 200 units, when the physical stock is only

120 units (80 having been issued since the last update at the end of the preceding day).

Outputs

Typical outputs from a stock control package include:

❑   *Stock enquiry* - details concerning a stock item may be displayed on screen, or printed;

❑   *Stock out report* - a list of stock items which have reached a level of zero;

❑   *Re-order report* - a list of stock items which have fallen to their re-order level, together with supplier details and recommended re-order quantities;

❑   *Stock list* - a full or limited (for example, within a certain stock code range) list of stock items, giving details of quantities held and their value. The value may be calculated using the cost or sale price, depending on the costing method used by the business;

❑   *Outstanding order report* - a list of all purchase orders not yet fulfilled and the dates ordered. This may be used to chase up orders when stocks are falling dangerously low.

This is not an exhaustive list and some packages offer many other analytical reports which can help a business to maintain an efficient customer service and plan future production and purchasing more effectively.

A stock control case study

The Astex Homecare chain of DIY stores has branches all over the country and each branch maintains stocks of thousands of items used in the home. These items range from building materials such as sand and cement to bedroom furniture, fitted kitchens, bathroom suites, ceramic wall and floor tiles, lights and light fittings, garden materials such as plants, plant pots and garden furniture, nails, screws, paint, wallpaper and numerous other common household goods.

Each branch has its own small computer system dedicated to dealing with the *point of sale* (POS) terminals located at the customer tills. The POS terminals are used to record purchases and provide customer bills by scanning the bar code on each purchase using a hand-held scanner. The stock number contained in the bar code is fed by the POS terminal to the local computer which returns the description and price to be printed on the customers' receipts as well as the bill totals.

Each branch maintains its own stock file on the local computer but ordering stock is controlled by a mainframe computer at the Astex head office. Each Astex branch is laid out according to a *merchandise layout plan* (MLP) in which the store is organised into a large number of four foot sections, each having its own MLP code. Each item of stock is allocated to one MLP section and its computer record contains the MLP code together with the minimum and maximum stock level for that particular section of the store. When an item has been sold, the relevant information is transmitted automatically by the local computer to the mainframe at head office. The head office computer determines from the MLP data whether the item needs to be re-ordered from a supplier. It uses the MLP information regarding minimum and maximum stock levels in order to determine how many of a particular item to order.

Overnight, while the stores are closed, the head office computer transmits suggested ordering information back to the individual branches where order sheets are printed out on local laser printers, so that they can be checked manually by the appropriate personnel before stock is ordered. This manual monitoring of computer-generated information allows the information system to cope with unexpected situations and prevents the occurrence of gross errors. About ninety percent of all orders can be made electronically using communication links to the computers used by suppliers. Other suppliers not linked to the central Astex computer are contacted manually by telephone.

The security of the Astex information systems are ensured in two major ways. Firstly, because of the importance of the local computer system for producing customer bills, a backup processor is always available for use in the event of the primary processor failing. Secondly, access to the various users of the computer systems is provided on several different levels. Each person who uses the computer system has his or her own access code which provides access to only those areas he or she is authorised to use. These measures are essential to maintain the security and reliable operation of such large-scale systems.

Sales order processing and invoicing

Sales order processing

Sales order processing is concerned with the handling of customers' sales orders. It has three main functions:

- ❑ validation of orders. This means checking, for example, that the goods ordered are supplied by the business or that the customer's credit status warrants the order's completion;

- ❑ to identify quantities of individual items ordered. A customer may request several different items on the same order form. An item will probably appear on many different order forms and the quantities for each need to be totalled to provide lists (picking lists) for warehouse staff to retrieve the goods;

- ❑ to monitor back orders. If an order cannot be fulfilled it may be held in abeyance until new stocks arrive. The system should be able to report all outstanding back orders on request.

The efficient processing of customer orders is of obvious importance to the success of a business and in whatever form an order is received, the details should be immediately recorded. Preferably, the details should be recorded on a pre-designed order form which ensures that all relevant details are taken. The order details should include:

- ❑ the date the order is received;

- ❑ the customer's order number;

- ❑ a description of each item required including any necessary stock references or codes;

- ❑ the quantity of each item ordered;

- ❑ the price per item excluding VAT;

- ❑ the total order value excluding VAT;

- ❏ any discount which is offered to the customer;
- ❏ the VAT amount which is to be added to the total price;
- ❏ the total order value including VAT;
- ❏ the delivery date required.

Invoicing

The invoice is the bill to the customer, requesting payment for goods or services supplied by the business. The following section describes typical package facilities which allow the integration of the sales order processing and invoicing systems.

Package requirements and facilities

To be effective, the sales order processing system needs to have access to the customer file (sales ledger) for customer details and to the stock file, so that prices can be extracted according to stock item codes entered with the order. This latter facility means that the system may also be integrated with invoicing.

Files

- ❏ *Customer file.* When a customer account number or name is keyed in with an order, the package usually accesses the customer file and displays the address details, so that the operator can confirm the delivery address or type in an alternative address if this is required. The process also ensures that all orders are processed for registered customers;

- ❏ *Stock file.* As stock item codes are entered from an order form, the system accesses the price and displays it on the screen for confirmation by the operator. Access to the stock file also ensures that only valid stock codes are used;

- ❏ *Completed order file.* This is used for the generation of invoices after an order's completion;

- ❏ *Back order file.* This is needed to ensure that orders which cannot be fulfilled immediately are kept on file and processed as soon as goods become available.

Transactions

- ❏ *Sales order* - details concerning an individual order, including customer number, items required (by item code), quantity of each item, delivery date, discount allowed and the date of the order.

Outputs

- ❏ *Invoice* - an invoice can be generated by using the details of customer number, stock codes and quantities from the order, together with information retrieved from the customer and stock files;

- ❏ *Back order report* - a report can be requested detailing all unsatisfied orders. This is useful for planning production schedules or generating special purchase orders;

- ❏ *Picking list* - a summary of the quantities required of each item ordered. These are used by warehouse staff to extract the goods needed to make up orders for delivery;

❏ *Sales data* - details of each customer's order need to be extended to include the financial ledgers (sales, purchase and nominal ledger). Such integration should not usually be attempted all at once but full integration does reduce the number of inputs necessary and automates many of the updating procedures described in this chapter.

Payroll

The task of calculating wages for a large company having hundreds or even thousands of employees is an enormous task. It involves taking into account some or all of the following factors:

❏ number of hours worked;

❏ amount of overtime;

❏ bonus payment;

❏ sickness leave;

❏ type of employee (for example, waged or salaried, shop floor or management);

❏ deductions (for example, national insurance contributions and union fees);

❏ holidays;

❏ tax code;

❏ tax rate;

❏ cash analysis.

The gross pay is calculated from the hours worked and hourly pay rate, for weekly paid employees, and is a standard sum for salaried employees. Added to this gross payment are any allowances from overtime or bonuses, for example. Tax is calculated and subtracted from the total earnings and other deductions such as national insurance, union fees and pension contributions are also taken from it. Thus the total calculation is quite complicated, and it will probably be different for each employee. Producing payslips manually is therefore very time consuming and prone to error, so computers are particularly well suited to the task. Most computerised payroll systems use batch processing in which long-term employee information held on a master file is used in conjunction with a transaction file containing recent information such as hours worked and overtime details. The transaction file changes from week to week or month to month but most of the information on the master file either does not change at all or changes only occasionally. If employees are paid weekly, at the end of each week details of hours worked, bonus payments, overtime payments and deductions are recorded on a payroll transaction file which contains a record for every employee. This sequential transaction file is then sorted into employee number order so that it is in the same order as the payroll master file. The two files are then used by the computer to calculate and print the payslips, and to update the master file which must keep track of such things as tax paid to date, total national insurance contributions and holiday and sickness leave for each employee for the current tax year. A *systems flowchart*, as illustrated in Figure 35.1, is often used to describe business data processing systems such as this.

The systems flowchart shows the computer operations involved in a payroll run. Payroll systems normally use batch processing when the majority of the employees need to be paid. This lends itself to the use of magnetic tape devices (the flowchart does not specify the medium) which are restricted to sequential access. The payroll data is first stored on the payroll transaction file using keyboards as the input devices.

Each employee's pay information is stored in a separate record identified by employee number. Because the master file records are stored on tape in order of employee number, the transaction file must also be sorted into the same order. This is to avoid having to search for matching master file and transaction file records for each employee - because both files are in the same order, the next record in each file should be for the same employee. The sorted transaction file must be validated by the computer before processing the payroll data to produce payslips. This process performs various checks on the transaction file to ensure that only correct data will be processed. Any errors detected at this stage must be corrected before the payslips are generated.

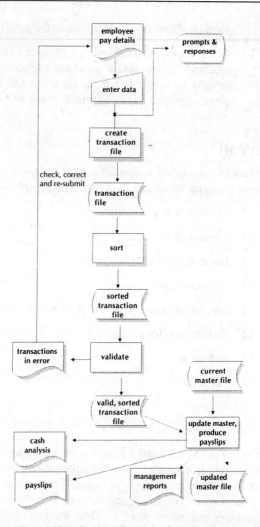

Figure 35.1. *Systems flowchart for payroll system*

Finally, the validated and sorted transaction file is processed against the payroll master file in order to produce the payslips. In addition to updating the master file, the payroll system might also produce summary reports for the management personnel of the company, and, if employees are paid by cash rather than by cheque or transfer to a bank account, a *cash analysis* might be produced. The cash analysis calculates exactly how many of each currency denomination will be required for all the pay packets, so that the correct money can be obtained from a bank. Each payslip would also have a corresponding breakdown for a single pay packet to make it easier for the cashiers to make up the pay packets.

A large company will probably use a mainframe computer for the task of processing the payroll information. Data entry will often be carried out using key-to-tape systems by a number of data entry clerks, and the output of the payslips will probably be by means of pre-printed stationery used on a line printer for speed. Backing storage will normally be in the form of magnetic tape or magnetic disk, but sequential *batch processing* will almost invariably be used. Of course, small companies having only a few employees might use a microcomputer system for the payroll, or even produce the payslips manually without the use of a computer at all.

Booking systems

Travel agents

If you go to a travel agent to book a seat on a major international airline, the travel agent will need to check the airline for the availability of the flight that you require. This normally involves communicating with the airlines computer to obtain up-to-date flight information. Remember that the same thing can be happening from all over the world: numerous travel agents could be accessing the same airlines computer at the same time, several of them even trying to book seats on the same flight that you want.

To cope with this type of demand, the airline will use a mainframe computer allowing on-line communication with each travel agent via the public telephone network. Each travel agency will have one or more terminals connected by modem to the airlines computer. Flight reservations will be performed in *real-time*, that is, the mainframe's flight and passenger information will be updated immediately to prevent the possibility of double-booking a seat on a particular flight. This ensures that the information that the travel agent obtains will be completely accurate and reliable. This form of processing, where a master file is updated immediately, is called *transaction processing* (see Chapter 16).

The process of reserving a seat on a flight is further complicated by the fact that several airlines might have scheduled flights to your destination, each offering different flight times, facilities and costs. Rather than contacting each one separately, a process that could take a considerable amount of time, the travel agent links into a wide area network(WAN) which connects the main computers of the different airlines. This allows the agent to choose the most appropriate flight for you and book it immediately. Though each airline in the system might have a different passenger reservation information system, the network software presents the same information format to the travel agents and takes care of transferring data in the correct format to the individual computer systems of the airlines.

When you have decided on your choice of airline and flight, your details are entered at the travel agent's terminal. While this is happening, other travel agents are prevented from accessing that particular flight record. On completion of the reservation, the flight record becomes available again. Booking cancellations and changes are handled in the same way. Your ticket, which will have been produced by the airline's computer, is usually sent out to you a few days prior to the departure date. Individual airline's computers also produce passenger lists automatically for use at the departure airports.

An airline's master passenger reservation and flight information file will be held on a high-capacity magnetic disk drive. For backup purposes, in case the master file is in some way lost or partly erased, or the disk drive fails, a separate disk drive will be used to hold an exact duplicate of the master file, and this duplicate file will be updated at the same time as the other master file. This duplication is necessary because the master file will be in constant use, night and day, and there will be no opportunity to stop updating it in order to make a backup on magnetic tape. For the same reasons of security, there will also be a duplicate main computer immediately ready to be used if the other one fails for some reason. Because of the importance of the fast response time required of the system, it will almost certainly be used exclusively for passenger booking purposes, and it will have been designed to operate without break, 24 hours a day, every day of the year.

Similar real-time systems are used by holiday firms, some of which are able to offer thousands of holidays all over the world. Travel agents must have access to accurate information regarding the availability of all the holidays on offer. Again it is important to ensure that exactly the same holiday is not sold to more than one customer, so the booking file held on the holiday company's main computer must be completely up-to-date.

Hotel booking

Hotels frequently use booking systems for keeping track of room reservations made by guests. These systems generally provide additional facilities relating to hotel management, typically keeping track of guests accounts and producing hotel room usage information.

When someone reserves a room in the hotel, a record is created in the guest file. The file contains three types of data:

❑ details of the guest, such as name, address, telephone number;

❑ room details, such as type (single, double etc.), number, period of occupancy;

❑ charges incurred by the guest during the stay at the hotel. For each charge, the item code, cost and date will be recorded.

The first two types of data are entered at the time the reservation is made; items and services bought by the guest during his or her stay, such as telephone calls, drinks, newspapers and extra meals, are recorded as and when they occur. When the guest leaves, the hotel system calculates the total bill and prints out an itemised list that the guest can check.

A hotel management system such as this can easily be implemented with a microcomputer system, though large hotel chains might also have a large central computer at their headquarters for general accounting purposes (such as producing financial reports covering the whole chain of hotels, and for payroll calculations).

Library systems

Dotherstaff College is a split site college of further and higher education. Each site has a large library which has recently been supplied with a microcomputer network for a library automation system called Alice, produced by a software company called Softlink. The software has a number of interlinked modules covering all aspects of typical library operation.

❑ Catalogue and Classification - managing the book database;

❑ Circulation - managing borrowers;

❑ Enquiries - information retrieval;

❑ Acquisition - ordering books;

❑ Reports and utilities- producing reports of publishers' details, author details and library usage figures;

❑ Periodicals- managing the ordering of magazines.

Catalogue and classification

This module is mainly used for the addition of new titles to the book database. Book details can be created, edited and deleted, as well as allowing the file to be browsed through, or searched.

Circulation

The circulation module is used for managing borrowers' details. To borrow a book from the library a borrower must produce his or her ticket on which there is a unique bar code. This bar code is scanned by a librarian and the borrower's record then appears on the screen. When the bar code of the book is scanned, the code is stored in the borrower's record. To return a book, the bar code of the book is scanned or typed in and the book is automatically removed from the borrower's record. The system also allows the display of all books currently borrowed by any person. Periodically, about every two weeks, the borrower file is searched for overdue items so that reminders can be generated automatically.

Enquiry

The enquiry module is used by staff and students to search the book database for books satisfying certain criteria. For example, a user can type in the name of an author and obtain a list of all books in the library written by that person. The title of a book, or part of the title can be entered and a list of books closely matching the title will be displayed. Alternatively, one or more keywords can be used to produce a list of books which contain the keywords in the title. The book information retrieved by an enquiry is summarised on the screen in several sections containing such things as the book titles, subjects covered and author(s). Any book selected from the list can have its full details displayed on screen or printed. This type of enquiry facility can save a great deal of time searching shelves or catalogues for specific information.

The network used for the library information system currently supports about 20 terminals, but it is also linked to the main college networks which provide access to other software such as word processors and spreadsheets.

Management applications

Management information systems (MIS)

Although computers can perform routine processing tasks very efficiently, it is generally recognised that limiting a compute'rs use to the processing of operational information constitutes a waste of computer power. An MIS is designed to make use of the computer's power of selection and analysis to produce useful management information.

An MIS has a number of key features:

- ❏ it produces information beyond that required for routine data processing;
- ❏ timing of information production is critical;
- ❏ the information it produces is an aid to decision-making;
- ❏ it is usually based on the database concept (explained in Chapter 26).

The claims for MIS are sometimes excessive. It is rarely the complete answer to all a company's information needs, but when successfully implemented, it provides a valuable information advantage over competitors.

Decision support systems (DSS)

A DSS aims to provide a more flexible decision tool than that supplied by a MIS which tends to produce information in an anticipated, pre-defined form and as such, does not allow managers to make ad hoc requests for information. DSS tend to be narrower in scope than MIS, often making use of general-purpose software packages. Examples of DSS include electronic spread-sheets, such as Microsoft Excel and relational database management systems such as Access and Paradox. The main features of these and other packages are described in some detail in Chapter 12. Additionally, *financial modelling* (Chapter 36) and statistical packages are considered to be DSS tools. A major benefit is the independence they allow for information control by individual managers and executives. When, for example, a sales manager requires a report on sales figures for the last three months, a microcomputer with database package may provide the report more quickly than a centralised data processing department.

Application objectives

A number of general objectives can be identified as being of relevance to most applications, in most organisations:

❑ Improved *operational efficiency*. *Speed* and *accuracy* of operations should be radically improved. This is not automatic as the computer-based system may be badly designed and the staff may be ill-trained, but given proper design and implementation, administrative systems will normally be more efficient.

❑ Better *control of resources*. Administrative systems such as those for financial control and the control of resources such as staff and raw materials, benefit particularly from the rapid production of up-to-date information by computer.

❑ Improved *productivity*. Redundancy does not always follow computerisation, particularly if the organisation is an expanding business. Computer-based systems should permit large increases in the volumes of business which can be handled without the need for extra staff.

❑ Improved *security of information*. With proper physical security, clear operational procedures to restrict access to computer facilities to those properly authorised, and with sophisticated use of software control mechanisms such as passwords, information can be made more secure than equivalent manual systems.

❑ Opportunities to *share data*. This is most likely where database systems and networked computer systems are employed.

❑ Improved *quality of information* for *decision taking* at the operational, strategic and corporate levels in an organisation. *Operational decisions* concern day-to-day operations, such as handling of customer orders or delivery of new stocks. At the *strategic level*, decisions may relate to issues such as production planning and the selection of suppliers. *Corporate decision* examples include the setting of prices, targeting of markets and the manufacture of new products. Most systems generate a range of management information reports, drawn from the routine processing of transactions and these are primarily of use at the strategic level, but may also help with corporate decisions. Accounts software, for example, produces reports on outstanding debts, potential bad debtors, dates when payments to suppliers are due and analysis of sales patterns.

❑ Improved *external image*. An organisation can improve its external image by the improved presentation of correspondence and by an improved service to its customers or clients, but badly designed procedures can also make life more difficult for them.

❑   Improved *working conditions*. This is highly debatable in respect of an office environment, but computer-based manufacturing systems usually provide a less dirty and dangerous environment for employees, as much of the work is done by robots and other computer-controlled machinery.

Selecting an appropriate system

Whether batch processing, one of the on-line types, or distributed processing (Chapter 16) is appropriate depends on a number of factors:

❑   the type and size of organisation. Large organisations generally have larger volumes of data to handle, than do small ones. Batch processing is efficient in the sense that it is a concentrated activity and if transactions can be accumulated and handled together, then it may be more efficient than dealing with each transaction as it arises. On the other hand, delay may prevent achievement of an important objective, such as the provision of up-to-date management information. Distributed processing, through computer networks, is an increasingly popular option for a medium or large organisation, because it gives local control to branches and allows data to be shared and communicated across the whole organisation;

❑   the activity (for example, financial accounts, hotel booking);

❑   the objectives of the activity (see previous section).

As explained in Chapters 16 and 17, a batch processing system provides numerous opportunities to ensure the accuracy of data, as it passes through the system. In this way, the type satisfies one of the main objectives of many systems and if this were the only criterion for selection, all systems would use batch processing. Of course, there are other criteria which must be applied to the selection process, including: system purpose(s); size and type of organisation; other objectives, such as security, speed, or the provision of extra management information. For example, an airline's passenger reservation system cannot be effective unless files are updated at the time each reservation is made and transaction processing is found to be appropriate. An organisation's stock control system may need to reflect stock changes on the same basis as the airline reservation system, particularly if delivery has to be immediate. Discount stores, such as Argos, sell a huge range of consumer items and some are expensive; it is not desirable to hold high stock levels, because this ties up large amounts of cash, so the stock records need to be updated as goods are delivered and sold. In some organisations, stock movements (stock received and stock issued) do not have to be instantly reflected in stock records, because delivery times to customers can be longer, perhaps up to several weeks. If the goods are not of high value, then it may be convenient to hold larger stocks, which ensure the satisfaction of customer demand. For example, if the stock record for an item shows 1000 units and 50 units is the maximum customer requirement, then a physical stock level which is only 800 units, is not an immediate problem.

The size of the organisation is also a significant factor in determining the most appropriate type of data handling system. A small plumbing firm, perhaps consisting of two partners and a couple of employees is unlikely to include anyone to keep the accounts; this will probably be the job of one of the partners, who will only have time to do the work at weekends. Thus, customer invoices and payments are dealt with in a batch, perhaps every week. As a small firm, a major objective will be to collect customer debts as quickly as possible and the computerised system can help to do this, in the limited time that the partner has to deal with such matters.

Chapter 36

Modelling and Simulation

The term *modelling* is used in information technology for computer applications which, for example, are used to investigate, analyse or plan a complex activity, or to *simulate* a complex process. Some models are concerned with investigating financial systems using a software tool such as a *spreadsheet* program. For example, a manufacturing company might use a spreadsheet-based model to determine the minimum number of items the company must produce in order to make a profit.

Other computer models are concerned with representing physical systems. For example, before a new chemical plant is built, its designers often will first model the complex arrangement of pipes and other equipment using a 3-D computer graphics program, and also simulate its operation with other types of software. In this way many potential problems can be identified and solved before construction work is started. This chapter begins by describing the nature and purpose of mathematical models and simulations. Some of the areas that have benefited from modelling and simulation are discussed in the next section. There are then some spreadsheet-based examples of simulations, followed by an investigation of the application of 3-D computer graphics programs to modelling.

Mathematical models

Physical models are usually simplified versions of actual objects or objects that may be constructed at some later date. Thus, a car manufacturer might produce a scaled-down model of a new car to investigate its wind-resistance characteristics. Though the model accurately represents the shape of the car, it is much easier to construct than a full-sized working version. Producing a model therefore provides a convenient and cheap method of investigating certain aspects of the final product. A *mathematical model* takes modelling a stage further: it provides a means of investigating something without the need to make a physical model. Mathematical models are symbolic representations of things that we want to know more about. For example, a mathematical model of the distance travelled by a body accelerating from rest is

$$s = \frac{1}{2}at^2$$

where s is the distance travelled, a is the acceleration of the body and t is the time period. This mathematical model now allows us to investigate the effects of different accelerations and different time periods on the distance travelled by the body, without having to build a working model. Using this model it can be predicted that a body uniformly accelerating at 5 metres/sec^2 for ten seconds will have travelled

$$\frac{1}{2} \times 5 \times 10^2 \text{ metres,}$$

that is, 250 metres. Of course not all mathematical models are as simple as this. Some mathematical models attempt to describe much more complex things such as human behaviour or weather patterns. Such complex models involve defining the relationships between the many variables of the system being modelled, and they almost invariably require the use of very powerful computers to investigate them.

Simulation

In computer science, *simulation* refers to the use of computers to model and investigate systems which involve some changing process. Thus a computer simulation will generally incorporate a mathematical model of the system of interest. The purpose of a computer simulation often is to enable experimental measurements to be made or to predict behaviour. Simulation can provide an experimental system for designers to investigate behaviour under a variety of different circumstances, or it may be used to provide a teaching aid for the system being simulated.

The prime reason for developing a simulation is that the cost of experimenting with the actual system is prohibitive, and since simulations are themselves expensive, there must be very sound economical reasons for justifying their use. For example, it is much cheaper and quicker to test a large number of design variations of a nuclear reactor by using a simulation rather than by building prototypes. More possible reasons for simulating a complex system are:

❑ *Testing* - it is necessary to test the system to destruction, that is, identify the factors that will cause it to fail and a complex device might be too expensive to use for the investigation.

❑ *Safety* - it is too dangerous or expensive to use the actual equipment. An example is teaching an aircraft pilot to respond to a range of emergency situations.

❑ *Prediction* - an accurate model is needed of an existing system so that its future behaviour can be predicted accurately. A good example of this is weather forecasting.

❑ *Speed and flexibility* - the system might require frequent modification and development. For example, in control systems electronically-based instruments can be simulated by a computer. These so-called virtual instruments allow devices, such as meters and indicators, and other electronic components, to be represented by software which is cheaper and easier to modify or replace than physical devices.

Simulation parameters

A mathematical model of a system usually consists of a linked set of formulae in which the result of one formula may affect others. These formulae will generally use one or more key factors, or *parameters*; altering the value of a parameter will generally alter the overall behaviour of the system. A number of different types of parameters can be identified:

❑ *Controllable inputs*. These are factors, or *variables*, which are under the direct control of the system designers. For example, in a stock control simulation where items of stock are continually being sold to customers and received from suppliers, two of the controllable inputs are likely to be the re-order quantity and re-order level. In a traffic lights simulation, the timing of the red/green cycle is also under the control of the system designers.

❑ *Non-controllable inputs*. These are factors which are not under the direct control of the system designers. For example, in a simulation of a supermarket checkout queue, the arrival rate of customers is an input variable which cannot be controlled, but there will be some statistical information regarding its characteristics. Similarly in a traffic lights simulation, the arrival and departure rates of vehicles at the junction are not directly under the control of the designers. These types of variables frequently have characteristics which can be described using probability.

❏ *Seasonal variations*. Some factors, again not under the control of the system designers, can vary significantly according to the time of day, the day of the week, or the season of the year. For instance, traffic density is usually heavier in the morning when people are travelling to work and in the evening when people are returning home, than at other times of the day. Supermarkets often attract more customers at the weekend and just before bank holidays, than on other days.

Monte Carlo simulation

One common technique used in simulation is called the *Monte Carlo* method which uses random numbers to solve problems. The method is particularly suitable for problems which involve statistical uncertainty. For example, when you throw a die, you are never certain which number is going to show: there is an equal probability of each of the number 1 to 6 appearing. A computer program could be used to generate a random number in the range 1 to 6 in order to simulate a die being thrown. This is a simple application of the Monte Carlo method.

Most high-level programming languages and spreadsheet programs provide random number generators. However, the random number function usually will return a fraction between 0 and 1, but this can be converted into the required range quite simply. For instance, if we multiply the random number by 6, add one and ignore the fractional part of the number, we will have a random number between 1 and 6. Thus if the random number was 0.3245 then when multiplied by 6 it gives 1.9470. Adding 1 gives 2.9470, and ignoring the fractional part gives us our random number 2. The queue simulation example later in this chapter uses random numbers produced by a spreadsheet to simulate traffic arriving at traffic lights.

Applications

Mathematical models and simulation are used in many areas including:

Marketing. This involves activities related to getting goods from the producer to the consumer. Marketing research involves the use of surveys, tests, and statistical studies to analyse consumer trends, to identify profitable markets for products or services and to produce sales predictions. Such research and forecasts require mathematical models of social behaviour and consumers' needs for various products. The cost implications of predicted demands for goods can also be modelled so that a company can be fully prepared to cope with the production, distribution and sale of the products.

Sociology is a social science that deals with the study of human social relations or group life. Quantitative sociology, which attempts to analyse sociological phenomena using mathematics, ranges from the presentation of large amounts of descriptive statistical data to the use of advanced mathematical models and computer simulations of social processes. One popular area of investigation is identification of the factors that are mainly responsible for people succeeding or failing in their chosen occupations.

Social psychology is a branch of psychology concerned with the scientific study of the behaviour of individuals as influenced, directly or indirectly, by social factors. Social psychologists are interested in the thinking, emotions, desires, and judgements of individuals, as well as in their outward behaviour. Numerous kinds of research methods and techniques are being used in social psychology. In recent years accurate mathematical models of social behaviour have been used increasingly in psychological studies. Such models allow predictions of social behaviour to be made, given a system of social relationships.

Educational psychology involves the application of scientific method to the study of the behaviour of people in instructional settings. Different theories of learning help educational psychologists understand, predict, and control human behaviour. For example, educational psychologists have worked out mathematical models of learning that predict the probability of a student making a correct response to a multiple-choice question. These mathematical theories are used to design computerised instruction in reading, mathematics, and second-language learning.

Weather forecasting involves reporting, predicting, and studying the weather, including temperature, moisture, barometric pressure, and wind speed and direction. In addition to their regular and special services to the public, weather services conduct research projects. In their meteorological investigations, primarily concerned with forecasting techniques and storm behaviour, these agencies make use of the findings from studies of mathematical modelling of the general circulation of the atmosphere, advances in radar meteorology, high-speed computer methods, and earth-orbiting artificial satellites.

Fluid mechanics is a physical science dealing with the action of fluids at rest or in motion, and with applications and devices in engineering using fluids. Fluid mechanics is basic to such diverse fields as aeronautics, chemical, civil, and mechanical engineering, meteorology, naval architecture, and oceanography. Turbulent flows cannot be analysed solely from computed predictions and depend on a mixture of experimental data and mathematical models for their analysis, with much of modern fluid-mechanics research still being devoted to better models of turbulence. The nature and complexity of turbulent flow can be observed as cigarette smoke rises into very still air. At first it rises in a stable streamline motion but after some distance it becomes unstable and breaks up into an intertwining eddy pattern.

Population biology is the study of populations of animals and plants. A population is a group of interbreeding organisms in a specific region - for example, the members of a species of fish in a lake. Populations are analysed in terms of their variability, density, and stability, and of the environmental and other processes and circumstances that affect these characteristics. Among such key features of a given population are birth and death rates; the distribution of ages and sexes; behavioural patterns of competition and co-operation; predator-prey, host-parasite, and other relationships with different species; food supplies and other environmental considerations; and migration patterns. To analyse populations biologists try to develop mathematical models of the group under study that incorporate as many of these variables as possible. Such models enable scientists to predict what effect a change in any one factor may have on a population as a whole.

Catastrophe theory is the term for an attempt to develop a mathematical modelling system for dealing with abruptly changing natural events. One such physical 'catastrophe', for example, could be an avalanche resulting from a gradual build-up of snow. In the area of human relations, a 'catastrophe' could be someone suddenly losing his or her temper after being patient for a long period. Catastrophe theory was primarily intended to be useful for describing events in the biological and social sciences.

Science education. Laboratory experiments to determine the characteristics of falling bodies, colliding balls, pendulums and projectiles can all be simulated quite easily by a computer. Students can investigate the effects of changing various parameters such as the weight of the pendulum, or the speed of colliding objects, or the angle at which an object is projected, or any one of a number of other factors that affect the experiment of interest.

Medical education. Medical diagnosis is a very complex activity and very difficult to learn. Though the typical symptoms of most ailments are well-known, the manner in which a given illness manifests itself varies from patient to patient. This means that physicians must acquire the ability to assign the correct level of importance to each recognisable symptom in order to make a correct diagnosis.

Computers can help with this task by simulating illnesses and associated symptoms. The computer model of the illness can be set up so that the symptoms vary each time the same illness is simulated. The computer might present a case study of a patient, supplying the student with the type of information gained from tests and by questioning the patient. The student is then required to arrive at a diagnosis of the ailment and suggest appropriate treatment. The student's diagnosis and suggested treatment can then be compared with the correct ones stored in the computer in order to provide feedback concerning the accuracy of the student's analysis. In this way, students can very quickly 'experience' many different manifestations of a particular illness, a situation which could be very difficult to organise using actual patients.

Computers can also be used to show the effects of drugs on the human body. How long a drug remains active in the bloodstream and the concentration of the drug after repeated doses are very important factors. However, because of the complexity of the human body and the great number of factors which contribute to the effects of a particular drug, predicting the effects of a drug is very difficult. Computer simulations which use complex theoretical models of the human body can allow students to experiment with typical drug dosages and observe the resulting effects. A common approach is to present the student with a number of screens of text and/or graphical information. After this information has been assimilated, the student is then in a position to understand the purpose of the simulation and what information must be supplied. By providing typical drug characteristics and dosages, the student can observe the predicted affect of the drug as simulated by the computer. Finally, the student completes a multiple-choice test which is marked by the computer. Any weaknesses in the student's understanding of the material can thus be identified and remedied by suggesting that the student repeats certain parts of the simulation program.

With the enormous increase in desk top computing power over recent years, it is now feasible to produce computer programs which use graphics to allow students to explore the human body in great detail. Software simulates the structure and function of the nervous, circulatory, immune and other systems of the body using multimedia. Though they are not used as replacements for actually dissecting cadavers, these products can give students a useful grounding in physiology and anatomy.

Queuing theory. This deals with the analysis of the waiting lines that occur in many areas of modern life. Whenever something is in demand, there is the possibility of a queue of some description forming, resulting in restricted access to resources, or losses in time, money and patience. Efforts to avoid and control congestion are therefore of great interest to providers of services which can cause queues, and this has led to the study of waiting lines using mathematical models and simulation. An area which has benefited greatly from queuing theory is that of time-shared computer systems in which each user is given a small amount of processing time and users waiting their turn are put in a queue; the computer decides which job will be serviced next and for how long using a scheduling algorithm based on queuing theory.

Instrumentation. Computer measurement systems frequently involve monitoring a physical system, analysing the data gathered and displaying the results. Traditionally, many such systems have used hardware components, such as filters, frequency analysers, meters and LED displays, but computers can be used to replace many of these devices. *Virtual instruments* allow many physical devices to be simulated using a computer. A virtual instrument uses software components to process the data measured externally to the computer, and to present results of processing using realistic representations of instrument panels containing meters, switches, digital and other types of displays. (See Figure 36.1). Graphically based programming languages allow complex processing tasks to be programmed by connecting together symbols which represent electronic devices.

Figure 36.1. *Example of a virtual instrument*

The advantage of this approach is that new devices can be constructed, tested and modified without the need to produce costly, purpose-built hardware devices.

Three-dimensional models. Many software products are available for simulating the structure of solid objects. These programs allow designers to create three-dimensional drawings of objects which can be viewed from any angle, rotated, and modified using a wide variety of software tools. Many 3D drawing programs also allow objects to be animated. For example, detailed computer models of buildings are used as the basis of *fly-throughs* in which a simulated camera navigates through the building, going from room to room, zooming in and out. Simulations such as this, animated or otherwise, allow complex objects to be visualised prior to production, thus speeding up and reducing the design process.

Figure 36.2. *3D model of a building*

Modelling and simulation using spreadsheets

In this section we look at the use of spreadsheet for performing a break-even analysis to investigate a manufacturing business, to simulate a stock control system and to simulate traffic arriving at traffic lights. Here we limit explanations to special functions that are required for simulation purposes and to the formulas that are required for the various calculations involved.

Financial planning - break-even analysis

The prime objective of most organisations is the achievement of profit. In order to make a profit the organisation must earn sufficient revenue from the sale of its products to exceed the costs that it has incurred in operating and producing. It is usually a relatively simple task to calculate revenue: simply determine the number of goods which have been sold and multiply this quantity by the price per item. The calculation of cost is slightly more complicated owing to the fact that the organisation incurs a variety of different costs in producing its products.

Fixed costs remain constant irrespective of the number of items produced. Examples include rent on the premises or local council rates. Therefore, as production rises the fixed cost per item reduces. Other costs, however, increase with production. These are called *variable costs*. Raw materials are an example of variable costs since as more items are produced, more raw materials are required. Combining fixed and variable costs gives the organisation its total costs and it is these which must be exceeded by its total revenue before it can make a profit. Clearly then, an organisation may make a loss if its output is low, but as it produces and sells more it will eventually move through a *break-even point* into profit. As the name suggests, the break-even point is where the organisation neither makes a loss nor a profit – it simply breaks even. Management are obviously very interested to know the level of production required to exceed the break-even point and make a profit. Combining the revenue and cost figures in order to determine the break-even point is called *break-even analysis*, and a graphical representation of the figures is termed a *break-even chart*. An example of a break-even analysis and the equivalent chart are shown in Figures 36.3 and 36.4, respectively. The formulas used in the spreadsheet are shown in Table 36.1.

	D	E	F	G	H	I
7	UNITS PRODUCED	FIXED COSTS	VARIABLE COSTS	TOTAL COSTS	REVENUE	PROFIT
8	0	=$G$4	0	=E8+F8	=D8*$G$5	=G8-H8
9	100	=$G$4	200	=E9+F9	=D9*$G$5	=G9-H9
10	200	=$G$4	300	=E10+F10	=D10*$G$5	=G10-H10
11	300	=$G$4	350	=E11+F11	=D11*$G$5	=G11-H11
12	400	=$G$4	450	=E12+F12	=D12*$G$5	=G12-H12
13	500	=$G$4	600	=E13+F13	=D13*$G$5	=G13-H13
14	600	=$G$4	800	=E14+F14	=D14*$G$5	=G14-H14
15	700	=$G$4	1050	=E15+F15	=D15*$G$5	=G15-H15
16	800	=$G$4	1350	=E16+F16	=D16*$G$5	=G16-H16
17	900	=$G$4	1700	=E17+F17	=D17*$G$5	=G17-H17
18	1000	=$G$4	2100	=E18+F18	=D18*$G$5	=G18-H18

Table 36.1. *Formulas for break-even analysis in Figure 36.3*

	PRODUCED	FIXED COSTS	E COSTS	TOTAL COSTS	REVENUE	PROFIT
8	0	500	0	500	0	500
9	100	500	200	700	270	430
10	200	500	300	800	540	260
11	300	500	350	850	810	40
12	400	500	450	950	1080	-130
13	500	500	600	1100	1350	-250
14	600	500	800	1300	1620	-320
15	700	500	1050	1550	1890	-340
16	800	500	1350	1850	2160	-310
17	900	500	1700	2200	2430	-230
18	1000	500	2100	2600	2700	-100

Figure 36.3. *Break-even analysis*

Figure 36.4. *Break-even chart*

The UNITS PRODUCED and VARIABLE COSTS columns of the spreadsheet are constant values. FIXED COSTS are copied from the Fixed Costs(FC) parameter cell. The TOTAL COSTS column is the sum of FIXED COSTS and VARIABLE COSTS. The REVENUE is calculated by multiplying the units produced by the Unit Cost(UC) parameter. Finally, the profit is found by subtracting the TOTAL COSTS from the REVENUE.

The break-even chart, shown in Figure 36.4, graphs the three costs and the revenue figures; the break-even point is where the TOTAL COSTS curve crosses the REVENUE line. Profit occurs to the right of the break-even point, and you can see that in this case, when the fixed costs are at £500 and the selling price is £2.70, the break-even point occurs when just over 300 items are produced. Interestingly, the graph also shows that maximum profit occurs when between 600 and 700 items are produced and that at about 1000 items the company again breaks even.

Stock control simulation

Suppose that Agros is a large retail outlet which sells a wide range of household materials. It has a computerised stock control, or *inventory*, system which deals with obtaining, storing and supplying the goods it offers to the general public. Agros provides free catalogues containing descriptions of items which customers can obtain by visiting one of their outlets. The items shown in the catalogue are kept in a warehouse attached to the outlet. It is of vital importance to Agros to ensure that it has a full range of items in stock so that customers can immediately obtain those that they require.

If an item is out of stock, the potential customer might decide to shop elsewhere thus causing Agros to lose the sale, and possibly future sales too. Agros attempts to prevent this situation by ordering quantities of those items that are in danger of being sold out. However, the time taken for the items to arrive from the suppliers may be several days, by which time the goods still could have sold out. Moreover, if the demand for an item is overestimated, and there are a large number of the item in the warehouse, Agros again loses money because each item incurs a warehouse storage cost.

Agros must try to achieve a balance between over-ordering and under-ordering goods. This would be an easy problem to solve if Agros knew exactly what the demand for a particular item is likely to be at any one time, but unfortunately this is never the case. Possibly the best prediction of demand will still involve a large amount of uncertainty. For example, past experience might provide an estimate of the average demand per day for an item, but the actual demand on a particular day will probably fluctuate fairly randomly. A possible means of investigating this type of system is therefore a Monte Carlo simulation in which demand is simulated using a random number generator such as that described in the previous example.

Before showing how a spreadsheet can be used for such a simulation, a number of terms commonly used in stock control systems, are described.

Demand – the quantity of a product that customers are willing to purchase.

Opening stock – the number of items of stock immediately available for purchase at the start of trading on any day.

Closing stock – the number of items of stock that remain in the outlet at the close of trading on any particular day.

Re-order quantity – the number of items of stock ordered from a supplier at any one time.

Re-order level – the minimum number of items held in stock before the item is re-ordered. As soon as the level of stock reaches this level, or drops below it, the re-order quantity is ordered from the supplier.

Carrying costs – the cost of storing an item waiting to be sold.

Stock out costs – the financial loss incurred when the demand for an item exceeds the stock level. In other words, a company loses money when it cannot supply an item to a customer because that item is out of stock. The term *Loss of Goodwill* also applies to this type of loss, because the disappointed customer might not use the outlet in the future.

Order costs – the cost to the company of making an order or a re-order quantity of a product; this in addition to the actual cost of buying the items from the supplier. Each time an order is generated, there is an order cost.

Lead time – this is the time it takes to receive an item from the supplier once the order has been generated.

The simulation shown in Figure 36.5 (see Table 36.2 for formulas) illustrates the effects of the stock control parameters, shown at the top of the spreadsheet, over a period of fourteen days.

Parameters

AVERAGE DEMAND(AD)	5 per day	REORDER-LEVEL(RL) 5 items
CARRYING COST(CC)	£2 per day	REORDER QUANTITY(RQ) 8 items
ORDER COST(OC)	£10 per order	
LOSS OF GOODWILL(GW)	£5 per item	
OPENING STOCK(OS)	5 items	LEAD TIME(LT) 2 days

DAY	OPENING STOCK	DEMAND	CLOSING STOCK	NUM ORDERED	ORDER COSTS	CARRYING COSTS	STOCK OUT COSTS	TOTAL COST
1	5	0	5	8	£10.00	£10.00	£0.00	£20.00
2	5	6	0	8	£10.00	£0.00	£5.00	£15.00
3	8	5	3	8	£10.00	£6.00	£0.00	£16.00
4	11	3	8	0	£0.00	£16.00	£0.00	£16.00
5	16	3	13	0	£0.00	£26.00	£0.00	£26.00
6	13	5	8	0	£0.00	£16.00	£0.00	£16.00
7	8	3	5	8	£10.00	£10.00	£0.00	£20.00
8	5	2	3	8	£10.00	£6.00	£0.00	£16.00
9	11	6	5	8	£10.00	£10.00	£0.00	£20.00
10	13	4	9	0	£0.00	£18.00	£0.00	£18.00
11	17	2	15	0	£0.00	£30.00	£0.00	£30.00
12	15	3	12	0	£0.00	£24.00	£0.00	£24.00
13	12	3	9	0	£0.00	£18.00	£0.00	£18.00
14	9	4	5	8	£10.00	£10.00	£0.00	£20.00
15	5	5	0	8	£10.00	£0.00	£0.00	£10.00
			Totals		£80.00	£200.00	£5.00	£285.00

Figure 36.5. *Stock control simulation*

The columns in the table have been calculated as follows:

❑ OPENING STOCK - On the first day of the simulation period this is the value OS which appears in the parameter table. On the second day it is the closing stock value for the first day, that is, the number of stock items left after close of business the previous day. On the third and subsequent days it is the closing value for the previous day plus any stock that was ordered two days previously. Thus, for day four, the opening stock (10) is the sum of the third day's closing stock (2) and the quantity ordered on the second day (8).

❑ DEMAND - This is produced using a random number generator which produces a random number between half the average demand and one and a half times the average demand. For example, if the average demand is 6 items per day, a random number between 3 and 9 is generated. This represents the actual demand for the item on a particular day, and this is where the uncertainty factor is introduced.

	DAY	OPENING STOCK	DEMAND	CLOSING STOCK	NUM ORDERED	ORDER COSTS	CARRYING COSTS	STOCK OUT COSTS	TOTAL COST
11									
12	1	=OS	=INT(AD/2*(1+2*RAND()))	=IF(F12<G12,0,F12-G12)	=IF(H12<=RL,RQ,0)	=IF(I12>0,OC,0)	=H12*CC	=IF(H12=0,GW*(G12-F12),0)	=SUM(J12:L12)
13	2	=H12	=INT(AD/2*(1+2*RAND()))	=IF(F13<G13,0,F13-G13)	=IF(H13<=RL,RQ,0)	=IF(I13>0,OC,0)	=H13*CC	=IF(H13=0,GW*(G13-F13),0)	=SUM(J13:L13)
14	3	=H13+I12	=INT(AD/2*(1+2*RAND()))	=IF(F14<G14,0,F14-G14)	=IF(H14<=RL,RQ,0)	=IF(I14>0,OC,0)	=H14*CC	=IF(H14=0,GW*(G14-F14),0)	=SUM(J14:L14)
15	4	=H14+I13	=INT(AD/2*(1+2*RAND()))	=IF(F15<G15,0,F15-G15)	=IF(H15<=RL,RQ,0)	=IF(I15>0,OC,0)	=H15*CC	=IF(H15=0,GW*(G15-F15),0)	=SUM(J15:L15)
16	5	=H15+I14	=INT(AD/2*(1+2*RAND()))	=IF(F16<G16,0,F16-G16)	=IF(H16<=RL,RQ,0)	=IF(I16>0,OC,0)	=H16*CC	=IF(H16=0,GW*(G16-F16),0)	=SUM(J16:L16)
17	6	=H16+I15	=INT(AD/2*(1+2*RAND()))	=IF(F17<G17,0,F17-G17)	=IF(H17<=RL,RQ,0)	=IF(I17>0,OC,0)	=H17*CC	=IF(H17=0,GW*(G17-F17),0)	=SUM(J17:L17)
18	7	=H17+I16	=INT(AD/2*(1+2*RAND()))	=IF(F18<G18,0,F18-G18)	=IF(H18<=RL,RQ,0)	=IF(I18>0,OC,0)	=H18*CC	=IF(H18=0,GW*(G18-F18),0)	=SUM(J18:L18)
19	8	=H18+I17	=INT(AD/2*(1+2*RAND()))	=IF(F19<G19,0,F19-G19)	=IF(H19<=RL,RQ,0)	=IF(I19>0,OC,0)	=H19*CC	=IF(H19=0,GW*(G19-F19),0)	=SUM(J19:L19)
20	9	=H19+I18	=INT(AD/2*(1+2*RAND()))	=IF(F20<G20,0,F20-G20)	=IF(H20<=RL,RQ,0)	=IF(I20>0,OC,0)	=H20*CC	=IF(H20=0,GW*(G20-F20),0)	=SUM(J20:L20)
21	10	=H20+I19	=INT(AD/2*(1+2*RAND()))	=IF(F21<G21,0,F21-G21)	=IF(H21<=RL,RQ,0)	=IF(I21>0,OC,0)	=H21*CC	=IF(H21=0,GW*(G21-F21),0)	=SUM(J21:L21)
22	11	=H21+I20	=INT(AD/2*(1+2*RAND()))	=IF(F22<G22,0,F22-G22)	=IF(H22<=RL,RQ,0)	=IF(I22>0,OC,0)	=H22*CC	=IF(H22=0,GW*(G22-F22),0)	=SUM(J22:L22)
23	12	=H22+I21	=INT(AD/2*(1+2*RAND()))	=IF(F23<G23,0,F23-G23)	=IF(H23<=RL,RQ,0)	=IF(I23>0,OC,0)	=H23*CC	=IF(H23=0,GW*(G23-F23),0)	=SUM(J23:L23)
24	13	=H23+I22	=INT(AD/2*(1+2*RAND()))	=IF(F24<G24,0,F24-G24)	=IF(H24<=RL,RQ,0)	=IF(I24>0,OC,0)	=H24*CC	=IF(H24=0,GW*(G24-F24),0)	=SUM(J24:L24)
25	14	=H24+I23	=INT(AD/2*(1+2*RAND()))	=IF(F25<G25,0,F25-G25)	=IF(H25<=RL,RQ,0)	=IF(I25>0,OC,0)	=H25*CC	=IF(H25=0,GW*(G25-F25),0)	=SUM(J25:L25)
26	15	=H25+I24	=INT(AD/2*(1+2*RAND()))	=IF(F26<G26,0,F26-G26)	=IF(H26<=RL,RQ,0)	=IF(I26>0,OC,0)	=H26*CC	=IF(H26=0,GW*(G26-F26),0)	=SUM(J26:L26)
27									
28					Totals	=SUM(J12:J2?	=SUM(K12:K?	=SUM(L12:L27)	=SUM(M12:M?

Table 36.2. *Formulas for stock control simulation*

❏   CLOSING STOCK - the number of items remaining in the warehouse/storeroom at close of trading on that day.

❏   NUM ORDERED - the number of items ordered that day. This will be either the re-order quantity, if the closing stock level is equal to or below the re-order level, or zero if the CLOSING STOCK level is greater than the re-order level.

❏   ORDER COSTS - each time the item is re-ordered, there is an order cost incurred.

❏   CARRYING COSTS - there is a charge for each item in stock at the close of trading on each day. Thus, on day 5, CLOSING STOCK was 9 and the order costs at £2 per item means that the CARRYING COSTS amount to £18.

❏   STOCK OUT COSTS - a fixed cost is incurred for each item out of stock that a customer was willing to buy. This is calculated by subtracting OPENING STOCK from DEMAND and multiplying the result by the LOSS OF GOODWILL cost shown in the parameter table.

❏   TOTAL COSTS - calculated by summing ORDER COSTS, CARRYING COSTS and STOCK OUT COSTS.

The column totals for the four costs calculated are shown below the appropriate columns.

Note that the OPENING STOCK parameter is a constant value that can be changed in this particular simulation only by changing the formulas in the OPEN STOCK column. Each time the spreadsheet is recalculated (by pressing F9 in Excel) new DEMAND random numbers are generated for each day, and the resulting costs are displayed. This allows investigation of the effects of changing the various parameters, for example, the investigation of the effect on the total costs of increasing the re-order level, or of reducing the re-order quantity, or the effect of changing both of these parameters together.

Simulating vehicles arriving at traffic lights

At a road junction controlled by traffic lights, vehicles arriving at the junction form a queue when the lights are on red. The size of the queue depends on two factors: the length of time the lights remain on red and the rate at which vehicles arrive at the junction. When the lights turn to green, the queue reduces as vehicles pass through the junction. At the same time, however, vehicles are still arriving at the junction while the lights are on green. In this simple simulation (Figures 36.6 and 36.7), we use four *parameters*, which affect the size of the queue:

1.   The average rate of arrival of vehicles at the lights. We assume that if the average rate is say, A, then during any stop period the actual rate is modelled by generating a random number between A/2 and 3A/2. For example, if the average arrival rate is 4 vehicles per minute, then we generate a random number between 2 and 6 and use this as the actual arrival rate for one instance of the lights being on red. We generate a new value for the actual arrival rate the next time the (simulated) lights turn to red.

2.   The average rate of departure from the lights. We use the same scheme as for the arrival rate: if the average departure rate is L vehicles per minute, then we generate a random number between L/2 and 3L/2 to represent the actual departure rate for one instance of the lights being on green. We generate a new value for the actual departure rate the next time the lights turn to green.

3.　The length of time (in minutes) the lights are on red. This affects the build-up of the vehicle queue, since the longer the lights are on red, the greater is the number of vehicles that will arrive at the junction and join the end of the queue.

4.　The length of time (in minutes) the lights are on green. This controls how many vehicles can leave the queue.

Figure 36.6. *Traffic lights queue simulation*

The figure shows a spreadsheet with the following content:

Microsoft Excel - mod and Sim.xls.xls

File Edit View Insert Format Tools Data Window Help

Traffic lights simulation

Parameters

Arrival rate	AR	5 per min
Leave rate	LR	10 per min
Stop period	ST	3 min
Go period	GO	4 min

CYCLE	ELAPSED TIME[min]	RED		GREEN			QUEUE
		Rate	Arrive	Rate	Depart	Arrive	
1	7	4	12	11	44	16	0
2	14	4	12	11	44	16	0
3	21	2	6	12	48	8	0
4	28	5	15	11	44	20	0
5	35	4	12	10	40	16	0
6	42	6	18	5	20	24	22
7	49	6	18	10	40	24	24
8	56	6	18	5	20	24	46
9	63	5	15	6	24	20	57
10	70	4	12	13	52	16	33

Chart1 \ Taffic lights sim / breakeven chart / Breakeven

Traffic lights queue length

Figure 36.7. *Chart for traffic lights queue simulation*

A complete cycle of the lights is one stop (i.e. red) period followed by one go (i.e. green) period. The simulation calculates the size of the queue after each of these cycles. As an example, suppose that the average arrival rate at the lights (called AR on the spreadsheet) is 5 vehicles per minute, the average departure rate (LR) is 20 vehicles per minute, the lights are on red for 3 minutes *(ST)* and green for 4 minutes *(GO)*, then for the first cycle, assuming that there were no vehicles waiting, the calculation might go as follows:

1.   Vehicles arriving when lights are on red : $3 \times R1 = 3 \times 2 = 6$ to the nearest whole number (assuming R1 was 2), where R1 represents a random number between 1.5 and 4.5

2.   Vehicles leaving the junction when lights are on green : $4 \times R2 = 4 \times 5 = 20$ to the nearest whole number (assuming R2 was 5), where R2 represents a random number between 2 and 6.

3.   Vehicles arriving at the junction while the lights are on green : $4 \times R1 = 4 \times 2 = 8$ to the nearest whole number.

Therefore, the queue length after one cycle of the lights is given by

4.   Vehicles arriving(red) – Vehicles departing(green) + Vehicles arriving(green)

     $= 6 - 20 + 8 = -6.$

The negative number indicates that it was possible for six more vehicles to go through the lights than actually arrived at the junction. This would give a queue length of zero. A positive value would mean that a queue of vehicles still remained after the lights turned back to red, and this would be used as the initial queue size for the next cycle. The formulas used in the spreadsheet are shown in Table 36.3. The Excel spreadsheet uses two important functions:

❏   `RANDBETWEEN (bottom, top)` produces a random integer greater than or equal to *bottom* and less than or equal to *top*. If this function is not available, the standard `RAND ()` function can be used as follows: `INT (RAND () * (top-bottom+1) + bottom)`. The `INT` function rounds down the value inside the brackets to the nearest integer; the complete expression again produces an integer between *top* and *bottom* inclusively.

❏   `IF(condition, true, false)` tests the specified *condition* and executes the *true* expression if it is true and the *false* expression otherwise. The `IF` function is required to check whether the queue length is negative, indicating that no vehicles were left in the queue at the end of the green period. If the queue length is negative, it is set to zero.

Note that the simulation parameters have been given names (AR, LR, ST and GO) in order to clarify their use in the formulas. The spreadsheet recalculation facility has been set to manual so that function key F9 must be pressed in order to generate a new set of random numbers and for their effects to be shown. The graph automatically reflects the change in the queue after each recalculation.

Once the simulation spreadsheet has been created, the effects of changing the parameters can be investigated. This allows the parameters to be set to values which reduce the probability of a large queue of vehicles forming. The parameter that is least likely to change frequently is the departure rate of vehicles, and the arrival rate is not under the direct control of the system designer; however, the timing of the signals is under the control of the designer and this type of simulation provides the opportunity of doing detailed analysis of how crucial the timing is likely to be in the reduction of large traffic jams. The principles used in this study could equally be used to investigate other types of queues, for example, supermarket checkouts or entrances and exits to football stadiums. Finally, note that this simulation could be improved in a number of ways. For instance, more accurate models could be devised for the arrival and departure rates, or perhaps another parameter representing the number of available lanes could be introduced, or the time of day could be taken into account, since this would affect the volume of traffic.

	E	F	G	H	I	J	K	L
	CYCLE	ELAPSEDTIME(min)	RED Rate	Arrive	GREEN Rate	Depart	Arrive	QUEUE
11								
12	1	=(ST+GO)*E12	=INT(AR/2*(1+2*RAND()))	=ST*G12	=INT((LR/2*(1+2*RAND())))	=GO*I12	=GO*G12	=IF(H12+K12-J12>=0,H12+K12-J12,0)
13	2	=(ST+GO)*E13	=INT(AR/2*(1+2*RAND()))	=ST*G13	=INT((LR/2*(1+2*RAND())))	=GO*I13	=GO*G13	=IF(H13+K13-L12-J13>=0,H13+K13-L12-J13,0)
14	3	=(ST+GO)*E14	=INT(AR/2*(1+2*RAND()))	=ST*G14	=INT((LR/2*(1+2*RAND())))	=GO*I14	=GO*G14	=IF(H14+K14-L13-J14>=0,H14+K14-L13-J14,0)
15	4	=(ST+GO)*E15	=INT(AR/2*(1+2*RAND()))	=ST*G15	=INT((LR/2*(1+2*RAND())))	=GO*I15	=GO*G15	=IF(H15+K15-L14-J15>=0,H15+K15-L14-J15,0)
16	5	=(ST+GO)*E16	=INT(AR/2*(1+2*RAND()))	=ST*G16	=INT((LR/2*(1+2*RAND())))	=GO*I16	=GO*G16	=IF(H16+K16-L15-J16>=0,H16+K16-L15-J16,0)
17	6	=(ST+GO)*E17	=INT(AR/2*(1+2*RAND()))	=ST*G17	=INT((LR/2*(1+2*RAND())))	=GO*I17	=GO*G17	=IF(H17+K17-L16-J17>=0,H17+K17-L16-J17,0)
18	7	=(ST+GO)*E18	=INT(AR/2*(1+2*RAND()))	=ST*G18	=INT((LR/2*(1+2*RAND())))	=GO*I18	=GO*G18	=IF(H18+K18-L17-J18>=0,H18+K18-L17-J18,0)
19	8	=(ST+GO)*E19	=INT(AR/2*(1+2*RAND()))	=ST*G19	=INT((LR/2*(1+2*RAND())))	=GO*I19	=GO*G19	=IF(H19+K19-L18-J19>=0,H19+K19-L18-J19,0)
20	9	=(ST+GO)*E20	=INT(AR/2*(1+2*RAND()))	=ST*G20	=INT((LR/2*(1+2*RAND())))	=GO*I20	=GO*G20	=IF(H20+K20-L19-J20>=0,H20+K20-L19-J20,0)
21	10	=(ST+GO)*E21	=INT(AR/2*(1+2*RAND()))	=ST*G21	=INT((LR/2*(1+2*RAND())))	=GO*I21	=GO*G21	=IF(H21+K21-L20-J21>=0,H21+K21-L20-J21,0)

Table 36.3. *Formulas for traffic lights queue simulation*

✍️Exercises

1. Describe three distinct areas that make use of computer models. Explain the purpose of each model and its benefits compared to alternative methods.

2. Develop a computer-based model to simulate customer queues at supermarket checkouts.

   (i)   Explain the factors governing arrival rates and time taken to process purchases.

   (ii)   Identify other factors which may need to be taken into account when developing the model.

   (iii) Carefully describe the rules for the operation of the model and how they have been represented in the spreadsheet.

   (iv)   Explore the effects on queue lengths of changing key variables, such as average arrival rates, service rates and number of checkouts open.

   (v)   Use a graph to show how the queue length at a typical checkout fluctuates over a period of time.

   (vi)   Evaluate the effectiveness of your simulation, commenting on any inadequacies and ways in which it might be improved.

Industrial and Control Applications

In recent years, computerization of industrial and control applications has become common-place and essential to the success of a modern industrial economy. This chapter examines this increasingly important area of computing.

Computer-aided design (CAD)

With the use of a graphics terminal and mouse, or similar device, a designer can produce and modify designs more rapidly than is possible with a conventional drawing board. Ideas can be sketched on the screen, stored, recalled and modified. The computer can also be instructed to analyse a design for comparison with some specified criteria. Drawings can be rotated and tilted on the screen to reveal different three-dimensional views. CAD is used in the design of ships, cars, buildings, microprocessor circuits, clothing and many other products. With the use of CAD a manufacturer has a distinct advantage over non-computerized competitors, in terms of speed and flexibility of design.

Computer-aided manufacture (CAM)

A number of areas of computer use can be identified in the manufacturing process.

❑ Industrial robots and process control;

❑ Computer numerical control (CNC) of machine tools;

❑ Integrated CAD/CAM;

❑ Automated materials handling;

❑ Flexible manufacturing systems (FMS).

Industrial robots

Basically, a robot replaces the actions of a human arm and consists of 3 main elements, a me-chanical arm with wrist joint, power unit and microprocessor or central controlling computer. To be called a robot, it must be able to react, albeit in a limited way, to external events and alter its course of action according to a stored program. Such sensitivity to the environment is pro-vided by sensors, for example, to recognize stylized characters and differentiate between shapes. The main areas of use are in spot welding, paint spraying, die casting and to a lesser but increasing extent, assembly. Use of robots can provide significant benefits for industry, its em-ployees and the population in general:

❑ operation in environments unsuitable for the health of workers;

❑ performance of tasks, particularly those which are repetitive, at a consistent level of quality, which is generally high, and without fatigue;

❑ lack of human weaknesses generally allows robots to be many times more productive and, apart from small specialist companies, car manufacturers could not

> stay in business without the use of extensive automation;

> ❑   labour costs are drastically reduced and the capital costs of robots are recoverable through increased production and a consequent fall in the unit costs of production (the cost of producing a single unit of a particular product).

Clearly, there are potential drawbacks to the use of robots, although the degree of disadvantage depends largely on how much human control is retained. For example, an aircraft can be landed virtually without pilot intervention, but it would be placing rather too much faith in a system's reliability and ability to deal with exceptional circumstances, to fly without a pilot. Thus, the consequences of an automated systems failure need to be taken into account when determining the level of reliance to be placed on it and the fallback procedures which need to be employed. Social disadvantages of using robots are examined in the chapter on Social and Organizational issues.

Computer numerical control (CNC)

CNC operation of machine tools has been widespread for some years because the repetitive nature of machining tasks lends itself to simple programming. However, as is the case with robots, the use of microprocessors allows the machine tool to vary its actions according to external information. The actions of the machine can be compared with a design pattern held by the computer. Any significant variations from the pattern are signalled to the machine tool which, through the microprocessor, reacts appropriately (known as Computer Aided Quality Assessment - CAQ). Other information regarding tool wear or damage can be picked up by sensors and communicated to the human supervisor who takes remedial action.

Integrated CAD/CAM

In fully integrated CAD/CAM systems, the designs produced using CAD are fed straight through to the software which controls the CNC machine tools, which can then produce the design piece. The CAD software checks the compatibility of the design with a component specification already stored in the computer.

Automated materials handling

A fully automated materials handling system consists of a number of sub-systems:

❑   stock control;

❑   part or pallet co-ordination;

❑   storage and retrieval;

❑   conveyor control.

Installation generally proceeds one sub-system at a time, each being fully tested before proceeding with the next sub-system. A materials handling system, controlled by a central computer, allocates storage locations in the warehouse, automatically re-orders when a pre-determined minimum level is reached, retrieves parts as required by the factory and delivers them by conveyor belt to the waiting robots or CNC machines.

Flexible manufacturing systems (FMS)

Such systems are beneficial where production batches are small and necessitate frequent changes in the sequence and types of processes. The aim of FMS is to remove, as far as possible, the need for human intervention (other than a supervisor or machine minder) in the production process. The main elements of FMS are, CNC machine tools (with diagnostic facilities), robots, conveyor belt and central computer with controlling software. In simple terms, the computer has information on parts, machine tools and operations required. The robots serve the CNC machines by presenting them with parts to be machined and loading the correct machine tools from racks.

Control systems

As the name suggests, a *control system* controls the operation of some process. The human body, for example, contains a temperature control system which maintains it at a constant temperature. If your body becomes too hot, it produces perspiration which cools it down, and if you become too cold you warm yourself by shivering. A muscle control system operates whenever you try to catch a ball: your senses provide constant data regarding the position of the ball and the position of your body so that you can adjust the position of your hands to coincide with the trajectory of the ball. A domestic central heating system is a control system in which the temperature of the air in a house is regulated, for example, by means of a boiler pumping hot water through radiators. The output of the boiler is controlled by thermostats which sense the temperature of the air in their vicinities, switching the boiler on when the temperature drops below a required level, and switching it off when that level has been attained. In computer control systems, a computer is the component of the control system which uses data from sensors in order to maintain the outputs of the system at certain levels.

Many control systems involve the use of *measurement systems* to provide data concerning the current output of the system, so that the output can be increased or reduced to maintain it at a certain level. In engineering, measurement systems are used in many different ways and for many different purposes. Sometimes a measurement system is simply required to monitor some process by obtaining data about it. For example, a rotating vane anemometer might be used to provide wind speed data for an athletics meeting. Some measurement systems are used to ensure that a device is operating according to specification for safety or quality reasons. An example is a microwave leakage tester, which measures microwave emissions from commercial microwave appliances and displays the strength of the emissions on the integral meter. Other measurement systems provide data for control systems. For example, in a computer-controlled car engine management system, a measurement system provides information regarding the composition of exhaust gases for the microprocessor which automatically adjusts the engine settings to keep emissions within required limits.

Control systems are used to monitor and control physical systems automatically. Such systems almost invariably use devices called *transducers* to convert from one form of energy into another. Most transducers used in computer control systems convert some form of energy into electrical signals that can processed by a computer, or they convert signals from a computer into a form that can be displayed or converted into mechanical movement. Here are some examples of such transducers:

- ❏ *Thermistor* - the electrical resistance of the material used in a thermistor varies according to the temperature of the material.

- ❏ *Strain gauge* - the electrical resistance of the material used in a strain gauge varies according to the mechanical strain applied to the material.

❑   *Seven-segment display* - converts digital information into readable characters.

❑   *Stepper-motor* - this converts electrical pulses into small, controlled angular movements of the shaft of an electric motor.

❑   *Loudspeaker* - this converts electrical energy into sound.

The first two are examples of input transducers, and the other three are output devices.

Another important feature of control systems is *feedback*. Feedback is the process of regulating the system by using output information to control the input, thereby keeping the output within certain limits. This usually involves using the computer to compare the input signal, or signals, with some critical values. If the input signals show that the quantities being measured need to be adjusted, output signals are used to activate devices which affect the quantities. For example, a control system for maintaining the temperature of a vat of liquid at a constant 20 degrees Centigrade will use a sensor to monitor the temperature of the vat and a heater to increase its temperature if it cools below the required value. A computer program could be used to compare the actual temperature of the vat, as supplied by the sensor, with the desired temperature; a temperature lower than that required will result in the computer issuing an output control signal to activate the heating element. Figure 37.1 illustrates the main features of a control system.

Figure 37.1. *Components of a control system*

A control system for heating water

An example of a control system which illustrates the concepts discussed above is the domestic water heater (see Figure 37.2). The insulated water tank contains a combined *heating element* and *thermostat*. The thermostat is simply a heat activated switch which is off when the temperature of the water reaches a certain level, and is on when the water temperature is below that level. The heating element is connected to the electricity supply via the thermostat so that while the temperature of the water is below a certain level, the heating element is on, otherwise it is off. The control box contains the connections between the heater, the thermostat and the power supply.

Figure 37.2. *Immersion heater control system*

In this simple control system for regulating the temperature of the water in the tank, the thermostat is the transducer, heat generated by the heating element is the output and *feedback* is provided by the resulting temperature of the water. The thermostat switches the heater off when the water reaches the required temperature. When hot water is drawn from the tank, cold water enters and reduces the temperature of the water. This reduction in temperature is detected by the thermostat which activates the heater, thus heating the water until it again reaches the required temperature. Thus the output (heat) provides feedback to the transducer so that the water temperature can be regulated. Of course, this simple control system does not require a computer to control it but, if there were such a requirement, a computer could easily be used. The mechanical thermostat could be replaced by a different transducer providing a voltage proportional to the temperature of the water. This signal could be monitored by a computer and compared with the required temperature of the water. The computer could easily control a relay to switch the heater on when the temperature falls below a pre-determined minimum value and switch it off when the temperature exceeds a pre-determined maximum value. The computer controlled version is shown in Figure 37.3.

Figure 37.3. *Computer-controlled water heating system*

In this version the water temperature is detected by a sensor immersed in the water. A voltage proportional to the water temperature is transmitted to the computer which determines whether it is necessary to turn on an electronic switch to activate the heating element.

Computer control system components

Because PCs are so popular and now provide powerful, cost-effective solutions to many processing problems, more PCs are being used in both process monitoring and control applications. Consequently, many plug-in devices have been developed to simplify these tasks, and software has also kept pace with development needs. The components of a typical PC-based control system are:

- ❏ Sensor(s) to monitor the process.

- ❏ Signal conditioning module to convert sensor signals to meet input/output specifications. As well as being the front end for a DAQ board, these also isolate the computer from the environment.

- ❏ Data acquisition board (DAQ) which plugs directly into the PC. Input and output transducers can be connected directly to them (depending on the type) or through signal conditioning modules. These boards often can perform a variety of functions, including analogue to digital conversion, digital to analogue conversion and digital input/output.

- ❏ Interface software which facilitates control and communication through the DAQ board.

The heat regulating system described in the next section illustrates how these components combine to form a computer control system.

A heat regulating system

Since the signal from any temperature sensing device, whatever the type of transducer employed, is a continuously varying (that is, *analogue*) signal, it must be amplified using a signal conditioning unit and then converted into a *binary* signal using an *analogue-to-digital converter* (ADC) before it can be used directly by a computer.

The analogue signal from the sensor unit is converted to binary signals by the ADC. ADCs take as input a voltage in a certain range and produce a number of parallel binary outputs which represent the current input voltage. A typical ADC will provide eight binary outputs corresponding to the input voltage. So, if the input range is –5V to +5V , a binary output of 0 corresponds to –5V, an output of binary 127 corresponds to 0V and +5V is represented by 255 in binary. Figure 37.4 illustrates an ADC producing a binary output of 240 corresponding approximately to an input of 4V.

Figure 37.4. *Operation of a typical ADC*

Let us suppose, for example, that a certain microprocessor-controlled washing machine allows the selection of a large range of water temperature settings. Such an appliance might use a system similar to that just described to convert water temperatures between 0°C and 100°C to a binary signal. If the ADC produces an 8 bit binary output corresponding to an input voltage in the range 0V to 5V, the temperature range 0°C to 100°C will be represented by a binary signal in the range 0 to 255 (that is, 00000000 to 11111111 in binary) such that binary 0 represents 0°C and binary 255 represents 100°C. Since a temperature transducer is unlikely to generate the voltage range required by the ADC, namely 0V to 5V, it must first be conditioned. Thus after the transducer signal had been conditioned, a temperature of 25°C would produce about 1.25V and this would translate to binary 63 (00111111). Figure 37.5 illustrates the use of an ADC contained within a PC data acquisition (DAQ) board in a simple system intended to maintain a tank of liquid at a certain temperature.

Figure 33.5. *PC control system using a DAQ board*

The DAQ board also allows the PC to output a digital control signal to operate a power switch which activates the tank's heating element.

The figure shows a temperature sensor immersed in a tank of warm liquid. The sensor contains a thermal transducer and an electronic circuit that produces as output an analogue signal in the form of a voltage proportional to the temperature of the liquid in the tank. The output from the sensor unit is converted to binary by the ADC. A computer program then compares the temperature of the liquid, as represented by the binary signal, with the required temperature of the liquid and activates the heating element switch accordingly. Note that the temperature sensor unit, switch and ADC all require a power supply to function.

Control systems applications

Computer control systems are used in a wide variety of application areas, including:

- ❏ Process monitoring and control - see *Process Control Systems* later in this section;

- ❏ Data logging - gathering and recording data;

- ❏ Quality control - testing products to ensure that they fulfil specific standards of quality;

- ❏ Machine control - for example, controlling the machines used in manufacturing processes. Includes the use of robots (see later).

The following sections describe the application of computer control in motor vehicles, chemical processes and manufacturing. To simplify the illustrations, the signal conditioning and converting components of the systems are not shown.

Control systems used in cars

Some modern cars, particularly in the USA, have a cruise control that allows a driver to set the speed of the car to be maintained automatically by pressing a button. A microprocessor is used to monitor the speed of the car, from data provided by a sensor, and continuously compare it with the required speed. If the car starts to slow down while going up a hill or speeds up going down a hill, the microprocessor activates a control that changes the car's speed. Figure 37.6 illustrates this idea.

Figure 37.6. *Cruise control for a car*

The microprocessor uses *feedback* provided by the speed sensor to determine whether the car is travelling at the required speed. Some systems have sensors which use the rotation rate of the wheel drive shafts to determine the speed of the car, while others use microwave technology to measure the Doppler shift of a signal bounced off the road. If the microprocessor detects that the car is travelling slower than the required speed, it increases the delivery of fuel to the engine. This speeds the car up so that the difference between the actual speed and the required speed is reduced. The microprocessor continuously reacts to speed changes as they occur and adjusts the fuel delivery to keep the car travelling at a nearly constant speed. The driver, by braking or accelerating, can override the cruise control and assume normal control of the car at any instant.

Early versions of this type of control were achieved using complicated electromechanical devices, but the advent of cheap microprocessors rapidly caused them to be replaced with computer-based machines. The great advantage of using a microprocessor in this type of application is that its function can be duplicated by a more powerful computer system used for the purpose of designing and evaluating the final system before putting it into production. This reduces the time taken to produce a workable system and allows its performance to be thoroughly investigated and modified easily before testing it in a car.

Another application of control systems in cars is the *anti-locking brake system,* usually known as *ABS.* These devices prevent locking of the wheels during braking so that:

❑ The vehicle does not tend to swerve during braking;

❑ The vehicle can still be steered during braking;

❑ Stopping distances are reduced;

❑ Tyre damage during emergency braking is eliminated;

❑ Less physical effort is required of the driver in emergency situations.

Cars with an ABS fitted are therefore considerably safer in hazardous conditions than those having ordinary braking systems. Figure 37.7 illustrates the components of one type of ABS system.

Figure 37.7. *Anti-locking brake system (ABS) on a car*

The rotational speed of the wheels, continuously measured by the wheel speed sensors, are transmitted to the ABS control unit. The control unit processes the rotation data for each wheel separately and if a wheel is in danger of locking, it sends a signal to the brake valves to reduce the braking effect for that wheel. If the braking effect on a wheel is too weak, the control unit increases the braking effect, still ensuring that the wheel does not lock.

The wheel sensors measure the rotational speed of the wheels from the pulse-generating wheels which revolve at the same speed as the road wheels. The pulse-generating wheels generate a voltage in the sensor proportional to the speed at which they are revolving.

The ABS control unit contains two microprocessors which perform exactly the same functions of using the wheel rotation information to control braking. Two microprocessors are used for safety: they continuously monitor and test each other to ensure that the ABS system is operating correctly. If a fault in the ABS system is detected by one of the microprocessors, the system shuts itself down and normal manual braking is made available.

Engine management systems

Engine management systems use a microprocessor to monitor and control the operation of a car's engine. Though devices to control such things as exhaust emissions, fuel supply and ignition timing have been available for years, recent regulations regarding pollution control have resulted in new computer-controlled systems which integrate a number of functions and use feedback to continuously regulate the operation of the engine. These systems sample exhaust gases to provide feedback to the computer system which modifies the engine settings to keep emissions within required limits. A modern engine management system can provide system support for such things as:

- ❏ ignition timing;
- ❏ fuel injection;
- ❏ exhaust gas recirculation;
- ❏ engine idle speed.

Process control systems

The term *process control* is applied to systems which involve the automatic control of manufacturing, material handling, or treatment handling of processes. Such processes were controlled mechanically or manually in the past, but the advent of microprocessors allowed digital control systems to take over. Microprocessor-based control systems allowed process control to become more efficient and profitable by providing a means of responding to changes much more rapidly than was previously possible. Process control systems are typically found in industries that produce chemicals, steel, aluminium, food, beverages, petroleum products etc. For example, suppose that a certain chemical process requires that a concentration of a particular chemical is maintained in a tank from which fluid is being drained at the same time as other chemicals are being added. A sensor in the tank provides continuous information to a microprocessor regarding the concentration of the chemical concerned (see Figure 37.8). The output to be controlled here is the concentration of the chemical in the tank. The difference between the required concentration and the concentration as measured by the sensor is compared by the controller. If the difference between the two becomes too large, the controller opens the flow valve until the difference is reduced to an acceptable level. The process has been controlled when the concentration of the chemical is maintained at the required level. Note that there may be several processes interacting with each other, with each separate controller keeping its particular process under control.

Figure 37.8. *Chemical process control*

Robotics

Since 1962, when General Motors of the USA first used a robot commercially on one of its production lines, they have been used profitably for a wide range of tasks. The word robot was first coined by a Czechoslovakian playwright called Karel Capek who in 1921 used the Czech word robota, meaning worker, to describe a human-like machine which served humanity in one of his plays. Later, Isaac Asimov, a very popular science fiction writer, was the first person to use the word robotics to refer to the science of robots. Though as yet robots are not advanced enough to need them, Asimov's well-known Laws of Robotics may be required in the not too distant future. His three laws state that:

1.   *A robot must not harm a human being or, through inaction, allow one to come to harm.*

2.   *A robot must always obey human beings unless that is in conflict with the First Law.*

3.   *A robot must protect itself from harm unless that is in conflict with the first or second laws.*

Asimov's fictional robots had very advanced positronic brains which gave them the power to reason like humans, but the robots in use today are much more rudimentary machines usually used for fairly simple and repetitive tasks. It will be some time before intelligent, humanoid robots are more than just an interesting theme for novels.

According to the Robot Institute of America, a robot is a *reprogrammable, multifunctional manipulator designed to move material parts, tools or specialized devices through variable programmed motions for the performance of a variety of tasks.* However, there are many very different types of machines that are covered by this definition. Most robots have an arm with a number of joints linking the sections. Joints rotate or slide or combine the two movements, as illustrated in

Figure 37.9. *Example of robot arm*

Figure 37.9. Until recently, nearly all robots were mounted on a stationary base and were therefore fixed in one position. However, with the availability of low-cost computers able to cope with the added problems caused by providing mobility, manufacturers now provide robots which can move in a number of different ways. Most mobile robots are restricted to moving on a track either on the ground or on an overhead gantry, but there are some robots with wheels used as household assistants. Some robots have been equipped with legs so that they are able to walk over uneven terrain, but there are many problems associated with making such machines, and they are still in the very early stages of development.

The advantages of using robots

Some of the reasons for using robots in industry are:

❏   Although robots are very expensive, when the cost is averaged over several years, the cost per hour of using a robot is much less than using human labour. One of the main reasons for this is that robots, unlike people, do not need such things as holidays, sick leave (except when they break down), medical benefits or pensions.

❏   Robots work nearly 100% of the time at their tasks, whereas people have to be given tea breaks and lunch breaks and time off for other reasons.

❏   Robots do not make mistakes resulting from tiredness or lack of attention because they repeat the same operations in exactly the same way every time almost without fail.

❏   Robots can work much faster and with more accuracy at some tasks than human workers can. This results in the production of more and better quality articles.

❏   Certain manufacturing operations take place in conditions hazardous to humans but harmless to robots. For example, robots are not affected by red hot flying sparks in a steel forge, or by toxic fumes given off by certain types of paint.

Because robots can be programmed to perform many different sequences of movements, a single robot can be used to perform a wide variety of tasks, whereas a machine made to perform a specific task is limited to doing that one thing.

Uses of robots

Robots have been used for many years to do simple tasks in factories, such as picking up items at one location and feeding them to a machine at another fixed location. Another common use of robots is spray painting. Here, a spray paint nozzle is attached to the robot arm which is programmed to move through a sequence of movements to carry out the painting operation. Many robots are also used for spot welding in the automobile industry. These robots use welding guns to weld car chassis and body frames together at a number of programmed points.

More sophisticated robots, called *adaptive robots*, which are able to sense their environment and use this data to modify their behaviour, are used for more complex tasks such as: the assembly of small products; the inspection of automobile bodies travelling along an assembly line so that faulty assembly of components can be recorded and later corrected; and welding metal along seams which cannot be precisely aligned beforehand. These applications have resulted from the development of computer controlled vision systems which allow the robot to recognize simple shapes.

Measurement systems

In general, measurement systems have three component parts:

1.   A sensor, or *transducer,* as it is frequently termed, responds in some measurable way to the quantity of interest. For example, in a hot wire anemometer, the transducer is a thermistor (see later) whose electrical resistance changes according to air movement.

Figure 37.10. *Input and output signals for a hot wire anenometer*

2.   A *signal conditioning* device which converts the physical response of the transducer
into a form suitable for operating a display device. In the hot wire anemometer example mentioned previously, the signal conditioner is an independently powered
electrical circuit which converts the resistance changes of the thermistor into an electrical signal suitable for driving a digital or analogue wind-speed display. Some
conditioning circuits are *amplifiers* which convert small electrical signals into signals
which can drive a display. In computer control systems, the output from the measuring device must be converted into a form suitable for input to a computer. Since a
computer processes binary data, an *analogue-to-digital converter* will often form an
additional signal conditioning stage. Figure 37.11 illustrates these types of conditioning devices. Signal conditioning circuits are also called *signal converters* and *signal
processors.*

Figure 37.11. *Three types of signal conditioning devices (a) signal converter, (b) amplifier, (c)
analogue to digital converter*

3.   A *display* which takes the signal from the conditioning element and presents it in a
form which can be interpreted by an observer. For example, the output from an amplifier could be used to deflect the needle of a meter or it could be converted into a digital
signal to be displayed as figures on a computer screen or another type of digital
display.

Figure 37.12 illustrates a complete measurement system consisting of a transducer, a signal
conditioner and a display element.

Figure 37

Chapter 38

The Internet

The Internet is a world-wide network composed of thousands of smaller regional networks scattered throughout the globe. A common set of communication protocols enables every computer connected to the Internet to interchange information with every other computer so connected. On any given day it connects roughly 20 million users in over 50 countries. Over the last 25 years, the Internet has grown to include government and educational institutions, and, more recently, commercial organisations.

Figure 38.1 shows the estimated coverage of the Internet in 1995. The countries in black have facilities to connect to the Internet, though the number of people with Internet access in these countries varies widely. Countries in white may have access to e-mail, local isolated networks, or no facilities for connection to networks at all. No single person or organisation owns the Internet. There are companies which help manage different parts of the networks which tie everything

Figure 38.1. *Internet world coverage*

together, but there is no single governing body which controls what happens on the Internet. The networks within different countries are funded and managed locally according to local policies.The Internet began in early 1969 under the experimental project ARPAnet. ARPA (Advanced Research Projects Agency, later known as the Defence Advanced Research Projects Agency) wanted to demonstrate the feasibility of building computer networks over a wide area such that the loss of a number of hosts on that network did not disrupt it. So ARPA initially interconnected four computers and linked them with Internet Protocol (IP), and the Internet grew from there. In the 70s and 80s US universities began to link with DARPAnet so that it could be used for academic research and in 1991 the U.S. government lifted its ban on commercial use of the Internet. The considerable business opportunities provided by the Internet ensure that it will continue to grow.

Today the Internet is a huge collection of different, intercommunicating networks funded by commercial, government and educational organisations. It has developed to handle larger volumes of data, software has become more powerful and user-friendly, and the types of services available have grown. The Internet now links more than 150 countries. All types of computers make up the hardware connected on the Internet. They vary from PCs, Macintoshes and UNIX workstations to minicomputers, mainframes and supercomputers. Anyone who wants to have access to the enormous amount of information available regionally or around the world can use the Internet. They can access electronic libraries, receive periodicals, exchange ideas, read the news, post questions with newsgroups, examine the weather (from reports or satellite photos), obtain the latest stock market prices and currency exchange rates, and access public government information on trade, laws, research and other subjects. It is likely that in the very near future, every school will be connected to the Internet, an Internet connection in your house will be no more unusual than a telephone line and, if you run a business, the Internet will be a vital tool (see E-commerce later).

Connecting to the Internet

Figure 38.2 shows a PC connected to the Internet via a remote service provider which is itself a LAN (Local Area Network). The PC connects to the service provider using a modem and the telephone system. The service provider is directly connected to the Internet by means of a *router,* a computer which provides the link to special data transmission lines required to access the Internet. A large organisation might have its own direct link to the Internet, but many private users rely on commercial service providers for the connection, for which they must pay a subscription. Some service providers do not charge a subscription but generate revenue from advertising and a percentage of telephone call charges received from subscribers who take advantage of the telephone help lines they run for their clients.

Uses of the Internet

The Internet is essentially a tool for transferring information between computers. This can be achieved in numerous ways and for various purposes. For example, *E-mail* is a convenient, quick and cheap alternative to the postal system for business and personal correspondence; *File Transfer Protocol (FTP)* allows large amounts of information to be transferred between two computers very conveniently; *Usenet,* the world-wide collection of interest groups, or *Newsgroups*, allows groups of people with similar interests to exchange views and information. Another important

Figure 38.2. *PC connected to a server for access to the Internet*

use of the Internet is the remote control of computer systems via *Telnet*. The *World-Wide Web* provides a uniform means of accessing and transferring information in the form of hypermedia documents. Accessing these documents does not require any particular machine or operating system. These and other Internet services are discussed in the following sections. A rapidly expanding application of the Internet is e-commerce, or on-line trading, between businesses and between businesses and consumers; this topic is examined at the end of this chapter. Note that programs used on the Internet can be classified as being either *server* or *client*. Server programs operate at Internet sites where the particular Internet service being used is provided; the program which is used to access a site, on a home PC for example, is the client program. For instance, a Web server at a Web site processes requests made by client programs called Web *browsers*.

The World-Wide Web

Abbreviated to the Web and WWW, this is the fastest growing Internet service. Though the World-Wide Web is mostly used on the Internet, the two terms do not mean the same thing. The Web refers to a world-wide collection of knowledge, while the Internet refers to the physical side of the global network, an enormous collection of cables and computers. The World-Wide Web uses the Internet for the transmission of hypermedia documents between computer users connected to the Internet. As with the Internet, nobody actually owns the World-Wide Web. People are responsible for the documents they author and make available publicly on the Web. Via the Internet, hundreds of thousands of people around the world are making information available from their homes, schools, colleges and workplaces. The aim of WWW is to make all on-line knowledge part of one interconnected web of documents and services.

The World-Wide Web began in March 1989, when Tim Berners-Lee of the European Particle Physics Laboratory (known as CERN, a collective of European high-energy physics research-ers) proposed the project as a means of distributing research results and ideas effectively throughout the organisation. The initial project proposal outlined a simple system of using net-worked hypertext to transmit to members of the high-energy physics community. By the end of 1990, the first piece of Web software had been introduced on a NeXT machine. It had the capa-bility to view and transmit hypertext documents to other people on the Internet, and came with the capability to edit hypertext documents on the screen. Since then many people throughout the world have contributed their time writing Web software and documents, or telling others about the Web.

The World-Wide Web is officially described as a wide-area hypermedia information retrieval initiative aiming to give universal access to a large universe of documents. What the World-Wide Web (WWW, W3) project has done is provide users on computer networks with a consis-tent means to access a variety of media in a simplified fashion. With the aid of a popular software interface to the Web, called a *browser* (described later), the WWW has changed the way people view and create information. The first true global hypermedia network, it is revolu-tionising many elements of society, including commerce, politics, and literature.

Hypertext and hypermedia

The operation of the Web relies mainly on *hypertext* as its means of interacting with users. Hy-pertext is basically the same as ordinary text - it can be stored, read, searched, or edited -with an important exception: hypertext contains links to other places within the same document or to other documents. A Web browser indicates text links by the use of colour or by underlining. For example, Figure 38.3 shows part of a document called Writing Java Programs which contains three underlying links to other documents, the second one being The Anatomy of a Java Application.

This latter document in turn contains a link to a third document called The Hello World Applet. The first document would be retrieved from the WWW using a browser and the user, by point-ing and clicking with a mouse on a link, will cause the browser to retrieve the appropriate document automatically, no matter where it is located.

Hypermedia is hypertext with a difference - hypermedia documents contain links not only to other pieces of text, but also to other forms of media, namely sounds, images, and movies. Im-ages themselves can be selected to link to sounds or documents. Hypermedia simply combines hypertext and multimedia.

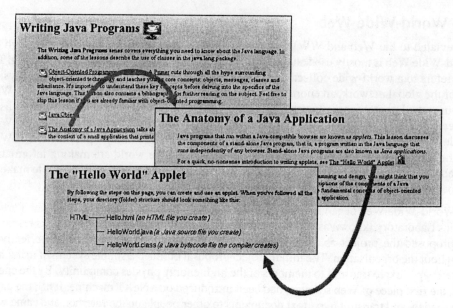

Figure 38.3. *Three linked hypermedia documents*

Figure 38.4 shows a browser displaying a hypermedia document with three buttons which, when clicked with a mouse, would demonstrate sound, graphics and video files.

Figure 38.4. *A hypermedia document being displayed by a Netscape browser*

The appearance of a hypermedia document when it is displayed by a browser is determined partly by the browser which provides a certain amount of control over such things as text fonts and colours, but mainly by the language used to encode the document. This language is *Hyper-Text Mark-up Language* (HTML). HTML is described in more detail in a later section of this chapter.

Web browsers

These are graphical interface client programs to help users to navigate through the Web, to transmit and to receive information from other users or information providers. By using a browser, the user does not have to know the format and location of the information: he or she simply jumps from site to site by clicking on hypertext links. Examples of commercially available browsers are Netscape's *Navigator*, Microsoft's *Explorer* (Figure 38.5).

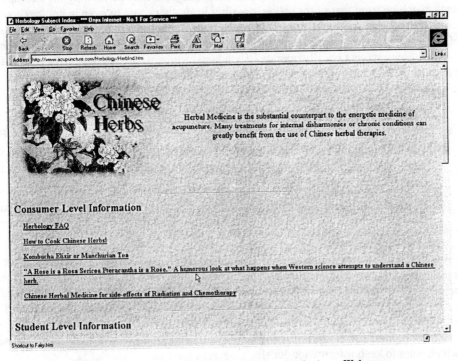

Figure 38.5. *Microsoft's Explorer browser displaying a Web page*

Although there are many different ways to represent a document on the screen, it is often called a *page*. Usually, those responsible for creating a given collection of interrelated documents also create a special document which is intended to be viewed first - one that contains introductory information and/or a master menu of documents within that collection. This type of document is called a *home page* and is generally associated with a particular site, person, or named collection. The example document has underlined hypertext phrases. These phrases are hyperlinks (or links) - typically, clicking on one of them with a mouse will cause another document to appear on the screen, which may hold more images and hyperlinks to other places. There is no single way to represent text which is linked to other things - some browsers underline, others use special colours, and many give the user a variety of options. Images which are part of the document and are displayed within the page are called *inline images*.

There is usually a toolbar at the top or bottom of the screen. This contains buttons which perform frequently used operations. For example, a set of navigation buttons is provided because a user might go to many different pages by selecting links in hypertext and there needs to be some method of retracing one's steps and reviewing the documents that have been explored.

How the Web works

Web software is designed around a distributed client-server architecture. A Web client (called a Web browser if it is intended for interactive use) is a program which can send requests for documents to any Web server. A Web server is a program which, upon receipt of a request, sends the document requested (or an error message if appropriate) back to the requesting client.

Using a distributed architecture means that a client program may be running on a completely separate machine from that of the server, possibly in another room or even in another country. Because the task of document storage is left to the server and the task of document presentation is left to the client, each program can concentrate on those duties and progress independently of each other. Since servers usually operate only when documents are requested, they put a minimal amount of workload on the computers on which they run. Here is an example of how the process works:

1.   Running a Web client program, such as a browser, the user selects a hyperlink in a piece of hypertext connecting to another document - Java Programming for example.

2.   The Web client uses the address associated with that hyperlink to connect to the Web server at a specified network address and asks for the document associated with Java Programming.

3.   The server responds by sending the text and any other media within that text (pictures, sounds, or video clips) to the client, which the client then renders for presentation on the user's screen.

The World-Wide Web is composed of thousands of these virtual transactions taking place per hour throughout the world, creating a web of information flow. Web servers are now beginning to include encryption and client authentication abilities, allowing them to send and receive secure data and be more selective as to which clients receive information. This allows freer communications among Web users and ensures that sensitive data is kept private. In the near future, it will be harder to compromise the security of commercial servers and educational servers which want to keep information local.

The language which Web clients and servers use to communicate with each other is called the *HyperText Transfer Protocol* (HTTP). All Web clients and servers must be able to 'speak' HTTP in order to send and receive hypermedia documents. For this reason, Web servers are often called HTTP servers.

HTML - The Hypertext Markup Language

The standard language the Web uses for creating and recognising hypermedia documents is the Hypertext Mark-up Language (HTML). Figure 38.6 shows part of the underlying HTML document which produces the page being displayed by the browser shown in Figure 38.5.

An important characteristic of HTML is its ease of use. Web documents are typically written in HTML and are usually named with the suffix *.html* or *.htm*. HTML documents are nothing more than standard 7-bit ASCII files with formatting codes which contain information about layout (text styles, document titles, paragraphs, lists) and hyperlinks.

```
<HTML>
<HEAD>
   <TITLE>Herbology Subject Index</TITLE>
</HEAD>
<BODY BACKGROUND="Back.gif"

<CENTER><TABLE WIDTH="100%">
<TR>
<TD ALIGN=CENTER><IMG SRC="Herb.gif" HEIGHT=233 WIDTH=340
</TD>

<TD><FONT SIZE=+1>Herbal Medicine is the substantial counterpart
to the energetic medicine of acupuncture. Many treatments for
internal disharmonies or chronic conditions can greatly benefit
from the use of Chinese herbal therapies. </FONT></TD>
</TR>
</TABLE></CENTER>

<CENTER><P>
<HR SIZE=2 WIDTH=30%></P></CENTER>

<H2>Consumer Level Information</H2>
<UL>
<H4><A HREF="Herbology.htm">Herbology FAQ</A> </ H4>

<H4>A HREF="Cook.htm">How to Cook Chinese Herbs!</A> </H4>

<H4><A HREF="Man.htm">Kombucha Elixir or Manchurian Tea</A> </ H4>

<H4><A HREF="Fairy.htm">&quot;A Rose is a Rosa Sericea Pteracantha
is a Rose.&quot; A humorous look at what happens when Western
science attempts to understand a Chinese herb.</A></H4>
<H4><A HREF="Chemo.htm"Chinese Herbal Medicine for side-effects of
Radiation and Chemotherapy</A></H4>
</UL>
<CENTER><P>
<HR SIZE=2 WIDTH=30%></P></CENTER>
<H2Student Level Information</H2>
<UL>

.........
```

Figure 38.6. *An HTML document*

Note the *tags* indicated by keywords enclosed between < and >. Most tags are of the form
`<tagname>`........ `</tagname>`, with the text being controlled by the tag appearing between
the two parts. For example, text enclosed between `<H2>` and `</H2>` is shown as a type 2 heading by the browser, and text between `<B>` and `</B>` is shown as bold type. Hypertext links are
indicated by `<A....>` and `</A>`. An example of a hypertext link is

`<A HREF="Cook.htm"How to Cook Chinese Herbs!</A>`

This tag causes the browser to show 'How to Cook Chinese Herbs!' as a hypertext link by displaying it in a different colour from ordinary text, and the page to be loaded from the same web
site directory as the current document has the file name 'Cook.htm'

Images, such as the picture in the top left-hand corner of the displayed page shown in Figure

38.5, use the `<IMG..>` tag. The tag

```
<IMG SRC="Herb.gif" HEIGHT=233 WIDTH=340>
```

indicates, among other things, that the source of the image to be displayed is to be found in the same directory as the parent document under the filename, 'Herb.gif'. The file extension '.gif' is the standard format for Web page inline graphics.

One of the major attractions of using HTML is that every WWW browser can 'understand' it, no matter what machine the browser is being run on. This means that Web page developers do not need to worry about producing different versions for different computer platforms.

Uniform Resource Locators

The World-Wide Web uses what are called Uniform Resource Locators (URLs) to represent hypermedia links and links to network services within HTML documents. It is possible to represent nearly any file or service on the Internet with a URL. The first part of the URL (before the two slashes) specifies the method of access. The second is typically the address of the computer which the data or service is located on. Further parts may specify the names of files, the port to connect to, or the text to search for in a database. A URL is always a single unbroken line with no spaces.

Sites which run World-Wide Web servers are typically named with a "www" at the beginning of the network address.

Here are some examples of URLs:

```
http://www.nc.edu/nw/book.html
```

Connects to an HTTP server and retrieves an HTML document called 'book.html' in a directory called 'nw'

```
file://www.nc.edu/sound.au
```

Retrieves a sound file called 'sound.au' and plays it.

```
file://www.abc.com/picture.gif
```

Retrieves a picture and displays it, either in a separate program or within a hypermedia document.

```
file://www.bcd.org/dd/
```

Displays the contents of directory 'dd'.

```
ftp://www.wer.uk.co/pub/file.txt
```

Opens an FTP connection to www.uk.co and retrieves a text file.

```
gopher://www.hcc.hawaii.edu
```

Connects to the Gopher at www.hcc.hawaii.edu.

```
telnet://www.nc.edu:1234
```

Telnets to www.nc.edu at port 1234.

```
news:alt.hypertext
```

Reads the latest Usenet news by connecting to a news host and returns the articles in the "alt.hypertext" newsgroup in hypermedia format.

Most Web browsers allow the user to specify a URL and connect to that document or service. When selecting hypertext in an HTML document, the user is actually sending a request to open a URL. In this way, hyperlinks can be made not only to other texts and media, but also to other network services. Web browsers are not simply Web clients, but are also full-featured FTP, Gopher, and telnet clients (see later for a discussion of these Internet services).

WWW search engines

The WWW is a vast, distributed repository of information, and more is being added to the Web each day. However, the only consistent characteristics of the information available are the manner in which it is coded, that is, in HTML, and the way in which it can be located, that is, by using URLs.

To access this huge bank of information, dispersed over the entire world, and locate specific information on a certain subject, there are numerous information retrieval utilities which provide access to databases of Web page details. These *search engines* allow Web users to enter search criteria in the form of keywords or phrases and they retrieve summaries of all database entries satisfying the search criteria. Of the many information retrieval services available, some of the most well known include *Excite*, *Lycos* and *Yahoo*.

Figure 38.7 shows the Yahoo search engine being used to find information on shiatsu.

Figure 38.7. *A keyword entered in the Yahoo search engine*

The search produced short summaries of numerous Web pages containing the keyword shiatsu, the first few of which are shown in Figure 38.8. Clicking on any of the links shown as underlined headings would cause the browser to retrieve the appropriate page which might also have links to further pages containing related information.

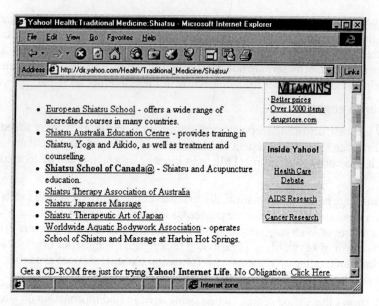

Figure 38.8. *A partial list of the result of searching for the keyword 'shiatsu'*

Gopher

Gopher is an Internet-wide tool used to search for and retrieve text-based information stored at Gopher sites throughout the world. One way to picture Gopherspace is to think of each Gopher site as a page in an extremely large index of information. Gopher resources include research results (both governmental and commercial), special-interest groups and databases of almost any kind of documented information.

A Gopher *client* is a software package which allows you to search this master index for information which meets your criteria. There are Gopher clients available for most computers. With its user-friendly menu-based interface, Gopher spares the user the need to learn many computer commands. In effect, Gopher presents the Internet as if it were all part of a single directory system. There are numerous programs specifically designed to access Gopher sites, but general purpose Web browsers, such as Explorer, will also handle Gopher. Figure 38.9 shows Explorer displaying a Gopher directory at the University of Minnesota in the USA where Gopher was created.

As can be seen, the directory contains a mixture of different types of files, including text documents (for example, 'About Gopher'), further directories of files (for example, 'Gopher News Archive'), and video clips (for example, 'Gopher T shirt on MTV movie').

Figure 38.10 shows the information received by the browser when the link to the first document, 'About Gopher', was selected.

Because information held on Gopher servers is accessed through menu hierarchies, which is time consuming if many levels of menus have to be negotiated, a widely available tool called *Veronica* is used to search 'Gopherspace' for keywords. Veronica uses a database which has been compiled from Gopher servers - almost every item offered by a Gopher server is indexed by Veronica. Veronica uses Gopher client programs to act as user interfaces, allowing searches to be performed and presenting the results of searches. In this respect, they operate in much the same way as search engines available through Web browsers.

Figure 38.9. *A Gopher directory displayed by the browser*

Figure 38.10. *A text document retrieved from the Gopher menu*

WAIS (Wide Area Information Servers)

WAIS is a networked information retrieval system. Client applications are able to retrieve text or multimedia documents stored on the servers. and request documents using keywords. Servers search a full text index for the documents and return a list of documents containing the keyword. The client may then request the server to send a copy of any of the documents found. Although the name Wide Area implies the use of the large networks such as the Internet to connect clients to servers distributed around the network, WAIS can be used between a client and server on the same machine or a client and server on the same LAN.

Currently, there are a large number of servers running and topics range from recipes and movies to bibliographies, technical documents, and newsgroup archives.

The information which is provided by WAIS is not limited to ASCII text only. With WAIS you can also get multimedia information like pictures, graphics, sounds and even video. WAIS uses natural language queries to find relevant documents. The result of the query is a set of documents which contain the words of the query. The documents which provided the most hits with the given query are placed at the top of the list of documents. WAIS databases can be accessed using specific WAIS client programs, or alternatively Gopher, Telnet and Web browser client programs.

E-mail

The most used application of the Internet is electronic mail, or *e-mail* as it is widely known. E-mail is primarily used to send and receive text-based messages such as personal or business letters, orders, reports and statements.

To use Internet e-mail, access to a computer which is connected to the Internet and has e-mail software is required. Most commercial Internet service providers include e-mail facilities in their subscriber services. Subscribers are given an identifying code called an e-mail *address*. The service provider collects and forwards mail sent from that address and holds mail to be received by that address until able to deliver it. The service provider thus acts like a post office, and in fact there is a close analogy between the way which e-mail is implemented and the traditional manual postal system (which is disparagingly termed snail mail by e-mail devotees). The same principles apply to e-mail users who do not rely on commercial service providers - messages are automatically forwarded from users to their destinations and incoming mail is stored on their service provider's computer until the user is able to accept it.

The process of composing and sending an e-mail message is as follows:

1. The message to be sent is composed (usually off-line) using some form of text editor.

2. A *mailer* program is used to connect to the Internet and transmit the message to its destination computer. The mailer examines the code containing the address to which the message is to be sent and makes a decision regarding how the message should be routed to the destination before sending it on its way.

3. The message is automatically passed from computer to computer until it arrives at the recipient's *mailbox* which is generally a special directory used for storing messages which are waiting to be read.

4. The recipient accesses his/her mailbox and removes any messages which have arrived.

Because e-mail is delivered by electronic means, it is much faster than the manual system, taking minutes or seconds rather than days to arrive at practically any destination in the world. Though the technology which makes e-mail possible is complex, from a user's viewpoint e-mail is simple to use and extremely useful.

FTP

File Transfer Protocol (FTP) provides the facility to transfer files between two computers on the Internet. There are thousands of FTP sites all over the Internet with data files, software, and information for almost any interest. Figure 38.11 shows an FTP program being used to provide a link between a PC and a remote computer.

The file directory structures of both machines are being displayed in adjacent windows, allowing files to be selected and transferred between the two machines.

Some FTP programs require typed commands to accomplish file-handling operations, but modern programs usually provide convenient graphical user interfaces such as the one illustrated.

Though there are other methods of transferring files between computers on the Internet, FTP allows such tasks to be performed quickly and easily. It is worth noting, however, that in order to access a remote host computer in this way, you need to have:

The host name, that is, the Internet name of the computer system to which you hope to connect. This will be used by your FTP software to establish a link to the host. A typical host name might be of the form *ftp.layton.com.*

Figure 38.11. *An FTP program being used to link to computers*

A valid login name and a password which will allow you to access the host. These are obviously for security purposes - many computer systems on the Internet contain confidential information which only authorised personnel should be able to access. However, unrestricted files which are available on host computers can often be accessed by using the special visitor password *anonymous.*

In Figure 38.11, the user has already provided an acceptable login name and password, through the FTP software, and consequently has been given access to the host system.

Closely associated with FTP, *Archie* is a program which periodically searches all FTP sites on its master list, and stores the filenames it finds in a central database. This information is then made available to users to retrieve via FTP. This, in common with other types of search engines found on the Internet, provides a convenient method of locating items of information which could be in an FTP site anywhere in the world.

Telnet

Telnet allows you to use a remote computer system from your local system. For example, an employee of an organisation which is on the Internet and supports Telnet working, could use the firm's computer system from home. The employee would simply Telnet the employer's computer system using his/her home PC and, once connected, could run programs available on the remote system. The Telnet software provides an interface window through which commands can be issued and results displayed.

This *virtual terminal* allows the remote computer to be controlled as if it were the local computer. Any task which can be performed on a workstation connected directly to the remote computer can also be done using a Telnet connection.

Usenet

Usenet is a large collection of newsgroups, of which there are many thousands. Newsgroups allow people with common interests to exchange views, ask questions and provide information using the Internet. Almost anything you care to find can be found as a newsgroup, which acts like a community bulletin board spread across millions of computer systems world wide. Anyone can participate in these groups, and moderation ranges from strict to none. Everything imaginable is discussed, from selling and trading goods and services, to discussing the latest episode of a popular TV show. Subscribers can read news articles, and reply to them - either by posting their own news articles, or by sending E-mail to the authors.

Since Usenet news is not limited to any political or geographic boundaries, it provides the possibility of being able to interact with an enormous number of individuals.

A program called a *newsreader* allows access to a newsgroup and the articles available for reading, retrieval of articles of interest and the posting of articles for others to read. Each article has a header which summarises the contents of the article, and the newsreader can be configured either to read all available article headers or those which meet certain criteria.

Figure 38.12 shows a Microsoft Windows newsreader displaying a selection of headers for a newsgroup devoted to the Internet language Java.

The shaded item with the document symbol to the left has been retrieved so that the complete article (shown in Figure 38.13) could be read. The author of the article is posing the question 'setBackground???' in the hope that someone with a similar interest in Java will know the answer to the full question shown below and post it to the newsgroup.

As mentioned earlier, there are now well over 13,000 different newsgroups with many new ones adding to the list every day. To give you an idea of the range of interests represented, Figure 38.14 shows a number of recent additions.

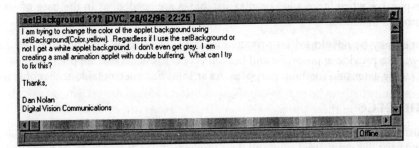

Figure 38.12 *A Newsreader program showing a selection of article headers for the newsgroup comp.lang.java*

setBackground ??? (DVC, 28/02/96 22:25)

I am trying to change the color of the applet background using
setBackground(Color.yellow). Regardless if I use the setBackground or
not I get a white applet background. I don't even get grey. I am
creating a small animation applet with double buffering. What can I try
to fix this?

Thanks,

Dan Nolan
Digital Vision Communications

Figure 38.13. *The body of the article corresponding to the shaded header in Figure 38.12*

comp.lang.pl1
comp.lang.tcl.announce
comp.os.linux.m68k
comp.os.ms-windows.apps.compatibility.win95
comp.os.ms-windows.apps.utilities.win95
comp.os.ms-windows.networking.win95
comp.os.ms-windows.setup.win95
misc.industry.insurance
rec.autos.makers.ford.explorer
rec.games.computer.quake.misc
rec.music.arabic
rec.music.artists.mariah-carey
rec.sport.softball
soc.culture.breton
soc.culture.nicaragua
soc.genealogy.slavic
soc.support.loneliness
uk.business.telework
uk.comp.training
uk.org.mensa

Figure 38.14. *A selection of newsgroups*

IRC

IRC, or *Internet Relay Chat*, is a multi-user talk program. IRC allows several people to simultaneously participate in a discussion over a particular channel, or even multiple channels. There is no restriction to the number of people who can participate in a given discussion, or the number of channels which can be formed over IRC.

All conversations take place in real time and IRC has been used extensively for live coverage of such things as world events, news and sports commentary. It is also an extremely inexpensive substitute for long distance calling.

Intranets and Extranets

An intranet is a private Internet which uses Internet software and the TCP/IP protocols. Its appearance is that of the Web and the familiar browser is its user interface. 'Out of the box' Web servers provide a convenient and relatively cheap method of developing internal network requirements and many organisations have built intranets as part of their overall Internet strategy. Employees are usually familiar with the Web and require little training to access the resources they need on the company intranet.

Web tools, such as HTML editors, are relatively cheap and application development only becomes expensive when large and complex databases are needed, as in the case of an on-line store's product database.

An intranet may be developed on private corporate LANs or WANs but organisations frequently wish to provide appropriate and limited access to clients and suppliers and develop an outward facing extension for those purposes. As an intra/Extranet, outside access only requires

E-commerce

Many businesses including, for example, supermarkets, travel agents, wine merchants, booksellers and car sales companies now sell their products through e-commerce web sites. With a computer, Internet connection and Web browser, consumers can visit these virtual stores and view, select and pay for goods which can often be delivered within 24 to 48 hours. Until the 1960s it was common practice for shops to make home deliveries or orders taken over the telephone and Internet shopping has the potential to reduce the volume of traffic visiting, for example, out of town shopping centres. It is extremely unlikely that demand for conventional 'bricks and mortar' will disappear because Internet shopping provides no social interaction and many consumers will wish to view and handle many types of goods before buying.

More formally, e-commerce can be defined as *"conducting business transactions over electronic networks"*. E-commerce is fundamentally changing the way business operates. Because of e-commerce, businesses of all sizes are changing their internal operations and their relationships with suppliers and customers. When properly implemented, e-commerce can improve the efficiency of all stages of the business process, from design and manufacture to retailing and distribution.

E-commerce is playing a major role in the establishment of a global economy. The major catalyst for the expansion of international electronic retailing is the Internet. Its users, the number of which is rapidly increasing, can communicate with the Web sites of countless organisations all over the world, and it is through these *World Wide Web* sites that companies can provide 'on-line stores'. The Web-based on-line stores are accessible by Web browsers, such as Microsoft Explorer and Netscape Communicator and a standard feature of all modern home computers. An Internet store provides all the facilities that the customer needs, including a product catalogue, a 'virtual shopping basket' and a secure credit card payment system (see later).

Business to business e-commerce

Business to business e-commerce is well established and one of the fastest growing areas. Many office equipment and consumables suppliers, for example, are able to take orders on-line and provide direct delivery to business customers. Because transactions such as the submission and settlement of invoices are all conducted electronically, the participating businesses enjoy significant cost savings.

Benefits of e-commerce for business

Businesses can benefit tremendously from e-commerce in many important ways, reducing costs and improving efficiency. For instance, expensive printed catalogues and service guides can be replaced by a single, up-to-date electronic product database that is accessible at all times. Many businesses use mail shots to inform customers of new products or special offers, a time consuming and expensive exercise. Instead the latest information can be held on the company web site and existing customers can obtain up-to-date information on new products or services at any time. A business can maintain closer contact with its customers and suppliers, and direct communication allows improved pre- and post-sales support.

Direct selling shortens the supply chain so delivery times and costs are reduced. Staffing costs can be a fraction of those for conventional sales outlets. For example, Web site software can handle routine sales transactions automatically, leaving sales staff to deal with more complex orders.

E-commerce also provides opportunities for entirely new products and services. These include network supply and support services, web site design and hosting, and various types of on-line information services.

Business to consumer e-commerce

Business to consumer e-commerce, or electronic retailing, is expanding rapidly as businesses become informed of the new opportunities it presents for market expansion. Physical products, information and various services are all available for purchase over the Internet. For example, consumers can buy cars, books, CDs, wine, stock market information and computer software from numerous Internet shops.

Benefits of e-commerce for consumers

Consumers can gain considerable benefits from electronic commerce. The range of products that can be bought on-line is continually being extended. There are virtual stores all over the Internet offering a wide range of goods, including books, wine, newspapers, cakes, computer hardware, software and even cars. Similarly, numerous services are available on-line. These include education, entertainment and information services.

There is the convenience of 24-hour home shopping and access to a wider range of goods and services than is conventionally available within their locality. A conventional shopping chain rarely offers its full product range at every shop, whereas a virtual shop can make its full product range available globally. The consumer is given global choice. If a product or service is available from a number of suppliers, the consumer can choose without regard to geographical location.

Consumers may benefit from lower prices because electronic commerce drastically reduces transaction costs. A transaction involving human interaction may be measured in £s, but the same transaction carried out electronically can cost a few pence.

Orders may be fulfilled more quickly. Direct supply from manufacturer to customer can also be effected with mail order or telephone order catalogues, but the human and paper-based transactions are more costly and involve longer delays than is possible with e-commerce. For products that can be delivered electronically, such as software, video and newspapers, the time delay between order and delivery can be reduced to an absolute minimum, and intermediaries in the traditional supply chain are entirely redundant.

By bringing products and services to the home, electronic commerce also has the potential to benefit the disabled, the elderly and those living in remote areas.

Social and employment costs of e-commerce

Clearly, some of the above benefits will not apply to all consumers and there will be social costs as well.

- ❑ If residents of rural communities choose to shop on the Internet local stores may be unable to compete and have to close. Not everyone will have, or wish to have, access to the Internet and such closures will bring serious social deprivation to some.

- ❑ Many aspects of electronic shopping are automated and fewer staff are needed to process orders. Much customer support can be provided through the Web site, which further reduces staff requirements. Of course, e-commerce will also create jobs, but the skills and working practices are very different from those in many traditional businesses.

- ❑ E-commerce businesses may have access to global markets, but they may also be subject to global competition. This means that the business must be able to respond much more quickly to changes in consumer demand and to the activities of its competitors. Working practices, therefore, tend to demand a much more flexible and multi-skilled approach than is usual in traditional business.

E-commerce relies entirely on the operation and effectiveness of electronic systems and there are greater demands for people with suitable technical skills. Rapid delivery is considered to be a vital requirement if an e-commerce business is to keep its customers jobs in distribution are likely to increase.

An organisation's network needs to be secure against unauthorised access to maintain the integrity and confidentiality of its resources and protect the privacy of any clients whose details they hold. There are general security issues which apply to all networks, closed and open, but here we are concerned with the particular problems thrown up by the Internet and the new security measures developed to cope with those problems.

Internet security threats

Viruses and hostile applets

A computer virus is program code designed to create nuisance for users, or more seriously, to effect varying degrees of damage to files stored on magnetic media. Files downloaded from *bulletin boards* on the Internet may be infected and uncontrolled use of these services is likely to result in the receipt of viruses.

A feature of all viruses is that they replicated themselves. Once into the computer's memory, it transfers from memory onto any integral storage device, such as a hard disk and commonly conceals itself in the boot sector (and sometimes in the partition sector where it is less likely to be traced), from where it can readily infect any other media placed on line in that computer system, whether it be stand-alone or networked. Naturally, any write-protected media cannot be infected.

Some virus codes are merely a nuisance, whilst others are developed specifically to destroy, or make inaccessible, whole filing systems.

Boot sector virus

This type of virus stores itself in the boot sector of the hard drive and so is activated when the system is started up. From there the virus can carry out various types of damage to files on the hard drive and copy itself to any disks accessed from floppy drives. Some are able to change their form to avoid detection by virus detection software. One such virus, Hare, only affects Windows 95 systems and is picked up from Usenet News on the Internet. It activates when an infected machine is booted on the 22nd August or the 22nd September and overwrites the contents of the hard disk.

Macro virus

This is probably the most common type of virus, new ones being reported almost daily. It embeds itself in documents created with general-purpose packages, such as Microsoft Word and Excel, each of which provides its own *macro language* (a type of programming language). The language can be used to automate certain procedures, such as formatting a document in a particular way, or customising the package for a specific application. Macro viruses have the following features.

- ❑ Once a macro virus has infected a machine, it embeds itself in all documents subsequently created with that machine.

- ❑ Macro viruses may change or delete file contents, or prevent subsequent saving or opening of a file.

- ❑ It spreads quickly because so many people use these packages and exchange files on portable media, such as floppy disks and increasingly via e-mail as attachments..

- ❑ Some macro viruses are of the 'Trojan' variety. They do not reproduce themselves, but destroy or corrupt the data in the infected document as soon as it is opened.

Largely because of the widespread use of Internet e-mail, the macro virus now presents the greatest threat of system infection.

Trojan horse virus

Named after the wooden horse at the siege of Troy, this type of virus does not reproduce itself, but pretends to be a real application program. Ironically, one such program claims to remove viruses, but in fact introduces viruses into a computer system.

Hostile Applets

An applet is a small, self-contained application written in the Java programming language and executable by all modern browsers.

Virus and hostile Applet protection

Ant-virus software can be installed on individual machines on a network, but additional protection needs to be provided at network server level. A variety of package solution exist to check incoming e-mails for infected attachments. If an infected attachment is found the user is sent the e-mail, minus the attachment and with a warning that the e-mail was infected. To keep track of new viruses and quickly develop 'cures', IBM has developed a technology called the Immune System for Cyberspace. Company networks which are connected to the system automatically send any viruses they receive to IBM's automated lab which develops 'cures' and distributes them to the company networks.

Many products developed for Internet-delivered viruses also include protection against hostile Applets.

Service attacks on Internet servers

There are numerous ways in which the service provided by an Internet server can be damaged.

❏   Ping of death. 'Ping' stands for Packet Internet Groper which is an Internet utility used to check whether an IP (Internet Protocol) address is on-line. This is confirmed if the packet sender receives a response. By using a very large 'ping' packet, the volume of data can overwhelm an Internet server and cause it to crash.

❏   E-mail 'bombs' can be created by duplicating and sending a message duplicated hundreds of times or by attaching large files which fill up the Internet server's space and clog the system.

❏   SYN flooding. A 'SYN' is the first part of the TCP (Transmission Control Protocol) packet for an Internet connection request. Such requests are received and handled by Internet servers. When flooded with requests for connections to invalid IP addresses, the server SYN queue becomes full and cannot handle further requests.

Nuisance attacks

'Spam' e-mail (Internet junk mail) is the most common type of nuisance attack and although no damage is done, it can be extremely annoying for users when their mailboxes are filled with unwanted communications. Legislation has been introduced in the USA to combat the problem, but there are numerous software products to protect Internet Service Providers and their users from 'spam' e-mail. The main method of protection filters out e-mails from the IP (Internet Protocol) addresses of well-known sources of 'spam'.

Internet security measures

Firewall protection

Firewalls are considered essential for the protection of corporate networks, such as intranets, from external networks such as the Internet. A firewall protection system may use both hardware and software components. Its purpose is to checks all packets before they enter or leave the intranet, stopping any that do not pass the relevant security standards. Most firewalls are concerned with checking incoming messages from the Internet, but they can also be used to screen out Internet sites which the organisation does not want to be accessible by staff. This may be because they contain objectionable material or because they will cause staff to waste time.

E-mail encryption

An e-mail transmission over the Internet is transferred from server to server on the way to its destination and the only way to maintain the confidentiality is to use encryption. The S/MIME (Secure/Multipurpose Internet Mail Extension) encrypts the standard MIME message and adds a digital signature (see later). To use this security system requires that sender and recipient must both have e-mail software which can handle S/MIME.

Payments through secure servers

Unlike e-mail transmissions, credit card payments can be made direct to a particular Internet server which can be secured with both hardware and software. The growth of electronic retailing is dependent on customer confidence in the security of Web-based transactions. In fact, credit card payments over the Internet can be more secure than using the telephone or post. Security is achieved with the use of Secure Servers by the vendors or third party businesses that receive and process transactions on their behalf. The banks and credit card companies specify the physical and software security measures for a Secure Server. In the UK, card authorisation and processing is handled by Streamline.

The secure server is in effect the Web-based equivalent of the Streamline terminal used in conventional retail outlets. A modern Web browser will indicate when a 'secure environment' is entered, normally at the point when credit card details need to be provided. In addition to this *automatic* reassurance to the customer that the transaction is safe, your Web pages can be designed to reinforce customer confidence by explaining what a 'secure environment' actually is.

The Web-based retailer takes payment before the product or service is delivered to the customer, so is in the same position as a conventional retailer who takes credit details over the telephone or by post.

Finally, e-commerce transactions are subject to the same framework of domestic and international rules as traditional means of shopping including, for example, existing rules on "distance selling", advertising and customer credit.

S-HTTP (Secure HyperText Transport Protocol)

This extension of the standard HTTP supports the encryption of both client (browser) and server transmissions and is essential for the security and confidentiality of commercial transactions over the Internet. When making a payment to an Internet store, the normal IP address of, for example, http://www.ourshop.com, becomes s-http://www.ourshop, indicating that the user is now connected to a secure server.

Encryption and authentication

Authentication of both client and server sides of a connection is important for network security and the confidentiality and integrity of data passing between them. Apart from password solutions, authentication can be effected with the SSL and SET protocols (widely used to protect the confidentiality of credit card payments made over the Internet) and digital signatures.

Secure Sockets Layer (SSL)

SSL (Secure Sockets Layer) is the de facto standard for encryption between client browsers and Internet servers. The identity of the server is always authenticated, but authentication of the client is optional. An electronic 'handshake' between server and browser authenticates the server and enables the client to be confident that a secure and private link has been established. Optionally, the identity of the client can be authenticated if he or she has a digital certificate issued by a Certificate Authority. To allow the client and server to be confident that a message has not been altered during transmission, a digital fingerprint is transmitted with the message. The digital fingerprint is a 'hash' value generated from a computation carried out on the data (a 'hash function'). The same hash function is applied to the message upon receipt and if it generates the same digital fingerprint, the message cannot have been altered.

Before a transmission from the client browser, it sends a request to the Internet server, and in return receives the server's public encryption key and other cryptographic details. The browser generates its own random key and encrypts it with the server's public key. Now the browser's random key can only be decrypted with the server's private key. The encrypted random key is sent to the server, which uses its private key to decrypt it. The server returns a message, encrypted with the browser's original random key. If the browser is able to decrypt the message with its original random key, the server is authenticated.

Secure Electronic Transactions (SET)

Like Secure Sockets Layer (SSL), the Secure Electronic Transaction (SET) protocol was developed (jointly by Visa and MasterCard) as a method to secure bankcard transactions over open networks, including the Internet. Compared with SSL, SET places greater importance on the validation of *both* parties to the transaction.

Although SSL allows the customer's browser to authenticate the Merchant's Web server, it does not assure the Merchant that the user of a credit card is in fact the owner of the card. Of course, this weakness also applies to transactions conducted by telephone or post. SET uses digital signatures to enable merchants to verify the identity of buyers. SET also protects customers by providing a mechanism for the credit card number to go directly to the card issuing bank for verification and billing without the merchant seeing it. Another limitation of SSL is that, outside the US, it is only available with a maximum 40-bit encryption key, which allows relatively weak encryption.

The SET protocol authenticates all aspects of a transaction by controlling the interactions that take place between all parties including, for example, credit card holders, Merchants and card issuing banks. SET provides greater confidentiality, greater transaction integrity and less opportunity for fraud than SSL or any other secure payment system.

When a SET virtual store customer has finished shopping, that is, accumulated all required items into the virtual shopping basket, the Merchant's Web server displays the completed order for the customer's review and approval. After approval, the customer chooses to use a bankcard for payment. Before transmission from the customer's computer, the payment details are encrypted using a randomly generated encryption key. Then, using the Merchant's public key received from the Web server, the key is itself encrypted, effectively placing it inside a "digital envelope". The digital envelope can only be 'opened' with the Merchant's private key, known only to the Merchant. Upon receipt, the Merchant's server opens the digital envelope and uses the enclosed key to decrypt the message.

SET also authenticates both parties to the transaction with a distinct public/private key pair to create a "digital signature". This digital signature Authentication is further strengthened by the use of certificates issued by a trusted third party Certificate Authority (CA).

Before they can shop at SET sites, cardholders must register with a CA to obtain the necessary digital certificate. The certificate provides the digital signature needed to prove a cardholder's identity in e-commerce transactions. The certificate can be held, along with other payment information, on the customer's PC, using encryption software called an electronic wallet – see below.

Virtually all the major players in electronic commerce, including Microsoft, Netscape, Visa, and MasterCard have endorsed SET. Acceptance in the US has been slow, but SET is the most widely used protocol for electronic transactions within Europe.

Digital signatures

Before transmission from the client computer, the message is encrypted using a randomly generated encryption key. Then, using the public key received from the Web server, the key is itself encrypted, effectively placing it inside a "digital envelope". The digital envelope can only be 'opened' with the server's private key, known only to the server. Upon receipt, the server opens the digital envelope and uses the enclosed key to decrypt the message.

This authenticates both parties with a distinct public/private key pair to create a "digital signature". This digital signature Authentication is further strengthened by the use of certificates issued by a trusted third party Certificate Authority (CA).

✍️Exercises

1. Distinguish between the *Internet* and the *World Wide Web*.
2. (i) What is the purpose of a *browser*?
   (ii) Give two examples of the use of *hyperlinks*.
   (iii) Distinguish between *hypertext* and *hypermedia*.
   (iv) What does *HTML* stand for and what is its purpose?
3. Give a well-known example of a *URL* (Uniform Resource Locator).
4. What is the purpose of a *search engine*? Name three.
5. Define the terms *Intranet* and *Extranet* and suggest applications of each for an organisation.
6. A business is making extensive use of e-mail and the Internet in general and has experienced some minor problems from nuisance viruses. It is concerned that it may be suffer real damage from viruses in the future.
   (i) What is a computer *virus*?

(ii) Describe the main types of computer virus.

(iii) Explain the measures which can be taken to minimise the risk of virus damage.

(iv) What is a hostile *applet*?

7. An Information Service Provider (ISP) has been receiving numerous complaints from its users concerning a slowing down of Internet access. Its servers are also tending to crash more frequently. The ISP suspects that it may be being subjected to '*ping of death*', '*SYN flooding*' or '*e-mail bomb*' attacks.

Explain each of the italicised terms.

8. The business is also planning to set up an Extranet to provide restricted Internet access to its Intranet, primarily for staff working away from the main office. The Intranet is to be protected with the use of *firewalls* and *encryption*.

Define the italicised terms.

9. The business is planning the development of an e-commerce site to sell its products over the Internet. It does not have the *secure server* facilities demanded by the merchant banks, for the acceptance of on-line credit card payments and plans to use the services of a *Payment Service Provider* (PSP).

(i) What is a *secure server* and why is it an essential part of an e-commerce site?

(ii) What does *S-HTTP* stand for and what is its significance for an e-commerce consumer?

(iii) What advantage has the SET protocol over the SSL protocol for the business?

(iv) Explain the function of a Payment Service Provider.

5. Explain the term *digital signature* and consider its significance for the conduct of business electronically.

Chapter 39

Organisational and Social Issues

The introduction of a computer to an organisation cannot be effective if computerisation simply means the transfer of manual files to computer storage and the automation of some of the existing clerical procedures. To achieve the full potential of computerisation, an organisation needs to implement certain changes which will affect its staff and its form of management. This chapter examines the functions of Information Technology Services and the roles of its staff, the possible effects of computerisation on staff in other functional areas and the implications of distributing computing power. In many organisations, a separate department has overall responsibility for computer system provision and operation.

Information Technology (IT) Services

Apart from small firms, most organisations need specialist staff to develop, introduce, maintain and update the various systems which make use of information technology. The term 'information technology' covers all computer-based information processing systems, plus those which make use of data communications, such as computer networks, fax machines, photocopiers and telephone systems. The responsibilities of IT Services are, therefore, much broader than those traditionally held by wholly centralised computer services or data processing departments. The development of cheaper and more powerful microcomputer systems, which can be networked with one another, as well as with larger mini and mainframe systems, has resulted in computer facilities being distributed more widely. For this reason, IT Services needs to provide a much more flexible service and support user systems at the point of use. For example, users of network workstations need support when equipment, such as a shared printer, breaks down or they may require help in the use of software on the network. This contrasts with a centralised department, which holds all the computer equipment, carries out all computer processing and restricts user access to specialised applications, run through dedicated terminals. IT Services may be known variously as Computer Services, Management Information Services or less commonly now, the Data Processing Department.

Role of IT Services

IT Services fulfils a servicing function for the whole organisation. In larger organisations, there is a centralised computer facility, possibly in the shape of a mainframe or mini-computer system, with the responsibility for major applications, such as payroll and stock control. User departments may have access to the centralised facility through attached terminals or networked microcomputers. Individual members of staff may also use stand-alone microcomputer systems or portable devices, such as notebooks and personal digital assistants (PDAs). IT Services staff need to support users in the use of these distributed facilities, as well as control the operation of any centralised system. IT Services provides facilities to satisfy both *operational* and *managerial* information needs.

Operational requirements

Each functional area has its own operational information needs. For example, Wages and

Salaries need payroll details and payslips, and Sales Order Processing require the production of customer invoices. Common examples of routine operations include:

- ❑ keeping stock records
- ❑ sales accounting and purchase accounting;
- ❑ payroll;
- ❑ invoicing and production of delivery notes;
- ❑ routine costing;
- ❑ filing of customer orders.

Managerial requirements

Routine processing work forms the bulk of the activity within IT Services, but there is an increasing demand for management information. This includes assistance with functions which require management involvement and thinking, but which can be partially automated or assisted by computers. Examples of such functions include:

- ❑ production planning;
- ❑ short term and long term forecasting;
- ❑ setting of budgets;
- ❑ decision-making on financial policies;
- ❑ marketing decisions and sales management;
- ❑ factory maintenance and management;
- ❑ price determination;
- ❑ selection of suppliers.

Function of IT Services

Figure 39.1 shows the typical functions within an IT Services department.

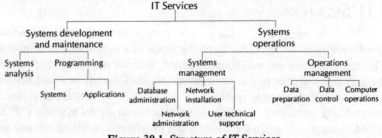

Figure 39.1. *Structure of IT Services*

Systems development

This function relates to the development of new computerised systems and the maintenance of existing ones. This function is staffed primarily by *systems analysts* and *programmers*. In small organisations, hybrid skills are often needed, so job titles such as *analyst programmer* may be used.

Systems analysis

Systems analysis is a process used in the design of new systems, as requested by corporate management. Systems analysis follows stages of *investigation, design* and *implementation*. Each stage should involve close consultation with potential users, in the various functional areas of the organisation, to ensure that their information and operational requirements are met.

The design stage should produce a *system specification* which, rather like an architect's plans for a building, details all necessary materials and procedures needed to fulfil the specification. The specification should detail the necessary clerical procedures, hardware requirements and the inputs, processing and outputs required of the computer software.

After implementation of a system, it will require continual monitoring and probably, occasional modification, when the operational or information requirements of users change. This maintenance task is the responsibility of the systems analysts,

Programming

Programming lacks some of the creative aspects of systems analysis and involves the use of a programming language (for example, C++, COBOL, Visual BASIC) to code the necessary computer programs. The program requirements are detailed in the *program* or *software specification*, which forms part of the system specification prepared by systems analysts.

Most programmers who work in an IT Services department are likely to be *applications programmers*, responsible for the development or modification of applications, such as stock control or payroll. Systems programmers are concerned with the development of operating systems and utilities (Chapter 13), which are normally developed by large computer manufacturers or software companies, such as Microsoft. An IT Services department may also employ *systems programmers*, but they are likely to have a more limited role than applications programmers. Much software is now in commercial package form, but not all applications can be satisfied by such means and applications programmers continue to be needed for tailoring of programs specifically for their employer. The growth of network use has created the need for *network programmers*, who have specialist knowledge of such systems.

Apart from specialising in systems, applications or network programming, a programmer is likely to be skilled in the use of one or more programming languages. An organisation seeking to employ programmers will specify the language or languages they require.

System operations

This broad function is concerned with the operational, rather than the developmental aspects of the IT systems. It is divided into *systems management* and *operations management*.

Systems management

This function deals with the general operation of all the IT systems and is not directly concerned with particular applications. There are a number of separate areas within this function: *network installation*; *network administration*; *user technical support*; *database administration*.

Network installation and administration

Computer networks (Chapter 10) are a feature of most organisations and tasks of selecting, purchasing and installing the hardware and software, both systems and applications, may be carried out by specialist staff in this area. Staff employed in this area need to be familiar with the network operating system (Chapter13) and its utilities. They are responsible for setting up and managing network user accounts, controlling passwords, managing printer queues, allocating and maintaining and backing up network storage and monitoring the performance of the network.

User technical support

The distribution to users, of computer resources through networks, desktop and portable computer systems has hugely expanded the need for IT user support. Users often have access to a range of different devices, such as printers, scanners, plotters and fax modems and apart from needing initial training in their use, they also require occasional support when things go wrong. Support staff may also give guidance in the use of software and help trouble-shoot problems which users will inevitably encounter at some stage. User technical support is extremely important if users are to use IT resources efficiently and for the benefit of the organisation.

Database administration

If applications are implemented through a database system, then specialist staff, known as database administrators, are employed to control access to the database by applications and ensure consistency in the use of data within it. Systems analysts and programmers involved in the development of database applications need to work closely with the responsible *database administrator* (DBA).

Operations management

This function, led by an operations manager, has three main areas of responsibility: *data control*; *data preparation*; *computer operations*; *media library*. These responsibilities relate particularly to centrally controlled applications.

Data control

Data control staff are responsible for the co-ordination and control of data flowing through the operations section. For example, data received from Salaries, to update the payroll master file and produce payslips, have to be controlled to ensure their accuracy and completeness at all stages of processing. The methods of control are described in Chapter 17.

Data preparation

Batch processing systems require the transcription and encoding of data gathered from source documents, such as order forms or invoices, onto magnetic storage. The input is then effected directly from the magnetic tape or disk on which the data has been accumulated. On-line, transaction processing systems, do not usually require this data preparation stage.

Computer operations

Computer operators are responsible for the day-to-day running of the computer hardware. In the case of mainframe computer systems, their responsibilities include the loading and unloading of magnetic tape reels or magnetic disk packs, according to the on-line requirements of applications currently in use. For example, before a payroll run, the media containing the master and transaction files have to be loaded onto the relevant devices, so that they can be accessed by the computer which is running the payroll program. The computer hardware is under the control of operating system software (Chapter 13) and an operator needs to communicate with the operating system regarding jobs to be processed and to deal with error conditions which may arise. A separate terminal is normally dedicated as an *operator console* and access to it is restricted both physically and through software-controlled passwords.

Implications of decentralising computing power

The combined technologies of computing and telecommunications have facilitated the decentralisation of computer power through wide and local area networks and stand-alone microcomputer systems. The main benefits for an organisation may be as follow:

❑ The delegation of some information processing control to branch level management, hopefully results in systems which respond to local requirements. The control of information processing systems are thereby the responsibility of those who use them; .

❑ More rapid, up-to-date information at the local level, because it is processed locally;

❑ The rapid distribution of centrally produced information via network systems;

❑ Provided that the local systems are linked to a central facility, then information which is locally produced can be transmitted and stored so as to be available at a corporate level. Overall control is not lost, but enhanced.

The above benefits are not automatic and may have certain implications for an organisation:

❑ New hardware and software needs to be purchased, which is compatible with any existing centralised facility;

❑ Local management and workers need to be trained in the operation of any new system introduced, if the maximum benefit is to be obtained. The use of microcomputers with, for example, database and spreadsheet packages requires extensive training and this can be expensive;

❑ A complete re-appraisal of specialist staffing may be necessary, including, for example, the recruitment of systems analysts already familiar with the design and implementation of distributed systems;

❑ Specialist personnel, including programmers and operators, may be required at the local level;

❑ Decentralised systems present new problems in terms of controlling the security of information and the additional risks must be considered and covered.

Computers and employment

The rapid advances in computer and micro-electronic technologies have occurred during periods of considerable change in the Western economies and although many different factors have conspired towards the generally higher levels of unemployment, computerisation has undoubtedly played a major role. No attempt is made in this text to relate particular numbers of employed or unemployed to computerisation and discussion will centre on the identifiable effects of computerisation on employment patterns and prospects. Computerisation requires consideration of a number of possible effects/implications:

❑ re-training;

❑ re-deployment;

❑ de-skilling;

❑ changes in working practices;

❑ re-grading and changes in career prospects;

❑ redundancy;

❑ changes in working conditions (health and safety).

Each of the above can be identified in different types of job.

Office work

Computerisation is common in most areas of office work, for example, word processing, electronic messaging, and accounting systems. Additionally in some specialised areas such as banking, automatic tellers are replacing humans for routine banking transactions and staffing requirements are likely to reduce quite drastically as new automated services such as telephone banking expand.

Re-training

Generally, an organisation will choose to make full use of its existing staff, rather than search for new staff who already have the skills required. Depending on the nature of the job, the re-training needed may be radical or quite minor. For example, a typist has keyboard skills which are quite readily transferrable to the task of word processing and re-training needs centre on the concept of text editing, mailing lists and the use of floppy disks and printers. The aim is to give the operator the knowledge, skill and understanding to make maximum use of the facilities provided by a word processor. Word processing is a general skill which can be applied in different ways in different organisations. Similarly, the use of a software package for sales accounting or stock control needs knowledge and skills, some of which are transferable to other packages. Familiarity with computers in general and expertise in the use of some packages, provides an individual with the confidence to quickly pick up skills for new applications as they arise.

Re-deployment

Computerisation generally reduces manpower requirements but increases the opportunities for business expansion. Re-deployment means moving staff from one area of work or responsibility to another, generally with retraining and is a common consequence of computerisation in any area of work.

De-skilling

The judgement as to whether or not a job is de-skilled by computerisation is a rather subjective one. For example, does a wages clerk using manual methods require a higher level of skill than a data entry operator? The answer is probably yes, although a trade union may argue otherwise in the interests of improved job re-grading. On the other hand it is generally accepted that higher level skills are required to use a word processor than a typewriter.

Changes in working practices

Staff may be required to carry out a wider range of tasks as a result of computerisation. For example, in smaller offices a clerk may be required to answer customer enquiries and carry out data entry at a terminal. Flexibility rather than specialisation is often the key to the introduction of new technology. The lines of demarcation in the newspaper industry had to disappear before computerisation could take place.

Re-grading and career prospects

Sometimes, improvements in job gradings are introduced in order to encourage staff to accept computerisation. At the same time, career prospects in office work are generally diminished. In the banking industry, the prospects for managerial jobs have diminished drastically in the last two decades and currently, few clerical staff who did not enter the job with a degree have prospects for managerial posts.

Redundancy

Computerisation of office work inevitably reduces the manpower requirements for an existing level of work, but redundancy does not always result, usually because computers are introduced in response to an expansion in the business of an organisation.

Health and safety

Anxiety and stress frequently result from subjection to frequent and rapid change. Many staff, particularly older members, may feel anxious about the security of their jobs or possible redeployment and may become unhappy about personal contact being replaced by a computer screen. As they get older, many people prefer continuity rather than constant change and computerisation usually means radical and frequent change. Anxiety can also result from a fear of falling behind, a common malady amongst people working with computers, because the changes and advances are so rapid.

Ergonomics

Certain health and safety problems can result from computer usage and ergonomically designed equipment and working environments can help minimise the hazards. A number of health and safety concerns are recognised in relation to VDU screens: exposure to radiation; induction of epileptic fits; mental and physical fatigue; eyestrain, eye damage and visual fatigue; muscular strain. Suitable working practices and well-designed equipment can largely avoid such dangers, for example, gentle lighting, lack of screen flicker and hourly breaks for VDU operators. Other concerns relate to the design of office furniture and the general office environment, including temperature and noise levels.

Manufacturing industry

Most of the factors described in relation to office work apply equally to factory work, but the following additional points are worth mentioning.

❑ *Job satisfaction.* Shop floor workers who supervise and service the machines have a cleaner, less dangerous job than traditionally skilled machinists. It may be surmised that young people, without the experience of the old skills, will look more favourably on such supervisory jobs than the older workers.

❑ *New job opportunities.* If automated systems such as Flexible Manufacturing Systems (FMS) are to be successful, then the number of jobs in factories using FMS must inevitably decrease. Opportunities lie in the creation of a new range of jobs, many of which are in software engineering and in the design of automated systems. The Japanese experience is that new, highly-skilled jobs are created in the development and design fields in companies manufacturing automated equipment and commercial machinery, whereas both skilled and unskilled jobs are lost in the companies using this equipment. The Japanese experience is being mirrored in the UK.

❑ *Increased unemployment.* Many older, skilled workers have been made redundant because of the loss or de-skilling of their jobs through automation. On the other hand, the redundancies may have occurred without automation because of loss of competitiveness.

Computers and society

There is general agreement that computers and related technologies will bring great social changes, but there are wide differences of opinion about what they will be, the rate at which they will occur and the extent to which they are beneficial. It must be emphasised that many of the following points are highly subjective and open to debate.

The *benefits* include:

❑   increased productivity;

❑   higher standard of living;

❑   cleaner and safer working conditions;

❑   shorter working hours;

❑   more leisure time.

The *costs* include:

❑   polarisation of people into two groups - the technologically advantaged and disadvantaged;

❑   increasing crime and delinquency rates;

❑   the threat of a totalitarian state;

❑   invasion of privacy.

The remainder of this section looks at an important area of concern regarding the future impact of computers on society, namely tele-working. Some of the effects are already apparent.

Tele-working - the office at home

At present, millions of office workers travel by car or public transport to their respective places of work. Nearly all organisations carry out their business from centralised offices because information needs to be exchanged, usually on paper documents and decisions need to be made, which requires consultation between individuals. Through the use of telecommunications (most importantly, the Internet) and centrally available computer databases, some forward-looking organisations allow their staff to work from home, using a computer terminal. There are a number of advantages to be gained from home-based work.

Advantages of tele-working:

- ❑   savings in travel costs;
- ❑   no necessity to live within travelling distance;
- ❑   flexible hours of work;
- ❑   equality between men and women. Bringing up children can be a shared activity;
- ❑   savings for the organisation in terms of expensive city-centre offices.

Disadvantages of tele-working:

- ❑   loss of social contact;
- ❑   need for quiet workroom at home. This can be difficult in a small flat;
- ❑   the difficulty of office accommodation is compounded when two or three members of a family all work from home;
- ❑   loss of visible status for senior staff in terms of a plush office and other staff to command.

Privacy, computer fraud and copyright

Computer Misuse Act (1990)

The Act identifies three categories of offence:

- ❑   Unauthorised access to computer material.
- ❑   Unauthorised access with intent to commit or facilitate commission of further offences.
- ❑   Unauthorised modification of computer material.

The Act is deals with the general crime of 'hacking'. The first category of offence deals with unauthorised access to a computer system, its programs and data. An offence is committed if a person performs any computer function with the <u>intent</u> of securing unauthorised access to any program or data held in any computer. The second category covers the offence of persistent hacking. The third category of covers the alteration of data to which a hacker has gained access. These crimes are punishable by prison sentences.

Computer fraud and protection measures

Computer fraud is invariably committed for financial gain, but unlike some forms of fraud, the perpetrator(s) will make considerable efforts to prevent discovery of any loss by the victim. The rewards for such efforts may be complete freedom from prosecution, or at least a delay in discovery of the fraud and a consequent chance of escape. Unless proper controls and checks are implemented, computer systems are particularly vulnerable to fraudulent activity, because much of the time processing and its results are hidden. The following section examines some methods for committing fraud and the measures which can be taken to foil them.

To extract money from a financial accounting system requires its diversion into fictitious, but accessible accounts. To avoid detection, appropriate adjustments must be made to ensure that the accounts still balance. Sometimes, fraudulent activity may involve the misappropriation of goods rather than cash. Frequently, the collusion of several people is necessary to effect a fraud, because responsibility for different stages of the processing cycle is likely to be shared. Some common methods of fraud are given below.

❑ Bogus data entry. This may involve entering additional, unauthorised data, modifying valid data or preventing its entry altogether. Such activity may take place during the data preparation or data entry stages.

❑ Bogus output. Output may be destroyed or altered to prevent discovery of fraudulent data entry or processing.

❑ Alteration of files. For example, an employee may alter his salary grading in the payroll file or adjust the amount owing in a colluding customers account.

❑ Program patching. This method requires access to program coding and a detailed knowledge of the functioning of the program in question, as well as the necessary programming skill. By introducing additional code, in the form of a conditional subroutine, certain circumstances determined by the perpetrator can trigger entry to the subroutine, which may, for example, channel funds to a fictitious account.

❑ Suspense accounts. Rejected and unreconciled transactions tend to be allocated to suspense accounts until they can be dealt with; fraud may be effected by directing such transactions to the account of someone colluding in the crime. Transactions can be tampered with at the input stage to ensure their rejection and allocation to the suspense/personal account.

An organisation can minimise the risk of computer fraud by:

❑ controlling access to computer hardware; in centralised systems with a limited number of specialist staff access can be readily controlled. On the other hand, if power is concentrated in the hands of few staff, then the opportunities for undetected fraud are increased. Distributed systems or centralised systems with remote access, for example through the Internet, may increase the number of locations where fraud can be perpetrated;

❑ auditing of data and procedures; until hard copy is produced the contents of files remain invisible and a number of auditing techniques can be used to detect fraudulent entries or changes.

❑ careful monitoring of the programming function; program patching can be controlled by division of the programming task, so that an individual programmer does not have complete responsibility for one application program. Unauthorised alterations to existing software can be detected by auditing utilities which compare the object code of an operational program with an original and authorised copy.

Copyright, Designs and Patents Act (1988)

A computer program can now obtain the status of literary work and as such, retains protection for 50 years from the first publishing date. Computer software is now covered by the Copyright Designs and Patents Act 1988 and infringements include:

❑ the pirating of copyright protected software;

❏ the running of pirated software, in that a copy is created in memory;

❏ transmitting software over telecommunications links, thereby producing a copy.

The major software producers have funded an organisation called FAST (Federation Against Software Theft) which successfully lobbied for the inclusion of computer software into the above-mentioned Act.

The law also covers material published on the World Wide Web, including images and materials used as part of a Web site's design. For example, you would be committing an offence if you copied images of products from a manufacturer's on-line brochure. An offence is also committed if you place a link in your own Web site to another site which contains copyright material, without the copyright holder's permission. It is wise to assume that material is copyright protected unless there is a statement to the contrary.

Data Protection Acts (1984 and 1998)

The Data Protection Act of 1984 states that a business or other organisation which holds personal information on their computer system must register with the Data Protection Registrar, the body that administers the act. The registration process requires identification of the classes of data held and the purposes for which they are to be used. For example, a business may hold personal data which includes information on lifestyle and income which it uses to target its marketing campaigns. A new UK Data Protection Act, passed in 1998 and which came into force on 1 March 2000, specifically concerns the processing of personal data on the Internet. The main provisions of each Act are given in the following sections.

Data Protection Act (1984)

Since the 1960s, there has been growing public concern about the threat that computers pose to personal privacy. Most countries, including the UK, have introduced legislation to safeguard the privacy of the individual. The Younger Report of 1972 identified ten principles which were intended as guidelines to computer users in the private sector. A Government White Paper was published in 1975 in response to the Younger Report, but no legislation followed. The Lindop Report of 1978 was followed by a White Paper in 1982 and this resulted in the 1984 Data Protection Act. Apart from public pressure concerning the protection of personal privacy, a major incentive for the Government to introduce the Act stemmed from the need to ratify the Council of Europe Data Protection Convention. In the absence of this ratification, firms within the UK could have been considerably disadvantaged in trading terms through the Conventions provision to allow participating countries to refuse the transfer of personal information to non-participating countries. The principles detailed in the Younger Report formed the foundation for future reports and the Data Protection Act. They are listed below.

❏ Information should be regarded as being held for a specific purpose and should not be used, without appropriate authorisation, for other purposes.

❏ Access to information should be confined to those authorised to have it for the purpose for which it was supplied.

❏ The amount of information collected and held should be the minimum necessary for the achievement of a specified purpose.

❏ In computerised systems which handle information for statistical purposes, adequate provision should be made in their design for separating identities from the rest of the data.

❏ There should be arrangements whereby a subject could be told about the information held concerning him or her.

❏ The level of security to be achieved by a system should be specified in advance by the user and should include precautions against the deliberate abuse or misuse of information.

❏ A monitoring system should be provided to facilitate the detection of any violation of the security system.

❏ In the design of information systems, periods should be specified beyond which information should not be retained.

❏ Data held should be accurate. There should be machinery for the correction of inaccuracy and updating of information.

❏ Care should be taken in coding value judgements.

The White Paper which followed the Younger Report identified certain features of computerised information systems which could be a threat to personal privacy:

❏ The facility for storing vast quantities of data.

❏ The speed and power of computers make it possible for data to be retrieved quickly and easily from many access points;

❏ Data can be rapidly transferred between interconnected systems.

❏ Computers make it possible for data to be combined in ways which might otherwise not be practicable.

❏ Data is often transferred in a form not directly intelligible.

The 1984 Data Protection Act sets boundaries for the gathering and use of personal data. It requires all holders of computerised personal files to register with a Registrar appointed by the Home Secretary. The holder of personal data is required to keep to both the general terms of the Act, and to the specific purposes declared in the application for registration.

Terminology
The Act uses a number of terms which require some explanation:

❏ Data. Information held in a form which can be processed automatically. By this definition, manual information systems are not covered by the Act.

❏ Personal data. That which relates to a living individual who is identifiable from the information, including any which is based on fact or opinion.

❏ Data subject. The living individual who is the subject of the data.

❏ Data user. A person who processes or intends to process the data concerning a data subject.

Implications

The requirements of the Act may result in an organisation having to pay more attention to the question of security against unauthorised access than would otherwise be the case; appropriate education and training of employees are also needed to ensure that they are aware of their responsibilities and are fully conversant with their roles in the security systems. The Act also provides the right of a data subject (with some exceptions) to obtain access to information concerning him or her. Normally, a data user must provide such information free of charge or for a nominal charge of around £10.

From the individuals point of view, the Act can be said to have a number of weaknesses:

❑ Penalties for infringement of the rules are thought to be weak and ineffective.

❑ There are a number of exemptions from the Act. Some holders do not need to register and there are exceptions to the right of access to ones own file. There are also limits to confidentiality.

The Registrar is appointed by the Home Secretary and cannot therefore, be wholly independent.

Data Protection Act (1998)

"An Act to make new provision for the regulation of the processing of information relating to individuals, including the obtaining, holding, use or disclosure of such information." [16th July 1998 Data Protection Act].

The Act defines 'data' as information which is automatically processed, or is gathered with that intention, or is held in a structured filing system which is not automatically controlled. In other words, the Act covers manual filing systems which were not covered in the 1984 Act.

The Act also refers to:

❑ the "data controller" as the person or persons who determine the purposes to which the personal data is put and the manner in which it is processed;

❑ the "data processor", meaning any person (other than an employee of the data controller) who processes the personal data;

The terms "data subject" and "personal data" retain the same meanings as stated in the 1984 Act.

The 1998 Act additionally refers to "sensitive personal data", meaning personal information relating to racial or ethnic origin, political opinions, religious or similar beliefs, trade union membership, physical and mental health, sexual life, offences or alleged offences and court proceedings for such offences.

There are a number of exemptions to registration, for example, when the data is held for national security, crime prevention or detection and certain tax purposes.

Index

ICT 2000 CD ROM from
Leighton Educational Multimedia Ltd,
The Teleport, Doxford International
Business Park, Sunderland, Tyne and
Wear, SR3 3XD. Tel   0191 525 2400
Fax   0191 520 1815

Geoffrey Knott - Nick Waites   May 1999
Single Site Licence £120 inc. VAT
Single user Licence £19.99 inc. VAT

ICT 2000 is a comprehensive CD ROM reference providing detailed information on a broad range of computer-related topics. All of the material is in HTML format so that it can be accessed immediately using either Netscape Navigator 4 or Internet Explorer 4. If neither Netscape Navigator 4 nor Internet Explorer 4 is available, Internet Explorer 4 can be installed from the CD ROM. A screen shot of ICT 2000 is shown below.

Produced in HTML format, ICT 2000 is ideal for use on a network. Universities, Colleges and Secondary schools will find it an invaluable resource for their students whether they are on the premises or involved in distance learning. The material provides excellent coverage of a range of important computing courses, including AS/A2 Level Computing and ICT, GCSE Information Technology, GNVQ Intermediate and Advanced Information Technology and BTEC National Computing. ICT 2000 provides in-depth coverage of the following major areas of computing:

Fundamental principles	Systems analysis
Hardware	Databases
Software	Computers in action
Software engineering	Multimedia
Computer files	Internet
Information system controls	Programming skills
Data processing	

These main areas are broken down into more than seventy detailed topics ranging from the principles of numbering systems and boolean algebra to practical introductions to three popular programming languages and a complete HTML 4.0 reference. The text is supplemented by over four hundred diagrams, numerous tables and complete program listings. Over one thousand index entries and a keyword search facility provide rapid access to any topic or sub-topic.

A demonstration version can be viewed by visiting www.ict2000.co.uk

Information Technology GNVQ Intermediate

Geoffrey Knott - Nick Waites September 1998   320 pp
ISBN 1901888 12 6 Soft Cover £13.95

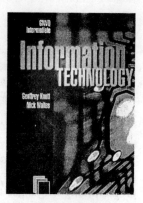

This book has been created with two main purposes in mind: to present the basic knowledge demanded by the GNVQ Intermediate in Information Technology as clearly as possible, and to provide detailed instruction for the practical skills necessary to use a range of modern software. Consequently it is also suitable for anyone interested in acquiring basic literacy in IT, and especially for those who need a gentle introduction to using popular software. The book addresses the requirements of the mandatory units of the Information Technology Intermediate level, for both the 1995 Specification and the Pilot Programme started in 1997, namely:

1995 Specification	Pilot Programme started 1997
Introduction to Information Technology	Presenting Information
Using Information Technology	Handling Information
Organisations and Information Technology	Information Technology Systems
Communications and Information Technology	Programming

The structure of the book reflects the objectives outlined earlier by being divided into two sections. The first eleven chapters comprise a Knowledge Resource of necessary theory. Each chapter ends with a number of self-test questions to test the reader's retention of essential facts. The remaining chapters comprise a Skills Resource of tutorials. These tutorials lead the reader through numerous practical exercises covering word processing, spreadsheets, databases, presentation graphics and programming. The tutorials are based on the following popular software:

Microsoft Word 97   Microsoft Excel 97   Microsoft Access 97   Microsoft Powerpoint 97

Borland Turbo Pascal version 7

Those tutorials covering Microsoft Office 97 applications are in the form of detailed instructions taking the reader step-by-step through the procedures required to produce typical documents. Designed to establish basic skills, the tutorials make full use of screen shots to show the reader what to expect at each stage of the production of a document. Turbo Pascal is used to introduce basic programming concepts. A number of simple examples progressively cover the essentials of developing and testing programs. Complete assessment schemes for both the 1995 Specification and the Pilot Programme are stored on the CD ROM which accompanies the book.

Information Technology GNVQ Advanced

Geoffrey Knott - Nick Waites August 1997   768 pp
ISBN 1901888 01 0   Soft Cover £16.95

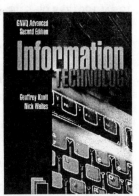

The new edition of this very popular book has been extensively
revised and updated and chapters covering the Internet and program
testing have been added to an already comprehensive text. The book
covers the 8 mandatory units of the

Information Technology GNVQ Advanced level

namely:

- Information Technology Systems
- Systems Analysis
- Using Information Technology
- Software
- Organisations and Information Technology
- Database Development
- Communications and Networking
- Information Technology Projects and Teamwork

It also provides in-depth coverage of two important optional Units:

- Program Design
- Programming

The book is divided into three parts

Knowledge Resource

The underpinning knowledge required for all of the Units

Skills Resource

Supporting the practical aspects of the course

Study Programme

Over 20 assignments designed to cover fully the Performance Criteria specified for the
Mandatory Units of the course.

Computer Studies Fourth Edition

Geoffrey Knott - Nick Waites September 1998   704 pp
ISBN 1901888 09 6   Soft Cover   £19.95

Core Units

Information Systems, Introduction to Programming, Computer
Systems, Quantitative Methods

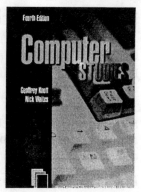

Programming Stream

Concepts and Practice Units

The Fourth Edition of Computer Studies has been completely revised and updated to keep
students aware of the most recent changes and developments in this subject.

Each chapter is followed by exercises designed to test the reader's retention of facts and
understanding of ideas and techniques developed within the text.

The Assignment Programme at the end of the book provides assessment coverage of all the
BTEC Units listed above. Unit tables at the beginning of the Assignment Programme list the
assignments, and for each one, the Principal Objectives it covers and the chapters which are of
particular use for its completion.

Although the book meets the particular requirements of BTEC National Courses in Computer
Studies, it is also suitable for Higher Education programmes which do not assume prior
knowledge of the subject.

GCSE Information Systems

Nick Waites August 1994   320 pp
ISBN 0 907679 71 4   Soft Cover   £11.50

GCSE Information Systems has been written specifically for the National Curriculum
Attainment Target 5: Information Technology Capability. The material presented in the book
covers the syllabus extensions for students who wish to obtain a **GCSE in Information
Technology** .The text, which covers all aspects of information technology and information
systems, includes:

- basic computer operation principles
- hardware devices
- the different types of software problem solving techniques

- ❑ elements of programming in BASIC, Pascal and Logo
- ❑ systems analysis and design
- ❑ applications of computers
- ❑ social issues relating to computers
- ❑ glossary of commonly used computing terms

The text is supplemented with numerous diagrams and self-test questions and answers are provided at the end of each chapter. A number of model GCSE examination questions have also been included. These features combine to provide an excellent general introduction to computing for GCSE students or for people who out of interest, simply wish to learn more about this important subject.

Information Processing Third Edition

Geoffrey Knott - Nick Waites July 1997 352 pp
ISBN 0 907679 97 8 Soft Cover £15.95

The new edition of this popular text demonstrates the importance of computerised Information Processing in modern organisations. The text has been extensively revised to keep students aware of the most recent changes and developments. It assumes no previous knowledge of the subject and is suitable for National, Advanced, Higher National and undergraduate programmes which have an Information Processing requirement. Business, Finance and Management courses will find the text highly relevant. The text also meets the requirements of Members of the Association of Accountancy Technicians (AAT), who are studying for **Paper 6, Elements of Information Systems**. Each chapter is followed by exercises designed to test the reader's retention of facts and understanding of ideas developed within the text.

An Introduction to Pascal

James K Morton June 1993 160 pp
ISBN 0 907679 47 1 Soft Cover £10.95

This book has been specially written for those studying Pascal for the first time and assumes no prior knowledge of programming. The format of the book provides the student with a logical, step by step learning experience proven to be successful in practice.

The material included covers the programming requirements of BTEC National and First Awards, City & Guilds Modular Courses and GCE Advanced Level Computing syllabuses. BTEC National/First Award and City & Guilds students will find their requirements met by the material contained in chapters 1 to 5; Advanced Level students should include chapter 6 in their course of study. Undergraduate and HNC/HND students requiring a working knowledge of Pascal will find this an invaluable text. Chapters 1 to 5 provide the material necessary for a good, general understanding of the Pascal language and Chapter 6 provides a platform for those students intending to pursue programming at a professional level.

The book contains a wealth of complete, ready-to-run programs along with numerous end-of-chapter programs, exercises and assignments designed to enhance understanding of the material presented in each chapter.